NEW YORK UNIVERSITY SERIES IN SELECTED ECONOMIC WRITINGS

M. Ishaq Nadiri
Chairman, Department of Economics
and
Jay Gould Professor of Economics
New York University

•

General Editor

BOOKS IN THE SERIES

Selected Economic Writings
of William J. Baumol
Edited by Elizabeth E. Bailey

•

Selected Economic Writings
of Fritz Machlup
Edited by George Bitros

•

Selected Economic Writings
of Oskar Morgenstern
Edited by Andrew Schotter

The publication of this work has been aided by a grant from the Andrew W. Mellon Foundation

Selected Economic Writings of William J. Baumol

Edited by
Elizabeth E. Bailey
Adjunct Associate Professor
of Economics
New York University
Research Head of Economic Research Department
Bell Laboratories

M. Ishaq Nadiri
General Editor

New York • New York University Press • 1976

Acknowledgments

Grateful acknowledgment is made to the following for permission to use essays which appeared in their publications:

American Economic Review

Bell Journal of Economics and Management Science

Economic Journal

Econometrica

Economica

Harcourt, Brace and Jovanovich

Journal of Economic Literature

Journal of Political Economy

Management Science

Prentice Hall Publishers

Princeton University Press

Public Opinion Quarterly

Quarterly Journal of Economics

Rand McNally Publishers

Review of Economic Studies

Review of Economics and Statistics

Southern Economic Journal

Swedish Journal of Economics

University of Pennsylvania Press

Weidenfield and Nicholson Publishers

Library of Congress Catalog Card Number: 75-34649

ISBN: 0-8147-1005-0

Manufactured in the United States of America

GENERAL EDITOR'S PREFACE

Our publication of the selected scientific writings of several eminent economists is not only a gesture of appreciation for their contribution to economic theory and policy but also a convenient means to bring their important contributions to the attention of the readers. This volume is one of three volumes pertaining to the works of Professors William J. Baumol, Fritz Machlup and Oskar Morgenstern. They bring together contributions in a wide area of economic theory and policy. These three prolific authors have dealt with an extremely broad range of topics including fundamental methodological issues, the history of economic theory, the theory of demand, utility theory, theory of games, business decision process and pricing rules, externalities, economic dynamics, theories of inflation, unbalanced growth, monetary theory, theory of international trade and finance, sources of economic growth and economics of knowledge, mathematical and nonlinear programming and economic statistics. Each of the articles contributes to the literature and many of them were controversial at the time of their appearance. Though their styles and the problems with which they concern themselves differ considerably, they share an interest in rigorous economic theory, in the process of change, in the history of doctrine. However, the authors employ different techniques in building their models and in analyzing issues of economic policy; and in the process contribute new and important technical insights.

The editors of these volumes are not off the mark in their emphasis on the important contributions that these authors have made to economic science. They have done a very real service for the profession in providing an overview of the writings of these three distinguished authors in a one volume format.

M. Ishaq Nadiri
Jay Gould Professor of Economics
New York University

PREFACE

There are several distinct talents that an economist can have: he can be an original and creative thinker and model builder; he can be a master expositor who has the ability to explain complex issues incisively on an intuitive level; or he can be a policy analyst who is conscious of the real world and its relationship to economic theory. Few economists develop even one of these talents to the extent necessary to make a major contribution to economic science. William J. Baumol has mastered them all.

The multiple talents of this economist are evident in each of the papers in this volume. The papers span theory, application, and policy, and cover the fields of welfare economics, economic dynamics, mathematical programming, theory of financial and business behavior, and doctrinal history. The selections are arranged chronologically within fields; we discuss them by tracing several of Baumol's most compelling ideas over time and across fields.

His earliest contributions were in assessing the impact of external effects in our economy. The paper "Community Indifference" formed the core of his Ph.D. dissertation. The work delineates conditions under which economic agents are or are not led by their self interest to act in a manner that is consistent with the maximization of the welfare of the group taken as a whole. In cases where activities of members of a community depend or impinge upon one another, it is shown that governmental action in the form of pricing and taxation policies may well benefit the individual agents by helping them attain their own ends.

The functioning of economic systems subject to external effects was later studied in the context of decentralization of decision making in planned economies and in business firms when there are externalities in production. The circumstances under which prices can act as an automatic motivation mechanism, and those under which other allocation rules must be imposed, are outlined in "Decomposition, Pricing for Decentralization and External Economies." Both it and "The Dual in Nonlinear Programming and its Economic Interpretation" offer lucid interpretations of duality theory as it relates to economics. These papers are among several articles which did much to hasten the spread of mathematical programming techniques among economists. The papers, although difficult, exhibit the clear exposition of technical material that has made Baumol without peer in his ability to disseminate mathematical models and methods to the profession.

More recently, Baumol has become interested in externalities as a key issue in environmental policy. In "On Taxation and the Control of Externalities," attention is directed to those externalities, such as pollution, where negotiation between the polluters and those who are harmed by the pollutants is not feasible. As a matter of theory, it is proved that, under pure competition, optimal resource allocation results if a Pigouvian tax is levied upon the polluter. No compensation to or taxation of those affected by the externality is required. A practical two-step policy procedure using standards and charges is advanced. The procedure, while not a theoretical ideal, is designed to insure that pollutants are reduced to any prespecified level in an economically efficient manner.

The recognition that economic agents must often settle for second-best is evident as well in "Optimal Departures from Marginal Cost Pricing." Since marginal cost pricing results in financial losses to firms with increasing returns, pricing principles are derived which have the feature that they achieve viability for the firm at the least social cost. The article is a prime example of Baumol's interpretive skill and his ability simultaneously to review, contribute to, and popularize an area of economics research.

Baumol's pioneering work in dynamic analysis contains several recurring themes. One message, illustrated in "Pitfalls in Contracyclical Policies: Some Tools and Results," is that common sense may be a dangerous and misleading tool when applying economic theory to the policy arena. Dynamic and external effects can so complicate the economic interrelationships that practical judgment may prove unreliable. Another message to be learned from incorporating economic dynamics into analytical models is that it is dynamics, not statics, which explains many current social problems. For example, "The Dynamics of Urban Problems in its Policy Implications" describes a feedback phenomenon under which deterioration in public services may lead to an exodus of wealthier families from urban areas which, in turn, erodes the tax base and leads to further deterioration—thus, the urban decay.

The article "Macroeconomics of Unbalanced Growth: The Anatomy of Urban Crisis" contains one of Baumol's most influential ideas. The idea, which encompasses both dynamic effects and welfare theory, is that technical change and productivity gains are at best sporadic in areas of the economy that provide personal services such as education, performing arts, fine cuisine, and police protection. Thus, we can expect these activities to exhibit rising costs relative to those of the technically progressive industries. More specifically, wages adjust across markets and tend to follow the rate of productivity increases in the productive sector; hence, there is continual financial strain in the provision of those services where productivity is constant. A practical application of this unbalanced growth hypothesis is discussed in "On the Performing Arts: The Anatomy of their Economic Problems."[1]

In addition to important contributions in welfare theory, dynamic analysis, and mathematical programming, Baumol is renowned for his work in the modeling of business and financial activity. His special talent is in expanding traditional models to include the sorts of business objectives, investment decisions, and transactions costs that actually occur in reality. Where optimality is possible, he provides decision makers with the appropriate marginal tools for use in their decision making processes. Where optimality is not possible, sensible "Rules of Thumb and Optimally Imperfect Decisions" are suggested that can be used in meeting governmental responsibility and in the running of business enterprise.

In the paper "On The Theory of Oligopoly," oligopolistic firms are portrayed not as maximizers of total profit, but instead as maximizers of gross revenue (or sales, as

[1]This paper, and several others in the volume, display Baumol's interest in the economics of cultural activities. This interest doubtlessly stems at least in part from the fact that he is, in private life, a painter and sculptor of considerable skill.

businessmen would call them) subject to the constraint that profits be at some acceptable level. The more realistic model of business objectives is shown to imply behavioral predictions that have more plausibility than those which arise under the pure profit objective. Baumol's most widely cited paper, "The Transactions Demand for Cash: An Inventory Theoretic Approach" adds a realistic element to models of budget management in firms and households. It recognizes that there are transactions costs in converting assets into cash, and explores ways in which these costs affect corporate and individual decision making.

In "Input Choices and Rate-of-Return Regulation: An Overview of the Discussion" Baumol reviews the proposition that rate-of-return regulation gives the monopoly firm an incentive to use to much capital relative to labor in production. This paper, which interleaves graphical methods of explanation and proof with mathematical techniques, also provides such substantial extensions of the theory that it has become a major building block for further work in the area.

The final section of this volume includes two papers which emphasize doctrinal aspects of economics. The first "The Classical Monetary Theory: The Outcome of the Discussion" contends that allegations that the classics (such as Walras, Pareto and Wicksell) had mishandled monetary theory are largely unfounded. The paper "The Transformation of Values: What Marx 'Really' Meant", seeks to convince the reader that many of the traps that economists have fallen into while trying to reconcile the relevant portions of Volumes I and III of *Das Capital* were deliberately set by Marx himself: for although Marx had his transformation analysis worked out before Volume I was completed, he quite deliberately withheld treatment of the issue there.

This brief guide to Baumol's selected writings has only touched the surface of a rich terrain. It is the papers themselves which provide the ultimate proof of the variety, depth, and importance of the writing of this influential scholar.

Acknowledgments

I am grateful to my colleagues, Ishaq Nadiri, Richard Quandt, Andrew Schotter, Peter Steiner, and Edward Zajac for their extremely helpful comments and suggestions, and to Florangela Arango for her preparation of the index.

Elizabeth E. Bailey
Little Silver, N.J.
March, 1976

CONTENTS

PART ONE

WELFARE ECONOMICS

[1]

Community Indifference

In seeking to develop propositions of universal applicability, writers on welfare economics have always encountered a stumbling block in the problem of interpersonal comparisons of well being. Even when viewed with a predominantly utilitarian bias, judgment of the desirability of any phenomenon was usually precluded by the absence of an objective standard which would permit the counter-balancing of the desirable with the undesirable effects.

Recently Mr. Kaldor[1] proposed a device which, it was hoped, would resolve this difficulty in many cases. Roughly, under the terms of Mr. Kaldor's suggestion, any potential innovation should be subjected to the following test. All persons who would suffer deleterious effects as a result of the innovation would be asked how much (in money terms) they should consider the minimum amount necessary to compensate them for the inconvenience to which the innovation put them. Similarly, all persons who would benefit from the innovation would be asked to estimate how much money they should be willing to give up rather than forego the benefits to be obtained. The innovation would be judged socially desirable so long as the latter sum was greater than the former. Of course, in practice, the market would in many cases permit these quantities to be estimated conveniently without the difficulties suggested by the above wording.

The essence of Mr. Kaldor's innovation is found in the assertion that the community can be considered to be indifferent to an innovation (its real income can be considered unchanged) " . . . if supposing that those who are worse off were exactly compensated for their loss by those who are better off, this re-distribution of incomes would leave the real income of everyone the same as before."[2] Observe that the condition does not require that the compensation actually be made.

In the words of Dr. Hicks, " A ' permitted reorganization ' must be taken . . . to mean one which will *allow* of compensation being paid, and which will yet show a net advantage. The position is not optimum so long as such reorganization is possible."[3] It is Dr. Hicks' opinion that this suggestion has rendered secure the objective foundation of welfare economics, having completely answered the objections of Prof. Robbins[4] and Mr. Harrod.[5] In Dr. Hicks' opinion, welfare economics is now rendered acceptable to the positivist so that it is no longer true that " One's welfare economics will inevitably be different according as one is a liberal or a socialist, a nationalist or an internationalist, a christian or a pagan."[6]

Now it is true, as Dr. Hicks suggests, that where a " permitted reorganization " is possible the community could, so to speak, do better for itself. The absence of such a possibility is clearly necessary in order that the situation be in some sense optimum. We have achieved this much tautologically by approving a change which harms no one and is desired by some. But this negative result by itself is an inadequate foundation for an economics of welfare which is usually required to answer such specific questions as: Is a certain tax desirable under the circumstances? or, should the corn laws actually have been abolished? But caution is here required in applying Mr. Kaldor's principle, for while it contains a necessary condition it is by no means sufficient founda-

[1] Nicholas Kaldor, " Welfare Propositions in Economics," *Economic Journal*, Sept., 1939, pp. 549–52

[2] Kaldor, " A Note on Tariff and the Terms of Trade," *Economica*, November, 1940, pp. 377–8.

[3] J. R. Hicks, " The Foundations of Welfare Economics," *Economic Journal*, December, 1939, p. 706. My italics.

[4] Lionel Robbins, " Interpersonal Comparisons of Utility : A Comment," *Economic Journal*, December, 1938, pp. 635–41.

[5] R. F. Harrod, " The Scope and Method of Economics," *Economic Journal*, September, 1938, pp. 389–97

[6] Hicks, op. cit., p. 696.

tion for an economic optimum. Thus I believe it is quite possible to conceive of " permitted reorganizations " which (it can be argued on utilitarian but non-economic grounds) leave the community as a whole in a worse state than before. And I maintain, moreover, that only by assuming some criterion for the interpersonal comparison of utility can we always distinguish the sheep from the goats—the desirable from the undesirable " permitted reorganizations ".

It is the contention of this paper that the approach suggested by the community indifference method, while advancing us in some respects, does not always eliminate the problem involved in interpersonal comparison of utility, and that the device described above is consistent with the complete elimination of this difficulty only in a limiting case which had long been recognized. In sum, it is maintained that application of the criterion requires somewhat more caution than the original expositions may have implied. I shall attempt to show, moreover, that in those cases where the criterion is valid with respect to its ethical frame of reference, the method of community indifference yields satisfactory results only to persons of utilitarian or quasi-utilitarian bias, and that the recommendations of the welfare economist must still rest ultimately upon the system of morality and ethics to which he adheres.

II. The applicability of Mr. Kaldor's device is, I believe, weakened by one crucial characteristic, namely that it does not require that persons injured by some economic phenomenon must *actually be compensated* in full by those who have gained from it. It is true that if, upon the establishment of any such innovation, not only were a survey made of the money value of gains and losses, but compensation was actually paid, then we would be justified in concluding from this transaction that no persons had lost and at least some persons had gained. In fact, we would be returning to Pareto's criterion : " Consider any position whatsoever, and suppose there is a very small departure from it, consistent with the circumstances of the case. If, as a result, the well being of everybody in the group is augmented, it is evident that the new position is preferable to everyone in the group, and *vice versa*, it is undesirable if the well being of everyone is diminished. The well being of some may, moreover, remain constant without affecting our conclusions . . . . It is these considerations which lead us to define a position as representing one of maximum ophelimity if it is such that it is impossible to depart from it by a small quantity in such a manner that all the ophelimity enjoyed by the individuals concerned increases or remains constant."[1]

But what if the compensation suggested (but not required) by Mr. Kaldor's criterion is not in fact made ? Are we justified in assuming that because the money measure of a gain to one set of individuals is greater than the money measure of the loss to a *different* set of individuals, that society as a whole has indeed benefited ? To take a crude illustration, let us assume that all the persons who gain from an innovation are very rich whereas all the losers are in a highly impoverished state. Is it then reasonable to assume that the subjective value of money does not vary from one group to the other ? I think it is clear that under the assumption of the utilitarian ethic to which most economists (including myself) are to some extent subject, the fact that the richer group has gained (in money terms) slightly more than the poorer group has lost is meagre evidence that there has indeed been a balancing between satisfactions and dissatisfactions. Indeed, it seems very likely that the same amount of money might well represent a much greater loss to the poorer group than the corresponding gain to the richer.[2]

[1] Vilfredo Pareto, *Manuel d'Economie Politique*, 2nd edition, pp. 617–8. My translation. Cf. however Wicksell's objections as to the insufficiency of this criterion, *Lectures on Political Economy*, Vol. I, pp. 82–3.

[2] Compare Marshall, *Principles of Economics*, 8th edition, p. 130, " . . . a pound's worth of satisfaction to an ordinary poor man is a much greater thing than a pound's worth of satisfaction to an ordinary rich man. . . ."

It turns out then that Mr. Kaldor's criterion in its most general sense has not eliminated the problem of interpersonal comparison of utility. It has only subjected utility to the measuring rod of money, a measuring rod which bends, stretches, and ultimately falls to pieces in our hands. It is my belief, then, that we are not entitled to say that merely because one group is *willing* to compensate another for any inconvenience caused to the latter, the positivist economist can lend this transaction his unqualified approval.

Though related to it, this is not the same point as that made in T. de Scitovszky's article[1] which points out that because of Mr. Kaldor's resort to this flexible yardstick, his criterion as originally stated may give inconsistent results when the gain from an innovation is compared to the loss from the elimination of that same innovation. Thus both the innovation and its elimination may turn out to be " permitted reorganizations ". This results from the possibility that the distribution of " wealth " may be so different in these two cases that in either case those who gain from the change will be more than able to compensate those who lose by it. The arguments of this note are meant to apply even to the restricted criterion proposed by Mr. de Scitovszky which would permit no conclusions to be drawn in those cases where the original criterion led to this type of inconsistency. For it is the contention of this note that a rubber yardstick is not necessarily trustworthy where its elasticity is insufficient to permit the conclusion that one distance is both greater and smaller than another.[2]

The difficulty stems from the fact that we have not discovered, at least as yet, any " objective " criterion for an optimum distribution of income, and in any problem in the field of welfare economics we are therefore forced to take the distribution of income as data about which the economist has no basis for any sort of recommendation. As soon as a redistribution of income is involved in some innovation, the economist is prevented from passing judgment upon the desirability of that innovation since he is unable to tell whether the change in distribution of income is good, bad or indifferent, or whether the importance of this latter effect is of sufficient magnitude to vitiate any other considerations which may have led to recommendation or rejection of the proposal.

One of the uses that has been suggested[3] for Mr. Kaldor's device is that it enables us to distinguish an increase from a decrease in total production. Thus we may on occasion be enabled to say, for example, that a reduction in tariffs will increase a nation's productive capacity[4]. This is, of course, subject to the proviso that we define an increase in the nation's production to mean any change which falls within the category of Dr. Hicks' " permitted reorganizations ". This transformation seems to

[1] " A Note on Welfare Propositions in Economics," Review of Economic Studies, November, 1941, pp. 77–88.

[2] Mr. de Scitovszky does, however, briefly consider the point now being argued. He states, " . . . it might be argued that the abolition of the corn laws should not have been advocated by economists in their capacity of pure economists without advocating at the same time the full compensation of landowners out of taxes levied on those favoured by the cheapening of corn. Yet in a sense, and regarded from a long run point of view, such propositions are not independent of value judgments between alternative income distributions either. For, going out of their way to preserve the existing distribution of income, they imply a preference for the *status quo*." (Op. cit., p. 79).

But, of course, it is not my argument that the *status quo* should be preserved, or that the economist *should*, in fact, always recommend full compensation. But I do claim that *qua* positivist he can only differentiate between an improvement and a deterioration in general welfare. When compensation is, in fact, made in order to be able to distinguish an improvement in the general case and indeed to decide what should be done about compensation, he must resort tacitly or explicitly to his political postulates which include among them a criterion for interpersonal comparison of utility. It is, in fact, my contention that the criterion under discussion is the one which exhibits a predilection for the distributive *status quo*, in that it is weighted by the " compensating power " of the individuals involved.

[3] This point was brought to my attention by Prof. Robbins.

[4] Cf. Mr. Kaldor's discussion of the classical argument on the repeal of the corn laws, " Welfare Propositions in Economics," p. 550.

fall outside the range of the problems of welfare economics, regardless of the attitude one may have concerning the method of tautology. For clearly it is precisely the argument of this paper that we are not justified in taking an increase in production, so defined, to constitute (necessarily) an unmixed blessing. To a statement professing no more than a prediction as to the course of this " production", the welfare economist may be justified in responding, So what.

Yet we cannot leave the matter thus. Mr. Kaldor's criterion does provide the ground for an important advantage which stems from a recognition that welfare can conveniently be said to depend on two elements, the level of production and the distribution of the product. Granting that, as maintained above, there exists no positive ground for preferring any one distribution as against another, Mr. Kaldor's suggestion would lead to increased emphasis on and consideration of the residual problem, production, on which we are not so circumscribed.

But even this is not straightforward. If there were but one homogeneous product we should know exactly what was meant by an increase or decrease in production. However, this is not so clear in the multi-commodity economy, and Mr. Kaldor's criterion is offered to fill the breech. Although it enables us to pass final judgment on problems of welfare economics only in the special cases considered above, it is necessary to enable us to pass any judgment at all in many of these problems, even after we have decided on some standard for an evaluation of the distributive system.[1]

III. The applicability (to utilitarians) of this proposed criterion of welfare economics is thus, I believe, roughly circumscribed to where it amounts to no more than the older and previously well recognized criterion requiring that some people gain and no one loses from an innovation before the economist's blessing can be bestowed upon it. There remains the question of whether, thus limited, the principle is of universal validity and independent of ethical preconceptions. Can we indeed agree with Dr. Hicks' implication that this principle will be equally acceptable to " . . . a liberal or a socialist, a nationalist or an internationalist, a christian or a pagan " ?

What I take Dr. Hicks to imply is that this principle enables two different persons, irrespective of each one's ethical bias, to take a given set of data, engage in a set of formal manipulations with this data, and in those cases where the criterion does apply, arrive at identical conclusions as to the desirability or undesirability of the phenomenon under consideration. This is, of course, subject to the proviso that both individuals are willing to accept the facts as given and are both agreed as to the formal manipulations permitted by the rules of logic. But can we in fact accept Dr. Hicks' implication ? Surely it is possible that Professor Robbins' Brahmin[2], not being afflicted with the peculiar preconceptions of neo-Benthamism, might resent the type of arrangement whereby the untouchable in question found his material status improved while he, the Brahmin, was in no way benefited.[3]

Moreover, I see no way of reconciling our criterion with the preconceptions of Auguste Walras, for example, who in defending the morality of a concept of value based on the scarcity of goods and services (note that he felt called upon to defend it), wrote, " Limitation of certain useful things is undoubtedly part of the universal order, and worthily plays the role assigned to it by the author of nature. If God had wanted all

[1] It should not be taken that I am here arguing that Mr. Kaldor implied in his original note that welfare was unaffected by distribution. That is clearly not the case. I maintain merely that the severe limitations on a welfare economics with no basic premises as to the desirability of a system of distribution bear more emphasis than the wording of the articles here considered suggest.

[2] Op. cit., p. 636.

[3] It may be objected that our criterion can be interpreted so as to avoid this stricture, for we might say that the displeasure suffered by the Brahmin at the increase in proximity of the other's station to his own means that while the untouchable gained, the Brahmin necessarily lost in the transaction, so that our criterion is only partly satisfied.

our wants to be supplied by unlimited quantities of goods, he would undoubtedly have been able to arrange this : and since He made other arrangements, one must believe that He had a purpose in so doing . . . "[1]. It is, I believe, sufficiently clear that where some proposal sanctioned by our criterion were to come in conflict with what someone with preconceptions similar to Walras' believed to be the universal order, there would exist no basis for agreement despite common acceptance of the facts and rules of formal manipulation.

I doubt whether it is necessary to cite examples from the philosophers[2] to further corroborate these views.

We have, I believe, no choice but to return to Professor Robbins' view that, " The analysis of the effects of a small tax on particular prices and quantities of particular products[3] would rest upon scientific demonstration. But according as Maine's Brahmin or Bentham, Hitler or St. Paul, laid down the postulates of interpersonal comparison[4], the valuation of these effects in terms of social welfare would be diferent."[5]

May it not sometimes be better, then, to begin by setting out our " political postulates " boldly and proceeding from there ? If nothing else, this procedure would relieve us of the burden of (unattainable) proof and replace it in the lap of the positivist philosopher.

New York and London. WILLIAM J. BAUMOL.

[1] Auguste Walras, *De La Nature de la Richesse et de l'Origine de la Valeur*, Nouvelle edition, 1938, p. 128. My translation.

[2] For example, see Nietzsche, *Beyond Good and Evil*, Chapter VII, Section 225.

[3] And, I might add, upon particular people or groups of people.

[4] Or indeed the very definition of social utility.

[5] Robbins, op. cit., p. 637.

[2]

The Community Indifference Map: A Construction[1]

I

Before we can feel at all satisfied with the use of community indifference technique, even allowing for restrictions on its interpretation,[2] we must be able to show how one can construct the map given all the information about the tastes of the members of the community which indifference analysis considers admissible, i.e. the indifference maps of all the individuals constituting that community.

I do not pretend that the construction here presented is the only one possible. I do believe, however, that it comes as close as possible to the views implicit in the standard welfare analysis. Within limits it also results in an apparatus which is applicable to the analysis of the market and some problems in the theory of value in general, and also, presumably, to questions of international trade.[3]

Unfortunately, I have not been successful in attempting to simplify the argument, and must therefore beg the reader to bear with me through some fairly heavy going.[4]

In the diagram I assume for simplicity that we are in a two-commodity world, but the discussion, as will be seen, is perfectly general in this respect. I also assume:

(1) that the totality of the goods in existence at any given time is uniquely distributed (allocated) among the members of the community by the market;

(2) that within the relevant range none of the goods in question is consumed to satiety, i.e. any consumer prefers to have more of any good;

(3) that the demand side of the market for finished products is in every sense perfect; and

(4) that there are no external economies or diseconomies of consumption, i.e. that the satisfaction any consumer derives from a given set of commodities is in no way affected by anyone else's consumption.

Assumption (1), which is crucial, can perhaps be better viewed as the resultant of the premises that the market structure and the economic functions and initial holdings of wealth of every individual are given. Thus, when a specific set of outputs is produced by the community, there will be a unique function undertaken by, and remuneration accruing to each individual, and that remuneration will presumably be spent (exchanged) by him in a way perfectly determined by his scale of preferences and the state of the market (which itself depends on the behaviour and tastes of other consumers). But we are running ahead of our story.

[1] My sincere thanks are due to Dr. Finch, Mr. Hahn and Mr. Graaff for their most valuable advice and criticism.

[2] See my paper "Community Indifference," this journal, Vol. XIV, No. 1, 1946–7.

[3] I believe I have been able to show this by example in an unpublished paper. Here we do come upon Mr. Little's objection (I. M. D. Little: "A Reformulation of the Theory of Consumer's Behaviour," *Oxford Economic Papers*, January, 1949) that unless we are dealing with problems of welfare economics, as I was when I developed this construction, we would need some sort of "community behaviour curves" analogous to his consumer behaviour curves, rather than indifference curves.

[4] Professor Scitovszky in "A Note on Welfare Propositions in Economics," Review of Economic Studies, 1941, does present a more elegant method which can be applied to the constructions of the community indifference map in a two-person community (by superimposition of their indifference maps with one of the maps overturned), but the method here employed applies to a community with any finite number of members.

Suppose, for illustrative purposes, that there are two individuals in the community. Let[1] the relevant portions of their individual indifference maps be indicated in Figs. IB and IC, and let the total quantities of x and y in the community be indicated in Fig. IA. Then by assumption (I), to every point in Fig. IA (e.g. point Aa) there correspond unique points Ab and Ac in Figs. IB and IC respectively, representing the quantities of x and y which fall into the hands of each of the members of the community. The abscissa and ordinate of Aa are, of course, respectively equal to the sum of the abscissæ and the sum of the ordinates of Ab and Ac.

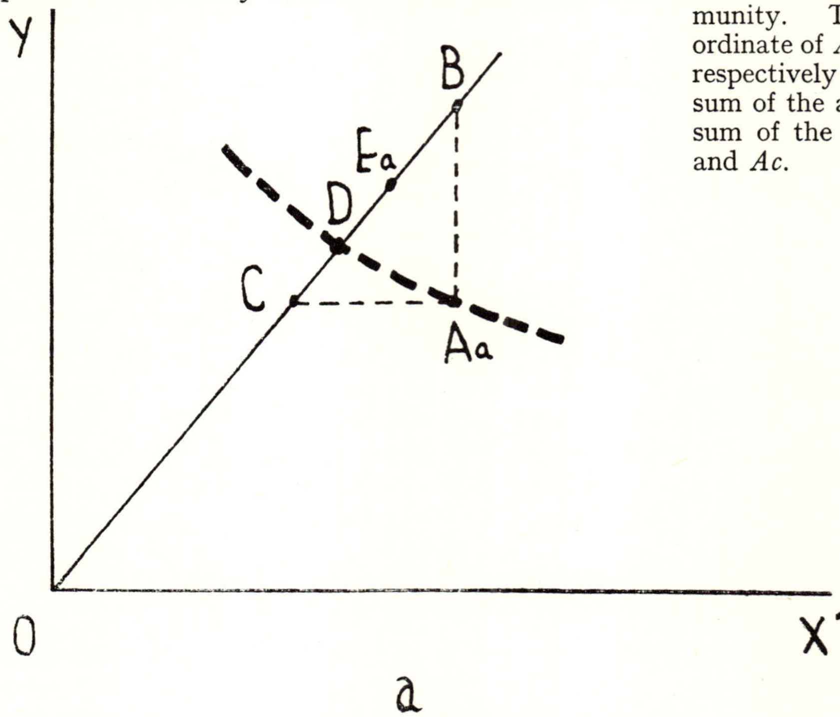

FIG. IA

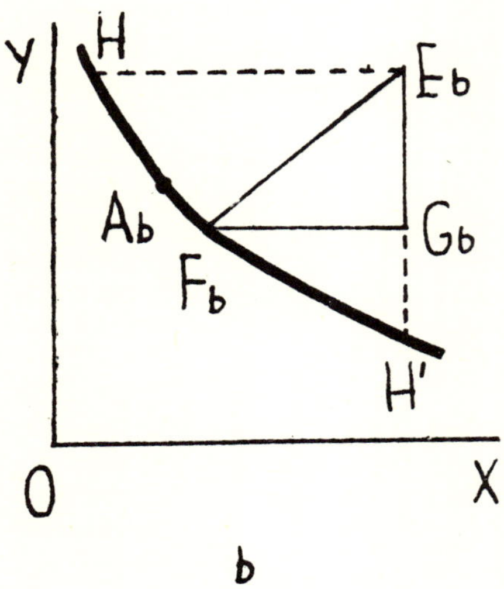

FIG. IB

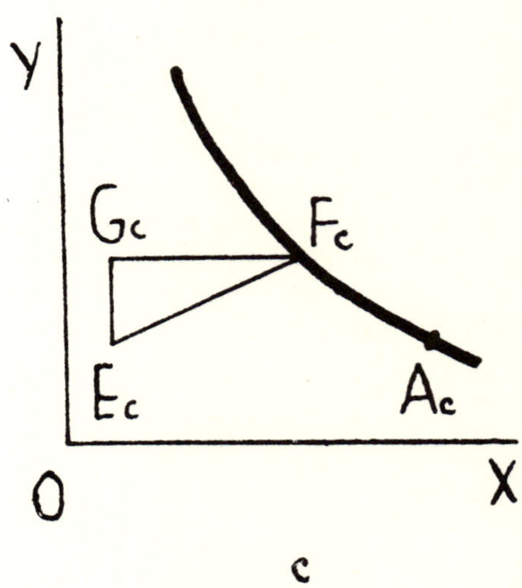

FIG. IC

[1] The reader may prefer to follow the discussion of the next few pages in the more general and somewhat neater algebraic form given in a note at the end of this paper.

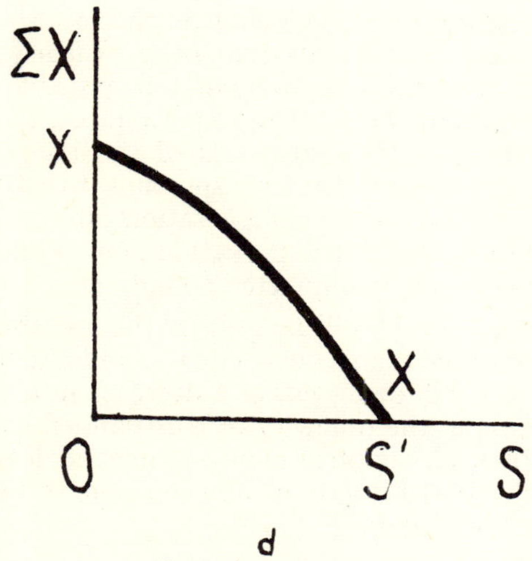

FIG. 1D

We may argue that the community may always be taken to prefer a larger to a smaller quantity of all commodities, for if the larger quantity were so distributed as to leave those who gain unable to compensate those who lose,[1] a return to the initial total quantities of each good can be arranged without loss to anyone concerned. This can be done by exchanges plus the temporary creation of stocks of the increments of the various goods. A strictly equal division of all the increments will then certainly (by assumption (2)) leave everyone better off. But this final arrangement could have been made by means of exchange among consumers, and by assumptions (3) and (4) would have been made at some stage in our perfect buyer's market. Thus an allocation of an increased quantity of all resources which does not leave the community better off is not possible if the allocation is determined by a market of the sort we are here considering. This proposition may be strengthened by analogous reasoning to cover the case where only some commodities increase in quantity, all others remaining fixed.

We may now proceed with the construction of our community indifference map. Draw the (individual's) indifference curves through *Ab* and *Ac*. In Fig. 1A draw any straight line *OL*, through the origin which does not go through point *Aa*. Then if point *B* is the point on *OL* either directly above or to the right of *Aa* (thus representing an increase in total holding of y with no change in quantity of x held, or vice versa), it follows that the community is better off on any point on *OL* further from the origin than is *B*. Similarly, if point *C* is the point on *OL* just to the left of or below *Aa*, the community must prefer *Aa* to the situation represented by any point on *OL* nearer to the origin than *C*. From this we may conclude (if we accept continuity) that there will be a point *D* on *OL* lying between *B* and *C* such that the community will be indifferent between *D* and *Aa*. From this, incidentally, follows the negative slope of the community indifference curve.

To find *D*, and here we come to the really tedious part of the proceedings, take any point *Ea* on *OL* between *B* and *C*. Let *Eb* in Fig. B and *Ec* in Fig. C represent the corresponding allocations to the members of the community.

In comparing two points, i.e. *Aa* and *Ea* in Fig. 1A, our problem is to find whether compensation can profitably be paid, just be paid or not be paid at all to those who lose in the change, out of the gains of those who benefit. Compensation may be paid in any commodity or combination of commodities.

Let us define an *individual's compensation offer* (positive or negative) as any set of commodities which taken from (given to) him after a change from which he gains (loses) will just offset his gain (loss). We then define a *compensation offer* to be *any* aggregate of individual compensation offers summed over the members of the community, e.g. if in a two-commodity (beer, tobacco), two-individual (1 and 2) community, the gainer, 1, is willing to offer (among other compensations) two gallons of beer and one pound of tobacco, and the loser, 2, is willing to accept one gallon of beer and

[1] This may occur, for example, if everyone receives goods of a sort for which he has little desire compared to those he had before.

C

one and a quarter pounds of tobacco in compensation for a given change, the totality of this information constitutes what is here called a compensation offer. Clearly, with any given change an infinite number of such compensation offers may be possible, and our problem is to find if *any* of these is acceptable, or more than acceptable, i.e. if any of these enables gainers to satisfy the compensation demands of the losers. Finally we define the *net compensation offer* of any commodity corresponding to any compensation offer to be the algebraic sum of the individual compensation offers of that commodity. Thus in the above illustration the net beer compensation offer is one gallon and the net tobacco compensation offer is minus one-quarter pound.

Now, the net compensation in any one commodity, y, will be greater the less the net amount offered of every other commodity, for other things being equal, a reduction in the net amount of some other commodity, x, offered means either a decrease in the quantity of x offered by the gainers, or an increase in the quantity of x demanded by losers, or both. Each person concerned must then either offer more or demand less of some other commodity than previously in order that his gain or loss continue to be just offset by his individual compensation offer (or demand).

If a compensation offer is to be acceptable, then in no case may the *net* compensation offer of any good fall below zero, i.e. compensation offers in *each* good must exceed or equal compensation demands.[1] It follows from this and the argument of the previous paragraph, that the total net quantity of y offered as compensation will be at a maximum, subject to the condition that the offer be acceptable only when the *net* quantity of every other commodity offered is zero.[2] The change in question must then leave the community better off, indifferent or worse off as the maximum net amount of y offered as compensation exceeds, equals or falls short of zero. For if it equals or falls short of zero, *all* other net offers being equal to zero, no other acceptable compensation offer can be arranged, since any increase of the net quantity of (say) x offered must involve a further decrease in the net offer of some other commodity.

The question is then: how can this maximum net offer of y be determined? We proceed to show that what is required is that the quantities of x and y offered (demanded) by each individual be such that his marginal rate of substitution of y for x (the ratio between the marginal utility of x and of y to him) be equal to that for any other individual. For if individual 1's marginal desire for x (as compared to his marginal desire for y) is greater than that of individual 2, and if 1 decreases and 2 increases his offer of x by exactly the same small amount, the offsetting decrease in 2's offer of y will be less than the offsetting increase in 1's offer of y. Thus where the marginal rate of substitution of x for y is not equal for all persons, the total net offer of y cannot be at a maximum since the net offer of y may be increased while the net offer of x remains unchanged.

[1] A minor qualification must be added here if there are inferior goods present. In the process of compensation payment the payers' desire for these may increase and the recipients' demand for them may fall, so that it may actually pay the recipients of compensation to give some of these inferior goods to the payers in return for increased compensation payments in other goods. Such an (acceptable) offer might be taken to involve a negative net compensation offer of the inferior good. If, however, we reinterpret the net compensation offer to mean the quantity of a good offered (no matter by whom) minus the quantity of that good demanded (no matter by whom), when payments and demands are of such a magnitude as to leave the recipient indifferent between his present and his initial state, then it may readily be verified that the argument holds without further modification.

[2] Note that this does *not* imply that no one offers or demands any commodity other than y. Clearly we do not want to prejudge the choice of commodities in which compensation will be paid; indeed it may be impossible to arrange for compensation in one commodity alone (e.g. in tobacco if all the losers are non-smokers), whereas it might be payable in some other commodity or combination of commodities. The net shoe compensation being zero means that shoe demands are just satisfied, and not that no shoes are offered or demanded at all.

The marginal rate of substitution is, of course, given by the slope of each individual's indifference curve at the relevant point. Consider the slope $S(Fb)$ of any point Fb on the individual's indifference curve which he may reach from Eb by paying or receiving an appropriate amount of compensation (Fb must then lie between H and H'). The amount of x here offered by the person in question is represented by $FbGb$ ($FbGb$ parallel to the x axis and perpendicular to $GbEb$).

Let Fc be the point on the indifference curve through Ac in Fig. 1C having the same slope $S(Fb)$. If Fc is a point which may be reached from Ec by receiving (paying) an appropriate amount of compensation, let the amount of x which must be paid to reach Fc from Ec be $FcGc$. Then $[FbGb - (+)\ FcGc]$ is the net amount of x offered corresponding to this slope of the indifference curves. Compare the net offer of x corresponding to every other relevant slope, S, of the indifference curves, similarly, and plot these against S in Fig. 1D (curve xx'). Let S_1 be the point at which xx' cuts the x axis. Then S_1 is the slope for which the total net offer of x is zero, and since the offers of y corresponding to S_1 are so chosen as to involve equality of marginal rate of substitution of y for x, the sum of these offers must be the maximum acceptable net offer of y. If, for the sake of illustration, $S_1 = S(Fb)$, then the maximum net payment of y will be $[GbEb - (+)\ GcEc]$.

If the algebraic sum of these lengths, taking distance below the relevant indifference curves to be negative, is positive, as in the case shown in the diagram, the community must be taken to prefer Ea to Aa, and we now know that D, the point of indifference with Aa on OL, lies between C and Ea. Repeating this process for a point H between C and Ea, we may locate D by successive approximation. The case where the sum of the lengths GE is negative may be handled analogously, and, of course, if that sum happens to be zero we need go no further; Ea must be the point (D) of indifference with Aa, on OL. The community indifference curve through Aa is obtained by connecting up points D on every upward sloping line, OL, through the origin, and the other community indifference curves may be constructed analogously.

II

It seems appropriate to add something on the possibility of the intersection of community indifference curves.[1] It may at first seem that this arises out of the possibility that the xx' curve in Fig. 1D crosses the axis more than once, i.e. that there is a multiplicity of payment arrangements possible consistent with our criterion, and that the result may vary depending on which of these we examine. But (provided the number of crossings, i.e. possible compensation arrangements, is finite) the community indifference criterion theoretically permits us to handle this case quite easily; for this criterion requires that we ask whether there is *any* way in which compensation is more than or is just payable. Thus, if for *any* of the intersections of the xx' curve with the axis, compensation is more than payable, point Ea is superior to Aa. If the "most favourable" point just permits payment of compensation the community is indifferent between Ea and Aa, etc. This is akin to another spurious source of indeterminacy—is it not possible that compensation could be paid in tobacco but not in beer? The answer (on which the construction is based) is that we must employ the "most favourable" commodity or combination of commodities, i.e. that permitting the greatest payment of compensation.

How then does intersection of community indifference curves arise? The essence of the matter arises out of the peculiarity of the basic definition of community

[1] See Scitovszky, op. cit.

indifference as I attempted to show in an earlier note.[1] However, the whole thing can be brought out much more clearly with the aid of Professor Samuelson's powerful device, the utility possibility curve.[2] Again, considering our economy composed of two individuals, let us indicate in Fig. 2 the state of welfare or utility of one individual, X, along the x axis, and that of the other, Y, along the vertical axis. It is not necessary for our purpose to be able to measure utility or welfare, for we insist merely that the index whereby we measure utility increases when the individual in question feels himself better off, decreases when he feels his welfare diminished, and otherwise remains unchanged.

Suppose now that in a given situation the possible combinations of the welfare of individuals X and Y, obtainable by modification of the system of distribution and nothing else, is shown by line AA'. The line is drawn in such a way that if the welfare position of X is given by ox, then xT is the best that can be done for Y under the circumstances. This is the utility possibility curve referred to above.

Suppose now that some change occurs such as the removal of a tariff, and that as a result our utility possibility curve shifts from AA' to BB' where the two lines intersect at P. Is the change in question desirable?

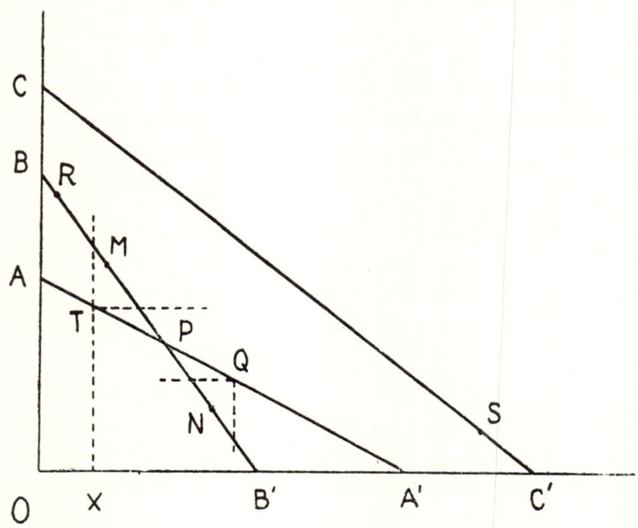

FIG. 2

If the initial situation is given by T, then the change is taken to be an improvement if there exists on the new utility possibility curve *any* point such as M which leaves both X and Y better off than before. For if there exists any such point it is always *possible* to make the change in a way which leaves both parties better off, i.e. by moving from T to M. Mr. Kaldor's community indifference criterion is that the possibility of a movement from T to M makes a change from T to any point on BB' an improvement, even a change to point N, which involves a loss to Y. This tacitly assumes all points on any utility possibility curve to be equally desirable, i.e. that the utility possibility curves are taken to be the indifference curves of the social welfare function. For then, if there exists any point such as M on BB' which is superior to point T by Pareto's criterion (i.e. it is an improvement from the point of view of both parties), then any other point on BB' must be superior to T.

If the change-over in question involves a movement from a point like T to a point like N, then by Kaldor's criterion the change from AA' to BB' is an improvement since there is a point M on BB' superior to T. But the change back from BB' to AA' is also an improvement since there is a point Q on AA' which is superior to N. Thus by Kaldor's criterion both the change and its elimination represent improvements. To eliminate the difficulty Scitovszky proposes to call the change an improvement

[1] See footnote [2], page 189.
[2] *The Foundations of Economic Analysis*, Chapter VIII, especially p. 243, et. seq. Cf. also his " Evaluation of Real National Income," *Oxford Economic Papers*, January, 1950.

only if the change from the first point is an improvement on Kaldor's criterion, and if, at the same time, the change back is undesirable on Kaldor's criterion. Thus if the change is from T to, say, R, it is an improvement on Scitovszky's criterion, since the movement from T to any point on BB' is an improvement on Kaldor's criterion, as before, but the movement from R to AA' is undesirable, since there are no points on AA' which leave both X and Y better off than they are at R. On the other hand, on the Scitovszky double criterion we can pass no judgment on a movement from T to N. Indeed, if my argument about the tacit assumption behind the Kaldor criterion is correct, the difficulty is not yet taken care of, for if all points on AA' are taken to be equally desirable and all points on BB' are equally desirable, we cannot, as we do, have point M on BB' superior to point T on AA', and at the same time point Q on AA' superior to point N on BB'. Thus, where the utility possibility curves intersect there is an implicit contradiction in the use of Mr. Kaldor's criterion; this because the curves are used as indifference curves. It is this implicit contradiction which seems to be the basic source of the intersection of community indifference curves. For there is no reason why the utility possibility curves corresponding to different situations should not intersect, and since these provide the implicit criterion of equivalent distributions of welfare on which the community indifference curves are based, it becomes possible for one situation to be simultaneously better and no better than another.[1]

THE ALGEBRAIC (m COMMODITY n PERSON) ARGUMENT

Let x_i represent the quantity of the ith commodity held by the community so that any set of goods held is given by $X = (x_1, \ldots, x_m)$. Given any such set $A = (a_1, \ldots, a_m)$, it is our object to find all other sets $D = (d_1, \ldots, d_m)$, such that the community is indifferent between A and D. To do this we seek a family of sets of quantities of the commodities (lines) such that:

(*a*) on every such line there is one and only one point D having the required property;

(*b*) every possible combination of commodities is included in one and only one set in the family (every point in the positive " octant " lies on one and only one such line); and

(*c*) there is a method for locating D on every line to any required degree of accuracy in a finite number of steps. We may then, by finding the points D corresponding to a sufficiently large number of the lines in our family, map out the locus of the D which is, of course, the community indifference hyper-surface through point A.

We assume (justification in terms of our basic definition being given in the text):

Proposition (1): for any two sets of commodities $C = (c_1, c_2, \ldots, c_m)$ and $B = (b_1, \ldots, b_m)$ B is preferred to C by the community if $c_i \leqq b_i$ $i = 1, \ldots, m$ and $c_j < b_j$ for some j.

The family of sets of quantities of commodities which will be shown to have

[1] The contradiction can, of course, be eliminated by confining the use of the criterion to changes which involve non-intersecting utility possibility curves, e.g. a change which moves the curve from BB' to CC' which may be defined an improvement. But even this leaves difficulties. Thus a change to point S on CC' represents an improvement in the position of X, and a deterioration in the position of Y as compared to the situation represented by point R. We can then only choose between S and R if we are prepared to follow Bergson and take a stand on how we believe welfare should be distributed.

the required properties is the family of lines through the origin and the positive "octant" given by the $m - 1$ equations:

$$k_i x_m = x_i,\ k_i > 0 \qquad i = 1, \ldots, m - 1 \qquad (1)$$

we obviously have:

Proposition (2): one and only one such line, L, goes through every point in the positive octant. Also,

Proposition (3): there can be no two points between which the community is indifferent on any such line, L; for assume C and B to be two such points. If $c_m = b_m$ then by (1) the points are identical. If on the other hand they are not equal, say $b_m > c_m$, then $b_i > c_i$ for all i (since $k_i > 0$) so that, by Proposition (1), B is preferred to C.

Now consider a line L given by (1) and not going through our given point, A. There must then be a u, $1 \leqq u \leqq m$ such that, for this line,

$$k_u a_m \neq a_u, \text{ i.e. } 1 \neq \frac{k_u a_m}{a_u} \qquad (2)$$

The m conditions $a_i = x_i$ determine m points on this line given by:

$$P_i = \left(\frac{k_1}{k_i} a_i, \frac{k_2}{k_i} a_i, \ldots, \frac{k_{m-1}}{k_i} a_i, \frac{a_i}{k_i}\right) \qquad (3)$$

I shall now show that there is one and only one point C among the P_i having the property:

$$c_i \leqq a_i \text{ for all } i, \qquad (4)$$

so that by (2) and Proposition (1), C is clearly inferior to A from the point of view of the community.

Proof: Let v be that value of u for which $\frac{k_u a_m}{a_u}$ in (2) assumes its maximum value.

(*i*) If $\frac{k_v a_m}{a_v} < 1$ then the point $P_m = (k_1 a_m, \ldots, k_{m-1} a_m, a_m)$ of the P_i in (3) clearly satisfies (4).

(*ii*) If $\frac{k_v a_m}{a_v} > 1$, then

$$\frac{k_v a_m}{a_v} \geqq \frac{k_i a_m}{a_i} \qquad (5)$$

for all i by definition of v, so that $Pv = \left(\frac{k_1}{k_v} av, \ldots, \frac{av}{kv}\right)$ in (3) satisfies (4), since we have from (5)

$$1 = \frac{\frac{k_v}{k_v} a_v}{av} \geqq \frac{\frac{k_i}{k_v} a_v}{a_i}, \text{ i.e. } \frac{k_i}{k_v} a_v \leqq a_i \text{ for all } i.$$

Thus there is a point, C, in the set (3) on line L, inferior to A.[1]

[1] Uniqueness is easily shown as follows: Let P_v and P_w both satisfy (3) and (4). Then $\frac{k_v}{k_w} a_v \leqq a_w$, by (4). If $\frac{k_v}{k_w} a_v < a_w$ then $\frac{k_w}{k_v} a_w > a_v$, contradicting the assertion that P_w satisfies (4). If, on the other hand $\frac{k_v}{k_w} a_w = a_v$ then $\frac{a_v}{k_v} = \frac{a_w}{k_w}$ and $P_w \equiv P_v$.

Similarly it can be shown that there is a unique point, B, satisfying (3) which is clearly superior to A. Thus if we assume continuity we have:

Proposition (4): There is a unique point D, on L between C and B such that the community is indifferent between A and D.

There remains but one step in our programme, i.e. the location of D on L. To do this we first take any point E between B and C on line L, given by (1), and attempt to find whether E is preferred to A, A is preferred to E, or whether the community is indifferent between them.

Let x_{ij} be the quantity of the jth commodity possessed by individual i. Then for every point $X = (x_1, \ldots, x_m)$ there are by assumption (1) in the text $(n-1)(m)$ functions.

$$x_{ij} = f_{ij}(x_i, \ldots, x_m) \qquad i = 1, \ldots, n-1,\ j = 1, \ldots, m \quad \ldots\ldots (6)$$

and the conditions

$$\sum_i x_{ij} = x_j \qquad j = 1, \ldots, m \quad \ldots\ldots (7)$$

uniquely distributing the m commodities among the n members of the community. (6) and (7) then give us the holdings a_{ij} and e_{ij} of every commodity, j, by each individual, i, at points A and E respectively. Now the ith individual's indifference map may be viewed as a function,

$$c_{im} = \phi_i (c_{i1}, \ldots, c_{im-1}, e_{i1}, \ldots, e_{im}, a_{i1}, \ldots, a_{im}) \quad \ldots\ldots (8)$$

giving the quantity, c_{im} of the mth commodity which i must give or receive, at E, after he has given c_{ij} of commodity j, in order to make him indifferent between E and A.

We desire to maximise Σc_{im}, subject to

$$\sum_i c_{ij} = 0 \qquad j \neq m \quad \ldots\ldots (9)$$

for reasons given in the text. This requires

$$\frac{\partial\left[\sum_i \phi_i - \sum_{ij} \lambda_j c_{ij}\right]}{\partial c_{ik}} = 0 \qquad k = 1, \ldots, m-1;\ i = 1, \ldots, n; \text{ or,}$$

$$\frac{\partial \phi_i}{\partial c_{ik}} = \lambda_k \quad \ldots\ldots (10)$$

for all i, $k \neq m$ where λ_k is a Lagrange multiplier. Condition (10) requires that the marginal rate of substitution of k for m be the same for all individuals, i. There is no point in going into the second order conditions needed to assure us that (9) and (10) give a true and unique maximum, though we may note that the second partial derivatives of (10) are all positive if diminishing marginal rates of substitution are assumed for all individuals' indifference maps, in which case the point is certainly not a minimum. (9) and (10) then give us nm conditions to solve for the nm compensation offers, c_{ij}, and we have by our basic definition:

E is preferred to A if $\Sigma c_{im} > 0$

A is preferred to E if $\Sigma c_{im} < 0$ and

the community is indifferent between A and E otherwise.

Thus, by successive approximation we can find the point D on L of Proposition (4) to any desired degree of accuracy. By rotating L we may then map out the community indifference hyper-surface through A, and our construction is complete.

Princeton University. WILLIAM J. BAUMOL.

[3]

THE ECONOMIC JOURNAL

DECEMBER 1958

THE CARDINAL UTILITY WHICH IS ORDINAL[1]

DESPITE the frequent disclaimers,[2] the phrasing of many of the discussions of the Neumann–Morgenstern utility index continues to invite reading into them the mistaken view that the utility index is, or is intended to be, just another device for measuring neoclassical introspective utility, and differs from the latter only in being defined exclusively for risky propositions. As one who once fell into this trap, I am perhaps oversensitive to this matter. In this paper, I attempt to make clear the nature of the N–M index and its distinction from the measure which plays so great a role in the neoclassical literature. I shall show, in fact, that in the neoclassicist's sense, the N–M index turns out to be just an ordinal measure.

First, let us try to see what use its inventors and their successors have made of this important device. It is *not* the purpose of the Neumann–Morgenstern utility index to set up any sort of measure of introspective pleasure intensity.[3] Such a measure of "strength of feelings" is totally unnecessary in the theory of games for which the N–M utility theory was constructed. Rather the utility measure was set up for purposes of calculation, or rather of prediction (in the subtler sense of the word) to permit the theorist to *determine in the absence of the player* which of several risky propositions the player will *prefer*. For the solution of a duopoly game must predict which strategy each player will choose (prefer), and the theory must therefore be able to predict how each player will rank risky[4] strategic decisions.

The theory makes this prediction not by measuring subjective utility but by assuming preference patterns for the individual, patterns which have sometimes been described as "rational." It is assumed (in any of several

[1] I am heavily indebted to William Bowen, Robert Dorfman, Robert Kuenne and Richard Quandt for their very helpful comments and suggestions.

[2] See, *e.g.*, Milton Friedman and L. J. Savage, "The Expected Utility Hypothesis and the Measurability of Utility," *Journal of Political Economy*, Vol. 60, 1952, esp. p. 473.

[3] This is documented in and should have been made clear by Ellsberg's excellent "Classical and Current Notions of 'Measurable Utility,'" ECONOMIC JOURNAL, Vol. LXIV, September 1954.

[4] Indeed the theory is constructed to a large extent to pave the way for the analysis of the "mixed strategy" into which the player himself introduces elements of risk partly to cloud his opponent's foresight.

sets of axiom systems) that the person's preferences are so structured that a limited number of observations will reveal his ranking of all the other relevant alternatives.

More specifically, suppose we are given two lottery tickets, one of which offers the prize *A* with probability *P* (so that there is probability $(1 - P)$ of being subjected to the loser's penalty, *B*). Let the corresponding elements of the other lottery ticket be *A′*, *B′* and *P′*. If this individual's mind works as required by the N–M axioms we should be able to predict correctly which of the lottery tickets he will prefer (choose) without having asked him his opinion of the two alternatives. Rather, as is shown in the Appendix, we need only inquire about his attitudes toward the prizes and penalties, *A*, *B*, *A′* and *B′*, and even these need be *ranked* only against an arbitrarily chosen imaginary lottery ticket which is used as a standard of comparison. In fact, these assertions hardly require proof—we have assumed that the person's mind works in such a consistent predictable pattern.

Then where does the " cardinal utility measurement " enter this matter? The answer is that the word " cardinal " has been used, misleadingly, to mean two entirely different things. One denotation is the introspective absolute marginal pleasure measurement which I have heard one well-known game theorist indignantly call " metaphysics." The other, game theoretic, use of the word " cardinality " is entirely operational. The prediction as to which of the two lottery tickets will be chosen is most conveniently made with the aid of a numerical calculation. We are given the person's ranking of the prizes and intend to predict from these data which ticket he will choose. We want to find numbers (cardinal utility measures) which permit us to make this prediction.

The problem is like that of finding two pieces of cloth in a shop which together are large enough to cover our table at home. We wish to predict which two pieces will do this without having to take them home, try them and return them for exchange if they turn out to be too short. Numbers can help us here. We know that a table 3 yards long can easily be covered by two cloths whose lengths are $1\frac{1}{2}$ yards and $2\frac{1}{4}$ yards. Similarly, Neumann and Morgenstern have shown us how to find numbers which can help us to predict the person's ranking of the two lottery tickets. This clever device is essentially what is meant by their cardinal utility measure.

But note that this is not cardinal utility in the old-fashioned sense. Not a word has been said about successive increments of some item yielding diminishing (or increasing) marginal joy. Indeed, in the old-fashioned sense the N–M index is a sheep in wolf's clothing—it is nothing but an ordinal measure, after all! For it has been used to predict, but to predict only *rankings* of lottery tickets!

What specifically is meant, then, when N–M utility is called " cardinal "? This (and the equivalent assertion that the measurement is unique up to a linear transformation, or that it permits two degrees of freedom) refers only to the predictive power of the index. This is best brought out by contrast with two less-powerful types of measurement scale.

The weakest type of index (one which conveys very little information) is one which serves only to *associate* items in two different collections. For example, persons in a newspaper group photograph are sometimes identified by placing a number next to each face and the same number beside the corresponding name in a list printed underneath. Here we set up the linguistic convention that any one man's name and face are given the same number. The numbers themselves do not matter and can be transformed in any way we like (we can exchange any number for another), provided no two faces bear the same number.

A ranking conveys somewhat more information, and in order to be able to transmit these data the numbers which measure them must be more circumscribed. To take the standard illustration, harder minerals are given higher numbers. The same information can be conveyed by any other set of numbers provided that we satisfy the linguistic convention that of two rocks the one with the higher number in the initial numbering also bears the higher subsequent number.[1] We say that the index which measures, or rather describes, a ranking is unique up to a monotone transformation.

Finally, we come to " cardinal measurement " which conveys still more information than did either of the other types of measure. It permits us, from what we know about two items in isolation, to *predict* something about them in combination. For example, our index of cloth length permitted us to predict whether two pieces of cloth of given lengths would cover a table whose dimensions are known without actually laying the pieces of cloth end to end. Here we have still less choice in the numbers which can convey the information. On the linguistic convention that we *add* lengths [2] the numbers which we assign to the lengths of any two pieces of cloth must add up to the number which we assign to the length they can cover together. This leaves us no more than two choices [3] (two degrees of freedom)

[1] Clearly other linguistic conventions might do—*softer* minerals might be given higher numbers.

[2] Here again we might use other conventions. Any process which uniquely assigns a third number to any two will do the trick. We might, for example, use logarithmic rulers with slide-rule scales and get used to multiplying lengths—10 in. and 5 in. = 50 in. But the point is that to convey information we must start off with some sort of language. We must first set up our linguistic conventions in any convenient way and then find the numbers which correctly convey the information in this language.

[3] Actually a length measure conveys even more information than this, and so we have only one choice in assigning numbers to lengths—we can only decide on a unit of length—whether we will measure in centimetres or in inches. The point is that in length we have a well defined zero. Mathematically, zero is defined as a number which when added to another leaves the latter unchanged. A non-existent piece of cloth (a piece of zero length) has an analogous (the mathematician calls it " isomorphic ") property. Hence in measuring length we have only one degree of freedom, the choice of unit of measurement, and a length measure is said to be unique up to a proportionate transformation. When measuring utility or temperature (without an absolute zero) we have two degrees of freedom—the choice of unit and the zero (freezing of water or some other point as in Fahrenheit measure), and hence these measures are said to be unique only up to a linear transformation.

in assigning these numbers. Once we call *A* " 3 yards " and *B* " 4 yards " we are forced to call *A* and *B* together " 7 yards," we are forced to call *A* and *B* and another piece like *A* " 10 yards " and so on. Similarly, in N–M utility measurement we want to assign to lottery-ticket prizes utility numbers which, when they are processed arithmetically in accord with the linguistic convention chosen,[1] will assign a utility number to the lottery ticket that ranks that lottery ticket correctly in relation to other possible tickets. And here again, once we pick such utility numbers for any two alternatives we are left no choice on the numbers to be assigned to other alternatives. This, then, is the sense in which the N–M utility measure is cardinal—it is richer in that it conveys more information than does an ordinary ranking obtained, for example, by directly asking any individual to state all his preferences. In effect, it is an economy device which requires an interviewer only to ask the subject to state *some* of his preferences—his ranking of lottery ticket prizes. With the aid of the N–M utility index (if it is applicable to this person) the interviewer can then *deduce* by himself the person's ranking of all other alternatives from the answers he has already received. But it must be emphasised that the N–M index still conveys information *only* about the individual's preference ordering.

But, it has been objected, the argument so far has only purported to indicate what its authors intended of the utility measure. Is it not possible that the index can do more, and measure marginal joy (or compare increments of satisfaction) as well? It is, after all, illegitimate to argue that Columbus failed to discover America by documenting his intention to find a new sea route to India.

Despite Professor Robertson's attempt to ascribe marginal subjective utility measurement powers to the index,[2] I shall argue that no such interpretation will do here. Such an interpretation must confuse marginal utility with another closely related concept, the marginal rate of substitution. We have long known that ordinal utility is perfectly compatible with the discovery of the *ratios* of the marginal utilities of two items (their marginal rate of substitution for one another). It is not the same to say that for me the marginal utility of apples is declining (a statement which to me has no operational meaning) and to say that I will offer successively smaller amounts

The linguistic convention employed by Neumann and Morgenstern is that utilities can be added actuarially, *e.g.*, given a lottery ticket which promises a prize *A* with probability of $\frac{1}{3}$ and the alternative *B* with the probability of $\frac{2}{3}$, the ticket's utility will be evaluated at $\frac{1}{3}$ the utility of *A* plus $\frac{2}{3}$ the utility of *B*. In the appendix to this article I show when this convention can convey the information required of it, *i.e.*, numbers assigned in this way will rank lottery tickets correctly in accord with a person's preferences.

We can then say that the N–M index is cardinal in the mathematical sense that it yields numbers which can in turn meaningfully be multiplied by probability numbers and added. But this addition is meaningful just in *predicting rankings* correctly, which is all it is intended to do.

[2] See D. H. Robertson, " Utility and all What? " ECONOMIC JOURNAL, Vol. LXIV, December 1954, esp. pp. 671 and 674–5.

of money for additions to my stock of apples. It would be completely naïve to try to measure the subjective old-fashioned " cardinal " joy of apple possession in money terms because money itself is not calibrated in utility terms and its utility cannot be assumed constant.

But an attempt to interpret the N–M index as an old-fashioned cardinal measure is naïve in precisely this way. The N–M construction, instead of asking " how much more money for an additional apple?", validly takes as its behavioural criterion " How much higher must be the probability of winning some prespecified prize in order to compensate me for not receiving an additional apple? " In effect, it deals not with the marginal utility of (say) income, but with the ordinalist's substitute, the marginal rate of substitution between (the ratios of the marginal utilities of) income and the probability of winning the prespecified prize. As it should be, this is good cardinal measurement only in the game theorist's useful sense. Only if we are prepared to assume that we know the behaviour of the denominator of the *MRS*, the marginal subjective utility of an increase in the probability of winning,[1] can we go on to make deductions about the marginal *subjective* utility of apples from N–M index data.

In any event, the N–M theory and this assumption are totally irrelevant for one another. The N–M index can serve its purpose (prediction of the ranking of lottery tickets) perfectly well without any such premise. Contrariwise, while an assumption of constancy (or some other known pattern) of the subjective marginal utility of the probability of winning, P, can give us a neoclassical index of subjective marginal utility, it can do so without recourse to any of the N–M apparatus. We need only multiply the marginal rate of substitution of apples for P by the marginal utility of P to obtain a figure for the marginal utility of apples.

William J. Baumol

Princeton University.

Appendix

The Neumann–Morgenstern Utility Measure

It may be worth deriving the statements on the N–M utility index which are made in the text, since no simple statement seems to be available in the literature.

[1] It may appear from the notation of the N–M index that this marginal utility is assumed to be constant. For, writing L for the standard lottery ticket, we have in the notation of the Appendix

$$U(L) = U[P : E, D] = PU(E) + (1 - P)U(D)$$

by the N–M linguistic convention (3), where $U(E)$ and $U(D)$ are the two constants whose choice is permitted by the index's two degrees of freedom. Hence the N–M marginal utility of P,

$$\frac{dU(L)}{dP} = U(E) - U(D) = \text{a constant}$$

In this theory there is, however, no reason to interpret the value of $dU(L)/dP$ as an index of the change in the individual's subjective pleasure. The constancy of $U(E) - U(D)$ is of no more significance than the use of a constant monetary unit—the dollar—when items are ranked in terms of money (which surely does not commit us to a belief in a constant subjective marginal utility of money).

First let us list a set of assumptions sufficient to assure predictability of the person's preferences:

To do this it is convenient to employ the following notation: For any alternatives A and B let $A \text{ I } B$ mean A is indifferent with B and for any alternatives A and B and any (probability) number P where $0 \leq P \leq 1$, let $[P : A, B]$ represent a lottery ticket which offers the probability P of obtaining prize A, and $1 - P$ of obtaining prize B. Using this notation, we may now list five assumptions about an individual's preference structure which suffice to assure that his preferences among lottery tickets will be predicted correctly by an N–M utility index:

> *Assumption 1. Transitivity:* If for this person $A \text{ I } B$ and $B \text{ I } C$, then $A \text{ I } C$.
>
> *Assumption 2. Continuity of Preference as a Function of P:* For any three outcomes E, A and D, if E is preferred to A and A is preferred to D, there exists a (probability) number P_a such that $0 < P_a < 1$ and $A \text{ I } [P_a : E, D]$.
>
> *Assumption 3. Independence:* If $A \text{ I } B$ then $[P : A, C] \text{ I } [P : B, C]$ for any C and any probability P. This states that if two investments involve equal probabilities of attaining outcomes which are different but are in themselves equally valuable, the two investments will be equally attractive.
>
> *Assumption 4.* For any alternatives E and D, and any probability numbers r and r', if E is preferred to D, then $[r : E, D]$ is preferred to $[r' : E, D]$, if and only if $r > r'$. This states that other things being equal, we will always prefer the investment opportunity with the greater probability of a favourable outcome.
>
> *Assumption 5. Compound Probability Arithmetic:* For any alternatives E and D and any probability numbers P, P_a and P_b,
>
> $$[P : [P_a : E, D], [P_b : E, D]] \text{ I } [r : E, D],$$
>
> where r is a probability number given by $r = PP_a + (1 - P)P_b$. This requires some explanation. The first bracketed expression represents a compound lottery ticket which offers the probability P of winning. If the ticket holder wins, however, rather than a definite prize he obtains another lottery ticket $[P_a : E, D]$. If he loses, he is given, instead, the inferior lottery ticket $[P_b : E, D]$, with the same prizes but poorer odds. What is the probability of eventually coming out of all this with the grand prize, E? There is a probability P of winning the better lottery ticket which offers E with probability P_a, so the probability of getting E in this way is PP_a. However, if he loses the first draw, a loss which will occur with probability $(1 - P)$, the ticket holder still has the probability P_b of getting E, so that there is a probability $(1 - P)P_b$ of his obtaining E in this way. The total probability of obtaining E is then $PP_a + (1 - P)P_b$.

We may now interpret this last assumption to say that the person's psychology is such that he will evaluate a compound lottery ticket in terms of the probabilities of winning the ultimate prizes.

It has sometimes been asserted that " rational persons " will behave as these five assumptions require, but we need not get into this dispute here.

Let us now choose some lottery ticket to be used as a standard against which other alternatives can be evaluated. It is convenient (but not necessary) to assume that this ticket offers to the winner eternal bliss (E) and to the loser damnation (D), so that any alternative, A, which we bring to be evaluated against this standard ticket will presumably be no better than E and no worse than D.

By assumption 2, for any such A, there will be a probability number $P_a (0 < P_a < 1)$ such that $A \text{ I} [P_a : E, D]$. We can now prove the following theorem: Given any two lottery tickets $[P : A, B]$ and $[P' : A', B']$ and a person whose preferences never violate assumptions 1–5, if we obtain (say by his introspection) the four probability numbers P_a, $P_{a'}$, P_b and $P_{b'}$ chosen so that

$$(1) \qquad A \text{ I } [P_a : E, D], \text{ and } B \text{ I } [P_b : E, D], \text{ etc.}$$

then from these numbers it is possible to predict which of the two lottery tickets will be preferred.

Proof: We begin by evaluating our first lottery ticket in terms of E and D.

$$[P : A, B] \text{ I } [P : [P_a : E, D], [P_b : E, D]] \quad \text{(by assumption 3)}$$

$$\therefore \qquad [P : A, B] \text{ I } [r : E, D] \quad \text{(assumptions 1 and 5)}$$

where r is the probability number $PP_a + (1 - P)P_b$. Similarly, the second lottery ticket can be evaluated in terms of E and D as

$$[P' : A', B'] \text{ I } [r' : E, D] \text{ where } r' = P'P_{a'} + (1 - P')P_{b'}.$$

Therefore, by assumption 4, the individual must prefer $[P : A, B]$ to $[P' : A', B']$ if and only if

$$(2) \qquad r = PP_a + (1 - P)P_b > P'P_{a'} + (1 - P')P_{b'} = r',$$

and he will be indifferent between these tickets if and only if $r = r'$. But by hypothesis, P, P' are numbers given by the terms of the two lottery tickets, and P_a, P_b, $P_{a'}$ and $P_{b'}$ were found out by observing or questioning our individual. r and r' can then be evaluated directly and the higher of these two numbers must, by assumption 4, correspond to the preferred lottery ticket. Q.E.D.

Let us now see how the N–M index is constructed and prove that it can be used to predict correctly the choice of lottery ticket. As already indicated, we employ the following linguistic convention (definition) for evaluating the "utility" of a lottery ticket in terms of the utilities of its prizes:

$$(3) \qquad U[P : A, B] = PU(A) + (1 - P)U(B)$$

That is, if $P = \frac{3}{4}$ so that the odds of winning are 3 to 1, then we evaluate the utility of the lottery ticket at $\frac{3}{4}$ the utility of victory plus $\frac{1}{4}$ the utility of defeat. But we note that this is only a convention. To show that it is usable we must first indicate how these utility numbers can be found and then we must prove that they must always assign a higher utility number to the preferred lottery ticket.

To see how the utility of any alternative, A, can be found we first assign arbitrary "utility" numbers

$$(4) \qquad U(E) > U(D)$$

to eternal bliss (E) and damnation (D) in our standard lottery ticket. Now we can find $U(A)$ by recalling (1) and defining

$$(5) \qquad U(A) = U[P_a : E, D], \; U(B) = U[P_b : E, D], \text{ etc.}$$

so that by (3)

$$U(A) = P_aU(E) + (1 - P_a)U(D), \text{ etc.}$$

Hence by finding P_a in (1) the utility number $U(A)$ can be computed.

Finally, I give a proof of the statement that these utility numbers rank lottery tickets correctly so that $U[P : A, B] > U[P' : A', B']$ if and only if the former is the preferred lottery ticket, *i.e.*, if and only if (2) holds.[1]

[1] The proof can easily be extended to the case of indifference.

Proof: The utility of the first lottery ticket is

$$
\begin{aligned}
U[P:A,B] &= PU(A) + (1-P)\,U(B) && \text{(by convention (3))}\\
&= PU[P_a:E,D] + (1-P)U[P_b:E,D] && \text{(by (1) and (5))}\\
&= P\{P_aU(E) + (1-P_a)U(D)\} + (1-P)\{P_bU(E) + (1-P_b)U(D)\} && \text{(by (3))};
\end{aligned}
$$

which, multiplying out and rearranging terms

$$
\begin{aligned}
&= \{PP_a + (1-P)P_b\}U(E) + \{P(1-P_a) + (1-P)(1-P_b)\}U(D)\\
&= \{PP_a + (1-P)P_b\}U(E) + \{1 - PP_a - (1-P)P_b\}U(D)\\
&= rU(E) + (1-r)U(D) \qquad (6)
\end{aligned}
$$

Similarly the utility of the second lottery ticket is

$$
U[P':A',B'] = r'U(E) + (1-r')U(D) \qquad (7)
$$

Thus comparing (6) and (7) we see that since by (4) $U(E) > U(D)$, the first lottery ticket will have the higher utility number if and only if $r > r'$. But we have just seen (2) that this condition also guarantees that that lottery ticket will be preferred. Thus we have proved that convention (3) will always assign a higher utility number to the preferred lottery ticket as we require.

[4]

ON THE PERFORMING ARTS: THE ANATOMY OF THEIR ECONOMIC PROBLEMS*

By W. J. BAUMOL *and* W. G. BOWEN
Princeton University

I. *The Setting*

Romanticism long ago fixed in our minds the idea that there is something inevitable about the association between artistic achievement and poverty. The starving artist has become a stereotype among whose overtones is the notion that squalor and misery are noble and inspiring. It is one of the happier attributes of our time that we have generally been disabused of this type of absurdity. We readily recognize that poverty is demeaning rather than inspiring—that instead of stimulating the artist it deprives him of the energy, time, or even the equipment with which to create or perform.

While we have come to accept the idea that artists are often impecunious, even a cursory encounter with the facts of the matter usually proves surprising. One may or may not see something shocking in the fact that the median total income in 1959 of males classified by the census as actors was $5,640; that for musicians and music teachers the comparable figure was $4,757; and that for dancers and dancing teachers, $3,483.[1] But one must recognize that these figures include income from all sources, some of them (e.g., truck driving, lobster fishing, waiting on tables) rather unrelated to the performer's art.[2] A detailed and specific investigation of economic conditions in the performing arts was conducted by Senate and House Committees in 1961 and 1962, and the volumes of *Hearings* which resulted are very

* This paper is based on a study being prepared by the authors for the Twentieth Century Fund, through the administrative channel of Mathematica. The study is still in progress, and this paper is nothing more than a brief introduction and a statement of certain theoretical ideas. The Fund has facilitated our work, not only by making generous financial provision for the extensive job of data collection and analysis which has been necessary, but also by helping to secure the cooperation of organizations and individuals and by allowing us full freedom to proceed as we wish. In the volume which will emerge from this study, we shall acknowledge our debt to the many people whose patient assistance has been essential to our work.

[1] U.S. Bureau of the Census, U.S. Census of Population: 1960, Subject Reports, *Occupational Characteristics,* Final Report PC(2)—7A, Table 25.

[2] As the Department of Labor's career guidance publication stresses: "Many performers . . . supplement their incomes by teaching, and thousands of others have to work much of the time in other occupations." (U.S. Dept. of Labor, Bureau of Labor Statistics, "Employment Outlook in the Performing Arts," Bulletin No. 1300-65, 1961, p. 214.) The BLS goes on to warn: ". . . the difficulty of earning a living as a performer is one of the facts young people should bear in mind in considering an artistic career" (*loc. cit.*).

revealing.[3] At that time the minimum weekly salary for Off-Broadway actors was $45 per week (it is currently $60); and what makes this figure significant is that most Off-Broadway actors are at the minimum. In such circumstances it is not difficult to see why Joseph Papp, producer of the New York Shakespeare Festival, was able to report that "banks and landlords consider him [the actor] a credit risk without visible means of support."[4]

Mrs. Helen Thompson, of the American Symphony Orchestra League, presented figures indicating that in 1961-62 the average salary paid to musicians in the twenty-six major orchestras in this country was $4,512; if the four highest-paying orchestras are excluded, the average for the remaining twenty-two major orchestras (again as of 1961-62) falls to $3,500.[5]

Dancers are in even worse financial circumstances, as illustrated by the case of a leading modern dance company whose members normally receive $25 after a trip which frequently includes four days of travel, a day of rehearsals, and a public performance.

In the main, performing artists are employed by organizations—by orchestras, opera and dance companies, producers and impresarios, resident theater companies—and the underlying economic pressures which manifest themselves in low performer salaries are transmitted through these organizations. Inadequate financial flows to these groups can threaten not only the welfare of individual performers but also the very existence of the institutions serving the entrepreneurial and managerial functions in the field of the performing arts. And, notwithstanding the publicity that has been given to the alleged "cultural boom" in America, we continue to hear frequently of theatrical groups which collapse, of opera houses whose seasons are in danger, and performing arts organizations of all kinds for whom financial emergency seems to have become a way of life. It is this situation and the threat that it poses for the cultural prospects of our society which constitutes the setting for the study we have undertaken.

The first objective of our study is to explain the strained economic circumstances which beset performing companies, to determine whether they are attributable mainly to fortuitous historical circumstances, to mismanagement or poor institutional arrangements, or whether there is something fundamental in the economic order which accounts

[3] U. S. House of Representatives, *Hearings Before the Select Subcommittee on Education of the Committee on Education and Labor,* "Economic Conditions in the Performing Arts," 87th Cong., 1st and 2nd Sess., 1962 (cited hereafter as "House Hearings"). U. S. Senate, *Hearings Before a Special Sub-Committee of the Committee on Labor and Public Welfare,* "Government and the Arts," 87th Cong., 2nd Sess., 1962.

[4] House *Hearings,* p. 111.

[5] House *Hearings,* p. 47.

for these difficulties. On the basis of our analysis we hope to produce some conditional forecasts of the financial future of the performing arts, the prospective costs, the operating revenues likely to be associated with various levels of activity, and the proportion of the resultant financial gaps which one can expect to be met from current sources of contributed income.

This session is intended to deal with theoretical matters and, while much of our work has been empirical, we welcome this opportunity to try to describe the basic economic relationships which seem to us to underlie the financial problems of the performing arts.

II. *Basic Economic Characteristics of Nonprofit Organizations*

Before we turn to the special economic properties of the performing arts, it is useful to devote some discussion to the economics of nonprofit-making organizations in general, for only in this way can the difficulties which beset the performing arts be seen in perspective.

Nonprofit organizations as a group share at least two characteristics: (1) they earn no pecuniary return on invested capital and (2) they claim to fulfill some social purpose. These two features are not wholly independent. Any group which sought to fulfill no social purpose and earned no financial return would presumably disappear from the landscape. Moreover, its goals themselves often help explain why no money is earned by such an organization. While an automobile producer may take pride in the quality of his cars, he is much less likely to regard product quality per se as an ultimate objective of the enterprise than is the head of a nonprofit organization. Nor is the auto producer likely to be nearly as concerned about the social composition of his clientele.

The significant point is that the objectives of the typical nonprofit organization are by their very nature designed to keep it constantly on the brink of financial catastrophe, for to such a group the quality of the services which it provides becomes an end in itself. Better research, more adequate hospital facilities, more generous rehearsal time, better training for those engaged in these activities—all these are not merely incidental desiderata. They are fundamental goals in themselves, and with objectives such as these, the likelihood of surplus funds is slim indeed. These goals constitute bottomless receptacles into which limitless funds can be poured. As soon as more money becomes available to a nonprofit organization, corresponding new uses can easily be found, and still other uses for which no financing has been provided will inevitably arise to take their place. Any lively nonprofit organization always has a group of projects which it cannot afford to undertake and for whose realization it looks hopefully to the future. Once this fundamental fact is grasped, it is hardly surprising that such groups feel themselves constantly strapped. It becomes clear that they are simply built that way.[6]

Nor is it just through its quality aspirations that the social goals of the nonprofit enterprise contribute to its financial difficulties. The concern of the typical nonprofit organization for the size and composition of its clientele often causes operating revenue to be lower than would be the case if services were priced to satisfy a simple profit-maximization goal. Since such a group normally considers itself to be a supplier of virtue, it is natural that it should seek to distribute its bounty as widely and as equitably as possible. The group is usually determined to prevent income and wealth alone from deciding who is to have priority in the consumption of its services. It wishes to offer its products to the needy and the deserving—to students, to the impecunious, to those initially not interested in consuming them, and to a variety of others to whom high prices would serve as an effective deterrent to consumption. In short, a low price for the product of a nonprofit group is normally an inevitable consequence of its objectives, and indeed sometimes becomes an article of faith. The ancient doctrine of "just price" is imbedded in the operations of these groups and carries with it all the difficulties which inevitably accompany an attempt to put it into practice.

The desire to provide a product of as high a quality as possible and to distribute the product in a manner other than that which maximizes revenue combine to produce a situation which is unusual in yet another respect. For such an enterprise a substantial increase in the demand for its product may well worsen the organization's financial health! Marginal costs may well exceed marginal revenues over the relevant interval. An increased number of student applications, an increased number of hospital patients, an increased number of orchestral performances may well increase the size of the contributions required for solvency. More generally, it follows that, contrary to widespread impressions, the much publicized cultural and educational "booms," whatever their composition, may in many cases prove a very mixed financial blessing.

Yet even in such circumstances the organizations cannot simply refuse to expand their activities in response to an increase in demand. By such a refusal the organization would renege on its fundamental

[6] The fact that any nonprofit organization can always find uses for a temporary excess of funds—and indeed may be embarrassed to report to its contributors that it has some money left at the end of the year—makes it very difficult to determine its cost functions. If an auto producer finds that a sudden increase in demand has swollen his receipts, he is only too happy to report higher profits; a nonprofit enterprise, however, may well use the extra revenue in a way which, in effect, deliberately raises it costs.

objectives, and, incidentally, it might even produce a loss in private and community support.

III. *The Performing Arts in Particular*

It is apparent that all of the standard problems of nonprofit organizations which have just been discussed beset the performing arts. It is not surprising, therefore, that the survival of the great majority of its organizations requires a constant flow of contributions. We can then easily understand why the arts find themselves in their present unhappy financial circumstances. But, up to this point, our discussion has offered no portents for the future. Here we don the inherited mantle of the dismal scientist and argue that one can read the prospects of the arts tomorrow in the economic structure which characterizes them today. The evidence will suggest that the prospects offer no grounds for complacency—that there are fundamental reasons to expect the financial strains which beset the performing arts organizations to increase, chronically, with the passage of time.

To understand the prospective developments on the cost side, it is necessary to digress briefly and consider in general terms the implications of differential rates of growth in productivity within the economy for the relative costs of its various outputs.[7] Let us think of an economy divided into two sectors: one in which productivity is rising and another where productivity is stable. As an illustration, let us suppose that where technological improvements are possible they lead to an increase in output per man-hour of 4 percent per annum, but that output per man-hour remains absolutely constant in the stable productivity sector. If these sectors are assigned equal weights in the construction of an economy-wide productivity index, the aggregate rate of increase in output per man-hour will be 2 percent per annum. For the moment let us assume that there is only one grade of labor, that labor is free to move back and forth between sectors, and that the real wage rate rises *pari passu* with the aggregate rate of change of productivity, at 2 percent per annum. Finally, let us suppose that the money supply and the level of aggregate demand are controlled in such a way that the price level is kept stable. Assuming that there are no changes in the shares of capital and labor, this means that money wages will also increase at the rate of 2 percent a year.

The implications of this simple model for costs in the two sectors are straightforward. In the rising productivity sector, output per man-

[7] There is, of course, nothing new in the following observations on the effects of differential rates of productivity change on costs and prices. See, e.g., Tibor and Ann Scitovsky, "What Price Economic Progress?" *Yale Rev.*, Autumn, 1959. Only its application to the state of the arts is novel.

hour increases more rapidly than the money wage rate and labor costs per unit must therefore decline. However, in the sector where productivity is stable, there is no offsetting improvement in output per man-hour, and so every increase in money wages is translated automatically into an equivalent increase in unit labor costs—2 percent per annum in our example. It should be noted that the extent of the increase in costs in the stable productivity sector varies directly with the economy-wide rate of increase in output per man-hour. The faster the general pace of technological advance, the greater will be the increase in the overall wage level and the greater the upward pressure on costs in those industries which do not enjoy increased productivity. Faster technological progress is no blessing for the laggards, at least as far as their costs are concerned.

It is apparent that the live performing arts belong to the stable productivity sector of our economy. The legitimate theater, the symphony orchestra, the chamber group, the opera, the dance—all can serve as textbook illustrations of activities offering little opportunity for major technological change. The output per man-hour of the violinist playing a Schubert quartet in a standard concert hall is relatively fixed, and it is fairly difficult to reduce the number of actors necessary for a performance of *Henry IV,* Part II.

Moreover, from the standpoint of long-term developments, the essence of the matter is not absolute or relative levels of productivity at a given date but the rates of change in productivity over time. This means that even if the arts could somehow manage to effect technological economies, they would not solve their long-term cost problem if such savings were once-and-for-all in nature. In order to join the ranks of the rising productivity industries, the arts would somehow have to learn not only to increase output per man-hour but to continue to do so into the indefinite future. Otherwise, they must at some juncture fall behind the technologically progressive industries and experience increases in costs which stem not from their own decisions but from the inexorable march of technological change in other parts of the economy.

True, some inefficiencies of operation are to be found in the field, and their elimination can help matters somewhat. Moreover, performing arts organizations can reduce the rate of increase in their unit costs by permitting some deterioration in the quality of their product—by fewer rehearsals, the use of more poorly trained performers, shoddy costumes and scenery. But such a course is never popular with organizations dedicated to quality, and, furthermore, it may lead to loss of audience and community support. Nevertheless, it is not an uncommon "temporary" expedient, imposed by the realization that the cutting of corners may be the only alternative to abandonment of the enterprise.

There is one other important avenue for cost saving open to the performing arts which has so far not been considered. We refer to wages paid performers. In the simple model sketched above, we postulated a situation in which a single, market-clearing wage was paid to all persons regardless of the industry in which they were employed. In actual fact, the live performing arts constitute a rather special labor market—a market in which the need for great native ability and extensive training limits the supply, but in which the psychic returns to those who meet these tests often offers a very substantial inducement to remain in the field. For these reasons, the performing arts are relatively insensitive to general wage trends, especially in the short run. It is largely for this reason that performing arts organizations in financial difficulty have often managed to shift part of their financial burden back to the performers—and to the managements, who also are generally very poorly paid by commercial standards. The level of the incomes in this general field must be considered remarkably low by any standards, and particularly so in light of the heavy investment that has often been made by the artists in their education, training, and equipment. And it is surely explained at least in part by the willingness of those who work in these fields to sacrifice money income for the less material pleasures of their participation in the arts.

However, there are limits to the financial sacrifices society can extract from the performers in exchange for psychic returns. One may reasonably expect that rising incomes in other sectors will ultimately produce untoward effects on the supply of talent. At what point this will occur depends partly on the income elasticity of the demand for psychic income. As the general level of real income rises, it may well be possible to persuade performers to accept a lower relative position in the income hierarchy. However, there are symptoms which suggest that, in some specialized areas, effects involving both quantity and quality are already being felt, though, overall, excess supply continues to be one of the market's most notable characteristics.

In sum, the cost structure of the performing arts organizations promises them no easier future. One might anticipate, therefore, that this structural problem would produce discernible effects on pricing policy. Certainly, in most of the industries in which productivity is stable, we would expect the price of the product or service to rise relative to the general price level. And there is a widespread impression that the arts have indeed behaved in accord with this anticipation—that ticket prices have been soaring. Yet our preliminary evidence suggests strongly that this view is incorrect and is largely a product of money illusion. Indeed, our preliminary data indicate that the rate of increase of ticket prices has barely managed to keep up with the price level and has lagged substantially behind increases in costs.

One might undertake to account for the surprisingly modest rate of increase in ticket prices in terms of a revenue maximization model—on the hypothesis that arts organizations believe the demand for their product to be highly elastic. We suspect, however, that a more valid explanation is the role of a doctrine of just price in the objectives of these organizations.

The tendency for increases in prices to lag behind increases in costs means simply that arts organizations have had to raise larger and larger sums from their contributors—and our analysis leads us to expect this trend to continue. Thus our analysis has offered us not only an explanation for the current state of affairs; it has also provided us with a basis for speculation about the future. What it has shown will not, we are afraid, be reassuring to those to whom ready availability of the arts constitutes an important objective of society. If our model is valid, and if, as may be suspected, there are limits to the amounts that can be obtained from private contributors, increased support from other sources will have to be found if the performing arts are to continue their present role in the cultural life of this country and especially if it is intended that they will expand their role and flourish.

[5]

INFORMED JUDGMENT, RIGOROUS THEORY AND PUBLIC POLICY

WILLIAM J. BAUMOL*

Princeton University

I. DIVIDING UP THE JOB

It has long been considered to be the better part of discretion to leave day by day and even year by year formulation of recommendations for public policy to the practical economists—men of long experience and great good judgment whose intimate acquaintance with the pertinent facts and whose reasoned approach is recognized and admired. The division of labor between the economist of this variety and the pure theorist (so far as public policy is concerned) has been somewhat like that described in the old saw about the pacific married couple in which the wife made only the unimportant decisions—she settled routine housekeeping issues such as the place for their vacation, and the make of their next automobile, while his were the world shaking decisions—what stand the family should take on the Soviet Union's relations to Cuba, on the proper amount of federal aid for urban mass transportation, etc.

Similarly, the welfare theorist has willingly accepted responsibility for the more fundamental policy matters: the building of pure models, the formulation of defensible definitions, the determination of just what one is entitled to say on policy without stepping outside one's role as economist, and even a painful and searching examination of the possibility that the economist might not be entitled to say anything at all on these subjects (except in the happy but possibly rare circumstance which can be judged with the aid of the Pareto criterion).

Meanwhile, the applied economist has simply gone ahead and given his advice, either because he was pleasantly unaware of the welfare theorist's fundamental doubts, or because he was prepared to sacrifice logical niceties to pressing current social needs. And it is difficult to take issue with this course so long as the theorist's doubts were grounded on considerations which on their face seem far removed from the exigencies of public needs. It is all very well to undertake a searching examination of the foundations of welfare economics, and in the long run a great deal that is of considerable value may emerge from such a study. But in the meantime, public policy cannot wait. Decisions must be made—whether with the aid of reasoned judgment, or willy-nilly by default, or as a by-product of political maneuver, these decisions will somehow be made. Given this, if the applied economist can in any way make himself useful, if he can provide advice which has probability or even plausibility in its favor, surely it should be offered though imperfections may somewhere mar its foundations.

No doubt most theorists will readily admit all this and it would be grossly unfair to depict them as quibbling naysayers who seek to undermine confidence in the pronouncements of their colleagues. Any such allegation is effectively belied by the willingness of many of our most prominent theorists to offer their own views on current matters to Congressional committees and before other public forums.

* This paper was originally given as an invited lecture at the 1964 meeting of the Southern Economic Association. I would like to acknowledge my gratitude to the National Science Foundation whose grant to our project, "The Dynamics of the Firm," greatly facilitated the completion of this paper. I also want to acknowledge my debt to my colleagues, Professors Bowen and Goldfeld, for their extremely helpful comments and suggestions.

But it is too much to expect this amicable state to continue without disturbance. The welfare theorist is and should be by nature a trouble maker who disturbs calm waters. His constitution requires him to question what is accepted and to cast doubt on standard operating procedures. And if he raises a sufficient number of questions, it is not unlikely that eventually he will strike pay dirt—he will hit upon issues which are not so easily dismissed. That is precisely what has occurred in the last few years. A number of theorists have produced results which raise very serious doubts about the reliability and utility of practical judgment in a number of important areas of public policy. These more or less abstract theorems seem to imply that plausible reasoning is a very dangerous thing, and that policy makers may, in many cases, be well advised to disregard the reasoned and apparently illuminating views of members of our profession. The allegations challenge the very usefulness of our discipline—in a word, from our point of view they are dynamite. And as such, it is a bit surprising that they have not received far more attention outside the literature of pure theory.

The remainder of my paper will be devoted to a description of these disturbing propositions, and to an evaluation of their implications for the practical economist's role. The theorems themselves are, of course, not new—they have been discussed in the standard journals over the course of the last few years. But so far as I know they have not previously been evaluated systematically and in a body.

II. SOME THEOREMS FOR SKEPTICS

Although it would be possible to cite other recent theoretical results which might raise doubts about many of the economist's judgments, it will suffice for our purposes to describe three such propositions and to point out the sorts of difficulties posed by each. One of these theorems examines the policy implications of external economies and diseconomies and shows that the simple policy measures which had been thought appropriate in their presence may have unpleasant unforeseen consequences. A second and probably more significant theorem (or set of theorems) raises serious questions about some of the economist's standard anticyclical policy proposals. But perhaps most significant and of widest applicability is the Lipsey-Lancaster *second best* theorem which appears capable of yielding a rich harvest of havoc.

In discussing these results I will not follow the order in which they were just listed. We begin then with the relatively well-known theorem of the second best.[1] In brief, this theorem states, on the basis of a mathematical argument, that in a concrete situation characterized by *any* deviation from "perfect" optimality, partial policy measures which eliminate only some of the departures from the optimal arrangement may well result in a net decrease in social welfare. Thus if, for example, an optimal allocation of resources requires that a system of 5000 supply-demand equations be satisfied, there is no reason to believe that people would be better off if 3900 of these conditions were met than if only 2400 of them were satisfied.

This result may at first glance appear rather abstract and its significance fairly remote, but as a matter of fact its (rather unfortunate) implications are demonstrably pertinent. As a general consideration it must first be recognized that the conditions to which the theorem applies are precisely those which constitute the environment of public policy. In our enonomy it can be taken for granted that arrangements are not all perfectly optimal. Moreover, ameliorative policy measures never attempt to be all encompassing—they

[1] See Lipsey and Lancaster [5]. Their formulation yields a somewhat stronger result than James Meade's original version, in which the relevance of a subset of the optimality conditions is not necessarily precluded in a non optimal situation.

typically seek to deal, one at a time, with departures from the ideal, and thereby they fall subject to the strictures of the Lipsey-Lancaster theorem.

There are standard illustrations of the ways in which such measures can go wrong. In England and France, for example, it is commonplace to consider some variant of marginal cost pricing as a guide for nationalized industries. But a little thought suggests that, in a world where many industries do not set prices at the level of marginal cost, the conversion of a few industries to this type of pricing procedure need not improve the public welfare. According to much of the literature, a major source of misallocation of resources is the restrictive policy of the monopolist and the quasi-monopolist who produces too little of his product in comparison with the outputs of other industries. But suppose only one of several monopoloid industries is nationalized and its prices reduced to competitive levels. The disparity between the output of this industry and that of the remaining monopolists is then likely to be increased. Competitive behavior imposed on a few industries in a world of monopolistic elements is likely to increase overallocation of resources to the quasi-competitors and, hence, the underallocation of resources to others.

A second standard application of the Lipsey-Lancaster analysis (and there are many more) is Professor Viner's caveat on Customs Unions—the observation that such unions may easily drive us further from achievement of the benefits of universal free trade. Thus, consider two countries E_a and E_b both of which export some commodity and a third country I which imports this item. If I levies a tariff on imports of this good, no matter from where it originates, it may be expected to obtain the commodity from the source having the greatest comparative advantage—the country which can offer the best terms. Suppose this is country E_a. Imagine, moreover, that in the course of time I's and E_b's diplomats negotiate a customs union. Tariffs on exports from E_a then remain unamended, while those on exports from E_b are removed. Suddenly the price of E_b's product may fall in the importing country and so the customs union will then have diverted trade from E_a, the country with the comparative advantage, to E_b, the exporter with the tariff advantage.

It is worth noting in passing that both the applications of the second best theorem which have just been described made their appearance in the literature well before Lipsey and Lancaster formulated their result, as these authors are most careful to point out. But this in no way reduces the significance of their generalization. For what that finding does, or at least appears to do, is to remove effectively one of the most obvious guideposts to the judgment of the applied economist—the view that it is generally a good thing to amend the anatomy of the economy in any way that makes it approximate more closely the structure of an ideal arrangement. If it is not necessarily good to increase the size of free trade areas, if markedly deleterious consequences can follow from an increase in the number of industries which behave competitively, in sum, if no good may be accomplished by behaving every day in every way better and better, how much more treacherous becomes the task of him who would offer cogent economic advice.

The second of our theorems—that on policy for externalities—can be dealt with rather more briefly, for it is not so very different in character from the applications of the Lipsey-Lancaster proposition. Much of the literature of welfare economics asserts by implication and often states explicitly that the level of an activity which yields external benefits will, in the absence of regulation, fall below its ideal level, so that appropriate public policy must expand such activities, e.g., by subsidizing them, and correspondingly it should seek to limit activities which impose external costs. This proposition is extremely plausible, for it rests on the argument that the individual who undertakes an activity which produces external disadvantages will, in his private calculations, ignore the costs to others, and so he will carry his efforts to a point where all their costs (both those borne by himself and those imposed on others) will outweigh the benefits of his activities at the margin. He will carry his activity to a point beyond that where marginal social costs and benefits are equal.

It is important to observe that the simple rule which tells us always to expand activities that yield external benefits is extremely convenient for policy purposes. Normally, we have no way of measuring the magnitude of an externality, much less of comparing one externality with another. We do, however, know some specific activities which almost certainly yield external benefits and others which probably impose external costs. Certain plants pollute the air or neighboring rivers and so produce external costs. Others provide technical know-how or otherwise make it easier for organizationally unrelated firms to operate. We are in no position to put a reliable dollar figure on the costs imposed on society by the former's smoke, or to compare it in magnitude with the advantages offered to others by the technological training provided by the latter.

Yet the simple standard welfare theorem, nevertheless, appears to permit the policy maker to act, to change things, perhaps not by ideal amounts, but at least in the right direction. The classical role tells him to reduce the output of the smoke producer and to increase the activity of the firm which provides technical skills to others, perhaps to tax the former and to subsidize the latter. A guess at the levels of the tax and the subsidy may yield results which are imperfect, but which surely move us in the right direction.

Or do they? In a recent and important note, Buchanan and Kafoglis[2] raised doubts about the validity of the standard externalities theorem. They pointed out that the theorem is valid only in the context of a sort of partial analysis, which does not carry over into the more general case (as they indicated by several counterexamples). In a subsequent discussion[3] I developed the argument further and derived the following results:

1. That the standard welfare theorem can be shown to be valid if and only if there is no more than one activity in the pertinent portion of the economy which yields external benefits or costs! In any but this totally uninteresting case, the level of an external benefit generating activity may well *exceed* its ideal magnitude, etc.

2. That the presence of externalities is very likely to yield a social welfare function which is characterized by a multiplicity of maxima. That is, instead of having a single well-defined peak, the surface which represents the social welfare function geometrically is likely, as a consequence of the externalities, to exhibit a number and plausibly a very considerable number of little hills. As a result, it becomes very difficult for the policy maker to judge the direction in which things should be headed—whether a move toward a nearby bump really serves the larger interests of the economy or whether it moves it away from the really significant peaks in the social welfare function.

There is no need to repeat here the slightly technical arguments underlying these assertions. Our interest here is rather in their implications for policy, and it can be seen that, once more, these implications are apparently unfortunate. They rob the applied economist of another criterion which appeared to enable him to make effective use of his limited information. It would seem that no longer can he confidently tell us to subsidize an industry which

[2] See Buchanan and Kafoglis [3].
[3] See Baumol [2].

he recognized to be beset by external economies. To act at all he should be able to measure externalities in various industries, he should be able to compare them, and most demanding of all—he should be able to trace how the magnitudes of these externalities vary with the scale of the activities which produce them so that, perhaps step by step, he can plan an effective approach to the ideal-output combination. For this purpose, then, he must, in effect, be prepared to describe in detail the entire social welfare function, or at least a considerable portion of its (multidimensional hyper) surface, an achievement which quite obviously and quite thoroughly exceeds our present conceptual powers. Intuition, judgments and observation combined into a heuristic procedure for dealing with externalities would then appear to have failed and would seem capable of counseling measures which are the very opposite of those required by the circumstances.

We come, finally, to the third set of our skeptical theorems, one which we have saved until last since its implications may prove to be the most disturbing to advice-giving economists. For these last results invade the central region of their activities—economic stabilization policy. In brief, these theorems assert that contracyclical monetary and fiscal policies, if they are to be dependably stabilizing, must be very carefully controlled in their terms, in their timing and magnitude, and that very slight miscalculations on these matters can transform a set of policies which seem to be stabilizing into a mechanism which unobtrusively but effectively aggravates the cycle, increasing its frequency and its amplitude. Moreover, the sort of analysis which could avoid such difficulties would require mathematical calculations based on models very similar to those used by engineers in designing steering instruments for airplanes, self-regulating chemical blending machinery or any other sort of automatically regulated process. But such a dynamic model must correspond closely to the facts, and must, therefore, emerge from an econometric analysis far more powerful than any we have so far been able to achieve.

It is not difficult to indicate why stabilizers can backfire badly. Any dynamic mechanism in which current events depend on occurrences in the past is likely to exhibit inertia. Thus, if some policy measures succeed in ending a deflationary price movement the matter may not simply terminate there. The very process which reverses the direction of price change may now easily send the price level into an inflationary phase, or the resulting price rise may be sharper and sooner than it would had no tinkering occurred. Attempts to offset the inflation may in turn bring on an earlier and more severe price fall than would otherwise have been experienced. In sum, while each stabilizing measure achieves the short run results which are expected of it, their effects may cumulate and impose on the economy a sequence of fluctuations which are distressingly sharp and frequent.

The sequence of events which I have just described is only meant to be illustrative. There are many other far more subtle time sequences whose consequences are all too similar. And, it must be emphasized, such results can be produced by policies which are to all appearances rational *and successful,* and by miscalculations which are apparently very small. Contracyclical policy just seems to be an extremely tricky and treacherous business. These difficulties arise whether the policies in question are discretionary (as has been shown by Friedman[4]) or automatic, as has been demonstrated by Phillips and independently (but somewhat belatedly) by myself.[5]

[4] See Friedman [4].

[5] See Phillips [6] and Baumol [1]. It should be emphasized that these results apply directly only to policies which undertake to reduce the magnitude of economic fluctuations and not to measures intended to stimulate long-run economic growth.

In these matters plausibility becomes wildly unreliable as a guide to good policy. Thus, for example, I have shown that in a world operating in accord with the Samuelson multiplier-accelerator model, fluctuations are likely to be aggravated by either of the two following types of stabilization policy, each of which is reasonable on its face:

Policy 1. If economic activity is increasing, automatically decrease the volume of government activity.

Policy 2. If national income is below the full employment level, increase governmental activity by an amount proportional to the shortfall.[6]

There is no need to push the discussion of our three unpleasant theorems any further. Their apparent import is all too clear. They are designed to guarantee that the advisor's lot is not a happy one. For even his most extensive experience, his most clearsighted judgment, his most subtle intuition may now leave us with the uneasy feeling that the decision maker might do as well by tossing a coin. But we shall see presently that while things may be black, they are not quite as black as all that. . . .

III. WITH SUCH A FRIEND WHO NEEDS AN ENEMY?

But first it may be well to pause briefly and examine why the contribution of pure theory to the work of the advising economist seems predominantly to have been so negative. As a matter of fact, the preceding discussion exaggerates matters. The propositions we have examined were, of course, all selected just because of the difficulties they raise and they therefore constitute a very biased sample, one which can hardly fail to suggest that pure theory has produced nothing but impediments to the work of the economist-advisor.

But while such a view is somewhat of an overstatement it is not entirely groundless. There is a fundamental reason to expect that a body of theory like that provided in economics should be able to indicate what *cannot* legitimately be concluded about reality more readily than it can point to the things that *do* follow.

The basic reason for this bias stems from the necessary oversimplification and artificiality of the economist's models. Our analytic tools simply cannot cope with a representation of reality which incorporates all of its complexities. That is why theory (and implicitly, any kind of thinking) makes use of models. Such a construct provides a subject which is more easily dealt with. If we are fortunate, our model will provide us with not too misleading a picture of the facts and yet will be simple enough for our instruments of analysis. But very often we must give up one of these goals to a considerable extent and, quite legitimately, the theorist will usually sacrifice realism to avoid being left with a model which is completely beyond his instruments of investigation.

Now such a model can often be used to derive policy conclusions which are demonstrably effective *within its artificial world*. We are assured that if reality were like that model then the measures in question would be efficacious. But since we have good reason to suspect the representativeness of the model, we are not likely to have much confidence in policy proposals for which it serves as primary justification.

The model can, however, provide more persuasive *criticism* of a policy measure. Suppose, for example, that policy X is al-

---

Thus, the widespread support of the recent tax cut by members of the profession can be defended by regarding that act as an attempt to increase the rate of growth rather than as a contracyclical measure.

[6] Also, in the context of this model it turns out that a really effective stabilization policy seems to have no obvious intuitive appeal. This ideal policy requires that governmental expenditure be regulated (perversely) by the level of total economic activity two periods earlier—that if there were a depression two periods earlier the government accumulate a tax surplus currently, and if inflation prevailed two periods ago there be a deficit currently—this no matter what the current state of the economy!

leged always to improve the balance of payments. If in a simple international trade model it can be shown that this policy produces no such effect, one is driven to suspect that it may not work elsewhere, or at least that there is some flaw in the logic which has been mustered in its favor.[7]

These asymmetric powers of the analytic model are clearly illustrated by my argument indicating the dangers of automatic contracyclical policies. In that discussion I used as my instrument the Samuelson multiplier-accelerator model. Now, no one to my knowledge has ever suggested that this model is an adequate representation of the complex mechanism which underlies business fluctuations in practice. Hence, the "effective policy" which I was able to derive with its aid seems to me to have absolutely no presumption in its favor. But the fact that several standard and plausible contracyclical measures turn out to produce most untoward effects in a multiplier-accelerator world offers us good grounds for mistrusting them, at least until other evidence in their favor can be produced.

It is, therefore, no accident that the theorist has been more effective in telling the policy maker what he cannot legitimately do than in providing him with good affirmative advice. Though this is not likely to increase his popularity, there is little he can do to change matters.

IV. WHITHER POLICY? (OR, HOW SERIOUS ARE THE STRICTURES?)

To return to our central theme, I had argued in earlier sections that the theorems which constitute our central subject matter are extremely important and that they have serious implications for the task of the economic advisor. But just how serious are these consequences? Are they as destructive and stultifying as a first reading may suggest?

It is easy to argue that the significance of the theorems is readily exaggerated—that there exist situations in which the formal conditions for the theorems are satisfied and yet their consequences can in good conscience be ignored. For example, picture a world in which pure competition prevails universally except in one industry in the United States and on an isolated island which trades with nobody else. Considered uncritically, the Lipsey-Lancaster theorem would suggest that there is no good reason to advocate competitive behavior for the one deviant American industry. For even if such a change were effected, the requisite optimality conditions would still not be satisfied everywhere. And the second best theorem tells us that two unsatisfied optimality conditions need be no more reprehensible than one.[8]

But such a conclusion is surely unacceptable. If two economies are completely insulated from one another by circumstances beyond the influence of policy, it is clearly advantageous for either of the societies to do the best it can with its own resources—to see that its own optimality conditions are satisfied, no matter what may be happening elsewhere. And if the theorem has little import where such complete isolation occurs, Marshall's dictum might lead us to suspect that there are intermediate cases—circumstances involving varying degrees of imperfect isolation, in which the significance of the theorem is commensurately small.

Thus there appears to be one sort of circumstance in which the Lipsey-Lancaster theorem and, for that matter, our other propositions need be regarded with only moderate apprehension. For each of our

[7] However, it can be argued, cogently, that if a reasonable policy fails to produce the effects anticipated of it when it is tested with the aid of a simplified model, this casts as much doubt upon the applicability of the model as it does on the validity of the proposal. This very significant point about the logic of model evaluation was suggested to me by Professor Goldfeld.

[8] This illustration was suggested to me in conversation by Andrew Whinston who, I understand, has produced a formal critique of the second-best theorem.

theorems relies for its results on the complexities produced by interdependence in the system—the implications of one optimality condition for another, the effects of one externality on a second or the influence of the course of the current cycle on future business fluctuations. And where the interconnection in question is extremely weak, it is plausible that it will not serve as a serious source of trouble.

In fact, there are probably a great many interrelationships within the economy that are weak enough to be ignored. Thus, for all practical purposes, the demand for most goods is likely to be dependent only on the demands for a few other items, at least judging by the relatively small number of statistically derived interrelationships that turn out to be significant. It may, then, be possible to partition the economy more effectively than some might have suspected.

A second circumstance which moderates the consequences of our theorems can perhaps be described as the case of "clear and present danger." Where some particular economic phenomenon is flagrantly obnoxious—where its consequences are patently unacceptable by society—where perhaps the very survival of the economy is threatened—it is undoubtedly good policy to ignore secondary interdependence considerations and, shouting "damn the torpedoes," proceed full steam ahead! The economy suffering from a great depression, the metropolis which is trapped by a process of cumulative deterioration, the underdeveloped nation whose growth is choked off by rising population—none of these can afford to take cognizance of the consequences of their counter measures for other less-immediate problems. A policy devised to cope with a vast economic crisis may indeed aggravate some future recession as our contracyclical policy theorems have demonstrated. A conference on world trade which tries to stem the tide of autarchy will undoubtedly fail to achieve the Lipsey-Lancaster optimality requirements of universal free trade. The provision of a social good such as national defense when a country is threatened, deals with only one externality at a time—and provides more only of that one external-benefit-yielding commodity, in disregard of the need for caution pointed out by the externalities theorem. Yet in all these cases reason clearly sides with those who choose to act. And, once again, if there are extreme cases where decisiveness is so obviously desirable, there will surely be intermediate circumstances where the grounds for decision, while not quite so patent, are nevertheless persuasive even to sophisticated observers, and examples should not be very hard to find.

Thus we have a second class of condition which can contain the destructive powers of our skeptical theorems. One can muster still others which are perhaps less powerful or less universal, but are, nevertheless, at least sometimes effective. For example, it should be recalled that in our theorems it has been convenient to distinguish carefully between improvement and optimality. Specifically, the externalities theorem tells us that the classical policy proposals for dealing with externalities may well cause us to move away from the *optimal* output arrangements. But it cannot deny that the classical remedies will effect *improvements.* If it can be shown that the marginal welfare product of some activity is positive (as will be the case where external benefits are present in a competitive equilibrium) then an increase in the level of that activity must assuredly *increase* social welfare even though the activity has already been expanded beyond its optimal level. True, in this process we may only obtain a very small improvement and perhaps thereby we may sacrifice very large potential benefits which only an optimal decision can bestow. But whether this is so or not we cannot determine in the present state of knowledge, and perhaps we will never know. Is it not then reasonable policy to give up a hopeless quest for the optimum and to adopt reasonable and well-defined policy measures which are at least capable of effecting improvements? It is not the businessman alone who may be well-advised to abandon maximization in favor of satisficing.[9]

There is yet another reason for going ahead with partial policy measures which defy the Lipsey-Lancaster interdict. This arises out of the nature of the political process which rarely permits really radical and comprehensive upheavals in public policy. Though our ultimate objective is compliance with every one of an extensive set of optimality conditions, one must begin somewhere. Within such a dynamic framework, the costs which may perhaps be incurred by the satisfaction of only a partial set of optimality requirements may in the long run prove worthwhile provided that this stage only represents an intermediate station on the way to the enactment of more comprehensive measures. Such a strategy can backfire, and the success of partial moves may sometimes simply induce complacency among the makers of policy who are led to feel that further measures merit lower priority. However, these considerations are matters of political strategy rather than welfare theory.

Ultimately, to judge the pertinence of the skeptical theorems to particular policy issues we require a vital piece of information which is, unfortunately, unavailable. We need some reliable indication of the relevant probabilities. Though it must be granted that satisfaction of one additional marginal optimality condition can reduce welfare, we would do well to determine how likely is it to produce that effect, and how likely is it that this consequence will be serious. This unfortunately, we do not know, and there seems to be no *a priori* way to get at the matter. It is easy to demonstrate that the answers to our probabilistic questions are highly sensitive to the shape of the relevant functions and to the choice of reference points. Small changes in these can substantially affect the probability that a partial measure will yield untoward effects, and it can materially influence the gravity of these consequences. The answers to our basic questions, then, are likely to vary substantially from application to application and may have to await a marked increase in the amount and quality of our information about the pertinent functions.

From all of this we can conclude that the skeptical theorems do not threaten to put the policy maker or his advisor out of business. There is still plenty to be said and done in the areas and much of it can legitimately proceed largely unhampered by these propositions. But the preceding discussion should not be taken to offer carte blanche to those who would ignore the theorems. On the contrary, it is my view that the theorems emerge with much of their power intact and that the advisor who chooses to ignore them does so at the public's peril. I urge the reader to reconsider the propositions carefully and to decide for himself how often, in practice, they have casually been neglected, and how serious may have been the consequences.

[9] The reader is reminded that the preceding discussion applies peculiarly to our externalities theorem and not to our other skeptical propositions.

REFERENCES

[1] Baumol, William J., "Pitfalls in Contracyclical Policies: Some Tools and Results," *The Review of Economics and Statistics*, February 1961.

[2] ———, "External Economies and Second-Order Optimality Conditions," *The American Economic Review*, June 1964.

[3] Buchanan, James M. and Milton Z. Kafoglis, "A Note on Public Goods Supply," *American Economic Review*, June 1963.

[4] Friedman, Milton, "The Effects of a Full-Employment Policy on Economic Stability: A Formal Analysis," *Essays in Positive Economics* (Chicago, Ill.: University of Chicago Press, 1953).

[5] Lipsey, Richard and Kevin Lancaster, "The General Theory of Second Best," *Review of Economic Studies*, December 1956.

[6] Phillips, A. W., "Stabilization Policy in a Closed Economy," *Economic Journal*, June 1954.

[6]

MACROECONOMICS OF UNBALANCED GROWTH: THE ANATOMY OF URBAN CRISIS*

By William J. Baumol

There are some economic forces so powerful that they constantly break through all barriers erected for their suppression. Such, for example, are the forces of supply and demand which have resisted alike medieval efforts to abolish usury and contemporary attempts to control prices. In this paper I discuss what I believe to be another such mechanism which has colored the past and seems likely to stamp its character on the future. It helps us to understand the prospective roles of a wide variety of economic services: municipal government, education, the performing arts, restaurants, and leisure time activity. I will argue that inherent in the technological structure of each of these activities are forces working almost unavoidably for progressive and cumulative increases in the real costs incurred in supplying them. As a consequence, efforts to offset these cost increases, while they may succeed temporarily, in the long run are merely palliatives which can have no significant effect on the underlying trends.

The justification of a macroeconomic model should reside primarily in its ability to provide insights into the workings of observed phenomena. Its aggregation of diverse variables usually deny it the elegance and the rigor that are provided by microeconomic analysis at its best. Yet macro models have succeeded in explaining the structure of practical problems and in offering guidance for policy to a degree that has so far eluded the more painstaking modes of economic analysis. This article hopes to follow in the tradition—the structure of its basic model is rudimentary. Yet it can perhaps shed some light on a variety of economic problems of our generation.

1. *Premises*

Our model will proceed on several assumptions, only one of which is really essential. This basic premise asserts that economic activities can, not entirely arbitrarily, be grouped into two types: technologically progressive activities in which innovations, capital accumulation, and economies of large scale all make for a cumulative rise in output per

* The author is professor of economics, Princeton University. He wishes to thank the Ford Foundation and the National Science Foundation whose grants greatly facilitated completion of this paper. The basic hypothesis was originally developed jointly with William G. Bowen in the study of the performing arts conducted for the Twentieth Century Fund. In this paper there is no attempt to document the illustrative empirical observations though in every case the data have been examined and appear to support the assertions.

man hour and activities which, by their very nature, permit only sporadic increases in productivity.

Of course, one would expect that productivity would not grow at a uniform rate throughout the economy so it is hardly surprising that, given any arbitrarily chosen dividing line, one can fit all goods and services into one or the other of two such categories in whatever way the dividing line is drawn. I am, however, making a much stronger assertion: that the place of any particular activity in this classification is not primarily a fortuitous matter determined by the particulars of its history, but rather that it is a manifestation of the activity's technological structure, which determines quite definitely whether the productivity of its labor inputs will grow slowly or rapidly.

The basic source of differentiation resides in the role played by labor in the activity. In some cases labor is primarily an instrument—an incidental requisite for the attainment of the final product, while in other fields of endeavor, for all practical purposes the labor is itself the end product. Manufacturing encompasses the most obvious examples of the former type of activity. When someone purchases an air conditioner he neither knows nor cares how much labor went into it. He is not concerned one way or the other with an innovation that reduces the manpower requirements for the production of his purchase by 10 per cent if the price and the quality of the product are unaffected. Thus it has been possible, as it were, behind the scenes, to effect successive and cumulative decreases in the labor input coefficient for most manufactured goods, often along with some degree of improvement in the quality of the product.

On the other hand there are a number of services in which the labor is an end in itself, in which quality is judged directly in terms of amount of labor. Teaching is a clear-cut example, where class size (number of teaching hours expended per student) is often taken as a critical index of quality. Here, despite the invention of teaching machines and the use of closed circuit television and a variety of other innovations, there still seem to be fairly firm limits to class size. We are deeply concerned when elementary school classes grow to 50 pupils and are disquieted by the idea of college lectures attended by 2000 underclassmen. Without a complete revolution in our approach to teaching there is no prospect that we can ever go beyond these levels (or even up to them) with any degree of equanimity. An even more extreme example is one I have offered in another context: live performance. A half hour horn quintet calls for the expenditure of $2\frac{1}{2}$ man hours in its performance, and any attempt to increase productivity here is likely to be viewed with concern by critics and audience alike.

The difference between the two types of activity in the flexibility of their productivity levels should not be exaggerated. It is a matter of degree rather than an absolute dichotomy. The jet airplane has increased the productivity per man hour of a faculty member who is going from New York to California to give a lecture. Certainly the mass media have created what may be considered a new set of products that are close substitutes for live performance and by which productivity was increased spectacularly. In addition, there are, as the reader will recognize, all sorts of intermediate activities which fall between the two more extreme varieties. Yet, the distinction between the relatively constant productivity industries and those in which productivity can and does rise is a very real one, and one which, we shall see, is of considerable practical importance.

In addition to the separability of activities into our two basic categories I shall utilize three other assumptions, two of them primarily for ease of exposition. The reader will recognize, as we proceed, that neither is essential to the argument. The first of the incidental premises consists simply in the assertion that all outlays other than labor costs can be ignored. This assertion is patently unrealistic but it simplifies greatly our mathematical model. A second, far more important, and more realistic assumption is that wages in the two sectors of the economy go up and down together. In the long run there is some degree of mobility in all labor markets and consequently, while wages in one activity can lag behind those in another, unless the former is in process of disappearing altogether we cannot expect the disparity to continue indefinitely. For simplicity I will in the next section take hourly wages to be precisely the same in both sectors, but the model is easily complicated to allow for some diversity in wage levels and their movements.

A final inessential assumption which is, however, not altogether unrealistic, asserts that money wages will rise as rapidly as output per man hour in the sector where productivity is increasing. Since organized labor is not slow to learn of increases in its productivity it is likely to adjust its wage demands accordingly. This assumption affects only the magnitude of the absolute price level in our model, and does not influence the relative costs and prices that are the critical elements in the analysis.

2. *A Model of Unbalanced Expansion*

Assume that the economy is divided into two sectors, sector one, in which the productivity of labor is constant, while in sector two output per man hour grows cumulatively at a constant compounded rate, r. Thus we have for the respective values of outputs Y_{1t} and Y_{2t} in the two sectors at time t:

$$Y_{1t} = aL_{1t} \quad (1)$$

$$Y_{2t} = bL_{2t}e^{rt} \quad (2)$$

where L_{1t} and L_{2t} are the quantities of labor employed in the two sectors and a and b are constants.

We suppose wages are equal in the two sectors and are fixed at W_t dollars per unit of labor, where W_t itself grows in accord with the productivity of sector 2, our "progressive" sector, so that

(3) $$W_t = We^{rt}. \qquad (W = \text{some constant})$$

We may now derive several properties of such a system. First and most fundamental is *Proposition 1:* The cost per unit of output of sector 1, C_1, will rise without limit while C_2, the unit cost of sector 2, will remain constant.
proof:

$$C_1 = W_t L_{1t}/Y_{1t} = We^{rt}L_{1t}/aL_{1t} = We^{rt}/a$$

$$C_2 = W_t L_{2t}/Y_{2t} = We^{rt}L_{2t}/bL_{2t}e^{rt} = W/b.$$

Note that the *relative* costs will behave in this manner whether or not wages increase in accord with (3) for we have

$$C_1/C_2 = (L_{1t}/Y_{1t})/(L_{2t}/Y_{2t}) = be^{rt}/a.$$

In practice, we would expect in these circumstances that market demand for the output of sector 1 would decline. Suppose, for example, the elasticity of demand for the two outputs were unity in terms of prices which were proportionate to costs. Then relative outlays on the two commodities would remain constant, i.e., we would have

$$\frac{C_1 Y_1}{C_2 Y_2} = \frac{We^{rt}L_{1t}}{We^{rt}L_{2t}} = \frac{L_{1t}}{L_{2t}} = A(\text{constant}).$$

Hence the output ratio of the two sectors would be given by

$$Y_1/Y_2 = aL_{1t}/bL_{2t}e^{rt} = aA/be^{rt}$$

which declines toward zero with the passage of time. Thus we have *Proposition 2:* In the model of unbalanced productivity there is a tendency for the outputs of the "nonprogressive" sector whose demands are not highly inelastic to decline and perhaps, ultimately, to vanish.

We may inquire, however, what would happen if despite the change in their relative costs and prices the magnitude of the relative outputs of the two sectors were maintained, perhaps with the aid of government subsidy, or if demand for the product in question were sufficiently price inelastic or income elastic. Then we would have

$$(b/a)\ Y_1/Y_2 = L_1/L_2e^{rt} = K.$$

Let $L = L_1 + L_2$ be the total labor supply. It follows that

(4) $$L_1 = (L - L_1)Ke^{rt} \quad \text{or} \quad L_1 = LKe^{rt}/(1 + Ke^{rt})$$

and

$$L_2 = L - L_1 = L/(1 + Ke^{rt}). \tag{5}$$

Hence, as t approaches infinity, L_1 will approach L and L_2 will approach zero. Thus we have *Proposition 3:* In the unbalanced productivity model, if the ratio of the outputs of the two sectors is held constant, more and more of the total labor force must be transferred to the nonprogressive sector and the amount of labor in the other sector will tend to approach zero.

Finally, we may note what happens to the overall rate of growth of output in the economy if the output ratio for the two sectors is not permitted to change. We may take as an index of output a weighted average of the outputs of the two sectors:

$$I = B_1Y_1 + B_2Y_2 = B_1aL_1 + B_2bL_2e^{rt}$$

so that by (4) and (5)

$$I = L(KB_1a + B_2b)e^{rt}/(1 + Ke^{rt}) = Re^{rt}/(1 + Ke^{rt})$$

where

$$R = L(KB_1a + B_2b).$$

Therefore

$$\begin{aligned} dI/dt &= R[re^{rt}(1 + Ke^{rt}) - Kre^{2rt}]/(1 + Ke^{rt})^2 \\ &= rRe^{rt}/(1 + Ke^{rt})^2. \end{aligned}$$

As a result, the percentage rate of growth of output will be

$$(dI/dt)/I = r/(1 + Ke^{rt})$$

which declines asymptotically toward zero as t increases. We have, then, arrived at *Proposition 4:* An attempt to achieve balanced growth in a world of unbalanced productivity must lead to a declining rate of growth relative to the rate of growth of the labor force. In particular, if productivity in one sector and the total labor force remain constant the growth rate of the economy will asymptotically approach zero.

3. *Discussion of the Propositions*

The logic of the entire analysis can be restated rather simply in intuitive terms. If productivity per man hour rises cumulatively in one sector relative to its rate of growth elsewhere in the economy, while wages rise commensurately in all areas, then relative costs in the nonprogressive sectors must inevitably rise, *and these costs will rise cumulatively and without limit.* For while in the progressive sector productivity increases will serve as an offset to rising wages, this offset must be smaller in the nonprogressive sectors. For example (ignoring nonwage costs) if wages and productivity in the progressive sector both go up 2 per cent per year, costs there will not rise at all. On the other hand, if in the nonprogressive sector productivity is constant, every rise in wages must yield a corresponding addition to costs—a two per cent cumulative rise in wages means that, year in year out, costs must be two per cent above those of the preceding year. Thus, the very progress of the technologically progressive sectors inevitably adds to the costs of the technologically unchanging sectors of the economy, unless somehow the labor markets in these areas can be sealed off and wages held absolutely constant, a most unlikely possiblity.

We see then that costs in many sectors of the economy will rise relentlessly, and will do so for reasons that are for all practical purposes beyond the control of those involved. The consequence is that the outputs of these sectors may in some cases tend to be driven from the market. If their relative outputs are maintained, an ever increasing proportion of the labor force must be channeled into these activities and the rate of growth of the economy must be slowed correspondingly.

4. *Some Applications*[1]

These observations can be used at once to explain a number of observed phenomena. For example, there is evidence that an ever increasing portion of the nation's labor force has been going into retailing and that a rising portion of the cost of commodities is accounted for by outlays on marketing. Now there have been several pronounced changes in the technology of marketing in recent decades: self service, the supermarket, and prewrapping have all increased the productivity per man hour of the retailing personnel. But ultimately, the activity involved is in the nature of a service and it does not allow for constant and cumulative increases in productivity through capital accumulation, innovation, or economies of large-scale operation. Hence it is neither mismanagement nor lack of ingenuity that accounts for the relatively constant productivity of this sector. Since some sort of marketing effort is an inescapable element in economic activity, demand for this service is quite income elastic. Our model tells us what to expect in this case—cumulatively increasing costs relative to those of other economic activities, and the absorption of an ever growing proportion of society's resources by this sector—precisely what seems to have been observed.

Higher education is another activity the demand for whose product seems to be relatively income elastic and price inelastic. Higher tuition charges undoubtedly impose serious hardships on lower-income stu-

[1] Some of the ideas in this section arose out of discussions with Eugene Beem of Sperry and Hutchinson.

dents. But, because a college degree seems increasingly to be a necessary condition for employment in a variety of attractive occupations, most families have apparently been prepared to pay the ever larger fees instituted in recent years. As a result higher education has been absorbing a constantly increasing proportion of per capita income. And the relatively constant productivity of college teaching leads our model to predict that rising educational costs are no temporary phenomenon—that they are not a resultant of wartime inflation which will vanish once faculty salaries are restored to their prewar levels. Rather, it suggests that, as productivity in the remainder of the economy continues to increase, costs of running the educational organizations will mount correspondingly, so that whatever the magnitude of the funds they need today, we can be reasonably certain that they will require more tomorrow, and even more on the day after that.

But not all services in the relatively constant productivity sector of the economy face inelastic demands. Many of them are more readily dispensable than retailing and education as far as individual consumers are concerned. As their costs increase, their utilization tends therefore to decrease and they retreat into the category of luxury goods with very limited markets or disappear almost completely. Fine pottery and glassware produced by the careful labor of skilled craftsmen sell at astronomical prices, though I am told the firms that produce them earn relatively little profit from these product lines which they turn out primarily for prestige and publicity, obtaining the bulk of their earnings from their mass production activities. Fine restaurants and theaters are forced to keep raising their prices, and at least in the case of the latter we know that volume is dwindling while it becomes ever more difficult for suppliers (the producers) to make ends meet.

An extreme example of an activity that has virtually disappeared is the construction (and, indeed, the utilization) of the large and stately houses whose operation even more than their construction allows for little in the way of enhanced productivity, and whose rising costs of operation have apparently decreased their salability even to the wealthy.

These observations suggest something about the likely shape of our economy in the future. Our model tells us that manufactures are likely to continue to decline in relative cost and, unless the income elasticity of demand for manufactured goods is very large, they may absorb an ever smaller proportion of the labor force, which, if it transpires, may make it more difficult for our economy to maintain its overall rate of output growth.

The analysis also suggests that real cost in the "nonprogressive" sectors of the economy may be expected to go on increasing. Some of the services involved—those whose demands are inelastic—may continue viable on the free market. Some, like the theater, may be forced to leave this market and may have to depend on voluntary public support for their survival. Our hospitals, our institutions of private education and a variety of other nonprofit organizations have already long survived on this basis, and can continue to do so if the magnitude of contributions keeps up with costs. Some activities will either disappear or retreat to a small scale of operation catering primarily to a luxury trade. This fate may be in store for restaurants offering true *haute cuisine* and it is already the case for fine hand-worked furniture and for clothes made to measure. Some activities, perhaps many of the preceding among them, will fall increasingly into the hands of the amateurs who already play a considerable role in theatrical and orchestral performances, in gastronomy, in crafts such as woodworking and pottery. Finally, there is a considerable segment of nonprogressive activity that is dependent on tax support. Some of the problems that go with this position will be considered in the remainder of this paper.

In all the observations of this section there is one implicit underlying danger that should not escape the reader: the inherent threat to quality. Amateur activity has its virtues, as an educational device, as a good use for leisure time and so forth. But in a variety of fields it offers a highly imperfect substitute for the highly polished product that can be supplied by the professional. Unbalanced productivity growth, then, threatens to destroy many of the activities that do so much to enrich our existence, and to give others over into the hands of the amateurs. These are dangers which many of us may feel should not be ignored or taken lightly.

5. *On the Financial Problem of the Cities*

One of the major economic problems of our times is the crisis of the larger cities. Together with their suburban periphery the cities are attracting ever greater segments of our population. Yet at least the core of the metropolis is plagued by a variety of ills including spreading blight as entire neighborhoods deteriorate, increasing pollution of its atmosphere, worsening traffic, critical educational problems, and, above all, mounting fiscal pressures. The financial troubles are perhaps central to the entire issue because without adequate funds one cannot hope to mount an effective attack on the other difficulties. More than one reform mayor has taken office determined to undertake a radical program to deal with the city's difficulties and found himself baffled and stymied by the monstrous deficit which he discovered to be hanging over him, a deficit whose source appeared to have no reasonable explanation. There seems in these cases to be no way to account for the growth in the city's financial needs—for the fact that a municipal budget far above that which was roughly adequate a decade earlier threatens to disrupt seriously the city's most vital services today. Where the political process is involved it is easy to blame growing costs on inefficiency and corruption but when they take office, reform administrations seem consistently puzzled by their inability to wring out the funds they require through the elimination of these abuses.

A critical element in the explanation becomes clear when we recognize how large a proportion of the services provided by the city are activities falling in the relatively nonprogressive sector of the economy. The bulk of our municipal expenditures is devoted to education which, as we have already seen, offers very limited scope for cumulative increases in productivity. The same is true of police, of hospitals, of social services, and of a variety of inspection services. Despite the use of the computer in medicine and in traffic planning, despite the use of closed circuit television and a variety of other devices, there is no substitute for the personal attention of a physician or the presence of a police patrol in a crime-ridden neighborhood. The bulk of municipal services is, in fact, of this general stamp and our model tells us clearly what can be expected as a result. Since there is no reason to anticipate a cessation of capital accumulation or innovation in the progressive sectors of the economy, the upward trend in the real costs of municipal services cannot be expected to halt; inexorably and cumulatively, whether or not there is inflation, administrative mismanagement or malfeasance, municipal budgets will almost certainly continue to mount in the future, just as they have been doing in the past. This is a trend for which no man and no group should be blamed, for there is nothing that can be done to stop it.

6. *The Role of Static Externalities*

Though these may be troubles enough for the municipal administrator, there are other compelling forces that plague him simultaneously. Among them are the general class of externality problems which have so long been the welfare economist's stock in trade.

Since the appearance of Marshall's and Pigou's basic writing in the area a most significant development has been the growing impact of external costs on urban living. No longer are road crowding and smoke nuisance only quaint cases serving primarily as textbook illustrations. Rather, they have become pressing issues of public concern—matters discussed heatedly in the daily press and accorded serious attention by practical politicians. Newspapers devote headlines to an engineer's prediction that the human race is more likely to succumb to its own pollutants than through a nuclear holocaust, and report with glee the quip that Los Angeles is the city in which one is wakened by the sound of birds coughing.

Now there are undoubtedly many reasons for the explosion in external costs but there is a pertinent observation about the relationship between population size in a given area and the cost of externalities that seems not to be obvious. It is easy to assume that these costs will rise roughly in proportion with population but I shall argue now that a much more natural premise is that they will rise more rapidly—perhaps roughly as the square of the number of inhabitants. For example, consider the amount of dirt that falls into the house of a typical urban resident as a result of air pollution, and suppose that this is equal to kn where n is the number of residents in the area. Since the number of homes in the area, an, is also roughly proportionate to population size, total domestic soot-fall will be equal to soot per home times number of homes $= kn \cdot an = akn^2$. Similarly, if delays on a crowded road are roughly proportionate to n, the number of vehicles traversing it, the total number of man hours lost thereby will increase roughly as n^2, since the number of passengers also grows roughly as the number of cars. The logic of the argument is simple and perhaps rather general: if each inhabitant in an area imposes external costs on every other, and if the magnitude of the costs borne by each individual is roughly proportionate to population size (density) then since these costs are borne by each of the n persons involved, the total external costs will vary not in proportion with n but with n^2. Of course I do not maintain that such a relationship is universal or even that it is ever satisfied more than approximately. Rather I am suggesting that, typically, increases in population size may plausibly be expected to produce disproportionate increases in external costs—thus pressures on the municipality to do something about these costs may then grow correspondingly.

7. *Cumulative Decay and Dynamic Pareto Optimality*

Economic theory indicates yet another source of mounting urban problems. These are the processes of cumulative urban decay which once set in motion induce matters to go from bad to worse. Since I have discussed these elsewhere I can illustrate the central proposition rather briefly. Public transportation is an important example. In many urban areas with declining utilization, frequency of service has been sharply reduced and fares have been increased. But these price rises have only served to produce a further decline in traffic, leading in turn to yet another deterioration in schedules and another fare increase and so on, apparently *ad infinitum*. More important, perhaps, is the logic of the continued flight to the suburbs in which many persons who apparently would otherwise wish to remain in the city are driven out by growing urban deterioration—rising crime rates, a growing number of blighted neighborhoods, etc. Once again, the individuals' remedy intensifies the community's problems and each feeds upon the other. Those who leave the city are usually the very persons who care and can afford to care—the ones who maintain their houses, who do not commit crimes, and who are most capable of providing the taxes needed to arrest the process of urban decay. Their exodus therefore leads to further deterioration in urban conditions and so induces yet another wave of emigration, and so on.[2]

It is clear that these cumulative processes can greatly increase the financial pressures besetting a municipality and can do so in a variety of ways: they can increase directly municipal costs by adding to the real quantities of inputs required for the upkeep of buildings, to maintain levels of urban sanitation, to preserve the level of education attained by an average resident, etc.; they can reduce the tax base—the exodus of more affluent urban inhabitants cause a decline in the financial resources available to the city; and with the passage of time the magnitude of the resources necessary to arrest and reverse the cumulative processes itself is likely to grow so that the city may find it increasingly difficult to go beyond programs that slow the processes slightly.[3]

[2] As is to be expected, such dynamic processes may be monotonic or oscillatory, stable or unstable. As examples we might expect the public transportation scheduling problem to grow monotonically while automotive road crowding may be inherently oscillatory. More specifically, let f represent frequency of public bus departure and p be the number of bus passengers. We would expect the relevant relationships to be something such as

$$p_t = a + bf_t \quad \text{(demand for public transport) and}$$
$$f_{t+1} = w + vp_t \quad \text{(lagged public transport supply response)}$$

so that

$$f_{t+1} = w + av + vbf_t$$

in which the coefficient vb is presumably positive. On the other hand, if D represents average delay on some road and A is the volume of automotive traffic, the corresponding relationships would be

$$D_t = a' + b'A_t \quad \text{(delay grows with traffic volume) and}$$
$$A_{t+1} = w' - v'D_t \quad \text{(delays today lead to lower traffic tomorrow)}$$

so that we have a negative coefficient $-b'v'$ in the difference equation

$$A_{t+1} = w' - a'v' - b'v'A_t.$$

Since monotonic and oscillatory time paths correspond respectively to positive and negative variable coefficients in a first-order difference equation, our result follows. An intuitive explanation is fairly simple in each case: increased automotive traffic today causes delays and so may reduce traffic tomorrow. But a decline in number of passengers which causes a deterioration in service leads to still another fall in volume.

As stated, the time path in each case may be stable. But in the latter case, even though the declines will not be unbounded, the limit toward which they tend may be very low and totally unacceptable as a matter of public policy.

[3] I have argued that the cumulative processes involve what may be considered dynamic externalities. Each passenger who uses public transportation less frequently imposes the increased likelihood of poorer schedules not only on himself but on others as well. As a result these processes will yield results that do not maximize social welfare. For the private and social marginal rates of transformation between present and future will then differ from one another. The individual will tend to cut down on his use of public transportation by an amount greater

8. *Conclusion—The Financial Problems of the Large City*

The story is perhaps completed if we add to the preceding observations the fact that each city is in competition with others and with its own surrounding areas for industry and for people with the wherewithal to pay taxes. No city government acting alone can afford to raise its tax rates indefinitely. Even if they were politically feasible, mounting tax rates must eventually produce diminishing and perhaps even negative returns as they depress the tax base further.

We can now quickly pull the pieces of our story together. We have just seen that our municipalities are perhaps unavoidably subject to a variety of growing financial pressures: the limited sources of tax funds, the pressures imposed by several processes of cumulative decay, the costs of externalities which seem to have a built-in tendency to rise more rapidly than the population. These phenomena imply that the activities of the municipality will have to be expanded if standards of city life are to be maintained. But the funds available for the purpose are extremely limited. And over all this hangs the shadow cast by our model of unbalanced growth which has shown that the costs of even a constant level of activity on the part of a municipal government can be expected to grow constantly higher.

The picture that has been painted is bleak. It suggests strongly that self-help offers no way out for our cities. All of this would then appear to offer stronger theoretical support for the Heller-Pechman proposal that the federal government can provide the resources necessary to prevent the serious crisis that threatens our larger urban communities and whose effects on the quality of life in our society may become one of the nation's most serious economic problems.

References

1. W. J. Baumol and W. G. Bowen, *Performing Arts: The Economic Dilemma*. New York 1966.
2. Jean Fourastié, *The Causes of Wealth*. Glencoe, Ill., 1960.
3. Tibor and Anne Scitovsky, "What Price Economic Progress?" *Yale Review*, Autumn 1959, *49*, 95–110.

than that which is optimal because he himself does not bear all of the costs of his action. There is a marginal rate of transformation between the utility derived from public transportation today and that obtainable from transportation tomorrow. If relative prices do not equal that marginal rate of transformation a misallocation of resources is likely to result. The consequences may even be what might be called Pareto-nonoptimal. That is, everyone may be harmed. For example, when automobile traffic becomes sufficiently bad it may become clear that everyone will be better off if passenger cars are banned completely from the downtown area in order to make possible a faster, more efficient public transportation system.

Macroeconomics of Unbalanced Growth: Comment

Macroeconomics of Unbalanced Growth: Comment

These few remarks should not be interpreted as a rejoinder, for a rejoinder is neither intended nor necessary. Rather, I take the opportunity to clear up a few misunderstandings about the nature of my hypothesis, which Alice Vandermeulen has dubbed "Baumol's Disease"— misconceptions which have characterized a number of comments on my paper and for which limitations in my original exposition are surely responsible.

1. The primary objective of my article was to explain the rising costs of a number of outputs of what I call the "nonprogressive industries." In particular, I sought to account for the spectacular rise in the cost of municipal services. The allegation that the quality of some of these services is rising is a moot question although it certainly may not be uniformly false. However, it is beside the point for the issue I was raising. If my analysis offers some ground for believing that the cost of education will continue to rise more rapidly than the general price level for the foreseeable future, it is comforting to believe that this may be accompanied by some improvement in educational standards but that fact, if it is a fact, does not reduce the size of the prospective bill that must be paid if we are to provide some given number of days of schooling per child, a goal the community is not likely to surrender lightly.

2. I certainly agree tht it would be folly to rule out categorically the possibility of cost-saving innovation in urban services. Subsequent events have belied spectacularly such prognostications for agriculture and for the operation of the kitchen. Perhaps no technological revolution has increased productivity more spectacularly (in terms of audience size per performer) than have the electronic media in the case of the performing arts. Yet because the quantity of labor is so closely correlated with the quality of the final product in so many of the urban services, we have strong grounds on which to expect that they will characteristically tend to lag behind the remainder of the economy in the productivity benefits which they enjoy as a consequence of innovation.

And, as a result, I persist in the view that the extraordinary rates of cost increase that we observe throughout the nonprogressive sector is a matter of their technology—the special role of the labor input in determining the quality of their end product.

3. Having predicted a cumulative cost rise for the output of the "nonprogressive sector" of the economy I did not intend to go further and attempt a generalized forecast of the activities that compose it. I meant to suggest a variety of possibilities: that some, like the construction of stately homes, would tend to disappear; that others, such as very fine restaurants, would be reduced to a small number catering almost exclusively to the very affluent; that some, like handmade furniture and pottery, would fall into the hands of amateur craftsmen; and that some, such as education (at least up to this point) would continue to be demanded but would, as a consequence, eat up an ever-growing portion of G.N.P. I do *not* believe that any one type of time path will characterize the behavior of every output of the nonprogressive sector in the future any more than it has until now. But each of the possibilities involves some consequences which some of us may consider unpalatable and which, at the very least, merit explicit consideration by the policy maker.

4. Of course the Heller-Pechman plan is not the appropriate means for dealing with those who impose external costs upon society, nor has anyone claimed that it is. Clearly, those whose activities produce these costs should, where possible, be made to pay for them. That is still generally the best way to deal with the matter. Nor did I intend by my reference to the Heller-Pechman plan to prejudge whether the community will indeed choose to preserve our cities, at least in the form in which we now find them. I meant only to indicate that *if* society makes such a decision it must recognize that cumulatively rising costs may well force some such financing measure upon it. I may add, incidentally, that since smaller geographic entities must also supply services that are, typically, produced in the nonprogressive sector, decentralization may constitute no cure for Baumol's Disease. I think symptoms of this are already accumulating.

5. A final word on Professor Bell's lovely example on our response to the rising costs of barber services: the growth of self-service in the process of shaving. Surely this is a beautiful illustration of one of the consequences I have drawn from my model, the growing inducement for amateur activity. We see it all about us: in cuisine, in dramatic presentations, in orchestral performance, in the making of pottery and furniture—and in beard removal!

William J. Baumol*

* Professor of economics, Princeton University

Macroeconomics of Unbalanced Growth: Reply

By WILLIAM J. BAUMOL*

There is no doubt that Michael Keren is right and that the point is important.[1] In the initial discussion of my model, I simply misinterpreted the rising relative cost of the urban public services to mean that it will become harder for society to provide them. As Keren shows, the rising productivity elsewhere in the economy that is the source of the increasing opportunity cost of the services, also automatically means that the community will be able more easily, if it wishes, to pay for these services, despite their rising cost.

The implications of Keren's point are worth spelling out. The basic argument of the original analysis still remains valid: the financial problem of the cities increases (in part) because the costs of the services rise more rapidly than the general price level. This may well lead to cumulative deterioration in the quality and quantity of the services, even though it is not forced on the economy by lack of resources.

Because of their rising relative costs, the community may in fact *want* less of some or even most of these services. But the danger is that the nature of the political process and the tax system will also force it to accept a decline in even those services which the public would in fact prefer to expand, an expansion which, as Keren shows, society will well be able to afford. The problem is to find means by which the rising resources of the community can be channelled into *those* public services at a rate that grows more rapidly than their costs.

* Princeton University.

[1] My error has also been pointed out by several others, though sometimes not so clearly as in Keren's note. See, e.g., illuminating papers by David Bradford and by L. K. Lynch and E. L. Redman.

REFERENCES

D. Bradford, "Balance on Unbalanced Growth," *Zeitschrift fur Nationalokonomie*, 1969, *29*, 291–304.

I. K. Lynch and E. L. Redman, "Macroeconomics of Unbalanced Growth: Comment," *Amer. Econ. Rev.*, Sept. 1968, *58*, 152–55.

[7]

ON THE DISCOUNT RATE FOR PUBLIC PROJECTS

BY WILLIAM J. BAUMOL

William J. Baumol is Professor of Economics at Princeton University. "At stake in the choice of an acceptable discount rate is no less than the allocation of resources between the private and public sectors of the economy." On the basis of this observation, Professor Baumol discusses the principles which lead to the choice of an appropriate public discount rate concept. He asserts that "the correct discount rate for the evaluation of a government project is the percentage rate of return that the resources utilized would otherwise provide in the private sector." In discussing this basic proposition, Professor Baumol investigates the nature of opportunity costs and why they differ under certain circumstances. He focuses on the role of taxes in creating a disparate pattern of opportunity costs in the private sector. When a public activity draws resources from a number of sectors in the economy, "the correct social discount rate . . . will be a weighted average of the opportunity cost rate for the various sectors from which the project would draw its resources."

After discussing the difficulties in estimating an appropriate public discount rate caused by externalities and the problem of second best, Professor Baumol concludes "that with the help of the principles and data now available, one should be able to arrive at reasonable approximations for the social rate of discount. Certainly it should be possible to derive figures considerably more defensible than the conventional calculations that are all too often utilized to justify projects, not all of which are clear in their economic merit."

1. SIGNIFICANCE OF THE DISCOUNT RATE

It is generally recognized that the discount rate is a critical datum for the evaluation of any proposed Government project.* Even where there is little basic disagreement about the investment's prospective costs and benefits, the choice of discount rate figure may make the difference between acceptance and rejection. A project which seems to yield substantial net benefits when evaluated at a 3 percent rate may well appear extremely wasteful if the rate is 5 percent.

Yet, despite the critical nature of this parameter, in some calculations it is assigned a value almost cavalierly, with little attempt to show that the selected figure is not chosen arbitrarily and capriciously.** One sometimes encounters discount figures in cost-benefit calculations whose sole justification seems to be that similar figures were used in the past. Of course that can never be an acceptable argument, first because the earlier figure may have had as little justification as the one presently employed and, second, because changing circumstances change the appropriate value of the discount rate.

At stake in the choice of an acceptable discount rate is no less than the allocation of resources between the private and the public sectors

*Further discussion of this issue is found in the paper by Krutilla in this volume.

**Further discussion of this issue is found in the papers by Hirshleifer & Shapiro in this volume, and Searl in vol. 3 of this collection.

of the economy. The discount rate, by indicating what Government projects should be undertaken, can determine the proportion of the economy's activity that is operated by governmental agencies, and hence, the proportion that remains in the hands of private enterprise.

Moreover, even given the decision on resource allocation between the private and the public sectors, the choice of discount rate can affect profoundly the type of projects undertaken by Government agencies. When the discount rate is low this will encourage highly durable investments, the bulk of whose benefits will become available only in the distant future. Thus, when the economy is beset by urgent and immediate investment needs a relatively high discount rate will tend to be appropriate.

With so much at issue it is well worth exploring in some detail the principles that should be employed in arriving at a discount figure, and the rationale that underlies them. This paper undertakes to do so without heavy reliance on the jargon of technical economics.

2. The Basic Criterion: Opportunity Cost

The observation that the discount rate is the arbiter of the allocation of resources between private and public enterprise is the key to the principles which underlie the choice of an acceptable discount figure. The right discount rate becomes that number which indicates correctly when resources should be transferred from one sector to another.

More specifically, suppose one is considering the construction of a dam which will employ x man-hours of labor, y tons of cement, and z kilowatt hours of electricity. In an economy in which the level of employment is high, if those resources are made available to the Government they must be transferred out of the private sector. Just as in the guns versus butter case, each item added to the public sector involves some corresponding reduction in the volume of resources in private hands.[1]

We may now establish a rather obvious criterion to test the desirability of the proposed resource transfer. If the resources in question produce a rate of return in the private sector which society evaluates at r percent, then the resources should be transferred to the public project if that project yields a return greater than r percent. They should be left in private hands if their potential earnings in the proposed government investment is less than r percent. The logic of this criterion is self-evident. It states no more than the minimal dictate of efficiency: Never take resources out of a use where they bring in (say) 9 percent in order to utilize them in a manner which yields only 6 percent!

The standard which has just been described is the concept economists call *opportunity cost.* We have stated, in effect, that the proper

[1] On the other hand, if any resources used by the Government project would otherwise be totally unemployed, now and in the future, their use obviously incurs no opportunity cost in the private sector. In an economy such as that of the United States since World War II employment of resources has usually been so high that this consideration is often largely irrelevant to the facts of the matter, except when a project is designed specifically to make use of idle resources, e.g., to provide jobs to the unemployed. However, some types of project, or projects undertaken in particular sectors of the economy may well utilize a relatively large proportion of resources and particularly labor, that might otherwise go unusued. For a discussion of this phenomenon and its consequences see [5] and also the paper by Haveman in this volume.

criterion on which to judge the desirability of a governmental project, from the point of view of the general welfare, is the value of the opportunities which the private sector must pass by when the resources are withdrawn from that sector. A government project is desirable if and only if the value of the net benefits which it promises exceeds the cost of the lost productive opportunities which that investment causes.

It follows almost immediately that *the correct discount rate for the evaluation of a government project is the percentage rate of return that the resources utilized would otherwise provide in the private sector.* That is, the correct discount rate is the opportunity cost in terms of the potential rate of return in alternative uses on the resources that would be utilized by the project. An example will readily show why this must be so. Suppose these resources are capable of returning our hypothetical 9 percent in the private sector. Consider three proposed government projects: Project *A* which offers an average rate of return of 12 percent, project *B* whose expected return is 9 percent, and project *C* whose anticipated yield is 7 percent. It should be obvious that if we discount the returns of project *C* at the opportunity rate of 9 percent we will end up with a negative net present value figure (i.e., 7 percent discounted at 9 percent comes out to less than the principal invested). If we discount project *B*'s expected returns at 9 percent we will obtain a zero figure for the present value of net benefits (the returns will just cover the cost of the investment). Only project *A*, when discounted at 9 percent, will be assigned a positive net benefit figure. Thus the discount rate calculated at the opportunity rate works just as it should: it passes projects whose yield is greater than its resources could earn in the private sector and turns down projects whose benefits are not equal to the earnings the resources could provide in private hands.

The same illustration also shows immediately how an incorrect choice of discount figure—one not equal to the opportunity rate—can result in decisions harmful to the general welfare. For example, consider two extreme possibilities in terms of our hypothetical figures—a discount rate that is much too high (say, 15 percent) and one that is much too low (say, 5 percent). At the excessive 15 percent figure the usual cost-benefit criterion would reject all three projects, even project *A*. The Government would then fail to undertake an investment that clearly represents an efficient use of society's resources. On the other hand, a 5 percent discount rate would, on a cost-benefit criterion, lead to the construction of all three projects. Thus even investment *C* would be undertaken even though it uses resources that should better be left in private hands. For it takes resources from employments in which they return 9 percent and puts them into an occupation in which they bring in only 7 percent, a palpable 2 percent net loss to the community.

The upshot is perfectly clear. Any discount rate that is clearly above or clearly below the opportunity cost rate is indefensible because either of these will lead to decisions that reduce the general welfare. We must turn therefore to an investigation of the opportunity cost rate of resources, for once we have determined this we will have the requisite information for the choice of discount rate to be used in the evaluation of Government projects.

27-877—69—vol. 1——33

3. Reasons for Differences in Opportunity Costs*

Matters would be relatively simple if any batch of resources withdrawn from the private sector were to incur the same (percentage) opportunity cost as any other batch. If an opportunity cost of r percent were to apply throughout the economy, to determine the social disocunt rate one would simply proceed to estimate this number, r, and the resulting figure would then be the discount rate.

Unfortunately, for a variety of reasons, the magnitude of the opportunity cost varies with the source from which a project's resources are obtained. As we will see, resources which might otherwise have been used by a corporation will generally incur a higher opportunity cost than do resources drawn from direct consumer use.

In some sense, differences in opportunity costs of resources taken from different sectors of the economy are all a manifestation of imperfections in the market. In principle, if capital could flow without restriction to any sector of the economy where its earnings would be increased and all returns on capital were to accrue to its investors, resources would be forced by the market process to yield the same rate of return in every use. The standard argument is easily summarized. Suppose in such an economy that there were two industries, one of which returned k percent on capital while the other yielded some higher return, say $2k$. In that case investors would find it profitable to withdraw funds from the first of these industries and put them to work in the second. But the growing scarcity of capital in the first industry would tend to reduce its outputs, raising its prices and (therefore) its rate of return. Similarly, in the second industry the influx of capital would expand production, and force prices and returns downward. This transfer of capital would continue so long as any substantial difference in the two rates of return persisted. The flow of capital would cease only when the rate of return in the first industry had risen sufficiently and that in the second had fallen enough to make the two rates of return equal. At that point, clearly, capital withdrawn from the one sector would have exactly the same rate of return as capital withdrawn from the other—their opportunity cost rates would be identical.

Why does such equalization generally not occur in practice? There are two broad reasons: First, part of the return to capital may not accrue to the investor. A prime example of this is provided by taxation which siphons part of that return off to the Government, and since the burden of taxation varies from industry to industry, from the corporate to the noncorporate sector, and so forth, it means that opportunity costs will vary accordingly. A second broad reason for such variation lies in impediments, such as monopoly, to the influx of capital into some productive activities.[2] Specifically, we will consider three broad sources of such divergence because they must be taken into explicit account in the determination of the social rate of discount. These elements are the following: (a) taxes, (b) risk, (c) divergence between private and social benefits (externalities). Let us examine them in turn.

[2] For the relevance of monopolistic elements to the social discount rate calculation, see [2], p. 791, footnote 2.

*Further discussion of this issue is found in the paper by Hirshleifer & Shapiro in this volume.

4. The Role of Taxes: Analysis

As already indicated, the burden of taxes will vary from industry to industry, from one class of producer to another, depending on its mode of organization—that is, corporation, partnership, or do-it-yourself production by the consumer himself.

However, let us, to begin with, assume for simplicity that there are only two classes of producer: The corporation, which pays a 50-percent corporate income tax, and the private individual who produces certain items for his own use, and who pays no taxes on this production process. Assume also that there are available for sale riskless Government bonds offering a rate of return of, say, 5 percent.

In our example, it is easy to determine the opportunity cost of resources withdrawn from the corporate sector. Corporations must yield to their investors an after-tax return of 5 percent. For otherwise investors would be unwilling to provide any funds to the corporations and would instead put all their money into the safe Government bonds. But the required after-tax return of 5 percent on corporate capital means that these firms must earn 10 percent on capital *before* payment of the 50 percent corporate profit tax. In other words, the presence of special taxes on the output of this sector means that resources invested in it must produce goods and services valued at a level sufficiently high to yield a 10 percent return. The corporation can then engage only in the production of consumers' or producers' goods whose purchasers value them sufficiently to pay a price that yields a 10 percent return on corporate investment. A withdrawal of resources from the corporation, then, will cause a reduction in output whose opportunity cost in terms of consumer valuation is given by that figure: 10 percent.

Notice in evaluating resources from the corporate sector in this way, it does not matter whether the resources are used by the firm to produce consumers' goods or producers' goods (e.g., machinery). So long as the output in question is supplied by a corporation, the resources used in its manufacture will have a 10 percent opportunity cost. The relevance of this consideration will be clear presently.

Let us turn now to the more difficult problem, the opportunity cost of resources withdrawn from the other productive sector in our imaginary economy, the do-it-yourself consumers.

Since goods produced by consumers for their own use do not provide a rate of return that is measurable directly it is necessary to find some indirect means by which their opportunity cost can be inferred. Fortunately there is a straightforward way in which this can be done. When a consumer voluntarily purchases one of the bonds available in our imaginary economy he is indicating that their 5 percent rate of return compensates him for giving up the use of that money in his do-it-yourself operation. Put another way, if this investment in his own production were worth more than 5 percent to him he would not buy the bond, while if his investment in his own work were worth less than 5 percent to him he would purchase more bonds than he does. Thus without any conscious calculation on his part, a consumer's security purchases reveal something about what the rate of return of investment in the production of goods for his own consumption is worth to him—the opportunity cost incurred when a dollar's worth of resources is prevented from going to him and is transferred to a Government investment project.

What about consumers who do not buy any bonds? It follows from the preceding discussion that their opportunity cost must be at least as high and probably higher than it is for bond purchasers.[3] To a man who chooses *not* to purchase bonds at 5 percent, the purpose for which he uses his money must by definition be worth more than 5 percent. This is no less true for a man who fails to purchase bonds because "he cannot afford them." That phrase merely implies that his consumption dollar means a great deal to him—perhaps even survival itself, and is therefore certainly more valuable than 5 percent.

We may summarize by saying that the opportunity cost of present consumption to nonbondholders must be at least as great as the figure for bondholders, and that to bondholders the opportunity cost of resources is indicated by the rate of return on their bondholdings.

In practice, of course, there is a broad spectrum of earnings tax conditions, among which are included the untaxed do-it-yourself productive process and corporate production with its (roughly) 50 percent profits tax. We have seen that the opportunity cost of resources from the untaxed sector (assuming the absence of risk and other such complications) is, roughly, r percent. In the corporation, half of whose earnings are taxed away, the opportunity cost rate is $2r$, where r is the bond rate of interest. Similarly, if the earnings of a partnership in a particular industry were reduced by, say, one-fourth through taxation, that firm would also have to earn enough before taxes to yield r percent after taxes to its investors. This company's pretax rate of return, call it s percent, must then satisfy the relationship

$$s-(1/4)s=r, \text{ that is, } (3/4)s=r \text{ or } s=(4/3)r.$$

This figure, which obviously lies between r and $2r$, will then be the opportunity cost rate for resources withdrawn from a firm paying 1/4 of its earnings in taxes.

5. Taxes and the Social Discount Rate: General Principles[4]

We may then generalize our results as follows:

(*a*) For production that is not subject to taxation the opportunity cost rate will generally be no lower than, and as an approximation, be equal to the r percent rate of return on riskless bonds.

(*b*) For production whose returns are taxed at a rate such that the fraction $1/k$ of the returns *remains* after taxes, then the opportunity cost rate for resources withdrawn from this sector will be kr percent. Thus, in the preceding example, $1/k$, the fraction of the partnership's pretax returns remaining after taxes, is ¾. Therefore, the opportunity cost rate for its resources is $kr=4/3r$ percent.

[3] In particular, the do-it-yourself producer may not only invest his own money in his productive activity, but may in fact borrow to help in its financing. In that case his productive activity must to him be worth at least as much as the rate of interest on the funds that he borrows, for otherwise he would not be willing to pay that amount for a loan. Since the rate of interest on loans to an individual can be expected to exceed the yield on a government bond of comparable life, the basic proposition enunciated in the text still holds for such a borrower—the opportunity cost of resources coming from him must be at least as high as the bond rate of interest (and it may well be significantly higher).

[4] This section draws heavily on an unpublished note [13] by Prof. David D. Ramsey of the University of Missouri. That note pointed out some shortcomings in an earlier version of my analysis [2].

What can be done with the diverse opportunity cost figures for resources drawn from different sectors in calculating a single discount rate for the evaluation of a Government project? The answer is simple. Suppose the Government is to withdraw some resources from the one type of productive activity and some from the other. Suppose, for example, 20 percent of these resources would have come from do-it-yourself production yielding a 5-percent return, and 80 percent from the corporate sector with its 10 percent opportunity cost yield. Then the Government project will offer a net benefit to society if on the whole it can produce a rate of return equal to their weighted average:

$$(20/100) \times 5\% + (80/100) \times 10\% = 9\%.$$

More generally, we have as a third rule:

(*c*) The correct social discount rate for a project will be a weighted average of the opportunity cost rate for the various sectors from which the project would draw its resources, and the weight for each such sector in this average is the proportion of the total resources that would come from that sector.[5]

The preceding rule, incdentally, will be seen to hold where there are differences in opportunity cost rates whatever their origin, whether produced by variation in the tax treatment of different economic sectors, or differences arising from any other source. The three rules (*a*), (*b*), and (*c*) also hold for an economy with many more than the two sectors in our simple illustration.

Before turning to the next general topic, it should be emphasized that the preceding analysis was couched entirely in terms of productive sectors and had nothing to do with the distinction between consumption and investment goods. A corporation can produce either or both of these two types of output and the same opportunity cost rate will apply to both. This means, if the analysis is valid, that the correct social discount rate will tend to be considerably higher than it would appear to be on the basis of some of the more standard modes of calculation[6]

[5] The weighted average expression for the social discount rate can be derived by the following elementary argument. Let k dollars be invested in the Government project and let v be its value (including benefit flow) one year later. Suppose, if the project had not been built, that the proportion p of the investment would have been employed in an activity yielding r percent, and that the remainder, $(1-p)$, would have been used in an investment with an s percent yield. In total, at the end of the year the alternative use would then have yielded the total value

$$pk(1+r)+(1-p)k(1+s)=k[1+pr+(1-p)s] .$$

The Government's use of the k dollar investment will therefore be socially preferable to the private use if and only if

$$v>k[1+pr+(1-p)s], \text{ i.e., } k<\frac{v}{1+[pr+(1-p)s]} .$$

Thus, the discount rate is given by $pr+(1-p)s$, the weighted average of the returns in the two sectors described in rule (*c*) in the text. This argument obviously also applies directly to the case where resources are taken from more than two economic sectors.

[6] See, for example, Krutilla and Eckstein [8] and Eckstein [3]. On the other hand, I suspect that the radically different discount rate calculation recommended by Harberger [4] will yield results very similar to those that would be obtained by the methods proposed in the text. There also seems to be no conflict between these methods and the views expressed in the Joint Economic Committee's report ([7], pp. 13–14), which are deliberately (and, no doubt, wisely) vague on this issue, stating "while advocating the opportunity cost of displaced private spending as a correct conceptual basis for the Government discount rate, the subcommittee does not presume to advocate a precise method for calculating this rate. . . . We agree with the Bureau of the Budget's reluctance to 'adopt . . . the rate of return on private investment foregoing alone because government funds are withdrawn from both consumption and investment.' " The text of this paper obviously recognizes the relevance of the distinction between consumption and investment but maintains that the proper role of consumption in the discount rate of calculation is not quite what it is sometimes taken to be.

which, in terms of our simple example again, would employ the bond rate r for the discounting of all relevant consumers' goods production and the corporate rate only to (corporate) investment. An illustration will make the difference clear. Suppose the opportunity cost rates for our two sectors were the figures in our previous illustration (5 and 10 percent), and suppose the resources to be employed in the proposed project would otherwise have been divided into the following proportions:

	Percent
Consumers' goods production by consumer sector	20
Consumers' goods production by corporate sector	70
Producers' goods production by corporate sector	10

Since the conventional calculation applies the 5 percent bond discount rate to all consumers' goods, its weighted average calculation of the social discount rate would be

$$[(20+70)/100]\times 5\%+[10/100]\times 10\%=5.5\%.$$

But, as has been shown, even consumers' goods produced by the corporate sector must yield a 10-percent return on investment, and hence the correct weighted opportunity cost rate must be (as before)

$$[20/100]\times 5\%+[(70+10)/100]\times 10\%=9\%,$$

a very substantial difference.[7] It may be noted, incidentally, that the orders of magnitude of the figures are not totally unrealistic.

A final conclusion to be derived from the analysis is the implication that the appropriate discount rate may vary from one proposed Government project to another.* If they derive their resources from different sectors or vary in the proportions in which they draw upon the different sectors, then their opportunity costs may vary. Consequently, it may sometimes be possible to reduce the opportunity cost rate for the project by careful planning of the means by which its resources are obtained. In particular, as has already been noted, a project designed to draw heavily on resources which would otherwise be unemployed will for this reason incur an opportunity cost that is particularly low.

[7] The recommended procedure does of course conflict with the approach that has been taken in a number of highly reputable studies. It is therefore important to be very clear about the case for taking the opportunity cost of consumers' goods produced by a corporation to be dependent on the corporate income tax. The argument can be put very simply: assume that without a corporation tax all consumers' goods are associated with an r percent opportunity cost rate. Then the imposition of such a tax will lead the corporate sector to reduce its outputs and hence to raise the marginal utility of these goods to their consumers. Therefore a reduction of c units of corporate output of consumers' goods after the tax has gone into effect will incur a greater loss of consumer utility than the same c units of decrease in output would have caused before the tax. Hence if the opportunity cost was r when there was no tax it *must* exceed r percent after the tax has taken effect.

The argument clearly runs into all sorts of complications in practice in a world of risk and imperfect competition. But if the corporations were perfect competitors in a riskless economy it would apply precisely. Then the imposition of a tax would lead a sufficient number of firms to leave the production of any consumers' good to raise the pretax rate of return to $2r$ where r is the pure rate of interest. The marginal cost of a unit of output (excluding marginal return to capital) would, in equilibrium, equal price minus $2r\Delta k$ where Δk is the incremental capital needed to produce the output, and hence the opportunity cost per unit of capital moved out of this productive activity must then be $2r$.

Note that this argument is independent of the incidence of the tax, i.e., it must hold whether or not price has gone up by the amount of the tax, or has even gone up at all.

*Further discussion of this issue is found in the paper by Hirshleifer & Shapiro in this volume.

6. The Role of Risk*

Risk will also typically vary from industry to industry and from firm to firm. This produces further differences in reported rates of return. A risky industry may be expected to offer comparatively high profit prospects in order to be attractive to investors. That is why returns on stocks are typically higher than bond yields and why the rate of interest on a corporate bond is normally higher than that on a comparable Government security.

The nature of the issue this poses for the calculation for a social discount rate as well as its resolution can be brought out clearly with another simple example. Suppose two firms which are in all other aspects alike produce respective rates of return before taxes of 10 and 12 percent. The 2-percent excess in the return of the riskier firm is, in effect, an insurance premium to compensate investors for the greater gamble involved in offering funds to the less safe of the two companies. The question then is whether resources withdrawn from the second firm incur an opportunity cost of 12 percent, or whether the true (riskless) opportunity cost is merely 10 percent as it is for the other firm.

One may argue that in fact the two companies yield the same real rate of return to their investors. Since the latter's 2 percent higher return merely covers investors' risk, as already noted, the real loss to investors of withdrawal of a unit of resources will therefore be equal.

However, a number of noted economists (see, e.g., Arrow [1], Hirshleifer [6] and Samuelson [14]) have argued with considerable cogency that the risk for the investment in an individual project taken by itself does not necessarily correspond to the risk it contributes to society's investment as a whole.[8] A bankrupt firm which continues to operate in the hands of its receivers is a loss to its investors but not to society. More important, because in the economy a very large number of projects are underway at any given time, the insurance principle, that is, the statistical "law" of large numbers, applies to them if their prospects for success are largely independent. It is true that because a recession can produce serious consequences for a large number of investment projects simultaneously, the prospects for their success are not completely unrelated. But if, as an approximation, we ignore this complication it can be shown that the larger the number of projects involved the smaller the risk contributed to total social return by any one of them. Taken as a whole, from the viewpoint of society, they become virtually riskless.

This is essentially the principle on which a life insurance company operates. It cannot tell when any one of its policyholders will expire and, taken by itself, the risk of insuring him is enormous. But when it insures a large body of policyholders the operation becomes *virtually riskless*. That is, barring calamities such as epidemics or wars,

[8] It should be noted, incidentally, that risk affects governmental as well as private investment projects. For example, many abandoned canals were no doubt built in the anticipation that their use would continue much longer than it did. And just as bankruptcy may prevent the completion of a private investment project, a change in administration after an election may result in the abandonment of some unfinished public undertaking.

*Further discussion of this issue is found in the paper by Hirshleifer & Shapiro in this volume.

the insurance company can forecast with virtual certainty how many of its policyholders will die in any given year, and the residual risk approaches zero as the number of policyholders increases.

Viewed in this way, we must conclude that while the risk involved in any individual investment project is apt to be substantial for the supplier of capital, it may be negligible from the point of view of society as a whole.[9]

Only one more step is needed to see what these considerations imply for the role of risk in the evaluation of the social discount rate. Going back to our illustration, consider once again the 12-percent rate of return of our riskier firm. The 2-percent differential between this return and that of the safer company represents, as we saw, no net gain to the investor who is merely compensated thereby for his risk relative to investment in the other company. But since to society either firm's investment program is virtually riskless, it follows that the social rates of return of the two are *not* equal. One produces a riskless 12 percent while the other yields a riskless 10 percent. This means that the corresponding social discount rate of resources drawn from these two firms would be a weighted average of these two rates, in accord with rule (c) of the preceding section.

Specifically, it means that in the social discount rate calculation there should be no deductions for a risk component in the rates of return observed in practice. When a corporation produces a before-tax yield of 16 percent, 6 percent of which might be judged as a risk premium, from the point of view of the social discount rate the corresponding opportunity cost rate is 16 and not 10 percent. For here risk plays the same role as taxation in its effects on the social rate of return. Private risk forces the firm to invest only in opportunities which offer a yield of 16 percent. The social opportunity cost is therefore correspondingly high.

We conclude that the correct discount rate is a weighted average, over all tax and risk circumstances, of the rates of return that would otherwise be earned by the resources to be used in a Government project. As already stated, rule (c) then holds, at least approximately, for variations in rates of return resulting from differences in risk as well as from disparities in tax rates.

7. Externalities *

There is one other element important for the social discount rate calculation, though we may treat it rather briefly. It is a matter that has been given considerable emphasis in the economic literature, and justly so. This is the issue of externalities—the differences between social and private costs and benefits of an investment program, of which risk compensation is a special case, as we have just seen.

The point is easily made with the aid of the most standard of illustrations of an externality. The firm whose output pollutes the atmosphere obviously provides a net social return significantly lower than

[9] I have made this point elsewhere in a slightly more formal manner (see [2], p. 794–5). Note that on this point my position differs somewhat from that of the Joint Economic Committee ([7], pp. 13–14) which calls for a special allowance in the discount rate applied to a particular public project for the risk to which that project is subject. On the argument in the text, the *incremental* risk contributed by any one such project may plausibly be considered negligible, and hence requires little or no discount rate adjustment.

*Further discussion of this issue is found in the papers by Davis & Kamien, and Kneese & d'arge in this volume.

the figure given by the yield on its capital. Similarly, the company that produces external benefits; perhaps training of the underprivileged, yields a social product greater than is indicated by its financial returns. In calculating the social discount rate, corresponding adjustments naturally have to be made in the discount figure. The polluting firm's rate of return figure has to be adjusted downward in order to base the calculation on its true social yield, and a corresponding upward adjustment is required to obtain the true social opportunity cost of the company whose operations provide training to the unskilled.

This principle is one that would no doubt be accepted by virtually all economists. Yet one must not overlook some reservations relating to its implementation. First, one must recognize difficulties that beset the evaluation of externalities. The cases where investigators have succeeded in providing some quantification of external costs and benefits are extremely rare. Many types of externality (that is, the impairment of health that is caused by pollutants) simply are not readily translated into financial terms; for example, into a numerical evaluation of their consequences for the social rate of return. Even where such a translation is possible, the effects are typically so widely diffused among the population that an estimate of their aggregate value becomes very difficult. These remarks are of course not meant to question the validity of the principle under discussion—the need to adjust the discount rate for the *social* costs and benefits of the resources concerned. It does however suggest that anything but the roughest sort of implementation of this principle will not be very easy.

A second comment on the externalities issue is the fact, not often alluded to in the literature, that governmental projects can also produce externalities. Army trucks pollute the air as effectively as private vehicles, and government work also can, as a byproduct, teach skills to ghetto residents. This means that in judging the desirability of a proposed Government project adjustments for externalities must be made on both sides of the ledger—the estimated yields of both the private and the governmental projects competing for resources must be revised in order to arrive at *net* social contribution.

8. Subsidy for the Future

There is one argument in the literature which has been used to maintain that the weighted average rate of return such as that proposed in rule (c) yields too high a social discount rate. This view maintains that private citizens tend systematically not to invest enough from the viewpoint of the Nation's future. It concludes that the discount rate should be kept very low in order to induce an increase in investment today, as a contribution to the Nation's welfare tomorrow.[10] A low discount rate will clearly lead to approval of a large number of governmental investment projects, and the greater the number of

[10] This view is clearly associated with the work of Pigou. See [12], part I, chapter II. Among others, Marglin also seemed to take such a stand in an earlier paper [10]. In a more recent discussion [11] his position is hedged considerably more. He argues "that individuals may not have unique preference maps, that instead preferences may depend on the role they play. . . . The preferences with respect to present and future which individuals hold in their political life as citizens may differ from the preferences they hold in their economic roles as consumers and producers." (Pp. 15–16). However, he does not indicate whether he believes the difference between the two follows any consistent pattern, one way or the other.

investment projects undertaken, the greater is the contribution to the Nation's prosperity.

Such a position is, however, questionable in several respects. First of all, there is no basis for the presumption that a transfer of resources from the private to the public sector will necessarily produce a net increase in the amount of investment undertaken by the economy. The increase in the amount of governmental capital construction is very likely to be offset, at least in part, by a decline in private investments in plant and equipment.

Surely, if society's investment for the future is considered to be inadequate the appropriate remedy is to institute simultaneous inducements to both private and public capital formation.[11] As we have seen, an arbitrarily low discount rate on public projects is certainly not the instrument for that purpose. Such artificially low discount rate on public projects introduce serious inefficiencies into the investment process by causing the withdrawal of resources from areas of use in which their yield is high and leading to their transfer to areas in which their return is low. This is a most peculiar way to encourage more effective investment in the future.

In any event, those who maintain that there is inadequate provision for the future draw incorrect general inferences from irrelevant particular cases. It is difficult to quarrel with the conservationist's view that the destruction of irreplaceable natural resources imposes a heavy cost on our posterity. The destruction of a portion of a canyon, the extinction of a species of wildlife, the erosion of soil all are matters of serious concern because once done they cannot be undone, and this is precisely the legitimate ground on which conservationists urge increased care in avoiding depletion of our resources.[12]

But it is not legitimate to jump from the valid point that one generation has no right to use up wastefully the resources that cannot be replaced by its successsors, to the questionable conclusion that each generation is constrained to engage in overall efforts to support its posterity beyond the level that is indicated by the free market. For that is precisely what is involved in a program of low discount rates or any other program of special inducements to investment.

The basic issue is whether it is desirable to subsidize in this way the commitment to the future of resources which could otherwise serve society today. Considerable real investment is already provided by the private sector and by the program of government projects which can pass the standard cost-benefit test utilizing the discount rate that

---

[11] This viewpoint is also taken by the Joint Economic Committee report ([7], p. 11). There are of course important cases where it is considered socially desirable to stimulate governmental output of goods and services which cannot be provided effectively by the private sector. Education, elimination of pollution and national defense are all services whose supply, it is generally felt, should not be left exclusively in the hands of the private sector. In such cases Government subsidy, and in some cases complete Governmental financing, is entirely appropriate because of the external benefits contributed by these activities. But this only requires us to take explicit account of such externalities in our cost-benefit calculations. It does not justify a particularly low *discount rate* on the Government project which would distort the allocation of resources between short- and long-term investments. If we need more expenditure on education now—better books and better teachers—a reduction in the discount rate would not provide them. It would only stimulate the construction of durable school buildings, the long-term investment portion of educational-expenditure.

[12] Paradoxically, in practice a low discount rate will probably increase the destruction of such resources. In the past low discount rates have been used to provide a cost-benefit justification for precisely those engineering projects which have constituted, at least according to conservationists, the most serious threats to national parklands, recreation areas and other such resources.

has already been described. Is there any justification for a program of subsidies designed to produce an even greater overall commitment of resources to the future?

A little thought shows that the grounds for such a program are tenuous at best. Our economy is characterized by a long run rate of growth of GNP of the order of 3 to 4 percent per year, compounded, and in recent years the growth rate has been even greater. Per capita income has risen persistently throughout our history and there is every reason to expect the rise to continue. We are therefore wealthier than our predecessors and it can quite safely be predicted that our successors will be richer than we. In effect, then, the subsidization of a program of added investment amounts to an inducement for the transfer of additional resources from the poor to the rich. It would take inputs whose product would be available for consumption today and make them available tomorrow when the supply of consumer goods is likely to be so much more abundant than it is at present.[13]

It should be made clear that the preceding discussion is not meant to imply that there is no need for increased activity by the public sector. The crisis of our cities, the problems of the impoverished and the underprivileged minorities and a variety of other critical issues may well require for their resolution governmental activity on an increased scale. But these all call for investments whose yield is obtainable quickly, not long-term investments, the bulk of whose benefits will become available in the more distant future. Advocacy of a very low discount rate in these circumstances is tantamount to the view that these immediate problems are not very pressing, and that society's resources are better transferred to the service of the future generations who in any case will surely be wealthier than we.

9. The Problem of the Second Best

One technical problem besets the analysis of the social discount rate presented in this paper. This is the well-known problem of the second best. We have seen how taxes, risk, and externalities produce discrepancies in the rates of return earned by various parts of the private sector. This means that capital simply is not allocated optimally within that sector. Society could obviously benefit by a transfer of capital from areas in which its social rate of return is relatively low to other parts of the economy offering a higher social return.

It is, then, not necessarily true that the rules of optimal investment procedure for the public sector are applicable, unless they are simultaneously put into operation in the private portion of the economy as well. For it has long been shown (see [9]) that if an optimality rule is enforced in one sector of the economy alone it can actually make matters worse.

In the present case, however, it does not seem plausible that this problem will be very serious. By the nature of the opportunity cost test, it calls for a transfer of resources only from a use in which its yield is relatively low to one where its return is comparatively high. This implies that the social welfare can be expected to increase in the

[13] This argument is based on Tullock [15]. For a similar position, see also the Joint Economic Committee report [7], p. 11.

process, assuming of course that there has been adequate adjustment for differences between private and social returns, so that the yield and opportunity cost figures take into account the more indirect contributions of the resources in question.

10. Concluding Comment

There always remains a formidable task of implementation even after the basic principles in an area have been enunciated. But a rational decision process does require examination of those principles. It is primarily to this task that this paper has addressed itself. It has proposed what is, in appearance, a relatively simple formula for the evaluation of the social discount rate, the weighted average of the rates of return in the various productive sectors from which resources would be withdrawn for the government project under consideration.

But the simplicity of this expression is deceptive. It is not easy to determine in practice from what productive sector a given project will be drawn, or even from where governmental investment as a whole obtains its resources. What one seeks in trying to obtain this information is the catalog of the decrements in the outputs of the various portions of the private sector which would result from a governmental investment program. When the matter is put in this way, its difficulties should be obvious.

Nor is it easy to judge the rate of return figures for the various sectors of the economy. A corporation offers different nominal rates of return on its various types of debt and equity and, as the recent literature on corporation finance has brought out so forcefully, it is not easy to arrive on the basis of these figures at a single number representing the rate of return on the company's capital. Perhaps a reasonable rule of thumb is the traditional weighted average of the rates of return on a firm's stocks, its bonds, and its other securities, where each of these sources of funds is weighted by the proportion of the company's total finances which it contributes.

In sum, the calculation of the social rate of discount is not something that can be left simply to traditional practices and conventions. The underlying principles should enable us, by a reasonable process of approximation to arrive at operational procedures that represent a significant improvement over current procedures. I have sought to emphasize the complications in order to avoid the impression that all the issues have been settled and can readily be reduced to routine. But I believe firmly that with the help of the principles and the data now available one should be able to arrive at reasonable approximations to the social rate of discount. Certainly it should be possible to derive figures considerably more defensible than the conventional calculations that are all too often utilized to justify projects not all of which are clear in their economic merit.

REFERENCES

[1] K. J. Arrow, "Discounting and Public Investment Criteria," in A. V. Kneese and S. C. Smith, eds., *Water Research*, Baltimore, 1966.

[2] W. J. Baumol, "On the Social Rate of Discount," *American Economic Review*, September 1968, pp. 788–802.

[3] Otto Eckstein, *Water Resources Development: The Economics of Project Evaluation*, Cambridge, Mass., 1961.

[4] Arnold Harberger, "Statement," in *Hearings Before the Subcommittee on Economy in Government of the Joint Economic Committee of the Congress of the United States*, July 30–August 1, 1968, Washington, 1968.

[5] R. Haveman and J. V. Krutilla, "Unemployment, Excess Capacity, and Benefit-Cost Investment Criteria," *Review of Economics and Statistics*, Vol. 49, No. 3, August 1967.

[6] Jack Hirshleifer, "Investment Decisions Under Uncertainty: Applications of the State-Preference Approach," *Quarterly Journal of Economics*, May 1966, *80*, 252–77.

[7] Joint Economic Committee, *Economic Analysis of Public Investment Decisions: Interest Rate Policy and Discounting Analysis*, Washington, 1968.

[8] J. V. Krutilla and O. Eckstein, *Multiple Purpose River Development, Studies in Applied Economic Analysis*, Baltimore, 1958.

[9] R. Lipsey and K. Lancaster, "The General Theory of the Second Best," *Review of Economic Studies*, 1956, *24*, 11–32.

[10] S. A. Marglin, "The Social Rate of Discount and the Optimal Rate of Investment," *Quarterly Journal of Economics*, February 1963, 77, 95–112.

[11] ———, "The Discount Rate in Public Investment Evaluation" (unpublished) December 1968.

[12] A. C. Pigou, *The Economics of Welfare*, 4th ed., London, 1932.

[13] D. D. Ramsey, "On the Social Rate of Discount: Comment," 1968 (unpublished).

[14] P. A. Samuelson, "Principles of Efficiency: Discussion," *American Economic Review*, Proc., May 1964, *54*, 93–96.

[15] Gordon Tullock, "The Social Rate of Discount and the Optimal Rate of Investment: Comment," *Quarterly Journal of Economics*, May 1964–78, 331–36.

[8]

Optimal Departures From Marginal Cost Pricing

By WILLIAM J. BAUMOL AND DAVID F. BRADFORD*

The need for this paper is a paradox in itself and indeed it might be subtitled: *The Purloined Proposition or The Mystery of the Mislaid Maxim*. For the results which it describes have appeared many times in the literature and have been reported by most eminent economists in very prominent journals. Yet these results may well come as a surprise to many readers who will consider them to be at variance with ideas which they have long accepted.

The proposition in question asserts that, *generally, prices which deviate in a systematic manner from marginal costs will be required for an optimal allocation of resources, even in the absence of externalities.* The reason for the difficulty into which marginal cost pricing is likely to fall is rather well known. What is not widely recognized is that there exists a highly sophisticated and well-developed body of literature indicating what should be done in such circumstances.

To see how the problem arises, consider an economy in which all industry has been nationalized and in which the central planning agency is dedicated to the maximization of social welfare. Suppose, accordingly, that it is decided to set all prices *equal* to marginal costs and to make up any deficits by subsidy out of the governmental treasury. If these funds are derived by excise taxes this is obviously a decision to make some prices depart from marginal costs after all. Or if it is obtained by an income tax, it is the price of labor which is forced away from its marginal cost. Any tax, except a Pigouvian poll tax—which might perhaps more felicitously be called an "inescapable tax"—will unavoidably affect some price. There is no way out of it. Any level of tax revenue which the government is determined to collect, whether as a means to make up a deficit resulting from a marginal cost pricing arrangement or for any other purpose, must in practice produce some price distortion.

Once this difficulty is recognized it becomes clear that one is dealing with a problem in the area of the second best. We are now faced with a problem involving maximization *in the presence of an added constraint*. Resource allocation is to be optimal under the constraint that governmental revenues suffice to make up for the deficits (surpluses)[1] of the individual firms that constitute the economy.

* The authors are members of the department of economics, Princeton University. We are grateful to the National Science Foundation whose grant greatly facilitated completion of this paper. We must also express deep appreciation to our colleagues, Charles Berry, Stanley Black, William Branson, and W. Arthur Lewis, and to Ralph Turvey, whose comments and suggestions helped enormously in the development of its ideas.

[1] Presumably, as a practical matter, there is an asymmetry between the problems posed by surpluses and those resulting from deficits. The real difficulty arises when we try to collect resources to cover the deficits without distorting consumers' and producers' choices. Since it is not possible in practice to levy lump sum taxes whose magnitude is independent of the decisions of those who pay them, we are forced to consider second-best solutions to the tax problem. A surplus can presumably be distributed more easily in a "lump sum" manner. One can, for example, distribute shares in future surpluses to all members of the economy on the basis of their incomes at some point in the past, or one can simply divide them equally among all individuals.

It should be emphasized also that the deficit problem need not arise only in the case of decreasing costs where

The theorems which have been developed to deal with this issue derive added interest from the fact that they are (virtually) the only concrete prescriptions for any second-best problem which have so far appeared in the literature. The discussion of this paper differs from the earlier writings in several ways. First, it deals with an important case not explicitly covered in most of the other papers in the area: quasi-optimal pricing when commodity prices throughout the economy are all adjusted as far as is possible. Second, it attempts a simplified exposition which is, of course, possible only at a cost in terms of loss of generality. Third, it brings together, explicitly, all three strands of the discussion: the welfare theoretic, the regulatory, and the public finance contributions. Finally, as far as we know, it offers the first overview of the extensive literature that has grown up in the area.

I. *Sources of the Analysis*

The preceding formulation of the problem suggests why the results described in this paper are not widely recognized. For they arise not out of the literature of welfare economics but from two more specialized fields—the theory of taxation and the analysis of public utility regulation.

The connection of the analysis with the theory of taxation is easy to understand. For the investigation, as it has just been described, is tantamount to a study of a system of optimal excise and income taxes. Only a small modification in our statement is needed for this purpose: instead of requiring the governmental revenue to equal the (algebraic) sum of the deficits of the firms constituting the economy, the revenue constraint can be generalized to require the tax system to bring in whatever revenues the government has decided it needs. The taxes which are optimal subject to this more general revenue requirement constraint then can be shown to follow the same necessary condition as that which replaces the marginal cost pricing rule in our previous discussion.

Similarly, there is a direct line between the more general welfare analysis and the theory of public utility regulation. For one reason or another, various public or regulated private monopolistic or partially monopolistic enterprises are operated under what amounts to a fixed profit constraint. Examples are turnpike authorities (required to cover costs and pay back invested capital), and regulated electricity, water, and telephone systems. The enterprises cited as examples are all firms that market a number of commodities. The turnpike sells easy driving between many different pairs of points, and, perhaps more important, at various times of day. Similarly, the telephone system sells ordinary telephone services for various uses over various distances and at various times, and, in addition, sells private wire, teletype, television signal transmission, and other services related to, but not identical with, telephone services as usually conceived. In each example the demands for the different services are very obviously strongly interrelated, and they are obviously produced under conditions involving common costs.

If we assume that the net revenue allowed these enterprises is less than the amount profit maximization would yield, some degree of freedom is introduced into the pricing of the commodities produced.[2] A wide variety of output combinations and

the revenue yielded by marginal cost pricing will fall short of the total costs of the firm. For example, in practice revenue requirements of the firm are often based on historical accounting cost figures which management feels it must recover. Similarly, governmental tax requirements may exceed any profits obtained from nationalized firms subject to diminishing returns when they price at marginal costs.

[2] Of course, some amount of freedom is also introduced into the choice of method of production. We assume throughout that good will, pride of service, patriotism or the shrewdness of regulators assure that whatever output combination is chosen is produced at minimum cost.

sets of prices can then be chosen, each of which would just meet the net revenue constraint. The problem, then, is to determine which of these is optimal (second best) from the point of view of the use of resources to serve consumer desires. A similar problem obviously arises in a nationalized industry which is required to earn enough to cover its costs.

II. *The Nature of the Theorem*

In this section we shall describe the rules indicating whether a particular price-output combination that satisfies the profit constraint is socially optimal, i.e., whether from the point of view of the economy it yields the most effective allocation of resources permitted by the constraint.[3] A solution to this constrained maximum problem will be called "quasi-optimal," because it is a second-best solution forced upon us by the revenue requirement.

A problem such as ours is usually framed in terms of the determination of appropriate output levels, but it can also be treated in terms of the choice of a price set for the outputs. Given the relevant demand functions, the choice of prices is tantamount to the choice of (salable) output levels. The two problems are, of course, formally identical, but, as we shall show, the pricing decision approach avoids a number of difficulties and yields a surprisingly simple optimality rule. In most conventional and familiar terms this rule asserts that Pareto optimal utilization of resources in the presence of an absolute profit constraint requires (considering substitution effects alone) that all outputs be reduced by the same proportion from the quantities that would be demanded at prices equal to the corresponding marginal costs. The rule takes an even simpler form in the event cross elasticities of demand are zero. It then requires that each price be set so that its percentage deviation from marginal cost is inversely proportionate to the item's price elasticity of demand. According to this result, the social welfare will be served most effectively not by setting prices equal or even proportionate to marginal costs, but by causing unequal deviations in which items with elastic demands are priced at levels close to their marginal costs. The prices of items whose demands are inelastic diverge from their marginal costs by relatively wider margins.

This result is surely not immediately acceptable through intuition. It strikes us as curious, if for no other reason, because it seems to say that ordinary price discrimination might well set relative prices at least roughly in the manner required for maximal social welfare in the presence of a profit constraint. Since the objective of the analysis can be described as the determination of the optimally discriminatory set of prices needed to obtain the required profit, some degree of resemblance is perhaps to be expected. The case studied here is, thus, in a sense the obverse of the problem of profit maximizing price discrimination, and while the two solutions bear some qualitative resemblance, it can be shown that they may in fact differ substantially in quantity.

The theorem can be reformulated and generalized in a number of ways. Instead of utilizing the producers' and consumers' surplus concepts with all their theoretical limitations, the analysis can be framed in terms of the Hicksian compensating variation. Or a Pareto optimality approach can be utilized, both of these procedures obviating any need for interpersonal utility

[3] It is not suggested that profit-constrained firms will by themselves tend to institute such optimal policies. When profits are eliminated or reduced in importance, other objectives presumably guide decision makers. For one thing, they may be able to afford stupidity in production decisions as pointed out by Harvey Leibenstein. A well-known alternative goal is sales maximization, the implications of which have been discussed *ad nauseam* by one of the present authors. Other possibilities have been examined by Herbert Simon, Robin Marris, Oliver Williamson, Armen Alchian, and Reuben Kessel and by others. For a bibliography and an excellent discussion see Williamson.

comparisons. Similarly, the theorem has been extended to cover cases involving nonzero cross-elasticities of demand, to deal with input prices and the prices of intermediate goods, etc. Of course, once this is done the result loses some of its simplicity and the preceding statement requires considerable modification. But even then, surprisingly simple versions remain possible, as we shall see.

III. *The Formal Theorem*

In previous discussions, the basic theorem has been stated in a number of different ways. The objective itself has been described alternatively as: a) maximization of the sum of consumers' and producers' surpluses; b) determination of a set of prices from which it is *not* possible to change in a way that permits the gainers to compensate the losers; and c) maximization of the level of satisfaction of any one individual, given the utility level of each other individual (Pareto quasi-optimality). Each of these maximizations is, of course, constrained by the revenue requirement.

We will discuss the following four variants of the theorem, each of which gives a set of necessary conditions for quasi-optimal pricing:

1) If prices are quasi-optimal the ratio between the marginal profit yields of unit changes in the *prices* of any two goods will be equal to the ratio between their output levels.

2) For each product, the deviation of the quasi-optimal price from marginal cost must be proportionate to the difference between the product's marginal cost and marginal revenue (i.e., its marginal social welfare cost must be proportionate to its marginal contribution to the profit requirement). This result holds only in the case where cross-elasticities are all zero.

3) For each product, the percentage deviation of quasi-optimal price from marginal cost must be inversely proportionate to its price elasticity of demand. This result also holds only where cross-elasticities of demand are zero.

4) Quasi-optimal prices must yield outputs that deviate by (approximately) the same proportion from those which would result from pricing at the marginal costs corresponding to the quasi-optimal output levels. This last form of the proposition, which is the variant most frequently encountered in the literature, is more general than the second and third versions of the theorem.

In demonstrating these propositions we shall utilize a comparatively straightforward manner of proof which has not previously appeared in the literature.[4] To facilitate the exposition we start with a partial equilibrium approach. That is, we demonstrate that socially optimal pricing by a multi-product monopolist operating under a profit constraint is described by the preceding propositions. The monopolist is assumed able to set the prices of his final good outputs, but to purchase inputs at prices which remain fixed throughout the analysis. It will be clear that his optimal policy is the same as that which would be induced by the imposition of excise taxes equal to the derived divergence between output price and the marginal costs which would obtain if the outputs were to be produced by perfect competitors. This establishes the correspondence between the monopoly regulation and the excise taxation interpretations of the theorems.

If the monopolist is taken to be very large (e.g., if substantially all of the economy is operated by the government), or correspondingly, if the commodities taxed account for a large share of total output, the assumption of fixed input

[4] To simplify the exposition we have dispensed with some theoretical niceties in the proof presented here, especially in the definition of the objective function. These are discussed and the objective function is examined in greater detail in our forthcoming paper.

prices must clearly be relaxed. This has been recognized and dealt with in the literature (for a simple statement see A. C. Pigou (1947, pp. 105–09); a sophisticated treatment is found in M. Boiteux 1956). We do not go into detail on this problem, but we do show in a subsequent section that the same line of reasoning used in our proof can readily be extended to a general equlibrium model.

The demonstration proceeds as follows: Let $p_1, \ldots, p_n$ and $x_1, \ldots, x_n$ be the prices and outputs of the n commodities produced by the monopolist and, as indicated above, take as fixed the prices of his inputs. Let $Z(p_1, \ldots, p_n)$ be our (unspecified) measure of consumer benefit which is to be maximized subject to the profit constraint[5] $\Pi(p_1, \ldots, p_n) = M$ where the profit function has now been expressed in terms of prices rather than outputs. As usual in such constrained maximization problems, Z will be maximal subject to this constraint only if

$$(1) \quad \frac{\partial Z}{\partial p_i} = \lambda \frac{\partial \Pi}{\partial p_i}, \quad (i = 1, 2, \ldots, n)$$

That is the intuitively obvious first-order requirement that the marginal welfare gain from a given price change (price reduction) must be proportionate to its marginal profit cost.

[5] If the revenues permitted by regulation are based on total investment rather than being fixed in absolute amount, this constraint may require some modification. If (as is at least ostensibly the goal of regulation) gross profits are required to be no greater than the cost of capital, then net profits (over the cost of capital) will be zero and the constraint will hold as stated with $M = 0$. If, however, the profit rate is permitted to exceed the cost of capital and the firm's total capital varies with output levels we may end up with M, the total profit permitted by regulation, itself varying with output levels. Our formal results remain unchanged if in the profit constraint $\Pi = R - C = M$ (where R = total revenue and C = total cost) we use C^* to represent $M + C$ and rewrite the constraint as $\Pi = R - C^* = 0$. We can then express all of our results in terms of C^* instead of C. Economic interpretations are, however, clouded by this modification.

We can make the preceding equation much more explicit by examining more specifically the nature of the consumer benefit function $Z(p_1, \ldots, p_n)$. While we will not be able to say much about that function itself, we can be rather specific about its partial derivatives, which is all we need for our present purposes.

We need a basis on which to estimate the gain to consumers from price-quantity data. A one dollar reduction in the price of a commodity will enable a consumer who is presently consuming x units of that commodity to continue buying exactly his original bundle of goods with a budget that is smaller by x dollars than his original budget. Thus x dollars is a lower limit to the relevant compensating variation since this is the least he would be willing to pay for that price change, and he would probably pay more since the x dollar reduction in his budget accompanied by the one dollar reduction in the specified price would certainly permit him to buy his original bundle and might perhaps enable him to buy one which he prefers but which he could not previously afford. Similarly, if an individual is currently purchasing the respective amounts $x_1, \ldots, x_n$ of our n commodities at prices $p_1, \ldots, p_n$, the amount he would pay to confront instead prices $p_1 + \Delta p_1, p_2, \ldots, p_n$ will be at least $-x_1 \Delta p_1$. John Hicks (p. 330 ff.) shows rigorously in this same general manner that the *rate* of consumer gain per dollar *increase* in the price of any commodity is precisely the negative of the amount of the commodity initially consumed, times one dollar. We may then take as our expression for the derivative of the benefit function the compensating variation corresponding to the price change

$$\partial Z / \partial p_i = -x_i$$

Hence, substitution into the previous equation (1) yields

$$(2) \quad -x_i = \lambda \partial \Pi / \partial p_i$$

or, dividing by the corresponding condition for any other item j, we obtain

$$(2a) \qquad \frac{1}{x_i}\frac{\partial \Pi}{\partial p_i} = \frac{1}{x_j}\frac{\partial \Pi}{\partial p_j}$$

as the required condition for quasi-optimality.

Equation (2a), then, is the first of the four variants of the theorem described at the beginning of this section. This necessary condition for quasi-optimality requires marginal profit yields of price changes to be proportionate to output levels. It may perhaps claim the virtue that it is relatively operational. If the firm has some notion of the likely marginal profit yield of a change in any one of its product prices, management can readily check whether (2a) is approximately satisfied.

We can now proceed directly from (2) to a derivation of the other variants of the basic theorem. We use MR_i, MC_i, and E_i to represent, respectively, the marginal revenue, marginal cost, and price elasticity of demand of output i, and for simplicity assume that all cross-elasticities of demand are zero, though this is not necessary for the more general analysis, and is certainly not required for the preceding variant of the theorem.

Since[6]

$$(3) \qquad MR_i = p_i + x_i \partial p_i / \partial x_i$$

then

$$\partial \Pi / \partial p_i = (MR_i - MC_i) dx_i / dp_i$$
$$= (p_i + x_i \partial p_i / \partial x_i - MC_i) dx_i / dp_i$$

Substituting this into our basic condition (2) we have

$$-x_i dp_i / dx_i = \lambda(p_i + x_i dp_i / dx_i - MC_i)$$

or adding $(p_i + x_i dp_i/dx_i - MC_i)$ to both sides we obtain

$$p_i - MC_i = (1 + \lambda)(p_i + x_i dp_i/dx_i - MC_i)$$
$$= (1 + \lambda)(MR_i - MC_i)$$

This is the second form of the quasi-optimality theorem: the difference between price and marginal cost[7] should be proportionate to the difference between marginal revenue and marginal cost.

Next we may rewrite the preceding equation as

$$(4) \quad -\lambda(p_i - MC_i) = (1 + \lambda) x_i dp_i / dx_i$$

or

$$\frac{p_i - MC_i}{p_i} = \frac{1 + \lambda}{\lambda} \frac{1}{E_i}$$

since by the usual formula, $E_i = -(p_i/x_i)(dx_i/dp_i)$ which is the third form of the result.[8] Note that it implies that if all elasticities in question are equal, prices

[6] It is here that the zero cross-elasticities enter our exposition. In the more general case, of course, $MR_i = p_i + \sum_j x_j \partial p_j / \partial x_i$. In our forthcoming paper we have dealt in some detail with this more general case which clearly complicates the analysis but does not change its nature in any fundamental way.

[7] Some care must be exercised in interpreting the various forms of the theorem described here because marginal costs are not generally constant. Let $MC_i(q)$ represent marginal costs corresponding to the quasi-optimal output levels while $MC_i(M)$ represent the marginal costs corresponding to the equilibrium outputs when all prices are set equal to marginal costs. Then in our proposition we have $\Delta p_i = p_i - MC_i(q)$ and they are thus *not* necessarily equal to the $p_i - MC_i(M)$. That is, the propositions do not contrast quasi-optimal prices with the prices corresponding to a marginal cost pricing equilibrium as ordinarily conceived. They refer instead to the differences between the quasi-optimal prices and the marginal costs corresponding to the quasi-optimal output levels.

[8] It should be reemphasized that this form of the derivation deliberately ignores the supply side for the sake of expository simplicity. However, the analysis is easily extended to take supply into account, and this was done from the very beginning of the discussion, by Frank Ramsey and by A. C. Pigou in 1947. For example, Pigou states "Writing η (defined as negative) for the elasticity of demand in respect of pre-tax output, e_r for the corresponding elasticity of supply of the rth commodity and t_r for the ad valorem rate of tax on it, it can be proved that, in the conditions supposed (the optimum system of such taxes yielding a given revenue require) rates of tax . . . such that $t_r/(1/e_i - 1/\eta)$ has the same value for all values of r" (pp. 107–08).

should be set proportional to marginal costs.

For the final form of the proposition, write the deviation of price from marginal cost as Δp_i, i.e., set $p_i - MC_i = \Delta p_i$. Then equation (4) can be written after a minor rearrangement of terms as

$$\frac{dx_i}{dp_i}\Delta p_i = -\frac{1+\lambda}{\lambda}x_i$$

But the left-hand side of the preceding equation may be interpreted as an approximation to the change, Δx_i, in the ith commodity demanded which would result from a shift from the actual prices to current marginal cost levels. We thus obtain the last version of our theorem:

$$\Delta x_i = kx_i, \quad \text{where } k = (1+\lambda)/\lambda.$$

The more sophisticated discussions have generally emphasized this last form of the theorem, the assertion that quasi-optimal pricing requires (after compensation for income effects) a proportionate change in all purchases from the levels that would be observed if prices were set at marginal costs.[9] This interpretation has usually been preferred to the two variants that precede it because, as has been shown by M. Boiteux (1956), Paul Samuelson (1951), and others, this form of the theorem holds quite generally and does not depend on the simplifying assumptions needed to arrive at the two special forms of the theorem described before this last variant. Only our first relationship (2a), which requires the marginal profit yields of commodity price changes to be proportionate to their output levels, is of the same order of generality.[10]

IV. *Intuitive Rationale*

Though at first blush the rationale underlying the preceding propositions may not be entirely transparent, it is not too difficult to account for them intuitively. The last form of the theorem is perhaps the most helpful in offering us a grasp of the entire matter. We need merely think of the consequence of a deviation of price from marginal cost as a distortion of relative demand patterns. This immediately suggests the last form of the theorem for it implies that the damage to welfare resulting from departures from marginal cost pricing will be minimized if the *relative* quantities of the various goods sold are kept unchanged from their marginal cost pricing proportions. If we accept this plausibility argument, then the elasticity form of the theorem clearly follows. If we propose to (say) contract the demands for A and B each by precisely k percent, then if A's demand is much more elastic than B's, clearly A's price must be raised by a substantially smaller percentage than that of B.

A bit more light is shed on the matter by a simple graphic discussion that follows rather loosely an analysis first presented by Ursula Hicks (p. 167 ff) and developed

[9] In accord with the comments of fn. 6, this third form of the theorem should be read as follows: a change in prices from their quasi-optimal levels to *the corresponding marginal cost levels* should reduce all outputs in (approximately) the same proportions.

If we estimate demand changes on the assumption that the slope of each demand curve is constant over the relevant range, our proposition is valid for large as well as for small price changes. It now asserts that the divergence between price and marginal cost must be such that the estimated percentage changes in demand resulting from a drop in all prices to the given marginal cost levels are the same for all commodities.

[10] Note that application of the theorem in any of its forms does not rule out a two-part or a multi-part tariff. On the contrary, it tells us how to determine the quasi-optimal value for each of the multiplicity of prices that composes such a tariff. For example, when the consumer pays one charge for the rental of a telephone and another for each of his calls, this can be interpreted either as a two-part tariff or as a pair of prices for two distinct but related services each of which has a quasi-optimal price. This discussion is, of course, based on the observation that one cannot in reality impose a Pigouvian poll tax as one part of the multi-part tariff. Indeed, if such a lump sum tax were possible there clearly would be no need for the theorems under discussion. Marginal cost prices plus lump sum taxes could then satisfy the revenue requirement and yield an optimal allocation.

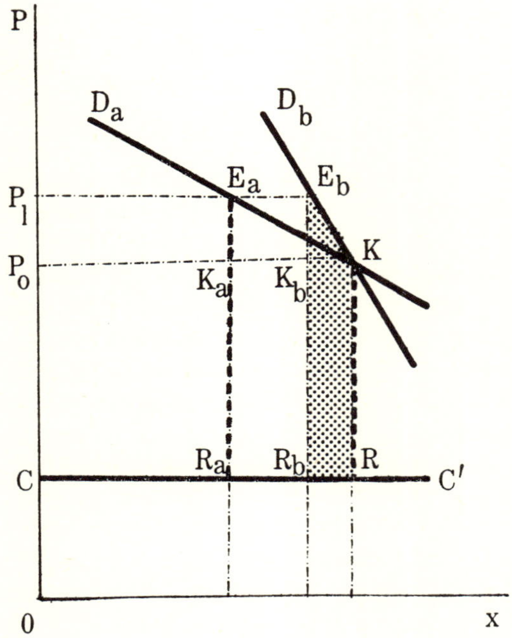

FIGURE 1

fully by William Vickrey in 1968. In Figure 1 consider the segments of two demand curves D_aK and D_bK through point K. Let us use the Marshallian measure of consumers' surplus to compare the psychic loss to consumers from a given price (tax) rise with the resulting increase in (tax) revenues. Then, if demand is in fact given by the less elastic curve D_bK and price rises from P_o to P_1, the loss of consumers' surplus will be $P_oKE_bP_1$. On the other hand, assuming for simplicity that marginal costs are constant at level OC, net revenue will be increased as a result of the price change by the quantity $P_oK_bE_bP_1$ minus R_bRKK_b. Thus the positive portion of the net revenue change, $P_oK_bE_bP_1$, may be considered to be offset by an approximately equivalent loss to consumers. This means that with the less elastic demand curve the rise in price will have caused a net reduction in net revenue plus consumers' surplus that is measured by the shaded area, R_bRKE_b.

Similarly, with the more elastic demand curve, D_aK, the rise in price from P_o to P_1 will decrease the sum of the revenue net of consumers' surplus by the greater area R_aRKE_a. In general, then (with marginal costs constant), a given price rise will exact a larger social cost in consumers' surplus not offset by increased revenues the more elastic the demand curve. That is essentially the reason for the theorem that calls for a relatively small deviation between the price and marginal cost of any commodity whose demand is comparatively elastic.

V. *A Simple General Equilibrium Model*

Our interest in conveying the central results of the literature discussed in our paper to a wide readership in an intuitively convincing fashion leads us to couch our argument of Section IV in terms of partial equilibrium analysis. It is desirable, however, to sketch out the way it all works in general equilibrium terms. A simple reinterpretation of the terms used in the derivation of the theorems will show that our proof is sufficient to establish the propositions in the special general equilibrium case in which there is only one input factor, labor, and all the productive activities are in the hands of the government. Accordingly, let $p_1, \ldots, p_n$, be the prices in terms of labor hours at which the n final outputs other than leisure, $x_1, \ldots, x_n$, all produced by the government, are sold to the consumer-laborers. The government is assumed to operate with a profit constraint in the form of a fixed number, M (which may be zero), of units of labor. In addition, of course, there is a production constraint, which we may write as[11]

[11] Notice that in putting this constraint in the form of an equality, we have ruled out production inefficiency. Although this is a plausible requirement and makes things easier, it is not always innocuous when more is meant by "consumer benefit" than attainment of Pareto optimality—the concept utilized here. See

(5) $$C = F(x_1, \ldots, x_n),$$

where C is the minimum labor input sufficient to produce the output vector, $x_1, \ldots, x_n$. The problem is to maximize "consumer benefit" subject to this production relation and the profit constraint,

(6) $$\pi = p_1x_1 + \ldots + p_nx_n - C = M$$

Now let us treat the government as an ordinary firm that imagines it can buy all the labor it wants at a price of one per unit. The additional labor it would have to buy to produce an additional unit of good is then the marginal cost of that good, both in the accounting sense and in the sense of its leisure opportunity cost, all other outputs held constant.

There will be, in general, a large set of price vectors compatible with both (a) clearing of the markets for goods and factors and (b) satisfaction of the government's profit constraint. It is useful to spell this statement out in somewhat more detail. If the aggregate labor sold is L, we can write the set of demand equations as

$$L = L(p_1, \ldots, p_n)$$
$$x_1 = x_1(p_1, \ldots, p_n)$$
$$\cdots\cdots\cdots\cdots$$
$$x_n = x_n(p_1, \ldots, p_n),$$

where, necessarily (Walras' Law),

$$p_1x_1 + \cdots + p_nx_n = L$$

For a set of prices to be market-clearing, the government must buy exactly the specified amount of labor and produce exactly the specified quantities of goods. By (5) and (6) "feasible price vectors" are those which satisfy the profit constraint conditions

$$L - F(x_1, \ldots, x_n) = M,$$

Peter Diamond and James Mirrlees for a proof that production efficiency will be called for under almost all "reasonable" assumptions about production, individual utility, and social welfare relations.

or, equivalently,

$$p_1x_1 + \cdots + p_nx_n - F(x_1, \ldots, x_n) = M$$

The task is to find among these an optimal price vector, where we have taken this to mean a vector which consumers in the aggregate would be unwilling (after costless negotiation among themselves) to bribe the government to change. The solution to this problem is found in the propositions set forth in Section III above. The entire analysis in that section continues to hold when the profit constraint as just described is used in place of the usual partial equilibrium construct.

VI. *The Taxed and the Untaxed Sectors*

Now we are equipped with a genuine, if very simple, general equilibrium apparatus, but one which in most respects can be manipulated in partial equilibrium terms. The key to this is the form in which we have expressed the production relation (as a cost function), the fixing of the government's profit constraint in terms of labor, and the corresponding choice of labor as price numeraire (so that the price of the single input factor, the "all other prices" of partial equilibrium analysis, is fixed at unity). In this model the government can be taken to tax the output of producers of the n non-leisure goods (where the tax is the difference between price and marginal cost), and hence these goods make up the "taxed sector." The untaxed sector here may reasonably be described as the production of negative labor input to the taxed goods-production sector, i.e., the production of leisure. In a rather trivial sense, in the latter sector marginal cost and price are always equal at unity.

It is illuminating at this point to reconsider "our" results in light of the following comment by Abba Lerner, who derives two special rules for quasi-optimality, each applicable to a special case:

> [One] rule [equalize tax elasticities] is

> appropriate where the shifting is only from a taxed to an untaxed sector, while the [other] rule [maintain proportionality of price to marginal cost] is appropriate where the shifting is only to another part of the taxed sector (as would be the case if all uses of resources could be, and were, taxed).
>
> What we need is a rule that is applicable whether the resources shifted by a tax remain in the taxed sector or go to the untaxed sector or are divided between the two sectors. [p. 285]

Documentation of the fact that a general rule for optimal excise taxation has long been available in the literature, and presentation of a simplified derivation of several forms of such a rule are precisely our objectives. It is easy to show that in those situations where Lerner recommends prices in proportion to marginal cost, our theorems do likewise; where Lerner recommends equalization of tax elasticities, so do our theorems; and where Lerner calls for something in between the two, our theorems provide an exact prescription.

In the case of the model which has just been described,[12] the statement that a tax change has as its only effect a shifting of resources from taxed to untaxed sectors is clearly equivalent to the assertion that the only output affected in the taxed sector is the one whose tax rate has changed. If the effect of varying any one tax is only to shift resources into the non-taxed sector then only own elasticities of the taxed goods, and not their cross-elasticities with one another, can be non-zero. In this case, Lerner and we (most directly in variant 3 of the theorem) conclude that the percentage deviation of price of any taxed commodity from marginal cost should be inversely proportional to its own price elasticity of demand.

We turn now to the next case where the alternative use of resources induced by tax changes can be said to be entirely in the taxed sector. This is obviously equivalent to the assertion that labor is perfectly inelastically supplied over a wide range of price vectors.[13] In this situation, Lerner and our theorems agree that prices proportional to marginal costs, i.e., relative prices equal to marginal rates of transformation between (non-leisure) commodities, is clearly optimal. This result follows easily for the case when cross-elasticities between (non-leisure) goods are all zero. Then, since a change in the price of a given good results in no change in either the purchases of other goods or of labor sold, it must lead to no change at all in labor expenditure on the good in question. That is, all goods must be demanded with equal, in fact, with unit elasticity. Our third form of the theorem states that in this case the relative deviation of price from marginal cost should be the same for all commodities.

More generally, admitting non-zero cross elasticities, the zero elasticity of labor supply means that any change in profit resulting from a price change comes purely from the change in labor cost of goods sold, since there can be no change in the

[12] Two things should be noted. First, when Lerner speaks of "tax elasticity" he is referring to what might better be called "own tax elasticity," that is, the relative change in the tax revenue (here, profit) collected on commodity x_i when the tax on x_i (divergence between price and marginal cost of x_i) is raised by one unit. The change in tax revenue collected on other commodities, which arises via cross-elasticity of demand, is not included.

Second, it should be observed that although the term "resources" is often not definable in general equilibrium models of the type described above (since choice is made from among alternative vectors of social aggregates of final goods, without reference to the underlying mechanics of production), in this simple case we may presumably equate them with "labor."

[13] Note that unless this inelasticity of supply results from some kind of artificial constraint, such as a legal maximum working day, or from a kink in the individuals' utility functions, commodity taxes will in this case *not* yield the same result as lump sum taxes. For if the inelasticity results from the offsetting of income and substitution effects, a doubling of prices will generally have a different effect from the subtraction of half (or any other portion) of the individuals' original labor income, leaving prices unchanged. This is obviously so because the (alternative) new price lines will not have the same slope and so they cannot be tangent to the same indifference curve at the same point.

total revenue received by the firm or government: the fixed quantity of labor offered in exchange for their products. We have, for all price vectors in question, by the inelasticity of labor supply at quantity L_0:

$$\sum_j p_j x_j(p) = L_0; \tag{7}$$

$$\text{i.e.,} \quad \sum_j p_j \frac{\partial x_j}{\partial p_i} + x_i = 0$$

for all i. Furthermore, as just noted, price changes can affect profits only through their effect on costs:

$$\frac{\partial \pi}{\partial p_i} = \frac{\partial}{\partial p_i}\left(\sum_j p_j x_j - C\right) \tag{8}$$

$$= 0 - \sum_j \frac{\partial C}{\partial x_j}\frac{\partial x_j}{\partial p_i}$$

Recall now the first form of "our" theorem which asserts that optimality requires, for all i,

$$-x_i = \lambda \frac{\partial \pi}{\partial p_i}$$

In the case now under consideration, this becomes by (8)

$$-x_i = -\lambda \sum_j \frac{\partial C}{\partial x_j}\frac{\partial x_j}{\partial p_i}$$

But by (7)

$$-x_i = \sum_j p_j \frac{\partial x_j}{\partial p_i}$$

Together these results imply that the first-order conditions can be written for all i,

$$\sum_j \left(p_j + \lambda \frac{\partial C}{\partial x_j}\right)\frac{\partial x_j}{\partial p_i} = 0$$

Since $\partial C/\partial x_j$ is the marginal cost of x_j, this asserts that prices bearing the proportion $-\lambda$ to marginal cost satisfy the first-order conditions.

In the more general case where shifting takes place both between sectors ($\partial C/\partial p_i \neq 0$) and within the taxed sector ($\partial x_i/\partial p_j \neq 0$, at least sometimes), an analogous algebraic chain of steps leads to the following first-order conditions, for all i:

$$\sum_j \left(p_j + \lambda \frac{\partial C}{\partial x_j}\right)\frac{\partial x_j}{\partial p_i} = (1+\lambda)\frac{\partial L}{\partial p_i} \tag{9}$$

Only by chance will these conditions be satisfied by prices proportional to marginal cost, or by prices deviating from proportionality by a simple function of own elasticity. In this we agree with Lerner. However, the theorems prescribe definite prices which do optimize, given the constraints, and there is no necessity to resort to a rough compromise between two polar rules. One rule prescribes for the polar situations as well as for intermediate ones. This does not mean that a more precise spelling out of Lerner's compromise would not yield the same (correct) conclusions: it means only that the task which remains is not to find the general rule. That is already accomplished by (9). Rather, it is only necessary to translate this rule into a form compatible with Professor Lerner's very illuminating intuitions.

VII. *The Case Where All Items are Taxable*

Finally, we must yet deal with the case, excluded from our discussion thus far, in which "*all* uses of resources" can be taxed. In view of our preceding agreement with Lerner that when tax changes result in resource shifts only within the taxed sector, prices proportional to marginal costs are optimal, our assertion that this is generally not the case when all goods are taxable may come as a surprise. The explanation is, however, relatively simple: overall marginal cost pricing will not, as a rule, yield the necessary revenue.[14] This

[14] We shall say that "overall marginal cost pricing" prevails when the price vector confronting consumers is a scalar multiple of the vector of first partial derivatives of the transformation function evaluated at the associated social total net output vector.

follows from a basic assumption of the entire analysis: that lump sum taxes are impossible. In terms of our general equilibrium this requires (by Walras law) that the net value of consumers' sales and purchases of all commodities, *including labor*, add up to zero. In that case, a proportionate tax, leading to a proportionate change in prices, will still leave the net consumer expenditures at zero and hence will yield no revenue to the government.

In formal terms, let P_i be the price of commodity i $(i=1, \ldots, n)$ facing the consumer, no longer expressed in labor terms, and let P_L be the price of labor. Following the sign convention that positive numbers represent net purchases of desired goods, negative numbers, net sales, let $a_1, \ldots, a_n, a_L$, be the vector of net transactions carried out by a consumer. Our no-lump sum tax assumption can be expressed as the requirement that $P_1a_1 + P_2a_2 + \ldots + P_na_n + P_La_L = 0$. (This implies, of course, that the aggregate net transactions vector, summed over all consumers, satisfies the same condition, expressed above as the condition on the demand functions $p_1x_1 + \ldots + p_nx_n = L$, where prices were expressed in labor terms.) Obviously, here it makes absolutely no difference to the consumer whether he faces prices $P_1, \ldots, P_n, P_L$ or prices ten times as high; only relative prices count. If the government were to collect the difference between these two price vectors (P and $10P$) as a tax, it would collect precisely $9(\sum_i P_ia_i + P_La_L)$, which is zero. A tax vector which is a scalar multiple of the price vector facing consumers will, under our zero-transfer assumption, *always* yield zero revenue.

With consumer budgets equated to zero, the vector of taxes thus cannot be proportional to consumer prices if there is to be any tax yield, and hence consumer prices cannot be proportional to marginal costs. Now we are back where we started. If the government wishes to obtain, say, a quantity M of labor for its own uses, and can only work with commodity taxes, it must get consumers to settle at an equilibrium with an aggregate net transaction vector $x_1, \ldots, x_n, -L$, satisfying $L - F(x_1, \ldots, x_n) = M$, i.e., such that the leisure given up for production exceeds that necessary to produce the other desired goods by M.

VIII. *An Analysis in Terms of Quantity Changes*

Some readers may find it instructive to see a derivation of the propositions carried out explicitly in a general equilibrium context and in terms of quantity changes rather than price changes. This is easily done within our present model if it is assumed that lump sum redistributions maintain a socially optimal distribution of alternative social totals of goods and leisure. Then we can employ a Samuelsonian social utility function relating social welfare to these totals, with the property that the tangent plane to any social indifference surface is also a "budget plane" associated with prices at which that point will be sustained as a competitive equilibrium. Thus prices can be written as a function of quantities. The analysis is made more transparent if we assume that there is a certain fixed total, $\bar{L}$, of labor time which must be allocated among production, leisure, R (for recreation), and government surplus, yielding the constraint:

$$F(x_1, \ldots, x_n) + R + M = \bar{L}$$

where $F(x_1, \cdots, x_n)$ is obviously the (labor) cost function for the output bundle $(x_1, \cdots, x_n)$.

The problem is to maximize over output-leisure bundles the social utility function, $U(x_1, \cdots, x_n, R)$, subject to this constraint, and subject to the constraint that exactly the required government surplus is obtained as profit:

$$\sum_{i=1}^{n} p_i x_i - F(x_1, \ldots, x_n) = M,$$

where the p's are equilibrium labor-prices associated with the chosen output-leisure bundle. Associating the Lagrange multiplier λ with the first constraint, and the multiplier, μ, with the second, we can write out the Lagrangian expression:

$$\begin{aligned} V(x_1, \ldots, x_n, R, \lambda, \mu) &= U(x_1, \ldots, x_n, R) \\ &\quad + \lambda[\bar{L} - F(x_1, \ldots, x_n) - R - M] \\ &\quad + \mu\left[M - \sum_{i=1}^{n} p_i x_i + F(x_1, \ldots, x_n)\right] \end{aligned}$$

Taking partial derivatives we obtain the first-order conditions:

$$\frac{\partial U}{\partial x_i} - \lambda \frac{\partial F}{\partial x_i} - \mu\left[\frac{\partial}{\partial x_i}\left(\sum_{j=1}^{n} p_j x_j\right) - \frac{\partial F}{\partial x_i}\right] = 0, \quad i = 1, \ldots, n$$

$$\frac{\partial U}{\partial R} - \lambda = 0$$

Dividing each of the first n conditions by the $(n+1)$st and noting that equilibrium of the consumer requires $\partial U/\partial x_i/\partial U/\partial R = p_i/p_r = p_i$ (since labor is the numeraire, its price unity) we have

$$p_i - \frac{\partial F}{\partial x_i} = \frac{\mu}{\lambda}\left[\frac{\partial}{\partial x_i}\left(\sum_{j=1}^{n} p_j x_j\right) - \frac{\partial F}{\partial x_i}\right].$$

Employing, with their usual meanings, the symbols MC and MR (the latter including the effect on revenue of variations in *all* prices), the preceding condition implies

$$p_i - MC_i = \frac{\mu}{\lambda}(MR_i - MC_i), \quad i = 1, \ldots, n$$

which is the second form of our theorem from which the other forms can be obtained exactly as before. Thus we have derived the results explicitly from a general equilibrium model. Note that the term "marginal revenue" is definable here because we have normalized prices to labor dimensions and have assumed behind-the-scenes income distribution, making determinate the effect on equilibrium prices of changes in any of the desired outputs. Note also that under these conditions, the second version of the theorem, proved in Section III for the case of independent demands, is shown to hold generally.

IX. *Notes on the History of the Discussion*

There is some point in going briefly into the antecedents of the discussion because this history makes it all the more difficult to understand why the propositions in question have achieved so little recognition by the profession. The general line of argument has appeared widely for the better part of a century. The formal theorems themselves date back more than forty years. As we will see, this work has appeared in some of our leading journals under the authorship of some of the luminaries of our profession and was clearly not limited to a backwater of the literature.

There is an informal proposition very closely related to the results under examination that has a long history going back at least to the 1870's. With the establishment of the Railway and Canal Commission in England in 1873, and of the discussion preceding the establishment of the Interstate Commerce Commission in the subsequent decade there arose a rich literature examining utility pricing in relation to the public interest. A number of authors advocated prices that vary directly with demand *in*elasticity ("value of service").[15]

[15] For some examples see A. T. Hadley (ch. 6); E. Porter Alexander (esp. pp. 2–5, 10–11) and W. M. Acworth (ch. 3, esp. pp. 57–60). Hadley, the American

The mainstay of the early discussion was an argument only loosely related to the formal propositions in which we are interested. In brief, it was maintained that a relatively low price in elastic markets, provided it covers more than incremental cost, may well permit lower prices in other markets and hence be beneficial to everyone. For (particularly if the firm is subject to a constraint on its overall profit) the opening of a market which makes any net contribution may permit or may even require a reduction in prices elsewhere.[16]

Discussion along these lines has since appeared throughout the literature of public utility economics. (See, e.g., James Bonbright, esp. chs. 5, 17–20.) The various forms of the proposition have also appeared at least implicitly in a number of the standard writings of economic theory, notably in Joan Robinson's work and that of W. Arthur Lewis.[17]

However, the formal mathematical propositions which are derived from optimality considerations and which are the subject of this paper, themselves have a substantial history. As propositions on optimal taxation they first appear in 1927 in Frank Ramsey's pathbreaking article on taxation.[18] Thus, more than a decade before the publication of Hotelling's historic discussion of marginal cost pricing, Ramsey had in another context provided at least implicitly a solution to the optimal pricing problem for an industry in which marginal cost prices do not cover total costs.

A. C. Pigou took up the Ramsey discussion in the following year in his book on public finance, providing a very lucid and rather extensive summary of the argument. It was independently approached by Ursula Hicks in her 1947 book on the same subject. Her analysis is largely diagrammatic and is based entirely on the Marshallian consumers' surplus, just as Ramsey's and Pigou's had been. However, as far as we have been able to tell, the formal anal-

economist who went on to become a president of Yale, is the author of what is apparently the classic discussion of the period, in which he coined the phrase "not charging what the traffic can *not* bear." There is in fact a hint of the argument much earlier than this in the work of Dupuit who advocates the separation of consumers into different classes each paying a different price, remarking "suppose that (railroads) offered nothing but first class tickets, what a loss for the public and for the companies" (pp. 124–27).

[16] "If the (New York to San Francisco) price is more than the *additional outlay* involved in doing it, as against leaving it alone, it is profitable to the railroad, and the business is moreover advantageous to the whole inland community served by the railroad. For it adds to the number of men employed along the line and . . . the more prosperous the road, the lower the local rates may be made" E. P. Alexander (p. 4) (author's italics). The author adds (p. 5) that between the limits of "unreasonable" profits and net loss, actual profit rates "should be adjusted in proportion to value of service rendered" (*inelasticity of demand*).

[17] See Joan Robinson (p. 207). Since she is dealing with a single product and does not utilize any explicit revenue constraint, the result she gives is not quite what is needed for our purposes but it is closely related to the theorem under discussion.

Lewis' statement (pp. 20–21), on the other hand, is precisely on target:

> The principle . . . is that those who cannot escape must make the largest contribution to indivisible cost, and those to whom the commodity does not matter much . . . get off lightly. . . . When there are escapable indivisible expenses to be covered the case for discrimination is clear. It secures an output nearer the optimum and levies the indivisible cost on those who get the greatest benefit (measured by their consumers' surplus). . . . Moreover, it is possible in some cases that the net result may be that everyone pays a lower price. . . . *If the undertaking is out merely to cover its costs* . . . reducing the price to some persons with elastic demands may increase the surplus over marginal cost which they contribute. . . . (emphasis added).

[18] The theorem seems to have made its greatest impact on the literature of public finance. A. C. Pigou (1928, pp. 126–28); (1947, pp. 105–09) reports Ramsey's results, offers an intuitive explanation and translates the theorem into elasticity terms. He also argues that except in the case of linear supply and demand functions the argument holds only if the taxes are small.

Ursula Hicks (pp. 167 ff) provides a very similar result on the basis of an elementary graphic argument. Yet even Richard Musgrave in his classic volume (p. 148) devotes only a footnote to the theorem and dismisses it as being "arrived at within the framework of the old welfare economics of interpersonal utility comparison " His characterization of the argument as part of the ability-to-pay approach is surely rather misleading. Cf. R. Bishop's comment on Musgrave, p. 212n.

ysis did not reappear until 1951 in an article by M. Boiteux which was the first to dispense with the notion of consumers' surplus. Apparently in the same year, Paul Samuelson submitted to the U.S. Treasury a closely related paper containing a generalization of Ramsey's results.[19] Samuelson's approach differs from that which we are discussing in that he employs no explicit revenue requirement. Instead he requires some preselected quantity of each output to be left unused by the private sector and made available to the government. His result, however, is essentially the same as those of the other contributors under discussion.

In 1952 there appeared a particularly simple derivation of the theorem in its most elementary form in a note by Alan Manne. His discussion assumes that cross-elasticities of demand are all zero and it measures and aggregates consumers' and producers' surplus in an unabashed Marshallian manner, but his derivation compensates for these simplifications by its great lucidity. Boiteux and Manne were also the first to present the analysis in the form of a discussion of public utility pricing. One year later Marcus Fleming provided an independent and illuminating derivation.

Meanwhile, Gerard Debreu had contributed analytic materials which led Boiteux to employ a Pareto optimality approach to the matter. On this basis Boiteux was then able to complete his definitive analysis of the subject. In Boiteux' classic 1956 article the analysis is, as a result, independent of any interpersonal comparison. The notions of consumers' and producers' surplus are dispensed with altogether. He is able to deal with goods whose demands are interdependent, with the pricing of inputs and intermediate goods as well as with outputs. It has also been emphasized by a subsequent writer (Jacques Drèze) that by his general equilibrium approach to the matter, Boiteux was contributing an explicit second-best solution, one of the few to be found to date in any area of welfare economics. Of course, no piece of analysis can answer every relevant question, and Boiteux left unsettled some matters of detail. There is a moderately mysterious role played in his analysis by the numéraire commodity; he has not dealt with problems of nonnegativity of outputs, etc. All this has left room for subsequent work by R. Rees, William Vickrey (*Testimony* and other unpublished work), the present authors, and by a number of others.[20]

[19] Samuelson's own brief description of the history of the analysis (1964) is worth reproducing:

> . . . Consider an optimal *laissez faire* situation that maximizes a social welfare function with zero government expenditure and taxes. Now introduce government services as a (vector) function of a small or large parameter y, $G(y)$. Suppose excise taxes (on goods or services) to be alone feasible, and introduce a (vector) pattern of excises $T(y)$ sufficient to provide resources for the G. What is the optimal $T(y)$ pattern to maximize the welfare function $W(y)=W(T, G)$? This is the problem set by Pigou to Frank Ramsey in the 1920's. Approximate answers were given by Ramsey, Boiteux (and in unpublished form by Hotelling and Hicks). In a pearl cast before the U.S. Treasury in 1950, I gave an exact solution for large and small programs; namely, that the optimal pattern is the one at which the response of all goods and factors to a further compensated-Slutsky price distortion would result in equal percentage (virtual) reductions.
>
> My literary wording is loose, but there is no need for approximative consumer's surplus at all. . . .

Though the reported date of the Samuelson memorandum may seem to imply some ambiguity about the order of appearance of this and the first Boiteux article, this issue is cleared up by Samuelson's explicit reference to the Boiteux article on page 5 of his memorandum in which he expresses his debt to the "brilliant analysis by M. Boiteux."

[20] Among those who have also written on the subject are Diamond and Mirrlees and Bishop. Recall in this connection Samuelson's reference to unpublished work by Hicks and Hotelling, on which more light is shed by the following excerpt from a letter which the authors received from Professor Hicks:

> It was just as well that you sent me the cutting from Samuelson [the preceding footnote], or I should have found it hard to recollect the matter. But with this refreshment it comes back. I think the story is as follows.

However, there is no need to go beyond Boiteux' work for a basis for the welfare discussion contained in this paper. The generalization to optimal pricing for an entire economy requires only one small modification in Boiteux' two-sector analysis. In his model there are two sets of firms, the first composed exclusively of perfect competitors, while the second are subject to the author's rules for quasi-optimal pricing. For our purpose we need merely take all firms to fall into the second category and our interpretation follows at once. In sum, it follows for the economy as a whole that unless marginal cost pricing happens to provide returns sufficient to meet the social (governmentally determined?) revenue requirement, a quasi-optimal allocation calls for systematic deviations of prices from marginal costs *throughout the economy* in the manner specified by the theorems that this paper has described.

X. *Concluding Comment*

We conclude our survey of the relevant literature as we began—at a loss to explain how a set of results flowing from the pens of so distinguished a set of authors and appearing and reappearing in the profession's leading journals, should so long have escaped general notice. This is all the more curious in light of the importance of the subject and the elegance of the theory.

As a theoretical matter, the theorem we have discussed seems fundamental not only for the analysis of public finance and the regulation of utilities, but also for some of the basic precepts of welfare economics. Earlier we spoke of the result as a proposition in the theory of the second best. But it is more than this. In a world in which marginal cost pricing without excise or income taxes is normally not feasible, the solution we have usually considered to characterize the "best" is none too good, because it is simply unattainable. In that case, the systematic deviations between prices and marginal costs that the theorem calls for may truly be optimal because they constitute the best we can do within the limitations imposed by normal economic circumstances.

In December 1946 (in the last week of my first visit to the United States) I stayed for a couple of days with Hotelling at Chapel Hill. I then told him that I had worked out (using a quite crude consumers' surplus method) that if a given sum had to be raised in excise taxes, the least-sacrifice way of doing it was the proportional all-round reduction in consumption, as compared with an optimum position. For if the burden of the tax is

$$\frac{1}{2}\sum q_{ij}dp_i dp_j$$

this is minimised subject to $G=\Sigma q_i dp_i$ if

$$dq_i = \sum q_{ij}dp_j = \lambda q_i$$

where λ is the Lagrange multiplier. Not much more than this, except that I had allowed (in the spirit of the old Hotelling article) that the q_{ij} could incorporate supply as well as demand reactions.

I remember he told me I ought to publish this, but I didn't—mainly, I suppose, because I was conscious of the qualifications to which Samuelson alludes in his paper, and which, if I had set them out in my style, would have whittled away the result so near to nothing.

Appendix

Comments On Lerner's Appendix

In the Appendix to his paper, Lerner asserts that our analysis over-emphasized demand elasticities. In addition, the Appendix contains a wider range of lesser criticisms. To deal in depth with all of these would require us to impose on the reader's time and patience. We propose to touch briefly on what appear to us to be the more important issues raised by Lerner, and trust that our failure to respond to other points will not be taken as a sign of general agreement.

Two criticisms appear recurringly in Lerner's Appendix and they are best disposed of at the outset. The first is that we have somehow used as a standard of welfare a measure of *consumers' loss*, and have left out any measure of *social damage.* Since our economy was taken to consist entirely of consumers, i.e., we use the terms "consumer" and "person with utility function" here interchangeably, we would use the two terms "consumers' loss" and "social damage" interchangeably as well. We would use neither without a grain of salt. The touchstone of quasi-optimality is plain and simple Pareto optimality, given the profit or tax revenue constraint. As is by now generally recognized, Pareto optimality cannot be comfortably equated with a "higher ethical good," and we apologize if we give the impression that a quasi-optimal price structure (for the monopolist) or tax structure was "good" in any sense other than Pareto optimality.

The second assertion that occurs in several places is that our analysis assumes constant marginal costs. This is simply incorrect. The only point at which marginal costs are taken to be constant is in our Section IV, the graphical presentation, which is intended solely as an aid to intuition. Elsewhere there is no assumption of any sort about marginal costs and none of the results depend on such an assumption. Lerner seems to suggest that our assumption that the prices of inputs are fixed can be equated to the premise that marginal cost is constant. We fail to see any connection between the two. Our assumption that input prices are constant is another, perhaps mistaken, compromise in the direction of intuitive appeal.[21]

Incidentally, the point of our footnote 7 is not, as Lerner suggests, to acknowledge in passing that marginal costs might in fact be variable. Rather, it is intended to point out that the marginal costs in question in the various forms of the theorem are *not* those which prevail in some initial situation before any taxes are imposed, but those which in fact rule at the solution values. Rather than apologizing for assuming marginal costs constant, we are, on the contrary, saying that marginal costs will very likely change as taxes are varied, so one must watch out and be sure to use the correct values in testing for optimality.

The basic task undertaken by Lerner in his Appendix relevant to the discussion here is derivation of our four forms of the "mislaid maxim" from his second rule. Since all four are derivable from either the first ($\partial\pi/\partial p_i=\lambda x_i$, all i) or the fourth ($\Sigma_j(\partial x_i/\partial p_j)(p_j-MC_j)=\gamma x_i$, all i) it is reasonable that he should be able to do this. It is nevertheless somewhat surprising that he did not in the process notice that his second rule takes into account only "own tax elasticity" and hence implicitly assumes the zero cross elasticities which he finds so objectionable in our second and third forms. It is probably because of this that he comes to the conclusion that our first form holds only when cross-elasticities are zero, which is simply incorrect.

Lerner's handling of our first form of the theorem (which, incidentally, is the one form we did *not* distill from the literature although since deriving it, we have seen essentially the same variant in Diamond and Mirrlees) is altogether curious. Almost paradigmatic of the economist's approach to a welfare problem, say, how large a park to build, is the following: "Clearly our rule should be, enlarge the park until the incremental social gain from enlargement by an additional unit is just balanced by the social loss from the space and other resources thereby foregone. But that is, of course, purely tautological. What we now need to do is clothe the concepts of social gain and social loss with operational measures. . . ." In this case Lerner goes backwards: "The equalization of the ratio between marginal yield and output level turns out to be an obscure way of expressing the equalization of marginal tax yield and marginal social damage—an equalization that minimizes the total social damage for a given total tax yield" (p. 289). We were, as it happens, especially pleased with the first form of the theorem which we think is new, precisely

[21] Analytically, it does serve to a set a price level so that the government profit constraint in pecuniary form is pinned down. In the case of more than one input factor it does, however, hide rather strong assumptions about the transformation function in a full general equilibrium treatment. In any event, the pecuniary variant of the government's budget constraint is perhaps not the most felicitous for use in such a treatment. The theorems in question are, however, in no way sensitive to these assumptions. Again we recommend perusal of the literature on this point.

because it seemed to promise more than the others a degree of operational applicability. Our feeling was that experienced tax officials (or monopoly managers) would have a much better chance of estimating at least roughly the magnitudes that enter that expression—the effect on the total tax take (profit) (including cross effects) of a change in a given tax (price) than econometricians would have of estimating the full matrix of cross elasticities, just as it seems plausible that a businessman may come close to maximizing profits even though he is pretty vague about quantities such as marginal cost and marginal revenue. If this is misplaced faith it doesn't matter, because the first form of the theorem, being equivalent to the others (and for more forms see our forthcoming paper), is at least no harder than they to put into practice. One thing is clear, the operational meaning of the first form is easier than the others (except, perhaps, for the fourth) to explain to a non-economist.

The derivations of the second and third forms of our theorem, like those of the first and fourth, make no use of and in no way depend upon constancy of marginal cost. The second and third variants do, however, involve an assumption of zero cross elasticities of demand among the goods whose prices are in question. Lerner is quite properly disturbed by the implication of extending this assumption to *all* goods. The demand relationship being traced out by variations in the price vector is simply the aggregate offer curve of the economy with the initial commodity vector of each citizen specified (generally at zero) and no net transfers. Independent demands for the individual goods are impossible here except in the trivial case in which the demanded vector is completely independent of the price vector, a vector which would in turn have to be the zero net transactions vector. The implication is not that the results are incorrect but that the second and third forms are not relevant when all goods are taxable and there are no net transfers.

Again, contrary to Lerner, the fourth form of the theorem is as general as the first, and more general than the second and third (*not* because it doesn't depend upon constant costs—they don't either—but because it does not assume zero cross-elasticities). Given the parenthetical word "approximately" its generality would seem assured. But we were willing to go farther than that, and took great pains to make precise in Section III, in the algebraic development of the fourth variant, what operationally was meant by "approximately" here. In footnote 9 we spell this out still further.

REFERENCES

W. M. Acworth, *The Railways and the Traders.* London 1891.

E. P. Alexander, *Railway Practice.* New York 1887.

R. Bishop, "The Effects of Specific and ad valorem Taxes," *Quart. J. Econ.,* May 1968, *82,* 198-218.

D. F. Bradford and W. J. Baumol, "Quasi-optimal Pricing with Regulated Profit and Interdependent Demands," forthcoming.

M. Boiteux, "Le 'revenue distribuable' et les pertes économiques," *Econometrica,* Apr. 1951, *19,* 112-33.

———, "Sur la gestion des Monopoles Publics astreints à l'équilibre budgétaire," *Econometrica,* Jan. 1956, *24,* 22-40.

J. Bonbright, *Principles of Public Utility Rates.* New York 1961.

G. Debreu, "The Classical Tax-Subsidy Problem," *Econometrica,* Jan. 1952, *20,* 100.

P. A. Diamond and J. A. Mirrlees, "Optimal Taxation and Public Production," mimeo. working paper 22, M.I.T. 1968.

J. H. Drèze, "Some Postwar Contributions of French Economists to Theory and Public Policy, with Special Emphasis on Problems of Resource Allocation," *Amer. Econ. Rev.,* June 1964, *54,* 1-64.

J. Dupuit, *Traité théorique et pratique de la conduite et de la distribution des eaux.* Paris 1854.

J. M. Fleming, "Optimal Production with Fixed Profits," *Economica,* Aug. 1953, N.S. *20,* 215-36.

A. T. Hadley, *Railroad Transportation.* New York and London 1886.

J. R. Hicks, *Value and Capital,* 2d ed, New York 1956.

Ursala Hicks, *Public Finance.* New York 1947.

H. Hotelling, "The General Welfare in Relation to Problems of Taxation and of Railway and Utility Rates," *Econometrica,* July 1938, *6,* 242-69.

H. Leibenstein, "Allocative Efficiency vs. 'X-Efficiency,' " *Amer. Econ. Rev.,* June 1966, *56,* 392-415.

A. P. Lerner, "On Optimal Taxes With an Untaxable Sector," *Amer. Econ. Rev.,* June 1970, *60,* 284-94.

W. A. Lewis, *Overhead Costs.* London 1949.

A. Manne, "Multiple-Purpose Public Enterprises—Criteria for Pricing," *Economica,* Aug. 1952, N.S. *19,* 322-26.

R. Musgrave, *The Theory of Public Finance.* New York 1957.

A. C. Pigou, *A Study of Public Finance,* (a) 1st ed., London 1928; (b) 3d ed., London 1947.

F. Ramsey, "A Contribution to the Theory of Taxation," *Econ. J.,* Mar. 1927, *37,* 47-61.

R. Rees, "Second-Best Rules for Public Enterprise Pricing," *Economica,* Aug. 1968, N.S. *35,* 260-73.

Joan Robinson, *The Economics of Imperfect Competition.* London 1933.

P. A. Samuelson, "Theory of Optimal Taxation," unpublished, approx. 1951.

———, "Principles of Efficiency—Discussion," *Amer. Econ. Rev. Proc.,* May 1964, *54,* 94-95.

W. Vickrey, *Testimony,* F. C. C. Docket No. 16258, Networks Exhibit No. 5, Appendix I. Washington 1968.

O. Williamson, *The Economics of Discretionary Behavior.* Englewood Cliffs 1964.

[9]

THE

QUARTERLY JOURNAL OF ECONOMICS

Vol. LXXXV | August 1971 | No. 3

ECONOMICS OF ATHENIAN DRAMA: ITS RELEVANCE FOR THE ARTS IN A SMALL CITY TODAY *

WILLIAM J. BAUMOL

Perhaps our cities have grown too large for efficiency in the supply of services and amenities to their inhabitants. At least this is a hypothesis one encounters fairly frequently in the literature of urban economics. In discussing this view some writers have suggested that even the arts do not need a large metropolis in order to survive. While today activity in the theater is centered in the biggest cities, in New York, in London, and in Paris, it has been suggested that the drama can, under appropriate circumstances, prosper in smaller communities. The case of ancient Athens has more than once been cited as an example.[1] Greek cities were certainly small towns by current standards, and yet the vitality of its drama and

* I must express my gratitude to the Ford Foundation, whose support of our urban project helped in the completion of this study. I must also thank for their help F. R. B. Godolphin of the Princeton Department of Classics, Lawrence Stone and Henry N. Drewry of the Department of History, as well as K. J. Arrow, my colleague Daniel S. Hamermesh, and my research assistant, Mrs. Sibyl Silverman. My very deepest gratitude must go to my friend and colleague Hourmouzis Georgiadis, for his enormous help in my attempts to arrive at a reasonable translation of the ancient currency.

1. Thus, e.g.: "Finally, still another argument frequently given [for policy to attract the middle classes to the central city rather than the suburbs] is based on increasing returns rather than externalities. It is argued that cultural amenities require for support a large interested public, and this can only come from the middle classes. The necessary size is perhaps not so obvious; Athens in its classical period had a population little bigger than San Jose, and presumably a much lower per capita income, even allowing for tribute payments." (Kenneth J. Arrow, "Criteria, Institutions and Function in Urban Development Decisions," in A. H. Pascal, ed., *Contributions to the Analysis of Urban Problems*; Santa Monica: RAND Corporation P-3868, Aug. 1968, pp. 49-50.)

its other arts is obvious enough. Does this not suggest that cultural activities can flourish without being surrounded by eight million neighbors? I will offer evidence that the circumstances of the Athenian theater were in fact very different from anything we can expect to find in our society and that the lesson of the Greek experience is of very limited significance for the arts today.

The real issue is the replicability of the Greek arrangements. Are the Athenian methods for the financing of the drama readily transferable to our society? By what means did the Greeks attract their audiences and would their methods work for us?

In this note I undertake to describe the relevant facts so far as they are known. Many readers will no doubt find them as surprising as I did. I must add that this foray into a field in which I have no qualifications involves even more than the obvious degree of presumption. One of the standard references tells us in its opening sentence that it undertakes "to treat of a subject concerning hardly a detail of which can any statement be made without the possibility of dispute. . . ."[2] To this we must add the near impossibility of providing a sensible interpretation of the prices and cost figures reported at various points in the discussion.

The economic difficulties of our own theater can usefully be subdivided into two (interrelated) categories: the limited audience, and the high and rising cost of live performance. It will be convenient to divide my discussion of the economics of the Greek drama accordingly.

I. The Greek Audience

The level of attendance at performances of the Greek drama is incredible by current standards. Though the size of the audience at any period is not in fact known, the Theater of Dionysus in Athens (actually built about 340 BC — after the golden age of Greek drama had passed) is estimated to have held some 15,000 to 20,000 spectators.[3] It is even possible that there were additional persons standing on the hillsides above the theater. Audience figures as high as 30,000 have been mentioned but seem implausible.[4] The population of all of Attica at the height of the Periclean Age may have included

2. Roy C. Flickinger, *The Greek Theater and Its Drama* (Chicago: University of Chicago Press, 1918), p. 1.
3. Albert A. Trever, *History of Ancient Civilization*, Vol. I (New York: Harcourt, Brace and World, 1936), p. 266.
4. Sir Arthur Pickard-Cambridge, *The Dramatic Festivals of Athens* (Oxford: Clarendon Press, 1953), p. 268.

40,000 adult male citizens, perhaps some 120,000 free women and children, and perhaps more than 100,000 slaves (though only figures for the free adult males seem to have a dependable basis).[5] It may be guessed that the city of Athens itself contained some 70 percent of those numbers during the period we are discussing.

The enormous size of the Theater of Dionysus becomes clear when we recognize that today no Broadway theater seats more than 2,000 persons. The total audience of all Broadway theaters together on a particularly good evening is on the order of 25,000 persons (with a total of some 33,000 seats available), which as a proportion of New York's eight million population is surely miniscule, comparatively.

A number of elements help to account for the apparently vast Athenian audience. First, it should be recognized that performances were not available throughout the year. One could not simply decide to attend a play next Saturday. In the city itself plays were given only on two occasions — during two festivals. The main performances occurred during the great festival of Dionysus (Bacchus), held annually, early in the spring (roughly, in March). In Athens proper there seems to have been only one other dramatic festival, the Lenaia (held in about January), during which plays were given fairly regularly.[6] Thus, in terms of audience-days per year, Athenian attendance at the theater was not all that large, say two or three days per adult male citizen, since there were about five performance-days per year, with an audience of, say, 20,000 each.[7] In New York City some six or seven million theater tickets are sold annually, so that even relative to its population it does not suffer so much by the comparison.

The number and types of performance at the main festival, the Great Dionysia, varied somewhat with the passage of time, but certainly an enormous number of plays was squeezed into a very few days. During the time of Pericles the festival normally ran for some seven days, four of which were devoted to drama. On the first of

5. See Trever, *op. cit.*, pp. 292–93 and compare H. Mitchell, *The Economics of Ancient Greece* (New York: Macmillan, 1940), pp. 19–20.
6. Pickard-Cambridge, *op. cit.*, p. 38.
7. Perhaps frequency of attendance was even higher. We have no way of knowing since we do not know either the population of the city itself or the number of persons who watched the performances from the hillsides above the theater. As we will see presently, it is plausible that social pressures made it difficult for any free adult male to absent himself from any of the (approximately) five days of performance per year. The number of days on which drama was presented was, incidentally, not the same every year. During wartime one day of performance was, at least sometimes, eliminated from the main festival of Dionysus.

these, five comedies were presented in succession; and on each of the next three succeeding days, three tragedies and one satyr play (a combination, rather scatological in content, of the contemporary tragic drama and an earlier dramatic form — the dithyramb).[8] The performances began at sunrise and lasted through the day. Later, during the Peloponnesian War, the day of comedies was canceled and instead the other three days of dramatic performance were lengthened by the addition of one comedy each evening.[9]

These three- or four-day marathons of drama must have required stamina of the audience, many of them sitting on backless stone (earlier, wooden) benches. Performances began promptly at sunrise and continued on until dusk. Aristophanes must have struck a sympathetic chord when in *The Birds* he listed as one of the advantages of flying the possibility of escaping "from the long-winded tirades of tragedy" to get home for dinner and back in time for the comic performances.

Thus, while the population of the city did not have dramatic performances available to it during most of the year, when the dramatic season did come it seems to have provided a surfeit. How then did the theater manage to keep its audience?

The answer, it would appear, lay in the religious character of the performance. The drama was able to draw so many spectators in fourth-century Athens for the same reason that permitted Bach to draw an audience for his music some 22 centuries later. Going to church simply was the right thing to do, and Bach's performance of his own music was just part of the ritual.

The sacred character of the performance in Athens even affected the Greek attitude toward the actor. Ancient Greece may well have been the only society before very recent times in which the actor was regarded with favor. ". . . the actors were active participants in a religious service and during the festival performances their persons were quasi-sacrosanct. As such, they were entitled to and received the highest respect. . . ."

It was considered essential that everyone attend the dramatic

8. The satyr play may have been introduced about 500 BC as a device to appease the more conservative members of the audience. It represented a return to the Dionysiac subjects from which the tragedy had largely departed. Performers in the satyr play wore goat ears, horns, tails, and hoofs, presumably "in imitation of Dionysus' attendant sprites." In the earlier dithyramb these performers "were sometimes called *tragoi*, which is the Greek word for 'goats.'" Still later, as the form of the play developed, "it came to be called *tragoidia* ('goat-song')" (Flickinger, *op. cit.*, p. 3).

9. Margarete Bieber, *The History of the Greek and Roman Theater* (Princeton: Princeton University Press, 1961), p. 97.

festivals. "Business was abandoned; the law-courts were closed; . . . even prisoners were released from jail, to enable them to share in the common festivities."[1] Boys and slaves were admitted if their tickets were paid for by their parents or owners. Pickard-Cambridge believes (though this has been questioned) that even women and girls were permitted to attend.[2] (!)

It was, indeed, considered so important that everyone attend the festival that the state provided a special fund that paid the daily admission fee (two obols[3] per day at the time of Demosthenes) for

1. Haigh, quoted by Flickinger, p. 120.

2. This is surprising because of the "oriental-like seclusion" of women in the Greek households and because the content of the comedies was decidedly scatological. In the older comedies a large phallic symbol was carried on a pole as part of the ritual procession, and the actor wore a large artificial phallus which subsequently was replaced by a "less indecent" variant. Flickinger remarks (p. 121) that a respectable woman would have invited divorce by being present at real scenes of the character of those they may have been permitted to witness in the Old Comedy and the satyric drama.

3. I may as well attempt at this point to do what I can to translate the currency. The basic coinage ran as follows: 6 obols = 1 drachma, 1 minna = 100 drachmae, 60 minae = 1 talent. Records for the building of a temple about two decades after Pericles indicate that the regular wage for all workers was 1 drachma per day, and jurors were paid 3 obols per day (Trever, p. 296). Thus, admission fees for one day's performances came to a third of a day's normal wages and were by no means nominal. As we will see later, standards of living in ancient Greece were very low even at the height of the Greek civilization. As a very crude standard of comparison, I will take a day's wage to have been worth $3 in current dollars. (This is slightly more than one quarter of what is now considered to constitute the poverty line for a family of four by the Department of Health, Education and Welfare.) Then, the daily admission price to the festival would have been about $1. Clearly, such a translation into dollars is largely fantasy, but it will serve as a convenient mnemonic device. In any event, since it has been suggested (Trever, p. 269) that 1 drachma sufficed to cover all the daily expenses of a family of four, the proposed convention, 1 drachma = $3, may not be excessive in terms of dollars of 1970 purchasing power.

After writing an earlier draft of this footnote, I came across Colin Clark's much more careful attempt to reconstruct the purchasing power of ancient currencies. Using dollars of 1925–34 purchasing power as his standard, Clark assigns the following values for the drachma at the dates indicated: 480 BC, $4; 400 BC, $2; 300 BC, $1.20. Since the price level in the United States has risen two to three times from 1925–34 until 1970, my conversion rate seems to be moderately consistent with his for the age of Pericles (about 460–430), though my rate gives somewhat fewer 1970 dollars to the drachma than his. (See Colin Clark, *The Conditions of Economic Progress*, London: Macmillan, 1951, p. 551.)

Professor Georgiadis has helped me to conduct some further checks of the suggested conversion rate. We have some figures for wheat prices in Periclean Athens indicating that 50 liters of wheat cost some 3 drachmas. Making a rough attempt to calculate a retail price equivalent for today gives us something less than $2 per drachma. On the other hand, utilizing a weighted average for the urban and rural work force for modern Greece, we arrive at an average daily wage that translates into a bit less than $4. If, as Clark suggests, the output per man-year in ancient Greece was higher than it is today, the drachma, one day's wage, should perhaps be valued somewhat higher. In any event, the choice within the range that seems plausible does not affect the discussion materially since I am concerned primarily with the *ratio* of the ticket price to the daily wage, the ratio between the subsidy to the festivals and the total budget of the state, etc. My attempt to find a reasonable conversion rate anyone who felt he could not afford it. There are even hints that potential members of the audience were bribed more substantially for attending.[4] Thus, state subsidy for the drama seems to have begun rather early.

II. Financing the Greek Festival

We turn next to the costs of the festival and the means by which they were met. The revenues were clearly not inconsiderable. Assume that the audience was in fact 15,000 per day and that each attendee paid his 2 obols admission. Over the course of the festival if admissions were collected for six days (including the two days in which no plays were performed) this would yield a gross of 5 talents or, at our arbitrary conversion rate of $6 per drachma, about $90,000.

The expenses of the festival are not entirely clear. The personnel involved in the dramatic portion included the author of the play, the chorus, which for the tragedy at different times consisted of twelve to fifteen persons, and the actors, who at the time we are considering, according to Flickinger,[5] generally numbered no more than four persons.[6] Of course, expenses were reduced substantially by the very small number of actors, and for that reason it is still considerably cheaper to produce a Greek drama than, say, a typical Elizabethan play.[7] Nevertheless, because of the sheer number of presentations, despite the small number of actors in each play, the combined size of the casts involved in the festival was enormous. "The number of participants was also astonishing. The dithyrambs alone needed 500 choreutai, with at least ten flute players. In each comedy there were about five actors and 24 choreutai with their flute players and sometimes citharists. In each tragedy, of which nine were presented, there were three actors, fifteen chorus members, and probably at last two musicians. In each of the three satyr

is intended only to convey a rough sense of order of magnitude, indicating that the drachma was worth neither 5 cents nor $50.

4. Pickard-Cambridge, pp. 270–73, and Mitchell, p. 364.

5. Flickinger, pp. 182–83.

6. This often required the actors to play several parts. Sometimes, moreover, a single part seems to have been divided among several actors. Thus, Flickinger suggests that the important role of Theseus in Sophocles' *Oedipus at Colonus* was "played in turn by each of the three actors!" (p. 181).

7. Moreover, the cast had grown only gradually to this size. In the earlier choral performances there was a chorus leader (coryphaeus), usually the poet himself, who answered questions posed by the chorus. Gradually he was given a more distinctive role and replaced by an actor. Aeschylus apparently introduced the second actor, and Sophocles the third (in about 470 BC) (Flickinger, pp. 166–67). It was only with Sophocles, whose voice seems to have been weak, that the poet ceased taking the leading roles.

dramas there were three actors, and chorus members with their flute player. There must have been 700–800 choreutai, 30–50 actors and 20–40 musicians. If we add the mute characters, choregi, chorus teachers, magistrates, judges and stage hands, the number of active participants must have been not much less than one thousand."[8] Today even grand opera rarely involves much over 300 performers. However, the figures refer to the entire festival, including some seventeen plays. If we subtract the 500 performers in the dithyrambs, this leaves us with some thirty performers per play. In any event, when plays went on the road after the Athenian festival, the companies were kept very small.

We do not seem to know how much the actors were paid. We do know that in the middle of the third century they were organized into a guild, called the "Dionysiac Artists," apparently a powerful organization. The guild members formed themselves into companies. A record for the years 272–69 BC of twenty-two companies, all members of the Athenian guild, lists exactly three actors' names for each company. The actors were normally paid by the state. They also took part in contests and may have been able to supplement their incomes with prizes.

Prizes, substantial in magnitude, were also offered to the playwrights. We do not know their amounts in the Athenian festivals. However, we do know that toward the close of the fourth century prizes of 10, 8, and 6 minae were presented to the dithyrambic victors at the festival of Piraeus, with one such prize to each contestant who had been selected to participate.[9] Recalling that a mina was equivalent to 100 drachmae, and that a drachma could cover a day's expenses for a family of four, we see that the poet could probably live comfortably for over a year on his prize money. (At our fictitious rates of exchange the first prize of 10 minae comes to $3,000.)

The finances of the festival involved, primarily, three different groups: the lessees of the theater, the government itself, and a very interesting institution, the choregus. The first of these was the only source of funds not amounting to pure subsidy. ". . . although the dramatic festivals were under the direct control of the state, the financial management was relegated to lessees, who agreed to keep the theater in repair and to pay a stipulated sum into the public treasury in return for the privilege of collecting an admission fee. During the fourth century BC the lessees of the Piraeus theater paid

8. Bieber, p. 53.
9. Flickinger, p. 269.

thirty-three minae [about $10,000 on our concocted exchange rate] annually. This system explains why the authorities, when they wished to enable even the poorest citizens to attend the dramatic exhibitions, did not simply throw open the doors to all. . . ."[1]

The state seems to have contributed the wages of the actors, their costuming, the honoraria of the poets, and the prizes, as well as the admissions subsidies that we have already noted.[2] These must have constituted some of the more substantial outlays on the festivals.

However, a very heavy burden also fell on the choregi. The highest state official involved in the festival had as one of his first duties the appointment of a number of choregi from among the wealthier citizens. These persons, in effect, were "volunteered" to bear a substantial portion of the expenses of the Dionysia. They paid for the training of the chorus, for their costumes, the wages of the singers and their trainer, perhaps also for the flute player, and were responsible for any special scenery that was needed. There is a speech listing the expenses of one choregus who may have been on the generous side. It lists 30 minae ($9,000) for choregia in tragedy in 410 and 50 minae ($15,000) for a dithyrambic chorus of men in 409. In another year his expenses for a comedy came to 16 minae (about $5,000 at our artificial exchange rate). In a country in which wealth was scare, these were very heavy sums.[3]

The choregi were selected from among the wealthy Athenian citizens in rotation. A citizen appointed to take on the position of choregus could ask to be excused on the ground that he had already assumed other public burdens, or he could suggest that it be taken on by someone else better able to do so. Under the law the person who was challenged in this way either had to assume the position of choregus *or had to trade estates with the challenger*.[4] However, citizens would characteristically take on the task more often and would spend more generously than they were required to.[5] This was fortunate from the point of view of the playwrights, the success

1. *Ibid.*, pp. 269–70.
2. Pickard-Cambridge, p. 91.
3. *Ibid.*, pp. 88–89.
4. Flickinger, p. 270.
5. The choregi had a very considerable incentive to contribute to the theater. Sponsors financed the plays of specific playwrights, and when the prizes were awarded, naturally, a great deal of the honor went not only to the author but also to the financial backer. When inscriptions of the festival prizes were prepared, the name of the financial sponsor was at least sometimes inscribed above that of the author of the winning play. For example, the name of Pericles is written above that of Aeschylus, who won the prize for the play *The Persians* in 472 BC. Moreover, financial supporters would sometimes back plays with a particular political slant coinciding with their own interests.

of whose production might be damaged severely by the niggardliness of a choregus.

In sum, the dramatic festivals were made possible by a two-part system of subsidy, involving generous grants by the state and lavish contributions by private citizens that were, in part, voluntary but whose philanthropy was enforced by law and custom.

III. The Magnitude of the Financial Burden

The fragmentary state of our financial information clearly makes it very difficult to draw any conclusions about the real strain that drama imposed on the Greek economy. Before turning to what little information we have on the public finances of the Athenian state, we may first consider some relevant general principles.

Live performance is, of course, very close to being a pure service activity. Because of the *comparative* difficulty in instituting labor-saving innovation in the services,[6] they rise cumulatively in relative cost as an economy's productivity and real income grows. We all know how rapidly the relative price of a haircut rises as we go from an underdeveloped country to a country of moderate wealth to a highly prosperous area. We have also seen the cost of household services rising with the growing prosperity of our economy. Our theater has suffered from just this problem. Cost per performance has risen cumulatively at a rate significantly exceeding the general price level (and the rate of increase in ticket prices, for that matter). For wages in the theater have gone up steadily along with the level of real incomes in our economy, while productivity of the actor in live performance has remained essentially unchanged — it takes as many man-hours today to produce a play of Sheridan's as it did in the eighteenth century. With man-hour productivity in the economy as a whole growing as much as 4 percent per year, the continued rise in the cost of theatrical performance becomes easier to understand.[7]

6. Cf. Victor R. Fuchs, *The Service Economy* (New York: National Bureau of Economic Research, 1968), pp. 50 *ff*. I emphasize the word "comparative" to avoid being misunderstood to be saying that productivity increases in the services are impossible.

7. In the United States one manifestation of this phenomenon has been the increasing length of runs of plays in the commercial theaters. One simply cannot afford to produce plays unless the period of time over which they can be expected to run increases along with the production cost. It is noteworthy, therefore, that in ancient Athens a play was normally performed only once, though a successful drama might be repeated in the provinces. Only after 386 BC, after the great age of playwriting was over, was provision made for revival of earlier dramas as part of the Athenian festivals (Pickard-Cambridge, p. 100).

Thus, the surprising poverty of the ancient Greeks suggests that the opportunity cost of services must have been much lower than it is today. That is, the relative cost, in terms of material consumption goods, of an hour of theatrical performance must have been miniscule compared to what it is currently.[8]

Some idea of the standard of living of the Athenian in the age of Pericles is offered by the nature of his food and shelter. The ordinary houses were built side by side with a common wall between them. Burglars found it easier to break through the walls than to pick the locks. The bedrooms were "mere cells." "The average Athenian was satisfied with the most meager fare — barley or wheat cake or porridge with a much diluted sour wine and relish (opsonion) of salt fish or onions to make it go down. The monotony might be relieved by goat's cheese, honey, green vegetables, and an occasional egg or bit of mutton, but meat was usually reserved for festival days."[9] Perhaps this passage, as one reader has commented, describes consumption patterns that were more Spartan than Athenian, but it is, nevertheless, suggestive.

Even the relatively affluent Athenians were not terribly wealthy. In figures on the distribution of wealth in fourth-century Athens only seventeen persons are reported to have possessed over 5 talents ($90,000 on our contrived standard). All of this suggests that industry and productivity were indeed at a stage at which the cost of performance was relatively low.[1]

Despite this, and despite the substantial contributions of the choregi, the public festivals made very great inroads on the public purse. The budget for the purpose has been estimated by Mitchell[2] at no less than 40 talents per year (about 3/4 million dollars on our conversion scale) out of a total annual budget on the order of 700 talents (about $12 million).[3] That is, the festival expenses came

8. Clark (p. 552) uses the data provided by the Edict of Diocletian (301 AD) to investigate relative costs of various types of goods and services in the ancient world. He concludes that "the purchasing power of the denarius was highest . . . over personal services . . ." (i.e., these were relatively cheap), as our discussion suggests.

9. Trever, p. 295. See also Mitchell, pp. 132 *ff*.

1. Yet, Clark estimates (p. 461) that ". . . the average production per man-year of the whole working community was still probably in the neighborhood of [$500 of 1925–34 purchasing power]. This is a good deal higher than that of present-day Greece or of most southern or eastern European countries."

2. Mitchell, p. 371.

3. In a letter, Professor Arrow comments rather persuasively that the subsidy figure seems very high. If half the total budget for the festivals were devoted to the roughly seventeen plays offered during the Great Dionysia, the reported figure comes to some $20,000 per performance. In a period of low real wages the figure is hard to believe.

Mitchell does, however, cite another writer who "reduces the estimate [of to well over 5 percent of the annual costs of the entire government, including the "military and naval forces." It is hard to imagine a contemporary government that is prepared to budget that high a proportion of its revenues for the arts. In New York City, for example, it would call for an annual subvention to the arts of some $250 million — more than twice the 1964–65 budget for all nonprofit organizations of fully professional performance in the United States combined!

IV. Concluding Comment: Relevance for Contemporary Urban Planning

This superficial survey of the economics of the Athenian theater offers us little reason to expect that in our modern economy a small community can serve as a center for the performing arts. Certainly the circumstances of the arts in Athens were vastly different from those in our society, and there is nothing to lead us to expect that we can replicate them. There seems little prospect of government subsidy on the vast relative scale provided by the Athenian state. It is hard to imagine our wealthier citizens agreeing to be appointed as involuntary philanthropists — and then vying in the generosity of their patronage.

Perhaps most important, we have no substitute for the religious associations of the Greek drama, which helped to make possible the large public subsidies and private subventions, and which brought huge audiences into the theater. Today, with no religious fervor to pack the houses and with television competing for the audiences, a community in which 5 percent of the population is drawn to a live dramatic performance is unusual indeed. The enormous proportion of the Athenian population that attended the theater is surely unattainable for today's cities.

Even if all this could somehow be duplicated, the rising relative costs of live performance mean that the opportunity cost of this support would have grown enormously since the time of Pericles. It would no doubt cost much more today in terms of goods and services foregone, i.e., relative to the general price level, to finance a given level of dramatic activity, and we can expect these costs to continue to grow cumulatively.

the festival's budget] to 40,000 drs. [$180,000], a very small sum" (p. 371, fn. 2). Actually even this amount is not all that small — it is nearly 1½ percent of the total expenditure of the Athenian state. Clark (p. 466) reports the revenue of the Athenian treasury at 6 million drachmae ($18 million) in 433 BC and states that "in 422 BC, a war year, this revenue was doubled." He adds that "the former figure represents 17 percent of the national income."

The sad fact is that, short of a revolution in attendance patterns, the minimum size of city needed to support a theater or a symphony orchestra seems very likely to grow even larger than it is today as rising real costs of performance make it necessary to look ever more widely for sources of support.

Princeton University and New York University

[10]

ON THE ECONOMICS OF THE THEATER IN RENAISSANCE LONDON*

Mary I. Oates and William J. Baumol

Princeton University and New York University, USA

Summary

The theater of Elizabeth and James (1576–1642) was entirely commercial, receiving virtually no subsidy from patrons. Though not always profitable, some theatrical entrepreneurs made fortunes and many actors lived comfortably. The profitability of runs of two weeks (today some 35 weeks are required) helps explain the many plays produced. The high attendance rate was necessary for prosperity of the theater in a city under 200 000. It was also probably helped by the Tudor inflation which apparently reduced real wages to their lowest level from the late Middle Ages to the present. Today, with real wages many times higher and attendance rates lower, such small cities cannot provide prosperous unsubsidized theater.

Introduction

The outburst of dramatic activity that included the work of Marlowe, Shakespeare, Jonson, and scores of others was relatively brief. It lasted somewhat less than seventy years, that is, from the second half of the reign of Elizabeth until, after a period of decline, Cromwell's associates finally closed it down in 1642. It was, for the most part, a vigorous and successful activity. The immediate issue we explore in this paper is how, in a community so small as London at the end of the sixteenth century, the commercial theater was able to thrive as it did. Our ultimate objective, however, is to throw light on two broader issues.

First, we hope to offer evidence on the influence of city size on the vitality of the performing arts, and on the doubts expressed by Professor Arrow (1968), among others, about the assumption that there are a great many significant activities that can be provided only by the large metropolis. The second of the

* We would like to thank the National Science Foundation whose grant assisted materially in this study. And we are deeply grateful to Professor G. E. Bentley for his careful reading of our manuscript and for his many useful suggestions that helped us to avoid a number of serious errors. We must also thank Kenneth Arrow, A. Walton Litz, Wallace Oates, C. Patrick O'Donnell Jr., Joseph Parvin, and Lawrence Stone, each of whom was extremely helpful to us at various stages of our work.

Swed. J. of Economics 1972

broad issues considered is the relationship between the level of real wages and the supply of services. It has been argued elsewhere (Baumol & Bowen, 1966) that rising real wages generally put personal services at a cost and, hence, a price disadvantage, because in these activities it is relatively difficult to introduce labor-saving innovations that offset increasing wage costs. One tends to think of the Elizabethan period as one of great prosperity and relatively high real wages. However, we will see that, although incomes were apparently rising for some classes, there is evidence suggesting that real wages toward the end of the sixteenth century were in fact extraordinarily low. It will be suggested that the *low level of real wages may have contributed substantially to the prosperity of the drama,* thus leading to the conclusion that general economic prosperity, with the increase in real wages that normally accompanies it, may actually depress some of those activities which are usually taken to contribute to "the quality of life".

1. Nature of the Data

Much of the information we have about the workings of the theater in Shakespeare's London rests on inference, some of it quite tenuous. The surviving plays occasionally refer to the workings of the theater: for example, after Hamlet's theatrical venture—his attempt to catch the conscience of a king—he asks Horatio whether his efforts have earned him a "fellowship in a cry of players", and Horatio replies, "Half a share". From such allusions, as well as from legal documents, scholars have deduced that the leading actors in a theatrical company held stock in the company, shared in its profits, and were called "sharers" or "fellows": the half a share to which Horatio refers represented, Professor Bentley tells us in a letter (October, 1970), the size of the player's original investment. Since information about the earnings of these entrepreneurs, who sometimes doubled as actors, is more difficult to come by, it is fortunate that a diary has survived kept by Philip Henslowe, financier of the Admiral's Men, the leading rivals of Shakespeare's company. This diary records such information as the dimensions of a theater that Henslowe ordered built, and, for each performance over most of a three year period, his own share of the daily receipts (half the gallery seats sold). However, we do not know enough about the number of persons admitted at each of the various prices to permit us to translate with any degree of accuracy Henslowe's share to figures for attendance and gross revenue. If we add to that complexity the suspicion that prices doubled on opening nights[1] and may have been higher for holiday occasions, the inaccuracies are, of course, compounded. The traveler, Samuel Kiechel, furnishes us with the only surviving record of

[1] Samuel Kiechel, a German traveler, said flatly in 1585 that the price for a new play was double that for a repeat performance (quoted by Rye, p. 88). See also Jonson, Induction to *Bartholomew Fair.*

gross receipts as such. Kiechel either noticed, or was told, in 1585, that The Theater was grossing £10–£12 per day for a new play (Rye, p. 88), and while the figure may have been a mere guess, it does accord fairly well with both the inferential data upon which we are otherwise dependent, and with the usual payment (£10) for a performance at court.[1]

Legal records can also be valuable. On the important issue of total audience size for all theaters on a given day, for example, the most dependable source is a sworn statement that was not challenged by the plaintiff's adversaries.[2] It names what is likely, therefore, to be a lower bound, 3 000. For the capacities of individual theaters we are in worse case: in contrast with the surviving evidence on the Greek drama, no Elizabethan or Jacobean theater buildings remain, so that we are dependent on documents such as Henslowe's specifications for the dimensions of a house. Using such figures Alfred Harbage has actually experimented to determine the possible number of standees and the seats one could have crowded into the available areas (1941, pp. 19–23). This is, essentially, the basis of current estimates of the number of places offered in each price range, the size of a capacity audience, and total revenue that it would have yielded.

For data on wages and prices in the economy generally we use the figures furnished by E. H. Phelps Brown and Shiela Hopkins that report wages of building laborers and building craftsmen in Southern England, which may not have been quite the same as wages paid to workmen in London. The few references to earnings in London that we have come across are a bit higher, but are generally consistent with the figures that we use.[3]

---

[1] For a slightly later period, the office book kept by Sir Henry Herbert, James' and Charles' Master of the Revels for the period 1622–1641 is useful, since Herbert agreed on one occasion to accept the profits from two "benefit" performances per year for the period 1628–32, the most profitable of which, played at Blackfriars, yielded £17 10*s*., and the least, at the Globe, £1 5*s*. After the "daily expenses" of the company, averaged and estimated by them at £2 5*s*., were deducted, Herbert netted an average of £8 19*s*. 4*d*., the average gross being thus £11 4*s*. 4*d*. (Bentley, 1941–68, I, p. 24). This figure, slightly higher than the £10 mentioned in the text reflects the higher profits of the 1630's, during which Prof. Bentley has players' bills as high as £20 for a single performance at Hampton Court or Richmond: because they had to go farther afield, they note, the additional bounty was justified since, as one accountant's item reads: "[We] lost our day at our house" (quoted in Bentley Letter).

[2] In 1612 the Waterman's Company, who represented the bargemen on the Thames, presented a legal brief which complained that the fashionable new theaters on the North Bank were attracting some 3 000 spectators a day, the grievance being that this clientele had formerly employed the watermen to convey them across the Thames for performances at the large public theaters on Bankside or for bear-baiting at the Paris Garden. John Taylor, who presented the plaintiffs' case, was himself a playwright, and so probably had a fairly accurate idea of total daily audience-size at the North-Bank theaters; at all events, as noted, the defendants did not contest his claim (Harbage, 1941, pp. 36–37).

[3] The figures on prices and wages were originally gathered by Thorold Rogers and William Beveridge. More recently E. H. Phelps Brown and Sheila Hopkins used these data to construct, with considerable care and all the appropriate reservations, indices of wages and prices of a "composite unit of consumables running from 1260 to 1954". The price figures are based, however, on institutional records which may or may not represent retail prices, and unfortunately, such historical records can be affected by "kick-backs" and other distorting influences. The price index is based on a calculation of "an aggregate price year

2. Interpretation of Elizabethan Prices

It will be helpful to have some sort of crude translation of Elizabethan money into current terms. Such a translation is unavoidably suspect since it must be based on imperfect data, and because patterns of consumption, working hours and conditions have changed over the four intervening centuries. Nevertheless, we offer our calculations for what they may be worth, since we feel that the only thing worse than an attempt to interpret the sixteenth and seventeenth century currency in modern terms would be failure to do so.

Even if we had all the information we would like, the translation from Elizabethan pounds to 1970 dollars would still not be unique because of the very large difference in the behavior of prices of different items over the centuries. The calculated relative purchasing power of the two currencies will therefore vary materially with the type of item whose purchase is used as the standard of comparison. For our purposes two such standards seem particularly pertinent: labor time and a market basket of commodities. With the aid of the former one can hope to evaluate, say, an Elizabethan ticket price in terms of today's incomes. It will indicate the current dollar ticket price which would require as many hours of work for its purchase as the one penny admission paid by the Elizabethan attendee. The second standard, the market basket of consumer's goods, indicates the relative amounts of consumption given up in exchange for a ticket then and now. In both these calculations we rely primarily on the Phelps Brown-Hopkins figures.

The labor time translation is the more direct of the two, though here there is also an ambiguity. One can translate in terms of daily or in terms of hourly wages, but since the length of the working day has changed substantially over the centuries, from perhaps 8–12 hours in 1600 to some 7 or 8 hours today, the results will not be the same. The daily wage comparison may give us a better feeling for the relative total incomes available in the two periods, while the translation in terms of hourly wages indicates the relative purchasing power of a given amount of labor time, then and now. For the period 1580–1629, we are given a daily wage of 1 shilling for a building craftsman and 8 pence for a laborer. In the United States in 1968 union wages in construction in five major cities averaged \$5.75/hour for a journeyman and \$4.50 for helpers and laborers (U.S. Department of Labor, Table 11). Assuming that they work a seven hour day, this gives us a daily wage of approximately \$40 and \$31.50 for the respec-

---

by year for a composite commodity, made up always of the same amounts of some of the main heads of consumption ... bread-stuffs, meat, cloth, and so on". The specific items included in each category are varied to reflect the available evidence on changes in consumption patterns. Unfortunately, the calculation excludes a number of important cost components, notably, rents and the prices utilized are described as "more wholesale than retail". Recent evidence (Kerridge, pp. 208–226) suggests that rents in Tudor and early Stuart England did not lag behind other prices, though this view has not been accepted by all economic historians. If Kerridge's views are valid, the inclusion of rent data in the Phelps Brown–Hopkins index would, if anything, have strengthened our conclusions.

Table 1. *1970 Dollar equivalent in terms of Elizabethan currency*

	Purchasing power $	Wages $	
		Daily	Hourly
1 penny	0.17	3.30	4.60
1 shilling	2.00	40.00	56.00
1 pound	40.00	800.00	1 120.00

tive categories. Either of these two pairs of figures then indicates that a daily wage of a shilling in 1600 can be translated into a daily wage of some $40 today, i.e., that one Elizabethan pound is worth about $800 in its ability to purchase days of labor. Since in 1970 the workday was not only more remunerative but also shorter, the translation of Elizabethan currency on the basis of hourly wages gives us still higher figures. Using a ten and a seven hour day as very rough estimates for the building industries in the two periods, the hourly wage equivalents are about 1.4 times as high as the daily figures.

The translation in terms of a market basket of goods uses the Phelps Brown–Hopkins price index. The average value of that index for the 50 year period 1576–1625 is 456. By 1950 the index had reached 3155. Using the U.K. "Price Index Number" (Department of Employment and Productivity, p. 115) to bring this figure up to date we find that between 1950 and 1969 the Price Index number went from 100 to 205. Guessing that it had risen to 215 by 1970 we obtain an extrapolation of the Phelps Brown–Hopkins series that gives us an index number of about 6 800 for 1970. This means that the market basket of consumables rose in cost by about 15 times over the period 1600–1970. To translate this into dollars requires only one more step. We have an estimate for the cost of a "median weekly family food basket" which indicates that a pound in the U.K. can purchase as much as $2.60 here.[1] Multiplying by this factor we conclude that a pound in 1600 could buy as much as £15 or about $40 today.

If we believe the calculation, the real daily wages of an American worker today are 20 times as high as those of an Elizabethan,[2] whose daily wage in

[1] See Bush. An extrapolation of some earlier United Nations figures gives a rate of exchange of about $2.90 to the pound. This obviously does not affect our calculations substantially.

[2] And the real hourly wage is about 28 times as high! The figures at first glance may seem implausible, but a simple calculation suggests that it is quite credible. Data furnished in the *Economic Report of the President* (1965, p. 227) indicate that since World War I productivity per man hour in the United States has risen rather steadily at an average rate of 2.5 percent per year and somewhat more rapidly since World War II. Assume that in 1800 productivity in the U.S. was still exactly the same as that in Elizabethan London but that, with the advent of the Industrial Revolution, it rose at an average rate of 2 percent between 1800 and 1910, then increasing 2.5 percent per annum thereafter. This suffices to produce the estimated increase in real wages.

What little information we have about working-class living conditions suggests that they were indeed minimal. "For Dekker ... workmen were 'Stinkards': herrings and onions, alas, were among the few foods they could afford to buy; bread was an expensive luxury" (Harbage, 1941, p. 56).

terms of 1970 dollars is seen to be only $2! As we will see later, he did not normally live on his wages alone, but the calculation is nevertheless rather disturbing.

Table 1 may serve as a handy summary of our results.

3. The Public and Private Theaters[1]

The Elizabethan and Jacobean Theaters fell into two types, very different in character and in mode of operation: the public and the private playhouses. Their difference will play a significant role in the subsequent discussion. The public theater was a mass entertainment enterprise. It offered some 200 performances per year, although it was often forced to suspend its operations during Lent and during the plague-ridden summer months. The audience capacity of a single theater has been estimated at 3 000,[2] which is more than twice that of the typical Broadway house, and more than a third larger than the largest of the Broadway theaters. Prices of admission began at one penny,[3] which in terms of other consumables foregone amounts to less than twenty cents, but as a proportion of a worker's daily wage is equivalent to more than three dollars. The best seats seem to have cost threepence, and a very few, "The Lords", 6 or even 12 (Harbage, 1941, p. 26).

---

[1] A fine introductory discussion of the structure of the Elizabethan theater is found in Bentley, 1961, Chapters 4 and 5. Most of our discussion of the private and the public theaters is based on Harbage, 1952.

[2] "There are only two known contemporary estimates of the capacity of Elizabethan public theaters, one made by a touring Dutchman named Johannes De Witt, who visited the Swan Theater in 1596, and the other by the Spanish Ambassador, who reported to his government about the size of the crowds at the Globe Theater at several performances of a smash hit play in the summer of 1625. Both men name the same capacity figure, 3 000" (Bentley, 1961, p. 130). See also note 3, above, which refers, of course, to total theatrical attendance on a given day.

[3] Since the period of great theatrical activity lasted over half a century of general inflation, most prices, including those of tickets, must have changed over the course of the period. Most of our data are based on Henslowe's figures for the decade of the 1590's, just before the middle of the period. The 1590's must not, however, be taken as a "representative" decade. It included a very serious outbreak of the Plague, several years of crop failure and some extraordinarily sharp price rises. We have evidence indicating that, while before 1600 the minimum price of admission was one penny, by 1625 this had doubled. Thus Harbage quotes Platter (another German traveler) to this effect:

"... Whoever cares to stand below pays one English penny, but if he wishes to sit he enters by another door, and pays another penny, while if he desires to sit in the most comfortable seats which are cushioned, where he not only sees everything well, but can also be seen, then he pays yet another English penny at another door (1599)."

The later figures we get from Bentley, who quotes an allusion from a play performed about 1625. Thrift, "a citizen", is speaking:

And I will hasten to the money box,
And take my shilling out again,
I'll go to th' Bull, or Fortune, and there see
A play for two pense, with a Jig to boot.

(*The Careless Shepherdess*, quoted in Bentley, 1941–68, VI, p. 111.) Thrift is attending a play in a "private" house. The "two pense" seems to refer to standing room at one of the two public theaters mentioned.

The private theaters, which began as boys' companies with exclusively juvenile casts drawn from the great choir schools, only assumed a degree of commercial importance in about 1600. No adult company that we know of played in a private house until 1608, when Shakespeare's company, the King's Men, purchased Blackfriars, formerly used by the boys of the Queen's Chapel (who served as a company of child performers). At first the profits from both seem to have been about equal. By 1634, however, the balance had swung in favor of the Blackfriars, although the company continued to play both there and at its public, i.e., open air, theater for the remainder of its existence. Even as early as 1612 Edward Kirkham, who was both a theatrical investor and Revels Office official, said that "they took in £ 1 000 in a winter more at the Blackfriars than they had formerly taken at the Globe" (Bentley, 1948, p. 47).

Figure 1 provides an overview of the level of dramatic activity in London over the entire period, and indicates the number of public and private houses in operation. The numbers are only approximate, several unimportant and short lived theaters having been omitted; in a few cases the date of construction is unknown, and some of the buildings were later converted into prize fighting arenas. Nevertheless, the graph is a reasonably good representation of the course of events in the London theater, and it shows strikingly how the private theaters which, as just noted, only began to operate on fully professional basis some years after 1600, constituted at least 25 percent of the theater's operating units after 1615, and eventually reached 50 percent of the total. Note also that the number of private theaters actually in operation at a given time does not reflect very accurately the demand for their services. In contrast to managers of the public theaters, which lay across the Thames, the North Bank entrepreneurs were continually threatened with eviction by their Puritan-minded neighbors in the City. These worthies frequently entered successful complaints in the courts, insisting that the houses were a neighborhood nuisance, not to mention a moral threat. In the second decade of the seventeenth century, for example, knowledgeable theatrical investors sank vast sums into the building of a private theater ("Rosseter's Blackfriars", or Puddle Wharf) to replace Whitefriars, the lease on which expired in 1613. Although work began to convert the house at Puddle Wharf into a theater, and plays were actually performed there ca. 1613–1616, the legal authorities finally insisted on its demolition. Such failure, however, did not deter the backers of the Phoenix in Drury Lane, which was used as a playhouse from 1616–1642. The very vehemence of the watchdogs of public morals points to a greater demand for these theaters than the existing ones could meet.

Jonson, Beaumont and Fletcher were among those who wrote at least partly for the private theaters. Performances at these theaters were, at least during the first half of our period, given only once or at most twice a week, and their season was short, probably fewer than 30 weeks a year. The buildings which, unlike the public theaters, were entirely enclosed, were also very small. Estimates run to a seating capacity of perhaps 400, though some of them were later rebuilt to hold an audience of somewhat more than 600 persons.

Admission prices started at six pence (Harbage, 1952, pp. 43–44) and went up to a shilling or even one and six. Most seats sold at a shilling and occupants of sixpenny seats were sneered at as "groundlings".[1] Since in terms of today's daily wages this is a price scale whose cheapest tickets sold at some $20.00, it is clear that the private theater was *not* the theater of the common man.

4. The Theater as Commercial Private Enterprise

The fact that each theatrical company had its noble patron may suggest that the drama was subsidized. In fact, this simply was not so. Neither governmental nor private philanthropy was ordinarily provided to the theater: "The role of the patron cost little or nothing ... What a company could normally expect from its lord was a document declaring that its members were his servants and should be respected accordingly, occasional intercession on their behalf, if they got into trouble, a payment when they performed before him (such as they would receive in similar circumstances from any other lord), and, occasionally, a 'badge' or livery—an allowance of cloth so that they might wear the colors of his house" (Harbage, 1952). Bentley adds that royal companies received payment for livery every other year (1941–1968, I, 53). Typically, for a performance at court or at the home of one of the barons, the company received £10, which is very slightly more than what in the earlier period of the Elizabethan theater seems to have been the normal gross from a performance at its own theater—some 8 or 9 pounds. The role of the patron was primarily the protection of the actors from harassment as "Roges, Vacaboundes and Sturdy Beggers",[2] and no benefits other than prestige and suits of clothing for the coronation seem to have accrued to Shakespeare's company when, from "the Lord Chamberlain's Men", they were transformed into "the King's Men" after James' accession.

That the ordinary, commercial drama was far from being subsidized is indicated by the sizeable fees a company had to pay to the Master of the Revels, a sort of censorship arm of the Lord Chamberlain himself. The fees the Master might collect varied: Henslowe records what appear to be regular monthly

---

[1] Jonson (1632) refers to "the *Faeces*, or grounds, of your people, that sit in the oblique caves and wedges of your house, your sinfull sixe-penny Mechanicks ..." (*Introduction to the Magnetick Lady*, Vol. V, p. 504).

[2] "all Fencers Bearewardes Comon Players in Enterludes & Minstrels, not belonging to any Baron of this Realme or Towardes any other honorable Personage of greater Degree ... whiche ... shall wander ... shalbee taken adjudged and deemed Roges Vacaboundes and Sturdy Beggers, intended of this present Act" *Act* 16 *Elizabeth*, c. 5, p. 5 (1572), quoted by Simpson, Vol. II, p. 240.

£3 payments, perhaps simply for the license to use his theater as a playhouse, while Herbert seems to have applied a sliding scale for the censorship of the plays themselves, depending on whether the scripts were old or new, or whether they contained "dangerous matter" (Bentley, 1941–1968, III, 265). One of the few cases of outright royal grants to a commercial company occurred during James' reign when he granted the King's Men several subsidies to keep them together during plague seasons (Thaler, pp. 86–87, and Cunningham, pp. 82–96). But the King's Men by this time were clearly the premiere London company; others were not so fortunate, and were forced either to take to the road, where they seldom made expenses, or to disband completely. Aside from these rather rare instances of royal patronage, the picture is, as Baldwin says, that of the acting company as a "monopoly under license or patent" (Baldwin, p. 286), a privilege for which the Revels Office might collect as much as £100 per year from a successful company.

Theatrical enterprise then was, essentially, an unsubsidized commercial venture. Certainly, most if not all of the theatrical entrepreneurs were in the business for money and there is little reason to believe that they were reluctant to sacrifice "artistry" where that was dictated by financial considerations. Alleyn, who was Henslowe's partner and one of the age's great tragic actors was also an accomplished bear-baiter, and the two built the Hope in 1614 with the intention of using it for baiting at least two days in six (Briley, p. 106).[1] As another example, we note that new plays were simply placed on order by Henslowe as business needs dictated. He kept a stable of authors and often utilized several playwrights to produce one piece, somewhat in the spirit of Hollywood's procedure at the height of its prosperity. Professor Bentley (letter cited above) reports on the basis of a review of all English plays known to have been written between 1590 and 1640 that well under half of the total were works of collaboration, but the number was nevertheless substantial. With the market requiring a company to produce as many as 40 new plays in a year there was little time to waste on playwriting. Marchette Chute reports: "Thomas Dekker, for instance, worked for four years for Henslowe at a rate of nearly a script a

[1] As Murray Bromberg has observed, Henslowe's methods were matched if not equalled by more "respectable" entrepreneurs. "There are repeated suggestions that [Christopher] Beeston [another actor-manager] was more shrewd than honest in his business dealings with the actors ... A Beeston's Diary would probably offer many parallels to Henslowe's Diary ... (II, 364)". The impressment of children for the boys' companies; the beating in 1606 of Thomas Woodford, backer of a rival juvenile company by an Edward Pierce, who was probably Master of Paul's Boys, over what may have been a business dispute (Hillebrand, p. 213); and, on the positive side, the comfortable retirements of Shakespeare, Burbage, and other members of the King's Men, several of whom had even bought "gentility" in the form of coats of arms, suggest parallels between these "aesthetic" entrepreneurs and the eager money-makers of the City. Briley documents Alleyn's bear-baiting activity by a quotation from Alleyn's diary: "Baighted before ye king a my men washt my shep & pd 2*d* a skore ... 0.1.0." 11 June 1622. The Henslowe-Alleyn partnership considered baiting profitable enough to use the Hope two days out of seven for baiting, the stage "being made to take up and downe when they please". (Quoted from a manuscript continuation of Stow's *Annales* (1631) by Sir Edmund Chambers, *ES* (1923), II, 374–5, and by Briley, p. 106.)

month, and Michael Drayton ... produced seventeen scripts for Henslowe in a single year."[1]

With such devotion to their business interests it is not surprising that some of those involved in theatrical activities made out very well. We know of a number of cases of financial success. Certainly, the Henslowe–Alleyn partnership prospered. They are reported to have provided for the foundation of the College of God's Gift in Dulwich an endowment of £10 000, for those days an enormous sum, comparable in terms of workers' daily earnings with some $8 million today. John Heminges, Shakespeare's fellow-housekeeper was said to be of "Greate Lyveinge wealth and power", and Richard Burbage is reported to have died with holdings worth £300 annually (Harbage, 1952, p. 24).

Nevertheless, these success stories are about as unrepresentative as those we encounter in the theater today. We know that Henslowe was perpetually bailing his lackeys out of debt, and that much of his power resulted from their financial dependence on him. Few of the theatrical companies survived very long. Only Shakespeare's company managed to go on for 50 years, and no more than three or four others were able to continue for 20 years (Bentley, 1961, p. 88). Despite (or perhaps because of) their high prices, the early private theaters were constantly in financial straits (Harbage, 1952, p. 45).

In sum, the Renaissance theater in London was very much a private enterprise, dedicated to the pursuit of profit and not subsidized either by government or private philanthropy. It was a risky business in which some did manage to make their fortunes. The natural question, then, is how, in a city so small as London in 1600, it was possible for the theater to survive at all, and how it was able to support so many new productions. Since the answer may lie in the frequency of attendance of the average Londoner and in the relative cost of a production we will, therefore, next examine these in turn.

London one immediately runs into a problem: just what does one mean by "London" in 1600?—only the area within the political boundaries of "the City" or also suburbs, such as Westminster, from which one could reach the theaters on foot? In fact, many of the demographers' estimates do not specify which entity they have in mind. We are, therefore, not quite sure what to make of Roger Mols' figures (p. 47) that report London's population to have been over 100 000 but under 200 000 toward 1600. Similarly, we cannot readily interpret

5. Size of the Elizabethan Audience

There simply are no good records on audiences and populations three or four centuries ago. In examining the specialists' guesses about the population of

[1] (Chute, p. 56). Baldwin (pp. 28–29), however, cites several instances of individual playwrights who worked under bond to particular companies to provide about two or three new plays a year. Shakespeare's output was almost exactly two plays per year which may have represented an informal agreement with his company.

Trevelyan's estimate (p. 142) that "... when Elizabeth died [the population of London] may already have touched 200 000." Harbage, though no specialist in demography, has, however, undertaken a painstaking calculation, based on bills of mortality and other related evidence, on the population of areas within fairly easy walking distance of the theaters. He arrives (1941, p. 38) at a figure of 160 000 for 1605. Since this figure is consistent with the other estimates we have been able to find, we may take it to be correct in order of magnitude.

For the audience figures we must also turn to Harbage. He calculates his figure from the number of theaters in operation, which we do know with some degree of certitude, from the average capacity of the theaters, which, as we have said, is a very crude guess at best, from Henslowe's figures for gallery receipts,[1] and from estimates of the number of places available at each ticket price, which Harbage calculates from the known dimensions of the theaters. As already mentioned, the only surviving contemporary estimates mention "3 000" as the capacity of two *different* public theaters (see note 8). The same figure as a rough estimate of "ordinary" *total* attendance at all the theaters in operation in 1612 may possibly include the Bear Garden (see note 3).

The estimated size of the daily average audience of all theaters in London taken together varies by date. In 1595 it is put at 2 500. By 1601 it may have grown to 3 000. For 1605 there is an estimate of 3 500 and for 1613 a figure of 3 000–4 000 (Harbage, 1941, pp. 36–38). Harbage multiplies these figures by six to obtain a weekly attendance figure.[2] From this calculation Harbage deduces that weekly attendance, in 1605, the period when he believes attendance relative to the population was at its peak was about 21 000 persons. Since the relevant population was apparently 160 000 this means that at this time about 13 percent of the population attended the theater every week.

To indicate whether this figure is particularly large we offer two comparisons. First, we consider attendance at the New York theater which seems to have reached its peak in about 1928, just before the advent of the talking picture. We have an estimate of weekly attendance in February of 1928–29 of 286 thousand persons (Moore, p. 149). At this time (interpolating between the 1920

[1] Among many other entries, Henslowe's diary records his share of the gallery receipts at the Rose Theater from 1594 through 1597. It indicates that this figure on holidays (about 50 shillings) and at opening performances (55 shillings) tended to be much higher than it was on an "ordinary day" (28 shillings) (see Harbage, 1941, Appendix B) [the figures are averages for the two "more normal" seasons, 1595–1596]. It is surprising that there was so little fall in receipts from the galleries during the winter season considering that even the twopenny seats, while protected from snow, were probably not heated. November and December receipts were low (about 22 shillings) compared with the overall average of some 27 shillings. February revenues, however, perhaps owing to pre-Lenten celebration, averaged a healthy 32 shillings. The high receipts at opening performances are undoubtedly, in part, a consequence of the higher prices charged on those occasions.

[2] The estimate may be somewhat low because it is based on the assumption that the ban on Sunday performances was, in fact, enforced. There is evidence that Sunday performances and even performances during Lent were winked at, at least under James (Henslowe, pp. xxvii).

and the 1930 census data) the population of New York City proper was slightly more than 6.5 million, and, to use a somewhat broader geographic unit, the total population of incorporated places within 20 miles of New York City Hall was slightly over 9.5 million (Laidlaw, p. 43). Thus, the weekly attendance figure is roughly 4.5 percent of the New York City population and about 3 percent of that of the metropolitan area, well below the 13 percent figure for Elizabethan London, but not so far below it as one might have suspected.

A second comparison is provided by Harbage himself who considers

> "... the oft-used analogy of theater attendance in Shakespeare's day and movie attendance in our own", and concludes that "eighty-five million Americans are said to go to the movies every week [1941] ... about 65 percent of our population, or 10 persons in 15. In light of this modern devotion to drama the Elizabethan Londoner begins to appear almost apathetic."[1]

Thus, theatrical attendance during the period we are considering was high[2] but not astonishingly high. The data also lead us to question the notion that (in contrast with all evidence on today's audience) the Elizabethan theater attracted as many persons from the lower income groups as is generally supposed. Performances took place in the daytime, during working hours, and this suggests that the activity was not designed primarily to attract an audience of laboring poor.[3] But there is a stronger reason for suspicion. The decline in the number of public theaters and the rapid rise in the demand for performances at "private" houses so soon after the innovation had been introduced (Figure 1) suggests that the market for theater was to be found primarily among the upper classes. The commercial instincts of the Jacobean entrepreneurs would hardly have led them toward private theaters with their small seating capacity and their very high ticket prices if the masses were a primary source of demand.

Perhaps the "Theater of a Nation" was mainly an Elizabethan phenomenon: it does appear that shortly after James' accession in 1603, by approximately 1610, the lower income groups were beginning to go back to prize fighting, bear-baiting, visits to madhouses, and public executions for their entertainment. It is also likely that Puritan scruples were beginning to take their toll. There was growing Puritan sentiment among the well-off urban middle classes that was shared to a much smaller degree by the country gentry and aristocracy, and, although those sharing this sentiment frowned on public spectacles of almost any sort, they were particularly hard on the "common stage". Whatever the

---

[1] Harbage, 1941, p. 42. Harbage does go on, however, to point out various reasons, convenience of location being one, why the analogy between motion pictures and Elizabethan drama is of limited validity.

[2] A reader has suggested that the size of the audience during the period in question may be conditioned in part by the fact that so many "Londoners" were transients. This, plus the fact that the range of services, like the range of commodities, was narrow, would no doubt have contributed to the demand for theatrical entertainment.

[3] But see Harbage 1941, p. 67 for an account of the way in which members of this class might have been less "regimented by time clocks" than they are now.

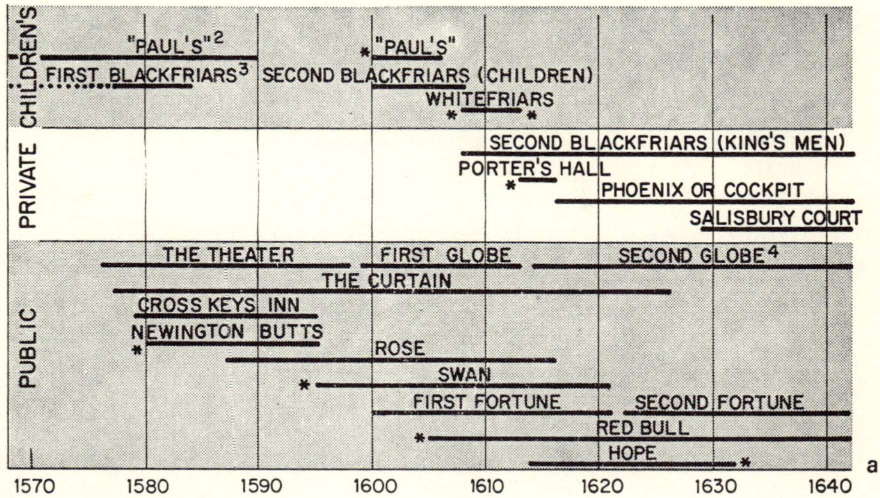

Fig. 1a. Life spans of London theaters 1575–1642.[1]
(* indicates approximate date)

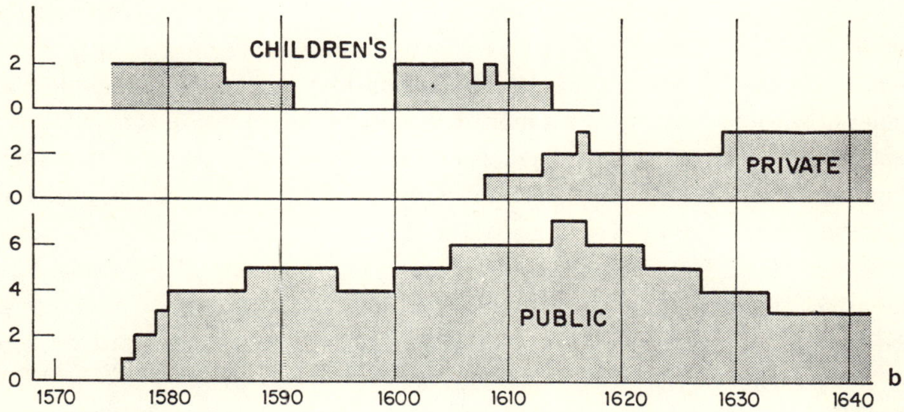

Fig. 1b. Number of theaters in use 1575–1642. Sources: Hillebrand; Chambers (1923) vol. II; Bentley (1941–68) vol. VI.

[1] Excludes the following theaters because of very problematic dates: The Bell Inn; The Bel Savage Inn; The Boar's Head; The Bull Inn; The Red Lion; Le Fevre's Riding Academy.

[2] Since no actual building has been identified, references to "Paul's" Theater rest upon accounts of activities undertaken by this boys' company, and the assumption that they must have had a fairly permanent playing place. See Hillebrand, p. 114. Children, including those of Paul's, continued to play sporadically in various "adult" houses until about 1616, when Hillebrand places their virtual disappearance from the London stage, p. 274.

[3] Both children's companies, the Boys of Paul's and the Children of The Chapel Royal (later the Children of the Queen's Revels, finally Children of the Revels) had begun public performances before 1575. The Chapel Children did not actually occupy the First Blackfriars until 1577, but must have used another playing place (denoted by a broken line) previously.

[4] Assumes the theaters did comply with the Parliamentary closing order of 1642. For surreptious performances following the order, see Bentley (1941–1968), VI, p. 173.

reason, by 1620 the theater's business interests were turning toward a smaller, more affluent audience.

6. Prices, Wages, and the Prosperity of the Theater

Live performance is a labor-intensive activity. Today some 30 percent of the budget of a Broadway play is devoted to the wages of the actors and musicians, and, when one includes payment to the author, to stagehands, carpenters, and the like, the figure is probably over 50 percent (Moore, p. 64). In the Elizabethan theater, as indicated in the appendix, the proportions do not seem to have been much different. In such an activity financial viability must then depend strongly on the level of real wages. When costs of labor are low the theater can more easily afford to take risks in its choice of plays, since even a rather short run can then show a profit. A relatively large number of companies can survive in a given market, and tickets can be offered at prices that are low in comparison with the cost of less labor-intensive goods and services.

The energy and expansionism of Elizabethan England are likely to foster the impression that it was a period of general prosperity in which most classes benefited. As we will see, the picture is considerably more mixed. At this point we are interested primarily in the real incomes of wage earners and the rural residents without secure land tenure, the copyholders and the tenants at will, from among whom one might expect the theater to have obtained its personnel. Here, the Phelps Brown–Hopkins indices can help us again. We have reproduced from the Phelps Brown–Hopkins articles graphs indicating the movement of prices, and of wages in comparison with prices, for the remarkably long period 1264–1954 (Figures 2 and 3). The authors themselves point out the dangers in such long-term comparisons, yet the broad general movements are probably not badly misrepresented.

The Tudor inflation is a phenomenon which excited a great deal of contemporary comment. By today's standards, the rate of price increase was very mild. The Phelps Brown–Hopkins figures indicate that during the 50 years 1576–1625, which encompass the period of greatest theatrical vitality, consumer prices rose only about 1.1 percent per annum.[1] Nevertheless, it is easy to see why Englishmen of the period were impressed by the rate of price increase. Figure 2, the graph of the Phelps Brown–Hopkins index of the price of consumables, shows that by the time Shakespeare began to write prices had been rising fairly steadily for about three quarters of a century. In the 1590's, with a series

[1] Any initial and terminal dates must be arbitrary to some extent. However, the results of our calculations are unlikely to be affected substantially by the choice of these dates since, as Figure 2 indicates, the inflation began much earlier and ended considerably later. For the entire period of the Tudor inflation, say 1510–1600, even though the price level increased eight-fold, the average annual price rise, as calculated by logarithmic least squares regression, using the Phelps–Brown Hopkins figures, was only 1.3 percent. Such is the power of compounding over long periods. Even during the catastrophic decade 1590–1600 the rate of increase was only 3.5 percent, pretty mild stuff by current standards.

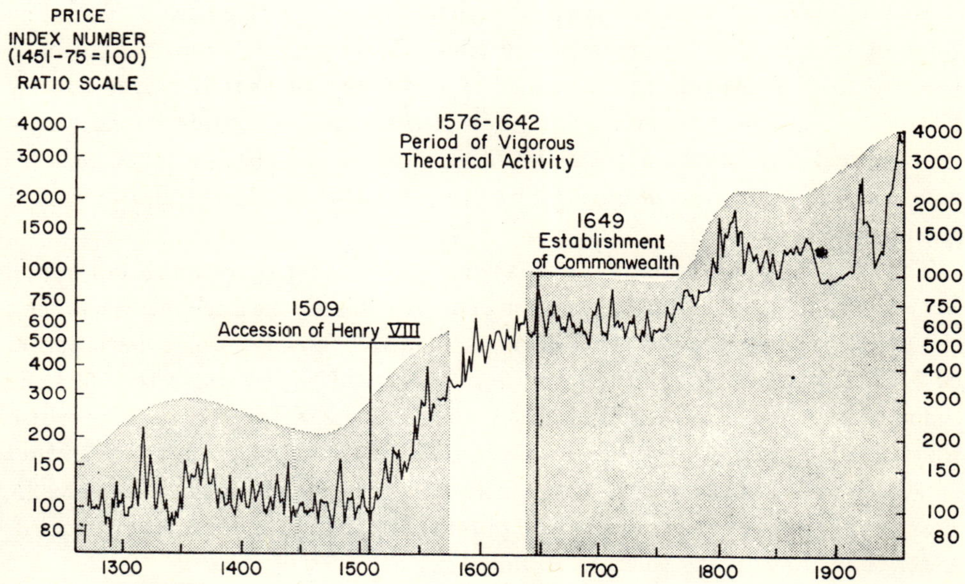

Fig. 2. Price of a composite unit of consumables in southern England 1264–1954. Reprinted by permission of *Economica*.

of bad harvests, prices really rose very sharply, the index going from a low of 356 in 1593 to a peak of 579 in 1598. Thereafter the index again drops, but by the 1630's it twice reaches the vicinity of 700.

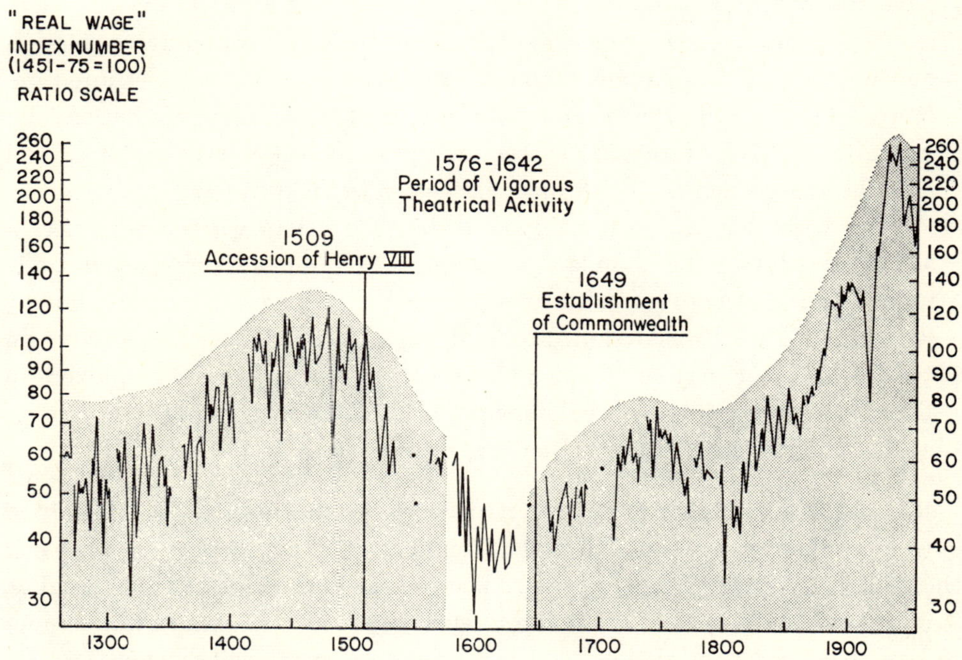

Fig. 3. Changes in the equivalent of the wage rate of a building craftsman expressed in a composite physical unit of consumables in southern England 1264–1954. Reprinted by permission of *Economica*.

Wages, on the other hand changed rather slowly over this period. The daily wage of a craftsman toward the beginning of our period is reported to have been 10 to 12 pence, rising to a range of 12 to 16 pence about half a century later. The common laborer's wage followed the same pattern, increasing from 8 pence to 10 to 12 pence in this interval. Thus wages may be taken to have gone up by 30 to 40 percent during a half century when the price index increased some 80 percent.

The Phelps Brown–Hopkins calculations confirm that there was a fall in real wages. The drop in purchasing power of wages was particularly severe during the great price upsurge of the 1590's, as Figure 3 shows. Using a base period of 1451–1475, coinciding roughly with the Wars of the Roses, after 1594 the index of purchasing power rises above 45 only once before 1629 (after which there is a long gap in the series). And in 1597, the year in which the *Merchant of Venice* may first have been performed, the index falls to its all-time low, 29, presumably representing a level of purchasing power more than two thirds lower than that during the late Middle Ages!

These figures must, as one historian has suggested, be treated with a great deal of scepticism:

> "It seems hardly possible that such a drop can have taken place without far greater outcry than we have record of. To accept the figures at their face-value would mean that urban workers were dying of starvation in thousands at the end of the 16th century and in the early Stuart period. Some factors have surely been left out of account: ... the building labourer may ... have received a supplement to his wages in the form of meals and accomodation on the job, and such payments in kind would cushion him against inflation. More important still, the urban labourer of the 16th century was not as fully urbanised as his 20th century successor, and would often have a plot of land or at least a garden on which he could cultivate his own food ...
>
> "But with this said it remains true that the urban worker did suffer a substantial fall in his standard of living ... Tudor workers lacked trade unions and political representatives to plead their case effectively, and the legislation of 1563 was designed to hold wages down rather than force them up. Cheap labor may have aided the prosperity of industrial employers in Elizabeth's reign. It meant real hunger and hardship for a substantial number of the working population." (Ramsey, pp. 137–38.)

Because it is so labor-intensive an activity the theater may have benefited even more than many of the "industrial employers" from the low real wages of the period. By giving opportunities to a sufficient number of new playwrights, it may have made it easier to find and encourage the ones whom we consider to have been great, as well as a host of others, to try their hands at the task.

We have evidence suggesting how the economics of the theater was affected by the wage levels. A change in real wages affects significantly the length of time a play must run before it can recoup the initial investment in rehearsal time, costumes and so forth. Today, it is estimated that a play generally has to run over 30 weeks in order to break even, at an average of 70 percent of capacity. For the period just before the onset of the Great Depression the estimated figures range from 5 1/2 to 8 weeks, and a calculation for 1913 for a comparable production sets the breakeven run at 4 weeks (all assuming attendance at 60 percent of capacity). (Bernheim, p. 206 and Poggi, p. 74.)

Harbage (1941, pp. 51–52) offers us some illustrations taken from Henslowe's *Diary* that permit a rough comparison: "*Julian the Apostate* with three performances was a failure; *Philipo and Hippolito* with twelve, an average success; and *Wise Man of West Chester* with thirty-two, a great hit." In other words, *a run of two weeks seems to have given a comfortable margin to the company.* Clearly, the figures are not perfectly comparable with the more recent data. The Elizabethan public theater had, easily, twice the audience capacity of our own. Moreover, several elements of production cost that are important today were less significant in Shakespeare's time. On the other hand, in terms of purchasing power, the admission prices to the Elizabethan public theaters were a fraction of today's. Yet it does seem fairly clear that a new play then represented a much smaller financial commitment than it does today. The profitability of a short run must be ascribed not so much to the magnitude of demand for the theater, but to low real wages, perhaps one twentieth of their current level in the United States.

Low real wages also permitted inexpensive ticket prices. The penny admission to the public theater was very cheap in terms of commodity purchasing power, even if it did amount to about a tenth of a day's wages. No doubt it helped to widen the audience. However, the growing importance of the private theaters, with their admission prices that are high by virtually any standards suggests that low ticket prices did not play an important role in the prosperity of the theater of James and Charles.

Burenstam Linder has drawn our attention to a more subtle connection between real wages and the demand for the arts. He points out that rising real wages increase the economic value of time. Hence, they raise the *relative* real cost of activities like theatrical attendance whose consumption time is high relative to their price. Low real wages will *always* produce a substitution effect that favors this type of activity.[1] Thus, the low real earnings of this period—

[1] *Proof*: let x_1 represent the individual's level of consumption of the service in which we are interested, i.e., theater; let r be his number of hours of labor-time and x_2 be the quantity he consumes of the Hicksian "all other goods". Since any consumption process takes time, the consumer will maximize the utility function

$$u(x_1, x_2, r)$$

subject to two constraints

$$p_1x_1 + p_2x_2 = m + wr \quad \text{(his budget constraint)}$$

perhaps (as already noted several times) one twentieth of their level today—may also in this way have contributed to the demand for the services of the theater, especially during the last two decades of the sixteenth century, when the new public theaters seem to have attracted at least some of the lower classes of wage earners.

There are other observations that may cause one to suspect that there is an association between the level of real wages and the viability of the drama. The theater of ancient Athens also flourished in a society in which real incomes were very low by our standards (see, e.g. Mitchell, p. 132 ff.). Greek theater, however, was very highly subsidized (Pickard–Cambridge, pp. 270–73), so that it is impossible to infer from the limited financial data available on the subject whether low wages really contributed a great deal to the success of the Greek drama. However, there is a more suggestive case. If we look again at Fig. 3, we see that there is one earlier period of unusually low real wages in English history. This occurs in the 1320's, and certainly wages do not seem to have been very high in the immediately preceding or the immediately succeeding decades. Now, it may largely be coincidence that this was the period of the Corpus Christi plays that represent the first known English instance of popular, secular drama, written in the vernacular (Chambers, 1903, I, pp. 108–109). These dramas were produced at the expense of the guild itself, which is to say, at the expense of the masters who supported it. The guild owned costumes, props, and pageant wagons, and provided acting personnel from among its own members. Since journeymen were probably paid their normal wages during rehearsals, and apprentices worked for food and lodging, the master absorbed whatever opportunity costs were incurred. Although the guilds did provide what amounted to subsidized drama, real wage rates in the half century before first

---

and

$$t_1x_1 + t_2x_2 + r = t \quad \text{(his time constraint)}$$

where p_1, p_2 and w are the respective prices of x_1, x_2 and r; t_1, t_2 and unity are their utilization times (with none of the coefficients necessarily constant); and m is non-wage income. Since time can be converted into income via changes in the value of r, the two constraints really amount to only one effective constraint. Eliminating r and collecting terms, they may be rewritten as

$$(p_1 + wt_1)x_1 + (p_2 + wt_2)x_2 = wt + m \tag{1}$$

which is a budget constraint of the normal Hicksian form, with Becker's "time prices", $p_i + wt_i$, substituted for the ordinary commodity prices, p_i.

Now a rise in real wage, w, will lower the relative time price of x_1 if and only if

$$\frac{d(p_1 + wt_1)/(p_2 + wt_2)}{dw} = \frac{t_1(p_2 + wt_2) - t_2(p_1 + wt_1)}{(p_2 + wt_2)^2} = \frac{t_1p_2 - t_2p_1}{(p_2 + wt_2)^2} < 0$$

i.e., if and only if $(t_1/p_1) < (t_2/p_2)$. The result now follows directly by the usual derivation of the Slutsky theorem. For there will be a substitution in favor of x_1 only if its relative (time) price falls when w increases, and this will be true, as we have just seen if t_1/p_1, the consumption time-price ratio, is relatively low for this commodity: this is not how we would normally characterize theatrical attendance.

the Black Death and then the Hundred Years War decimated the working population were so low, that the subsidies were not onerous.[1]

In sum, while we cannot conclude with any certainty that low real wages did play a critical role in helping to make the Elizabethan theater viable, all the evidence seems to suggest that it did not hurt then, or in earlier periods of flourishing dramatic activity.

7. Conclusions

One is never entitled to generalize from a single historical case, and the gaps in our information about the drama in Renaissance London make such an attempt all the more foolhardy. Nevertheless, from our information we can draw several negative conclusions which we believe to be still significant today.

First, the Elizabethan case offers little basis for the hope that professional live theater will be able to prosper in small communities in the foreseeable future without some sort of subsidy. At the beginning of the seventeenth century, several circumstances conspired to make it possible for the theater to finance itself. Real wages seem to have been unusually low—a considerable financial advantage to a labor-intensive activity such as the theater. Several economic classes, particularly the gentry, were attracted to London where they sought entertainment (see Fisher) and, apparently, the wealth of this class was rising,[2] making it easier for its members to purchase the more expensive tickets which even in the public theaters must have been important for the prosperity of the company. One may surmise that the large number of transients who visited London on business, for education at the Inns of the Court, or simply for a change from rural life, as well as the unusual interest in the arts and the hunger for entertainment that characterized the Renaissance also contributed to the size of the audience. Even then theater had to compete with cock fighting, boxing and other popular entertainments but these did not have the convenience and perhaps not the attraction of today's mass media. Low real wages may also have helped to attract audiences by permitting admission fees low in comparison with other prices and by generating a substitution effect favoring time-intensive activities such as theater attendance. These conditions (aside, perhaps, from the prosperity of the middle classes) are unlikely to be replicated

[1] It is generally thought that popular or folk, i.e., amateur, drama did survive the period of high real wages of the 15th century, and lasted down to Shakespeare's time (*vid.* the "craft" drama in *Midsummer Night's Dream*), but documentation is scanty.

[2] R. H. Tawney and Lawrence Stone are the leading proponents of the view that the real wealth of the gentry increased significantly during the Tudor period. This conclusion has, however, been disputed, particularly by Hugh Trevor-Roper. The importance of the higher priced tickets for the company reflected more than the obvious fact that these tickets are more lucrative than inexpensive ones. We have seen that in the smaller private theaters of the early seventeenth century *all* tickets were comparatively expensive. Without a wealthy clientele it would have been impossible for these theaters to operate using the financial arrangements they did.

in our economy. Certainly, with today's real wages differing by an order of magnitude from those of 1600, the financing of theatrical activity can be expected to remain correspondingly more difficult (compare, for example, the 30 with the 2 week breakeven runs for the two periods). From the fact that, despite all these favorable circumstances, the Elizabethan theater was a highly risky business, one can infer how much more difficult it would be for a self-financed professional theater to survive in a small community today.[1]

A second conslusion that can be drawn from our study is that economic prosperity does not automatically bring with it all the things that are usually taken to contribute to the "quality of life", and if it is accompanied by rising real incomes for all economic classes, it may be a positive detriment to such activities. Whether or not it was largely a coincidence, we have seen that several of the most celebrated periods in the history of the theater were also periods of low real wages, and we can also find periods of prosperity of a more general character, in which dramatic activity is not considered outstanding. The Roman theater, for example, is generally considered artistically inferior to the Greek, despite Rome's greater wealth, and, as we have seen, the unusually high real wages of the fifteenth century seem to have coincided with a long hiatus in theatrical activity that was either professional in organization or characterized by a willingness to experiment. It follows that one cannot simply assume that growth in GNP will bring with it a prosperous and innovative drama.

APPENDIX

Costs and Returns in the Theater of Elizabeth and James

Theatrical budgets from the first half of the eighteenth century have come down to us, but the data from the period studied in this paper are very fragmentary. This appendix summarizes our attempts to put together something resembling a budget from the available figures, from inference, and from a generous dose of guesswork.

Since many of our cost and revenue figures are calculated per-day or per-week of performance, it is first necessary to estimate the number of days and weeks that a successful company played in a typical year. We have already seen that for adult companies there were about six performances per week. We have data for the Swan Theater indicating that in 1610–11 it offered 208 performances; in 1611–12, 248; in 1612–13, 252; in 1613–14, 146; and in 1614–15, 46 (Baldwin, p. 334). The approximate average of these figures (leaving out the last, since in the autumn of 1615 the

[1] "(In 1968–69) the twenty-six regional theaters comprising the League of Resident Theaters had a combined operating deficit (before allowing for gifts or grants) in excess of $6 million. Grants and gifts covered all but $1.6 million. However, these uncovered deficits, added to previous years' deficits, left the regional theaters with accumulated deficits of just over $5 million, and these deficits have occurred despite the fact that actors, technicians, and other staff members in these theaters subsist on extremely meager earnings. Salaries for full-time employees of $50, $60, and $75 a week are common; the average salary for all full-time employees in these theaters, including managing and artistic directors and top actors was less than $150 a week [in 1968–69]. And for most of these employees, their work is only seasonal." (Fitchandler, p. 44.)

resident company moved to a new theater), 200 seems a reasonable estimate of the number of performances per year; the Swan figures also suggest how widely the number must have varied.

The cost of the Elizabethan theater seems to have included two major components: the cost of the building itself, and the earnings of its personnel. There was virtually no scenery and the cost of the costumes, though sometimes very high,[1] was held down by the fact that new costumes were not provided for every new production. It is true that some elaborate dramatic effects were employed – the First Globe burned down when sparks from a simulated cannonade set fire to the roof. But aside from such catastrophes, we may surmise that the cost of such effects did not amount to a great deal.

Initially, the theaters were constructed by investors in real estate who leased them to the companies at high rentals. Later, the more prosperous acting companies purchased or constructed their own theatrical houses. We have firm data about the costs of various theaters (Harbage, 1951, p. 23). The pathbreaking 1576 Theater cost £666 to construct – about $30 000 in terms of commodity purchasing power and over $500 000 in terms of modern daily wages. The Rose was built in 1587 at a cost of £816. We are not sure of the cost of the First Globe (1599) but it is estimated to have been comparatively low, £400–600. The First Fortune cost £520 to construct in 1600. By the time the Second Globe (1614) and the Second Fortune (1622) were built, costs had risen substantially, to £1 400 and £1 000 respectively, presumably at least in part as a result of the inflation.

There is evidence that rates of interest in our period ranged somewhere between 8 and 10 percent[2] as one might expect in an inflationary era. This means that if the theater buildings had been very durable and their use had been expected to continue indefinitely they should have rented for a little more than 10 percent of their building cost. In fact, rental charges were much higher than that. The 1576 Theater rented at £100, so that over £30 per year may be taken to represent amortization of the original £666 cost. We are told that the rent on the Rose amounted to the enormous sum of £346, as compared to the (roughly) £80 interest cost on the original capital. Rental on the First Globe is reported to have been an incredible £420–560 per annum, almost returning its original cost every year! It is easy to see why the theater was rebuilt almost immediately after its destruction by fire fourteen years after it was built.[3]

Before turning to the payments to the actors, we must consider the compensation of the playwrights, which on their own showing at least, was less than munificent.[4]

---

[1] Marchette Chute (p. 55) comments, "Stage costumes were expensive and accounted for a large part of the company's expenses. The taffeta for a single gown cost as much as the salary of a hired actor for fifteen weeks, and even a robe "for to go invisible" represented a considerable investment".

[2] See Kerridge, pp. 213–14. Figures as low as 6 percent are also mentioned.

[3] It is also easy to understand why some companies decided to construct their own theaters under these circumstances. The figures cited represent an annual rate of return on investment in the theaters averaging over forty percent! It is a bit harder to explain why, with such returns, competitive theaters were not constructed in order to drive down the rents. One conjecture is that it required a license which would not be granted for the construction of more theaters than the available acting companies were able to use (some companies did use two theaters—performing sometimes at one, sometimes at the other). The number of companies licensed to perform was indeed strictly limited. Financial difficulties were capable of reducing rents. When local residents prevented Burbage from using the Second Blackfriars as a theater for an adult company after he had purchased and reconstructed it for a total of £900 in 1596, he rented it out for 8 years for only £40 per annum.

[4] Prof. Bentley takes issue with the playwrights' complaints, pointing out that Chettle and Dekker earned more in a year than a curate or a schoolmaster (Bentley, 1971, Chap. V).

Ben Jonson complained to Drummond in 1619 that "of all his playes he never gained 2 hundreth pounds" and he may be fairly accurate, especially if he meant to exclude his numerous court masques (Jonson, 1925, 1, 148). By 1619 the canon of plays either entirely or mostly attributable to Jonson seems to have extended to about 14, although the figure may well have been higher. £10 was probably the top price for a new play, and Henslowe records a payment of 20 shillings to Chettle for a revision (Henslowe, 1961, p. 175). The playwrights (or teams of writers who manufactured many Elizabethan plays) appear to have been paid some £6–£10 per play. In Chapter V of his forthcoming book, however, Prof. Bentley points out that emoluments to playwrights seem to have been rising more rapidly than the general price level: he cites, as one example, the correspondence that appears in W. W. Greg. (ed.) *Henslowe Papers*, Articles 70, 71, 72, 84. This exchange between Robert Daborne and Henslowe (1613–1614) suggests that the playwright was earning approximately £20 per play (Bentley, 1971). As was noted in the text, an average success" might have been performed about twelve times, but a great many plays were performed only four or five times and some only once. This suggests that, with 200 performances per year, there may have been as many as 15 new productions per year. Consequently £120 per annum seems a fair estimate of the sum devoted to playwrights' compensation.

We come next to earnings in the company itself. There are estimates of the earnings of the actor-sharers. In Shakespeare's company these are said to have amounted to about £25–35 (Baldwin, p. 162), which is only about $1 000 to $1 300 per year in terms of 1970 purchasing power. Even the estimate of £55 per year (based on 1635 figures) given by Thaler does not come out much higher. It is noteworthy that these are figures for what was surely the most successful of the acting companies. However, if a leading actor were also a "housekeeper," i.e., part-owner of the building itself, he might expect additional income from the rental of the playhouse. It seems possible, too, that if he were a playwright as well (Shakespeare and a few others were involved in all three roles), he would realize the normal £6–£10 payment for his literary labors. Altogether, though low by today's standards, these compensation levels were reasonably good in comparison with contemporary wage rates. Assuming that the company performed 200 times per year on the average, a £25–35 annual payment per actor-sharer meant an earnings rate of 2 1/2 to 3 1/2 shillings per day, compared with 14 to 16 pence per day for a master craftsman in London. Taken as a whole, the actor-sharers in a single company seem to have earned in a year somewhere between £225 (the Rose in 1592–3) and £300 (average for the Globe in 1599–1608).

Data on wage costs of hirelings (the paid professional actors, musicians, etc. who were not sharers) record that in Henslowe's companies, which cannot have been atypical, they were paid from 5 to 10 shillings per week, and 6 shillings weekly appears to have been a typical wage.[1] The Henslowe diary does tell of an actor hired apparently for 10 shillings every week he played in London in 1597, on a two year arrangement. The contract was negotiated and signed by Henslowe's son-in-law, Edward Alleyn.[2] As for the number of hirelings ordinarily employed at one time by

---

[1] Thaler, p. 85. Gosson states that in 1579 the wages of a hireling were 6 shillings per week, which is probably accurate, since even though Gosson is hostile to the theater, the figures were a matter of public knowledge.

[2] The diary reports:
Md y^{t} this 8th of december 1597 my father philyp
hinchlow hiered as A Covenauant servant willyam kendall for
ij years after The statute of winchester w^{t} ij single penc

a single company, Ringler (p. 113) quotes the observant German traveler, Platter, as having reported "seeing on 21 September 1599, in the thatched playhouse across the Thames [the Globe], a performance of *Julius Caesar 'mitt ohngefehr 15 personen ... Agieren'*." Ringler goes on to observe that "since a member of the audience would not ordinarily be able to identify the individual actors who doubled in the various parts (49 in our only text), someone must have told Platter that the Chamberlain's company numbered 'about fifteen' in September, 1599." Ringler's detailed analysis of the text shows that "*Julius Caesar* can easily be produced by a company of sixteen actors, and cannot be produced with less than sixteen" (Ringler, p. 121). Since we know that at the time of the building of the Globe there were six actor-sharers, the number of hireling actors cannot have been more than ten and was probably closer to 7 or 8, since a few boy-apprentices were employed as well. It is well to remember of course that, as Bentley points out (1961, p. 90), the "hired men" often included "musicians, stage managers, wardrobe keepers and prompters, as well as minor actors", so that even Platter's statement is ambiguous for our purposes. It seems reasonable to surmise that including these other persons the total number of hirelings may have been as high as 15. This gives us an annual expenditure estimate for their wages of some £200 (15 hirelings × 33 weeks at, say, 8*s*./week).

The members of the last group in the company, the boy actors, were treated as apprentices. While they received no money, their keep was provided by the company at a cost which plausibly may be taken to have been somewhat less than £100 per year.

Having gone over the major cost categories we undertake next a rough estimate of receipts. With earnings perhaps slightly above £8 per performance and about 200 performances per year per company, we end up with a total revenue figure of some £1 600, that is, about sixty thousand dollars per year in terms of modern purchasing power.

Subtracting from this sum about £400 for rental of the theater, £300 per year as the compensation of the actor-sharers, £120 per year as payment of playwrights, and £200 per year for hirelings, and, say, £80 for the maintenance of the boy actors and payment to the roughly 20 gatherers (admissions collectors), this leaves over some £500 for miscellaneous expenses of which perhaps £50 or more went as tax payments to the Master of the Revels. The reader should notice that over 40 percent of the total cost is devoted to labor if we include the income of the actor-sharer and the payment to the playwright. This is very similar to the corresponding figure for today's theater,[1] despite the fact that today's productions are much more elaborate and require heavy outlays for stagehands, electricians, etc.

A to geue hym for his sayd servis everi
week of his playng in london xs & in ye
Cuntrie vs for the wch he covenaunteth for ye space
of those ij years To be redy att all Tymes to play in ye howse
of the sayd philyp & in no other during the sayd Terme

wittnes my self the writer
ofThis EAlleyn

(Henslowe, pp. 268–269)

The "two single pence" mentioned in this passage may be by way of "earnest money", a small amount customarily paid upon the signing of an agreement, as a means of signaling good faith.

[1] Indeed, the structure of Elizabethan theatrical costs as estimated and that of the more recent commercial theater is remarkably similar, as the following table shows.

Bibliography

Arrow, K.: Criteria, institutions, and function in urban development decisions. In A. H. Pascal (ed.), *Contributions to the analysis of urban problems.* Santa Monica, 1968.

Baldwin, T. W.: *The organization and personnel of the Shakespearean company.* Princeton, 1927.

Baumol, W. J. & Bowen, W. G.: *Performing arts: The economic dilemma.* New York, 1966.

Bentley, G. E.: Shakespeare and the Blackfriars Theater. *Shakespeare Survey no. 1*, pp. 38–50, 1948.

Bentley, G. E.: *Shakespeare, A biographical handbook.* New Haven, 1961.

Bentley, G. E.: *The Jacobean and Caroline stage.* (7 Vols.) Oxford, 1941–1968.

Bentley, G. E.: Letter to W. Baumol, Oct. 24, 1970.

Bentley, G. E.: *The profession of the dramatist in Shakespeare's time.* Princeton, 1971.

Bernheim, A. L.: *The business of the theater.* New York, 1932.

Briley, J.: Of stake and stage. *Shakespeare Survey*, No. 8, pp. 106–108, 1955.

Bromberg, M.: The reputation of Philip Henslowe. *Shakespeare Quarterly I*, 135–145, 1950.

Bush, K.: A comparison of retail prices in the United States, the USSR and Western Europe in April 1969. *Radio Liberty Research Paper*, no. 33, New York, 1969.

Carus-Wilson, E. M.: *Essays in Economic History.* (3 Vols.) Vol. II. London, 1962.

Chambers, E. K.: *The Elizabethan stage.* (4 Vols.) Vol. I. Oxford, 1923.

Chambers, E. K.: *The Medieval stage.* (2 Vols.) Vol. II. Oxford, 1903.

Chute, M.: *Ben Jonson of Westminster.* New York, 1953.

Department of Employment and Productivity, *Statistics on Incomes, Prices, Employment and Production*, June, 1969, No. 29, London, 1969.

Economic Report of the President, Washington, January 1965.

Fitchandler, Th.: Regional theater: filling the vacuum. *Cultural Affairs*, pp. 43–44, 1970.

Fisher, F. J.: The development of London as a centre of conspicuous consumption in the sixteenth and seventeenth centuries. *Transactions of the Royal Historical Society*, p. 30, 1948. Reprinted in Carus-Wilson, 197–207.

Gosson, S.: *School of Abuse.* London, 1579.

Harbage, A.: *Shakespeare's audience.* New York, 1941.

Harbage, A.: *Shakespeare and the rival traditions.* New York, 1952.

Henslowe, Ph.: *Henslowe's diary* (ed. R. A. Foakes and R. T. Rickert. Cambridge, 1961.

Hillebrand, H. Newcomb: *The child actors: A chapter in Elizabethan stage history.* Urbana, 1926.

Jonson, Ben: Conversations with Drummond. In *Works* (ed. C. H. Herford &

Table 2.

	Estimated % of total budget ca. 1600	% of itemized costs, Broadway Theater, 1960–1
Theatrical Rental	25	28
Playwright's Fees	7.5	8
Artists & Managerial	30–35	34

Broadway figures are taken from Moore, p. 155. Unfortunately, despite Moore's careful work, he was unable to obtain information about some 15 % of the relevant costs, which may or may not include salaries, playwright's royalties, etc. This may distort our percentage figures slightly, for example, perhaps reducing the rent figure from 28 to 23 percent of the total. More recent unpublished data for Broadway indicate that the theater rental figure has in fact risen and that the shares of the performers and the playwright have fallen.

Percy Simpson). (11 vols) Vol. I. Oxford, 1925.

Jonson, Ben: Induction to Bartholomew Fair. In *Works* (ed. C. H. Hereford & Percy Simpson). Vol. VI. Oxford, 1925.

Kerridge, E.: The movement of rent, 1540–1640. In Carus-Wilson, 208–226.

Laidlaw, W. (ed.): *Population of the City of New York, 1890–1930.* New York, 1932.

Linder, S. B.: *The harried leisure class.* New York, 1970.

Mitchell, E. H.: *The Economics of Ancient Greece.* New York, 1940.

Mols, R.: *Introduction á la démographie historique des villes d'Europe* du XIVe au XVIIIe siècle, tome troisième. Louvain, 1955.

Moore, Th. G.: *The economics of the American theater.* Durham, 1968.

Poggi, J.: *Theater in America.* Ithaca, 1968.

Phelps Brown, E. H. & Hopkins, S. V.: Seven centuries of building wages. *Economica,* N.S. 22, 195–206, Aug. 1955, Reprinted in Carus-Wilson, 168–178.

Phelps Brown, E. H. & Hopkins, S. V.: Seven centuries of the prices of consumables. *Economica,* N.S. 23, 296–314, Nov. 1956. Reprinted in Carus-Wilson, 179–196.

Pickard-Cambridge, A.: *The dramatic festivals of Athens.* Oxford, 1953.

Ramsey, P.: *Tudor economic problems.* London, 1963.

Ringler, W. A., Jr: The number of actors in Shakespeare's early plays. In Bentley (ed.) *The seventeenth century stage.* Chicago, 1968.

Rye, W. B.: *England as seen by foreigners, in the days of Elizabeth and James I.* London, 1865.

Simpson, P.: Actors and acting. In *Shakespeare's England: An account of life and manners of his age.* (2 Vols.) London, 1916–17.

Stone, L.: The anatomy of the Elizabethan aristocracy. *Economic History Review 18,* 1–38, 1948.

Tawney, R. H.: Harrington's interpretation of his age. Raleigh Lecture, *Proceedings of the British Academy 18,* 1–38, 1948.

Thaler, A.: Shakespeare's income. *Studies in Philology,* 82–96, 1918.

Trevelyan, G. M.: *English social history.* London, 1944.

Trevor-Roper, H. R.: The Gentry, 1540–1640. *Economic History Review,* Supplement 1, 1953.

US Department of Labor, Bureau of Labor Statistics, *Union Wages and Hours: Building Trades,* Bulletin No. 1621, Washington.

[11]

On Taxation and the Control of Externalities

By William J. Baumol*

It is ironic that just at the moment when the Pigouvian tradition has some hope of acceptance in application it should find itself under a cloud in the theoretical literature. James Buchanan has argued that its recommended taxes and subsidies may even increase resource misallocation in the presence of monopoly. Otto Davis and Andrew Whinston (1962) have, in effect, raised doubts about its applicability in the presence of oligopoly. And Ronald Coase has asserted that the tradition has not selected the correct taxation principle for the elimination of externalities, and may not even have chosen the right individuals to tax or to subsidize. In this paper I will suggest that these authors have led the discussion in our profession to focus on the wrong difficulties. In doing so they have, albeit inadvertently, drawn attention away from some of the most important limitations of the Pigouvian prescription as an instrument of policy and from consideration of the means that might prove effective in practice.

The main purpose of the paper is to show that, taken on its own grounds, the conclusions of the Pigouvian tradition are, in fact, impeccable. Despite the various criticisms that have been raised against it in the large numbers case, which is of primary importance in reality and to which Pigou's analysis directs itself, his tax-subsidy programs are generally those required for an optimal allocation of resources. Moreover, I will attempt to show that where an externality is (like the usual pollution problem) of the public goods variety, neither compensation to nor taxation of those who are affected by it is compatible with optimal resource allocation. Pigouvian taxes (subsidies) upon the generator of the externality are all that is required.

However, as is well known, the Pigouvian proposals suffer from a number of serious shortcomings as operational criteria when one seeks to implement them precisely as they emerge from the theory. I therefore discuss a modified approach that recommends itself more for its promise of effectiveness, than its theoretical nicety. It consists of two basic steps: the setting of standards, more or less arbitrarily, of levels of pollution, congestion and the like, that are considered to be tolerable, and the design of taxes and effluent charges whose rates are shown by experience to be sufficient to achieve the selected standards of acceptability. Such a system of charges will, at least in principle, effect any preselected reduction in,

* Professor of economics, Princeton University and New York University. I would like to express my gratitude to the National Science Foundation whose assistance helped materially in the completion of the paper and to my colleagues James Litvack, Wallace Oates, and David Bradford, to my students Mark Gaudry and Bryan Boulier, and to Peter Bohm, James Buchanan, Ronald Coase, Karl-Göran Mäler, Herbert Mohring, and Ralph Turvey who have given me many very helpful suggestions, and saved me from a number of serious errors. Mohring and J. Hayden Boyd have written an extremely illuminating paper dealing, among other relevant matters, with the portions of the Coase-Buchanan-Turvey arguments in the case where the polluters and their victims "can and do negotiate." Since the present paper concerns itself only with the "relevant" large numbers case where there is no negotiation, it deliberately makes no attempt to consider the interesting negotiation case examined so helpfully by Mohring and Boyd.

say, the pollution content of our rivers, at minimum cost to society. It automatically achieves an efficient allocation of the required reduction in emissions among the offending firms *even if they are neither pure competitors nor profit maximizers.* Thus, a persuasive case can be made for the use of taxes and subsidies to control externalities, even if they will not produce an optimal allocation of resources in the complex world of reality.

I. The Coase Argument in the Case Without Negotiation

Recommendations designed for the competitive case can clearly run into difficulties in the presence of monopolistic elements. Buchanan reminds us that, if a polluting monopolistic industry already restricts the outputs of its products below their competitive levels, the imposition of an effluent charge to restrict output still further is hardly likely to be appropriate. And Davis and Whinston (1962) show for the case of externalities under oligopoly that it is rather difficult to come up with an ideal set of taxes since in the small numbers case just about anything is possible by way of pricing and output levels. However, these arguments have little direct bearing on the Pigouvian analysis because it is couched entirely in terms of pure competition (on this see Stanislaw Wellicz' illuminating discussion), which, in view of the large numbers involved in virtually all of the externalities problems that worry us today, is entirely apropos.

Coase's arguments, buttressed by impressive legal erudition, are less easily dealt with. He offers us a number of illuminating observations, among them the interesting point (see his Section IV) that (in the relatively unimportant cases) where only a small number of decision makers is involved, a process of voluntary bargaining and side payments among those concerned by an externality may produce an optimal allocation of resources, even in the absence of liability for damage. This implies that where small numbers are involved, the imposition of a "corrective" Pigouvian tax may be too much of a good thing—it can produce a misallocation rather than eliminating it.

Coase suggests, however, that even in cases where there is no negotiation among the parties affected by an externality the Pigouvian taxes and subsidies may be the wrong remedy—that they may only modify the character of the misallocation of resources. Coase's central argument appears to be the following: Every social cost is inherently reciprocal in nature. The nearby residents who breathe smoke spewn by a factory must share with the management of the factory the responsibility for the resulting social cost. True, if the factory were closed up the social cost would disappear. But the same holds for its neighbors—were they to move away no one would suffer smoke nuisance. Put another way, just as the smoke emitted by the factory imposes at least a psychic cost on its neighbors, the latter's insistence on the installation of purification devices or a reduction in the pollution-producing activity imposes a cost on the factory.

This position, though at first glance very odd (the murder victim too, is then always an accessory to the crime), grows more persuasive as one considers it further. Coase does not raise the issue as a matter of distributive justice. Rather, he suggests, because of the reciprocal structure of the externality, the traditional taxes and subsidies are likely to lead to a misallocation of resources.[1] If it is socially less costly to

[1] Thus Coase starts out with

> . . . the case of a confectioner, the noise and vibrations from whose machinery disturbed a doctor in his work. To avoid harming the doctor would inflict harm on [be costly to] the confectioner. The problem posed by this case was essentially whether it was worthwhile, as a

remove the neighbors from the vicinity of the factory than to reduce the quantity of pollutants emitted by the plant (taking into account the location preferences of the current residents), surely the former is the course of action which is more desirable socially.

In that case, should not a tax sometimes be levied, at least in part on those who choose to live near the factory rather than upon the factory owners?[2] Otherwise might not too many persons be induced to move near the factory thus, incidentally, increasing the magnitude of the Pigouvian tax since the social damage caused by the smoke must then rise correspondingly?

A simple model shows readily that, properly stated, the prescription of the Pigouvian tradition is (at least formally) correct. An appropriately chosen tax, levied only on the factory (without payment of compensation to local residents) is precisely what is needed for optimal resource allocation under pure competition. No tax on nearby residents is required or, taken in real terms, is even compatible with optimal resource allocation. Thus the obvious and apparently common interpretation of the Coase position is simply invalid. We will see, however, that the issue Coase himself intended to raise was rather more subtle and his conclusions are not necessarily at variance with the Pigouvian prescription as I interpret it.

II. Analysis: Should the Victims of Externalities be Taxed or Compensated?

To formalize the argument we construct an elementary general equilibrium model designed to represent in most explicit form the conditions envisioned in the Coase argument, departing from it only by an assumption of universal perfect competition, including thereby the critical stipulation that costs of negotiated and voluntary control of externalities are prohibitive. In addition, we adopt the simplifying premises that there is only one scarce resource, labor, and that the externality (smoke) only affects the cost of production of neighboring laundries, rather than causing disutility for consumers. It is easy to show (see for example, fn. 5) that neither of these simplifications, nor the assumption that there are only four activities, affects the substance of the discussion. We utilize the following notation: Let

x_1, x_2, x_3, and x_4 be the outputs of the economy's four activities, I, II, III, and IV

R be the total supply of the labor resource available

x_5 be the unused quantity of labor (which is assumed to be utilized as leisure)

---

result of restricting the methods of production which could be used by the confectioner, to secure more doctoring at the cost of a reduced supply of confectionery products. [Section II, p. 2]

[2] If the factory owner is to be made to pay a tax equal to the damage caused, it would clearly be desirable to institute a double tax system and to make residents of the district pay an amount equal to the additional cost incurred by the factory owner (or the consumers of his products) in order to avoid the damage. [Coase, Section IX, p. 41] An even stronger statement on this subject occurs in Buchanan and Stubblebine (Section III):

> . . . full Pareto equilibrium can *never* be attained via the imposition of unilaterally imposed taxes and subsidies until all marginal externalities are eliminated. If a tax subsidy method, rather than 'trade,' is to be introduced, it should involve bi-lateral taxes (subsidies). Not only must B's behavior be modified so as to insure that he will take the costs externally imposed on A into account, but A's behavior must be modified so as to insure that he will take the costs 'internally' imposed on B into account. [italics added]

However, in a recent letter Buchanan commented:

> In my own thinking . . . I did not ever think of this sort of [double] tax at all, and it would have surely seemed bizarre to me to suggest that taxes be levied on both the factory and the laundries. What we were proposing was the Wicksellian public-goods approach. Suppose that existing property rights allow the factory to put out the smoke . . . There is a public goods problem here; the residents get together, impose a tax on *themselves* to subsidize the factory to install the smoke prevention device.

x_{ij} be the quantity of x_i consumed by individual j ($i=1, \ldots, 5$) ($j=1, \ldots, m$)

p_1, p_2, p_3, p_4, and p_5 be the prices of the four outputs and leisure

$u_j(x_{1j}, \ldots, x_{5j})$ be the utility function of individual j, and

$c_1(x_1)$, $c_2(x_1, x_2)$, $c_3(x_3)$ and $c_4(x_4)$ be the respective total labor cost functions for our four outputs

Here x_1 is an output whose production imposes external costs on the manufacture of x_2 (say, industry II is the oft-cited laundry industry whose costs are increased by I's smoke). To permit the full range of Coase's alternatives (moving of the factory's neighbors and elimination of smoke by the factory), each of these two products is taken to have a perfect substitute. The substitute for x_1 is x_3 whose production yields no externalities, but whose cost is different (presumably higher) than that of x_1. We may think of commodity III as identical with I, but produced in a factory equipped with smoke elimination equipment. Similarly, industry IV is taken to offer the same output as II but its operations have been relocated (at a cost) in order to avoid the effects of the externalities.[3] Thus, by changing the ratio between x_2 and x_4 the model can relocate as much of the laundry output as is desired.

All prices are expressed in terms of hours of labor so that, identically,

$$p_5 = 1 \tag{1}$$

[3] Since product III is a perfect substitute for product I and product IV is a perfect substitute for product II, the utility function for individual j can be written as $u_j(x_{1j}+x_{3j}, x_{2j}+x_{4j}, x_{5j})$. This is, of course, a special case of the more general utility function utilized in the text, and as the reader can verify, the conclusions are totally unaffected by the use of the particular form of the utility function just described.

Pareto optimality then requires maximization of the utility of any arbitrarily chosen individual, say m, subject to the requirement that there be no loss in utility to any of the $m-1$ other persons, i.e., given any feasible level for these other persons' utility. Thus the problem is[4] to maximize

$$u_m(x_{1m}, \ldots, x_{5m})$$

subject to

$$u_j(x_{1j}, \ldots, x_{5j}) \doteq k_j \text{ (constant)} \qquad (j = 1, 2, \ldots, m-1)$$

$$\sum_{j=1}^{m} x_{ij} = x_i \qquad (i = 1, \ldots, 5)$$

and the labor requirement (production function) constraint

$$c_1(x_1) + c_2(x_1, x_2) + c_3(x_3) + c_4(x_4) + x_5 = R$$

We immediately obtain our Lagrangian

$$\begin{aligned} L = {} & \sum_{j=1}^{m} \lambda_j[u_j(x_{1j}, \cdots, x_{5j}) - k_j] \\ & + \sum_i \nu_i(x_i - \sum_j x_{ij}) \\ & + \mu[R - c_1(x_1) - c_2(x_1, x_2) \\ & - c_3(x_3) - c_4(x_4) - x_5] \end{aligned} \tag{2}$$

where we may take $\lambda_m = 1$, $k_m = 0$.

We use the notation u_{ji} to represent $\partial u_j/\partial x_{ij}$ and c_{ik} to represent $\partial c_i/\partial x_k$ (or dc_i/dx_k, where appropriate).

Then, differentiating in turn with respect to the x_{ij} and the x_i we obtain the first-order conditions

$$\partial L/\partial x_{ij} = \lambda_j u_{ji} - \nu_i = 0 \quad (i = 1, \ldots, 5) \quad (j = 1, \ldots, m)$$

$$\partial L/\partial x_1 = -\mu(c_{11} + c_{21}) + \nu_1 = 0$$

$$\partial L/\partial x_i = -\mu c_{ii} + \nu_i = 0 \quad (i = 2, 3, 4)$$

$$\partial L/\partial x_5 = -\mu + \nu_5 = 0$$

[4] For a more sophisticated variant of this model, using the techniques of non-linear programming, see Robert Meyer.

Now, from consumer equilibrium analysis, we know that for any two commodities, a and b, and any two prices, p_a and p_b, we have $p_a/p_b = u_{ja}/u_{jb}$ $(j=1, \cdots, m)$ or $\omega_j p_i = u_{ji}$ for all i and some ω_j.

Hence, $\lambda_j u_{ji} = \lambda_j \omega_j p_i$, so that writing $s_j = \lambda_j \omega_j$ the first of our first-order conditions becomes $v_i = s_j p_i$ for all individuals, j. Consequently the value of s_j must equal the same number, $s = v_i/p_i$ for every individual, and that first equation of the first-order conditions now becomes simply $v_i = s p_i$ for all i. Substituting this expression for v_i into the other first-order conditions, we obtain

$$sp_1 = \mu(c_{11} + c_{21})$$

$$sp_i = \mu c_{ii} \qquad (i = 2, 3, 4)$$

$$(3) \qquad sp_5 = s = \mu \quad \text{since } p_5 = 1 \text{ [by (1)]}$$

By (3) we may then divide through the preceding conditions by $s = \mu$, and they therefore reduce just to[5]

$$(4) \qquad \begin{aligned} p_1 &= c_{11} + c_{21} \\ p_2 &= c_{22} \\ p_3 &= c_{33} \\ p_4 &= c_{44} \\ p_5 &= 1 \end{aligned}$$

In other words, the optimal price for the externality-generating product is equal to the (Pareto optimal) level of its entire social[6] marginal cost, $c_{11}+c_{21}$, while the optimal price for any item, i, which generates no externalities is simply its marginal private cost, c_{ii}. To obtain these prices in our world of pure competition, one need merely levy an excise tax on item I equal to c_{21} (labor hours) dollars per unit, just as the Pigouvian tradition requires. Assuming the appropriate concavity-convexity conditions hold, this will automatically satisfy the necessary and sufficient conditions for the Pareto optimal output levels.[7] In the competitive case, where negotiation is impractical, that is all there is to the matter. The generalization to the case of n outputs, each of them imposing externalities on a number of the others, is immediate.

It is important to observe that, *the solution calls for neither taxes upon x_2, the neighboring laundry output, nor compensation to that industry* for the damage it suffers.

One way to look at the reason is that our model (and the pollution model in general) refers to the important case of *public* externalities. The laundry whose output is

[5] The analysis can also take account of constraints on the availability of land at the relevant locations, which give rise to rents that equalize costs at all locations actually utilized. If S_a and S_b represent the availability of land near and away from the factory, respectively, presumably we would add to the labor constraint in the model the two additional land-use constraints $g_a(x_1, x_2, x_3) + s_a = S_a$ and $g_b(x_4) + s_b = S_b$, with the quantities of unused land, s_a and s_b perhaps entering the utility functions. It then follows, just as before, that the equilibrium conditions are now $p_1 = c_{11} + c_{21} + \rho_a g_{a1}$; $p_2 = c_{22} + \rho_a g_{a2}$; $p_3 = c_{33} + \rho_a g_{a3}$; $p_4 = c_{44} + \rho_b g_{b4}$; $p_5 = 1$; $p_a = \rho_a/\mu$; $p_b = \rho_b/\mu$; where ρ_a and ρ_b are the Lagrange multipliers for the new constraints and p_a and p_b are the (labor) prices of land at the two locations. Our previous conclusions are, thus, totally unaffected. Only the smoke producer's product sells for more than its marginal private cost of labor plus land.

[6] The social cost is not c_{21} alone but is the sum of the private and the external costs together (see the illuminating terminological discussion by D. W. Pearce and Stanley Sturmey). Note that the tax, implicitly, is a tax on *smoke* not a tax on x_1, the output of the smoke producing industry. For if s is the quantity of smoke and t the unit tax we may write $t = c_{21} = (\partial c_2/\partial s)(ds/dx_1)$ and obviously the firm can reduce its tax rate by decreasing the second of these terms, the smokiness of its product. This point has been emphasized by Charles Plott, who showed that a fixed tax per unit of x_1 might even conceivably increase s, if s were an inferior input.

[7] Moreover, measured in real terms this is the only tax arrangement that satisfies the optimality requirements, neglecting the possibility of a lump sum tax or subsidy which does not affect the marginal conditions. F. Trenery Dolbear has shown that it is generally not possible to find an optimal tax rate that compensates fully those who suffer the effects of the externality. Since no compensation is paid to industry II, the solution that is derived here does not run into Dolbear's problem. We also do not run into the problem of a multiplicity of solutions corresponding to the various points on Dolbear's contract curve because we are dealing with a world of pure competition with a given initial distribution.

damaged by smoky air does not, by an increase in its own output, make the air cleaner or dirtier for others. As with all public goods, an increase in one user's consumption does not reduce the available supply to others.[8] Hence, the appropriate price (compensation) to a user of a public good (victim of a public externality) is *zero* except, of course, for lump sum payments. Thus, perhaps, rather than saying there is no price that will yield an optimal quantity of a public good (externality), it may be more illuminating to say that a double price is required: a nonzero price (tax) to the supplier of the good, and a zero price to the consumer. Of course, no ordinary price can do this job, but a Pigouvian tax, without compensation to those affected by an externality, can indeed do the trick.

III. What Prevents an Excessive Influx of Neighbors?

When only smoke emission is taxed, with the tax level based on the magnitude of x_2, nearby laundry output, what will prevent too many laundries from moving near the smoky factory? The answer is that, when the tax on the externality producer is set properly, the externalities themselves keep down the size of the nearby population. Moreover, the level of the tax will control both the magnitude of smoke emission and thereby (indirectly), the size of the nearby population. A high tax rate will discourage smoke and hence encourage migration into the neighborhood. A low tax rate will encourage smoke and, hence, drive residents away. A tax on smoke alone is all that is needed to control the magnitudes of *both* variables. That is why, as shown by the mathematics of the preceding section, just a tax on the smoke producer is sufficient to produce an optimal allocation of resources among all the activities in our model.[9]

A diagram may help to make the point clearer. Figure 1 shows the response of our two industries' outputs to a change in the tax rate on the polluting industry, I. We see that as the tax rate varies, industry I's output response follows the curve RR'. Thus, if the tax level is t, the output of industry I will be x_{1t}. But, because of the externalities, the output of industry II, in turn, reacts to the output of I. This relationship is described by reaction curve PP'. With $x_1=x_{1t}$ we see that $x_2=x_{2t}$.

The tax rate on II can vary all the way from $t=0$, yielding output combination (x_{10}, x_{20}), to a prohibitive tax rate, t_p, that drives I out of business altogether, so that $x_1=0$ and $x_2=x_{2p}$. Obviously, the ratio x_1/x_2 then decreases monotonically as the tax rate increases and, assuming continuity, there will be some intermediate tax rate at which the two activities will be in balance. The tax will keep x_1 in check while the external cost imposed by x_1 on industry II will keep x_2 to the right relative level. There is no need for a separate tax on II to achieve this goal.

[8] In his discussion of these matters Coase seems at one point to skate awfully close to an error analogous to the confusion between pecuniary and technological externalities. He writes (section IX):

> The tax that would be imposed would . . . increase with an increase in the number of those in the vicinity . . . But people deciding to establish themselves in the vicinity of the factory will not take into account [the resulting] fall in the value of production which results from their presence. This failure to take into account costs imposed on others is comparable to the action of a factory-owner in not taking account the harm resulting from his emission of smoke. [p. 42]

This is analogous to the argument that where the supply curve of labor is rising an increase in output by firm *A* must produce externalities, by raising *B*'s labor costs. But, of course, this merely represents a transfer from *B* to his workers and is not a real net cost to society. For that reason, as is well known, pecuniary externalities do *not* lead to resource misallocation. Like a price change, the variation in taxes constitutes a pecuniary externality. Both have real consequences but they are merely "movements along" the production and utility functions, i.e., any given vector of inputs will be able to produce the same outputs as before the change in tax rates, and any vector of output levels will still be able to yield the same utility levels.

[9] See the Appendix for a discussion of an argument by Buchanan and Stubblebine which is related to Coase's.

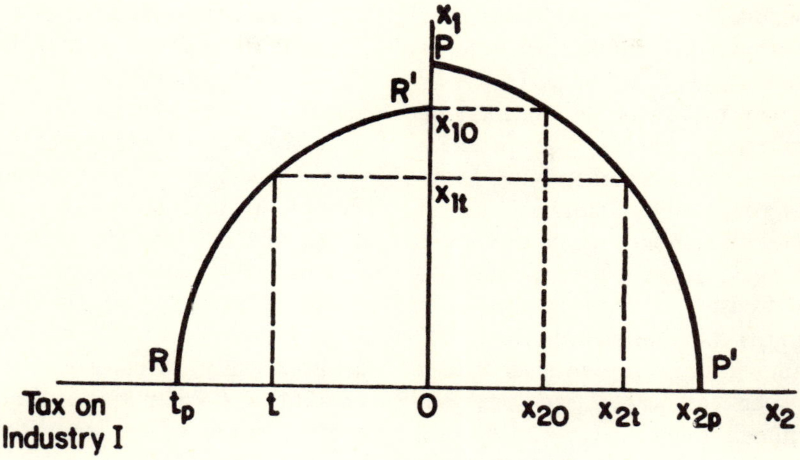

FIGURE 1

In order for this arrangement to work it is clearly necessary that the laundries *not* be compensated (at the margin) for the smoke damage they suffer. If they received in compensation an amount which varied with the magnitude of the smoke damage, that externality would not restrict the level of laundry activity near the factory. If the laundry operators' smoke costs were offset by damage compensation payments, obviously they would lose the economic incentive to eschew the vicinity of the smoky factory[10] and then Coase's tax on laundries would indeed be required to keep them away. But then the tax would be needed only to sop up the compensation payments which should never have been given in the first place.

IV. Multiple Local Maxima in the Coase Model

Coase's discussion is, however, right in pointing out the possibility that the economy may make the wrong choice between smoke elimination and laundry relocation: however the source of the problem, a multiplicity of local maxima, does not emerge clearly. Coase writes:

> Assume that a factory which emits smoke is set up in a district previously free from smoke pollution, causing damage valued at $100 per annum. Assume that the taxation solution is adopted and that the factory owner is taxed $100 per annum as long as the factory emits the smoke. Assume further that a smoke-preventing device costing $90 per annum to run is available. In these circumstances, the smoke-preventing device would be installed.
>
> . . . Yet the position achieved may not be optimal. Suppose that those who suffer the damage could avoid it by moving to other locations or by taking various precautions which would cost them, or be equivalent to a loss in income of, $40 per annum. Then there would be a gain in the value of production of $50 if the factory continued to emit its smoke and those now in the district moved elsewhere or made other adjustments to avoid the damage. [Section IX]

One curious feature of this example is its assumption that while smoke damage is $100, the cost of moving to other locations is only $40. Under these circumstances one

[10] Of course, as smoke cost increases in the neighborhood of the factory, rents will fall to some extent and serve as partial compensation to the laundries. However, this does not change the analysis fundamentally. It is analogous to the case of rise in the price of an input which, as is well known, will tend to reduce the output of competitive firms, even though prices of other complementary inputs fall as a result. As the discussion of footnote 5 shows, explicit consideration of the price of land does not change the character of the solution.

may well wonder why people living near the factory do not just move elsewhere on their own initiative. Moreover, this may not simply be a matter of the numbers he happens to have chosen. The problem arises whenever the cost of moving away from the factory is less than the cost of elimination of the smoke, which in turn is less than the cost of the smoke damage, as the logic of Coase's example requires.

It is perhaps more important to recognize that the example presents us with a choice between (at least) two local optima. As will be argued later, a multiplicity of maxima is generally rendered more likely by the presence of externalities so that this issue is not a pecularity of Coase's illustrations. The first of the two local optima in Coase's example (call it solution A) involves zero smoke emission and a full complement of residents near the factory. In the second optimum (solution B) no one remains in residence next to the factory and there is no restriction in smoke emission by the plant. Assuming that the (undesirable) initial position is the only other possibility, as Coase seems to suggest, which of these two will in fact be the global optimum depends on the cost of moving everyone away (m dollars) and the cost of elimination of the smoke (s dollars).

Assume with Coase that the initial cost of smoke damage is \$100, that $s<100$, but that $s<m$ so that it is cheaper to eliminate the smoke than to move the factory's neighbors. In this case, A is obviously the optimal solution. Since inhabitants surround the plant, and smoke emission, by assumption, cannot be changed by small amounts, the incremental social damage of an increase in smoke emission is \$100. Thus the correct Pigouvian tax is \$100 and, since $s<100$, with such a tax it will pay the factory to do the right thing by society—to install the smoke eliminator.

Now assume instead that $m<s<100$ (it is cheaper to move people than to stop the smoke). This time B is the optimal solution, and since under B no one lives near the factory, the incremental cost of smoke is clearly zero. Therefore the proper Pigouvian tax is zero, a value that induces the factory to continue smoking, and its neighbors will find it advantageous (since $100>m$) to exit (coughing) from the area. Thus the zero Pigouvian tax value automatically satisfies the requirements of solution B when B is optimal just as the \$100 Pigouvian tax leads to solution A when A is optimal.

Of course, if B happens to be the true global optimum and society mistakenly imposes the \$100 Pigouvian tax appropriate for (local) optimum A, the economy may well end up with the inferior equilibrium A. This is the usual difficulty one encounters whenever there is a multiplicity of maxima, a problem that Pigou so clearly recognized (pp. 140, 224).

V. Departures from the Optimum and Adjustments in the Tax

If there is a departure from the optimal solution, for whatever reason, the value of the Pigouvian tax need not change. If, for example, B is the global optimum so that the optimal tax is zero, that tax need not be increased if a few (misguided) individuals choose to move back near the factory so that additional smoke now incurs (say) \$50 in damage. *At the optimal solution* the marginal cost of smoke is zero, and the equilibrium Pigouvian tax remains zero—it does not increase to \$50.

Here we have arrived at the issue which, I now understand, was really Coase's main point in the portion of his article we are considering. He writes in a letter:

> . . . Let us assume your optimum tax is imposed. Now suppose that A establishes himself near the plant which produces the damaging emissions and thus

increases the amount of damage. Would your tax increase? My guess is that it would not (certainly if your tax system is right it should not). The tax system I was attacking was one which would in these circumstances, automatically lead to an increase in the tax as the damage increased.

This point is, surely, quite different from the issue he is usually interpreted to have raised (see the quotations in fn. 1, above, which suggest how the "usual interpretation" arose). It is, however, not inconsistent with the optimal solution derived in the previous section nor is it inconsistent with what I take to be the Pigouvian tradition.

But even on this issue Coase's strictures are not necessarily valid. Suppose that a regulator, having no way of calculating the *optimal* values of the Pigouvian tax is, however, able to determine the value of any marginal social damage at any point in time. *Faut de mieux* he therefore sets a tax rate equal to *current* marginal social damage on the smoke producer. This causes him to reduce his smoke, and so brings more laundries into the neighborhood. The tax is then readjusted to equal the new (higher) value of damage per puff of smoke, more laundries move in, and so on. Will this process of trial and error adjustments of the tax level, always setting it equal to current marginal smoke damage, converge to the optimum of Section II? That is, will the sequence of tax values converge to the optimal Pigouvian tax level, and will resource allocation approach optimality? That now seems to be Coase's main question.

Obviously, such a learning process always involves wastes and irreversabilities, just like the process of convergence of competitive prices to their equilibrium values in the absence of externalities. But if we follow the usual practice of assuming away these costs, one can show that the process may be expected to converge to the optimum, provided the equilibrium is unique and stable. That is, there is then nothing inherently different about gradually moving taxes and prices towards their equilibrium here, and the process of adjustment toward competitive equilibrium when there are no externalities.

Specifically, letting s_t represent the tax per unit on commodity 1 at time t, and G_i be the ith adjustment function we may set

$$(5)\quad \begin{aligned} dx_{1t}/dt &= G_1[p_{1t} - s_t - c_{11}(x_{1t})] \\ dx_{2t}/dt &= G_2[p_{2t} - c_{22}(x_{1t}, x_{2t})] \\ dx_{it}/dt &= G_i[p_{it} - c_{ii}(x_{it})] \quad (i = 3, 4) \end{aligned}$$

$$(6)\quad s_t = c_{21}(x_{1t}, x_{2t}) \quad p_{it} = f_i(x_{1t}, \ldots, x_{5t})$$

and where, as usual, we take

$$(7)\quad G_i(0) = 0$$

$$(8)\quad G_i' > 0$$

Going back to Section II, when optimality conditions (4) hold, we see by substituting them into (5) that all $dx_{it}/dt = 0$, i.e., (4) is indeed an equilibrium position for the dynamic system (5)–(8). Furthermore, any solution that does not satisfy (4) must involve at least one nonzero argument in the adjustment functions (5), and so no solution that fails to satisfy (4) can be an equilibrium.

It follows that if the dynamic system (5)–(8) is stable, and the solution to (4) is unique, the process with taxes set equal to *current* marginal damage and imposed *only on the polluter* will converge toward the optimum. One does not need to have calculated the optimal tax values from the beginning and stick to them.

The reason this process of simultaneous learning and adjustment does not work in Coase's example is that it involves (at least) two local maxima, as we have already noted. And in such a case, obviously, the adjustment mechanism may well take us to the wrong maximum. Unfortunately, as we will see presently, in the presence of externalities, a multiplicity of maxima is all too likely to be with us.

VI. Implementation Problems

Despite the validity in principle of the tax-subsidy approach of the Pigouvian tradition, in practice it suffers from serious difficulties. For we do not know how to estimate the magnitudes of the social costs, the data needed to implement the Pigouvian tax-subsidy proposals. For example, a very substantial portion of the cost of pollution is psychic; and even if we knew how to evaluate the psychic cost to some one individual we seem to have little hope of dealing with effects so widely diffused through the population.[11]

This would not necessarily be very serious if one could hope to learn by experience. One might try any plausible set of taxes and subsidies and then attempt, by a set of trial and error steps, to approach the desired magnitudes. Unfortunately, convergence toward the desired solution by an iterative procedure of this sort requires some sort of measure of the improvement (if any) that has been achieved at each step so that the next trial step can be adjusted accordingly. But we do not know the socially optimal composition of outputs, so we simply have no way of judging whether a given change in the trial tax values will even have moved matters in the right direction.

[11] For an excellent discussion of some of the work done in trying to implement Pigouvian taxes in practice, see Allen Kneese and Blair Bower, esp. ch. 6 and 8. The difficulty of determining the magnitude of the Pigouvian tax-subsidy level is one of Coase's major points, one that seems often to be overlooked in discussions of his paper. Thus Coase writes in a letter, "The view I expressed in my article was not that such an optimum tax system (levied solely on the damage producing firm) was inconceivable but that I could not see how the data on which it would have to be based could be assembled." An interesting approach to application for the small numbers case that is based on the decomposition principle of mathematical programming is presented by Davis and Whinston (1966).

These difficulties are compounded by another characteristic of externalities which has already been mentioned—the likelihood that in the presence of externalities there will be a multiplicity of local maxima (see Richard Portes, D. A. Starrett, and Baumol). Consequently, even if an iterative process were possible it might only drive us toward a local maximum, and may thus fail to take advantage of the really significant opportunities to improve economic welfare.

A simple model in the spirit of that of Section II can be used to show that the presence of "strong" externalities can be expected to produce a violation of the convexity conditions in whose absence one normally finds a multiplicity of local optima.

Let us assume (to permit the use of a two-dimensional diagram) that there exist only the first two of our four activities (the smoky output, x_1, and nearby laundry, x_2), and that their respective cost functions are, as before, $c_1(x_1)$ and $c_2(x_1, x_2)$. As a result, the equation of the production possibility locus is

$$c_1(x_1) + c_2(x_1, x_2) = R$$

For convenience let us use k as a parameter measuring the strength of the (marginal) externality.[12] Assume first that there are diminishing returns (increasing costs) in the production of the two outputs, and that there are no marginal external effects so that $k=0$. (At the margin industry I's output produces no smoke or smoke is harmless to industry II.) In that case it is easy to show that the production possibility locus must satisfy $dx_2^2/dx_1^2 < 0$, i.e., that the locus must assume the general shape AC_0B in Figure 2 with the concavity property required by the second-order conditions.

Now, suppose that the activity of in-

[12] E.g., k may be interpreted as $\partial^2 c_2/\partial x_1 \partial x_2$, i.e., the additional marginal resources cost of output 2 resulting from a unit increase in output 1.

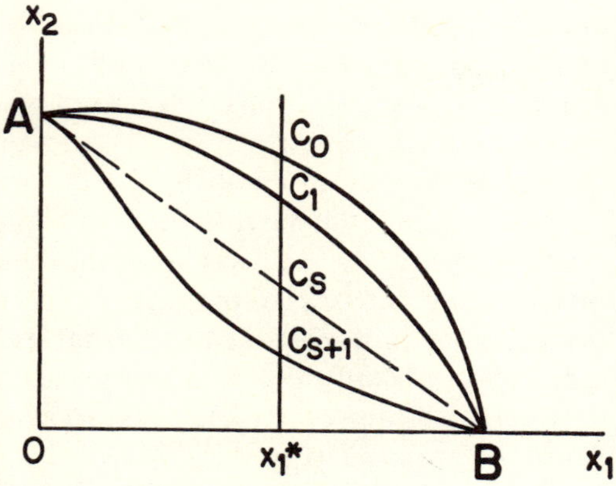

FIGURE 2

dustry I does produce some external damage ($k>0$). What happens to the production possibility locus? First I will argue that neither of its end points, A or B, will normally be affected. At point B, laundry output, x_2, is zero. Hence, no matter how much smoke is produced, there is no laundry output to be damaged. Point B is therefore invariant with the magnitude of k. Similarly, at A, the smoke creating output is zero. Consequently, no matter how smoky the process of producing output II may be (no matter how large the value of k) the total smoke emitted will be (output x_1) $\cdot$ (smoke per unit of output) $=0$, since the first of these factors is zero. Thus the position of point A remains invariant with the magnitude of k.

The effect on intermediate points such as C_0 on the locus is quite different. As k increases it takes increasing quantities of resources to produce a given volume of laundry. Thus, with any fixed value of x_1, say x_1^*, as k increases, the quantity of laundry that can be turned out with a given quantity of resources, R, must decline. Point C_0 will be pushed down to some lower point, C_1. With a still greater value of k it will be lowered still further. As smoke damage increases without limit it will take larger and larger quantities of resources to turn out a given quantity of laundry and eventually we approach a limit point γ on the horizontal axis, at which it is no longer possible to produce clean clothes with any finite quantity of resources.

Now draw in straight line segment AB whose position does not vary with k since neither A nor B does. It is clear that as k increases we will eventually come to some point C_s beyond which all remaining points in the sequence C_{s+1}, C_{s+2}, . . . lie below AB. Beyond this point, obviously, the second-order conditions must be violated, as the production possibility curve approaches the axes, AOB.

Thus we see that the presence of sufficiently strong detrimental externalities will generally produce a violation of the second-order conditions. Only in the presence of insignificant externalities can one have any degree of confidence that the convexity conditions will hold.[13]

It is easy to offer an intuitive reason indicating how the presence of externalities increases the likelihood of a multiplicity of maxima, a reason that suggests that the problem is very real and potentially very serious in practice. Where a particular activity reduces the efficiency of another it becomes plausible that the optimal level of that activity, at least at some particular locations, is zero. If there are one hundred possible locations for the plants of a smoke-producing industry the worst possible solution might be to place some plants in each candidate location. *Any* solution leaving at least some combination of smoke-free areas may be preferable, and may well constitute a local maximum.

To make the point more concretely, suppose we are dealing with an island separated by a ridge of mountains that pre-

[13] The analysis can be extended to the case of n activities and externalities that enter utility as well as production functions. The analysis here confines itself to externalities producing inefficiencies on the production side following a suggestion of Jacob Marschak that the argument is more persuasive if framed in these terms.

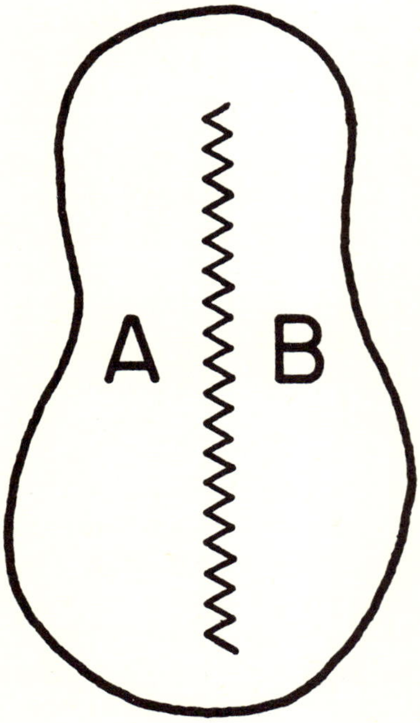

FIGURE 3

vent smoke from going from one side to the other (Figure 3). Let S_a and S_b be the volume of smoke-producing activity located on the two respective sides of the island, and let P_a and P_b be the corresponding number of residents living there. Let $S_a+S_b=S$ and $P_a+P_b=P$. Then, if the social cost of the smoke is great enough, there will obviously be at least two local optima: $(P_a=P,\ P_b=0,\ S_a=0,\ S_b=S)$ and $(P_a=0,\ P_b=P,\ S_a=S,\ S_b=0)$. For either of these arrangements keeps the smoke and the people apart. This does not mean, of course, that the two solutions are equally desirable. If A offers great scenic attractions while B is closer to raw materials we may expect the former of the two local maxima to be preferable. We cannot preclude the possibility of a third (interior) maximum, for once there is some industrial activity on each of the two sides of the island there may be some least cost distribution of people and industrial activity. But we see that we may well expect to encounter *at least* two local maxima. With more separated locations and more sources of externalities the number of combinations of zero-valued variables that constitute local maxima may well grow astronomically.

The presence of a number of local maxima clearly means that an "improvement" may merely represent a move toward some minor peak in the social welfare function and it can, therefore, impose serious opportunity losses on society. All in all, we are left with little reason for confidence in the applicability of the Pigouvian approach, literally interpreted. We do not know how to calculate the required taxes and subsidies and we do not know how to approximate them by trial and error.

VII. An Alternative Approach—Adjustment of Taxes to Achieve Acceptable Externality Levels

There is an alternative approach to the matter that seems perfectly natural. On issues as important as those we are discussing, given the limited information at our disposal, it is perfectly reasonable to act on the basis of a set of minimum standards of acceptability. If, say, we treat the sulphur content of the atmosphere as one of the outputs of the economic system, it is not unreasonable to select some maximal level of this pollutant that is considered satisfactory and to seek to determine a tax on the offending inputs or outputs capable of achieving the chosen standard. This is precisely the approach employed in the formulation of stabilization policy, where it is decided that an employment rate exceeding w percent and a rate of inflation exceeding ν percent per year are simply unacceptable, and fiscal and monetary measures are then designed accordingly.[14]

[14] As this discussion indicates, I join Wellicz in refusing to abandon externalities policy entirely to Little's "administrative decisions" (p. 184) or to Ralph Turvey's "applied economist" (p. 313). For further discus-

The advantages (as well as the limitations) of this approach are clear—unlike the Pigouvian procedure, it promises to be operational because it requires far less information for its implementation. Moreover, it utilizes global measures and avoids direct controls with all of their heavy administrative costs and their distortions of consumer choice and inefficiencies. It does not use the police and the courts as the prime instrument to achieve the desired modification of the outputs of the economy. Its effects are long lasting, not depending on the vigor of an enforcement agency, which all too often proves to be highly transitory. Unlike most other measures that have been proposed in the area it need not add to the mounting financial burdens of the state and local governments. Finally, it can be shown that, unlike any system of direct controls, it promises, at least in principle, to achieve decreases in pollution or other types of damage to the environment at minimum cost to society.[15]

One can expect an acceptability criterion procedure to be operational because policy makers think quite naturally in terms of minimum acceptability standards, and while it is no doubt an exaggeration to say that they can arrive at them easily, there are all sorts of precedents indicating that such standards can be decided upon in practice.

Though we are unlikely to be able to determine in advance precisely a set of tax values that will achieve the desired output standards, the output level achieved by a given tax arrangement is readily observed and, at least in principle, it is possible to learn by trial and error, continuing the direction of change of any tax modifications that turn out to bring outputs closer to their target levels. Since the procedure is a satisficing rather than a maximizing approach the possibility of a multiplicity of maxima is not relevant.

That is to say, one generally expects a considerable number of solutions to satisfy a particular set of acceptability conditions (various resource allocation patterns may be able to achieve a given set of reductions in pollution levels) *whether or not the second-order conditions are satisfied.* If several of these do so, then the essence of the satisficing approach is that one simply utilizes the first of the acceptable solutions that is discovered. One gives up any attempt to achieve any standard of optimality (other than minimization of cost[16] for a given degree of protection of the environment) and rests content with *any* solution that happens to satisfy the standards that have been selected.

sion see Baumol and Wallace Oates. For an earlier proposal that is very similar in spirit, see John H. Dales, ch. 6.

[15] This proposition has been suggested elsewhere (see, for example, Kneese and Bower, chs. 5 and 7; Larry Ruff, p. 79), and will be fairly obvious to anyone familiar with the analysis of the allocative effects of price changes and their efficiency properties. Specifically, suppose it is desired to reduce the pollution content of a river by k percent. Obviously a k percent reduction in the number of gallons emitted by each of the plants discharging wastes into the river will generally not be the desired solution. The theorem in question then asserts the following:

Given the production of any desired vector of final outputs by the plants along the river, a tax per gallon of effluent sufficient to reduce the overall pollution content of the river to the desired level will automatically achieve this decrease at minimum total cost to all plants combined.

The proof of the theorem is a straightforward exercise in constrained maximization (see Baumol and Oates). It works, of course, because the lower the marginal cost of reduction in pollution outflows of a particular plant, the larger the reductions it will pay it to undertake to avoid the corresponding tax payment.

What is surprising about the proposition, if anything, is that, unlike many results in welfare analysis, it does not require the firms along the river, or any other firms, to be perfect competitors, nor does it have to assume that they maximize profits rather than share of market or growth or some other target variable. All it requires is that the firms wish to produce whatever output they select at minimum cost to themselves.

[16] Of course it is conceivable that there may be more than one local *cost* minimum. In that case an effluent charge that yields an acceptable pollution level may not yield the global cost minimum. This may be something that practical policy simply has no way of avoiding.

Thus, the acceptability criterion approach does not dispose of the difficulties involved in finding a true optimum—rather it sweeps those difficulties under the rug. Even with pollution reduced to acceptable levels, there will remain the possibility that the (undiscovered) global optimum offers us a world far better than what we have managed to achieve—if only we knew how to attain it. But if we permit ourselves to be paralyzed by councils of perfection we may have still greater cause for regret.

It may be that with time we can learn to improve the workings of a set of standards of acceptability. If, say, it turns out to be unexpectedly cheap to attain the initial pollution standards, it may be reasonable to tighten the standards on the presumption that marginal costs will not yet have equalled the marginal social benefits. Successive modifications in the criteria based on experience and revaluation may produce results that on the whole are not too bad.

If firms are put on notice that the acceptability standards may well be modified in the future this may lead them to construct what George Stigler describes as more flexible plants,—plants which are designed to keep down the cost of response to changes in standards. Of course, flexibility itself is not costless. However, it may be precisely what is appropriate for a society which is only beginning to learn how to grapple with its environmental problems.

Appendix

Buchanan, Stubblebine and Taxation of Both Parties to an Externality

Buchanan and Stubblebine have raised objections to the Pigouvian solution similar to those offered by Coase (see fn. 2, above). Much of their discussion deals with the case where voluntary negotiation in the presence of externalities will lead automatically to a Pareto optimum. As already admitted, in this case a Pigouvian tax will only cause trouble. However, the authors also appear to offer an argument against the Pigouvian tax for the case in which negotiation is absent.

Their argument, if I understand it correctly, is that after industry I adjusts to a Pigouvian tax on its output, for that industry the marginal yield of an increase in x_1 is zero. However, for industry II, at the point γ the marginal yield of x_1 is $c_{21}<0$. There must, consequently, be potential gains from trade between the two industries. They state:

> So long as $[(\partial c_2/\partial x_1)/(\partial c_2/\partial x_2)]$ remains nonzero, a Pareto-relevant marginal externality remains, despite the fact that the full 'Pigouvian solution' is attained. The apparent paradox here is not difficult to explain. Since, as postulated, [II] is not incurring any cost in securing the change in [I's] behavior, and since there remains, by hypothesis, a marginal diseconomy, further 'trade' can be worked out between the two parties. . . . The important implication to be drawn is that full Pareto equilibrium can never be attained via the imposition of unilaterally imposed taxes and subsidies . . .
> [Section III, pp. 382–83]

No doubt this is true—in a competitive situation two interrelated industries can generally increase their joint profits ("gain from trade") by collusion at the expense of the general public. In the case under discussion, if the output of x_1 is reduced it is true that industry I will lose nothing and industry II will gain c_{21}. However, society as a whole will experience no net gain.

Since the analysis deals exclusively with resource *allocation* we must assume that the labor released by the reduced value of x_1 will be employed elsewhere to produce more of some other output or more leisure. Consequently, the goods or services represented by the t units in taxes must be redistributed to the general public either by remission of another tax, increased provision of government services or some other means.

We may now evaluate the consequences of a unit increase in the output of x_1 on the entire society by summing up the direct effects on each of the three groups immediately

	Industry I	Industry II	Consumers	General Public
Incremental gain or revenue	p		$u_1=c_{11}+t$	$t=c_{21}$
Incremental cost	$(c_{11}+t)=(c_{11}+c_{21})$	c_{21}	p	

concerned: industry I, industry II, consumers, and the consequences of the tax receipts for the general public (which encompasses all consumers and producers, including those already mentioned). These are shown in the table above Adding up the incremental gains and revenues we see that the net social gain is zero, precisely as optimality requires. There is only a redistribution from industry II to the general public.

In a recent letter Buchanan comments:

> As for the nonoptimality of a unilaterally imposed tax, the problem here is that income effects enter to make the benefit-receiving side change behavior so that still further adjustments would be necessary . . . Our point was that this new position would not be one of full equilibrium if income effects enter. The laundries would now find that they secure the benefits of cleaner air without cost to themselves. Presumably this would make them do more laundry. This change in behavior would in turn change the apparent optimal solution. Admittedly, the imposed solution qualifies as Pareto-optimal if further trading is prohibited. And here Pareto-equilibrium does take on a different meaning from Pareto-optimal. Gains-from-trade exist, as you agree and, once these take place, we are not in an optimal solution.

In this paper I deal with the case where trading fails to take place not because it is prohibited, but because (as seems characteristic of our most important externalities problems in reality) large numbers make trading virtually impossible to arrange (where have we seen automobile drivers pay one another to cut down their exhaust?). Moreover, one must distinguish between the role of Buchanan's income effect and that of "further trading." Of course, further trading can destroy the optimality of the results achieved by a Pigouvian tax. For, as just argued, in that case the two affected groups gain by exploiting the community. On the other hand, the "income effect"—the influx of laundries near the factory as clean air becomes cheaper is precisely the reason a tax on the smoke producer alone can lead *everyone* to behave Pareto optimally (see Section III).

REFERENCES

W. J. Baumol, "External Economies and Second-order Optimality Conditions," *Amer. Econ. Rev.,* June 1964, *54,* 358–72.

——— **and W. E. Oates,** "The Use of Standards and Pricing for Protection of the Environment," *Swedish J. Econ.,* Mar. 1971, *73,* 42–54.

J. M. Buchanan, "External Diseconomies, Corrective Taxes and Market Structure," *Amer. Econ. Rev.,* Mar. 1969, *59,* 174–7.

——— **and W. C. Stubblebine,** "Externality," *Economica,* Nov. 1962, *29,* 371–84.

R. H. Coase, "The Problem of Social Cost," *J. Law Econ.,* Oct. 1960, *3,* 1–44.

J. H. Dales, *Pollution, Property, and Prices,* Toronto 1968.

O. A. Davis and A. Whinston, "Externalities, Welfare and the Theory of Games," *J. Polit. Econ.,* June 1962, *70,* 241–62.

——— **and** ———, "On Externalities, Information, and the Government-Assisted Invisible Hand," *Economica,* Aug. 1966, *33,* 303–18.

F. T. Dolbear, Jr. "On the Theory of Optimum Externality," *Amer. Econ. Rev.,* Mar. 1967, *57,* 90–103.

A. V. Kneese and B. T. Bower, *Managing Water Quality: Economics, Technology, Institutions,* Baltimore 1968.

I. M. D. Little, *A Critique of Welfare Economics,* 2d ed., New York 1957.

H. Mohring and J. H. Boyd, "Analyzing 'Externalities': 'Direct Interaction' vs. 'Asset

Utilization' Frameworks," *Economica*, forthcoming.

R. A. Meyer, Jr., "Externalities as Commodities," *Amer. Econ. Rev.*, Sept. 1971, *61*, 736–40.

D. W. Pearce and G. S. Sturmey, "Private and Social Costs and Benefits: A New Terminology," *Econ. J.*, Mar. 1966, *76*, 152–57.

A. C. Pigou, *The Economics of Welfare*, 4th ed., London, 1932.

C. R. Plott, "Externalities and Corrective Taxes," *Economica*, Feb. 1966, *33*, 84–7.

R. D. Portes, "The Search for Efficiency in the Presence of Externalities," forthcoming.

L. E. Ruff, "The Economic Common Sense of Pollution," *Publ. Interest*, spring 1970, *19*, 69–85.

D. A. Starrett, "Fundamental Non-Convexities in the Theory of Externalities," Harvard 1971, unpublished.

G. J. Stigler, "Production and Distribution in the Short Run," *J. Polit. Econ.*, June 1939, *47*, 305–27.

R. Turvey, "On Divergences Between Social Cost and Private Cost," *Economica*, Aug. 1963, *30*, 309–13.

S. Wellicz, "On External Economies and the Government-Assisted Invisible Hand," *Economica*, Nov. 1964, *31*, 345–62.

[12]

chapter 8

Detrimental Externalities and Nonconvexities in the Production Set[1]

The preceding chapter showed that the conventional wisdom concerning the direction in which to modify output in the presence of externalities is likely, at least sometimes, to be misleading. The problem can arise whenever the relevant convexity conditions break down.

In this chapter, however, we will show that detrimental externalities of sufficient strength *will* produce a breakdown in the concavity-convexity conditions (the so-called second-order conditions) usually postulated for a social maximum, so that instead of a unique optimum, society may have the difficult task of choosing among a set, and, sometimes, a substantial set of discrete local maxima. Indeed, in a system otherwise characterized by constant returns everywhere (that is, a linear model), *any* detrimental externalities, however minor, can produce a nonconvexity. This problem is no mere theoretical curiosity. We will see that it produces some very real and difficult issues in the choice of policy.

Moreover, even in theory, prices and taxes cannot help with this matter. Prices and taxes (which, in general, influence the first-order maximum conditions) can affect the decisions of individuals and firms and thereby determine the location of the economy in relation to its production-possibility set. However, prices or taxes cannot change the shape of the possibility set itself to transform it from a nonconvex into a convex region, for that is essentially

[1] Our colleague, David F. Bradford, is a coauthor of this chapter, which draws heavily on W. Baumol and D. Bradford, "Detrimental Externalities and Non-Convexity of the Production Set," *Economica* XXXIX (May, 1972), 160–76.

a technological matter. Moreover, as we will see later in the chapter, in the presence of nonconvexities, these prices may also give the wrong signals —directing the economy away from the social optimum.

It is not our objective here to review in any detail the difficulties caused by nonconvexity. Some of these consequences have long been recognized and are widely known.[2] However, until the recent appearance of papers by Starrett, Portes, Kolm, and Baumol,[3] it was apparently not recognized that externalities themselves are a source of nonconvexity. These more recent writings suggest more than one connection between the two phenomena. However, one particularly straightforward relationship seems to have received little or no attention. With sufficiently strong interactive effects, nonconvexity follows from the simple fact that if *either* of two activities, one of which interferes with the other, is operated at zero level, no hindrance is suffered.[4] The goal of this chapter is to explore this phenomenon and to show how it is that sufficiently severe detrimental externalities and nonconvexity necessarily go together.

In the first three sections we show, with the aid both of illustrative examples and more general analysis, that detrimental externalities of sufficient magnitude must always produce nonconvexity in the production possibility set for two activities: one generating the externality and one affected by it. In the fourth section we show that the problem is reduced, but not generally eliminated, by the possibility of spatial separation of offender and offended. However, achievement of the "right" spatial separation turns out not always

[2] Pigou, for example, commented that ". . . if several arrangements are possible, all of which make the values of the marginal social net products equal, each of these arrangements does, indeed, imply what may be called a *relative maximum* for the [national] dividend; but only one of these maxima is the unequivocal, or absolute, maximum. . . . It is not necessary that all positions of relative maximum should represent larger dividends than all positions which are not maxima. On the contrary, a scheme of distribution approximating to that which yields the absolute maximum, but not itself fulfilling the condition of equal marginal yields, would probably imply a larger dividend than most of the schemes which do fulfill this condition and so constitute relative maxima of a minor character." *The Economics of Welfare*, London: Macmillan and Co., 1938 (4th ed.), p. 140.

[3] See D. A. Starrett, "Fundamental Nonconvexities in the Theory of Externalities," *Journal of Economic Theory*, 4, (April, 1972), 180–99; R. D. Portes, "The Search for Efficiency in the Presence of Externalities," in *Unfashionable Economics: Essays in Honor of Lord Balogh*, ed. Paul Streeten (London: Weidenfeld and Nicolson, 1970), pp. 348–61; S. C. Kolm, "Les Non-Convexites d'Externalité," CEPREMAP Rapport No. 11, mimeograph, 1971; and Baumol, "External Economies and Second-Order Optimality Conditions," *American Economic Review*.

[4] Note that this observation does not hold for externalities that Davis and Whinston (page 244) have termed "separable." Here, if industry 1's output affects the costs of industry 2, the latter's cost function would be of the form $f(x_2) + g(x_1)$. This implies that $g(x_1)$, the ill effects of industry 1 upon industry 2, would remain unaffected even if 2 were to go out of operation altogether! There is obviously no contradiction in such a premise, but it would seem to cast doubt upon the widespread applicability of the separable-externalities concept. See O. A. Davis and Andrew Whinston, "Externalities, Welfare, and the Theory of Games," *Journal of Political Economy* LXX (June, 1962), 241–62.

to be a simple matter. Section 5 contains some speculations about the way in which the number of local peaks in the production-possibility function grows with the number of interacting activities. In Section 6, we discuss the possibility of using Pigouvian taxes to sustain desirable behavior and, in a concluding seventh section, we review briefly the problems for social policy inherent in the sort of nonconvexity we have been analyzing.

An appendix contains a formal demonstration of the workability of Pigouvian taxes in this context. It is shown that, as long as individual production sets are convex, all socially efficient output vectors *can* be sustained as a sum of profit-maximizing output choices under taxes designed to equate marginal social and private costs.

1. A SIMPLE MODEL

Consider a two-output, one-input economy in which each output is produced by a single industry. To avoid compounding problems we shall assume that each industry has a convex technology in terms of its own inputs and outputs.[5] However, the presence of detrimental externalities means that increases in the output of one of the industries raise the other's costs of production, which is to say, the amount of input required to produce any given output. What we wish to show is that, if this detrimental externality is strong enough, then the social production set must be nonconvex.[6]

For consistency with the general analysis in the appendix, let us begin by carrying through this example following the practice of measuring inputs as negative outputs. As in the previous chapter, we consider an economy having three or more outputs that, for concreteness, we take to be leisure, electricity, and laundry. The shaded region of Figure 8–1a shows the production set (the set of attainable net output vectors) for the electricity industry, bounded by the ray *OE*. Figure 8–1b displays the production set for the laundry industry under two alternative assumptions about output in the electricity industry. The detrimental externality generated by electricity means that, for a given input of labor to laundry, less laundering will be

[5] Thus, if r_k is the quantity of input to industry k and y_k is its output, and if (r_k^*,y_k^*) and (r_k^{**},y_k^{**}) are two feasible input-output combinations (holding constant inputs and outputs in other sectors), then $0 < \alpha < 1$ implies that $[\alpha r_k^* + (1-\alpha)r_k^{**}, \alpha y_k^* + (1-\alpha)y_k^{**}]$ is also a feasible input-output combination. Convexity of a production set is sometimes referred to as *generalized nonincreasing returns*, which means that a convex technology cannot exhibit increasing returns to scale and that it obeys the laws of diminishing marginal rates of substitution among factors and among outputs, and diminishing marginal productivity of outputs by factors.

[6] In the notation of footnote 1, the social production set is the set of all vectors $(r_1 + r_2, y_1, y_2)$, such that (r_1, y_1) and (r_2, y_2) are *simultaneously* feasible for their respective industries.

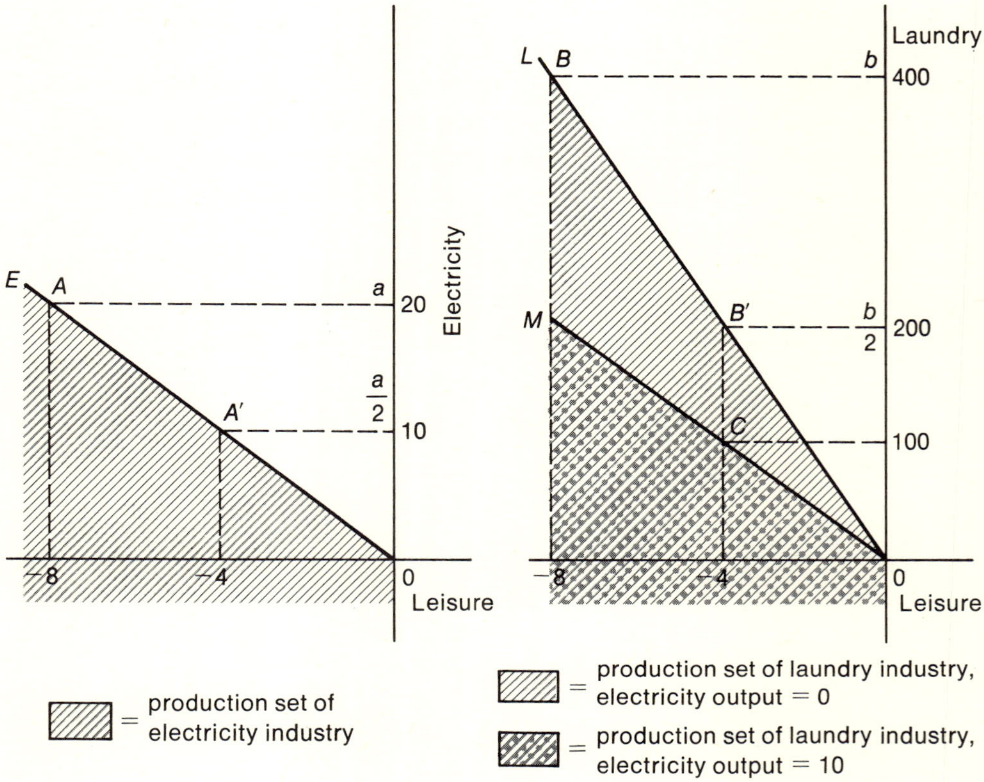

FIG. 8–1a & b

produced when electricity output is positive than when it is zero. Thus, in Figure 8–1b, *OM*, the ray serving as the laundry production frontier when some positive level of electricity is produced must lie below *OL*, the laundry frontier when no electricity is produced. To make things easy to follow, we have assumed constant returns to scale for each of the industries taken alone; hence the straight-line boundaries. We will now show that in this linear model any detrimental externality, however weak, can undermine the convexity conditions.

Consider two social production vectors on frontiers *OE* and *OL*, vector *A* on *OE* (−8 leisure, 20 electricity, 0 laundry) and vector *B* on *OL* (−8 leisure, 0 electricity, 400 laundry). Obviously both of these are technically feasible, as are (by constant returns to scale) the vectors A': (−4, 10, 0) and B': (−4, 0, 200), which are, respectively, half way to the origin from *A* and *B*. However, the vector $V = (-8, 10, 200)$, which is a convex combination of *A* and *B* because $V = A' + B' = 1/2\ A + 1/2\ B$, is *not* feasible technically. If we wish to give up 8 units of leisure altogether and insist on 10 units of electricity, requiring four of these units of leisure, the most we can obtain is 100 units of laundry (point *C*). More generally, if *L* is the amount of leisure devoted to the two outputs and a and b represent the respective outputs of electricity and laundry, if L is devoted exclusively to the one or the other, then the assignment of $1/2\ L$ to each output must necessarily provide less than $b/2$ of laundry output if there is any detrimental externality present. Point B' is never attainable under these conditions and nonconvexity *must* follow. Thus we have

Proposition One. In a linear model, *any* detrimental externality that occurs only when there are nonzero levels of each of two activities must produce a nonconvexity in the social possibility set.

2. AN ALTERNATIVE VERSION OF THE NONCONVEXITY ARGUMENT

Another way of looking at the matter may be helpful to the intuition. Figure 8–2 depicts an ordinary production-possibility frontier RAR' in the absence of externalities. Dropping our earlier assumption of a constant marginal rate of transformation between outputs, we take this curve to bound the convex feasible region $ORAR'$. Let us, for expository convenience, intro-

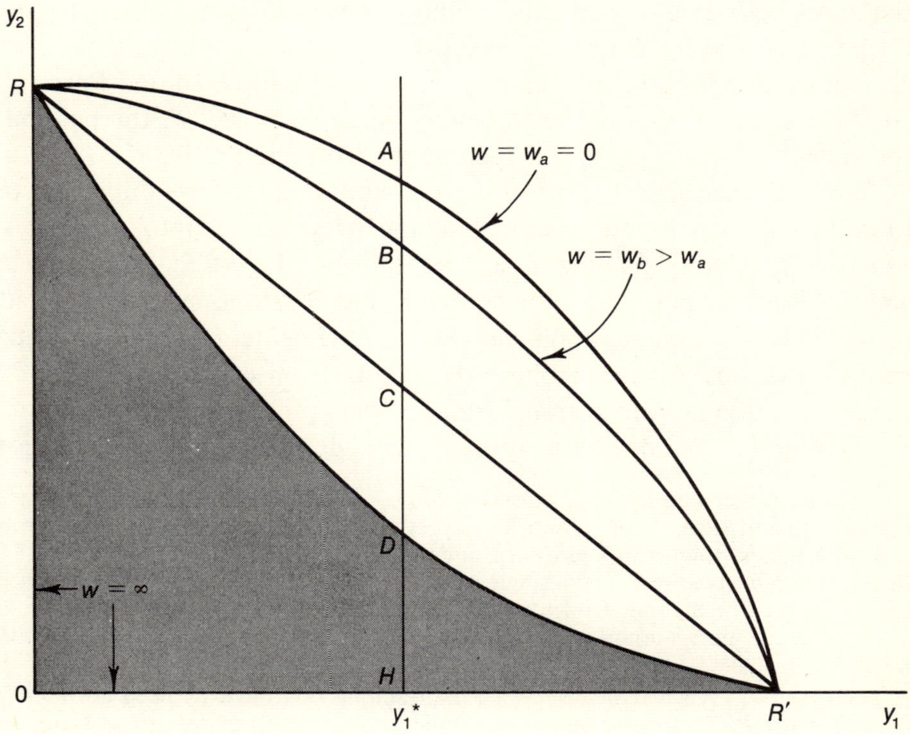

FIG. 8–2

duce a parameter w measuring the strength of the externality. In terms of our example, w can be taken to measure the mean addition to the resources cost of cleaning a given batch of laundry that occurs when an added unit of electricity output causes smoke to increase. By definition, then, along RAR', which corresponds to the absence of external effects, the value of w (call it w_a) is zero.

Consider what happens to the production-possibility locus as the value of w is increased. We will show that the position of the end points R and R' will be totally unaffected, but all other points on the locus will be shifted downward. Point R, where electricity production is zero, will be unaffected by a rise in the value of w; whatever the social cost of smoke, at that point there will be no increase in damage because, by assumption, there is no smoke produced in the absence of any electricity output. Similarly, the location of R', where laundry output is zero, is invariant with w, because at that point no resources are devoted to laundry production, and hence there can be no increase in the resources cost of laundry output. There simply is no laundry to be damaged so that the electricity industry can smoke away without causing any harm to the only other output in our model.

However, consider some intermediate level of electricity output, say y_1^*. Here an increase in w means that with a given amount of electricity and a given quantity of resources, a smaller quantity of clean laundry can be produced than before. Consequently, point A must shift downward to some lower point, B, and the entire possibility locus becomes something like RBR'. With further increases in the value of w, point A will be shifted lower still. If, at some value of w, it is pulled below line segment RCR', the possibility set becomes a nonconvex region, such as shaded region $ORDR'$.

This must certainly happen if the individual industries exhibit constant returns to scale, as in our example of the previous section,[7] so that the production possibility frontier is a line segment like RCR'. For then *any* downward shift in point C, with points R and R' stationary, must yield a nonconvexity. Thus, in the nonlinear case, a detrimental externality will produce a nonconvexity if it is sufficiently strong to offset the influence of the diminishing marginal rate of transformation between the outputs in question.

Even in the nonlinear case, if the external damage is sufficiently serious[8]

[7] Figure 8–2 can be connected directly to the interrelated individual production sets of Figure 8–1a and 8–1b. Points R and R', respectively, represent the social output vectors $(-8, 0, 400)$, that is, point B in Figure 8–1a, and $(-8, 20, 0)$, that is, point A in Figure 8–1a. With constant returns to scale and a single input, the production frontier, in the absence of externalities, must be the line segment RCR'. However, with electricity output at $y_1^* = 10$ in Figure 8–2, the most laundry we can obtain in the presence of the externality is $HD = 100$, not $HC = 200$.

[8] Of course, even if A lies below C, the resulting nonconvexity need not lie in the interior of curve RAR'. For example, the frontier may cut the vertical axis at some point R^* that lies below R, with a perfectly well behaved segment of the frontier connecting R^* and R'. This case certainly seems implausible.

(that is, for sufficiently high values of w), A *must* lie below C. For if the marginal smoke output is so great and so noxious that no quantity of resources can get laundry as clean as it would be in the absence of smoke, then A must fall all the way to the horizontal axis (point H). That is, in the limit, the possibility locus then must consist simply of the axis segments ROR'.

The simplicity of the preceding argument may belie its generality and rigor.[9] The point is that, with any pair of commodities at least one of which interferes with the production of the other, there will be no such interference if one or the other is not produced. On the other hand, if the interference is sufficiently great, the maximal output of the activity suffering the external damage will approach zero for *any* nonzero level of output of the other and a nonconvexity in the feasible set is unavoidable.

Note that this argument holds for such a pair of commodities no matter how many goods the economy produces; so that if there is a nonconvexity in the production set for *any* pair of commodities, the full n-dimensional production set in the n-commodity economy is also necessarily nonconvex.

Thus, we have

Proposition Two. If it is sufficiently strong, a detrimental externality that arises only when the level of each of two activities is nonzero must produce a nonconvexity in the social production set.

3. A FURTHER ILLUSTRATION

Some readers may prefer to deal with a concrete algebraic example explicitly relating a measure of the degree of detrimental externality to the "wrong" curvature of a production-possibility frontier of the type displayed in Figure 8–2. We therefore offer a case in which the separate production sets of the two industries are strictly convex. Let y_e be the output of electricity and y_ℓ the output of laundry services, r_e and r_ℓ be the amounts of labor (negative leisure) used by them, and suppose

$$r_e = y_e^2/2 \tag{1}$$
$$r_\ell = y_\ell^2/2 + w y_e y_\ell.$$

Thus each industry separately is subject to strictly diminishing returns to scale in terms of its own input. The coefficient w now measures the strength of the effect of electricity output on laundry costs; the effect is detrimental if $w > 0$. If a total of r units of labor is available for the two activities, we can

[9] For further discussion of the preceding argument as well as an ingenious examination of a great variety of other connections between externalities and nonconvexity, see Kolm, "Les Non-Convexites d'Externalité," CEPREMAP.

write the implicit equation for the laundry-electricity possibility frontier as

$$r = y_e^2/2 + wy_e y_\ell + y_\ell^2/2, \tag{2}$$
$$y_e \geqq 0, \qquad y_\ell \geqq 0.$$

We can deal with any such differentiable possibility locus in an obvious manner, calculating its second derivative and showing generally that when the externality parameter, w, becomes sufficiently large, that derivative must take positive values. The present illustration, however, permits us to show this result more directly. If $w = 0$ (no externality), (2) describes a quarter circle in a (y_e, y_ℓ) coordinate system. This boundary obviously has the "right" curvature. For small positive w, the boundary continues to be concave to the origin. However, when $w = 1$, (2) becomes the equation of a straight line $[(y_e + y_\ell)^2 = 2r]$, and, for larger values of w, nonconvexity of the production set occurs.

In the preceding example, the boundary between convexity and nonconvexity happens to involve a value of w, that is, $w = 1$, that is independent of the magnitudes of the outputs and that can, perhaps, be considered fairly large. More generally, however, the appearance of the nonconvexity will depend both on the magnitude of the externality parameters and on the values of y_e and y_ℓ. For example, suppose in the preceding illustration, we leave the electricity-cost function unchanged but make the laundry resource requirement function

$$r_\ell = y_\ell + wy_e y_\ell.$$

Then the production-possibility locus is given by

$$r = r_e + r_\ell = y_e^2/2 + wy_e y_\ell + y_\ell.$$

A straightforward but tedious calculation of the second derivative[10] shows that the production set will be convex if and only if

$$2w^2 y_\ell + wy_e < 1.$$

Clearly, for w or y_e or y_ℓ sufficiently large, this requirement will not be satisfied. In this illustrative example, the maximum feasible values of y_ℓ occur in the vicinity of $y_e = 0$. Here we have $y_\ell = r$ the total quantity of resource available, and it is not difficult to imagine values of w and r that will violate the preceding convexity requirement. If r is very large, say on the order of thousands or millions of units, even a very small value of the externality

[10] See Appendix A, which also presents a more general version of the arguments for the three-output production possibility locus using the differential calculus.

parameter, w, will violate the second-order conditions. For example, if r = 10,000, then any $w > 0.01$ will have this effect.

4. SPATIAL SEPARATION AS A PALLIATIVE[11]

A lower bound to the degree of nonconvexity in the social production set arising from detrimental externalities is provided by the possibility of separating the generators and their victims geographically, for instance, by moving the laundries from the vicinity of the electricity producers or vice versa. This is illustrated by the following example:

Assume once more that we have two outputs, this time call them 1 and 2, and that these can be produced at either of two locations, a and b, with respective output levels, y_{1a}, y_{2a}, y_{1b}, and y_{2b}. To begin with, we take all substitution relationships in the absence of externalities to be perfectly linear. Let us assume that, were there no externalities, it would pay to produce both

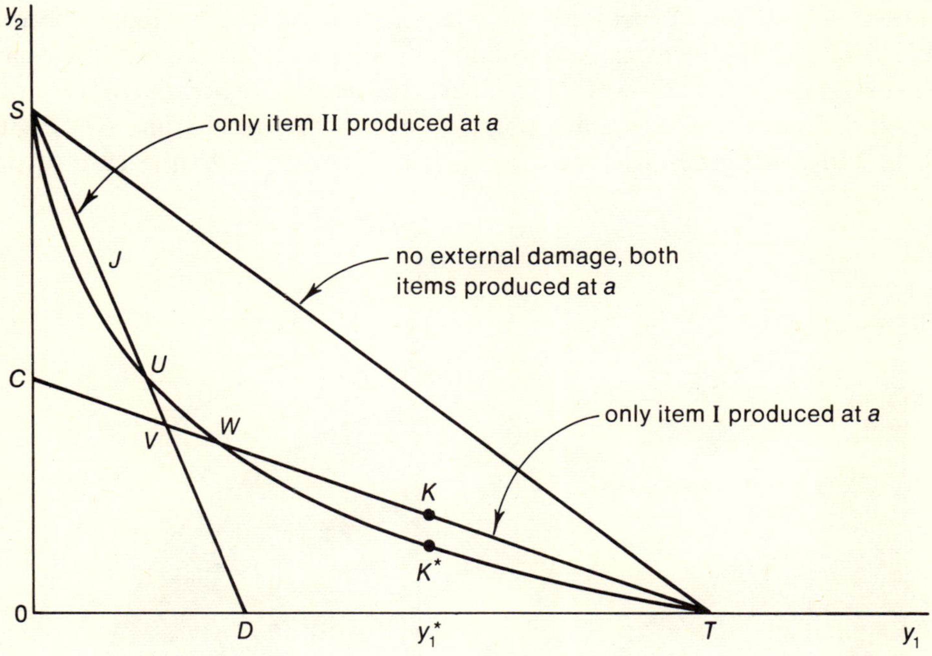

FIG. 8–3

items at the same location, say A. In Figure 8–3, line segment ST represents the production-possibility locus for our two items when external damage is

[11] For a very careful analysis of the location issue, see T. C. Koopmans and M. Beckmann, "Assignment Problems and the Location of Economic Activities," *Econometrica* XXV (January, 1957), 53–76.

zero and both are manufactured at the more economical location, *A*. *SD* represents the more restricted set of output levels[12] that remains possible if y_2 were still produced at *A* but the production of y_1 were moved to *B*. Because *B* is assumed to be a less suitable site, all of *SD* must lie below *ST*, with the exception of endpoint *S*, which corresponds to production of y_2 alone, which, by hypothesis, still occurs at *A*. Similarly, line segment *CT* represents the production possibilities when manufacture of y_2 is moved to *B* and that of y_1 takes place at *A*.

Now suppose that externalities generated by the production of y_1 at *A* grow serious, so that the locus corresponding to manufacture of both items at *A* shifts from the line segment *ST* to the convex locus *SUWT* by the process described in the discussion of Figure 8–2. Then, if society wishes to produce, say, quantity y_1^* of item 1, it can only obtain $y_1^*K^*$ of y_2 if both goods continue to be produced at *A*. However, by separating the two production processes, shifting the manufacture of item 2 to site *B*, the community can increase its output of commodity 2 to y_1^*K.

Obviously then, if we take into account the possibility of spatial separation of output processes, the production-possibility locus becomes *SJUWKT*. In no event can externalities force this locus to retreat closer to the origin than *SVT*. However, even here, the feasible region *OSVT* cannot be convex, because the boundary point *V* must lie below the line *ST*. Figures 8–4a and 8–4b generalize the argument of Figure 8–3 to the case of non-

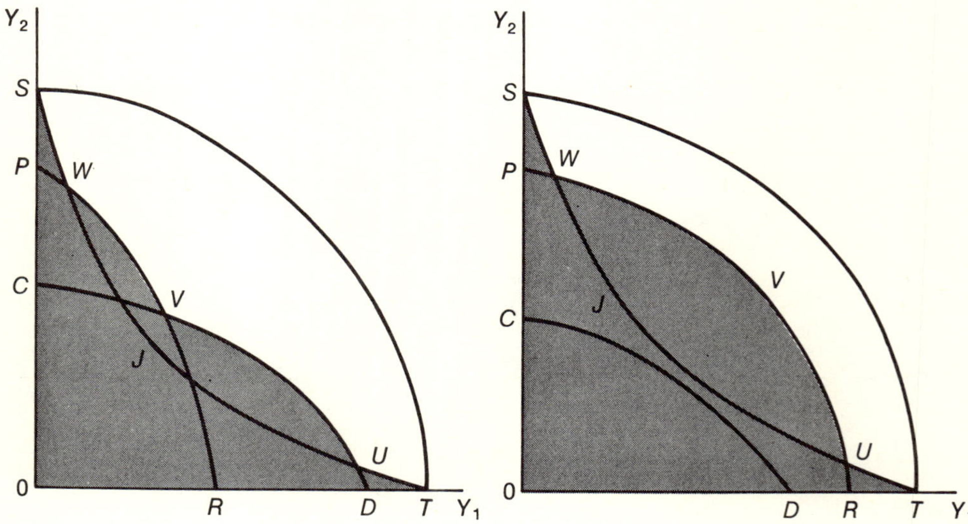

FIG. 8–4a & b

[12] This shrinking of the possibility set takes into account any resources that must be devoted to transportation as a result of the separation of activities.

linear substitution relationships in which it is no longer necessarily true that one location, *A*, is the best place for both outputs. Once again, *ST* is the possibility locus in the absence of externalities. The two possibility curves corresponding to the two ways of separating the two outputs geographically are *PR* and *CD*. These two curves need no longer have even a point in common with *ST* because along *ST* some of one or both items may now be produced at *B* as well as at *A*. Nor, as Figure 8–4b shows, need *PR* and *CD* intersect. They will limit the extent to which externalities can pull the possibility locus toward the origin, but they cannot prevent the appearance of a nonconvexity in the feasible region, as Figures 8–4a and 8–4b indicate. For suppose externalities transform the locus *ST*, along which the activities are not separated, into the curve *SJT*. The true possibility locus will now be *SWVUT*, yielding a feasible region *OSWVUT* (shaded areas) that is nonconvex.

In sum, these figures illustrate

Proposition Three. Sufficiently severe externalities make locational specialization economical. Separation limits the magnitudes of the nonconvexities resulting from externalities but does not prevent them.

The figures also bring out a disconcerting possibility.

Proposition Four. The location pattern that will be optimal socially may vary with the proportions among the various outputs that is desired by the community.

Thus, in Figure 8–4a, with fairly strong externalities the production possibility function is *SWVUT*. For output combinations along segment *WV*, all of y_2 is produced at *A*, all y_1 at *B*. Along segment *VU*, the specialization is reversed. The danger of an incorrect choice by planners in this context appears clear, particularly because in this area it may be very difficult and costly to undo an incorrect decision or one that was appropriate at the time it was made but no longer is.

5. THE TWO-LOCATION CASE: AN ALTERNATIVE GRAPHING

A somewhat different graphic representation of the two-location case from that in the preceding section may help to show how nonconvexities arise when geographic separation is possible, and will tie the discussion back to a topic discussed at the end of the previous chapter (Figure 7–5 of Chapter 7).

Suppose, once more, that there are two locations, *A* and *B*, and that it is proposed to establish at one or both of these two places two activities, at least one of which yields externalities detrimental to the other. We also still suppose that these are the only activities (other than leisure) under consideration, with y_{1a} and y_{1b} representing the quantities of the first item produced at the two locations, and y_{2a} and y_{2b}, the corresponding outputs of the other. To avoid any problems about variation in total outputs resulting from the differing effects of externalities when geographic patterns vary, let us assume that the investment plan calls for a fixed proportion between the *total* outputs of the two commodities, $(y_{1a} + y_{1b})/(y_{2a} + y_{2b})$. This leaves us, essentially with two degrees of freedom: $v_1 = y_{1a}/(y_{1a} + y_{1b})$, and $v_2 = y_{2a}/(y_{2a} + y_{2b})$, the respective proportions of the two outputs produced at location A.

This formulation permits us to utilize a box diagram to describe the effect of the externalities (Figure 8–5a). Along the two axes, we represent the values of v_1 and v_2, where clearly $0 \leq v_1 \leq 1$ and $0 \leq v_2 \leq 1$. Point E in the diagram with coordinates (1, 1) represents the case where both outputs are concentrated at location A and, similarly, the origin is the case where all activity takes place at B. The two other corners, C and D, are the arrangements under which the two activities are completely separated.

Now, if the externality were completely negligible or innocuous, a plausible social welfare function might very well have an interior maximum, as shown by the isoproduct curves in Figure 8–5a at point K. For example, having laundries next to electricity-generating plants will save on transmission costs, and having some of each type of plant at each location will avoid congestion costs and, perhaps, reduce the transportation costs of serving local customers. Depending on the geographic features of the two locations, the optimal scale of activity at the two locations will vary. In Figure 8–5a, the optimal solution point K involves the location of about two-thirds of each activity at A.

Now consider the opposite case, in which the emissions of one activity substantially reduce the efficiency of the other. In that case, when the emission cost becomes sufficiently great, total output will be maximized by separating the two activities completely. There will now be (at least) two local maxima. One of them will be point C, with all of output 2 located at A and all of item 1 production at B. The other local maximum will be D, where the locations are simply reversed. Figure 8–5b illustrates the isoprofit curves in such a case. Here O and E are both local minima, and the arrows indicate directions of increasing welfare. It is clear also that there can be intermediate cases when the social cost of the externality is more moderate, with the result that there exists some interior local maximum M, as well as the two corner maxima, C and D (Figure 8–5c).

The important point is that these sorts of relationships arise whenever one activity interferes with the efficiency of another, so that their separation can increase the efficiency of resource utilization. In any such case, a multiplicity of maxima is in the nature of things. It is plausible that the social wel-

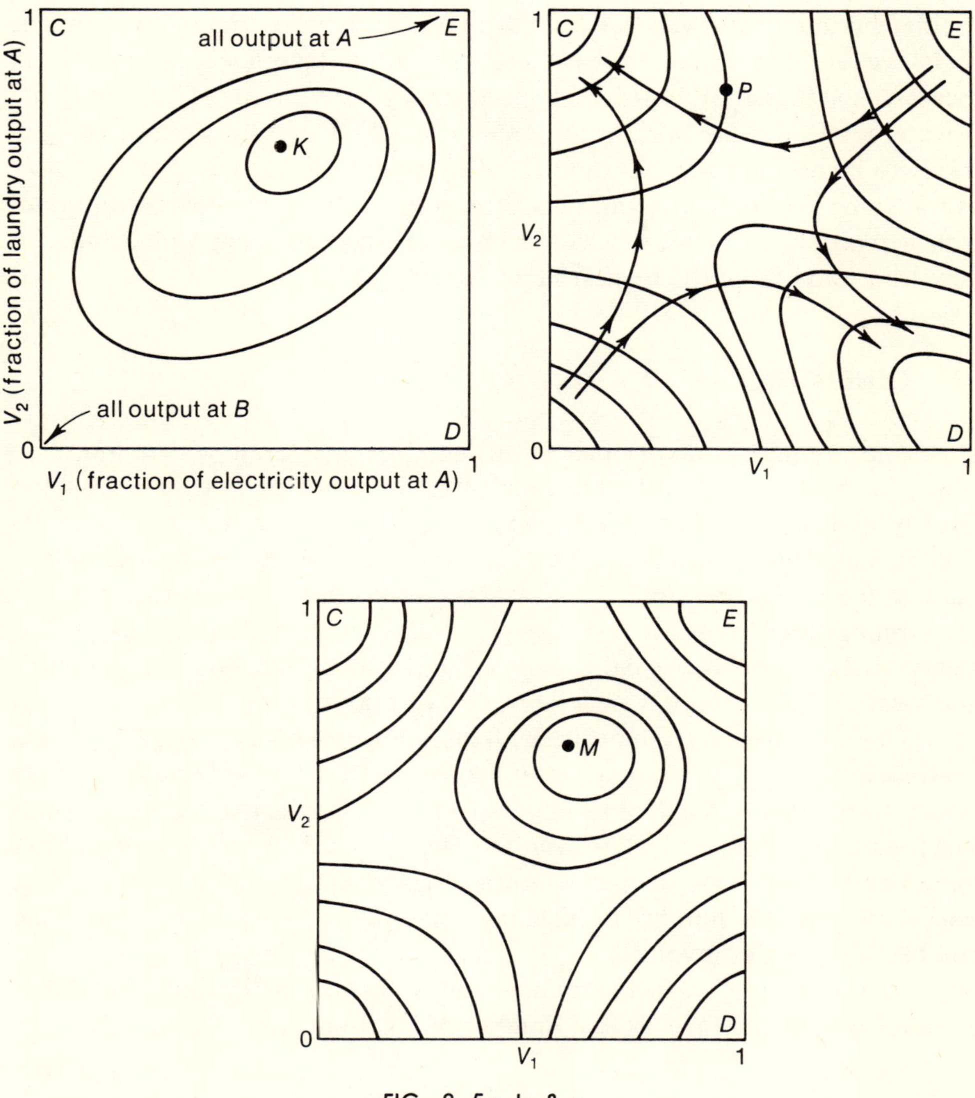

FIG. 8–5a, b, & c

fare function will exhibit at least two local maximal values of (y_{1a}, y_{1b}, y_{2a}, y_{2b}) occurring at (y^*_{1a}, 0, 0, y^*_{2b}) and (0, y^*_{1b}, y^*_{2a}, 0), (that is, at the solution points in which the two activities are carried on at different locations).

To return briefly to the subject matter of the preceding chapter, the diagrams indicate once again that, in the presence of a multiplicity of local maxima resulting from nonconvexity of the possibility set, the market-determined output of an activity that generates detrimental externalities may be *below* its optimal level, contrary to the impression that seems to be so widely held. For suppose (Figure 8–5b) that the social optimum is point *D* (all of y_1 produced at *A*, all of y_2 at *B*). With electricity output at *A* yielding harmful externalities, point *P* is a possible competitive equilibrium point. For with the indifference curve at *P* vertical, a small shift in laundry output will not change social welfare, but a small shift in electricity output from location *A* to *B* will increase social welfare (*MSC* of electricity greater than *MPC*—marginal private cost). Yet the socially optimal proportion of total output of electricity to be produced at *A*, as indicated by point *D*, is greater than it is at *P*, as was to be shown. The point, of course, is the well-known observation that, with a multiplicity of local maxima, a route that takes one uphill may, in fact, lead away from the highest point in the graph.

6. GENERALIZATION TO *n* ACTIVITIES

The arguments of the preceding sections have dealt with a world in which (including leisure) there are only three "activities." However, as was already indicated, generalization of the argument to a world of *n* activities is immediate.[13] In a world of *n* outputs, convexity can be guaranteed only if *each* of the partial possibility loci representing substitution between a pair of commodities is concave. Any single exception, like that in Figure 8–2, means that at least two local maxima become possible. Thus, the analysis holds whether the economy encompasses two outputs or *n*.

There is, however, one aspect of the matter that does require explicit analysis in terms of *n* commodities. One may well ask whether and to what extent the number of local maxima is likely to grow as the number of activities in an economy increases. Here we can offer only a few observations about some polar cases, none of them rigorous. They suggest, however, that in at least some cases the number of local maxima may grow *very* rapidly with the number of activities involved.

First, however, we deal with a case in which a proliferation of activities does not necessarily increase the number of local maxima.

Polar case a: if one activity imposes external costs on *m* other activities, even if the detrimental effects are very great, no more than two local maxima need result;[14] and

[13] Our discussion has also confined itself only to *detrimental* externalities. In principle, the presence of external benefits can also produce a multiplicity of local maxima, but here it is not so clear that the problem is likely to be serious. On this see Baumol, "External Economies and Second-Order Optimality Conditions," pp. 366–67.

[14] This does not preclude the possibility that there will be more than two maxima if the relevant functions violate the appropriate concavity-convexity conditions in the absence of externalities. Even where the maximum would otherwise be unique, externalities that are of intermediate strength may lead to three (or more) local maxima, characteristically two corner maxima produced by the externalities, and one interior maximum, a vestige of the unique maximum that would occur in the absence of externalities. An illustration occurs in Figure 8–5c. Complications such as these and the possibility of irregularities in the relevant hypersurfaces probably limit the profitability of a more rigorous discussion of the subject of this section.

Polar case b: a similar result holds when *n* activities each impose external benefits on one other activity. These results are suggested by Figure 8–6a, in which the smoke from electricity production is taken to increase

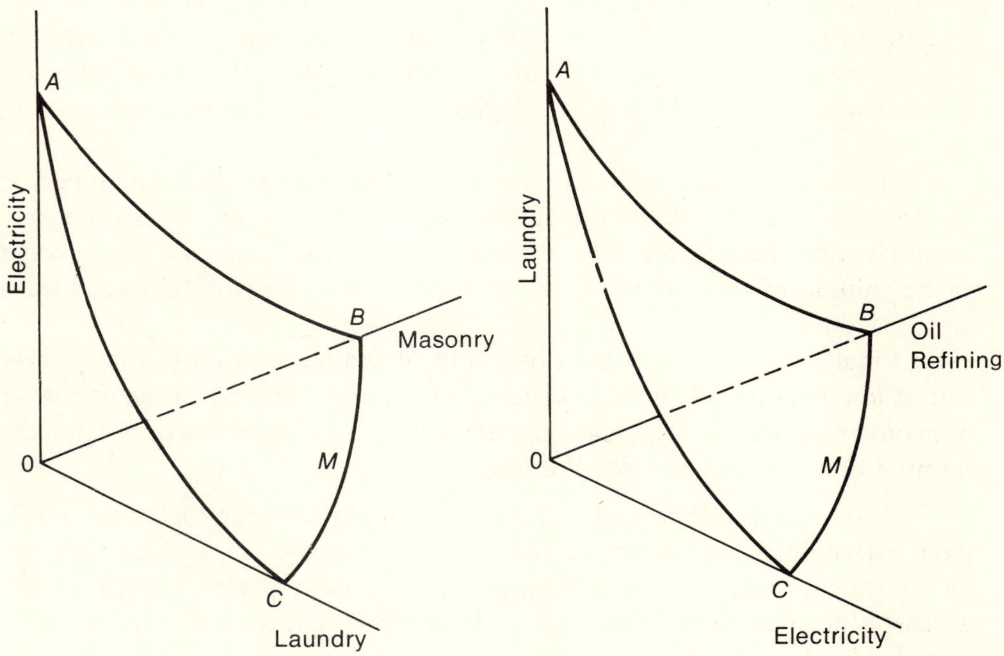

FIG. 8–6a & b

laundry cost and make it more expensive to produce deterioration-resistant masonry. The production locus will then tend toward the form indicated (surface *ABC*). Because laundry and masonry activity impose no adverse external effects upon one another, their production-possibility locus can be assumed to have the normal shape (concave to the origin) illustrated by curve *CB*. However, for the reasons indicated in the discussion of Figure 8–2, if smoke damage is sufficiently serious, the other two partial loci will have shapes like those of *AC* and *AB*. We may then expect two local maxima, one at *A* and perhaps another at a point such as *M*. The interpretation of Figure 8–6b is exactly the same and we merely pause to draw the reader's attention to the remarkable similarity of the diagram for the two-victim, one-polluter case with that for one victim and two polluters.

Next, we come to cases involving more complex patterns of interdependence and show that here the number of local maxima may indeed increase rapidly with the number of activities involved. We have

Polar case c: if each of *n* activities produces and suffers from very strong *mutually* detrimental externalities and spatial separation is not possible, some *n* local optima can be expected.

The reason is that, in the limit, as external damage becomes sufficiently great, it will be optimal (indeed, it will only be possible) to carry on just one of the n activities because the externalities resulting from any one activity effectively prevents the operation of any other. Clearly, there are exactly n possible choices of the activity to be continued. But each such solution, $y_i > 0$, all $y_{i'} = 0$ for $i \neq i'$ is a local maximum in the sense that it yields an output whose value is greater than is possible if we attempt to set some $y_{i'} \neq 0$ when $y_i > 0$. Hence, we do indeed have n local maxima, $y_i > 0$, $y_{i'} = 0$ $i \neq i'$, $i = 1, \ldots, n$.

If matters are not quite so serious, so that only a smaller number, k, of activities need be discontinued, it may be conjectured, somewhat surprisingly, that the number of local maxima actually will increase to the order of magnitude of the number of combinations of n activities chosen k at a time.

Finally, we deal with the possibility of spatial separation that, rather out of line with its role in our earlier discussion as a bound to the degree of nonconvexity, seems to increase the growth in number of maxima with the number of activities involved. We have

Polar case d: if there are n activities, each of which produces and suffers from externalities, and there are just n discrete locations into which they can be separated, then, if the externalities are sufficiently severe, we can expect at least $n!$ local maxima. Note that we have n candidates for the first location and, for each such choice, there remain $n - 1$ candidates for the second location, then $n - 2$ candidates for the third, and so on; this implies that there are altogether $n!$ different ways of achieving the desired isolation.

In practice, in some respects, this probably exaggerates the number of possibilities; in other ways, it understates them. There really is no fixed finite number of discrete locations, and so one will normally have more than n geographic areas in which to locate n activities. If that is the right way of looking at the matter, it is clear that the number of local maxima (that is, the number of ways of isolating each activity) will exceed $n!$ On the other hand, airborne pollution is known to travel over enormous distances. In that sense, we may have no hiding place from one another's emissions. We may then find ourselves back at the one-location case with its smaller number of local maxima but its higher levels of social damage.

7. CONVEXITY IN SOCIAL AND INDIVIDUAL FIRMS' POSSIBILITY SETS

In one respect the externality-induced nonconvexity poses a less-serious problem for social control than one might expect, for, as all of our examples indicate (see, notably, Figure 8–1)

Proposition Five. Nonconvexities in the social production-possibility set arising from detrimental externalities are entirely compatible with convexity in the sets over which individual producers make their choices.

This has an important theoretical consequence,

Proposition Six. Despite the presence of nonconvexities in the social production-possibility set as a result of detrimental externalities, it is possible through the use of prices and taxes alone to induce any individual firm to choose any designated point on its production-possibility frontier. We can thus use these devices to sustain any designated point on the social possibility frontier, despite its "incorrect" curvature.

This may be contrasted, for example, with the case of nonconvexity due to increasing returns to the scale of individual producers' production. There, if every firm's average costs decline continually with scale over some substantial range, a competitive producer confronted by a fixed price will either turn out zero output or some large quantity of output. Output combinations calling for intermediate levels of production of the good in question cannot be attained with the aid of the price mechanism alone.[15] But the nonconvexities with which we are now concerned affect only the *social* possibility set, and so they are perfectly consistent with the possibility that a producer can be induced to turn out any intermediate quantity of output by an appropriate choice of prices.

The general principle may be illustrated with the example of Section 3, involving two producers using their input fully, with input cost functions (1). If a fixed total quantity of the input is used, *any* pair of output choices by the two producers will be on the production-possibility frontier. It need, then, only be demonstrated that any attainable (y_e, y_ℓ) combination will be chosen by them at some specifiable set of prices. Let the prices p_e for electricity (y_e) and p_ℓ for laundry (y_ℓ) be chosen and let labor be given a price of unity. The profit functions of the two firms are then given, in accord with (1), by

$$\pi_e = p_e y_e - y_e^2/2 \tag{3}$$
$$\pi_\ell = p_\ell y_\ell - y_\ell^2/2 - w y_e y_\ell.$$

With the individual production sets being strictly convex in each firm's "own" decision variable, the profit functions are strictly concave in its own variables.

[15] Note, however, that intermediate output levels for the competitive industry are perfectly possible in these circumstances. In an industry producing two outputs, y_1 and y_2, if each firm's possibility set is nonconvex some firms will specialize in the production of y_1 and others will now produce only y_2. See Jerome Rothenberg, "Non-convexity, Aggregation and Pareto Optimality," *Journal of Political Economy* LXVIII (October, 1960), pp. 435–58, and see E. Malinvaud, *Lectures on Microeconomic Theory*, (Amsterdam: North-Holland Publishing Co., 1972) Chapter 7 for a more general discussion of nonconvexities in the large numbers case.

That is, the second derivatives of both profit functions are negative. Specifically,

$$\frac{\partial^2 \pi_e}{\partial y_e^2} = \frac{\partial^2 \pi_\ell}{\partial y_\ell^2} = -1.$$

Hence, the first-order conditions are sufficient, as well as necessary, for profit maximization by the individual firms. These first-order conditions are obtained directly by differentiation of (3) to yield

$$\begin{aligned} y_e &= p_e \\ wy_e + y_\ell &= p_\ell. \end{aligned} \tag{4}$$

Equations (4) are obviously invertible, which means that any desired pair of outputs (y_e, y_ℓ) can be obtained as a solution to (4) for some combination of prices. Thus despite the fact that, as shown in Section 3, for $w > 1$, (that is, for externalities sufficiently strong), this set of functions yields a nonconvex social possibility set, there is a unique pair of prices that induces the firms to produce any efficient output vector (y_e^*, y_ℓ^*) that is desired. This simple counterexample is in fact sufficient to prove our point here; that is, that nonconvexities in the social possibility set resulting from externalities *need not* result in nonconvexities in the private possibility sets and so may not prevent the price system from yielding any predetermined efficient vector of outputs.

Having dealt with the position of the firm in our world with a nonconvex social possibility region, we must next bring consumers into the picture. In Figure 8–7b, let II' be a social-indifference curve, so constructed that along it social welfare is constant and that its slope at any point equals the common slope of all consumers' indifference curves at the corresponding distribution of the two goods.[16] A social welfare maximum involving positive outputs of the two goods must be characterized by tangency of a social-indifference curve with the production-possibility frontier, as at point T in Figure 8–7b. As we have just suggested, so long as the only source of nonconvexity is the presence of detrimental externalities, such a point can be sustained as a tax-adjusted competitive equilibrium, in which producers are maximizing profits and individuals are maximizing their utilities in the small and in the large.

With this observation we are now in a position to offer some comments on the consequences of externality-induced nonconvexities for social welfare.

[16] See P. A. Samuelson, "Social Indifference Curves," *Quarterly Journal of Economics* LXX (February, 1956), 1–22 or W. J. Baumol, *Welfare Economics and the Theory of the State* (2nd ed.), (Cambridge, Mass.: Harvard University Press, 1965); Chapter 3, Section 9, and Appendix.

8. WHO NEEDS CONVEXITY?

It has long been recognized that the absence of convexity creates problems for public policy.[17] However, aside from the fact that earlier writers generally did not see that the externalities themselves tend to produce the nonconvexities that are the source of the problem, they may not have recognized the full extent of the complexity that besets the policy problem here both in theory and in practice.

Where the appropriate concavity-convexity assumptions are satisfied, it will be recalled that everything works out nicely in the competitive equilibrium case:

a. There will be a set of prices that determine an optimal budget line (hyperplane). In the differentiable case with an interior maximum, this budget line will simultaneously be tangent to the production-possibility locus and to a community-indifference curve at the optimal point. More generally, the budget hyperplane will constitute a separating hyperplane for the possibility set and the preference set at that point.

b. At that optimal point and at those prices, all consumers and all producers will be in equilibrium.

c. The value of total output at the optimal prices will be maximized at the optimal point. That is, the budget line described in **a.** will be the highest of the family of parallel budget lines that has any point in common with the production-possibility set. It is this property, the fact that maximization of value of output coincides with maximization of social welfare, that permits us to infer the Pareto optimality of the competitive equilibrium.

With the nonconvexities introduced by externalities, the preceding properties run into complications that increase, at least in principle, the problem of formulating rules capable of leading the economy to an optimal solution.

For simplicity in the following discussion we will assume that the production-possibility curve is strictly convex, (that is, that the possibility set has the simple smooth upper boundary *RR′* illustrated in Figure 8–7a). The reader can consider for himself the additional complexities that arise where this locus takes on a more irregular shape involving both concave and convex ranges.

As we can see in Figure 8–7a, with such a possibility set, no interior point on the possibility locus can be a point of maximum value at any positive output prices. Let the set of parallel lines labelled P_o, P_1, . . . be members of the family of price lines. Then it is clear that the point of tangency, *T*, between such a price line and the possibility locus must be a point of *minimum* output value, given production efficiency, (that is, P_o must be the lowest price

[17] See, for example, the quotation from Pigou at the beginning of this chapter.

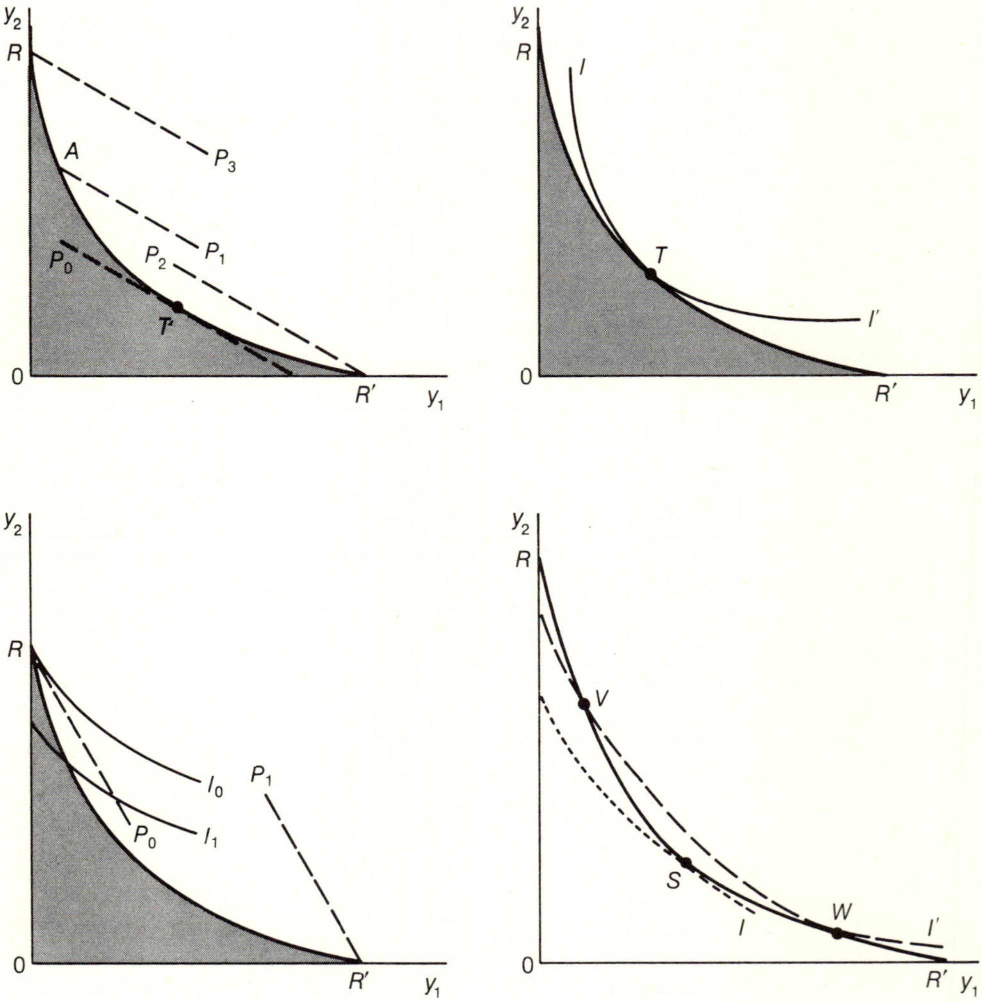

FIG. 8–7a & b, c & d

line along *RR′*). At any other interior point on *RR′*, such as *A*, obviously the output value will not be a maximum either. Only at *R* and at *R′* will we have two local value maxima. Which of these is the global maximum depends on the prices in question.

However, in this case it is *not* true that the social optimum must lie at one of the corner points. Figure 8–7b shows a well behaved interior optimum at *T*, the point of tangency of the possibility locus *RR′* and the social-indifference curve *II′*. All that is required is that the curvature of the indifference curve be greater than that of the possibility locus. Here, then, the social-optimum point obviously *cannot* be a point of maximum output value, because it does not lie on the highest price line passing through the possibility set.

Moreover, even if the social optimum occurs at a corner (Point R in Figure 8–7c), this still need not be the global *value* maximum. Thus, we observe in Figure 8–7c that if we use the prices corresponding to price line P_o tangent to the community indifferent curve I_o at the social optimum, then it is price line P_1R' through point R' that gives the maximum value of output.

We conclude,

Proposition Seven. With nonconvexity of the possibility set, the social optimum may or may not lie at a corner, but if the possibility frontier is convex (to the origin) throughout, there will be a local point of maximum output *value* at every corner of the possibility frontier (and nowhere else). *In neither case need the social optimum and the value maximum coincide*, as they would in the case where the usual convexity assumptions hold.

As a final curiosity, in Figure 8–7d we see a point of tangency, S, which is a point of *minimum* social welfare and, yet, which, after the imposition of Pigouvian taxes,[18] is a possible point of competitive equilibrium! After all, we assume that individual consumer and producer relationships have the convexity properties required by the second-order conditions. But at S, the first-order conditions for consumer and producer equilibrium must be satisfied, as we have just seen. Hence S now becomes a competitive equilibrium point.[19]

Note also that even if the point of tangency is like T in Figure 8–7b, it may only represent a local maximum. Thus, in Figure 8–7d, point W is such a tangency point, but any position on RR' to the left of V is better than W. And this is possible even when the social-indifference curves are entirely well behaved.

9. CONCLUSION: THE POLICY RELEVANCE OF EXTERNALITY-INDUCED NONCONVEXITIES

In sum, we can no longer utilize the familiar proof of the optimality of competitive equilibrium that depends upon convexity in the set of attain-

[18] One must keep in mind that in the competitive equilibrium under discussion here, Pigouvian taxes and subsidies have been imposed in order to induce consumers and producers to make their decisions in accord with the correct marginal rates of substitution and transformation. This point is important because our discussion is intended to show that, even after proper corrective taxes have been imposed, the nonconvexities problems remain.

[19] Whether S will be a point of *stable* equilibrium is not entirely clear. It depends in part whether Pigouvian tax-subsidy levels are adjusted when the economy leaves point A. It is our conjecture that if these tax values are not changed, with a suitable set of adjustment relationships S need not be unstable, but if taxes are varied continuously so that they are always equal to marginal social damage then S will generally be unstable. Thus, with a sufficiently sensitive taxing scheme we should at least be able to prevent the economy from settling at a welfare minimum point, such as S.

able output combinations to show that the actual output point attained as an equilibrium, in this case with appropriate corrective taxes (that is, taxes forcing producers to take externalities into account), must maximize the value of output at efficiency prices that are also market-clearing. Now that other attainable points may be more valuable at current prices, the equilibrium need no longer be Pareto optimal. Prices no longer can be depended upon to give the right signals. They do not tell us whether we are at a welfare maximum or minimum, whether a maximum is local or global, or in which direction the economy should move to secure an increase in welfare.

In short, in a world in which detrimental externalities are sufficiently severe to cause nonconvexities, efficiency prices are robbed of much of their normative usefulness. Although it remains true that an equilibrium that maximizes the value of output over all feasible outputs is Pareto optimal (this is assured by the convexity of preferences), it is no longer true that the availability of outputs that are more valuable (at current equilibrium prices) means that the current output is not Pareto optimal. Thus, in Figure 8–7b, point T is obviously the optimal output, but the most valuable output combination must lie either at R or R'. Notice that this problem arises even where the more valuable outputs can be obtained by infinitesimal (marginal) adjustments. More generally, *even if we know the entire set of feasible output points, equilibrium prices tell us nothing about the Pareto optimality of current output or the direction in which to seek improvement.* Although tax instruments may still be of some help in guiding the economy, as later chapters will suggest, the choice of the equilibrium point at which it is desired to have the economy settle must somehow be made collectively, rather than by automatic market processes.

PART TWO

ECONOMIC DYNAMICS

[13]

MORE ON THE MULTIPLIER EFFECTS OF A BALANCED BUDGET[1]

By William J. Baumol and Maurice H. Peston*

It seems to have become widely accepted among economic theorists that an increase in government expenditures on goods and services matched by an equal rise in taxes, will, subject to qualifications to be indicated presently, tend to result in a rise in national income equal to the tax-expenditure change.[2] In this paper we shall maintain that this argument is likely to be misleading in two respects. First, it suggests that there is something unique about the theory of the balanced budget multiplier which differentiates it sharply from other multiplier theory, in particular, because, as we shall see, the public's marginal propensity to save is alleged to be irrelevant for the process.[3] Second, the argument is misleading in that it appears by a feat of magic to be able to determine an empirical magnitude (the value of the multiplier) without the use of any empirical material. We believe that in this respect, though it involves correct deduction from its peculiar premises, the unit multiplier argument is really likely to be an irrelevant tautology because, as we shall argue, in practice there is very little assurance that unity is even a rough approximation to the multiplier associated with any balanced-budget expenditure program which a government may be expected to undertake.

Indeed, we have no reliable evidence on which to preclude even negative balanced budget multipliers or multipliers considerably in excess of unity. To a large extent this is the result of "leakages" in govern-

* The authors are respectively professor of economics and research assistant in economics at Princeton University.

[1] Most of the substance of this paper we owe to Professor Viner and Mr. Turvey. The former spent much time and effort in convincing one of us of the error of his views on this matter and a considerable part of our analysis can be traced to a rather obscure passage in the cited article by Turvey (pp. 284-86 [see end of this paper for all references]) where he had come to the same conclusions. While they both made highly useful suggestions on an earlier draft of this note they can, of course, not be held responsible for what happened to the baby after we adopted it, any more than can Professor Chandler who was our severest and most helpful critic. We must also express our gratitude for very useful comments to those who attended the faculty-graduate meetings of the economics departments of the University of California at Berkeley and Stanford University where this paper was given.

[2] For an extensive list of references see Samuelson's article, p. 140, footnote 5.

[3] But see Gurley's paper for a unified treatment which fits the balanced budget case directly into the general analysis.

mental expenditures, some of which have already been noted in the literature implicitly or explicitly. But we believe the full extent of their ability to affect the magnitude of the multiplier has not been recognized.

Our argument will be seen to apply equally well, *mutatis mutandis,* to all multiplier analysis, but it seems to us that the misunderstanding has been greatest in the balanced budget case.

We can perhaps best review the argument in question by quoting the following passage from Wallich (pp. 79-80), one of the original expositors:

> Suppose that national income is at a level of 130 billion dollars, and that this leaves without employment resources capable of producing ten billion dollars worth of goods and services. Now the personal income tax is raised to yield an extra ten billion dollars, and this money is employed, say, to build more roads, provide more free education, etc., previously idle resources thus finding employment. Incremental taxes and expenditures are so adjusted that the consumption and saving habits of taxpayers as a group are the same as those of the newly employed who are the recipients of incremental government expenditures. It is true that the additional tax reduces by ten billion dollars the purchasing power of those who are employed to begin with; this purchasing power, however, is not destroyed, but merely transferred to the hands of the newly employed. Since in their joint effect the additional taxes and expenditures are, by assumption, non-progressive, the consumption demand exercised by the newly employed will be the same as that which would have been exercised by the initially employed, had they not had to pay the tax. Aggregate private demand and private output therefore remain unchanged, but meanwhile there is an increase in government output equal to the ten billion dollars produced by the previously unemployed, which is paid for out of taxes and therefore is not dependent upon the level of aggregate demand. Thus national income has been raised to a total of 140 billion dollars.[4]

There are several well-known provisos attached to the argument:

1. The expenditure in question must involve a governmental purchase of goods and services rather than a transfer payment.[5] For a transfer payment merely redistributes income, and adds no governmental effective demand for output to that of the public.

2. The propensity to consume of the recipients of the expenditures

[4] Note that this argument attributes no peculiar powers to government. If it is valid, the same effect could, for example, be produced by a firm which simultaneously increased its saving and its investment expenditure by the same amount (*cf.* Samuelson, p. 151). It might be thought (as we did) that an equal change in imports and exports will also have a unit multiplier effect. But this is not so because, while a governmental balanced budget purchase will (at least initially) reduce the excess supply of goods available to the private sector, imports will increase supplies by just the amount they are decreased by the change in exports.

[5] See *e.g.*, Wallich, p. 82; Samuelson, pp. 142-43.

must, on balance, be the same as those of the payers of the tax.[6] Otherwise, even a transfer payment can affect national income if it takes money out of the hands of nonspenders and gives it to spenders. And governmental balanced-budget expenditure on goods and services will affect national income by changing private demands as well as by increasing the government's demands, and so increase national income by more or less than the amount the government spends.

3. The government's program must not affect the level of private investment. In particular it must not affect businessmen's views on the profitability of investment.[7] If, for example, they are led to fear increased governmental competition or if the taxes affect their incentives adversely, their reduced investment could offset some or even all of the expansionary effects of a governmental balanced-budget expenditure program. Similarly, businessmen's confidence in the program's ability to increase effective demand might further increase its effectiveness.

4. A closed economy is sometimes assumed. The reasons for this are not explained, though they are perhaps regarded as obvious.[8]

All of these qualifications already suggest that in practice a balanced budget might cause national income to go up by considerably more or less than the amount spent by the government. Later considerations will indicate that income might sometimes even be reduced.[9]

Though the effects of taxes have been mentioned in the literature and have already been referred to, there is somewhat more to be said in this connection. The unit multiplier argument takes the collection of T dollars in taxes to be equivalent to that much of a reduction in the public's income. For only then can it be argued simply that if taxpayers and expenditure recipients have the same marginal propensities to consume,

[6] See, *e.g.*, Haavelmo [1] p. 311; Wallich, p. 80; Samuelson, pp. 140, 141 footnote 6. It is also assumed by several of these writers that household saving is the only leakage in the system. Peston (pp. 129-30) has shown, however, (challenging Turvey on this point) that the balanced budget theorem is consistent with the existence of other leakages, and with indirect taxes in particular.

[7] See, *e.g.*, Wallich, p. 38; Samuelson, pp. 140, 141, footnote 6.

[8] See, *e.g.*, Haavelmo [1] p. 314; but see White, p. 357 for an explicit discussion. Another qualification which has received considerable attention in the literature involves the possibility of lags. Thus if there is a time lag between the receipt of the taxes and their disbursement, only the long-run multiplier will approach unity. See the papers by Haberler, Goodwin, Hagen and Haavelmo [2]. Other types of lag can be handled in the same way—for example there may be a lag between the time a businessman receives the money spent by the government on goods out of his inventory (when part of the money just adds to his liquid capital) and the time he hires labor, etc., to replace this inventory at which time that portion of the money first constitutes income.

[9] Most of the points raised in the next five paragraphs are made in considerably greater detail in White's valuable article where they are raised as part of a general discussion of the problems of empirical multiplier computation. But no mention is made of the consequences for the balanced budget multiplier theorem.

the government's tax expenditure program will not affect private consumption demands. But taxes are ordinarily not the poll taxes of pure income redistribution theory. Besides their income effect they usually also have some substitution effects and result in changes in plans other than what might be expected to follow from a simple change in income.

Perhaps most obvious is the case of a general sales tax which, in so far as it is a tax on consumption, may encourage saving at the expense of consumption. Thus a given increase in tax receipts, if obtained in this way, may reduce consumption expenditure more than would the same reduction in disposable income. We may suspect, therefore, that the government's expenditure of the same amount will not raise the public's consumption by as much as its taxes have reduced it. In this case, the multiplier will be less than unity.[10]

For the same reasons we may expect that a tax on savings or a (foreseen) capital levy which is matched by an equal governmental expenditure on goods and services may well have a multiplier effect greater than one as people rush out to increase their consumption in an effort to avoid the taxes. Death duties and capital-gains taxes too may conceivably cause less of a contraction in the public's expenditures than does a simple reduction of disposable income by the same amount. A tax on imports (tariff) may actually even increase consumer demand for domestically produced articles, particularly if the elasticity of demand for imports is very high. Even if the money is collected out of ordinary income taxes, the balanced budget multiplier cannot be presumed to be unity, for people's incentives to earn income may be affected.

Having examined the assumptions on the nature of the tax structure inherent in the unit balanced budget multiplier argument we shall now, in a similar way, question its premises on the nature of governmental expenditures. The passage from Wallich quoted above suggests that the sort of governmental expenditure program to which the unit balanced budget multiplier argument is meant to apply is typified by road building, free education and the like. But such programs usually involve, to at least a small extent, the purchase of items other than domestically currently produced goods and services. While they may involve no transfer payments, they will usually include some purchases on capital account rather than on income account, and they will usually have some import content. For example, road or school-building construction often

[10] In Turvey's model such a situation yields a multiplier of zero because he assumes a "money illusion" which leads people to keep their money expenditures unaffected by sales taxes. In other words, consumption is made a function of disposable income, which is defined as receipts from factor sales plus transfers minus income taxes; and indirect taxes are made a function of consumption.

involves the purchase of land which affects the seller by increasing his liquidity rather than his income. This may induce him to spend more, but presumably not as much as the amount by which the taxpayers have reduced their expenditure.[11] The result will be similar if some of the government's purchases involve imported ingredients or items obtained out of unwanted inventory, old buildings, etc.

The existence of these "leakages" in a governmental tax-expenditure program—the nonredistributional effects on private consumption, the purchase of items on capital account and of goods from abroad—is, of course, well known, though no attempt seems to have been made to take account of them in the literature. Possibly some of the writers had them in mind but considered them unimportant, since presumably none of them considered the unit multiplier figure as more than an approximation to the empirical magnitude in view of the recognized qualifications. The magnitude of the leakages may indeed be rather small, and it is very tempting to conclude that if 10 per cent of the government's balanced budget expenditure is "leaked," the multiplier will be reduced from unity to say about 0.9. However, we argue now that fairly small leakages can even produce a negative balanced budget multiplier.[12]

Suppose, for example, that T dollars end up being collected in taxes all of which are spent in various ways, many of which involve some sort of leakage. Let us say, then, that of this amount only E dollars end up being added to expenditure on domestic goods and services coming out of current production.[13] National income will then end up being increased by the E dollars of the increased income-creating expenditure, but it will be reduced by private expenditures foregone as a result of the $E - T$ dollar reduction in private disposable income. Taking c as the marginal propensity to consume, this reduction in private expenditure, as is well known, is represented by

$$c(E - T) + c^2(E - T) + \cdots + c^N(E - T) + \cdots = \frac{E - T}{1 - c} - (E - T)$$
$$= \frac{E - T}{s} - (E - T)$$

where s is the private sector's marginal propensity to "save," that is

[11] Of course, this does involve a change in private investment but not necessarily a change in the inducement to invest.

[12] For a result which is structurally the same as the following see Higgins, pp. 394-95.

[13] Note that T and E represent final taxes and income-creating expenditures. Actually, for example, T dollars may be collected as a result of a different amount, T^*, of new taxes being levied. For, by affecting the private sector's expenditures, the tax measure may affect the amount of taxes collected with any given tax structure. Similarly the legislated increase in expenditures may differ in magnitude from the increase actually attained, *e.g.*, because of the effect on employment compensation payments. For an analysis in terms of the taxes and expenditures initially undertaken, see Turvey.

to save, import and purchase items not currently produced or replaced.[14] Thus the total change in income, ΔY, will be given by the sum of this expression and the initial E dollar contribution to national income. This gives

$$\Delta Y = E + \frac{E - T}{s} - (E - T) = \frac{E - T}{s} + T.$$

The multiplier will then be

$$\frac{\Delta Y}{T} = \frac{E - T}{sT} + 1$$

which has a unit value in the special case where $E = T$.

Let k be the proportion of the tax not being added to income-creating expenditures so that $(1 - k)\ T = E$. Then our multiplier becomes

$$\frac{\Delta Y}{T} = \frac{(1 - k)T - T}{sT} + 1 = \frac{1 - k - 1}{s} + 1 = 1 - \frac{k}{s}.$$

Thus the multiplier will be positive, zero, or negative as the marginal propensity to save and import of the private sector is greater than, equal to, or less than k, the government's "marginal propensity to leak."

We can see now how misleading is Haavelmo when he argues that ". . . [Kaldor's] statement would seem to convey the idea that taxes equal to public expenditure can create employment only to the extent that they cut down on people's savings. This is not correct. We shall show below that public expenditures covered by taxes have an employment-generating effect which is *independent* of the numerical value of the propensity to consume."[15]

In line with what might be expected intuitively, our analysis indicates that a balanced-budget expenditure has an expansionary effect only if the government's "marginal propensity to leak" is less than the public's, that the expansionary effect will vary directly with the size of the public's marginal propensity to save, import, etc.,[16] and that the unit

[14] It will be noticed that c is not the straightforward marginal propensity to consume of elementary macro-theory. Rather it is the marginal propensity to consume currently domestically produced goods and services which are renewed. The significance of many of the leakages referred to in the text is that sometimes a consumption change involves a change in investment in the form of imports or inventory variation. This, however, is not necessary to ensure a balanced budget multiplier other than unity.

[15] Haavelmo [1] p. 312. The italics are Haavelmo's. See also the approving reference to this in Samuelson, p. 141, who objects to the conclusion only in the unstable case where $s = 0$.

[16] It is perhaps rather paradoxical to conclude that the magnitude of the balanced budget multiplier will be larger the greater is the marginal propensity to "save" of the private sector. The explanation is quite simple. Some of the money the government taxes away will not be returned to the public as income. The damaging effect will then be minimized if the public would have "saved" a large proportion of the income of which it has been deprived.

multiplier analysis is a direct consequence of the assumption that the government's marginal propensity to consume out of current domestic production of goods and services is unity. In this way we have removed the apparent peculiarity from the theoretical structure of the balanced budget multiplier which can now be seen to fit in directly with other multiplier analysis.

Furthermore, the analysis suggests that negative multipliers (or multipliers considerably greater than unity) are by no means out of the question.[17] We do not have adequate empirical information to assert that government's marginal propensities to import are typically smaller than those of the private sectors. Moreover, purchases on capital account may usually constitute a small proportion of public works expenditures but we really know very little about the magnitude of the private sector's marginal propensity to save or purchase on capital account against which this should be balanced. If we follow the usual multiplier analysis in assuming away any effects which occur outside the consumption sector, then business leakages are irrelevant. Of the remaining leakages certainly the average private propensity to save in this country has usually been rather small (about 1/20 to 1/10) and if the corresponding marginal propensity is anywhere in this neighborhood it might not take much in the way of governmental leakages for balanced-budget expenditure programs to exercise a contractionary effect on national income.

If the business sector were included in the discussion, we would add both to the induced expenditures and to the induced leakages. The average propensity to save would then no longer be negligible, but in this situation saving would only be a leakage if it were not undertaken to increase investment, *i.e.*, if it represented hoarding. This suggests that, if the public's marginal propensities to import and buy on capital account were the same as those of the government, the balanced budget multiplier might typically be rather close to zero. For the derivation of the usual proportion of the increased governmental revenue from excise taxation might, by discouraging consumption, tend to offset the small expansionary effect which works through the public's propensity to hoard. Of course, this sort of reasoning is always treacherous, and really insufficient to establish a presumption that the multiplier will in fact be low. Our aim is merely to indicate that on the information now available this possibility (among others) cannot be ruled out, and to suggest that *we really do not know much about its magnitude.*

In fact, there is no reason to believe that the magnitude of the balanced budget multiplier will remain unchanged with changing time and

[17] On this point the exposition in Baumol and Chandler is rather unsatisfactory. See pp. 349-51. But *cf.* p. 371, question 1.

circumstances. The following remark is presented primarily as an illustration of one way in which such variation may come about.

If it is true that the public's marginal propensities to save and import fall in a depression and rise at higher income levels, the expansionary effect of a governmental tax-balanced expenditure will tend to be reduced during periods of low national income and increased in more prosperous times. For, as we have seen, the higher the private sector's marginal propensity to "save," the lower will be the balanced budget multiplier. Thus an increase in balanced-budget expenditures may have untoward effects at all times, aggravating the cycle at both extremes.[18]

This result may perhaps be supported by an observation which involves the asset position of consumers. During a depression it is not unlikely that some people's consumption expenditure will be financed out of borrowing (which frequently takes the form of unavoidable arrears on rent payments, grocery bills, etc.). If it is assumed that these loans do not involve a decrease in consumption on the part of lenders, then, *ceteris paribus,* their repayment—in so far as it involves directly only an asset variation—will constitute a leakage in any expansion program. In other words, consumption out of a given income will be less than normal while consumers restore their net asset positions. It must be noted that often they do not have much choice in this matter. In addition, this consideration seems to lead to the conclusion that the sooner the expansion program gets under way, the larger will be its multiplier effect although other factors may be working in the opposite direction.

Of course, the government is not entirely powerless in these matters. By deliberately altering the composition of its purchases it can manipulate its "marginal propensity to leak." For example, a successful "Buy American" program could raise the balanced budget multiplier.

[18] A. G. Hart has suggested to one of the authors that the effect of investment on the balanced budget multiplier may work in the opposite way over the course of the cycle. The matched taxes and expenditures can reduce the liquid assets of business firms if they are designed to transfer purchasing power from nonconsumers to consumers. Many firms seem to be willing to invest out of borrowing only when it is supplemented by the flow of their own savings. In such a case their marginal propensity to invest may exceed unity. Thus any associated reduction in the earnings of business firms may, through its effect on investment, substantially reduce the magnitude of the balanced budget multiplier in prosperous, or even in moderately depressed times. In deep depression, argues Hart, investment will be at a minimum. Only absolutely unavoidable expenditures of this sort may be undertaken. Since the demand for investment will then be relatively inelastic the balanced budget multiplier will not be much affected by any reduction in disposable corporate income which results from an equal increase in governmental expenditures and taxes.

References

W. J. Baumol and L. V. Chandler, *Economic Processes and Policies* (New York, 1954).

R. M. Goodwin, "Multiplier Effects of a Balanced Budget: The Implication of a Lag for Mr. Haavelmo's Analysis," *Econometrica,* Apr. 1946, XIV, 150-51.

J. G. Gurley, "Fiscal Policies for Full Employment," *Jour. Pol. Econ.*, Dec. 1952, LX, 525-33.

T. Haavelmo [1], "Multiplier Effects of a Balanced Budget," *Econometrica*, Oct. 1945, XIII, 311-18.

——— [2], "Multiplier Effects of a Balanced Budget: Reply," *Econometrica*, Apr. 1946, XIV, 156-58.

G. Haberler, "Multiplier Effects of a Balanced Budget: Some Monetary Implications of Mr. Haavelmo's Paper," *Econometrica*, Apr. 1946, XIV, 148-49.

E. E. Hagen, "Multiplier Effects of a Balanced Budget: Further Analysis," *Econometrica*, Apr. 1946, XIV, 152-55.

B. Higgins, "A Note on Taxation and Inflation," *Can. Jour. Econ. Pol. Sci.* Aug. 1953, XIX, 392-402.

M. H. Peston, "A Note on the Balanced Budget Multiplier," *Am. Econ. Rev.*, Mar. 1954, XLIV, 129-30.

P. A. Samuelson, "The Simple Mathematics of Income Determination," in *Income, Employment, and Public Policy, Essays in Honor of Alvin H. Hansen* (New York, 1948).

R. Turvey, "Some Notes on Multiplier Theory," *Am. Econ. Rev.*, June 1953, XLIII, 275-95.

H. C. Wallich, "Income-Generating Effects of a Balanced Budget," *Quart. Jour. Econ.*, Nov. 1944, LIX, 78-91.

W. H. White, "Measuring the Inflationary Significance of a Government Budget," *Internat. Monetary Fund Staff Papers*, Apr. 1951, I, 355-78.

[14]

COMMUNICATIONS

Acceleration Without Magnification[1]

The literature on the acceleration principle is replete with assertions like this one in R. A. Gordon's excellent text, which appears under the heading "The Magnification of Derived Demand":

> The acceleration principle states that the derived demand for durable goods will vary with the absolute amount of change in the production of the finished goods or services produced by the durable goods. *Because of this relation*, fluctuations in the output of durable goods will be wider than in the finished goods and services produced with their aid. . . . (my italics)[2]

I do not believe that a magnification of fluctuations in investment relative to those in sales is formally deducible from the acceleration principle as usually defined. The two are not even directly related.

More specifically I maintain that while the acceleration principle is *consistent* with magnification, the latter is not *implied* by the former. This distinction can be explained as follows: Since the acceleration principle is a nonempty hypothesis it must make some assertions about the economy whose nonfulfillment would therefore contradict the principle. Such an assertion is *implied* by the principle. On the other hand, there are other assertions which will or will not conflict with the acceleration principle's predictions depending on the values assigned to the parameters in the expressions used to describe the principle. The principle is thus *consistent* with both realization and nonrealization of such phenomena, and its validity can never be challenged by any findings on such matters. In this note I maintain that magnification is a phenomenon of the latter variety, *i.e.*, that acceleration does not imply magnification.

The acceleration principle asserts that the level of investment, I, varies directly with (sometimes it is taken to vary in direct proportion with) the rate of growth of sales ds/dt. Thus the relationship

$$I = k\frac{ds}{dt} \tag{1}$$

[1] I am most grateful to R. A. Gordon, A. D. Knox, R. Turvey, and E. J. Zabel for their very helpful comments. I have drawn particularly heavily on Professor Gordon's suggestions.

[2] R. A. Gordon, *Business Fluctuations* (New York, 1952), p. 107. Similar assertions also appear for example in J. M. Clark's "Business Acceleration and the Law of Demand," *Jour. Pol. Econ.*, XXV, Mar. 1917, reprinted in Am. Econ. Assoc., *Readings in Business Cycle Theory*, (Philadelphia, 1944), p. 235 ff. and G. Haberler, *Prosperity and Depression*, 3d edition enl. (New York, 1946), pp. 85–96. I have even come across cases where the acceleration principle was simply defined as the magnification of derived demand. As a mere terminological innovation this cannot be objected to. But the authors seem to imply that the entire apparatus of the acceleration principle is formally deducible from magnification. I think, from what follows, it will be seen that this is an absurdity.

satisfies the requirements of the principle, and indeed, it is the strongest form in which the principle is ordinarily stated.

Magnification of fluctuations presumably means that any change per unit of time in final sales will be reflected in either a greater absolute or a greater percentage change per unit of time in investment, *i.e.*, that

$$\frac{dI}{dt} > \frac{ds}{dt}, \quad \text{or} \tag{2}$$

$$\frac{dI}{dt}/I > \frac{ds}{dt}/s. \tag{2a}$$

But neither (2) nor (2a) follow from (1) and therefore do not follow from any of the weaker versions of the principle. In fact there is no connection. For the acceleration principle relates the *level* of investment with the rate of growth of sales, and postulates no relationship between the *rate of growth* of investment and the rate of growth of sales. We can derive a relationship involving the rate of growth of investment by differentiating (1) to obtain

$$\frac{dI}{dt} = k\frac{d^2s}{dt^2}$$

which shows that investment will grow rapidly only when sales are accelerating rapidly. The acceleration of sales has at any moment no necessary connection with the rate of growth of sales since the magnitude of the second derivative of a function at any point is quite independent of that of the first derivative.

What then is the source of the idea that the acceleration principle necessarily implies magnification of fluctuations in derived demand? The illustration almost universally given[3] involves a sudden rise in demand from its formerly constant level. If this rise is of magnitude m, net investment will rise from 0 to km by equation (1). If $k>1$ this is clearly an absolute magnification, and the relative (percentage) rise is even greater since the percentage rise in net investment demand will be infinite (or rather, strictly speaking, it will be undefined, because the computation involves division by zero). But the sharp rise in investment demand is a consequence of the premise that sales have *accelerated* and not just risen rapidly—any upward move from a standing position involves acceleration. By itself this only argues that there is a point in the cycle (right after the trough in sales) when investment rises more rapidly than sales. That there should be some such point in an acceleration principle model is hardly surprising in view of the fact that the acceleration principle, at least as stated in (1), does imply that fluctuations in investment precede those in sales by one-quarter cycle. Since they are out of phase it is to be expected that sometimes the one and sometimes the other will rise more rapidly.

[3] See *e.g.*, J. M. Clark, *op. cit.*, pp. 239–40 of the *Readings*, Haberler, *op. cit.*, pp. 89–90. I rely for support of my universality assertion on the very considerable authority of A. D. Knox.

Indeed it is equally easy to find a phase of the cycle where the contrary is true, that is, where under the acceleration principle neither (2) nor (2a) can possibly hold so that magnification is completely ruled out. Since after the trough things begin to pick up, sales must be accelerating. Similarly just before the peak there must be a deceleration. This implies that if, indeed, *natura non facit saltum*, there is some intermediate point, the point of inflection, when sales will be neither accelerating nor decelerating, *i.e.*, when sales will be increasing at a constant arithmetic rate. Here the rate of change in the level of investment will clearly be zero. For example, if $s=1$ billion $t+$some constant, $ds/dt=1$ billion, so that by (1) $I=1$ billion k, and $dI/dt=(dI/dt)/I=0$, —hardly a magnification!

But the magnification allegation was not meant to apply to any one phase in the cycle. On the contrary it is stated about the cycle as a whole and asserts that the acceleration principle *requires* the amplitude of fluctuations in investment demand to be greater than that in final demand. I have found no argument which purports to support this more general contention, and in fact the assertion is false.

Suppose, for example, that sales behave perfectly cyclically and their time path is given by a sine curve

$$s = a \sin bt + w \tag{3}$$

where b determines the length of the cycle, a its amplitude, and w the mean value of sales. Thus if $b=1$ and t is measured in years the length of the cycle will be 2π or about $6\frac{1}{4}$ years. If $b=\frac{1}{2}$ it will take twice as long for bt to equal 2π, *i.e.*, t will have to reach 4π before $bt(=\frac{1}{2}t)$ equals 2π, so that the cycle will be somewhat less than 13 years long, etc. Since the sine function varies between $+1$ and -1 its amplitude is 2, and the amplitude of our function (3) will be $2a$.

To find the amplitude of the cycle in investment we obtain, by differentiating (3) with respect to t,

$$\frac{ds}{dt} = ab \cos bt$$

and substituting this into (1) gives

$$I = kab \cos bt.$$

This will obviously have amplitude $2kab$, since the cosine function also takes values between $+1$ and -1. We see then that the amplitude of the fluctuations in sales is $2a$, while that of the investment cycle is $2kab$. The latter will only exceed the former if $kb>1$.

Now k is "the relation" of the acceleration principle. It is usually assumed to be greater than unity since it represents the ratio of the value of the desired capital stock to the value of its annual output, and the desired capital stock is taken to be normally equivalent to several years output. Note that in any event this is an empirical proposition and is not a consequence of the acceleration principle. It is certainly not out of the question that in some sectors and in some circumstances k will be less than unity. But because it is unfavorable for my present position, let us take k to be somewhat greater than unity, say let $k=1.9$, and suppose that we have a cycle of fourteen years duration. Then $b<\frac{1}{2}$ and $kb<1$ so that the amplitude of fluctuations of investment will be less, absolutely, than those in sales.[4]

Of course in practice cycles tend to be of duration considerably shorter than 14 years so that the b in my model is in fact likely to be greater than unity, in which case the acceleration principle may well be *consistent* with absolute magnification.[5] But this only points up my basic conclusion, that ultimately the relatively wide fluctuations in private investment which are observed in the economy must be explained in terms of the magnitudes of the relevant parameters.

The acceleration principle has no inside track on such an explanation. Any theory which posits not too specific a connection between the time paths of sales and investment can, by an appropriate choice of parameters, be made to predict a greater amplitude in the movements of investment.

WILLIAM J. BAUMOL*

[4] All this has ignored such possibilities as the existence of excess capacity which would slow up net investment on the upswing, and the limits to negative investment which are imposed by rates of deterioration of existing assets. Both of these could, clearly, further decrease the amplitude of the investment cycle, as could an appropriate pattern of expectations, etc.

[5] And since w is positive there need be no conflict between the principle and relative magnification, *i.e.*, the assertion that the ratio of amplitude of investment of its mean value will be greater than that of sales.

* The author is professor of economics at Princeton University and a member of the firm of Alderson & Sessions.

[15]

Interactions Between Successive Polling Results and Voting Intentions

By William J. Baumol

Princeton University

Several years ago[1] Professor Simon arrived at an extremely ingenious solution to the old problem of the election which influences voting behavior and hence falsifies itself. Simon showed that on a rather plausible continuity assumption there will always exist a modified prediction which, rather than reporting current voting intentions, makes allowance for the effects on voting of the publication of the prediction so that this modified prediction will

[1] "Bandwagon and Underdog Effects of Election Predictions" *Public Opinion Quarterly,* Vol. XVIII, (Fall 1954) No. 3. Reprinted in Herbert A. Simon, *Models of Man,* John Wiley, New York, 1957.

be verified by the actual voting results. We will refer to this as a *self-confirming* prediction.

This note undertakes a simple extension of Simon's approach to the case where several successive repollings occur before an election as is usually the case. In such a situation each poll can affect voter intentions which in turn will affect the next poll result which will again affect voter intentions, etc. Thus there will be a sequence of changes in voter intentions and reported voter intentions, and we shall seek to show where this sequence can lead the actual election.

Simon has classified the effects of a prediction into two categories—bandwagon effects where a rise in the predicted vote for candidate *X* leads more voters to switch over to *X,* and underdog effects where the reverse is true. The case of bandwagon effects can be examined with the aid of the following diagram adapted from Figure 3 in Simon's paper.

FIGURE 1

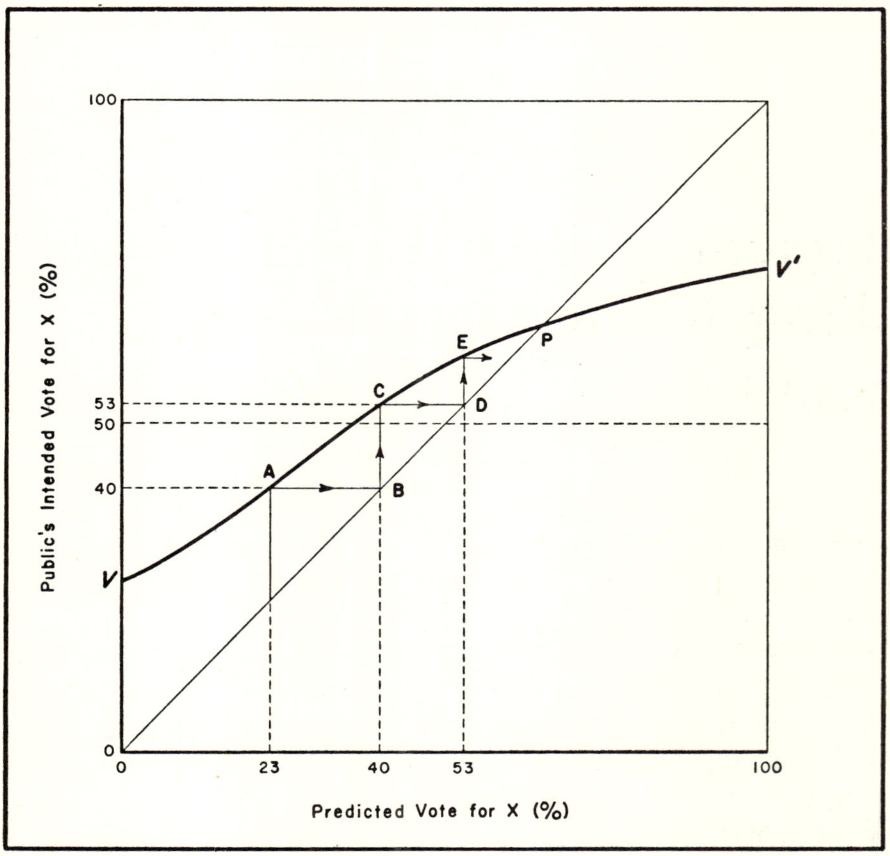

We can call the heavy line VV' a voter reaction curve. It shows how voters' plans will be influenced by the result of a poll. For example, point C on the curve shows that a poll which predicts a 40 per cent vote for candidate X will lead 53 per cent of the voters to cast their ballots for X.[2] This voter reaction curve can be described as a bandwagon case because of its positive slope— the larger the vote for X shown by the polls the greater the public's willingness to vote for him.

Suppose now that the initial poll shows a 23 per cent vote for X. This leads voters to increase their vote for X to 40 per cent (point A). The next poll will then show a 40 per cent vote for X. Diagrammatically this is found by moving horizontally from point A to point B on the 45° line, since any point on such a line shows the same values on both the vertical and the horizontal axis. The public's reaction to this reported vote shift will be shown by point C on the VV' line, i.e., X's vote will grow from 40 to 53 per cent. This will be reflected in the results of the next poll (point D) etc.[3]

Successive polls will move the vote closer and closer to P, the point of intersection of the 45° line with the voter reaction curve. This is also the point at which prediction (the height of the 45° line) and voter intention (the height of the reaction curve) coincide, i.e. it is the one self-verifying poll prediction. Thus in such a situation the predictions of a succession of polls will increase in accuracy simply because the movements in poll results and the induced movements in voter intentions will converge.

A second interesting result is that the outcome of an election can conceivably hinge not only on the results of the polls but also on the number of polls taken. In the case depicted in Figure 1 the results of one poll will raise candidate X's vote to 40 per cent but the second poll will switch enough voters to put him over the top. Further polls will then only increase X's lead.

Mathematics tell us that the convergence property need not hold universally, though a plausible argument suggests that it may generally hold in practice. It is geometrically possible for successive polls to move further and further away from the self-confirming prediction as Figure 2 readily shows. For example, the prediction that X will obtain 56 per cent of the vote will increase X's vote to 60 per cent, and the next poll, which shows this result, will raise X's vote to 70 per cent, and finally on the next round X will end up with 100 per cent of the vote! This extremely lopsided result is not an acci-

[2] This may seem like a queer example of a bandwagon effect because a poll showing a losing vote for X raises his vote from 40 to 53 per cent, but reflection may convince the reader that this is not so. The public's original votes are based partly on its original estimates of the candidate's chances. If originally many people had expected him to obtain only a 20 per cent vote, the 40 per cent vote forecast by the poll can convince marginal voters who rather like X that things are not as hopeless as they seemed, and they may consequently decide to switch to X. This leads me to a minor quibble with Simon who suggests that a 50-50 poll result will normally leave initial voting plans unaffected.

[3] The mathematically trained leader will recognize that we are dealing with a first order non-linear difference equation. For a more general discussion see my "Analyse Graphique de Modèles de Cycles Non Linéaires de Premier Ordre" in Centre National de la Recherche Scientifique, *Les Modèles Dynamiques en Économétrie,* Paris 1956. The work was originally done under the sponsorship of Professor Paul F. Lazarsfeld's panel project.

dent of the drawing nor is it just simply an illustration of how far things can go. By trying a few diagrams, the reader can convince himself that if successive polls do not move voter intentions and poll predictions toward a self-confirming prediction point like R[4] then candidate X must eventually, after a sufficient number of polls, end up with either 100 per cent or 0 per cent of the vote! This will occur only if all voters are prepared to be swayed in either direction by the bandwagon effect. Since 100 per cent of the votes for any one candidate are not even produced by the Kremlin, we may safely assume that the case shown in Figure 2 will not occur. This may mean that there is always some stable self-confirming prediction like point P in Figure 1 toward which sucessive poll results will tend to move.

FIGURE 2

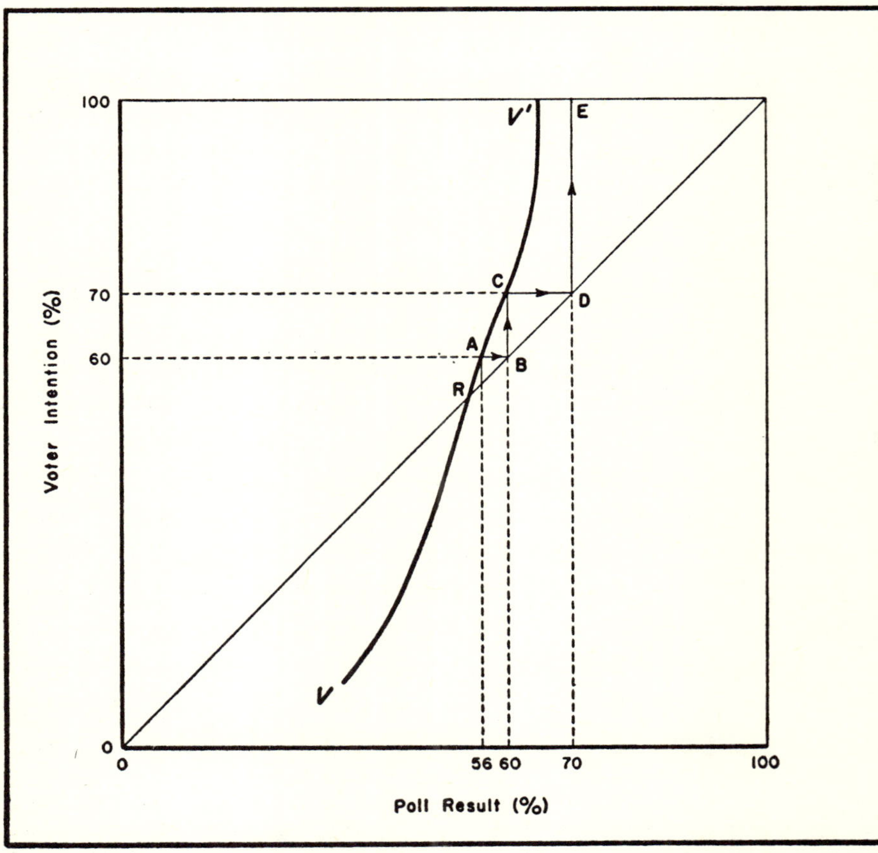

The reader may note that the difference between a stable point such as P in Figure 1 and an unstable one like R in Figure 2 is that in the former case VV' cuts the 45° line from above (going from left to right), i.e. that at the point of intersection the slope of the voter reaction curve is less than

[4] There may, of course, be several such points if VV' twists around the 45° line. Cf. Simon, *op. cit.*

that of a 45° line which, of course, has a unit slope. It can be proved that this again is a perfectly general result and a few drawings should convince the reader. The interpretation is fairly straightforward. The slope of *VV'* is the increase in the percentage vote for *X* per one per cent increase in the vote forecast for him by the polls. When this slope is less than unity it means that a one per cent increase in predicted vote will result in a less than one per cent *further* increase in the candidates vote through the bandwagon effect. In a stable situation this is the upper limit to the strength of a bandwagon effect. By maintaining that cases like that depicted in Figure 2 will not occur in practice, we have asserted that while the bandwagon effect can sometimes go above this upper limit it cannot do so indefinitely—successive pollings must eventually weaken the bankwagon effect to a point where this upper limit is observed.

Let us turn to the case of underdog effects—the case where the public is drawn to shift votes to a reportedly losing candidate. In such a case the voter reaction curve will have a negative slope (Figure 3). Then a *rise* in the

FIGURE 3

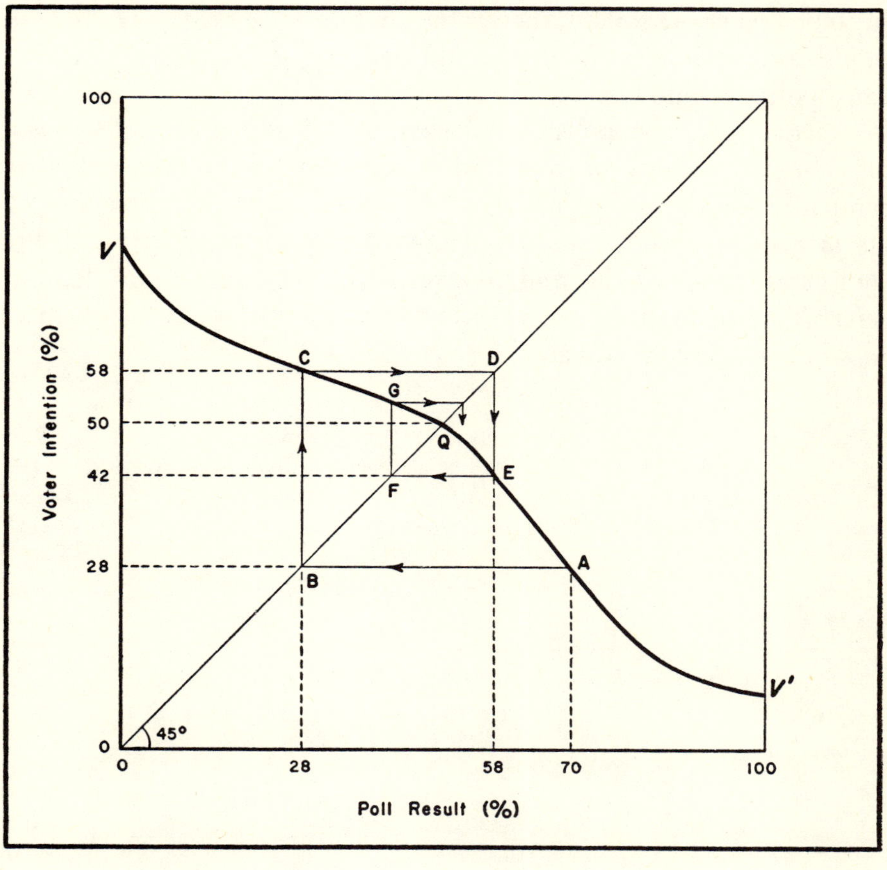

percentage vote for *X* shown by the polls will lead to a *decrease* in the per cent of voters who are his adherents.

Now successive polls will trace out the strange looking time path *ABCDEFG* etc. Thus if the first poll predicts a 70 per cent vote for candidate *X,* his adherents will fall to 28 per cent (point *A*). The next poll will now give him 28 per cent and as a result *X*'s vote will rise to 58 per cent (Point *C*) etc. The odd shape of the time path has the following interpretation: because of the underdog effect a poll which reports a high vote for some candidate will lead voters away from him which, when it is reported by the next poll, will favor the candidate and hence raise his vote again and so on. The underdog effect must then lead to oscillations—successive rises and falls in the proportion of votes predicted for *X* by successive polls. In the case shown in the diagram, because the slope of *VV'* is less (in absolute value) than that of the 45° line, the results of the poll will move closer and closer to the self-verifying prediction point, *Q*. However the reader can check that a more steeply falling *VV'* curve will lead to an unstable case.

The underdog case can involve results particularly sensitive to the number of polls taken. In the extreme case if the self-confirming prediction, *Q,* is a tie (a 50 per cent vote for *X*), then if the election were held after the first poll *X* would lose, if it were held after the second poll *X* would win, if after the third poll *X* would lose, etc.

In practice successive polls do not seem to exhibit the oscillatory behavior characteristic of a body of voters most of whom are motivated primarily by sympathy for the underdog. Thus it would appear that if either of the effects is present to any marked degree the bandwagon effect ordinarily predominates. Since in the underdog case the outcome of an election can conceivably be so highly responsive to the *number* of polls taken, this may perhaps be considered fortunate.

[16]

SPECULATION, PROFITABILITY, AND STABILITY

William J. Baumol *

PROPONENTS of flexible exchange rates have maintained that a completely free exchange market is very likely to be stable. In particular they have argued that any profitable speculative activity in this and other markets must necessarily be stabilizing. By this they appear to mean that it must, *ceteris paribus*, reduce the frequency and amplitude of price fluctuations. In this note, I dispute this allegedly universal proposition with the aid of a counterexample. Certainly this counterexample is not meant to suggest that profitable (or even unprofitable) speculation will never exert a stabilizing influence. How often and to what extent speculation is stabilizing remains a matter for empirical inquiry.

Perhaps a more important aim of this note is to indicate the sort of mathematical apparatus which is necessary for an analysis of the effects of speculation on stability. The techniques are precisely those which have been used in other stability analyses, and it is surprising that they do not seem to have been employed in this area. Because most of the mathematical analysis of speculation and stability has been conducted in static terms, it has failed to get to the heart of the stability question which, of course, refers to properties of the price *movements*.

Nature of the Arguments

It is easy to recapitulate the basic argument which maintains that profitable speculation is necessarily stabilizing. In Professor Friedman's relatively guarded words, "People who argue that speculation is generally destabilizing seldom realize that this is largely equivalent to saying that speculators lose money, since speculation can be destabilizing in general only if speculators on the average sell when the currency is low in price and buy when it is high." [1]

Certainly this position conflicts with what may, depending on the point of view, be described as our commonsense or our preconceived views. There is however a counter argument.[2] This maintains that speculative profits characteristically are earned by selling *after* the price peak has been passed and by buying after the beginning of the upturn. This is because speculators know they cannot foretell the future with accuracy, and so can only hope to identify price peaks and troughs in retrospect after the price trend has been well established. By doing so they give up any chance to skim off the cream but hope in return significantly to reduce their risks. The occurrence of such speculative patterns is not implausible. Certainly, for example, this aim is inherent in the idea of buying and selling in accord with the Dow Jones indicators and in some of the other investment formulas, though there may be some question about the extent to which these schemes succeed in realizing their goal.

The main point is that speculation of this variety involves purchases during the upswing and sales during the downswing. It will have some stabilizing influence in that, if profitable, it involves higher priced sales than purchases thereby forcing the higher prices down and vice versa. But it must also have a destabilizing influence in accelerating both upward and downward movements because speculative sales occur when prices are falling, and purchases are made when prices have begun to rise. For

* I am very much indebted to Professors Chandler, Dorfman, Friedman, and Viner for their comments.

[1] Milton Friedman, *Essays in Positive Economics* (Chicago, 1953), 175. Friedman adds in a footnote: "A warning is perhaps in order that this is a simplified generalization on a complex problem. A full analysis encounters difficulties in separating 'speculative' from other transactions, defining precisely and satisfactorily 'destabilizing speculation' and taking account of the effects of the mere existence of a system of flexible rates as contrasted with the effects of actual speculative transactions under such a system." For another such statement see Friedrich A. Lutz, "The Case for Flexible Exchange Rates," *Banca Nazionale Del Lavoro*, No. 31 (December 1954), 30–32. The argument goes back much further. For further references see James A. Ross, Jr., *Speculation, Stock Prices and Industrial Fluctuations* (New York, 1938), 127, footnote 1 and 134, footnote 19.

[2] See e.g. Ross, op. cit. 131, 134–38.

[263]

this reason the speculative activity may be profitable, yet be on balance destabilizing.[3]

Several questions must be answered before this argument can be accepted.

1. What precisely is the difference between a speculator and a nonspeculator? Are not those to whom the profit-makers sell and from whom they purchase also in some sense speculators? If so, the preceding argument breaks down, because it is not really true that speculation is on balance profitable in this situation. Rather, it just amounts to some more skillful speculators profiting at the expense of others.

2. The sort of speculative pattern just considered has both a stabilizing influence, in that its sales occur at a higher price than its purchases, and a destabilizing influence, in that it accelerates price movements. Can the destabilizing influence ever predominate?

3. Can the acceleration of downward and upward movements, even if it is the dominating influence, ever increase the amplitude and frequency of fluctuations, or will it simply result in lengthened price plateaus at the old peak and trough levels with a reduction in the time taken in moving from peak to trough?

I shall dodge the first question in the next few sections and only deal with it indirectly in the next to the last section. Certainly there are no absolute definitions available to the positivist to settle the matter once and for all. It may be pointed out that a similar problem exists for the argument which maintains that profitable speculation must be stabilizing. Indeed in a market which trades a fixed stock of items (e.g. securities) among a fixed group of traders it is a tautology that net money profit (meaning net cash withdrawal) of the group is zero. Whatever one group of traders gains another must lose, and it is necessary somehow to define the second group to consist of non-speculators. In most of the present paper this problem will be evaded by assuming that there exists a group of non-speculators on some unspecified definition and that its activities somehow result in cyclical behavior in the price of some commodity. The effect of the entrance of speculators into the market will then be examined.

It may be remarked, however, that for practical problems the answer to the first question may not be so very difficult. For the relevant dichotomy may not be between pure speculators and pure non-speculators, but rather it may involve conscious *vs.* unconscious speculators or professional *vs.* amateur speculators, or even pure speculators *vs.* those whose market behavior is not primarily influenced by speculative considerations. That professional or pure or conscious speculators can profit at the expense of the hybrid residual groups, and do so in a destabilizing manner is, I think, conclusively shown by the models which follow.

The purpose of the models is to the provide a construction which permits measurement of the amplitude and frequency of the price movements and thereby an unambiguous answer to questions 2 and 3.

Market in the Absence of Speculators

It is simply assumed here that the pattern of prices of the commodity in question is endogenously determined and that the time path of prices is perfectly cyclical, i.e., sinusoidal and of constant amplitude. This time path can be represented by a second-order difference equation,[4]

$$P_t = 2\,aP_{t-1} - P_{t-2} + k. \quad |a| < 1 \qquad (1)$$

It is also convenient to assume $a > 0$, for reasons which will be seen presently.

The solution of this equation is

$$P_t = c\cos qt + s\sin qt + R = p\cos(qt + r) + R \qquad (2)$$

where R is a constant which represents the mean level of prices; c, s, p and r are constants determined by initial conditions; and q is an angle given by[5] $\cos q = a < 1$.

As already mentioned, I assume that the behavior of non-speculative traders is of such

[3] The main point of this counterexample then is that while the Friedman argument takes account of the levels of the variables it neglects their time derivatives, and the time path is dependent on both. Note the analogy with Samuelson's criticism of the Hicks stability analysis, *Foundations of Economic Analysis* (Cambridge, 1947), 269–76.

[4] It should be noted that no other second-order linear difference equation with constant coefficients and no lower-order equation of this variety will produce the sort of time path which is described above.

[5] There are really two such angles, since $\cos q = \cos - q$ but it is easy to see that this choice makes no difference to the time path indicated by the solution.

a variety that this time path will result.[6] However, it is possible to give some sort of meaningful if unconvincing economic interpretation of equation (1). Aside from the inherent desirability of such an interpretation it will be needed to decide how to bring the speculative elements into the model.

Suppose the non-speculative excess demand function (quantity demanded minus quantity supplied as a function of price) is

$$E_t = K - UP_t + V(P_t - P_{t-1}) + W(P_{t-1} - P_{t-2}) \qquad (3)$$

where W is a positive constant; and V, U, and K are constants given by

$V = W(1 - 2a)$, which is positive for $a < \frac{1}{2}$,

$U = 2W(1 - a)$, and

$K = Wk$.

Direct substitution of these values into (3) together with the equilibrium condition $E_t = 0$ at once yields[7] our basic equation (1).

Equation (3) states that excess demand is dependent on current price and recent price trends. The dependence on current price is given by $A - UP_t$, where A is some positive constant. This says that an increase in price will result in a linear decrease in excess demand. The dependence on recent price trends is expressed in $K - A + V(P_t - P_{t-1}) + W(P_{t-1} - P_{t-2})$ and states that rising recent price trends make for high excess demands.[8]

[6] This involves some difficulties. It is well known that if the coefficient of P_{t-2} in (1) is ever so slightly different from -1 the price cycles will either explode or their amplitude will asymptotically approach zero. In the mathematician's language the values of the parameters of a linear difference equation which can produce cyclical behavior of constant amplitude is a set of measure zero. As Friedman points out, it is an invalid use of inverse probability to conclude from this alone that such a constant amplitude equation situation is unlikely to be encountered in practice. (See Friedman, op. cit., 292–93.) But this excuse is rather lame here. If I were looking for a convincing construction rather than a counterexample I would be driven to employ non-linear equations and models involving relaxation oscillations. See the final section below, for the reason I have not employed this type of model.

[7] Further, it is easy to show that (3) is the only excess demand equation of this form which yields (1).

[8] There is a fundamental difficulty here. Our non-speculators are influenced by price trends. Does this make speculators of the non-speculators? I know no really satisfactory answer. It can only be remarked that this influence need not be (conscious) and that, in any event, the above is only one possible interpretation of (1). We shall return to this problem below.

Speculative Behavior

It is now necessary to formulate a mathematical description of the speculative behavior postulated in the first section. The idea is that speculators will do the bulk of their buying right *after* the upturn and their selling right after the downturn. The trough and the subsequent upturn are characterized by a downward movement followed by an upward movement. If the trough is at t, $(P_{t+1} - P_t)$ and $-(P_t - P_{t-1})$ will then both be positive. Similarly if P_{t+1} is the price of the first period after a downturn, both of these expressions will be negative. At all other times these expressions will be of opposite sign. This suggests that a speculative excess demand function given by

$$\begin{aligned} E_{st+1} &= C[(P_{t+1} - P_t) - (P_t - P_{t-1})] \\ &= C(P_{t+1} - 2P_t + P_{t-1}). \end{aligned} \qquad (4)$$

where C is a positive constant, will have the desired properties. I shall prove that this is so. First note that (3) and (4) together with the equilibrium condition $E_t + E_{st} = 0$ give

$$\begin{aligned} 0 &= K - WP_t + 2WaP_{t-1} - WP_{t-2} \\ &\quad + C(P_t - 2P_{t-1} + P_{t-2}) \\ &= K - (W - C)P_t + (2Wa - 2C)P_{t-1} \\ &\quad - (W - C)P_{t-2}. \end{aligned}$$

From this follows

$$P_t = \frac{K}{W - C} + 2\frac{Wa - C}{W - C}P_{t-1} - P_{t-2}. \qquad (5)$$

If $Wa > C$ (so that certainly $W > C$), i.e., if speculative demand is not too large relative to non-speculative demand, both fractions in (5) will be positive and the second fraction will be less than unity. Thus the equation will be of precisely the same form as (1), and this too will involve a sinusoidal constant amplitude time path for price.

We now derive two properties of our model:

Property 1: Net speculative purchases of the commodity in question are given by a sinusoidal curve of constant amplitude and the duration of each cycle is equal to that of the cycle in prices. Maximum purchases occur one period after the upturn in prices, and maximum sales occur one period after the price downturn.

Property 2: The speculative behavior described by (4) is profitable provided the cycle is more than four periods long.

Proof of property 1: Since the form of (5) is precisely the same as that of (1), expression (2) is the solution of (5) for appropriate values of the constants in (2). That is, the time path of prices is once again given by (2). To see how this price behavior affects speculative excess demand, substitute expression (2) for P_t into the speculative excess demand function (4). We then have

$$\begin{aligned} E_{st+1} &= C[p\cos(qt+q+r) - 2p\cos(qt+r) \\ &\quad + p\cos(qt-q+r)] \\ &= C[p\cos(qt+r)\cos q \\ &\quad - p\sin(qt+r)\sin q - 2p\cos(qt+r) \\ &\quad + p\cos(qt+r)\cos q \\ &\quad + p\sin(qt+r)\sin q], \end{aligned}$$

so that,[9] collecting terms,

$$E_{st+1} = 2pC(\cos q - 1)\cos(tq+r). \quad (6)$$

Here $2pC(\cos q - 1)$ is a negative constant since the cosine of an angle is usually less than unity, and indeed, by elementary difference equation analysis we have from (5) $\cos q = \frac{Wa - C}{W - C} < 1$.

Comparing this result with (2) we see that $E_{st+1} = -D(P_t - R)$, where D is a positive constant. This proves the first property,[10] since it states essentially that speculative excess demands fluctuate inversely with prices *one period earlier* (note the time subscripts of E and P) and are inversely proportionate with the deviations of the past periods' prices from the mean price level.

Proof of property 2: Speculative profit during period t is the excess supply by speculators (quantity sold minus quantity bought)[11] multiplied by the price, i.e., it is, by (2) and (6)

$$\begin{aligned} -P_t E_{st} &= [p\cos(qt+r) + R] \\ &\quad [D\cos(qt-q+r)] \end{aligned}$$

where $D = -2pC(\cos q - 1) > 0$ [see (6)].

Thus profit over the cycle is the sum of these single period revenues taken over the entire cycle beginning at period T:

$$\sum_{t=T}^{T+\frac{360}{q}-1} [pD(\cos qt+r)(\cos qt-q+r) + RD\cos(qt-q+r)].$$

I assume here that $360/q$ is an even integer. Consider first the second term in this expression. Write $G = qT + q + r$. Then this second term is the sum

$$\begin{aligned} RD[&\cos G + \cos(G+q) + \cos(G+2q)\cdots \\ &+ \cos(G+180-q) + \cos(G+180) \\ &+ \cos(G+q+180) + \cos(G+2q \\ &+ 180) + \cdots + \cos(G+360-q)]. \end{aligned}$$

This sum is equal to zero because for any angle Q, $\cos Q = -\cos(180+Q)$. Turning now to the first term of the expression for profits over the cycle and taking $qt + r = Q$, the sum of any two consecutive terms may be written

$$\begin{aligned} &pD[\cos(Q+q)\cos Q + \cos Q\cos(Q-q)] \\ &= pD[\cos^2 Q\cos q - \sin Q\sin q\cos Q \\ &\quad + \cos^2 Q\cos q + \cos Q\sin Q\sin q] \\ &= 2pD\cos^2 Q\cos q. \end{aligned}$$

Total speculative profits over the cycle are then $pD\cos q \sum_{x=1}^{180/q} 2\cos^2(qT + 2xq + r)$ which is positive if $0 < \cos q$, i.e., if $q < 90°$, that is, if the cycle is longer than four periods.

Influence of Speculators on the Cycle

It remains only to see how the postulated speculation affects the frequency and amplitude of the fluctuations. I now derive two further properties of the model.

Property 3: The frequency of the fluctuations is increased by the postulated speculative behavior.

Property 4: The amplitude of the fluctuations is dependent on initial conditions and may or may not be increased.

Proof of property 3: There will be a com-

[9] The second line in the derivation is obtained by use of the standard formula for the cosine of a sum of two angles: $\cos(A+B) = \cos A \cos B - \sin A \sin B$ and the property $\sin(-A) = -\sin A$, $\cos(-A) = \cos A$.

[10] The property is really much more general in that it will hold for a much greater variety of time paths. It is easy to prove that if $P_t = f(t)$ and P_t attains a symmetric maximum or minimum at $t = T$, so that $f'(T-1) = -f'(T+1)$ then

$$dE_{st}/dt = 0 \text{ at } t = T+1.$$

[11] This is the same as quantity supplied minus quantity demanded since we are using an equilibrium model where total excess demand $E_t + E_{st} = 0$. Such a model is appropriate for most markets where there is organized speculation and the price rapidly adjusts to eliminate excess demands.

plete cycle every time tq in (2) increases by 360°. That is, the cycle will be of length $t = 360/q$ and hence of frequency $q/360$. In the absence of speculation write $q = q_N$. Here $0 < \cos q_N = a < 1$. In the presence of speculation write $q = q_s$ so that $0 < \cos q_s = \frac{Wa - C}{W - C} < 1$. Since the fraction $\frac{Wa - C}{W - C}$ is smaller than a, $\cos q_s$ is less than $\cos q_N$, i.e., $q_s/360 > q_N/360$. This really just confirms the intuitive notion that speculative purchases during the upswing and sales during the downswing will speed up the cyclical process.

Proof of property 4: This is obvious since, by (2), the amplitude of the fluctuations will be $2p$ whose magnitude depends on initial conditions. But a bit more can be said on this matter. Suppose that the speculators first observe the market in question to learn its behavior and then enter that market. The time path in the non-speculative market then provides the initial conditions. I shall now show by two illustrations that even so both increases and decreases in amplitude are possible.

First some preliminaries. From (2) we may write

$$P_t = c \cos qt + s \sin qt + R,$$

and

$$P_t = c' \cos q't + s' \sin q't + R$$

respectively for the non-speculative and speculative time paths, i.e., for the respective solutions of equations (1) and (5). It is to be noted that the constant R is the same in both solutions.[12]

Set $t = 0$ in both cases and assume that the corresponding P_0's are the same (the first initial condition). We obtain $c = c' = (P_0 - R)$. If this initial price is at the mean value of the prices, i.e., if $P_0 = R$ so that $c = c' = 0$, the time paths simplify to

$$P_t = s \sin qt + R \text{ and } P_t = s' \sin q't + R$$

whose amplitudes are $2s$ and $2s'$ respectively.

Now for our two cases illustrating the effects of speculation on amplitude:

[12] Proof: set $P_t = P_{t-1} = P_{t-2} = R$ in (1) to obtain $R(2 - 2a) = k$. Now make the same substitution in (5), getting $R[2(W - C) - 2(Wa - C)] = RW(2 - 2a) = K = kW$ by (3). Thus in both cases we have $R = k/2(1 - a)$.

Case 1: Speculation decreases amplitude. Let the second initial condition for the speculative case be given by the P_1 of the non-speculative time path. Then since $t = 1$ we have[13]

$$s \sin q = s' \sin q'$$

or

$$s / s' = \sin q' / \sin q$$

$$= \sqrt{1 - \left(\frac{Wa - C}{W - C}\right)^2} \Big/ \sqrt{1 - a^2} > 1.$$

Case 2: Speculation increases amplitude: Let the second initial condition be given by the peak (or trough) of the non-speculative time path so that $qt = 90$. Then

$$s' \sin q' (90/q) = s \sin q (90/q) = s \sin 90 = s$$

or

$$s / s' = \sin q' \, 90 / q < 1,$$

since $0 < q' / q < 1$. This result has a simple intuitive explanation. The two sine curves which portray the time paths of prices in the speculative and non-speculative situations

CHART 1

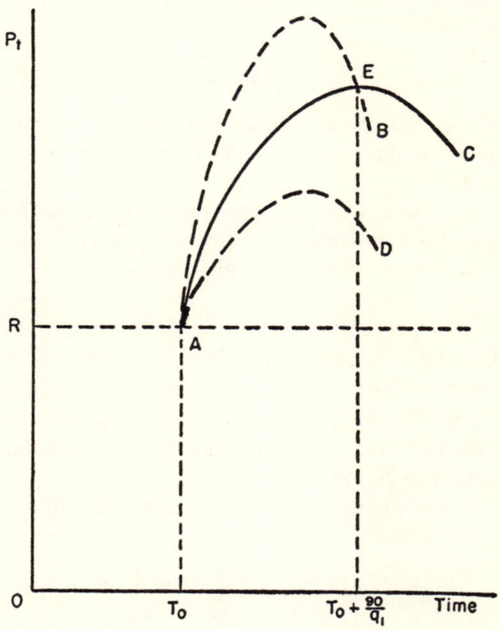

coincide at the mean price level, at A (Chart 1), and at the peak E of the (non-speculative) curve AC with the longer cycle. But at the

[13] The last line employs the relation $\sin B = \sqrt{1 - \cos^2 B}$ for any angle B.

latter point the other (speculative) curve, AB, since its cycle is shorter, must already be on its way down, i.e., its peak must be higher than that of the non-speculative curve.

A similar restatement is possible for case 1. Here the two curves AC and AD meet two consecutive periods near the midpoint of the cycle, i.e., they are roughly tangent in that vicinity. The speculative curve AD has the shorter cycle so it must reach its peak first and therefore its peak will be at a lower level. Both curves start climbing at the same rate so the one which has the longer time in which to climb will reach the highest level.

A Differential Equation Model

I outline briefly an analogous differential equation model because it permits me to illustrate another more impressive form which may be assumed by speculative destabilization. Again I posit price behavior in the absence of speculation to be perfectly periodic and of constant amplitude. It is then representable by the equation

$$P = R - a\ddot{P} \tag{7}$$

where $\ddot{P}$ is the second derivative of P with respect to time, and a and R are positive constants.

Equation (7) can be taken to be derived from the following not entirely implausible non-speculative excess demand function

$$E = 0 = R - P - a\ddot{P} \tag{8}$$

This says that the excess demand curve will be low near the trough when the second derivative is positive, and high in the vicinity of the peak. Such perverse behavior seems rather characteristic in some markets!

I now assume speculative excess demand to be given by

$$E_s = U(R - P) + W\dot{P},\ U > 0,\ W > 0,$$
$$\dot{P} \equiv \frac{dP}{dt}. \tag{9}$$

Roughly, this exhibits the features we desire because it has speculators concentrating their purchases when prices are simultaneously low ($P < R$) and rising ($\dot{P} > 0$). That is, they will be buying preponderantly during the beginning of the upswing, and, analogously, selling mainly during the beginning of the downswing.[14] It is also possible to show that this speculative activity can be profitable.[15]

By (8) and (9) the equilibrium condition $E + E_s = 0$ is now equivalent to

$$P(1 + U) = (1 + U)R + W\dot{P} - a\ddot{P}$$

or

$$P = R + \frac{W}{1 + U}\dot{P} - \frac{a}{1 + U}\ddot{P} \tag{10}$$

which can be written

$$R + 2r\dot{P} - s\ddot{P}.$$

This will have complex roots $r + \sqrt{r^2 - s} = r + qi$ and hence a cyclical time path provided $r^2 < s$, which will surely hold if $W^2 < a$, that

[14] This can be shown more rigorously. Differentiation of the solution (11) below, for P yields

$$\dot{P} = Ae^{rt}[r\cos(qt + B) - q\sin(qt + B)].$$

Substituting this and expression (11) for P in (9) gives us

$$E_s = Ae^{rt}[(Wr - U)\cos(qt + B) - Wq(\sin qt + B)],$$

i.e.,

$$E_s = -KAe^{rt}\cos(qt + B - E),$$

where $K = \sqrt{(Wr - U)^2 + (Wq)^2}$, $\cos E = -(Wr - U)/K$ and $\sin E = Wq/K$. Set $U > rW$ in (9) so that all of these are positive and therefore $0 < E < \frac{\pi}{2}$. Comparing the last expression for E_s with (11) we see that speculative purchases are inversely related to price and lag behind price movements but by less than one quarter of a cycle, as desired.

[15] *Proof:* Suppose first $W = 0$. By (9) speculative excess demand is now $E_s = U(R - P)$. In other words this is the case where speculative excess supply does not lag behind purchases. Now speculative profit over the cycle is given

$$\int_{t_0}^{t_0+2\pi/q} -PE_s\,dt = U\int_{t_0}^{t_0+2\pi/q} P(P - R)\,dt = U\int_{P>R} P(P - R)\,dt$$
$$+ U\int_{P<R} P(P - R)\,dt = UP_1\int_{P>R}(P - R)\,dt$$
$$+ UP_2\int_{P<R}(P - R)\,dt,\quad P_1 > R > P_2$$

(all positive constants) by one of the mean value theorems for integrals. Since we are assuming $W = 0$, by (10) $r = 0$. Then by (11) P is sinusoidal, so the portion of P above R is a mirror image of the portion below R. Therefore the last two integrals are equal in absolute value. The first integral is positive and the second negative, so that profit over the cycle is positive.

This proves our result for $W = 0$. But (9) shows that profit over the cycle, as expressed by the first integral in this footnote, is a continuous function of W. It follows that for sufficiently small W, i.e., if the lag in speculative demand is sufficiently small, the postulated speculation will be profitable.

is, provided the lag in speculative excess demand behind price movements is sufficiently small.

But there is an important difference between the solution of (10) and that of the non-speculative equation (7). The roots of the characteristic equation of (10) have a positive real part and the solution is

$$P = Ae^{rt}\cos(qt + B) + R, \ A \text{ and } B \text{ constants.} \qquad (11)$$

These fluctuations are no longer of constant amplitude. Rather their amplitude will grow at a geometric rate. Thus profitable speculation has demonstrated its destabilizing ability by knocking the system from its position of delicate constant amplitude balance into a time path of explosive fluctuation.[16]

A Real Non-speculative Cycle

It will be recalled that both our non-speculative cycle models have involved excess demands which are influenced by price trends as well as by prices. This raises some doubts whether the traders in question can legitimately be classed as non-speculators. In a letter to the author, Professor Friedman has suggested that perhaps a non-speculator can only safely be defined (if this is done in terms of his demand curve) as one whose purchases are directly influenced by current prices but not by past prices or price trends. In the absence of speculation, so defined, cyclical price movements can only result from real influences. It may perhaps be conjectured that such a cycle would not be subject to any destabilizing effects of profitable speculation, since the speculative influence on rates of price change would, by definition, not affect non-speculative behavior.

I shall now argue, however, that even in such a situation speculation which is apparently profitable can be destabilizing.

Suppose the supply S of some commodity varies sinusoidally, say, as the result of seasonal climatic changes, in accord with the equation

$$S = A - B\ddot{S} \ (A, B \text{ constants}). \qquad (12)$$

On Friedman's criterion the non-speculative demand function may take the form

$$D = K - VP, \qquad (13)$$

where K and V are constants and D and P respectively represent the quantity demanded and current price.

In the absence of speculation the equilibrium condition is $D = S$, which readily yields by substitution of

$$S = D = K - VP \text{ and } \ddot{S} = -V\ddot{P} \text{ into (12)},$$

$$P = \frac{K - A}{V} - B\ddot{P}.$$

This is of the same form as is (12) and involves constant amplitude sinusoidal price movements, as is to be expected.

What happens when speculation is imposed on this real cycle? The equilibrium condition (zero excess demand) is now

$$D - S + E_s = 0 \qquad (14)$$

where E_s represents speculative excess demand, and is given by equation (9) in the preceding section. Substitution of this expression and (13) into (14) yields

$$S = K - VP + U(R - P) + W\dot{P}$$

which may be rewritten

$$S = C - EP + W\dot{P} \ (C \text{ and } E \text{ constants}).$$

Substituting this and the corresponding expression for $\ddot{S}$ into (12) we obtain the third-order differential equation

$$C - A = EP - W\dot{P} + BE\ddot{P} - BW\dddot{P}.$$

Since complex roots come in pairs, at least one of the three roots of the characteristic equation must be real, and it cannot be negative since the terms are alternately positive and negative.[17] It follows that the time path of prices is changed by speculation from a cyclical

[16] It is clear that the same reasoning is applicable to a non-speculative market with damped or explosive fluctuation. The type of speculative behavior postulated in (9) could then increase the rate of explosion or reduce the rate of dampening because the coefficient of the $\dot{P}$ term is positive.

[17] No negative number can be the root of an equation like $X^3 - 3X^2 + 5X - 2 = 0$, since the substitution of a negative number for X will make every term negative, and the sum of four negative terms can clearly never be zero.

pattern of constant amplitude into an unstable, explosive movement.

However, we must see whether this speculation can be profitable. Here the matter is not quite so clear cut. In the short run, the time path may still be approximately cyclical, and the previous arguments apply. In the long run, the root whose real value is largest will determine the time path of P. If this is a complex root, again the analysis of the preceding section seems applicable. But if this root, r, is real, the time path of P will eventually approach $a\ e^{rt}$, where a is a constant. The speculator's excess demand as given by (9) of the previous section will then be

$$U(R - ae^{rt}) + Wrae^{rt}.$$

This will be positive for appropriate values of W and U. In other words, speculators will continue to buy on a rising market and, at least in terms of the value of their assets, this would appear to be profitable. However, it is clear that difficulties can arise if speculators try to cash in these profits or if they run out of funds with which to continue their purchases.

Stability of Unpegged Flexible Exchange Rates

I digress from my central theme to recapitulate a recent discussion by Professor Viner.[18] I have just maintained that even if exchange markets would otherwise be stable, speculation may act as a destabilizer. By contrast Viner has indicated that even if exchange rate speculation were stabilizing, the stability of flexible exchange rates is sometimes questionable. Together these two discussions then call into question much of the stability analysis of the proponents of flexible exchange rates.

Viner argues that the equilibrating forces which are ordinarily taken to be present in commodity markets cannot be expected to help stabilize unpegged exchange rates. In competitive markets, for example, the relative price of one consumers' good as against another is determined by costs of production and demands. If this price ratio is out of line with costs, capital will find it profitable to flow from the production of one item to the other and move prices back toward their equilibrium ratio in accord with the well known analysis.

But the peculiarity of the exchange market is that the cost of production of the commodities traded is, for all practical purposes, nil. Governments or the central banking systems can, at nearly zero cost, expand their currencies at will, and frequently they do not resist that temptation. Moreover, a currency ". . . has no price ceiling or price floor derived from any direct utility as a consumers' good or any indirect utility as an ingredient, a technical coefficient, in the production of producers' or consumers' goods." [19]

If, for example, one country inflates indefinitely, the exchange rate of its currency against others can fall indefinitely unless the foreigner himself inflates with equal success. By counterbalancing inflations, a precarious and rough constancy of exchange rates might be maintained, but in the absence of any pegging mechanism, the coincidence could end at any moment.

This means also that there is little reason to expect any consistent pattern of cyclical price movement on these exchanges. Rather, the time path can plausibly be expected to be erratic, responding to the political developments in the countries involved. This may appear to limit the applicability of the arguments of the earlier part of this paper, because these arguments examined the effects of speculation on perfectly cyclical price movements; but it is possible to interpret any one of the cycles discussed as a never-to-be-repeated erratic individual movement which may well approximate some actual exchange movements. These illustrations, as we have seen, are counterexamples to the assertion that profitable speculation is *necessarily* stabilizing. If interpreted as single erratic movements rather than strings of regular cycles, these counterexamples may carry rather more conviction for the exchange market case.

The Viner analysis also explains my employment of linear cycle models. It is fairly easy to construct a non-linear "relaxation" cycle model in which a constant amplitude is not the product of bizarre coincidence (see the foot-

[18] Jacob Viner, "Some International Aspects of Economic Stabilization," in Leonard D. White (ed.), *The State of the Social Sciences* (Chicago, 1956).

[19] Viner, op. cit., 291.

note 6 above). Characteristic of such a model is a sudden change in the basic relationships, as in the Hicks model, where attainment of full employment abruptly stops the working of the accelerator. In locating that turning point, the place where the relationships change, one has explicitly or implicitly built up a theory which explains the amplitude of the cycle. This would be very useful for our purposes, for such a theory would permit us to examine the effects of speculation on amplitude directly, and thus to grapple with an essential part of the stabilization question.

But this I have been unable to do because I can see no way of constructing a systematic explanation of turning points of truly flexible exchange rates. If, as I believe, Viner is right, exchange rate movements will be erratic and these turning points will be erratic, or rather, they will be explainable only in terms of the political circumstances of the countries in question.

[17]

Econometrica **26** (1958) 258–285; *North-Holland Publishing Co., Amsterdam*

TOPOLOGY OF SECOND ORDER LINEAR DIFFERENCE EQUATIONS WITH CONSTANT COEFFICIENTS[1]

BY WILLIAM J. BAUMOL

This article describes the geometric tools which can be employed for the qualitative analysis of second order difference equations. By showing how linear equations can be investigated by geometric methods it suggests how some nonlinear equations can also be handled with the aid of these tools. This is illustrated by a geometric restatement of the Hicksian (nonlinear second order difference equation) trade cycle model.

1. INTRODUCTION

FOR MANY PROBLEMS of economic dynamics linearity assumptions have proved unsatisfactory. This is because linearity sometimes seriously misrepresents the facts under analysis and because, in misrepresenting these facts it leads to conclusions characterized by undesirable properties.[2] But unfortunately most of our analytic apparatus fails us once nonlinearities make their appearance. Usually we have only two alternatives: algebraic methods of approximation to obtain quantitative conclusions, and geometric methods for qualitative analysis.

This paper deals with *linear* equations as a means for investigating the relevant geometry. It expounds results for difference equations which are already well known for differential equations.[3]

[1] My very sincere gratitude for their help is due to Mrs. L. Atiyah, Mr. R. G. Davis, Professor Robert Dorfman, Dr. Lawrence Markus, and other members of Professor Lefschetz' O. N. R. Project on nonlinear differential equations, and Professor Richard Quandt. I accept no responsibility for the term "topology" in the title and employ it in response to intimidation by the mathematicians.

[2] For example, a cycle produced by a linear model is virtually certain to explode or fade away. Roots must be of modulus precisely unity if these alternatives are to be avoided, and a root of modulus 0.99997 or 1.00001 will not do the trick though for practical purposes we may be content to observe that for a considerable time the system will act very much as if the cycle were stable. But our statistics are never fine enough to permit us to distinguish between a unit root and one which takes values so close to it. I have seen systems which yield unit roots but these roots have always been built into the model often unobserved by the author. In such a case it is usually possible to show that a slight amendment in one of the simplifying assumptions will eliminate the unit roots and so have profound qualitative effects on the system. As Solow has pointed out, since our premises are always necessarily more or less false, good theorizing consists to a large extent in avoiding assumptions like these, where a small change in what is posited will seriously affect the conclusions.

[3] See, e.g., Andronow, A. A. and Chaikin, C. E., *Theory of Oscillations*, Princeton University Press, Princeton, 1949, Chapter I; or Minorsky, N., *Introduction to Non-Linear Mechanics*, J. W. Edwards, Ann Arbor, 1947.

The *phase plane*[4] for a second order difference equation may be defined as a two dimensional graph which shows the relationship between the values of the relevant variable in two consecutive periods. From this we can trace thiough the time path of the variable from one period to the next, and as will be seen presently the graphics work out very much as they do in the familiar cobweb or the reaction curve diagrams.

Existence of the Second Order Phase Plane Relationship

The relationship which we have undertaken to plot on the phase diagram is[5]

$$Y_{t+1} = f(Y_t). \tag{1}$$

In the first order case this is given by the difference equation itself and clearly the general linear first order equation with constant coefficients[6]

$$Y_{t+1} = aY_t + b \tag{2}$$

is just such a relation. In the case of the second order equation the matter is less obvious and it may not be intuitively clear that any such expression can be deduced from the general equation

$$Y_{t+1} = aY_t + bY_{t-1} + c. \tag{3}$$

This is because there is no obvious way of eliminating the bY_{t-1} term. However this elimination can ordinarily be performed because (3) has a solution

$$Y_t = uX_1^t + vX_2^t + Z, \tag{4}$$

where u and v are constants whose values are determined by the initial conditions, X_1 and X_2 are the roots of the characteristic equation and Z is a particular solution. From (4) we also obtain

$$Y_{t+1} = uX_1^{t+1} + vX_2^{t+1} + Z, \tag{4a}$$

which together with (4) gives us two equations in Y_{t+1}, Y_t, and t. If between

[4] Strictly speaking, the relevant concept for an Nth order equation is an N dimensional phase space. The phase space for a first order equation is then one dimensional, i.e., just one straight line axis with numbers indicating where to go next period. For example the difference equation $Y_{t+1} = 2\,Y_t$ can be represented by $\begin{array}{ccccccccc} -4 & -2 & 0 & 2 & 4 & 6 & 8 & 10 & 12 \\ \hline -2 & -1 & 0 & 1 & 2 & 3 & 4 & 5 & 6 \end{array}$. Here if $Y_0 = 1$ we read from above the axis that $Y_1 = 2$, and move to where there is a 2 below the axis. Again reading above the axis there we see that Y_2 will be 4, etc. However, for most purposes it is more illuminating to diagram first order equations on a two dimensional plane with the numbers previously shown above the line moved to the vertical axis.

[5] As we shall see, it is sometimes convenient to express Y_{t+1} as a function of both Y_t and t, i.e., as $Y_{t+1} = f(Y_t, t)$.

[6] Note that the graph of (2) is always a straight line.

them t can be eliminated (although as we shall see it is not always desirable that this be done), we obtain, at least implicitly, the phase relationship (1) between Y_{t+1} and Y_t. This is essentially the procedure which we shall follow.

The Number of Degrees of Freedom

There is one more point to be noted. The graph of the general first order equation will be uniquely determined by (2). We have no degrees of freedom in drawing the curve. On the other hand the second order equation, (3), will, given any Y_t, yield different values for Y_{t+1} which depend on the magnitude of Y_{t-1}. This means that we have one degree of freedom in drawing our phase plane graph. Rather than a single curve $Y_{t+1} = f(Y_t)$ there will be a family of such lines. Given any historical value of Y which can be taken as an initial condition Y_0, (3) yields a unique relationship between the values of the variable for the next two periods. In other words, in the second order case one initial condition will determine which of a *family* of curves representing the equation will be followed by the movement of the variable Y_t.

2. THE COMPLEX ROOTS CASE

Where the roots of the characteristic equation are complex, the solution (4) can be written[7]

(5) $$Y_t = r^t\,[p \cos Qt + q \sin Qt].$$

This expression can in turn be rewritten

(6) $$Y_t = r^t K \cos (Qt + w)$$

where K and w are constants.

The Phase Plane Relationship (Complex Roots)

Expression (6) almost directly produces the relationship between Y_{t+1} and Y_t required for the phase plane representation. For we have

$$\begin{aligned} Y_{t+1} &= Kr^{t+1}\,[\cos (Qt + Q + w)] \\ &= Kr^{t+1}[\cos Q \cos (Qt + w) - \sin Q \sin (Qt + w)], \end{aligned}$$

and since for any angle A, $\sin A = \pm \sqrt{1 - \cos^2 A}$

$$\begin{aligned} Y_{t+1} &= Kr^{t+1}[\cos Q \cos (Qt + w) \pm (\sin Q) \sqrt{1 - \cos^2 (Qt + w)}\,] \\ &= r \cos Q\,[Kr^t \cos (Qt + w)] \pm r\,(\sin Q)\,\sqrt{(Kr^t)^2 - [Kr^t \cos (Qt + w)]^2}. \end{aligned}$$

[7] Until a later section I will take the difference equation (3) to be homogeneous, i.e., I assume $c = 0$.

By (6) the items in the square brackets are equal to Y_t so that the expression reduces to

$$Y_{t+1} = r\,(\cos Q)\,Y_t \pm r\,(\sin Q)\sqrt{(Kr^t)^2 - Y_t^2} \tag{7}$$

which is the desired relationship (1) between Y_{t+1} and Y_t.

The Phase Plane Diagram (Complex Roots)

The shape of the geometric representation of (7) may not be immediately obvious. Although a more direct approach is possible, it is convenient to divide this problem into two parts by examining in turn the two terms on the righthand side of (7). First we note that, letting Y^*_{t+1} denote the first term,

$$Y^*_{t+1} = r\,(\cos Q)\,Y_t$$

is a straight line through the origin of the phase plane diagram with slope $r \cos Q$. The shape of Y_{t+1} will be given by the vertical sum of this line with that representing the second term: that is, by $Y_{t+1} = Y^*_{t+1} + Y^{**}_{t+1}$ where

$$Y^{**}_{t+1} = \pm\, r \sin Q \sqrt{(Kr^t)^2 - Y_t^2}. \tag{8}$$

The shape of (8) then remains to be analyzed. Squaring both sides and rearranging terms gives

$$(Y^{**}_{t+1})^2 + (r \sin Q \cdot Y_t)^2 = (r \sin Q \cdot Kr^t)^2.$$

If we set $\overline{Y}_t = r \sin Q \cdot Y_t$ this becomes

$$(Y^{**}_{t+1})^2 + (\overline{Y}_t)^2 = (r \sin Q \cdot Kr^t)^2 = (Ar^t)^2. \tag{9}$$

Where $r = 1$ this will be recognized as the standard formula for the circle, with its center at the origin, $x^2 + y^2 = B^2$.

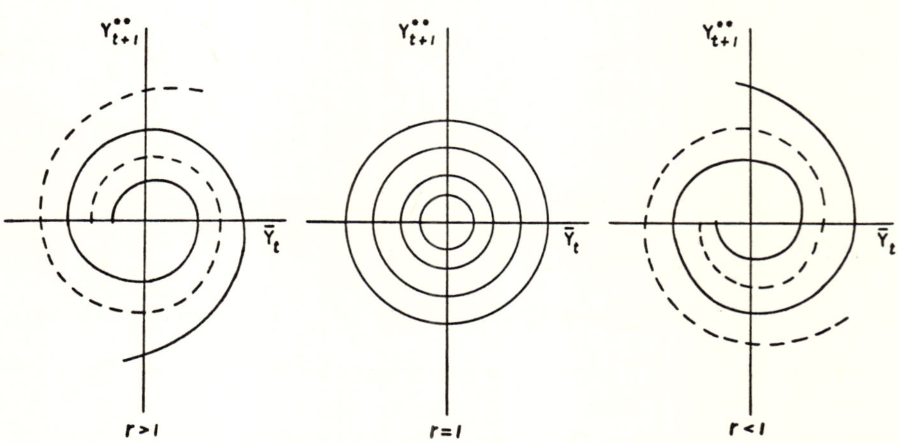

FIGURE 1

Suppose on the other hand $r > 1$. The formula (9) then says that the distance $\sqrt{(Y_{t+1}^{**})^2 + (\bar{Y}_t)^2}$ of the point $(\bar{Y}_t, Y_{t+1}^{**})$ from the center (the radius of the "circle") keeps growing larger and larger as t increases.[8] This means that the figure will spiral outward. Similarly with $r < 1$ it will spiral inward. We then have the relationship shown[9] in Figure 1.

As already noted, for different values of A there will be different curves so that in each case an entire family rather than a single curve will be involved. This is shown in the case of the circles but to avoid complication in the drawing of the spiral diagrams every member but two of the family of curves is omitted.

Transformation to the Y_{t+1}, Y_t Diagram

This then is the relationship between Y_{t+1}^{**} and $\bar{Y}_t$. But these are both only artificial variables invented to make the drawing easier. What we really want is the Y_{t+1}, Y_t graph. First, to get back to a graph which has Y_t instead of $\bar{Y}_t$ on its horizontal axis we note that the transformation $\bar{Y}_t = r \sin Q \cdot Y_t$ used to obtain (9) merely shrinks or stretches the horizontal axis depending on whether $r \sin Q$ is less than or greater than unity. For example, if it is less than 1, every value of Y_t is simply decreased proportionally to yield a $\bar{Y}_t$ smaller than itself. Thus to get from the graph which has a $\bar{Y}_t$ axis to one employing a Y_t axis we must merely unshrink or unstretch the diagram horizontally. This will turn the circle into an ellipse and deform the spirals analagously as shown in Figure 2.

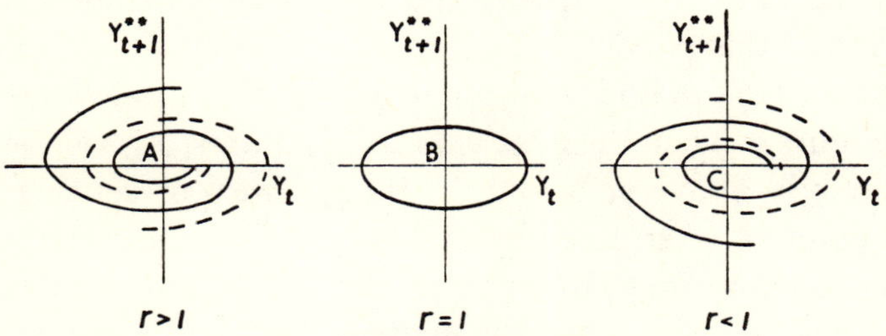

FIGURE 2

Figure 2 ($r \sin Q<1$)

Points A, B and C are referred to, respectively, as an *unstable focus*, a *center*, and a *stable focus*.

Finally, to get to a Y_{t+1} $(=Y_{t+1}^{*} + Y_{t+1}^{**})$ axis from the Y_{t+1}^{**} vertical axis employed in Figure 2 we must add the straight line $Y_{t+1}^{*} = r \cos Q\, Y_t$ to the Y_{t+1}^{**} values shown in Figure 2. In Figure 3 this line is superimposed

[8] Indeed, in polar coordinates (9) is given by $\varrho = Ar^t$.

[9] Movements along the spiral are always clockwise because above a 45° line through the origin $Y_{t+1}^{**} > \bar{Y}_t$ so that movement is to the right, and below the 45° line movement is to the left. (See section on phase line and time path below.)

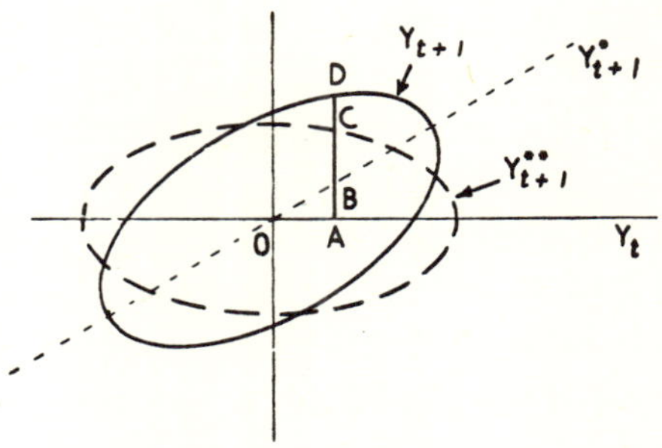

FIGURE 3

on the ellipse of Figure 2 (dotted lines). Their vertical sum is the new tilted ellipse shown in the solid line. This is obtained by picking points like A on the Y_t axis and noting that here $Y^*_{t+1} = AB$ and $Y^{**}_{t+1} = AC$ $(= BD)$ so that $Y_{t+1} = AD = AB + AC$. That then is the representation of the second order linear difference equation with complex roots on the phase plane. It consists of tilted ellipses,[10] and tilted elliptical spirals.

The Time Path (*Complex Roots*)

We can now see at once what will be the time path of Y. I will only draw it (Figure 4) for the elliptical case where the roots are of unit modulus ($r = 1$). The extension to other values of r is obvious and will only be considered explicitly in the illustrative application to the Hicks trade cycle model in the last section of this paper.

In the phase plane diagram, suppose the given initial value of Y_t is Y_0 as shown in Figure 4. Then the next value of Y, that is, Y_1, will be represented by a point directly above or below Y_0, that point representing $Y_1 = f(Y_0)$. This second point is determined by the two initial conditions in our second order difference equation system, since the two initial conditions give the values of Y_0 and Y_1 which are the coordinates of this point. It is in this way that we discover which of the family of ellipses in the phase diagram will determine the time path. Suppose then that point A in Figure 4 is this point with coordinates (Y_0, Y_1) and that it lies on the ellipse shown in the diagram. Now superimpose a 45° line, RR' on this graph. By moving horizontally from point A, whose vertical coordinate is Y_1, to point J on the 45° line, and then directly down to the horizontal axis we can locate Y_1 on that axis. Y_2 is now shown as $f(Y_1)$ by point B on the ellipse directly above Y_1, and above the 45° line. Continuing in this way we see that the time path of Y is given by $A\ B\ C\ D\ E$ . . . in Figure 4.

[10] This could have been shown directly in terms of the discriminant of the quadratic (7).

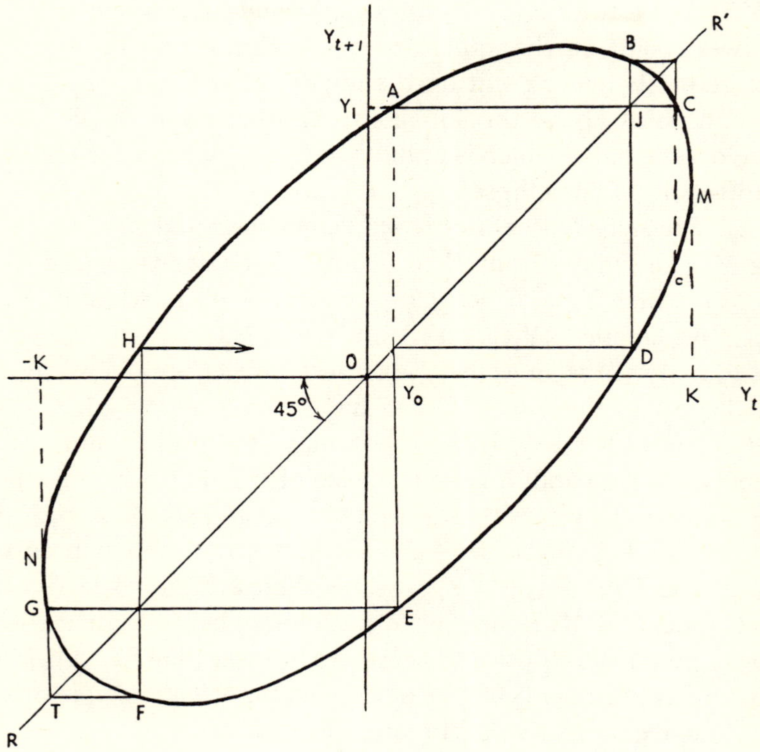

FIGURE 4

We can see as follows why from point A the time path moves to B rather than to D and why from B it moves to C rather than c, etc.

To do this I shall prove the following theorem: from any point on the time path which lies above the 45° line the next point on the time path will lie on the upper arc[11] of the ellipse. From any point which lies below the 45° line the next move will be to a point on the lower arc of the ellipse.

The time path is given by equation (6) from which our phase diagram is also derived. By symmetry we need only deal with initial points which lie above the 45° line and are therefore points of increasing Y (i.e., $Y_{t+1} > Y_t$ everywhere above the 45° line). Only the following two cases are possible and I shall show that the theorem holds in each case.

Case (i). The second point also lies above the 45° *line.* The coordinates of the two points are (Y_t, Y_{t+1}) and (Y_{t+1}, Y_{t+2}) where $Y_{t+2} > Y_{t+1} > Y_t$. Thus the second point lies above and to the right of the first. The slope of *NT which is the only segment of the lower arc of the phase line which lies above the* 45° *line* is everywhere negative (as can be shown via the expression for

[11] By "upper arc" of the ellipse I mean the upper arc connecting the two vertical points on the ellipse.

dY_{t+1}/dY_t in footnote 12). N is (by the assumed negative slope of Y^*_{t+1} (Figure 3)) the lowest point on the upper arc of the ellipse, so that every point on NT must lie below every point on the upper arc of the ellipse. Hence every move from a point above the 45° line to another point above the 45° line, since it involves a move which is uphill and to the right, must end at a point on the upper arc of the ellipse.

Case (ii). The second point lies below the 45° *line* and hence must involve declining Y. (The move from B to C or c.) Let t' be that (not necessarily integral) t for which $Y_t = K \cos (Qt + w)$ attains its maximum, K. Our two points can be labelled (Y_{t^*-1}, Y_{t^*}) and (Y_{t^*}, Y_{t^*+1}) with $Y_{t^*+1} < Y_{t^*} > Y_{t^*-1}$ so that by (6) t^* must be the largest integer $\leqslant t'$, i.e., the last date before Y begins to decline. We then have $t^* \leqslant t' < t^* + 1$. Since in $Y_t = K \cos (Qt + w) = K \cos (-Qt - w)$ we may by appropriate choice of w take Q to lie between zero and π. By out choice of t' Y_t is monotonically decreasing for $Qt + w$ in the interval between $Qt' + w$ and $Qt' + w + \pi$. And if $t = t^* + 1$ or $t = t' + 1$, where $t^* + 1 \leqslant t' + 1$, $Qt + w$ lies in this interval since $0 \leqslant Q < \pi$. Thus $Y_{t^*+1} \geqslant Y_{t'+1}$ where these are the respective ordinates of points C (or c) and M. Hence the former cannot be the ordinate of c which is on the lower arc of the ellipse and therefore is lower than M. Q.E.D. I conjecture that similar arguments can be developed for other multiple valued phase functions (see, e.g., Figures 11, 14, and 15 below).

Phase Line and Time Path

There are several basic relationships between the shape and location of the phase line and the nature of the time path of Y which are required for the analysis:

1. When a phase line is above the 45° line, Y_{t+1} is by definition greater than Y_t, *so that Y must always be increasing*, i.e., motion must be upward and to the right. The reverse holds below the 45° line.

2. If the phase line always has a slope greater than unity, the time path will be explosive upward or explosive downward and go ever further from the 45° line and certainly never cross it. On the other hand, if the phase line's slope is positive but less than unity the motion will approach the 45° line asymptotically but never cross it (damped movement toward equilibrium).

3. Where the phase line has a negative slope, Y_t will oscillate in the familiar cobweb pattern, as the reader may easily verify by drawing such a diagram.

4. If motion is to be periodic, it must involve rises in Y (the phase line above the 45° line) interspersed with falls in Y (phase line below the 45° line). Thus in periodic motion the time path must cross the 45° line. But we have just seen that this can never occur where the phase line has a positive

slope. Thus *where motion is periodic the phase line must ordinarily have a negative slope where it crosses the* 45° *line.*

5. Where the phase line is defined only for a limited range of Y, e.g., for the range Y_1Y_2 in Figure 5 there is often a simple interpretation of the consequences of an initial Y outside that range. To see this we turn back to the general expression (7) for the phase line in the complex roots case where we take $r = 1$.

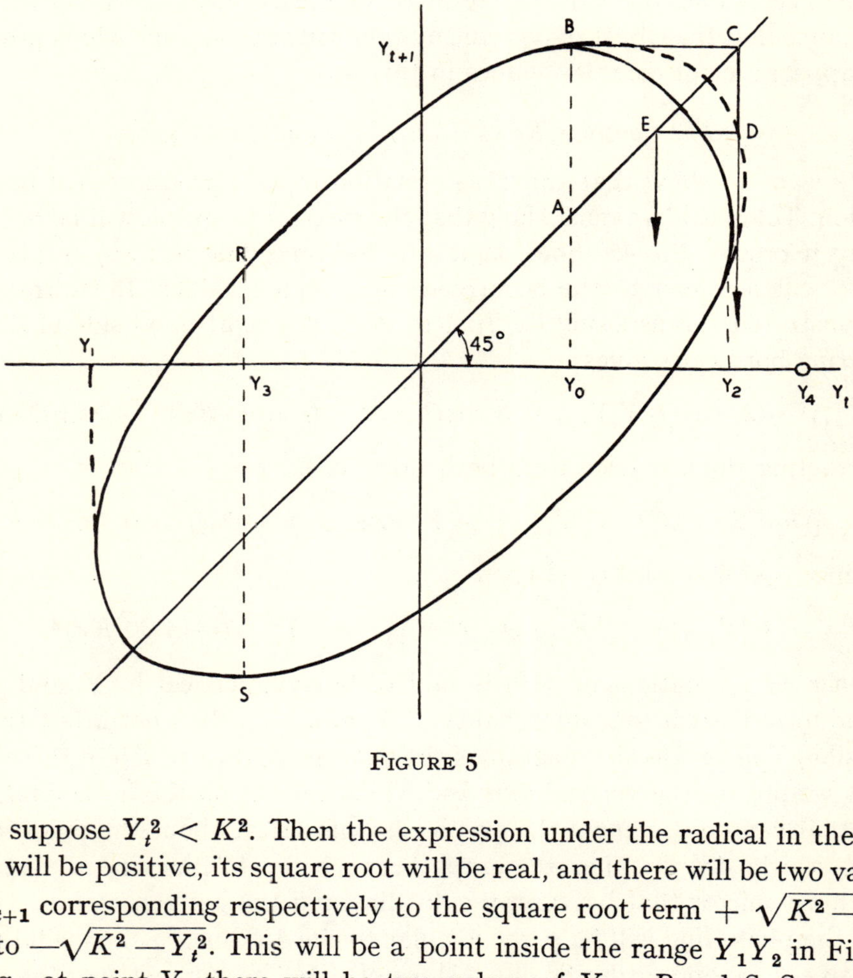

FIGURE 5

First suppose $Y_t^2 < K^2$. Then the expression under the radical in the last term will be positive, its square root will be real, and there will be two values of Y_{t+1} corresponding respectively to the square root term $+\sqrt{K^2 - Y_t^2}$ and to $-\sqrt{K^2 - Y_t^2}$. This will be a point inside the range Y_1Y_2 in Figure 5; e.g., at point Y_3 there will be two values of Y_{t+1}, R and S. Second, if $Y_t = \pm K$ the last term in (7) will be zero and there will be only one corresponding value of Y_{t+1}. This occurs at points Y_1 $(= -K)$ and Y_2 $(= K)$ in the figure. Finally, outside this range where $Y_t^2 < K^2$ the last term in (7) will be imaginary. That is why there is no representation of a phase line in the diagram which has only axes showing real magnitudes. We see, then, that a Y_t like Y_4 will produce a complex Y_{t+1}. For some phase lines such a point might even be reached from an initial position inside the real range

$Y_1 Y_2$. For example with initial point Y_0 the time path is traced out by broken line $A\ B\ C$ . . . where C is to the right of Y_2 so that we know that in the next period Y will be complex. This could have been avoided if the phase line extended further to the right underneath the 45° line as does the dotted figure, for then we would have had the real time path construction line $A\ B\ C\ D\ E$. . . . Correspondingly, to the left of the axis to prevent complex values the phase line must extend far enough to the left above the 45° line. Since in economics our variables ordinarily take on only real values we want assurance that the ellipse of periodic motion will have a shape which prevents the appearance of complex values in this way.

The Complex Roots Phase Line and Periodicity

We want to show that the phase relationship (7) produces real periodic motion. To do this we must show that the slope of its graph will be negative where it crosses the 45° line (point 4 of the preceding section) and that its shape will not lead to the occurrence of complex values. Both are easily demonstrated. Transposing the first term on the right-hand side of (7) and squaring both sides gives

$$(Y_{t+1})^2 - 2r\cos Q \cdot Y_t Y_{t+1} + (r\cos Q \cdot Y_t)^2 = (r\sin Q \cdot Kr^t)^2 - (r\sin Q \cdot Y_t)^2.$$

Subtracting the last term from both sides we have

$$(Y_{t+1})^2 - 2\,r\cos Q \cdot Y_t\,Y_{t+1} + r^2\,Y_t^2\,(\cos^2 Q + \sin^2 Q) = (r\sin Q \cdot Kr^t)^2$$

or, since $\cos^2 Q + \sin^2 Q = 1$,

$$(Y_{t+1})^2 - 2\,r\cos Q \cdot Y_t\,Y_{t+1} + r^2\,Y_t^2 = (r\sin Q \cdot Kr^t)^2. \tag{10}$$

When $r = 1$, relationship (10) is said to be symmetrical in Y_t and Y_{t+1}, for its form is such that interchange of Y_t and Y_{t+1} does not affect the expression. This means the diagram is the same no matter which of these variables we put on the vertical axis and which we put on the horizontal axis. But that can only occur if the graph is symmetrical about the point where it crosses the 45° line, i.e., the graph between the 45° line and the vertical axis must mirror that between the 45° line and the horizontal axis. If this is so the phase line will be perpendicular to the 45° line,[12] i.e., it will have a negative slope, more specifically, a slope of —1. The symmetry of the phase

[12] A more formal proof is obtained by setting $r = 1$ in (10) and differentiating totally to obtain

$$2[Y_{t+1} - \cos Q \cdot Y_t]\,dY_{t+1} + 2[Y_t - \cos Q \cdot Y_{t+1}]\,dY_t = 0$$

or

$$\frac{dY_{t+1}}{dY_t} = -\frac{Y_t - \cos Q \cdot Y_{t+1}}{Y_{t+1} - \cos Q \cdot Y_t}$$

and on the 45° line where $Y_t = Y_{t+1}$, this is equal to —1.

curve about the 45° line also suffices to preclude a time path which leads into complex values of the variable. This can be seen by referring back to Figure 5. The symmetry property means that corresponding to any point like B in the positive quadrant which lies above the 45° line and, incidentally, lies on a negatively sloping segment of the phase line, there must be another point D on the phase line which is similarly placed on the other side of the 45° line. It follows that any movement from a point like B to the 45° line at C must be followed by move CD. In other words there exists no point B on the phase curve from which the next move will be to a point on the 45° line to the right of the phase curve. No point can then be the stepping stone to a complex value of our variable, Y.

3. REAL ROOTS

The Equation of the Phase Lines

Having examined the phase plane representation of the second order equation whose roots are complex we turn to the real roots case, continuing on the assumption that the equation is homogeneous and positing, in addition, that the two roots are distinct. The solution is given by expression (4) above with $Z = 0$. Together with (4a) this yields by a simple calculation

$$Y_{t+1} - X_1 Y_t = vX_2^{t+1} - vX_1 X_2^t = v(X_2 - X_1) X_2^t$$

and similarly

$$Y_{t-1} - X_2 Y_t = u(X_1 - X_2) X_1^t.$$

Clearly the ratio of $Y_{t+1} - X_1 Y_t$ to $Y_{t+1} - X_2 Y_t$ is a non-constant function of t. But is there any function of the left-hand sides of the two preceding equations which does not depend on t? Such a function would, of course, be the phase graph relationship which we are seeking. To answer the question, square both sides of the first equation and raise both sides of the second to the $2a$ power, where a is a constant whose value is still to be decided on. Dividing one of the resulting equations by the other we find

$$(11) \qquad \frac{(Y_{t+1} - X_1 Y_t)^2}{(Y_{t+1} - X_2 Y_t)^{2a}} = k\frac{X_2^{2t}}{X_1^{2at}} = k\left(\frac{X_2^2}{X_1^{2a}}\right)^t$$

where $k = [(-1)\,(X_1 - X_2)^{(1-a)}\,\frac{v}{u^a}]^2 > 0.$

This is independent of t if and only if the parenthesis on the right-hand side equals unity, i.e., if

$$X_2^2 = X_1^{2a}.$$

Thus any number, a, which satisfies this equation will do. Clearly such a number is given by

$$(12) \qquad a = \log (X_2^2)/\log (X_1^2).$$

For this value of a the right-hand side of (11) is equal to k. This is the basic equation of the phase lines in the real roots case.

The Phase Diagram: $|X_1| > 1$ *and* $|X_2| > 1$

First consider the case where both roots are greater than unity in absolute value so that their logs are both positive. It involves no loss of generality to take $\log (X_2^2) > \log (X_1^2)$ so that, by (12), $a > 1$. Setting

(13) $$Y_{t+1} - X_1 Y_t = R \quad \text{and} \quad Y_{t+1} - X_2 Y_t = S$$

equation (11) becomes

(14) $$R = \pm KS^a$$

where $K = \sqrt{k}$.

The graph of this function with axes R and S is the family of curves of parabolic type shown in Figure 6. If, for example, a is an even integer, then for different values of K, AOB and COD will be typical curves given by

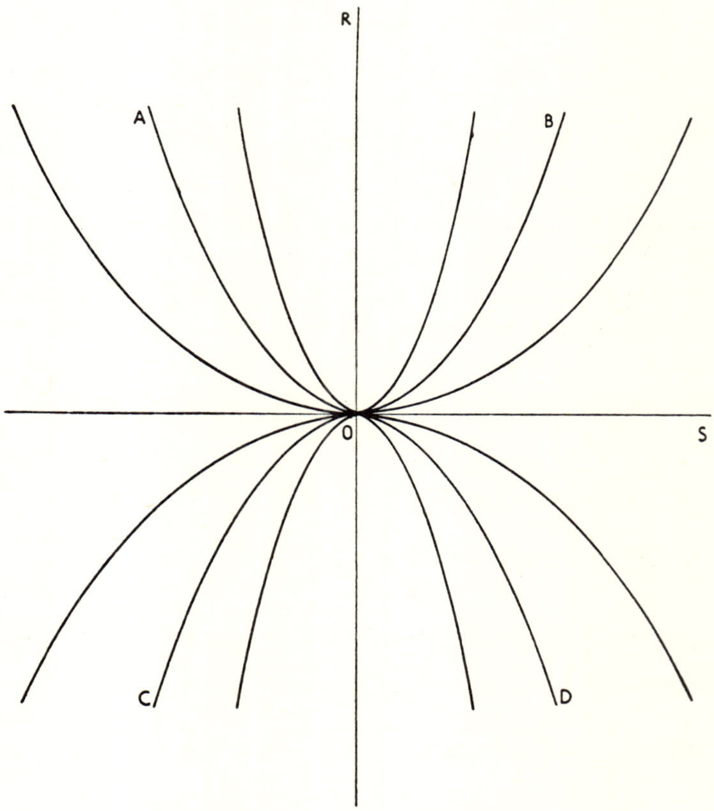

FIGURE 6

(14), while if a is an odd integer, COB and AOD will be among the graphic representations of the equation. Note that the curves all go through the origin, are tangent to the S axis ($dR/dS = \pm aKS^{a-1} = 0$ for $S = 0$), and asymptotically approach lines parallel to the R axis, i.e., their slope approaches infinity.

We must now transform this diagram with axes S and R into the phase diagram with axes Y_t and Y_{t+1}. This transformation is given by equations (13). These equations state that in the phase diagram the previous S axis ($R = 0$) is given by the straight line through the origin with slope X_1

(15) $$R = Y_{t+1} - X_1 Y_t = 0, \qquad [S \text{ axis}]$$

and similarly the R axis becomes

(16) $$S = Y_{t+1} - X_2 Y_t = 0. \qquad [R \text{ axis}]$$

Thus the transformation simply involves a rotation of the S and R axes with a corresponding distortion of the parabolic curves. For example, if both roots X_1 and X_2 are negative, lines (15) and (16) will both have negative slopes. The position of the old S and R axes in the phase plane is shown in Figure 7. It will be noted that since $|X_2|$ is greater than $|X_1|$ the line given

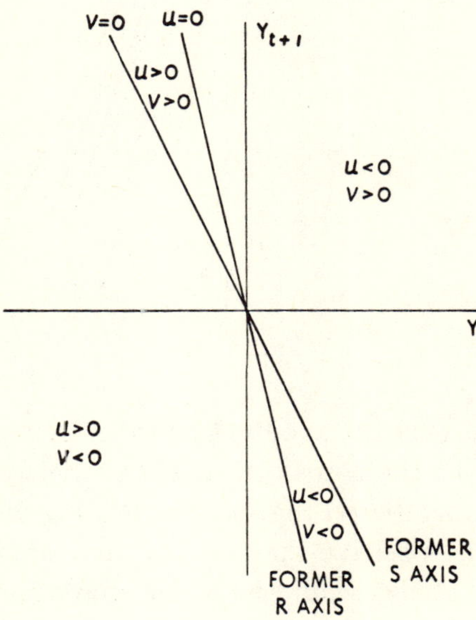

FIGURE 7

by (16), i.e., the old R axis, will have the greater slope in absolute value. Also, since the absolute value of both roots is greater than unity both lines will be steeper than a 45° line.

The distorted parabolas which result from this rotation of axes are shown in Figure 8. It will be noted that they are still tangent to the former S axis

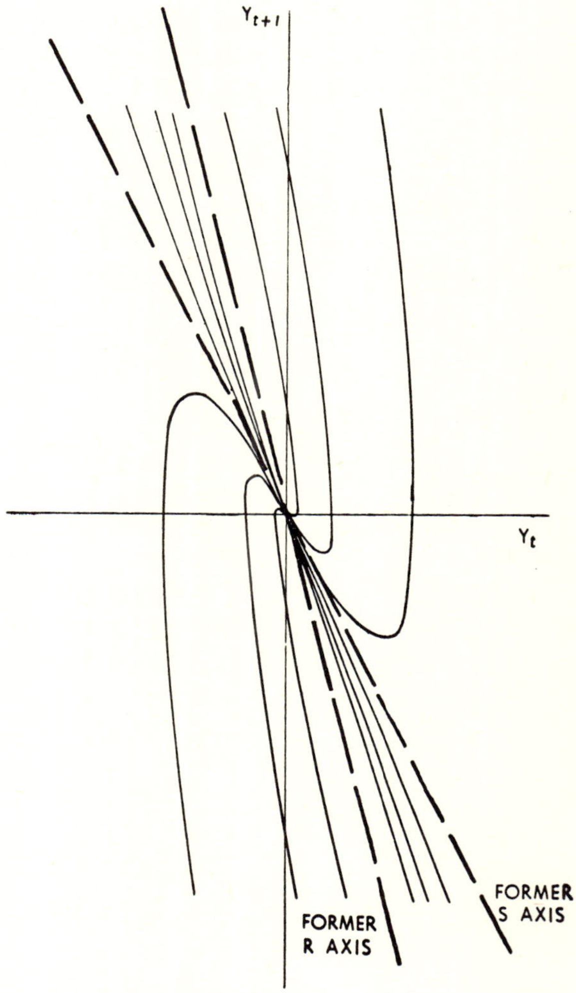

FIGURE 8

at the origin and still curl up about the former R axis, forming U shapes lying on their sides with the transformed R axis between the two branches of the U. It will be remembered that we are dealing with negative roots. If the roots X_1 and X_2 are positive the slope of the transformed R and S axes is positive and the parabolas would have the shape shown in Figure 9. The origin in both these diagrams is called a *node*. To see what these apparently odd shapes mean for the time path of Y a preliminary matter must first be settled.

The "Initial" Conditions and the Arbitrary Constants

Any two successive values of Y can be used to determine the values of the arbitrary constants u and v in the solution (4) of the difference equation.

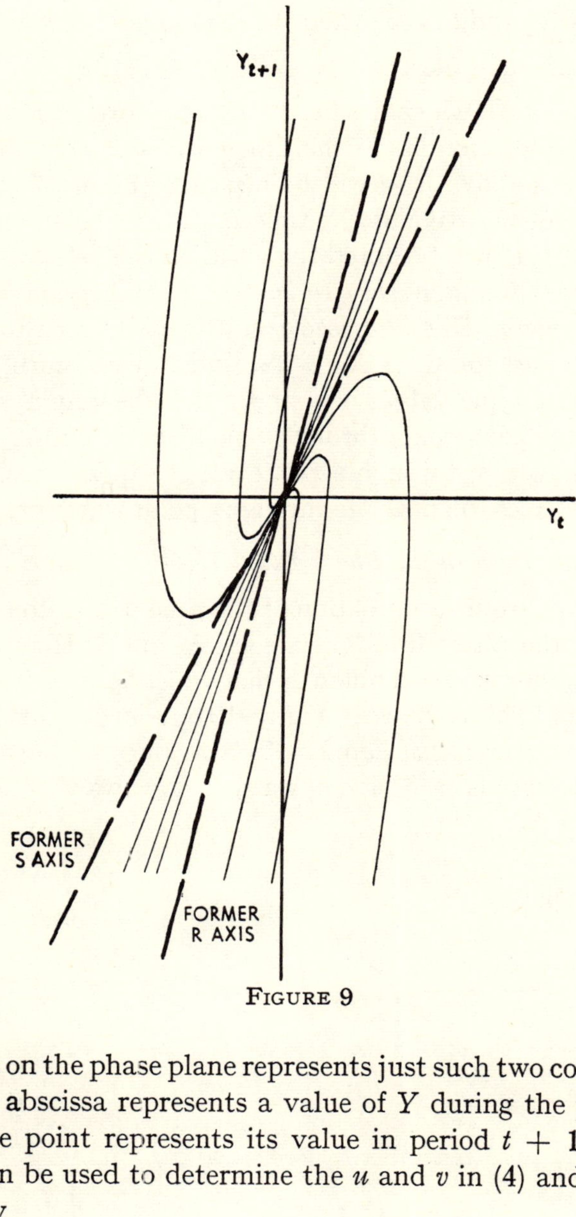

FIGURE 9

Now any point on the phase plane represents just such two consecutive values of Y since the abscissa represents a value of Y during the period t and the ordinate of the point represents its value in period $t + 1$. Still assuming $Z = 0$, this can be used to determine the u and v in (4) and (4a) by solving simultaneously

$$Y_t = uX_1^t + vX_2^t$$

and

$$Y_{t+1} = uX_1^{t+1} + vX_2^{t+1}$$

for u and v in terms of Y_t and Y_{t+1}. We obtain

$$(17) \qquad u = -\frac{(Y_{t+1} - X_2Y_t)}{X_1^t(X_2 - X_1)}, \qquad v = \frac{Y_{t+1} - X_1 Y_t}{X_2^t (X_2 - X_1)}.$$

Suppose $X_2 > X_1$ and t even. Then the denominators will be positive and u will be positive, zero or negative as $-(Y_{t+1} - X_2 Y_t) \gtreqless 0$, i.e., as $Y_{t+1} \lesseqgtr X_2 Y_t$. Then a time path which lies below the transformed R axis will involve a positive u in the solution (4). If the time path is on transformed R, u will be zero, and if it is above R, u will be negative (Figure 7). Similarly v will be positive, zero, or negative as the time path lies above, on, or below the transformed S axis. It will be noted that *"in between" the transformed R and S axes u and v are of like sign while in the rest of the diagram u is positive and v negative or vice versa.* This italicised result is easily seen to be unaffected by removal of the assumptions $X_2 > X_1$ and t even. Since any time path is associated with unique values of u and v this theorem has an important corollary: any time path going through a point between the transformed R and S axes will never go through a point outside these lines, and any time path outside these lines will never go through a point which lies between them.

The Time Path in the Phase Plane (Real Explosive Roots)

We can now divide our examination of the time path into two parts. First we consider just the phase lines "between" R and S. Here u and v are of like sign and behavior is very similar to that which follows from a first order difference equation. This is shown in Figure 10 by construction lines $A\ B\ C \ldots$ Here only one member of the family of phase lines is shown (heavy line). The positive roots case is explosive upward or downward while the negative

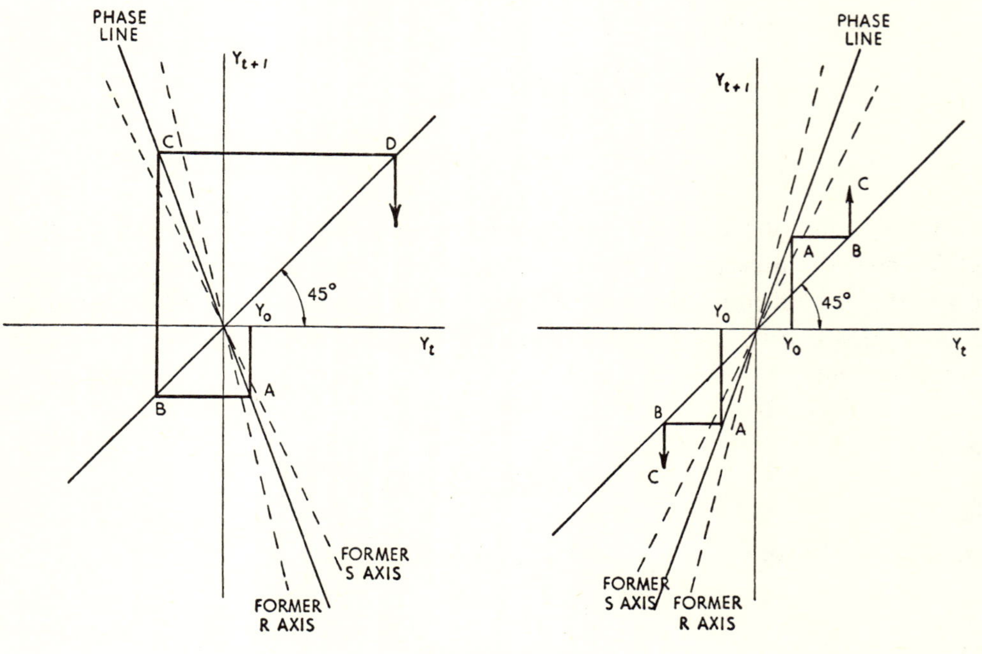

FIGURE 10

roots case involves explosive cobweb type cycles. This qualitatively unchanging behavior is to be expected because, as we have seen, we are dealing with the region where u and v, the constants in solution (4), are of the same sign so that both terms in the solution behave similarly and so their effects on the time path reinforce one another.

Next we can explore the portion of the phase lines outside the R and S lines. We show only a negative roots case. Consider as an illustration the time path given by the solution

$$Y_t = -4(-1.1)^t + (-2)^t$$

where $u = -4$, $v = 1$.

This yields the following table of values:

t	0	1	2	3	4
Y_t	—3.0	2.4	—0.8	—2.7	10.1
Y_{t+1}	2.4	—0.8	—2.7	10.1	—25.6

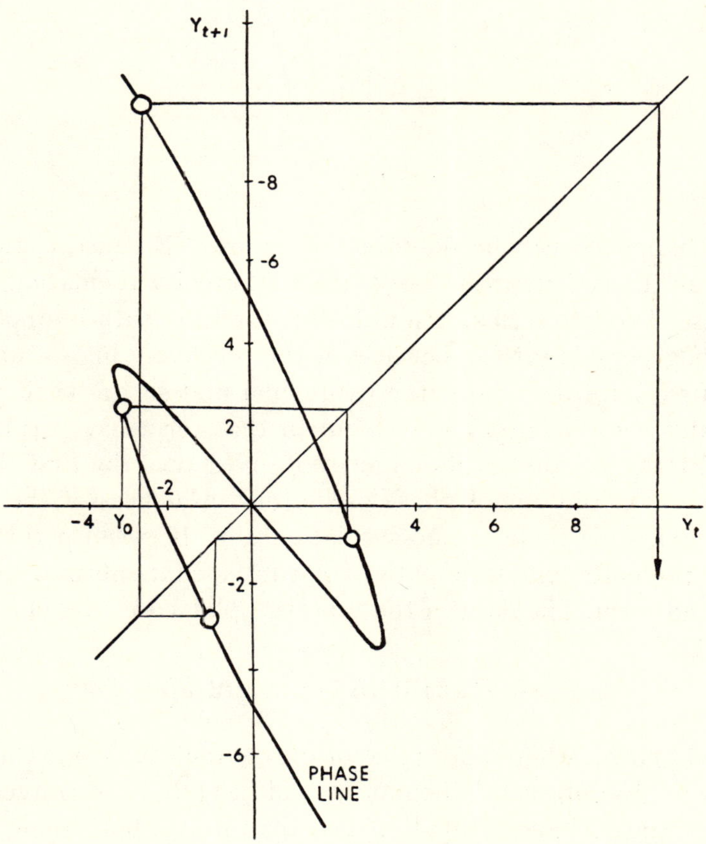

FIGURE 11

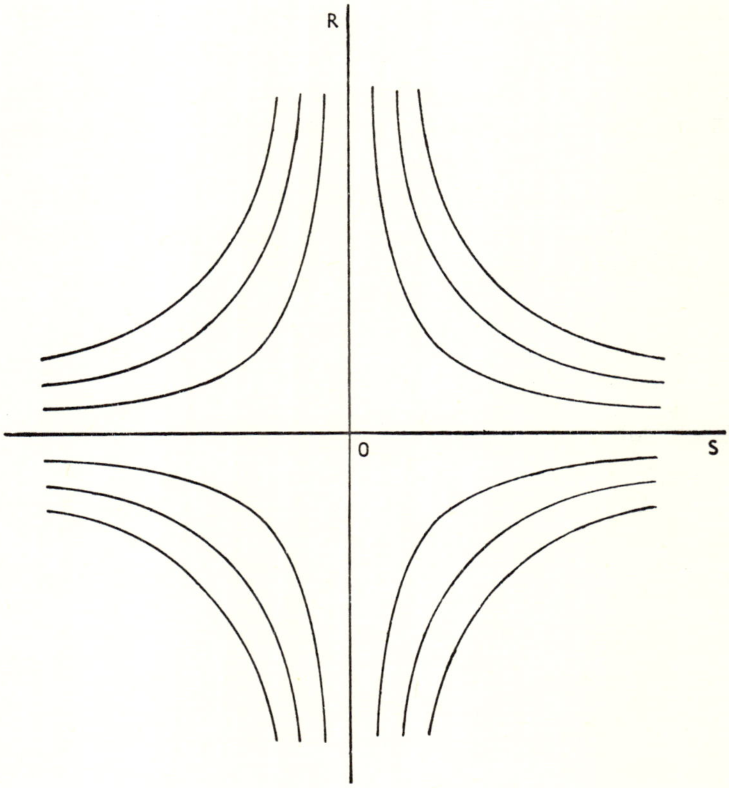

FIGURE 12

What has happened can be described as follows. Because u and v are of opposite sign the two terms in the solution (4) involve oscillations which are out of phase. The two terms then influence the time path in opposite directions. During periods 0 to 2, because of the relatively high absolute value of u, the first term dominates the expression and so the time path of (4) approximates the oscillatory movement of that term. By periods 3 and 4 the second term, because of its larger root, overtakes the first. In the process of transition the out of phase oscillatory influences of the two terms cancel out. There is therefore no oscillation of Y between periods two and three. But thereafter the time path of Y will be characterized by the cycle of the second term. The data in the table are plotted in the phase diagram of Figure 11.

The Phase Plane With Convergent Time Path

As is well known, where both roots of the characteristic equation are less than unity in absolute value the motion will be stable and converge toward equilibrium. Since X_1^2 and X_2^2 are both less than unity, both their logarithms will be negative and hence the exponent in (12) will again be positive. The

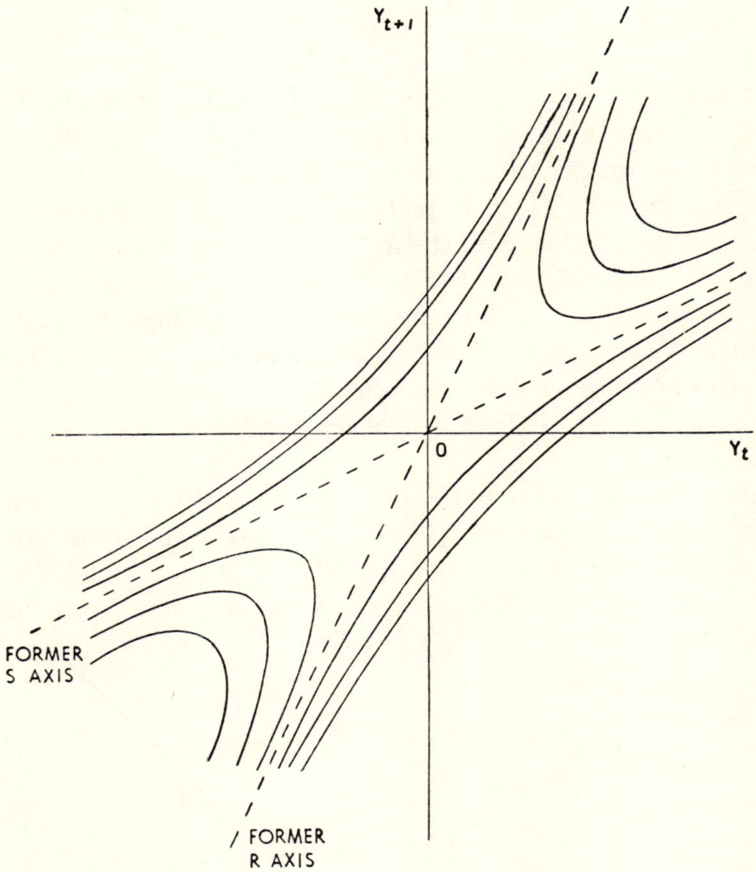

FIGURE 13

same analysis applies as in the case where both roots are greater than unity in absolute value. Only the slope of the transformed R and S lines in the phase plane will now be less than unity in absolute value with the S now steeper than the R.[13]

One Root Explosive, One Root Convergent

Where the roots are real but one is greater and one less than unity in absolute value the solution (12) still applies. It must be reinterpreted, however, because the exponent is now negative. If, for example, we take $X_1^2 < 1$ and $X_2^2 > 1$ then $\log X_1^2 < 0$ and $\log X_2^2 > 0$. The substitution (13) yields instead of (14), for appropriate choice of X_1 and X_2,

[13] This is because in (14) we require $a > 1$, where, by (12), $a = \log (X_2^2)/\log (X_1^2)$. With $X_1^2 < 1$ and $X_2^2 < 1$ both logs are negative and $a > 1$ implies $|\log (X_2^2)| > |\log (X_1^2)|$ which for such small X' s involves $X_2 < X_1$, where these are the respective slopes of the R and S lines by (13).

$$R = \pm KS^{-a}, \qquad a \geqslant 1$$

i.e.,

$$RS^{a} = \pm K.$$

This will be recognized at once as a family of quasi-rectangular hyperbolas as shown in Figure 12 where the curves in the northwest and southeast quadrants correspond to negative values of K. Again the transformation from the $R\,S$ plane into the Y_{t+1}, Y_t plane involves a rotation of the R and the S axes in accord with (13), with the R axis transformed into the line through the origin with slope X_2, etc. The result in the positive roots case is shown in Figure 13. Here the point of intersection of the $R\,S$ lines is called a "saddle point" and it is easy to see that the phase lines can be interpreted as contour lines of a three dimensional saddle point. One of the transformed axes (here taken to be the S axis) will have a slope less than unity and the other a slope greater than unity.

The interpretation of the phase lines in terms of the time path is again conveniently divisible into two parts, that between the transformed axes[14] and that outside these axes. Dealing with the latter first, we take two typical phase lines outside the R and S lines and get the time paths depicted in

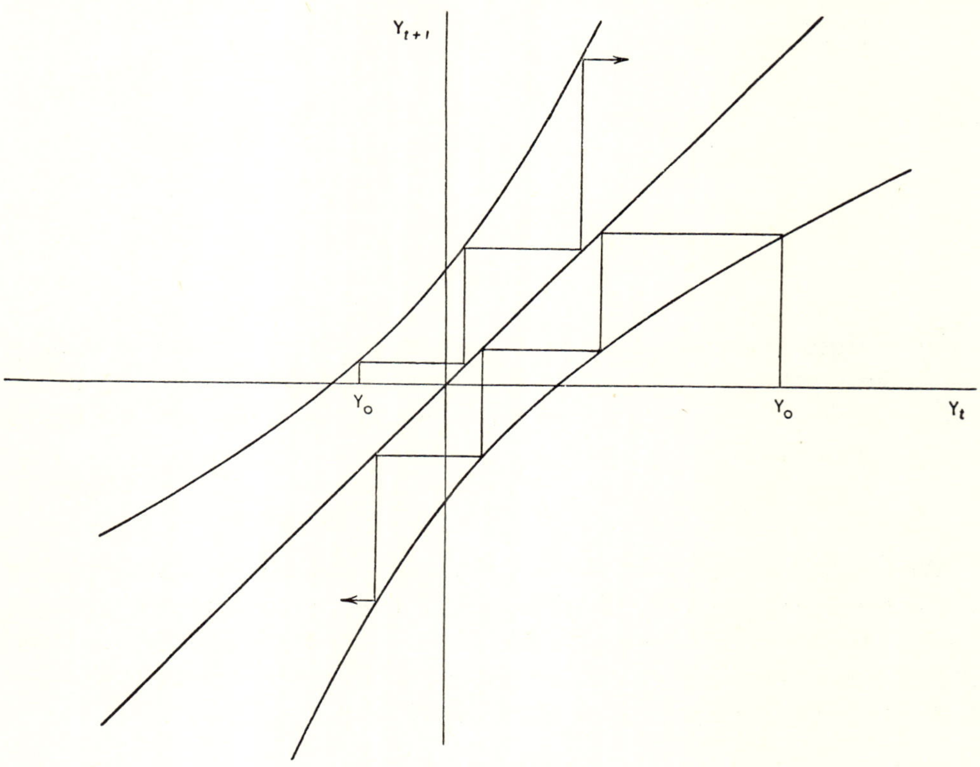

FIGURE 14

[14] We denote the area "between" the transformed axes as that which contains the 45° line.

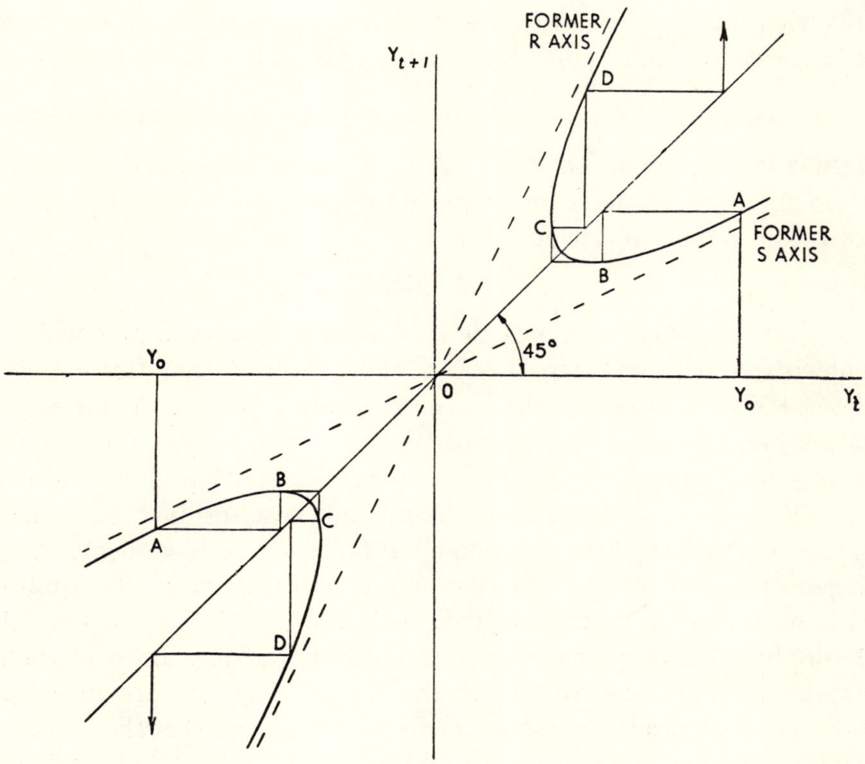

FIGURE 15

Figure 14. The phase line above the 45° line involves a time path which is uninterruptedly explosive upward, while the lower phase line dictates a downward explosion. It is easy to show from (17) by the methods previously employed that these phase lines involve arbitrary constants u and v of opposite sign in the solution (4). The time paths are of a variety which can be expected intuitively because if, e.g., $|X_1| < 1$ and $|X_2| > 1$, then X_1^t will be decreasing and X_2^t will be increasing in absolute value. If, however, these terms are given coefficients of opposite sign in solution (4) they will then be working in the same direction, in the one case upward, in the other downward and there is therefore no way in which the direction or nature of the movement can be reversed at any point.

Let us now consider the phase lines between the transformed axes and the corresponding time paths. These are shown in Figure 15. It is to be noted that the time paths $A\ B\ C\ D\ldots$ reverse themselves. They converge at first but then move outward again. Here the arbitrary constants of the solution are of like sign and the convergent movement represents the time during which the root of smaller absolute value dominates the time path. As we know the larger root will eventually swamp the rest of the solution and that is when the explosive movement occurs. We see then, as was expected, that in the saddle point case all movement ultimately becomes explosive.[15]

4. NON-HOMOGENEOUS EQUATIONS AND THE EQUILIBRIUM POINT

If the difference equation (3) has an equilibrium (stationary) solution, that solution obviously will have the property $Y_{t+1} = Y_t = Y_{t-1} = k$ (a constant). Substituting this in (3) yields

(18) $$k = ak + bk + c,$$

i.e., $k = c/(1-a-b)$. Thus, provided $1 - a - b \neq 0$, the equation will be consistent with a stationary state. It is a standard theorem that this equilibrium value k of Y is the same as the constant term, Z (the particular solution), in (4). Where equation (3) is homogeneous so that $c = 0$, the equilibrium value k is zero, so that the equilibrium point in the phase plane will involve $Y_{t+1} = Y_t = 0$, i.e., the origin will be the only equilibrium point.[16] This has been true of all the equations examined so far since we have dealt only with homogeneous cases. Where the equation is non-homogeneous, the equilibrium point is moved up from the origin to the point $Y_{t+1} = Y_t = k$ which lies on the 45° line. I shall show now that the entire phase diagram is at the same time shifted k units upward and to the right.[17] Thus the previous analysis applies unchanged to the non-homogeneous case except that the point which is a center, a focus, a node, or a saddle point will lie at (k,k) rather than at the origin and the rest of the graph will be moved correspondingly.

To prove this, apply the transformation

(19) $$Y_t = Y_t^* + k,$$

so that $Y_{t+1} = Y_{t+1}^* + k$, etc., to equation (3). This yields

$$Y_{t+1}^* + k - a(Y_t^* + k) - b(Y_{t-1}^* + k) = c,$$

i.e.,

$$Y_{t+1}^* - aY_t^* - bY_{t-1}^* + k - ak - bk = c,$$

or, by (18)

(20) $$Y_{t+1}^* = aY_t^* + bY_{t-1}^*.$$

(20) then is essentially the same as equation (3) with the non-homogeneous term equal to zero, that is, it is the homogeneous equation whose phase plane

[15] There is a trivial exception. The transformed S axis in Figure 15 is itself a phase line and movement along it clearly converges on the origin. Examination of (15) and (17) indicates that this is the case where there is a zero coefficient before the root of largest absolute value in the solution (4). For by (15) the slope of the transformed S axis ($R = 0$) is X_1, and therefore from the drawing in Figure 15 X_1 is the smaller root in absolute value. But the numerator of the expression for v in (17) is R (= 0).

[16] At any other point on the 45° line two consecutive values of Y will be the same but the next Y thereafter will be different.

[17] If k is negative this will, of course, mean moving downward and to the left.

representation has been described throughout this paper. To find the phase plane representation of the non-homogeneous equation we must then consider the effect of the transformation from Y^* to Y. This transformation (19) clearly involves the move k units to the right and k units upward which has already been discussed.

This representation can easily be extended to the more general case where the non-homogeneous part of the difference equation is a function of time $c(t)$ rather than a constant c. The particular solution, Z, in (4) is now a function of time, $k(t)$. Instead of a stationary equilibrium solution, the system now will usually permit only the moving equilibrium solution $Y(t) = k(t)$, which by substitution in (3) yields, instead of (18),

$$k(t+1) = ak(t) + bk(t-1) + c(t).$$

The rest of the argument of this section now follows. The center, node, or focus shifts from period to period, and not generally along the 45° line. At any date t that point will be given by $Y_{t+1} = k(t+1)$, $Y_t = k(t)$. The entire phase diagram shifts along with this point.

The time path followed by our variable can be traced out by employing for each date the appropriate phase diagram position, as shown in Figure 16.

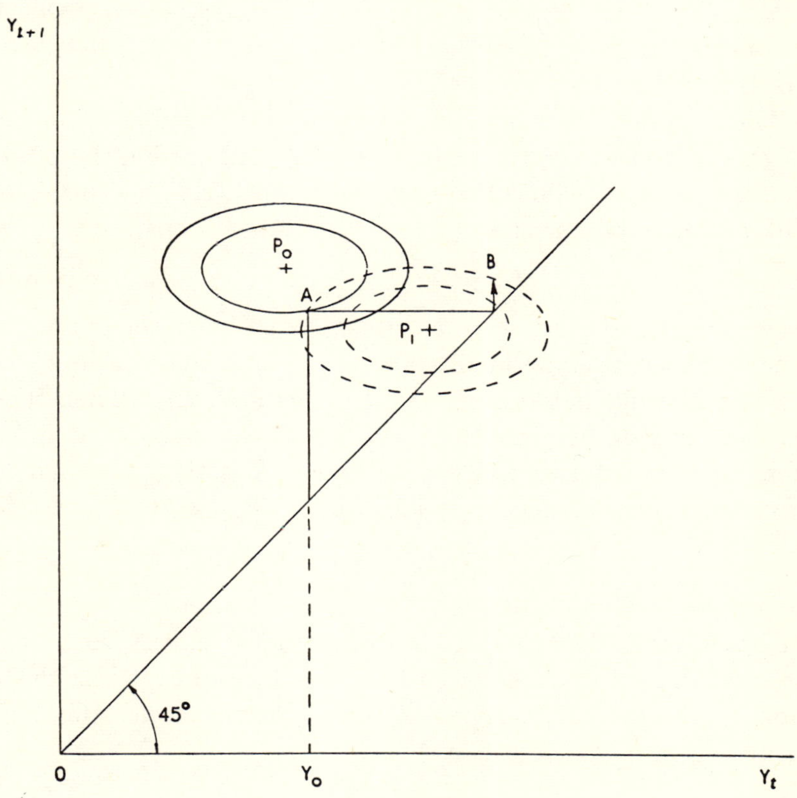

FIGURE 16

Here I depict the shift of only two of the ellipses in a family from period 0 (solid curves) to period 1 (dotted curves). The focus moves from P_0 to P_1 and the phase curves shift correspondingly. Suppose our initial point is A. Then the time path of Y will move to point B in the next period. Note that while A was a point on the inner curve in the previous period B does *not* lie on the transposed inner curve. Rather it lies on that transposed ellipse which also goes through the preceding point A (whose coordinates are the initial conditions generating B). In the case shown in the diagram this happens to be the outer curve. That is because it is the only curve which meets all three of the following conditions: (i) it satisfies the difference equation, (ii) its center lies at $Y_{t+1} = k(t+1)$, $Y_t = k(t)$, and (iii) its equation is satisfied by the initial conditions given by the coordinates of A.

It is obvious how the value of Y in succeeding periods in the variable non-homogeneous term case can be found in the same way. The diagrams are messy but the principle nevertheless remains simple.

5. ILLUSTRATIVE APPLICATION TO A NONLINEAR MODEL: HICKS' TRADE CYCLE

As Goodwin first pointed out, the Hicks' trade cycle model[18] is a second order *nonlinear* system. But it is of a simple variety since it consists of several connected linear segments, as I shall show in the simplified illustrative version of the model which follows.

In the Hicks model national income is, as usual, divided into consumption and investment (goods used by consumers and goods used in the production process). Also, as usual, Hicks takes the consumption, C_t, to be a fixed proportion of income in the previous period, Y_{t-1}, plus a constant:

$$(21) \qquad C_t = aY_{t-1} + b, \qquad a, b \text{ constants.}$$

However, the investment relationship will vary over the trade cycle. If we assume that there is an optimal economico-technological ratio, k, between capital stock, K_t, and national income (production), then when there is a down-turn in business activity there will be an excessive stock of capital. Equipment and inventories will not be replaced as they are used up and so net investment will be negative. This can be espressed by

$$(22) \qquad I_t = -w \qquad \text{for } K_{t-1} > kY_{t-1}$$

where w is a positive constant.

On the other hand when the capital stock is not in excess, as income rises investment will have to take place to keep the stock of capital at the desired proportion of income. This gives us the ordinary acceleration principle relationship

[18] J. R. Hicks, *The Trade Cycle*, Oxford University Press, New York, 1946.

(23) $$I_t = k(Y_{t-1} - Y_{t-2}) \qquad \text{for } K_{t-1} \leqslant kY_{t-1}.$$

Since, as already mentioned, income is divided into consumption and investment we have the usual identity

(24) $$Y_t = I_t + C_t.$$

Finally Hicks provides us with the restriction that real income must never exceed the full employment level

(25) $$Y_t \leqslant Y_e,$$

with equality holding whenever there is a computed value of Y greater than or equal to Y_e.

When there is excess capital, we have, substituting (21) and (22) into (24),

(26) $$Y_{t+1} = aY_t + b - w \qquad \text{for } K_{t-1} > kY_{t-1}.$$

This is a first order linear difference equation which is represented by the straight phase line RR' in Figure 17. Since its slope, a, the marginal propensity to consume, is presumably less than unity this line cuts the 45° line from above.

On the other hand when capital stock is not excessive, income is no longer given by (26). Instead, by (21), (23), and (24), we have

(27) $$Y_{t+1} = (a + k)Y_t - kY_{t-1} + b,$$

which is a second order linear equation with constant coefficients. Hicks assumes that it involves complex roots of modulus greater than unity, i.e., explosive cyclical movement.[19] Equation (27) will then be represented by

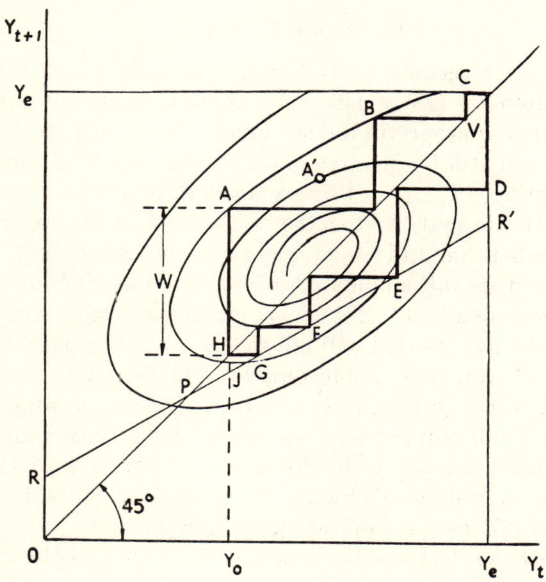

FIGURE 17

[19] *Ibid.*, pp. 91-94.

a family of spirals which move outward in a clockwise direction. These spirals are shown in Figure 17 only for the relevant range in which real income does not exceed its full employment level, Y_e.

We can now examine graphically the time path of real income. Let us begin with the upswing of the cycle when presumably capital stock is required to grow, so that (23) and hence (27) apply. We begin at some point A above the 45° line and move to B along an arc of the spiral representing (27). Finally at point C full employment income is attained. Now income can move no higher and stays in this position at most for two periods.[20] This is because investment will no longer be undertaken when income ceases to rise (equation (23)) so that the investment component in income (equation (24)) will suddenly drop to zero. By (21) and (24) income in the next period will be

$$Y_{t+1} = aY_e + b \tag{28}$$

(point D) which (unless a or b is very large[21]) will be less than the full employment income Y_e. Now, with the fall in income redundant capital will appear ($K_t > kY_t$) and in accord with (26) income will begin to move downward along RR'. Thus income will move down along the path EFG . . . toward "equilibrium point" P.[22] During this time, however, the capital stock K_t is reduced by an amount w per period. Thus income will keep falling until the capital which had been attained at full employment is cut down to size. This will occur s periods after the period e when full employment income had been attained, where s is the smallest integer for which

$$K_e - ws \leqq ky_e + s.$$

[20] When income first reaches its full employment level, Y_e the one period lag in investment postulated by (23) means that capital stock will not yet have reached the level kY_e which is appropriate for full employment output. Therefore investment in the next period will still be positive and (23) will still hold. Since income will just have risen by quantity $\Delta Y_{e-1} = VC$, investment demand in the next period will be given by $k\Delta Y_{e-1}$. If this quantity together with consumption demand, $aY_e + b$ add up to a quantity no smaller than full employment income, i.e., if $Y_e \leq aY_e + b + k\Delta Y_{e-1}$, income will remain at its full employment level one more period. On the other hand if induced investment demand, $k\Delta Y_{e-1}$, is insufficient to support a full employment output, income in the next period will fall to some intermediate level like that shown by point D in Fig. 17. But now this income level will not be given by (28). Instead it will be equal to $aY_e + b + k\Delta Y_{e-1}$. In practice, of course, our rigid assumptions must be modified. Then a full employment income may well last more than two periods because input shortages can delay the filling of investment orders so that it may take a long time before capital stock reaches its desired full employment level, kY_e, i.e., before (26) replaced (27) as the equation governing income.

[21] An a and b sufficiently large to cause trouble would imply an upward time path of national income even with zero investment!

[22] P is Hicks' lower national income equilibrium represented by line LL' in his Figure 12 (*ibid.*, p. 97).

Since the level of income cannot drop below the "equilibrium" level Y_b this means that this down-swing phase of the cycle will last at most until

$$K_e - ws \leqq kY_b,$$

i.e., for approximately

$$s = \frac{K_e - kY_b}{w}$$

periods. At the end of this time capital stocks will have been reduced to their desired level. Investment will therefore rise suddenly from $-w$ to 0. Provided that this rise in investment is greater than HJ, the fall in income which would otherwise have occurred in the next period (Figure 17), income will take a sudden jump since the negative investment component will have been eliminated. Income will rise perhaps (though not necessarily) to point A once more, and because income is increasing once again the time path will return to the spiral phase lines, to begin another cycle.

Before leaving this discussion several comments are appropriate.

1. There is some presumption that after the "second go round" every cycle will, in the absence of exogenous disturbances, be a precise duplicate of the cycle which preceded it, for income will always drop from the full employment level to the level of full employment consumption given by (28) (point D) so that we can take every cycle to start out from this point. Of course, if, as in the Hicks model and as has been the case historically, the full employment ceiling moves upward with the passage of time, this will no longer be true.

2. The graph shows how, as Hicks observes, some upswings may never reach the full employment ceiling. This will occur, for example, if the upswing begins at point A'.

3. In practice disinvestment doubtless declines gradually as capital stock approaches its desired level (so that w becomes a function $w(t - e)$ of the length of time elapsed since the last full employment period and, by (26), RR' will shift upward gradually).

4. The fall in disinvestment may never be large enough to produce an upturn, because it may never exceed HJ, the fall in income which would occur next period if disinvestment were to remain unchanged. In such a case we must depend on the Hicksian autonomous investment to produce an upturn. Autonomous investment will add another term $A(t)$ (where $A'(t) > 0$) to the investment functions (22) and (23). With the passage of time this investment will grow and shift RR' upward until some period T when the point on RR' with coordinates (Y_{T+1}, Y_T) lies above the 45° line and the upturn will then begin.

Princeton University

APPENDIX

Note 1. *The significance of the* 45° *line*

In the preceding discussion the 45° line has played a role analagous to that of the horizontal axis in the phase plane representation of differential equations. This is entirely a matter of convenience. Since we have been plotting Y_{t+1} against Y_t points above the 45° represent motion in the positive direction ($Y_{t+1} - Y_t > 0$). But had we instead drawn $\Delta Y_t = Y_{t+1} - Y_t$ on the vertical axis, thereby more closely following the differential equation procedure, all points above the horizontal axis would have represented increasing Y. In this way the 45° line would be divested of its special significance. The representation I have chosen, in accord with usage in the economic literature, is really more convenient in that it permits a simple construction to trace out the time path from one period to the next. With a ΔY_t axis it would be necessary to *add* this amount to Y_t at each step in order to obtain the value of Y for the next period. In effect, at each Y_t it would be necessary to draw a different 45° line from the horizontal axis in order to add ΔY_t to Y_t as shown in Figure 18.

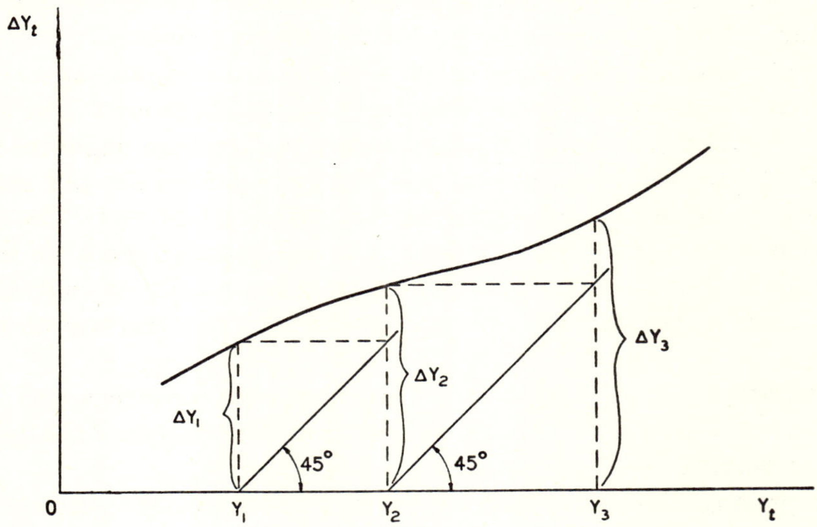

FIGURE 18

Note 2.

In differential equations it is possible to find the phase plane equation directly from the original equation as follows: The equation $\ddot{y} = a\dot{y} + by$ can be written $\dot{y} = x$, $\dot{x} = ax + by$, where $\dot{x} = dx/dt$, $\dot{y} = dy/dt$. Then $dx/dy = \dot{x}/\dot{y} = (ax + by)/x$. This is a first order homogeneous equation which can be integrated to yield the phase plane equation.

A similar procedure is not possible in the case of difference equations. We can rewrite $Y_{t+2} = aY_{t+1} + bY_t$ as $Y_{t+1} = X_t$, $X_{t+1} = aX_t + bY_t$ so that

$$\frac{\Delta X_t}{\Delta Y_t} = \frac{(a-1)X_t + bY_t}{X_t - Y_t}.$$

But we cannot interpret this as an approximation to dX_t/dY_t throughout the phase plane since, by definition, $\Delta Y_t \to 0$ only near the 45° line.

[18]

PITFALLS IN CONTRACYCLICAL POLICIES: SOME TOOLS AND RESULTS

William J. Baumol *

IT is not generally recognized by economists that where governmental contracyclical policies are concerned common sense is a particularly dangerous tool. Policies — automatic or not — which appear to be properly designed may very well turn out to aggravate fluctuations.[1] Miscalculations on delicate questions of timing or magnitudes can be crucial, and these matters may well be out of the range of competence of the good judgment and experience of most of the practical men who determine or advise on our monetary and fiscal policies.

This article describes tools which can be used to deal with at least some simple variants of these problems. Such tools can be particularly useful in indicating the nature of the pitfalls in the area. In particular, I will describe two rather plausible types of contracyclical fiscal policy and show that they can lead to some rather surprising results.

1. *The model and some contracyclical policies*. The discussion assumes that we are living in the world of the Samuelson accelerator-multiplier model.[2] It will be recalled that the time path of national income, Y_t, in that model is described by the second-order linear difference equation:

$$\begin{aligned} Y_t &= \text{consumption} + \text{acceleration investment} \\ &\qquad + \text{autonomous investment} \\ &\qquad + \text{net government outlay} \\ &= kY_{t-1} + c(Y_{t-1} - Y_{t-2}) + A + G_t \end{aligned}$$

where k is the marginal propensity to consume and c is the "relation" of the acceleration principle. In other words, we have:

$$Y_t - (k + c)Y_{t-1} + cY_{t-2} - A - G_t = 0 \quad (1)$$

or, writing $b = -(k + c)$,

$$Y_t + bY_{t-1} + cY_{t-2} - A - G_t = 0. \quad (2)$$

In employing this model I am, as is so often done, ignoring important monetary phenomena, such as changes in interest rates and the real balance effect. However, I do not believe that this materially affects my conclusions.

Let us now suppose that the government determines to regulate its net outlays, G_t, in a way which reduces the severity of the cycle in income generated by (2). Let us consider several possibilities.

a. *A policy to offset income trends*. Suppose the government decides to offset income trends by deficit spending ($G_t > 0$) when income has just been falling $[(Y_{t-1} - Y_{t-2}) < 0]$ and by collecting a budget surplus when income has been rising, and that the magnitude of this action is proportioned to the size of the change in income. This policy, which is designed to offset income trends,[3] is described algebraically by:

$$G_{t,1} = -a(Y_{t-1} - Y_{t-2}) \quad (3.1)$$

where a is a positive constant.[4]

Substituting from (3.1) into (2) and collecting terms we obtain:

$$Y_t + (b + a)Y_{t-1} + (c - a)Y_{t-2} - A = 0. \quad (2.1)$$

b. *A policy to adjust income levels*. Suppose the government determines always to compensate for the difference between effective demand, Y, and some desired (near full employment) level, E. That is, it seeks to move effective demand toward the full employment level.[5] If there is no lag in government response this yields:

$$G_{t,2} = w(E - Y_t) \quad (3.2)$$

* I should like to acknowledge my gratitude to Professor William G. Bowen for his helpful comments, and to the Ford Foundation, whose grant to my department helped in the completion of this paper.

[1] Several warnings on this problem have already appeared in the literature. See Milton Friedman, "The Effects of a Full-Employment Policy on Economic Stability: A Formal Analysis," *Essays in Positive Economics* (Chicago, 1953); and A. W. Phillips, "Stabilization Policy in a Closed Economy," *Economic Journal*, LXIV (June 1954). The extent of my debt to Professor Phillips' work should be perfectly clear. Also, as he has pointed out, engineers have long known about these dangers in automatic stabilization devices.

[2] P. A. Samuelson, "Interactions Between the Multiplier Analysis and the Principle of Acceleration," this REVIEW, XXI (May 1939), reprinted in American Economic Association, *Readings in Business Cycle Theory* (Philadelphia, 1944).

[3] Phillips (op. cit.) calls such a measure a "derivative policy," since net outlays are, in effect, based on dY/dt.

[4] This might, for obvious reasons, also be described as a counter accelerator policy.

[5] Phillips has called this a "proportionate policy."

where w is some positive constant. If there are one- and two-period delays in government reactions we have, respectively:

$$G_{t,3} = w(E - Y_{t-1}) \tag{3.3}$$

and

$$G_{t,4} = w(E - Y_{t-2}). \tag{3.4}$$

Substituting these expressions into (2), our basic income equation, we obtain respectively for the zero, one-period, and two-period lag cases:

$$Y_t + \left(\frac{b}{1+w}\right)Y_{t-1} + \left(\frac{c}{1+w}\right)Y_{t-2} - \frac{A + wE}{1+w} = 0 \tag{2.2}$$

$$Y_t + (b+w)Y_{t-1} + cY_{t-2} - A - wE = 0 \tag{2.3}$$

and

$$Y_t + bY_{t-1} + (c+w)Y_{t-2} - A - wE = 0. \tag{2.4}$$

It should be noted that equations (2.1)–(2.4) may be considered to approximate the much-discussed built-in stabilizers in our economy. For example, the fact that the government surplus tends automatically to rise (the deficit to fall) because tax payments as a proportion of income automatically go up when money incomes rise, and fall when money incomes decline, can be expressed by these relationships. Thus our analysis of (2.1)–(2.4) should shed some light on the contribution which these automatic stabilizers really make.

2. *Analytic tools: Iso-stability curves.* Let us now develop some tools to help us analyze the effects of these policies on the stability of our model's behavior.

In Chart 1 the axes represent the coefficients, b and c, of the difference equation:

$$Y_t + bY_{t-1} + cY_{t-2} + r = 0.$$

Ignoring the nonhomogeneous term, r, every such equation can thus be represented by some point in the diagram and vice versa.

As is shown in Appendix B, triangle UVW is the locus of all points representing difference equations whose characteristic root of largest absolute value is of modulus unity.[6] Hence, these are the equations on the borderline between damping and explosion, i.e., stability and instability. The smaller triangles nested within UVW represent equations with stable solutions; the smaller the triangle, the smaller the absolute value of its dominant root and hence the less explosive its time path. Similarly, the larger triangles outside UVW represent equations with unstable solutions; the larger the triangle, the larger the modulus of the dominant root.[7] These triangles, then, constitute the family of second-order difference equation iso-stability curves. It is clear that any change in the coefficients of a difference equation which is represented by a move in the direction of the origin must represent an increase in stability. In particular, stability must be increased by any leftward move inside the region bounded by the parabola SOS' (marked $b^2 = 4c$).

CHART 1

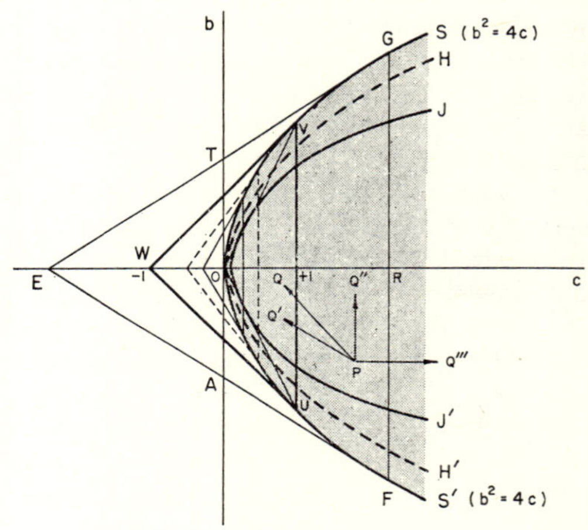

3. *Iso-frequency curves: Difference equations.* Parabola SOS' is the locus of all points which represent equations with multiple characteristic roots. All points inside this parabola involve complex roots and, hence, fluctuations. The family of iso-frequency curves, i.e., the loci of equations all of which yield a time path involving cycles of the same duration, must all lie within this shaded region. These iso-frequency curves are the parabolas such as HOH' and JOJ' which lie in this region. All of them are tangent to the b axis at the origin of the diagram, and

[6] In particular, UV represents complex root equations, WU represents equations with dominant unit root, and WV equations with dominant root $= -1$.

[7] Specifically, if triangle EFG is the locus of equations whose dominant root has modulus k, then we have $EO = OR = k^2$ and $AO = OT = k$.

they satisfy the equations $b^2 = 4k^2c$, where k is a number between zero and unity.[8]

In particular, the portion of the horizontal axis which lies to the right of the origin represents all equations whose cycles are four periods long. Points below the c axis represent cycles which are less frequent than this, up to the limiting case of lower arc OS' of the outermost parabola, $b^2 = 4c$. As we approach this arc the cycles become longer and longer, without limit, and their frequency approaches zero. Similarly, moving in the upward direction, we go toward arc OS and cycles whose length approaches two periods.[9]

In sum, any downward move within the shaded complex roots region reduces the frequency of cycles and is, in that sense, stabilizing.

4. *Evaluation of stabilization policies.* The preceding diagrams now permit a simple and quick analysis of the stabilization effects of the policies which were described in the first section.

First let us look at the trend-offsetting policy (3.1). For this purpose we compare (2.1), the income difference equation in the presence of such a policy, with equation (2), in which G is now taken to be a constant. We note that in (2) the first coefficient, $b = -(k+c)$, is negative, and the second coefficient, c, is positive. Hence this equation is represented by a point in the south east quadrant of Chart 1. I assume also that (2) generates a cyclical time path so that it must be represented by a point, say P, within the lower half of the area bounded by the parabola $b^2 = 4c$.

Now, in the equation (2.1), coefficient b has been increased to $(b+a)$, and c has been decreased to $(c-a)$.[10] This means, in terms of Chart 1, that the point representing our difference equation has moved upward and to the left by the same amount, a. It has moved from P to, say, Q. The leftward move is, as we have seen, definitely stabilizing; any such move must increase the rate of damping of the cycle. But the upward move is very likely[11] to involve an increase in frequency — that is, we are now likely to have more cycles in any given period of time than we would have in the absence of the trend-offsetting policy. Thus, such a measure may well turn out to be a mixed blessing.[12]

Let us see if our other policy alternative will do better. First comparing (2.2), our income equation in the case of a policy with zero lag in income adjustment, with the basic equation (2), we see that both b and c have been decreased in absolute value by the same proportion, $1/(1+w)$. That is, b will have been *increased* from its initial negative value whereas c will have fallen. The net result will thus be similar to that of the trend-offsetting policy, a north westward move in Chart 1 — increased damping but more frequent cycles. Only in this case, the unfortunate increase in cycle frequency will *always* result, despite the zero lag in government response![13]

In practice, of course, there are likely to be lags in government response to changes in economic data. As we shall now see, this is only likely to make things worse. Comparing (2.3) with (2) we see that a one-period lag in an income adjustment policy results in a rise in b to

[8] More specifically, if a cycle is of duration $2\pi/\theta$, we have $k = \cos\theta$.

[9] In the case of a difference equation it should be noted that a cycle less than two periods long is meaningless, since such an equation refers only to values of the variables at discrete points in time — one value per period — and since a cycle must have at least a high point and a low point, it must take on at least two such values, that is, it must occupy at least two time periods.

[10] This discussion ignores the effect of the various policy measures on the equilibrium income level via changes in the constant term of the equation. It is easy to add a constant amount of government expenditure to each of the policy equations to offset any effect on this constant term.

[11] The only possible exception is the case where the iso-frequency curve rises more sharply toward the left than does the vector PQ, whose slope is, of course, -1. This will only occur toward the extreme left of the shaded region. Specifically, since the equation of an iso-frequency curve is $b^2=4k^2c$, its slope is $db/dc = +kc^{-1/2}$, or, since $k = b/2c^{1/2}$, we have $db/dc = -b/2c$ which is less than unity only to the left of the lines $b = +2c$. This is the portion of the shaded region in Chart 1 to the left of lines OV and UO, the only region in which policy (3.1) does not increase the frequency of fluctuations.

[12] It will be noted that nothing is being said about the effect of these policies on the amplitude of the cycle in the short run. That is because this amplitude in a linear model is so much a matter of initial conditions. It is, at any rate, possible to show that the policies cannot be depended upon to reduce cycle amplitude except through their effects on dampening of oscillations. In the long run, of course, a more damped time path will eventually have a smaller amplitude.

[13] The effect will not be quite the same as that of the trend-offsetting policy because the move will no longer be represented by a line, PQ, of slope -1. Since both coordinates are reduced proportionately, in the present case the change will be represented by a vector, PQ', which is pointed directly toward the origin. We know in the present case that frequency will always be increased because the absolute value of the slope of vector PQ' is b/c while, as shown in footnote 11 above, that of the iso-frequency curves is $b/2c$.

$(b+w)$ and no change in c. There is thus a move due north from P to Q'' in the point representing our equation in Chart 2 — the policy

CHART 2

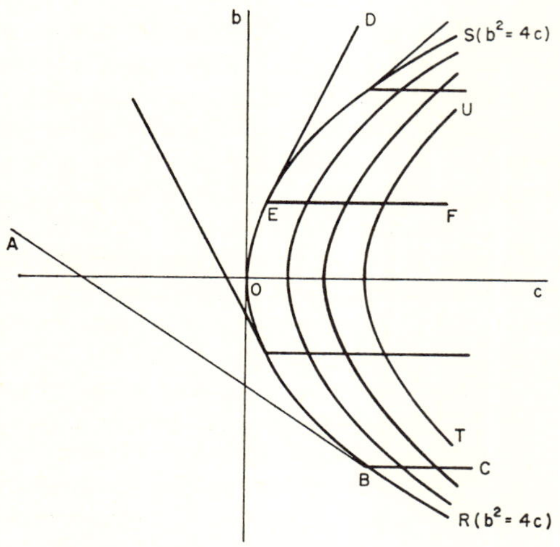

now serves only to increase frequency of fluctuations without any compensating increase in cycle damping such as accompanies the two measures which we examined previously!

A two-period lag can perhaps be considered as making things worse still. For it leaves b unchanged and *increases* c to $(c+w)$. The net result is a move directly to the right in Chart 1 from P to Q'''. There is an increase in explosiveness of the cycle and no change in frequency!

5. *Conclusion.* The results of this discussion may reasonably be considered somewhat frightening. Plausible and reasonable contracyclical policies turn out to be capable of increasing the explosiveness and frequency of economic fluctuations. In fact, none of the possibilities examined proved to be entirely harmless in these respects, even in the highly simplified world of the multiplier-accelerator model. There would, therefore, seem to be little ground for confidence in such measures in the far more complex and unpredictable world of reality.

This, of course, is not meant to imply that good automatic stabilizers cannot be invented.[14] The relatively crude model and blunt tools of this article can be of little help in designing such policies, but it is certainly easy to argue, in principle, that effective stabilizers can be found. What the analysis does show clearly is that the design of an automatic stabilization policy is a dangerous game which requires careful calculation and testing. Certainly it is not a game for amateurs, not even those whose mathematical skill is considerable or those whose good common sense and workaday knowledge of monetary and fiscal institutions has in so many other ways been invaluable to the community.

[14] But common sense remains a dangerous ally. In the present model, for example, a good stabilization policy is one which has effects opposite from those of (3.4), i.e., it moves us directly leftward from a point like Q''' in the direction of P in Chart 1. But such a policy $[G_t = -w(E - Y_{t-2})]$ calls for a government deficit exactly two periods after every inflationary occurrence (and the reverse in the wake of periods of depression) no matter what the length of the cycle, and even if the inflationary pressure has not yet disappeared!

APPENDIX A. ISO-STABILITY CURVES: DIFFERENTIAL EQUATIONS

A diagram analogous to Chart 1 can also be drawn for differential equations. In Chart 2 the angled straight lines such as ABC or DEF are the iso-frequency curves of second-order linear differential equations with constant coefficients, $y + b\frac{dy}{dt} + c\frac{d^2y}{dt^2} + r = 0$. That is, any such curve is the locus of all points representing equations the real portion of whose larger root has a given fixed value. In particular, the upper and right-hand segments of the axes, boc, constitute the locus of equations whose dominant root is zero, i.e., those which are on the borderline between stability and instability. Higher iso-stability curves, such as DEF, represent stable equations; lower curves, such as ABC, involve instability; and the higher the curve the greater its stability.[15]

Iso-frequency curves: Differential equations. Finally, the iso-frequency curves of differential equations are the parabolas such as RS and TU

[15] The horizontal segments of these curves (such as BC or EF) are of height $-k$ where k is the value of the dominant root. The sloping segments of these iso-stability curves (e.g., AB or ED) have slope $-1/k$ and the corners (the points of intersection such as B and E of the sloping with the horizontal segments) all lie on the parabola $b^2 = 4c$.

in Chart 2. These are all identical with the parabola $b^2 = 4c$ (*RS* in Chart 2) except that they are shifted to the right. The curve which represents a cycle of length $2\pi/k$ is shifted k^2 units to the right from *RS*. Hence, the further to the right such a parabola lies, the shorter, and thus more frequent, will be the cycles which it involves. It follows that moves toward the left must decrease the frequency of cycles, and will, in this sense, be stabilizing.

APPENDIX B. DERIVATION OF THE ISO-STABILITY LOCI

1. *Iso-maximal root loci*: second-order linear difference and differential equations.

A. *Real Roots.*

(1) *A General equation.* Let r_1 and r_2 be the roots of the characteristic equation:

$$x^2+bx+c=0. \text{ Set } r_1=k,\ r_2=\begin{cases}k-\epsilon \text{ for } k>0\\ k+\epsilon \text{ for } k<0\end{cases} \quad \text{(i)}$$

then

$$b = -(r_1+r_2) = -2k \pm \epsilon,\ c = r_1r_2 = k^2 \mp k\epsilon. \quad \text{(ii)}$$

Thus, eliminating ϵ, we have the equation of the straight line iso root $(r_1 = k)$ locus:

$$c = k^2-k(b+2k) = k^2-bk-2k^2 = -k^2-bk$$

or

$$b = -k-\frac{c}{k}. \quad \text{(iii)}$$

The intercepts of the equation are obtained by noting that

when $b = 0, c = -k^2$ and when $c = 0, b = -k$. (iv)

(2) *Difference equations.* Let r_1 be the root of largest absolute value. We must therefore have:

$$0 \leqq \epsilon \leqq 2|k|$$

because then and only then is r_1 the dominant root. Specifically, at the end points of this interval, if $\epsilon = 0$, $r_1 = r_2 = k$; and if $\epsilon = 2|k|$, $r_2 = (k-2k) = -k = -r_1$. Hence, by (ii), the iso-maximal root locus (iii) has the end points

$$c = k^2,\ b = -2k \quad \text{(v)}$$

and

$$c = -k^2,\ b = 0. \quad \text{(vi)}$$

To summarize, the iso-maximal root locus consists of two straight line segments, (iii). For $k > 0$ this has negative slope $-1/k$, and the end point (v) lies below the c axis. Similarly, for $k < 0$ it has a positive slope, and end point (v) lies above the c axis. The two segments meet on the c axis at point (vi).

(3) *Differential equations.* Let r_1 be the larger root. Then $\epsilon \geqq 0$ in $r^2 = k - \epsilon$ and the lowest point on the iso-maximal root locus (iii) is given by (vi).

If $r_1 > 0$ the line (iii) has the negative slope $-1/k$, while if $r_1 < 0$ this slope is positive.

(4) *Comment.* Points (v) lie on the parabola $b^2 = 4c$ since these are the cases $\epsilon = 0$, so that $r_1 = r_2$ (double roots).[16] Moreover at these points (iii) is tangent to that parabola, whose slope is $db/dc = 1/\sqrt{c} = 1/k$.

B. *Complex Roots.*

(1) *Difference equations.* Let the complex roots be $(v+wi)$ and $(v-wi)$ whose absolute value is $k = \sqrt{v^2+w^2}$. Then we have $c = (v+wi)(v-wi) = v^2+w^2 = k^2$ as the equation of the iso-maximal root locus. This is the vertical line which joins (iii) at points (v).

(2) *Differential equations.* The real part, k, of the complex root $-b/2 \pm i\sqrt{(4c-b^2)}/2$ is $-b/2$. Hence the locus equation is $b = -2k$. This is the horizontal line which joins (iii) at point (v).

2. *Iso-frequency loci.* Let r_1 and r_2 be the complex conjugate roots $-b/2 \pm i\sqrt{(4c-b^2)}/2 = v \pm ki$.

A. *Differential equations.* The solution is $ae^ve^{kit} + be^ve^{-kit} = e^v(c \cos kt + u \sin kt)$. This has period $(2\pi)/k$ or frequency $k/(2\pi)$. Thus an iso-frequency curve has the equation $k = \sqrt{(4c - b^2)}/2$ or $b^2 - 4c = -4k^2$, i.e., $b^2 = 4(c - k^2)$.

B. *Difference equations.* The solution is $R^t(c' \cos \theta t + u' \sin \theta t) = y(t)$ where $\cos \theta = v/\sqrt{v^2+w^2}$. By appropriate choice of the

[16] Also direct proof: If $c = k^2$, and $b = -2k$, then $b^2 = 4k^2$ and $4c = 4k^2$.

constants c' and u' we can take[17] $0 \leq \theta \leq \pi$. Then θ is a single valued function of $\cos\theta$. But $\cos\theta$ $= v/\sqrt{v^2+w^2} = -\frac{b}{2}/\sqrt{\frac{b^2}{4}+c-\frac{b^2}{4}} = -\frac{b}{2}/\sqrt{c}$ where we always take the absolute value of the complex root, $\sqrt{v^2+w^2}=\sqrt{c}$ to be positive. Hence an iso-frequency curve has the equation $-b/2\sqrt{c}=k$ or

$$b^2 = 4k^2c. \qquad \text{(vii)}$$

This is a family of parabolas all lying within the half plane $c \geq 0$, and symmetric about the c axis. Since $k = \cos\theta \leq 1$ the outermost parabola is the borderline of the complex region $b^2 = 4c$. For $k = 0$ the parabola degenerates into the non-negative portion of the c axis.

For $b \leq 0$ we have $\cos\theta = -b/2\sqrt{c} \geq 0$ so that $0 \leq \theta \leq \pi/2$; cycles will be at least $\frac{2\pi}{\pi/2} = 4$ periods long. For $b > 0$ the cycles will be less than four periods long. Hence the branch of a parabola (vii) which lies below the c axis is a different iso-frequency curve from that which lies above that axis. In particular, the lower branch of the outer parabola $b^2 = 4c$ is the case $\cos\theta = 1$ or $\theta = 0$, that is, of "cycles of infinite duration." The in-between case $b = 0$ (the c axis degenerate parabola) is $k = \cos\theta = 0$ or $\theta = \pi/2$: the four-period cycle. Finally, the upper branch of the outer parabola $b^2 = 4c$ involves cycles of two period duration.

[17] For if θ lies outside this interval we can set $\theta = m\pi + Q$ where m is some (positive or negative) integer and $0 < Q < \pi$. Then we have

$$y(t) = R^t[c' \cos(m\pi t + Qt) + u' \sin(m\pi t + Qt)]$$
$$= R^t[c' \cos m\pi t \cos Qt - c' \sin m\pi t \sin Qt + u' \cos m\pi t \sin Qt + u' \sin m\pi t \cos Qt]$$

and since $\sin m\pi t = 0$, $\cos m\pi t = (-1)^{mt}$

$$y(t) = R^t[(-1)^{mt} c' \cos Qt + (-1)^{mt} u' \sin Qt]$$

which differs at most by a factor of (-1) from the original solution in θ.

[19]

The Dynamics of Urban Problems and its Policy Implications[1]

W.J. Baumol

Sisyphus, King of Corinth, was repaid by the gods for his wickedness in life by a punishment that has fascinated observers from Homer to Camus. In the lower world he was forced to roll a large rock uphill; as soon as it neared the top the rock always rolled back down again.

Martin Nolan, 'A Belated Effort to Save our Cities'. The Reporter, Dec. 28 1967, Vol. 37 No. 11, p.16.

1 POLICY IMPLICATIONS OF A CUMULATIVE PROCESS

Among students of the subject it has for some time been recognised that a number of cumulative processes serve to compound the problems of the city; perhaps these dynamic relationships constitute the critical component of those difficulties.[2] For example, it is well known that urban deterioration and the exodus of the middle classes feed upon one another – the more rapid the migration to the suburbs the more quickly does the process of decay in the central city proceed, and vice-versa, each of those processes serving to stimulate and speed up the other. What has not generally been understood, however, is the policy implication of such a dynamic process. In fields such as engineering, which have long dealt with relationships of this variety, it is well known

1. I would like to thank the Ford Foundation and the Brookings Institution whose sponsorship of our project 'The Self-Sustaining City' facilitated greatly the completion of this paper. But above all I want to indicate my gratitude to the editors of this volume for another opportunity to express my deep admiration and affection for Lord Robbins, to whom I owe so much as a teacher and a friend. The paper, as a piece of theoretical reasoning applied to an economic issue of the utmost urgency, follows, I believe, the spirit of his teaching as much as anything I have written. Furthermore, it brings me back to the area of economic dynamics, a field in which Lord Robbins first aroused my interest more than twenty years ago.

2. See, e.g., Vernon, Raymond *The Myth and Reality of Our Urban Problems*, Cambridge, MIT-Harvard Joint Center for Urban Studies, 1962.

that malfunction in the system must often be treated by means which have no simple intuitive explanation, and that measures which seem appropriate in terms of common sense sometimes are shown by rigorous analysis to aggravate the problem, or, at best, to treat only its symptoms.

Precisely these complications arise out of the cumulative process which affects the cities. The intricacy of the relationships means that policy approaches, which seem on the basis of informed judgement to promise to come to grips with the problem, may or may not in fact turn out to do so. One simply cannot be sure, without a far more careful analysis, whether the measures that have been tried or proposed will in fact help the community toward a long-run improvement in its circumstances. It may even turn out that most of these policies are incapable of producing any significant long-run effects or that some of them can be absolutely harmful.

To illustrate the point, consider the cumulative problem of public transportation schedules – fewer passengers lead to a reduction in the frequency of departure, which in turn drives away still more passengers and so leads to a still poorer level of train service etc., etc. The most obvious policy measure in such a situation is a subsidy to the transportation authority to permit it to run more trains than it would otherwise find feasible financially. Suppose it is permitted to run ten trains a day more than it would otherwise have operated, and that in the absence of the subsidy the average number of trains run per day would have exhibited the following time pattern:

As a matter of fact, such cumulative processes and their consequences for the prosperity of individual localities have been recognised much earlier. For example, one finds them considered in writings on the local rate reforms in Great Britain in 1928 and 1929. Thus, in her discussion of these changes Lady Hicks writes, 'This disparity between the financial resources of districts has the disadvantage that since rates can be interlocally shifted, it tends to be cumulative . . . . Rates may be shifted by residential removal or by industrial removal . . . . This tends, moreover, to be concentrated on the better-paid workers, who can afford to move elsewhere and who are the most useful ratepayers. Those who remain are too often changed from an asset to a liability. In the meantime the high rates, or the fear of them, act as a deterrent to other entrepreneurs . . . This is an important aspect of the depressed-area problem.' Hicks, Ursula *The Finance of British Government, 1920-1936,* 1938, pp. 158-9. See also Plummer, Alfred 'The Reform of Local Taxation in Great Britain', *The Quarterly Journal of Economics,* Vol. XLIII, August 1929. I am grateful to my colleague Professor Lewis for pointing this discussion out to me.

year	1967	1968	1969	1970	1971
No. of trains	30	25	22	20	19 etc.

It can be shown that in the absence of a change in the underlying dynamics, the addition of the ten trains, say, in 1970 may well lead to the following time path

year	1967	1968	1969	1970	1971	1972	1973	1974
No. of trains	30	25	22	30	25	22	20	19 etc.

That is, the additional trains have served to postpone by three years the process of deterioration in train service, but they have not come to grips with the underlying problem nor have they improved the ultimate state of extremely poor service toward which the system is headed.

A physical analogy should suggest the nature of the problem. Consider a ball rolling down a child's slide in a playground, in which the bottom of the slide has been blocked off so that the ball will not fall to the ground. If one wishes to raise the height of the point at which the ball will utlimately come to rest it does no good to stop the ball in mid-passage and push it a few feet back up the slide. For while that will temporarily raise the position of the ball it does not affect the underlying dynamics of the arrangements. To achieve the true objective of this game – the raising of the final location of the ball – one must find ways to increase the level of the slide itself, and no amount of adjustment of the position of the ball can have that effect. The analogy to the train case should be clear – the addition of a few trains to a deteriorating schedule is like an upward push on the ball which moves it temporarily back up the slide. What is not so clear is the analogue of the low point on the slide and the means that can be used to raise it, in the case of the train schedule, or in the case of progressive urban deterioration.

To get at these parameters we must have recourse to a bit of mathematics, characterising the deterioration process in terms of an elementary mathematical model. Before turning to this model it should be emphasised that it is so oversimplified that its conclusions cannot pretend to offer any direct guidance to policy. Rather its policy implication is largely negative – it is intended to show that even in so simple a dynamic situation the formulation of appropriate policy measures is extremely difficult, and plausibility considerations constitute an extremely unreliable guide.

Turning now to our model, let us this time deal for variety of illustration with the dynamic process characterising the inter-relationship between per-capita income of urban residents, Y_t, *and* the state of deterioration of the city, D_t, however measured. Here we have a double relationship.

First, there is the fact that increased deterioration drives out wealthier residents and so lowers per-capita income, so that if the relationship is linear we have

$$Y_t = r - s\,D_t \qquad s > 0, \tag{1}$$

i.e., the greater the level of deterioration in period t the lower will be the per-capita income of the persons willing to remain in the city.

Second, we have the relationship in the reverse direction: a reduction in current income leads to further deterioration soon after the current emigration of wealthier inhabitants, so that in a simple linear case

$$D_t = u - v\,Y_{t-1} \qquad v > 0, \tag{2}$$

i.e. a reduction in yesterday's per-capita income (income in period $t-1$) leads to a higher level of deterioration today (period t).

Substituting from the second equation into the first we eliminate the variable D_t from the relationships and obtain the following first-order difference equation in the variable Y_t alone:

$$Y_t = r - su + sv\,Y_{t-1}. \tag{3}$$

This equation obviously determines completely the characteristics of the dynamic process – the future history of per-capita income in our city. To show this we represent this equation graphically in the standard difference equation diagram. Since it is a linear equation its graph will be a straight line, call it the time relationship line, RR' in Figure 1.

The time path of income is then found by following the path *ABCDF*... which, in the diagram, moves steadily toward the equilibrium

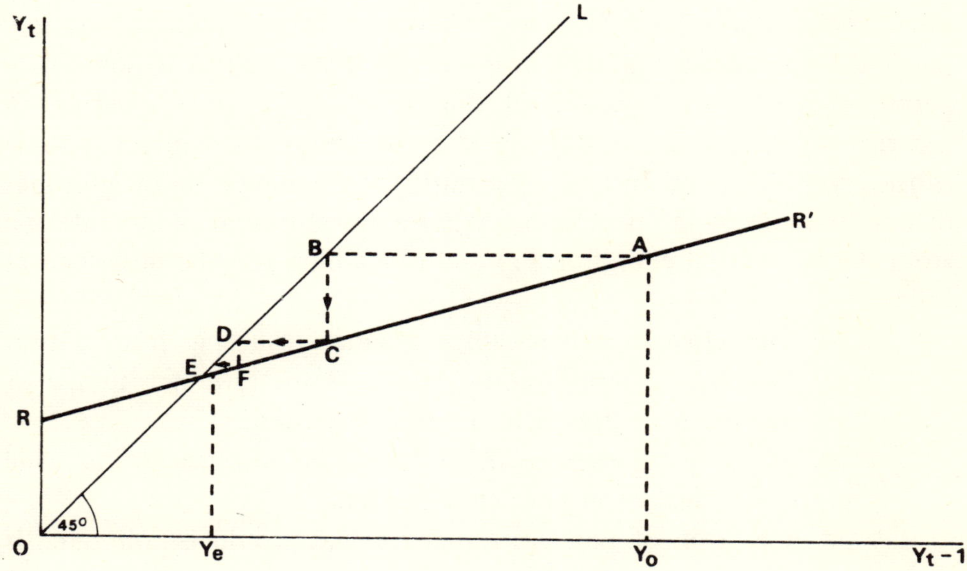

Figure 1

point, E, the point where the time relationship line RR' crosses the 45° line.

Now it will be noted that a supplement to per-capita income (or for that matter some slum clearance) which serves to offset to some extent the process of deterioration is, in effect, a backward move along the time path, say, from F back to A. It is like the uphill push on the ball on the slide in our earlier example, and it need have no long-run effect on the time path *because it has not changed the position of the time relationship line RR′ or that of the equilibrium point E.*

To see what is necessary to change the equilibrium point we must return to our basic equation (3). We note that at the equilibrium point, since it is on the 45° line, we must have $Y_t = Y_{t-1}$ so that we may call this equilibrium income, Y_e and write simply $Y_e = Y_{t-1}$. Thus from our equation (3)

$$Y_e = r - su + sv\, Y_e$$

or solving for Y_e

$$Y_e = (r - su)/(1 - sv).$$

Thus the co-ordinates of the equilibrium point depend entirely on the magnitudes of the four parameters, *s, v, r,* and *u,* and are entirely unaffected by D_t and Y_t, the magnitudes of our variables at any particular dates. The implication is clear – if we wish to do something about Y_e, the equilibrium level toward which the city's per-capita income is heading, an outlay on slum clearance or a direct income subsidy will not help. Instead, one must try to change the magnitudes of one or more of the parameters, whose interpretation can be inferred from the two initial equations (1) and (2), which may be described as follows:

s = The change in per-capita income resulting from a unit increase in deterioration, i.e. it is the rate of response of income to a change in urban living conditions,

v = The rate of increase in deterioration resulting from a one dollar decline in per-capita income,

r = The level of per-capita income that would be obtained if the city were totally unblighted,

u = The maximal rate of deterioration (with zero per-capita income).

Of course, since this oversimple model is hardly realistic, its policy implications should be treated with strong reservations. Yet even this model is sufficient to bring out the basic point that the magnitudes of the preceding parameters are not directly related to D_t and Y_t themselves. That is, if one does something to decrease blight or raise per-capita income, by itself this may have no effect on the long-run (low level) equilibrium point toward which the city is headed[3] In addition, and perhaps more important, it should be observed that *s, v, u,* and *r* are parameters whose magnitudes may not easily be subject to

3. While the effects of such once-and-for-all change will certainly be transitory in our present model, the practical implications of this result do require qualification. An influence that is transitory may nevertheless produce substantantial consequences that are felt for a considerable period of time. A measure whose influence is marked for several decades is not permanent in its effects; yet for practical purposes this may not matter. In formal terms, the full solution to our basic equation (3) is

$$Y_t = (Y_o - Y_e)(sv)^t + Y_e$$

where Y_o may be taken to be the current level of income and Y_t is the corresponding figure *t* years in the future. If a once-and-for-all outlay increases *Y* by $\triangle Y$, then *t* years in the future demand will still be increased by $Y\triangle(sv)^t$, an increase which will be negligible only if *t* is very large or if *s* and *v* are very small.

change. Certainly the haphazard pouring of money into a metropolitan area may have little effect on their values.[4] Thus, while this simple model cannot pretend to offer any specific basis for policy proposals, it does show that improvement of the long-run prospects of an urban community may require a set of approaches far more subtle and more carefully planned than had previously been imagined.

2 IMPLICATION OF NONLINEARITY

The argument to this point has assumed that the relationships are linear. Of course, there is no reason why this should be so in fact. There may here be operating, for example, some sort of diminishing returns whereby at a low level of per-capita income a relatively small increase in income attracts back to the city a substantial number of middle class families, but after some point one runs into the hard core of suburbanites so that there is a decline in the migration response to further income rises. In such a case the slope of the RR' curve decreases as one moves to the right. It might also be that at very low levels of per-capita income the response rate (slope of RR') is very small because some minimum level of average per-capita income is required before any substantial number of suburbanites are even willing to consider a return to the city. These remarks are, of course, not intended to imply that the empirical relationships do assume such shapes; the discussion is only intended to suggest how nonlinearities might arise, and to indicate the relationship between the slope of the RR' curve and the underlying economic facts.

In any event, under the conditions postulated, the RR' curve would assume the general shape depicted in Figure 2, though its relation to the 45° line need not be of the variety shown.

Now, in the situation illustrated in the graph there is a radical change from the linear case in the policy implications of the dynamic model. The position of the initial point, Y_O is no longer irrelevant to the location of the equilibrium position, and a once-and-for-all subsidy to

4. Here, however, we must distinguish a permanent subsidy from a once-and-for-all governmental investment (or one which is intended to last for a very limited number of years). A permanent subsidy which is designed to keep deterioration below what it would otherwise have been must produce a fall in the intercept of the equation (2), i.e., it must produce a decline in *u*.

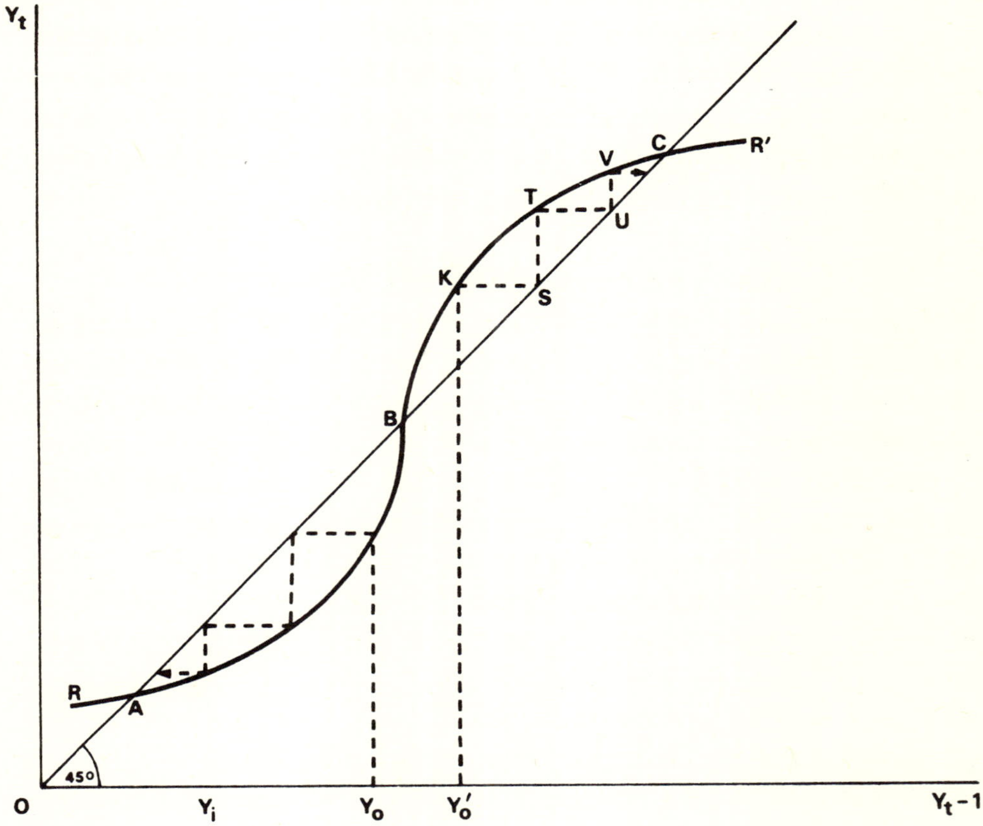

Figure 2

income (or a once-and-for-all programme of urban renewal), *provided it is of sufficient magnitude,* is capable of reversing the process.

This is very easily shown. It will be observed that in Figure 2 RR' has three points of intersection with the 45° line. However only two of these, A and C, are stable equilibria. From any starting point such as Y_O which lies between B and A the direction of movement will be downward toward lower equilibrium point A. There is no formal difference between this segment of the diagram and the relationships depicted in Figure 1

However, if a once-and-for-all income subsidy succeeds in pushing income beyond what we may consider the turning point B, say to point Y'_0 the situation changes completely. Now per-capita income growth begins to take care of itself and the time path, *KSTUV*, moves steadily upward toward point C. It will approach C asymptotically and, in the absence of exogenous shocks, will continue to rise forever.

In such circumstances, then, slum clearance, urban renewal and income subsidies may be the most effective policy measures but they will work only if they are sufficient in magnitude. For example, an increase in per-capita income from Y_i to Y_o will produce effects just as transitory as they would be in the linear case.

In any event, the conclusions derived from the nonlinear model of Figure 2 must be used with extreme caution. First, it is by no means true that *any* type of nonlinearity provides to the initial value of Y_o the means to reverse the dynamic process. Figure 3 shows several nonlinear time relationship curves with which no amount of manipulation of the initial income levels can reverse the dynamic process toward a higher equilibrium level.

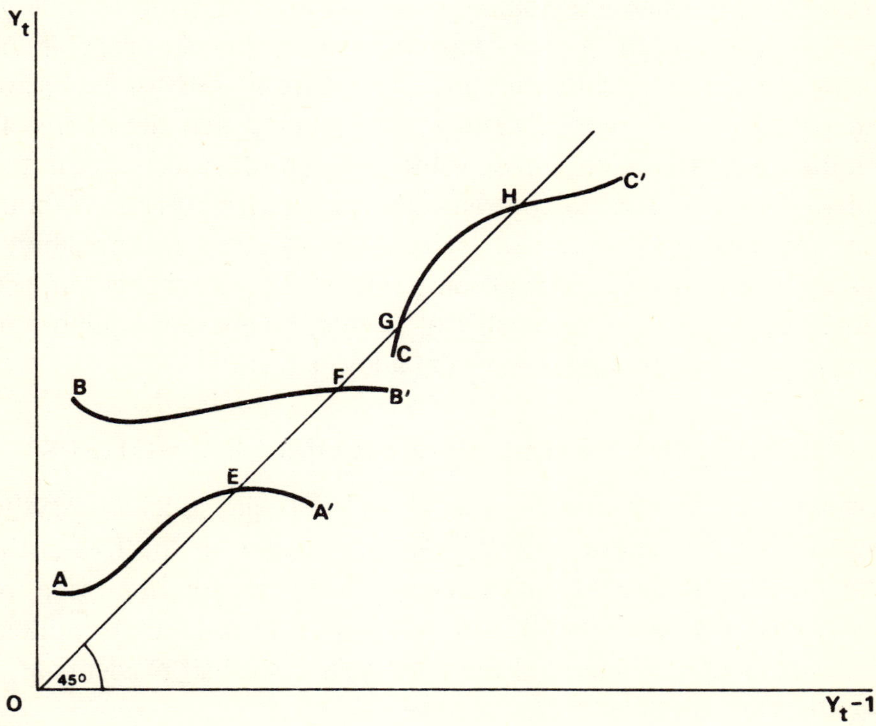

Figure 3

Since where the curves AA' and BB cross the 45° line their slopes are positive but less than unity, points E and F on these respective curves are stable equilibrium points whose qualitative implications are precisely the same as those of equilibrium point E in the linear case represented in Figure 1. And the multiple intersection point case represented by CC' involves an unstable intersection point G which cannot serve to raise income above that corresponding to the stable equilibrium point, H. Note also that AA' is very similar in shape to RR' in Figure 2 – thus, it is only the special position of RR' relative to the 45° line that accounts in the Figure 2 case for the power of a once-and-for-all change in the value of the variable to reverse the direction of movement. It follows that evidence of nonlinearity in the relevant relationships is not an adequate basis on which to justify the conventional approaches to urban problems. Only in the presence of the right sort of nonlinearity in the right position does an increase of expenditure on urban renewal offer any hope of a reversal in the dynamic process. It would clearly require very powerful evidence on whose basis we would undertake a careful estimation of the shapes of the relevant functions before one could conclude with any degree of conviction that the relevant nonlinearities were of the requisite variety.

In any event, even if the conventional means are capable of producing the desired results they may be far from the least expensive way to go about it. It must always be remembered that the nonlinear case requires a critical minimum expenditure to produce a change in the dependent variable sufficient to reverse the cumulative process. Without explicit investigation one cannot legitimately rule out the possibility that a shift in the time relationship curve, i.e. a change in the magnitude of its parameters capable of raising the relevant equilibrium point, may not provide similar results at a lower cost.

3 TOWARD SOMEWHAT MORE COMPLEX MODELS

It is easy to indicate directions in which our basic model can readily be expanded. For example, one can take cognisance of the role of the suburbs in the population movements. Suppose for the sake of simplicity that the total middle class population in some metropolitan area is fixed at level M and is divided between its urban residents M_{ut} and its suburban inhabitants M_{st}, so that

$$M_{st} + M_{ut} = M. \tag{4}$$

Suppose, moreover, that as in (1) the state of deterioration varies inversely (and linearly) with the number of urban inhabitants that belong to the middle class:

$$D_t = a_o - a_1 M_{ut}. \tag{5}$$

The Dynamics of Urban Problems and its Policy Implications

However, the suburbs after some point tend to become crowded so that some measure of crowding, C_t, varies directly with the number of suburban residents:

$$C_t = b_o + b_1 M_{st}. \tag{6}$$

Finally, suppose the number of middle class urban residents in the next period varies inversely with the current level of urban deterioration and directly with the current level of suburban crowding

$$M_{ut+1} = c_o - C_1 D_t + c_2 C_t. \tag{7}$$

We have by direct substitution of (5) and (6) into (7)

$$M_{ut+1} = (c_o - c_1 a_o + c_2 b_o) + c_1 a_1 M_{ut} + c_2 b_1 M_{st}$$

so that since $M_{st} = M - M_{ut}$

$$M_{ut+1} = (c_o - c_1 a_o + c_2 b_o + c_2 b_1 M) + (c_1 a_1 - c_2 b_1) M_{ut} \tag{8}$$

which is a linear different equation of the same form as (3),

$$M_{ut+1} = k_o + k_1 M_{ut}.$$

The analysis can be complicated further, to include a lower income population which divides itself between the city and some rural area.[5] Here we might take P_{rt} and P_{ut} to represent the number of persons in this group in the two areas. We may postulate, for example, that this group expands at an autonomously determined growth rate so that

$$P_{rt} + P_{ut} = P + kr^t. \tag{9}$$

In addition, in such a model instead of (5) one might have an urban deterioration function which varies inversely with M_{ut} and directly with P_{ut} so that

$$D_t = a_o - a_1 M_{ut} + a_2 P_{ut}. \tag{10}$$

Finally, in this model the number of poor in the city in period $t + 1$

may, for example, be taken to vary directly with the number of rural poor in period t and inversely with the number of urban poor in period t, i.e

$$P_{ut+1} = w_o - w_1 P_{ut} + w_2 P_{rt}. \tag{11}$$

Our model is now composed of equations (4), (6), (7), (9), (10) and (11) which can be collapsed into a two variable difference equation system consisting of the following two linear equations:

$$M_{ut+1} = (c_o - c_1 a_o + c_2 b_o + c_2 b_1 M) + (c_1 a_1 - c_2 b_1) M_{ut} - c_1 a_2 P_{ut}$$

$$P_{ut+1} = (w_o + w_2 P) - (w_1 - w_2) P_{ut} + w_2 k r^t. \tag{12}$$

It should be obvious that the model can easily be complicated further and that elements such as taxes, transportation, crowding and a variety of other relevant phenomena can easily be built into it. Our basic objective, however, is not to exhibit a number of increasingly complex models for their own sake. What is important is their policy implication.

It is well known that qualitatively there is absolutely no difference between the solution to a more involved linear system such as (12) and the rudimentary systems depicted in Figures 1 and 2. It follows that the addition of complexity is unlikely to change the basic policy conclusions of our analysis.[5]

4 CONCLUDING COMMENTS

Our analysis has been intended primarily as a means to convey a number of warnings:

1) That in a cumulative deterioration process such as that which characterises our cities, we can have no confidence without detailed

5. This suggests strongly the analogy between such formal models of the urban dynamic process and the mathematical models of ecology which depict the relationships of various biological species and the dynamic process resulting from their competition for available food supplies, etc. For an early and fascinating study in this area see Volterra, Vito, *Leçons sur la théorie mathématique de la lutte pour la vie,* 1931.

knowledge of the relevant functional relations that *any* long term effects can be achieved by the most obvious policy measures such as urban renewal projects, *no matter how large their scale.*

2) Even in cases where such programmes can effect a long-run improvement in the basic situation, they must still be sufficiently large in scale or their effects are still likely to prove entirely transitory.

3) Even where such programmes are capable of producing the desired results there is no *a priori* reason to presume that these direct approaches are the cheapest or most effective way to go about the matter.

This discussion also shows dramatically how a rather abstract analysis based on only limited empirical information can provide results relevant to pressing matters of policy by pointing out booby traps that are hardly obvious to the unaided investigator.

But while the basic model does serve the purpose for which it is intended, the questioning of facile policy proposals and apparently obvious approaches to difficult social issues, it does not quite so easily provide a set of reasonable alternatives. On its face the model is a vast oversimplification. one on which one would hesitate to base important decisions.

Perhaps even more important, it may not grapple with the right problem. As Arrow has pointed out so forcefully, in the area under discussion it is all too easy to pursue plausible objectives which in fact have little to do with the really important issues.[6] It does not help the urban poor if the middle classes are brought back to the city by a process that simply drives the impoverished further back into their ghettos. Nor is it clear that preservation of the cities is an appropriate objective if this can be achieved only at the expense of its inhabitants.

Obviously much more must be done before we can begin to provide

6. See Arrow, Kenneth J. 'Economic Criteria for Urban Renewal', (mimeographed), RAND Workshop on Urban Problems, Paper No. 14.

a model that captures these and the other economic problems. But even if our models are not yet ready to offer usable answers we have seen that they can be employed to expose the weakness in allegedly practical measures whose plausibility only serves to render them more dangerous.

PART THREE

MATHEMATICAL PROGRAMMING

[20]

Econometrica, Vol. 28, 3 (July 1960)

INTEGER PROGRAMMING AND PRICING

BY RALPH E. GOMORY AND WILLIAM J. BAUMOL

In this article Gomory's method of solution of integer linear programming problems is described briefly (with an example of the method of solution). The bulk of the paper is devoted to a discussion of the dual prices and their relationship to the marginal yields of scarce indivisible resources and their efficient allocation.

1. INTRODUCTION

IT HAS been known for some time that a method of solution of the general linear programming problem in which the variables are required to take integer values would also permit the solution of a considerable variety of other problems many of which are not obviously related to it.[1] For example, Markowitz and Manne [**13**] have shown that the difficult concave (nonlinear) programming problem (e.g., a cost minimization problem in which the total cost function is shaped like a hill) can, at least in principle, be approximated as an integer program which permits the determination of a global, and not just a local minimum. Nonconvex feasible regions can also, at least in principle, be handled by integer programming. Among the economic problems which are related to integer programming are the travelling salesman problem and problems in which fixed (inescapable) costs are present. A surprisingly wide range of problems including diophantine problems and the four color map problem[2] can be given an integer programming formulation. Some of these applications will be described in greater detail in section five of this paper.

Recently one of the authors of this article developed a method, which he calls the method of integer forms (MIF), for solving integer programming problems. In the next section the method of solution will be described in some detail. No proof that the algorithm arrives at the optimal integer solution in a finite number of steps will be described since it is rather lengthy and is being published elsewhere (see Gomory [**6**] and [**7**]. For an alternative approach see Land and Doig [**12**]).

The bulk of the paper, however, will be devoted to a discussion of the pricing problem in the integer programming case, that is, in the case where,

[1] For an excellent survey of the applications of integer programming see Dantzig [**3**].

[2] Integer programming methods have not succeeded either in confirming or rejecting such conjectures as the four color hypothesis. Rather, the technique permits the solution of individual problems *when solutions exist.* Thus, for any specific map, *if there exists a solution* to the four color map problem, integer programming can be used to find a solution, i.e., to assign four colors among the different territories in such a way that no two territories with the same color have a common boundary.

in economic terms, the inputs and outputs are "lumpy" (not perfectly divisible). We shall show that the MIF algorithm produces a dual problem whose solution also imputes shadow prices to the scarce inputs. These prices possess a number of the properties of the dual prices of ordinary linear programming. In particular, they possess one of the most important properties of ordinary dual prices—*they permit the construction of a decentralized decision making arrangement which, in principle, will achieve some of the possible efficient allocations of resources*. We shall see, however, that the price system no longer suffices to achieve *every* efficient allocation, and that, when the consumer side of the market is taken into account, the entire ideal output theorem of perfect competition runs into difficulties. These integer dual prices also possess a number of peculiar features. First, they will themselves be integers. Second, they are to some extent arbitrary and will vary with the procedure by which they are computed. Third, they will tend to impute a zero price to a number of resources to which the economist will want to assign a higher value. Fourth, the dual price of a resource will not always be equal to its marginal revenue product, and, in fact, the marginal revenue product of an input itself becomes a somewhat ambiguous concept.

Before actually describing the method of integer forms it seems worthwhile to state the result it produces, a result very similar to the one produced by the ordinary simplex method.

In the ordinary simplex method, starting with the integer inequalities in n original variables x_j

$$(1.1) \qquad \sum_{j=1}^{n} a^*_{i,j} x_j \leq Q_i \qquad (i = 1, \ldots, m,\ a^*_{i,j} \text{ integers})$$

and an objective function

$$z = a^*_{o,o} + \sum_{j=1}^{n} a^*_{o,j} (-x_j) \qquad (a^*_{o,j} \text{ integers}),$$

one introduces slack variables x'_i, one for each inequality, converting them into equations

$$(1.2) \qquad x'_i = a^*_{i,o} + \sum_{j=1}^{n} a^*_{i,j} (-x_j) \qquad (i = 1, \ldots, m)\ ,$$

where the $a^*_{i,o}$ are the Q_i of (1.1).

In the usual language of linear programming the x'_i in (1.2) are the "basic" variables, the x_j are the "non-basic" ones. In the simplex method one tries out in succession different sets of basic and non-basic variables, each time changing one variable from "basic" to "non-basic" and vice versa. Every such interchange of two variables is referred to as a "pivot step" of the simplex method. After a series of such steps (1.2) becomes (1.3)

$$(1.3)\quad \begin{cases} z = a_{o,o} + \sum_{j=1}^{n} a_{o,j}(-t_j)\,, \\ t'_i = a_{i,o} + \sum_{j=1}^{n} a_{i,j}\,(-t_j) \qquad (i = 1, \ldots, m)\,, \end{cases}$$

where the t'_i are the current basic variables and the $a_{i,j}$ are the coefficients used to express them in terms of the current non-basic ones, the t_j. The simplex method guarantees that eventually we can reach an expression (1.3) in which all the $a_{i,o}$, $i = 1, \ldots, m$, are nonnegative and also all the $a_{o,j}$, $j = 1, \ldots, n$, are nonnegative.

At this point we have obtained an optimal solution, for in order to maximize z all the non-basic variables (the t_j) must then be set equal to zero since every nonzero t_j must involve some subtraction from z (first equation in (1.3)). Each basic variable t'_i must now be equal to the appropriate $a_{i,o}$ since all other terms in the equations drop out. This, then, is the solution to the programming problem where it will be noted that, since all $a_{i,o}$ are nonnegative, all variables automatically get nonnegative values, as required. The $a_{o,j}$ also have economic significance, for, as will be noted later in this paper, they are the shadow prices of the dual problem.

In the method of integer forms one proceeds exactly as in the simplex method, only from time to time certain new variables and inequalities, which will be described presently, are added to the problem. The result is again a final set of equations

$$(1.4)\quad \begin{cases} z = a_{o,o} + \sum_{j=1}^{n} a_{o,j}(-t_j)\,, \\ t'_i = a_{i,o} + \sum_{j=1}^{n} a_{i,j}(-t_j) \qquad (i = 1, \ldots, m')\,, \end{cases}$$

with the $a_{i,o}$ and $a_{o,j}$ (except possibly $a_{o,o}$) nonnegative, and again the solution to the linear programming problem is obtained by setting $t'_i = a_{i,o}$. But this time there is a different number of equations, m', (where $m \leq m' \leq m + n$). These involve m' basic variables t'_i all of which were present in the original equations. There are still only n non-basic variables, t_j. However, while some of these are variables may appear in the original equations, others may be new variables added during the course of the computation. The essential point is that now *all the* $a_{i,j}$ *are integers*. Thus the solution is in integers.

2. THE METHOD OF SOLUTION

A geometric picture of the integer programming problem will give the reader an intuitive grasp of the method of solution. In Figure 1 we represent the feasible region, $OABCD$, of an ordinary linear programming problem. The dots within this region represent all feasible points both of whose coordinates are integers (the integer lattice points). The solution to the ordinary programming problem will occur on the boundary of the feasible region and in the diagram none of the boundary (other than the origin) goes through an integer lattice point. Suppose, however, that the feasible

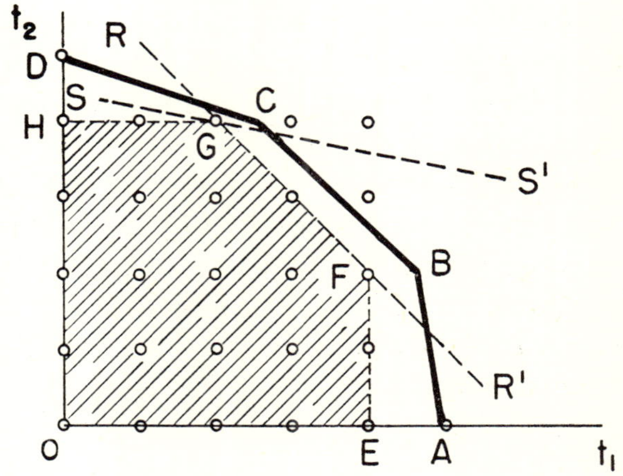

FIGURE 1

region could somehow be shrunk to the convex hull of the feasible lattice points (the shaded region). It is to be noted that this, too, would be the diagram of a linear programming problem—in fact, of the original problem modified by the addition of several supplementary linear constraints such as RR'. This new programming problem has two other important features: (1) it includes every integer feasible solution to the original program and (2) every basic (corner) solution of the new problem is an integer solution, for the boundary of the convex hull consists of linear segments which join lattice points. It follows at once that a (basic) optimal solution to the new programming problem must be an optimal integer solution to the original problem.

In practice it is difficult to cut the feasible region down to the convex hull of the feasible integer lattice points. The MIF method of solution does consist of a sequence of steps involving the addition of constraints to the original linear program and the subsequent solution of this expanded linear program. These constraints are chosen in a way which gives them the following properties: (1) they normally reduce the feasible region; (2) their graph (e.g., SS') ordinarily goes through at least one lattice point (point G in the figure) but it must be emphasized that *this lattice point need not lie in the feasible region*; (3) they never exclude from the new feasible region a lattice point which was originally feasible; and (4) they produce, in a finite number of steps, a new linear program whose solution is in integers and which is therefore the optimal integer solution of the original programming problem (if any such solution exists). It is to be noted that the feasible region of this final programming problem will include *OEFGH*, the convex hull of the feasible lattice points, and will itself be included in the original feasible region, *OABCD*. In this diagram it is clear that, with a suitable objective function, an optimal integer solution will occur, e.g., at point *G* at the intersection of the additional constraint lines *RR'* and *SS'*.

It remains now to describe the construction of these additional constraints. Consider any equation that occurs in the course of the solution of the problem which we write as

$$t_i' = a_{i,o} + \sum_{j=1}^{n} a_{i,j}(-t_j) \qquad (i = 0, \ldots, n) \tag{2.1}$$

in which we happen to have $a_{i,j} \geq 0$ for $j = 0, \ldots, n$. (Slack variables have been included in the set of variables t where necessary so that each constraint is an equation.) For later reference note that (2.1) *may be the objective (profit) function* $z = a_{o,o} + \Sigma a_{o,j}\ (-t_j)$, where z is the variable whose value is to be maximized (total profit). In other words, (2.1) need not be a constraint equation. For reasons which will later be emphasized, the t_i' are the current basic variables and the t_j are the current nonbasic variables.

Write $a_{i,o} = k + f_{i,o}$ where k is an integer and $0 \leq f_{i,o} < 1$. Inserting this in (2.1) and rearranging we have

$$\Sigma a_{i,j}t_j = f_{i,o} + k - t_i' . \tag{2.1a}$$

Since the $a_{i,j}$ are assumed ≥ 0, and the t_j are required to be nonnegative, the left hand side in (2.1a) must be a *nonnegative* number. The left hand side, however, differs from $f_{i,o}$ only by the integer $k - t_i'$. So the left side can only be one of the nonnegative numbers $f_{i,o}$, $1 + f_{i,o}$, $2 + f_{i,o}$, . . ., etc.

In every case

$$\Sigma a_{i,j}t_j \geq f_{i,o} \tag{2.2}$$

an additional inequality which must clearly be satisfied by any nonnegative integer solution to our original problem.

Further, since we require the t_j to be integers, any change in the $a_{i,j}$ by an integer amount to, say, $a^*_{i,j}$, where $a^*_{i,j}$ is also nonnegative, produces another valid inequality such as(2.2). For such a change in $a_{i,j}$ must change $a_{i,j}t_j$ and hence $\Sigma\, a_{i,j}t_j$ by an integer amount, so that $a_{i,o} + \Sigma\, a^*_{i,j}\,(-t_j)$ must still be an integer, call it t^*_i. Repeating our reasoning with t^*_i replacing t_i' and the $a^*_{i,j}$ replacing the $a_{i,j}$ we obtain

$$f_{i,o} \leq \Sigma_j\, a^*_{i,j}t_j\,, \qquad a^*_{i,j} \geq 0\,. \tag{2.3}$$

The strongest possible inequality which can be obtained by this process is clearly

$$(2.4) \qquad f_{i,o} \leq \sum_{j=1}^{n} f_{i,j} t_j \,, \qquad \text{all } f_{i,j} \geq 0 \,,$$

where the $f_{i,j}$ are the fractional parts of the $a_{i,j}$ in (2.2).

Note further that while in (2.1) we assumed $a_{i,j} \geq 0$ this restriction is unnecessary for the derivation of inequalities (2.4). For if in some original constraint we have, say, $a_{i,k} < 0$, since t_k is required to be an integer, we can *increase* the $a_{i,k}$ by some integral amount to obtain $a^*_{i,k} \geq 0$ and so, repeating this procedure for all other negative coefficients, we end up with an inequality of form (2.3) from which we can again obtain (2.4). These inequalities (2.4) or the corresponding equations

$$(2.5) \qquad s_i = -f_{i,o} - \Sigma f_{i,j}(-t_j) \,, \qquad s_i \geq 0, \text{ all } f_{i,j} \geq 0 \,,$$

where s_i is a slack variable, are the additional restrictions (corresponding to the equations of lines such as SS' in Figure 1) that are employed in solving the integer programming problem. Other restrictions can be obtained by adding together two or more equations or integer multiples of equations and then deducing a new restriction from the new combined equation. The class of possible restrictions is discussed in [**6**] where these restrictions are shown to form a finite group under certain simple rules of combination.

Several characteristics of (2.5) are to be noted: (1) s_i is itself required to be an integer for it is the of k—t' term of (2.1a); (2) if the optimal solution of the original programming problem contains any noninteger values it will not satisfy (2.5) so that (2.5) normally excludes some of the original feasible region;[3] (3) by the nature of its construction any feasible integer solution of the original programming problem will satisfy (2.5) so none of the original feasible lattice points is excluded by (2.5); finally, (2.4) is usually satisfied as an equality by some (not necessarily feasible) lattice point (so that here $s_i = 0$ in (2.5)).[4]

[3] For whenever the constants, $a_{i,o}$, in (2.1) are nonnegative, the solution obtained by setting all the non-basic t_j equal to zero is a feasible one. However, setting all t_j equal to zero in (2.4) violates that inequality except in the case $f_{i,o} = 0$. If any solution is noninteger so that $f_{i,o} \neq 0$, the formerly feasible point in which $t_j = 0$, all j, is thus excluded by the new inequality (2.4).

This also shows that constraint (2.5) normally cuts off some of the "top" of the feasible region in Figure 1 (SS' cuts out optimal point C) despite the direction of the inequality in (2.4) which seems to make it cut off a bottom piece. The explanation is that Figure 1 and (2.4) are expressed in terms of different variables. The t's in the figure are all in the current basis and hence, usually, positive while the variables on the R.H.S. of (2.4) are all initially nonbasic so that no constraint can decrease their (zero) values any further.

[4] For suppose all the f's in (2.5) are rational. Then that equation may be rewritten as $s_i' = F_{i,o} - \Sigma F_{i,j}\ (-t_j)$ where all the $F_{i,j}$ are integers. The greatest common

The algorithm for solving an integer programming problem is then: *step* 1, solve the original problem; *step* 2, if the solution is noninteger add any additional constraint (2.5); *step* 3, repeat this process until an integer solution (if any exists) is obtained. It should be noted that some of the additional constraints will become redundant and can be dropped so that no more than n additional constraints will ever be required at any one time.

It is also important from the practical point of view to realize that the sucessive reoptimizations usually require only a few steps.[5]

It will be noted that at any intermediate stage of this process there will usually be a number of possible constraints of the form (2.5). Any one of them can be used.[6] The solution process may be hastened, however, if in some sense the inequality (2.5) is chosen so as to make some sort of average $f_{i,o}/f_{i,j}$ as large as possible. The reason for this is most easily seen geometrically. In terms of Figure 1, our objective is to choose (2.5) is such a way that its associated graph SS' cuts off as much as possible of the "redundant" feasible region (the unshaded portion of the original feasible region). But at the old optimal point, C, all of the t_j in (2.5) were zero, i.e., this constraint is expressed in terms of the old *non*-basic variables. In other words, to move as far as possible from point C we require these formerly zero t_j to be *increased* as much as they can be. That is, we wish the hyperplane in these t_j obtained by setting $s_i = 0$ in equation (2.5) to be as far from the origin in their subspace as is possible. But $f_{i,o}/f_{i,j}$ is the nonzero coordinate of this plane on the t_j axis, so that by making these fractions as large as possible we bring this plane as far as we can from the origin.

In the illustrative computation below we shall employ only the roughest

divisor, G, of the $F_{i,j}$ $i \neq 0$, can be represented as an integer combination of these numbers so that we have $G = -\sum F_{i,j}\,(-t'_j)$ with the t'_j integers. If the $F_{i,j}$ have no common divisor we obtain $G = 1$ so that multiplying through by the integer $F_{i,o}$ and writing $t^* = t'F_{i,o}$ we have the integer solution $F'_{i,o} = -\sum F_{i,j}\,(-\overset{*}{t_j})$ for which s'_i and hence $s_i = 0$.

5 This is because the problem, before the additional constraint has been added, has been brought into optimal form, i.e., it is both primal feasible (all $a_{i,o} \geq 0$, $i \neq 0$) and dual feasible (all $a_{o,j} \geq 0$, $j \neq 0$) (see Section 6, below). After the constraint is added it is still dual feasible, and only one $a_{i,o}$, the $-f_{i,o}$, added is negative, consequently, using the dual simplex method, the problem can usually be brought back to optimal form quite rapidly.

6 The proof that the process terminates in a finite number of steps given in [**6**] actually requires that new inequalities be chosen by a certain rule. The proof can easily be extended so that the rule need be followed only once every p steps, p a fixed integer, and a free choice made the rest of the time. In actual computations so far what has been done was to choose a large f_o as described above. Some recent computations indicate, however, that the finiteness rule may have to be followed on larger problems.

approximation to this ideal by choosing that inequality (2.5) for which $f_{i,o}$ is as large as possible.

3. THE DUAL PRICES AND MARGINAL VALUATION

The solution to the integer programming problem which has just been described involves the solution to an ordinary linear programming problem which is identical with the original program except for the addition of several (at most n) "artificial" constraints. For convenience we may refer to this new program as the *augmented linear program*. Clearly, as to any linear program, there is a dual program which corresponds to this augmented program. Moreover, if the augmented program has a solution, i.e., if the original program has any integer solution, the dual problem, too, will have a solution which consists of the shadow prices corresponding to the constraints of the primal problem (where the primal problem is interpreted as that of selecting the optimal levels of several activities).

These dual prices are obtained just as they are in linear programming. If in the solution to an ordinary linear programming problem, the t_j in (1.3) is the slack of the kth constraint (the one involving the kth good), then the $a_{o,j}$ for that j is the shadow price of the kth good. In (1.4) the t_j may be slacks of original constraints or added ones, but the prices are determined in just the same way. Since in (1.4) *all* of the $a_{i,j}$ are integers, the prices will be integers.

Since these prices are the solution to an ordinary linear programming problem they will possess the usual characteristics of ordinary dual prices. They will be nonnegative; except in cases of degeneracy they will impute zero profits to any activity that is carried on at a nonzero level in an optimal solution and negative profits to all other activities; they will make the total imputed value of all "scarce inputs" equal to the value of the optimum output combination; zero prices will be imputed to inputs that are not used to capacity, etc.

In several respects, however, these integer programming prices will be peculiar. As just indicated, the prices will themselves be integers. More important, these prices will vary with the choice of additional constraints (2.5). Finally, we note that prices will be imputed not just to the scarce facilities of the original program: corresponding to each of the added constraints of the augmented program there will also be a shadow price. Before discussing the prices corresponding to these added constraints (call them the artifical capacity prices) let us see what happens to the prices of the original scarce facilities.

Some of these prices may have risen. For example, in Figure 2 suppose C is the optimal solution to the noninteger program, that T is the optimal integer solution and that SS' is the added constraint of the augmented program. Then the input associated with constraint AA' is not used to capacity at C but it is at T. Hence its price will be zero in the noninteger program and rise to some positive value in the integer program.

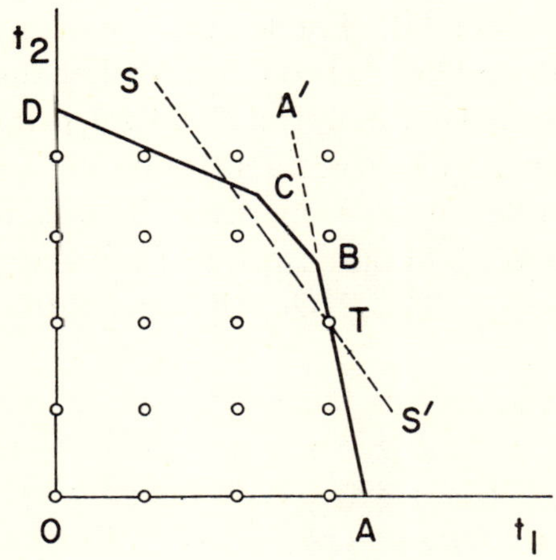

FIGURE 2

Many prices, however, which would be positive in a noninteger solution may be expected to fall to zero in the integer programming case. Thus the prices corresponding to constraint segments DC and CB are both positive when C is optimal, but they are both zero at the integer optimum T. The economic interpretation of these zero prices is easily given. If a warehouse has a capacity to store 36,463.4 cases of some item, an integer solution requires that the last 0.4 storage capacity be left empty—cases just do not come in fractional batches. But the calculation takes some of the warehouse's space to be idle, and hence labels it a free good—it is given a zero price.[7] Clearly this is not a fully satisfactory imputed price. We will return to this issue presently.

We see then that the requirement that the solution be in integers may increase some shadow prices and will normally reduce others. However, if we

[7] It is tempting to jump to the conclusion that "almost all" prices of original facilities will be driven to zero, for if, e.g., there is one capacity C, and one output each unit of which uses up X units of capacity, then between any two adjacent integer values of C/X, say n and $n + 1$, there will be a nondenumerable infinity of noninteger values of C/X for which it will be impossible to use up the capacity completely. In practice, however, this observation seems to be an exaggeration. Experience in problem solving shows that nonzero dual prices occur frequently. We seem to make up problems in a way which leads to this occurring. The same phenomenon is encountered elsewhere, say in the solution of linear difference equations where unit or multiple roots occur with a frequency which is surprising in view of the fact that the equations which possess such roots constitute a subset of measure zero of the set of all possible linear difference equations.

know that the capacities, Q_i, of the scarce facilities, including the capacities associated with the additional inequalities, are all nonnegative (as is proved in Appendix A) it is easy to show that the *arithmetic mean price* of the original facilities (when each price is weighted by the capacity of the corresponding facility) must fall. For let the augmented program have m original constraints and n additional constraints. Let the optimal noninteger prices be $P_1, \ldots, P_m$ and let the optimal integer prices be $P_1^*, \ldots, P_{m+n}^*$. Finally let the capicities of the scare facilities be $Q_1, \ldots, Q_{m+n}$. Then, since the additional constraints can never increase the maximum profit from the total output (equals the total imputed value of the scarce facilities), we have $\sum_{i=1}^{m} P_iQ_i \geq \sum_{i=1}^{m+n} P_i^*Q_i \geq \sum_{i=1}^{m} P_i^*Q_i$. Dividing through by $\sum_{i=1}^{m} Q_i$ we obtain the desired result.

There is a lower bound to this fall in average price. For suppose of the various constraints that could have been added in the augmented linear program we had chosen those which correspond to the boundary $EFGH$ of the convex hull of the lattice points (Figure 1). Since no constraint line SS' of our original augmented program has any points interior to this convex hull it can be added to the convex hull augmented program without affecting its solution. It follows that the convex hull augmented program consists of any other augmented program *plus some additional constraints.* It is then a direct consequence of the preceding theorem on average prices that the average dual price of the original capacities in any other augmented program will be greater than or equal to that of the convex hull augmented program. It is tempting to consider the latter to be the "true" integer programming prices since the convex hull of the integer lattice points represents the smallest convex body containing the entire integer feasible region (it can be shown though that even these prices may themselves not be uniquely determined. This is because what would be called degeneracy in ordinary linear programming is particularly likely to arise in integer problems). We would then say that the computed dual prices are usually overvalutions of the "true" dual prices. However, it will be shown, presently, that any such prices are themselves likely to be undervaluations of the marginal value product of a capacity.

So much for the prices of the original facilities. There remains the problem of interpreting the prices which correspond to the addition constraints (2.5). These may be viewed as a measure of the opportunity cost of indivisibility—e.g., the loss imposed on the businessman by a unit of the artificial capacity constraint which prevents him from seeking to stuff that last four tenths of a case into his warehouse. This interpretation, however, amounts to our thinking of these prices as the marginal revenue products of these inputs and we shall see now that, in the integer programming case, this concept runs into difficulties.

The basic difficulty involved in evaluating marginal revenue products in integer programming is that inputs come in indivisible units. For that reason we cannot speak, e.g., of the marginal profit contribution of a small change in input, i.e. we must deal with $\Delta R/\Delta X$ rather than dR/dX where ΔX is an indivisible unit of input X and R is total profit. But the dual prices represent dR/dX which may change over the range of a unit change in X.

More specifically, in Figure 3, we consider the effect of a unit decrease in the capacity, X, of the facility associated with constraint line UU where

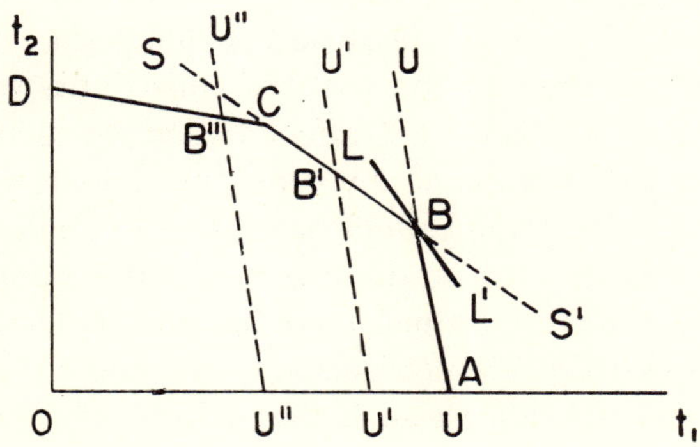

FIGURE 3

B is the original optimal point. Suppose this produces a shift to constraint line $U'U'$ which intersects CB at B'. This means that the new corner B' still lies on the intersection of the same constraint lines as before. The decrease in profits produced by the shift is strictly proportionate to the distance of the shift because the iso-profit lines such as LL' are all parallel straight lines. Hence dR/dX is constant over this range and equal to $\Delta R/\Delta X$ so that the dual price is equal to the marginal profit contribution of X as it would be in an ordinary linear programming problem.

But if a unit decrease in X shifts UU beyond $U'U'$ to $U''U''$ (past a corner, C, of the original feasible region) it is clear that dR/dX will change (more specifically, its absolute value will increase) beyond point C. In that case the marginal profit contribution of X, that is, $\Delta R/\Delta X$ will no longer be equal to dR/dX at the optimal point, B, which is the value of the computed dual price of X.

This argument also indicates, incidentally, why the value of the computed dual price will vary with the choice of additional constraint (2.1). Thus let SS' be the graph of such a constraint. Note that there is considerable choice in the slope of such a line, for so long as it goes through point B and has a negative slope less than that of the iso-profit line LL' it will still lead to the same optimal (integer) point B. But the value of the dual price of X, dR/dX at B, varies with the slope of SS' as we have just seen.

Normally, then, in integer programming there will be *three* marginal revenue product figures: dR/dX, $\Delta R/\Delta X^-$ where ΔX^- is a unit *decrease* in X, and $\Delta R/\Delta X^+$ where ΔX^+ is a unit *increase* in X.

For reasons which have just been indicated we shall normally have (in absolute value) $\Delta R/\Delta X^- \geq dR/dX$ (the dual price), that is, a unit decrease in X will reduce the objective function by no less than its dual price. It can be shown by numerical examples, however, that $\Delta R/\Delta X^+$ may be either greater or smaller than dR/dX. The reason is that an outward shift in one of the constraints can change the shape of the feasible region in a fairly unpredictable manner, because the change in this constraint can in turn cause a shift in some of the artificial constraints which are derived from it. This phenomenon does not affect the value of $\Delta R/\Delta X^-$ because when the feasible region is *reduced* any constraint which was initially valid will still be valid since its graph cannot lie inside the smaller feasible region.

There is one last matter to be discussed in this section. As mentioned before, the prices we have obtained have the unsatisfactory feature that they give zero prices to goods not normally considered free goods, goods that would be useful if available in larger quantities. The positive prices tend to be awarded instead to new "artificial goods" (capacities) whose limited availability shows up in the new inequalities. However, as a generalization of equation (A.1) of Appendix A to the n artificial constraint case shows quite clearly, the new inequalities are merely weighted sums (with nonnegative weights) of the old inequalities where we may use the symbols $g_{i,j}$ to designate the weight which is given the old inequality, j, in the expression for any new inequality, i. This suggests that the prices associated with the new inequalities might well be imputed or distributed back to the original goods (including some of those with zero prices) whose limited availability lies behind the scarcity of the artificial goods.

Appendix B is an attempt in this direction. The method proposed there can be described as follows. Let π_i represent the price of any artificial good i. In imputing back, we then add to the price, π_j, of any initial input good (capacity) j the amount $g_{i,j}\pi_i$. In other words, we obtain the recomputed prices

$$\pi'_j = \pi_j + \sum_i g_{i,j}\pi_i\,, \qquad \text{all } g_{i,j} \geq 0\,,$$

$$\pi'_i = 0\,,$$

for all artificial constraints i, where we note, incidentally, that we do not normally have

$$\sum_j \pi'_j = \sum_j \pi_j + \sum_i \pi_i\,.$$

These recomputed prices have the following desirable properties in common with ordinary linear programming dual prices, as is shown in Appendix B:

1. These prices are sufficiently high to eliminate the possibility of any profitable output, and an output will be produced if and only if it yields zero profits.

2. Any input with a zero recomputed price will be a free good in the true economic sense. That is to say, an unlimited increase in the stocks of this good will make absolutely no difference to optimum output levels.

Although the recomputed prices depend on the actual course of the calculation, as is shown in Appendix B, there is one case in which a type of uniqueness prevails.

3. If there is some set of n original inequalities such that these n alone determine the same integer solution as does the full set of inequalities, then, if all other inequalities are dropped, the recomputed prices for the reduced problem are unique, and are identical with the prices obtained by solving the reduced problem as an ordinary noninteger linear programming problem.

Aside from this, virtually nothing is known about the possible range of recomputed dual prices and the interpretation of this range.

The recomputed prices, however, will also have a number of unusual characteristics:

1. The converse of the preceding proposition 2 does not hold; that is, some free goods may not be given zero recomputed prices. This is because more than one subset of the constraint set may suffice to produce the ultimate optimal integer solution. In that case any one constraint which is not common to all such subsets can be considered redundant (i.e., to represent a free input) since elimination of that one constraint will make no difference to output levels. But it is not possible to eliminate all such constraints and so at least some of these must be chosen to receive a nonzero price. It should be noted that a similar situation can arise in an ordinary linear programming problem in cases of degeneracy.

2. Among the inequalities which make up the artificial constraints there may be included some of the final output nonnegativity conditions, $x_i \geq 0$. It follows that *some of the artificial constraint prices may be reimputed, in part, to some of these final outputs*. In other words, the process of price recomputation may well result in some changes in the prices of final outputs (activities) from the values given by the coefficients of the objective function. For purposes of the next section such a price change may conveniently be visualized as a per unit subsidy to the final outputs or activities affected.

4. PRICING, RESOURCE ALLOCATION, AND COMPETITION

Let us now see what role integer dual prices can play in welfare economics, and, in particular, in an arrangement for achieving an optimal allocation of resources through decentralized decision making.

Let us first note that the prices of the artificial constraints of the integer programming problem can be made very real to a firm by debiting them for the use of these artificial scarce resources. That is, if the fifth additional constraint involves the term $3t_7$, and the corresponding price is set at twelve dollars per unit, the firm would on this arrangement be charged 36 dollars for the use of this "scare resource" for every unit of output 7 it produced. Alternatively. the same resource allocation effect could be achieved by the use of "imputed back" prices as described in the previous section.

Suppose then that either a competitive market or a central planning authority were to compute the dual prices and output combinations necessary to maximize the value of total final output at any *fixed* set of commodity prices. It will be recalled that any such output combination must be an efficient output.[8] Moreover, if individual firms are charged for the use of both real and artificial scarce resources either directly at the computed dual prices or indirectly at these prices as imputed back to the original scarce resources, they will be forced to produce only the outputs contained in this efficient bundle since, by the usual properties of dual prices, each unit of any other output will incur a loss. If these outputs are then expanded as far as possible it follows that the firms must end up producing the efficient output in question.

We see then that every value maximizing (competitive) output will, by the usual argument, also be efficient, even in the integer programming case.[9] Unfortunately, the converse does not hold. There may be efficient outputs which are not competitive,[10] i.e., for which there exist no prices, P_i, at which this output combination maximizes the total value of output, $\Sigma P_i t_i$. This is easily proved by counterexample, as shown in Figure 4. Here the shaded triangle, OBC, is the convex hull of the feasible lattice points. Point A, with coordinates (2.1), lies in the interior of this triangle. But (because the feasible points are isolated) it is possible for such an interior point to be efficient. This is in fact the case with A for there is no feasible lattice point which "dominates" A, i.e., no point which lies directly above it, directly to the right of it, or above it and to its right. Now consider any straight line, such as PP' (equation $\Sigma P_i t_i = k$), through A. Any such

[8] For if the output combination Q were not efficient then there must, by definition, be some other output combination, Q', which contains larger outputs of some items and no smaller output of any item. Hence at the fixed prices the value of Q' must exceed that of Q, i.e., if Q is not efficient it cannot maximize the value of output.

[9] For the classic discussions of the problems of this section see Koopmans [**8**, Chapter 3], Arrow [**1**], and Debreu [**4**]. See also Dorfman, Samuelson and Solow [**5**, Chapter 14] and Koopmans [**9**, Essay 1].

[10] This has already been suggested by Koopmans and Beckman [**10**].

line must lie below either lattice point B or lattice point C. This means that there must exist another parallel line such as $P''P'''$ ($\Sigma P_i t_i = k^* > k$), which lies above PP' and goes through one of these corners of the convex hull triangle OBC. In other words, in the case in Figure 4, at the

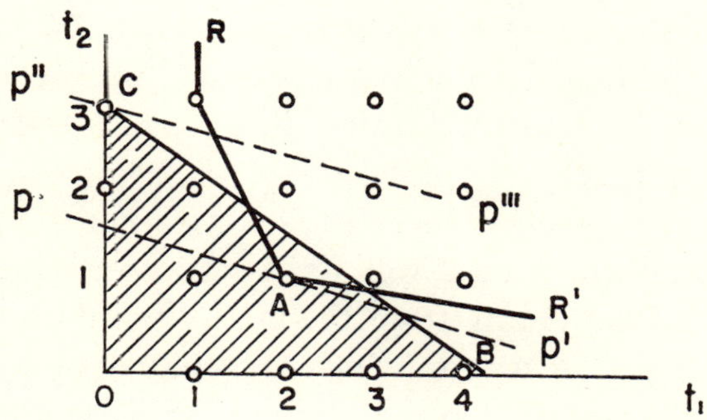

FIGURE 4

prices involved in the price (iso-output-value) lines shown, the value of output at point C exceeds that at A. And, similarly, at any other possible set of output prices the value of output at A will be smaller than that at B or that at C. This shows how there are, in the discrete programming case, likely to arise efficient outputs which are not competitive outputs and which cannot be enforced by the standard type of decentralized control procedure of the economic literature, in which the central authority makes only simple price decisions.

It is to be noted, however, that it is possible to find families of nonlinear or piecewise linear price curves such as RR' for which the value of output is maximized at A. This has a simple interpretation. The prices which are set up are discriminatory and vary with the magnitude of output. Output combinations which are close to A are given relatively high prices but as outputs move further and further from A prices are made increasingly unfavorable to the seller so that there are sharply diminishing returns to departures from A. In other words, an output, t_1, of any commodity at A is broken arbitrarily into a sum of sub-outputs $t_{11} + t_{12} + \ldots + t_{in} = t_1$ and each of the sub-outputs t_{1i} is assigned a different price, P_{1i} as just described. Such an arrangement could, in principle, be enforced by government fiat. But it is difficult to see much advantage to a decentralized control procedure when it becomes so complicated, and in any event it would never result from the spontaneous operation of competitive market forces which preclude the existence of different prices for different units of a homogeneous product.

The so-called basic theorem of welfare economics runs into even more serious trouble in integer programming. It is in this situation not generally possible to attain a Pareto optimal point by means of a price system.

This is obviously so for the case of interior efficient points such as A in Figure 4. For let RR' now represent a community indifference curve so that A is now the optimal feasible point. There obviously exists no line that separates the remainder of the feasible lattice points from the region socially preferred to or indifferent with A (the region above RR'). This means that with any fixed price arrangement producers will find it more profitable to manufacture either output combination B or C than to turn out the social optimum combination, A.

Moreover, even if the optimum point Q is a corner of the convex hull of feasible lattice points there may well exist no hyperplane which separates the feasible (producible) points from the lattice points which are preferred to or indifferent with Q. A way in which this may arise is illustrated in the following three dimensional diagram (Figure 5). Here the shaded region is

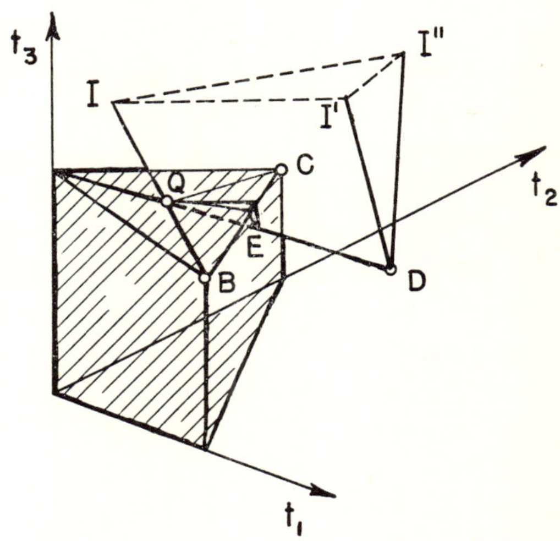

FIGURE 5

the convex hull of the producible (feasible) lattice points such as B, C and the optimal point Q. Similarly let $II'I''$ represent a portion of the convex hull of the lattice points which are preferred to or indifferent with Q. It will be noted that Q is indifferent with nonfeasible lattice point D. The segment QE of the line QD, which connects indifferent points Q and D, lies below triangle QBC which forms one of the faces of the convex hull of the feasible region. Q is the (unique) optimal point because no other feasible lattice point lies (on or) above "indifference surface" $II'I''$. It is obvious that no plane surface can separate the feasible lattice points in the figure from the lattice points preferred to or indifferent with Q since any such plane must either lie above point D which is indifferent with Q or it must be below feasible points B and C.

Let us summarize the results of this section:

1. Every competitive output combination is efficient and any such point can be attained by a system of fixed prices set by central authority, all other decisions being left to the individual firms in the economy. This is no different from the result for the ordinary linear programming case.

2. Unlike the ordinary linear programming case, however, not every efficient output can be achieved by simple centralized pricing decisions or by competitive market pricing processes.

3. Moreover, it is possible in the integer programming case that there exists no hyperplane which separates the feasible lattice points from those which are preferred to or indifferent with the optimal lattice point. In other words, there may exist no set of prices which simultaneously makes the optimal point, Q, the most profitable among those that can be produced and the cheapest among those that consumers consider to be at least as good as Q. That is, at any set of prices either producers will try to make, or consumers will demand, some other output combination.

It should be observed, in conclusion, that these limitations on the price system in the integer programming case should not be entirely surprising. For, as has already been indicated, cases of increasing returns to scale can, at least in principle, be reduced to integer programming problems. And in such cases it has long been recognized that the price system runs into difficulties.

5. NONCONVEX FEASIBLE REGIONS AND CONCAVE PROGRAMMING

Several of the nonnumber-theoretical applications of integer programming should be clear to the economist. The choice of magnitudes of indivisible outputs obviously calls for integer programming, though here ordinary programming methods will often do as an approximation (e.g., an answer which calls for a retailer to carry 47.9 automobiles in stock may reasonably be taken to indicate that 48 is the optimal car inventory). Such an easy compromise is not available in "yes or no" problems like the traveling salesman problem or the following problem of "choosing the largest harmonious expedition." Suppose an expedition is to be made up from n candidates with the condition that no two candidates who can't get along with each other are to be taken. Assigning a variable x_i to the ith candidate, we shall interpret a value of 0 to mean that that candidate is included in the expedition, a value of 1 to mean that he is excluded. The variable x_i is to be restricted to these two values. The problem of constructing the largest harmonious expedition then is the problem of minimizing $\sum_{i=1}^{n} x_i$, the number left out subject to restrictions

$$x_i + x_j \geq 1$$

for all pairs i,j of candidates who can't get along. The effect of each such restriction is to insist that at least one candidate in the i,j pair is left out. It is not hard to see that if the problem is solved as an integer programming problem, the variables in the minimum solution will not only be integers, but actually 0's and 1's, for if any larger integer is included in the minimal solution it could be decreased to 1 without violating any constraints. This would produce a solution with a still smaller objective function. Thus the problem can be solved as an integer programming problem, but it will be noted that an ordinary linear programming solution involving fractions, has no obvious meaning.

Less obvious are the more general applications of integer programming to nonconvex feasible regions and to concave programming problems. An example will now be described briefly.

It will be recalled that fixed costs are defined as costs which do not vary with the magnitude of some operation (at least within limits), and that these costs can therefore be escaped only by closing the operation down altogether. We will see now what computational problems expenses of this type can produce.

Figure 6 represents part of the profit function of a multi-branch firm showing how company profits will vary when the scale of operation of one of its branches, B, varies, the outputs of all other branches being given. This relationship is profit curve TRR'.

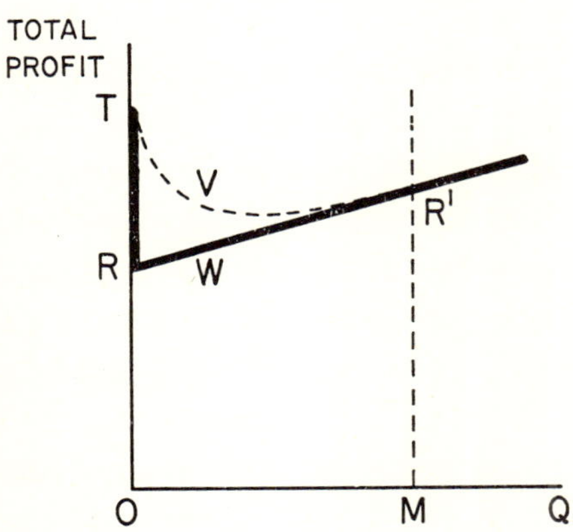

FIGURE 6

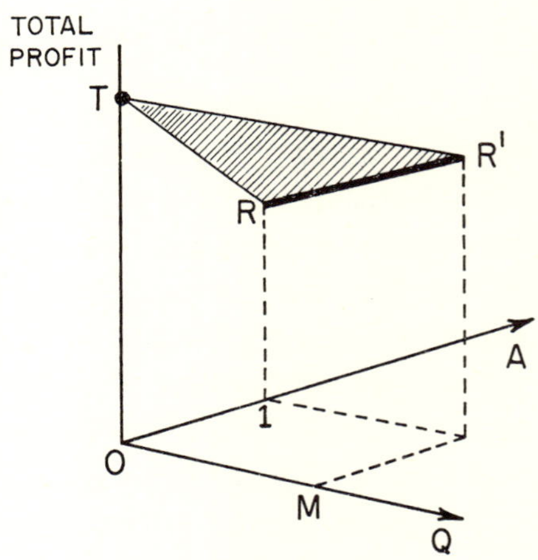

FIGURE 7

As the diagram shows, if this branch is kept in operation, the larger its output, Q, the larger will be the firm's profits (RR' slopes upill toward the right). But in the case shown, if the branch goes out of operation altogether, the fixed costs which it escapes are so large that company profits will suddenly jump from R to T. In fact (assuming that there is some upper limit, OM, to the demand for its product) even if the branch produces every bit that it can sell, the profit contribution of this branch will not suffice to cover the fixed cost, because point R', whose height represents profit at the maximum saleable output, lies below T, where OT represents company profit when the plant is closed down altogether.

We see, then, that point R' is a local maximum but T is the global maximum. However, any computation which tells us to go uphill along the profit curve will move us in the wrong direction. Even at a point like W which is very close to R there is not the slightest hint in the shape of the curve that profits can be increased by *reducing* output. This is a particularly nasty feature of the fixed charges problem. An ordinary increasing (marginal) returns profit curve (a convex objective function maximization problem), such as curved line TVR, will at least indicate the direction of the global maximum point when we get close enough to it—at point V going uphill takes us toward global optimum T, even if starting further to the right the "go uphill" rule would take us in the wrong direction.

It is, of course, only because we are dealing with a multi-branch firm that our problem is really difficult. As a result, even our graph is likely not to give us the right answer. Perhaps it is best not to close our branch B after all. Instead it might be better to close some other branch, C, and save the fixed charges at C, meanwhile serving C's former customers from B, for this increases the maximum demand for branch B's products and so permits us a higher move along our profit curve to the right of point R'. With a large number of branches the problem of examining the possibilities case by case, to decide how many and which to close, leads us into an enormous problem of permutations and combinations which rapidly grows astronomical. A more systematic computation is required.

A similar problem arises in the search for optimal investment criteria. Suppose, for example, that a country has limited investment funds to be divided between two competing projects. The first yields a low rate of return but has low fixed costs of entry into production, and the reverse is true of the second project. Which of the projects should be chosen will clearly depend on the magnitude of the fixed costs.

The role of integer programming in such a problem is easily represented schematically. For this computation it is necessary to introduce an artificial variable, A. In the three dimensional diagram, Figure 7, point T from the original profit function is placed where $A = 0$, while line RR' is moved to where $A = 1$. The three points T, R, and R' are then connected by the plane TRR' which can now serve as the feasible portion of an artificial *linear* programming objective function. But if we include the constraint $A \geq 0$ and $A \leq 1$ in the problem and require that A take only integer values it is clear that we can only have either $A = 0$ or $A = 1$. We can end up only at point T or on line segment RR', i.e., we must remain somewhere on the original profit curve TRR' of Figure 6. Thus by use of integer programming we have been able to substitute for our original fixed charges problem another ordinary linear programming problem which gives the same answers.[11]

In principle, this translation can be made for all of the company's branches at once and so the entire problem can be transformed into one large linear integer programming problem and thus be solved. Unfortunately, in practice this has not so far proved practical for even moderately large scale problems where the number of artificial variables which must be added can make the computation prohibitively time consuming and expensive.

6. THE SIMPLEX CALCULATION: A CONDENSED FORM

Before giving numerical examples of the integer programming computation it is convenient to call attention to a number of short cuts in the simplex computation in which we follow the work of A. W. Tucker.

The problem is set up in the form

$$(6.1)\qquad \begin{cases} \max z = a_{o,o} + a_{o,1}(-t_1) + \dots + a_{o,n}(-t_n) \\ \quad \text{subject to} \\ t_1' = a_{1,o} + a_{1,1}(-t_1) + \dots + a_{1,n}(-t_n)\,, \\ \cdots\cdots\cdots\cdots\cdots\cdots\cdots\cdots\cdots\cdots \\ t_m' = a_{m,o} + a_{m,1}(-t_1) + \dots + a_{m,n}(-t_n)\,, \end{cases}$$

with all of the variables required to take nonnegative values. First we note that if all the elements in the first column (the constant terms) are nonnegative a (basic) feasible solution is given by[12]

$$(6.2)\qquad t_1' = a_{1,o}, \dots, t_m' = a_{m,o}, t_1 = \dots = t_n = 0\,.$$

Thus the system is said to be *primal feasible* if for all $i \neq 0$ we have $a_{i,o} \geq 0$.

[11] Note that as described this is a "mixed" problem in which some but not all of the variables are required to be integer values. The MIF method does not apply directly to such problems. The difficulty can be evaded, at least in principle, by measuring outputs in very small units and taking their optimal *integer* values as approximations to their true optimal values. By making the units of measurement small enough this approximation can, in principle, clearly be made as close as possible, though we do not yet have enough computing experience with the MIF algorithm to know how rapidly it converges when dealing with the large numbers which are likely to result. There has also been some promising work on the mixed problem. Cf. Beale [**2**] and Gomory [**8**].

[12] We note again that in this computation the basic variables are expressed as functions of the variables outside the basis. This is the reverse of the more usual viewpoint. It permits us to solve directly for the values of the basic variables at the relevant corner, as shown.

Similarly, for obvious reasons, it is said to be dual feasible if the coefficients of the objective function $a_{o,j}$ are nonnegative.

It should be clear by inspection that if the system is transformed into a form that is both primal and dual feasible then (6.2) is also an optimal solution. The primal simplex method then proceeds by starting with the problem in primal feasible form and then transforming it by a sequence of steps in a way which leaves the $a_{i,o}$ nonnegative while increasing the $a_{o,i}$ until (6.1) becomes both primal and dual feasible.

To describe the simplex steps consider the following two illustrative constraint equations of the problem

$$t_1' = a_{1,o} + a_{1,1}(-t_1) + a_{1,2}(-t_2) + a_{1,3}(-t_3)\ ,$$
$$t_2' = a_{2,o} + a_{2,1}(-t_1) + a_{2,2}(-t_2) + a_{2,3}(-t_3)\ .$$

Suppose that the computations have reached a stage where there is to be a change in basis from c_1, c_2 to, say, c_1, t_3 (we say that we *pivot* on coefficient $a_{2,3}$, i.e., we replace c_2 by t_3 in the basis). Then we solve for t_2 by dividing the second equation through by $a_{2,3}$ and substitute the result into the first equation to obtain

$$t_1' = \left(a_{1,o} - \frac{a_{1,3}}{a_{2,3}}\,a_{2,o}\right) + \left(a_{1,1} - \frac{a_{1,3}}{a_{2,3}}\,a_{2,1}\right)(-t_1) + \left(a_{1,2} - \frac{a_{1,3}}{a_{2,3}}\,a_{2,2}\right)(-t_2)$$
$$- \frac{a_{1,3}}{a_{2,3}}\,(-t_2')\ .$$

More generally, the reader may readily verify that a pivot on element $a_{i,j}$ will replace element $a_{v,w}$ $(v \neq i,\ w \neq j)$ by

$$a_{v,w} - \frac{a_{i,w}}{a_{i,j}}\,a_{v,j}\ .$$

A slight extension of the argument leading to the preceding equation shows that any pivot step will lead to the following changes in the values of the coefficients in (6.1) (the elements of the matrix of the system):

(6.3)

a) The pivot element, $a_{i,j}$, will be changed to $a_{i,j}' = 1/a_{i,j}$.
b) Any other element $a_{v,j}$ in the pivot column j will be changed to $a_{v,j}' = -a_{v,j}/a_{i,j}$.
c) Any element $a_{i,w}$ in the pivot row i will be changed to $a_{i,w}' = a_{i,w}/a_{i,j}$.
d) Any other element $a_{v,w}$ will, by the preceding argument, be changed to $a_{v,w} - a_{i,w}a_{v,j}/a_{i,j}$.

One feature of the method we are using is that the same transformation (6.3) is applied to the objective function as to the constraints. This has the effect of expressing the objective function always in terms of the non-basic variables (the t_i) only, so that we always end up with an objective function of the form taken in (6.1). As a result, as soon as the system is transformed into both primal and dual feasible form the solution (6.2) is immediate.

The primal simplex method seeks to increase the value of the objective function, $a_{o,o}$, and so, like the dual simplex method, it pivots in a column with the first element negative, but unlike the dual method, it always pivots on a positive element. For with $a_{i,j} > 0$, $a_{o,j} < 0$ and $a_{i,o} \geq 0$ (by primal feasibility) it follows from (6.3d) that $a'_{,o} \geq a_{o,o}$ as required. The corresponding result for the dual simplex method in which we seek to reduce (minimize) the value of the objective function, is obvious.

The procedure used in the solution of the integer programming problem is, then, the following:

A. *The condensed form primal simplex calculation.*

1. Set up the matrix (simplex tableau) for a primal feasible system (6.1).

2. Choose a column, j, with the first element $a_{o,j}$ negative (in the illustrative computation we always choose the largest such element in absolute value).

3. Choose as the pivot that positive element in this column which minimizes $a_{i,o}/a_{i,j}$. (This element is chosen to keep the next matrix dual feasible. For suppose instead we chose as pivot $a_{k,j}$ such that $a_{k,o}/a_{k,j} > a_{i,o}/a_{i,j}$. Then by (6.3d) we would have $a'_{i,o} = a_{i,o} - a_{i,j}a_{k,o}/a_{k,j} < 0$.)

4. Transform the matrix in accord with (6.3).

5. Repeat steps 1–4 until the matrix becomes dual feasible so that optimal solution (6.2) applies.

B. *The addition of an MIF constraint.*

If solution (6.2) contains noninteger values, form an additional constraint (2.5). This is done by choosing a row j and writing an additional constraint with the same variables but whose coefficients are the *negative* fractional parts of the corresponding elements in row j. (In this computation we choose row j to be the one whose first element has the largest fractional part for reasons indicated at the end of Section 2, above.)

C. *The dual simplex calculation.*

The problem is now in dual feasible form (since the last step of the primal simplex computation put it in that form). However, it is no longer in primal feasible form since the new constraint (2.5) enters the negative element $-f_{i,o}$ into the first column. The new optimum is therefore found most conveniently by the dual simplex method which differs from the primal method only in the choice of pivot element. Here select we a *row* i whose first element $a_{i,o}$ is negative and from that row select we a *negative* pivot element $a_{i,j}$ which minimizes $-a_{i,o}/a_{i,j}$. Once the new optimal solution is found, if it contains noninteger elements we repeat steps B and C until an optimal integer solution is found.

7. EXAMPLE

$$\begin{aligned} \text{Maximize} \quad & z = 4x_1 + 5x_2 + x_3 \\ \text{subject to:} \quad & 3x_1 + 2x_2 \leq 10\,, \\ & x_1 + 4x_2 \leq 11\,, \\ & 3x_1 + 3x_2 + x_3 \leq 13\,. \end{aligned}$$

Introducing slack variables $\bar{x}_1$, $\bar{x}_2$, $\bar{x}_3$ we obtain the following sequence of simplex tableaux, where the asterisk indicates the pivot element and the arrow indicates the row from which the new inequality is formed:

	1	$-x_1$	$-x_2$	$-x_3$
$z =$	0	-4	-5	-1
$\bar{x}_1 =$	10	3	2	0
$\bar{x}_2 =$	11	1	4*	0
$\bar{x}_3 =$	13	3	3	1

TABLEAU 1

	1	$-x_1$	$-\bar{x}_2$	$-x_3$
$z =$	$13\frac{3}{4}$	$-2\frac{3}{4}$	$1\frac{1}{4}$	-1
$\bar{x}_1 =$	$4\frac{2}{4}$	$2\frac{2}{4}$*	$-\frac{2}{4}$	0
$x_2 =$	$2\frac{3}{4}$	$\frac{1}{4}$	$\frac{1}{4}$	0
$\bar{x}_3 =$	$4\frac{3}{4}$	$2\frac{1}{4}$	$-\frac{3}{4}$	1

TABLEAU 2

	1	$-\bar{x}_1$	$-\bar{x}_2$	$-x_3$
$z =$	$18\frac{7}{10}$	$1\frac{1}{10}$	$-\frac{7}{10}$	-1
$x_1 =$	$1\frac{8}{10}$	[illegible]/10	$-\frac{2}{10}$	0
$x_2 =$	$2\frac{3}{10}$	$-\frac{1}{10}$	$\frac{3}{10}$	0
$\bar{x}_3 =$	$\frac{7}{10}$	$-\frac{9}{10}$	$-\frac{3}{10}$	1*

TABLEAU 3

	1	$-\bar{x}_1$	$-\bar{x}_2$	$-\bar{x}_3$
$z =$	$19\frac{4}{10}$	$\frac{2}{10}$	$\frac{4}{10}$	1
$x_1 =$	$1\frac{8}{10}$	$\frac{4}{10}$	$-\frac{2}{10}$	0
$x_2 =$	$2\frac{3}{10}$	$-\frac{1}{10}$	$\frac{3}{10}$	0
$\rightarrow x_3 =$	$\frac{7}{10}$	$-\frac{9}{10}$	$-\frac{3}{10}$	1
$s_1 =$	$-\frac{7}{10}$	$-\frac{1}{10}$	$-\frac{7}{10}$*	0

TABLEAU 4 (L.P. optimal)[13]

	1	$-\bar{x}_1$	$-s_1$	$-\bar{x}_3$
$\rightarrow z =$	19	$\frac{1}{7}$	$\frac{4}{7}$	1
$x_1 =$	2	$\frac{3}{7}$	$-\frac{2}{7}$	0
$x_2 =$	2	$-\frac{1}{7}$	$\frac{3}{7}$	0
$x_3 =$	1	$-\frac{6}{7}$	$-\frac{3}{7}$	1
$\bar{x}_2 =$	1	$\frac{1}{7}$	$-1\frac{3}{7}$	0
$s_2 =$	0	$-\frac{1}{7}$*	$-\frac{4}{7}$	0

TABLEAU 5 (integer solution)

[13] In the original coordinates the inequality $s_1 \geq 0$ becomes the new integer inequality (see Appendix A) $-\frac{7}{10} + \frac{1}{10}(10 - 3x_1 - 2x_2) + \frac{7}{10}(11 - x_1 - 4x_2) \geq 0$, i.e., $x_1 + 3x_2 \leq 8$.

	1	$-s_2$	$-s_1$	$-\bar{x}_3$
$z =$	19	1	0	1
$x_1 =$	2	3	2	0
$x_2 =$	2	−1	−1	0
$x_3 =$	1	−6	3	1
$\bar{x}_2 =$	1	1	−2	0
$\bar{x}_1 =$	0	−7	4	0

TABLEAU 6 (all integer matrix)

APPENDIX A

SOME PROPERTIES OF THE ADDED INEQUALITIES

To fill the gap in the proof in Section 3 that the average price of the original capacities is reduced by the artificial constraints (2.5) we must show that the $Q_i \geq 0$. We can assume this for the Q_i of the original problem because of their capacity interpretation, but it remains to be shown for Q_i, $i > m$. We adopt a method of proof that brings out some interesting properties of the added inequalities.

If we express the new variables, t, in (1.4), above, in terms of the original variables x in (1.1) and substitute the result into the new inequalities, these inequalities are rewritten entirely in terms of the original variables. We will show now that they are then all-integer inequalities, i.e., all coefficients and constants are integers. To see this we will first assume that the inequality under consideration is the first new inequality to be added. It is derived from an equation

$$t_i' = a_{i,o} + \sum_{j=1}^{n} a_{i,j}\,(-t_j)$$

where the variables, t, are either x's or slack variables of the original problem. For each t_j on the right we substitute its original expression in terms of the x_j, i.e., if t_j is $x'_{k(j)}$ the kth slack, we substitute $Q_k - \sum_{i=1}^{n} \overset{*}{a}_{k,j}x_j$ $(= x'_{k(j)})$ and if t_j is some $x_{i(j)}$ we simply substitute $x_{i(j)}$. We thereby obtain an expression giving t_i' in terms of the x_j. As the expression for any variable in terms of the original non-basic variables is unique, this be one of the original all-integer equations if t_i' is a slack, or the expression $x_i = x_i$ if t_i' is one of the x's. In any event, the new right hand side is all integer. If the same process is applied to the new equation

$$(2.5) \qquad s_i = -f_{i,o} - \sum_{j=1}^{n} f_{i,j}(-t_j) = \left(u_{i,o} + \sum_{j=1}^{n} u_{i,j}(-t_j)\right) - \left(a_{i,o} + \sum_{j=1}^{n} a_{i,j}(-t_j)\right)$$

where the $u_{i,j}$ are the integer parts of the $a_{i,j}$, the result is again an all-integer right hand side. This is obviously so for the all-integer expressions involving the $u_{i,j}$, and we have just shown the same thing for the second parenthesis. We conclude that *the new inequality $s_i \geq 0$, is an all-integer inequality when it is expressed in the original variables.*

Looking at the substitution process in more detail, using J for the set of indices j whose t_j are original variables $x_{i,j}$, we have

$$s_i = -f_{i,o} + \sum_{j \varepsilon J} f_{i,j} x_{k(j)} + \sum_{j \varepsilon J'} f_{i,j} \left(Q_{i,j} - \sum_{k=1}^{n} a^*_{i(j),k} x_k \right) \tag{A.1}$$

or, assembling constant terms and the coefficients of the various x_k, the inequality $s_i \geq 0$ becomes

$$-f_{i,o} + \sum_{j \varepsilon J'} f_{i,j} Q_{i,j} \geq - \sum_{j \varepsilon J} f_{i,j} x_{k(j)} + \sum_{k=1}^{n} \left(\sum_{j \varepsilon J'} f_{i,j} a^*_{i(j)k} \right) x_k .$$

The left hand side contains only nonnegative terms except for $-f_{i,o}$, hence it is > -1. We have already shown, however, that all terms are integers. Hence the left hand side must be ≥ 0, and this left side is the Q_i of the new inequality.

In this argument we assumed we were dealing with the first added inequality. However, now that we have established this inequality as an all integer one with nonnegative Q_i we can go on without any difficulty to the second, third, etc.

We obtain one more piece of information by a similar argument. Suppose that the coefficients $a_{i,k}$, $i = 1, \ldots, m$, of some variable x_k are all nonnegative in the original problem, *then the coefficients of x_k are also nonnegative in the new inequalities*. For the coefficient is either

$$\sum_{j \varepsilon J} f_{i,j} \, a^*_{i(j),k}$$

or, if x_k is one of the $x_{k,j}$, $j \varepsilon J$, the same expression with the additional term $-f_{i,j}'$. If the $a^*_{i,j,k}$ are all ≥ 0, as we assume, this term, too, is > -1 and an integer and hence ≥ 0.

In particular, if the original inequalities involved only nonnegative terms, this is also true of the added inequalities if these are written in terms of the original variables.

APPENDIX B

IMPUTING BACK THE PRICES OF THE ARTIFICIAL CONSTRAINTS

It will be observed that each parenthesis on the right in equation (A.1) of Appendix A, if set ≥ 0, gives one of the original inequalities (1.1). Thus, *each of the new inequalities, $s_i \geq 0$, differs by a constant, $-f_{i,o}$, from a weighted sum of the original constraints.* (Note that this statement refers both to the explicitly given inequalities such as $Q_i - \sum_{j=1}^{n} a_{i,j} x_j \geq 0$ and to the implicit final output nonnegativity inequalities, $x_j \geq 0$.)

This suggests that the prices associated with the new inequalities can be distributed back to the original inequalities which compose them. This is not hard to do. To simplify the exposition we will first consider the case where only one new inequality has been added. This extends easily to the general case.

Suppose, then, that on solving the integer programming problem we obtain prices π_i for all the original goods (capacities) and for the artificial capacities. We already have "prices" for the final goods—these are the unit profits of the activities—the coefficients of the activity levels in the objective function.

To display this price information symmetrically we write the original inequalities augmented by the conditions, $x_j \geq 0$, together with the associated prices π_i:

$$\begin{array}{lll}
\sum_{j=1}^{n} a_{1j}^{*}, x_j & \leq Q_1 & \pi_1 \\
\sum_{j=1}^{n} a_{2,j}^{*} x_j & \leq Q_2 & \pi_2 \\
\vdots & & \vdots \\
\sum_{j=1}^{n} a_{m,j}^{*} x_j & \leq Q_m & \pi_m \\
\quad -x_1 & \leq 0 & \pi_{m+1} \\
\qquad -x_2 & \leq 0 & \pi_{m+2} \\
\qquad\quad \ddots & & \\
\qquad\qquad -x_n & \leq 0 & \pi_{m+n} .
\end{array}$$

The additional inequalities, as (A.1) shows, can be thought of as being obtained by adding together nonnegative multiples of the preceding inequalities and then reducing the right hand side by a certain constant to obtain the new integer inequality

$$\sum_{j=1}^{n} a_{m+n+k}^{*} x_j \leq Q_{m+n+k} \; \pi_{m+n+k} .$$

For simplicity let us suppose further that the integer solution has been obtained after the addition of our single new inequality. Extension of the method to the more usual situation will not require any additional effort.

We have then prices π_i, $i = 1, \ldots, m + n + 1$, and $m + n + 1$ inequalities

$$\sum_{j=1}^{n} a_{i,j}^{*} x_j \leq Q_j \qquad (i = 1, \ldots, m+n+1)$$

where we include the inequalities $-x_j \leq 0$.

The prices obtained from the solution have the usual linear programming property $\sum_{i=1}^{m+n+1} \pi_i \, a_{i,j}^{*} x_j \leq \pi_j x_j$,

i.e.,

$$\text{(B.1)} \qquad \sum_{i=1}^{m+n+1} \pi_i \, a_{i,j}^{*} \leq 0 \qquad (j = 1, \ldots, n)$$

with equality required for all j having $x_j \neq 0$, this last requirement of equality being equivalent to

$$\text{(B.2)} \qquad \sum_{i=1}^{m+n+1} \pi_i \, Q_i^{*} = 0$$

with Q_i^{*} the amount of the ith capacity or input good used up or, if i is a final good, Q_i^{*} represents the amount produced.

(B.1) represents the requirement that cost exceed or at best equal the value of the final good produced, and (B.2) asserts that at the prices π_i the value of input goods used equals the value of output goods produced. This is equivalent to the requirement that equality must hold in (B.1) in all cases where the final good, j, is actually produced in a positive amount, for

$$0 = \sum_{i=1}^{m+n+1} \pi_i Q_i^* = \sum_{i=1}^{m+n+1} \pi_i \sum_{j=1}^{n} a_{i,j}^* x_j ,$$

$$0 = \sum_{j=1}^{n} \left(\sum_{i=1}^{m+n+1} \pi_i a_{i,j}^* \right) x_j .$$

Since each parenthesis is ≤ 0, the only way for the zero total to be achieved is for $(\sum_{i=1}^{m+n+1} \pi_i a_{i,j}^*)$ to be zero for each nonzero x_j.

In this situation in the case of an input good it makes no difference in (B.2) if we use the Q_i^*, the amount used, or the Q_i, the amounts available, as these quantities will differ only for goods of price zero.

Let us now describe a procedure for imputing the prices of the artificial constraints back to the original constraints of which they are linear combinations. If we denote the row vector of coefficients $(a_{i,1}^*, a_{i,2}^*, \ldots, a_{i,n}^*)$ by R_i, we know by (A.1) that R_{m+n+1} is a nonnegative combination of the preceding R_i, i.e.

$$R_{m+n+1} = \sum_{i=1}^{m+n} g_i R_i .$$

(Here, because only one inequality has been added, the nonzero g_i are the f_j used in forming the new inequality.) (B.1) requires

$$0 \geq \sum_{i=1}^{m+n+1} \pi_i R_i = \pi_{m+n+1} R_{m+n+1} + \sum_{i=1}^{m+n} \pi_i R_i = \sum_{i=1}^{m+n} (\pi_{m+n+1} g_i + \pi_i) R_i .$$

This equation shows that if new (increased) prices $\pi_i' = \pi_{m+n+1} g_i + \pi_i$ are assigned to the original goods, and the additional inequality disregarded, i.e., given zero price, the condition of profitless production is still maintained. Also since $\sum_{i=1}^{m+n+1} \pi_i R_i = \sum_{i=1}^{m+n} \pi_i' R_i$, i.e., $\sum_{i=1}^{m+n+1} \pi_i a_{i,j}^* = \sum_{i=1}^{m+n} \pi_i' a_{i,j}^* =$ profit per unit of final good j for every j, the same final goods as before are made at zero loss, so the property (B.2) still holds with recomputed prices i.e., $\sum_{i=1}^{m+n} \pi_i' Q_i^* = 0$.

To obtain these prices in the case where more than one inequality has been added one takes the last added inequality, which represents a known weighted combination of earlier inequalities, and uses the explicit expression for this inequality to generate new prices just as above. Having thus gotten rid of this inequality one proceeds to the next to last, and so on until only original inequalities remain. The prices obtained by this process will have another desirable property:

Result (1). An original input good receiving a zero price will always be a free good in the sense that if unlimited amounts of it were available, the output of final goods would still not be affected.

To see this we consider the computation which has been gone through to obtain the original dual prices noting first that a nonartificial input with a zero recomputed price must always also have a zero dual price because the price recomputation process never lowers the price of such an item.

The original computation can be repeated step by step with the zero-priced inequality removed simply by regarding the slack x'_i of that inequality as an unrestricted variable rather than a nonnegative one.

When the computation has been completed the zero-priced slack variable x'_i, even if it is non-basic, must, as we have noted, have a zero dual price (zero coefficient in the top row). In either of these cases, despite the presence of an unrestricted variable, the final tableau still gives the old optimal solution to the problem because of the nonnegativity of the $a_{i,o}$ and $a_{o,j}$, provided only that we still know that those non-basic s_i having nonzero coefficients in the top row, i.e., nonzero prices before any redistribution of prices, are still required to be nonnegative. Now the nonnegativity of each s_i stems from its being given be an equation

$$s_i = -f_i - \sum f_j(-t_j) .$$

Since s_i is an integer, and *if the t_j are nonnegative*, we have $s_i \geq -f_i$, and hence $s_i \geq 0$. If, however, x'_i was among the t_j accompanied by a nonzero f_j, this reasoning fails, and we can no longer require $s_i \geq 0$ and the final tableau no longer gives an optimal solution. But if the ith inequality received a final redistributed price of 0, this undesirable situation can not have occurred. For if s_i received a nonzero price π, then, upon redistributing, the inequality with slack x'_i would have received an increase in price of πf_i and so its price could not be zero after redistribution.

The situation is somewhat more complicated if s_i is originally expressed in terms of other earlier s-variables whose nonnegativity has been endangered by the unrestricted sign of x'_i. However, the same argument, though it requires more words, does go through step by step.

Result (2). A second conclusion is the following. If there is some set of n original inequalities such that these n alone yield the same integer solution as does the full set of inequalities, then it is possible to redistribute prices in such a way that the prices of all input goods are simply the ordinary linear programming prices, i.e., the prices obtained for the goods if the program involving only these n inequalities were solved as an ordinary noninteger linear programming problem, omitted goods receiving zero price.

A consequence of result (2) is the fact that, in general, the converse of result (1) is not valid. It is not always true that if an inequality can be removed without changing the solution, i.e., if it represents a free good, that this good will receive a zero price. The connection is illustrated in Figure 8 in which L_1, L_2, L_3 represent constraints and the dashed line is an isoquant of the objective function. It is clear that restrictions L_1 and L_2 alone determine the solution P, and consequently, according to result (2), it is possible to redistribute prices so that L_1 and L_2 receive the ordinary (usually positive) linear programming prices that would result from an ordinary noninteger programming problem with L_3 omitted, and L_3 receives a zero price. However, in the problem L_2 is a free good in the sense that, since L_1 and L_3 also yield the same solution P, unlimited availability of the good involved in the restraint L_2 would not alter the solution.

This difficulty also arises in ordinary linear programming whenever several subsets of inequalities separately determine the answer. However, in ordinary linear programming this is comparatively rare since it must involve degeneracy (this is precisely what is meant by degeneracy). Such a situation is shown in Figure 9.

We now take up the proof of result (2). To obtain the prices in question we simply ignore the constraints other than the N singled out, and proceed to solve the problem first as an ordinary noninteger linear programming problem, and then as usual, by adding new inequalities to obtain the integer solution. At the solution point of the ordinary linear programming problem, all N inequalities are satisfied as equalities, i.e. all the slack variables are nonbasic (we may regard x as being the slack of the inequality $-x \leq 0$, for if we introduce an x', with $-x + x' = 0$, we have $x = x'$). This

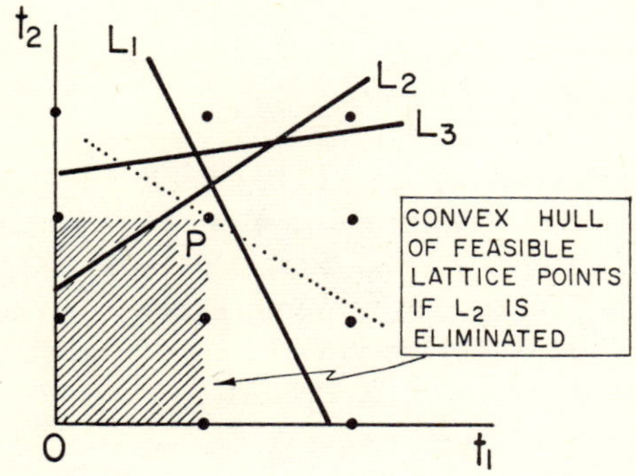

FIGURE 8

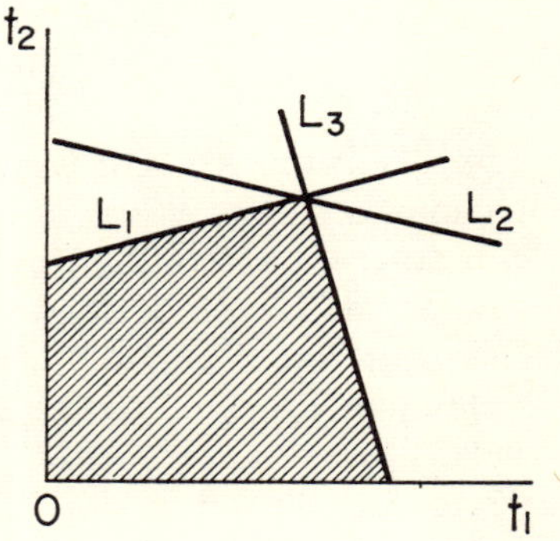

FIGURE 9

point may well not satisfy the inequalities that we are temporarily disregarding. This fact makes no difference, however, when it comes to generating the new inequalities whose validity is not affected. Of course when we reach the final integer solution, which is the same for the problem with or without these inequalities, the disregarded inequalities will be satisfied by hypothesis.

Now on redistributing the prices we distribute them back to exactly n inequalities, the original n inequalities. In other words we express each new variable in terms of the n slacks x'_j, $j = 1, \ldots, N$:

$$s_i = -g_{i,o} + \sum_{j=1}^{n} g_{i,j} x'_j \,. \tag{B.3}$$

Thus all the final non-basic variables are expressed this way.

If each non-basic variable (or the inequality it represents) receives a price π_i in the usual linear programming way, then, on distributing the prices back to the x'_j, they receive prices

$$\pi'_j = \sum_{i=1}^{N} \pi_i \, g_{i,j} \,. \tag{B.4}$$

To see that these are in fact the ordinary linear programming prices we note that the final set of equations can be augmented to express all the variables in terms of the non-basic ones. The basic variables are already given in terms of the non-basic ones, and the non-basic ones can certainly be given in terms of themselves. Having then an expression for all variables in terms of the non-basic ones, we substitute (B.3) for the s_i to obtain an expression for all variables in terms of the x'_i.

The z-equation of the final tableau

$$z = a^*_{o,o} + \sum_{i=1}^{n} \pi_i \, (-s_i)$$

becomes

$$z = \left(a^*_{o,o} + \sum_{i=1}^{n} \pi_i \, g_{i,o} \right) + \sum_{j=1}^{n} \left(\sum_{i=1}^{n} \pi_i \, g_{i,j} \right) (-x'_j) \,.$$

Note that the coefficient of $(-x_j')$ is the pr'ce given by (B.4). Now the expression for the variables in terms of the non-basic set x_j' is unique, so all the coefficients must be identical with those obtained in solving the n inequalities of an ordinary linear programming problem so that the ordinary linear programming price and the redistributed price coincide for input goods.

REFERENCES

[1] Arrow, Kenneth J.: "An Extension of the Basic Theorems of Classical Welfare Economics," *Proceedings of the Second Berkeley Symposium on Mathematical Statistics and Probability*, University of California Press, Berkeley, 1951.

[2] Beale, E. M. L.: "A Method of Solving Linear Programming Problems When Some but Not All of the Variables Must Take Integral Values." Statistical Techniques Research Group Technical Report No. 19, Princeton, N. J., July, 1958.

[3] Dantzig, George B.: "On the Significance of Solving Linear Programming Problems with Some Integer Variables," (Ditto) The RAND Corporation, Paper P-1486, September, 1958.

[4] Debreu, Gerard: "The Coefficient of Resource Utilization," *Econometrica*, Vol. 19, July, 1951.

[5] Dorfman, Robert, Paul A. Samuelson, and Robert M. Solow: *Linear Programming and Mathematical Analysis*, McGraw-Hill, New York, 1958.

[6] Gomory, Ralph E.: "Outline of an Algorithm for Integer Solutions to Linear Programs," *Bulletin of the American Mathematical Society*, Vol. 64, September, 1958.

[7] ———: "An Algorithm for Integer Solutions to Linear Programs," (mineographed) Princeton—I.B.M. Mathematics Research Project, Technical Report No. 1, November, 1958.

[8] ———: "A Method for the Mixed Integer Problem," in preparation as a RAND Corporation report.

[9] Koopmans, Tjalling C., ed.: *Activity Analysis of Production and Allocation*, Cowles Commission Monograph 13, Wiley, New York, 1951.

[10] ———: *Three Essays on the State of Economic Science*, McGraw-Hill, New York, 1957.

[11] Koopmans, Tjalling C. and Martin Beckmann: "Assignment Problems and the Location of Economic Activities," *Econometrica*, Vol. 25, January, 1957.

[12] Land, A. H. and A. G. Doig: "An Automatic Method of Solving Discrete Programming Problems," *Econometrica*, this issue.

[13] Markowitz, Harry M. and Alan S. Manne: "On the Solution of Discrete Programming Problems," *Econometrica*, Vol. 25, January, 1957.

MANAGEMENT SCIENCE
Vol. 11, No. 1, September, 1964
Printed in U.S.A.

[21]

DECOMPOSITION, PRICING FOR DECENTRALIZATION AND EXTERNAL ECONOMIES*†

WILLIAM J. BAUMOL‡ AND TIBOR FABIAN§

The decomposition procedure for the solution of large scale linear programs is described in an elementary manner with illustrative calculations. Its economic interpretation as a procedure for decentralized decision by the multi-division firm or the multi-sector economy is explained in detail. Decomposition is shown to provide internal prices for decentralized decision making in the presence of external economies or diseconomies. However, it is demonstrated that in many cases there exist no prices which will lead divisions to make independent decisions that are optimal from the point of view of the company (or the economy) as a whole.

Dantzig and Wolfe [2] and [3], have recently developed a computational technique, called the decomposition method, which in many cases permits the solution of linear programs of astonishing size. One particular applied analysis in which the authors of this paper are currently involved, uses this technique to deal with a linear programming problem containing more than thirty thousand constraints and several million variables!

The decomposition method can be given an economic interpretation which is illuminating in itself. This article deals with decomposition primarily as an instrument of economic analysis rather than a method of numerical calculation. It indicates how decomposition takes advantage of the economies of decentralized decision making either by divisions within a firm or by larger units in an economy.[1] The method includes in its operations a coordinating mechanism which prevents the decentralized decisions from working at cross purposes. This

* Received December 1963.

† We would like to acknowledge our great gratitude to the National Science Foundation whose grant to the study, "Dynamics of the Firm," was extremely helpful in the completion of this paper. We also wish to express our sincere thanks to Michel Balinski, Harold Kuhn, Edward Pearsall, Harold Shapiro, Philip Wolfe and Arthur Yaspan for their extremely helpful suggestions.

‡ Princeton University.

§ MATHEMATICA, Princeton, New Jersey and University of Pennsylvania.

[1] The interpretation of decomposition as a decentralized decision making process was suggested by Dantzig and Wolfe. See, e.g., Dantzig's recent volume [1]. They have also discussed this matter in other unpublished papers. It is also dealt with in Whinston's doctoral dissertation [12]. Also highly relevant here is the work of Gale on decentralized decisions. See [5], pp. 85–93.

mechanism employs as its instrument a generalized interpretation of the shadow prices of linear programming duality theory.[2] That portion of the decomposition process which arranges for decentralized decisions to work consistently toward an overall maximum necessarily offers an approach to the problems which arise out of the presence of external economies and diseconomies. For decentralized decisions do not automatically produce optimal overall results just because of this sort of phenomenon—the fact that a subdivision of the firm or the industry or the economy may not take into account the benefits conferred or the costs imposed by its activities on other subdivisions. Decomposition, then, can only work by maintaining control over these external economy or diseconomy problems and we shall discuss presently how this task is accomplished.

We must, however, be careful not to overstate the degree of autonomy of the divisional decision maker in the decomposition process. True, the calculation process is sufficiently localized that central management does not have to know *anything* about the internal technological arrangements of the divisions. But in the final analysis the output decisions are made and enforced by the central planner. Partly this is done by means of the persuasive powers of profit and pricing system. But at one stage of the operation a central decision, though based on divisional plans and proposals, must, at least in the linear case, be made and imposed directly on the divisions, as we shall see.

This article begins with a summary (without proofs)[3] of the decomposition theorems and procedures. It then digresses to describe the features of duality theory employed in the process, whose interpretation may be of considerable interest in and of itself. Finally, an economic interpretation of the decomposition process is given, along with some remarks on its implications for planning and control without detailed central direction in the presence of external economies and diseconomies. This discussion is equally applicable to the optimization problems of the large business firm which wishes to delegate some portions of its decision making process to its divisions, and to the work of the government agency which seeks to arrange for the activities freely undertaken in the private sector of the economy to be consistent with the common welfare.

1. Decomposable Structures: Illustration

Consider a company with two manufacturing subdivisions. Division 1 is able to produce either or both of two commodities whose outputs are represented by X_1 and X_2. Similarly, the three potential outputs of Division 2 are denoted by Y_1, Y_2 and Y_3. Both divisions make use of one company input resource whose

[2] Of course, the association of dual prices and decentralization is by now a commonplace of programming theory. See, e.g., Koopmans [7], pp. 93–97, [8], pp. 15–23 and Dorfman, Samuelson and Solow [4], pp. 59–63. However, externalities are not easy to treat in that analytic framework. Indeed, the standard programming approach in decentralized decision making guarantees only that the "right" commodities will be produced. But it offers no assurance that they will be manufactured in optimal amounts or that resources will be allocated optimally among the producers of these items.

[3] For derivations of the theorems see Dantzig and Wolfe, [2] and [3].

supply is limited to a quantity C_1. For example, C_1 might be the quantity of money capital available to the company as a whole. Division 1's output is also limited by the capacities C_2 and C_3 of two of its own resources—e.g., two specialized machines which are not needed by (or are not available to) the other division. Similarly, Division 2 has a limited capacity, C_4.

This problem can easily be restated in linear programming terms, letting

P represent total company profit

P_j represent the profit per unit of output j

and

a_{ij} represent the amount of input i required to produce a unit of output j,

where all P_j and a_{ij} are assumed to be constant, as is usual in linear programming. Then our problem has the formulation

$$\text{Max } P = P_1X_1 + P_2X_2 + P_3Y_1 + P_4Y_2 + P_5Y_3$$

subject to[4]

$$(1) \qquad a_{11}X_1 + a_{12}X_2 + a_{13}Y_1 + a_{14}Y_2 + a_{15}Y_3 \leqq C_1$$

$$(2) \qquad \begin{cases} a_{21}X_1 + a_{22}X_2 \leqq C_2 \\ a_{31}X_1 + a_{32}X_2 \leqq C_3 \end{cases}$$

$$(3) \qquad a_{43}Y_1 + a_{44}Y_2 + a_{45}Y_3 \leqq C_4$$

$$\text{all } X_i, \; Y_j \geqq 0.$$

Note the special structural characteristic of this program. Some of the constraints contain only the X variables and some contain only the Y variables. In more general terms, this sort of structure can be described in the schematic form shown in Table 1, where each of the A's represents a multiplicity of constraints.

The decomposition algorithm is applicable to any program which can be rewritten in this form. Fortunately, a number of important classes of problem in addition to the one described also happen to share this structure. Moreover, decomposition procedures can also be used in dealing with some other types of problem.

2. Outline of the Decomposition Procedure

Our multi-division company problem can help us to understand the entire decomposition procedure. The basic idea is very simple to follow if it is envisioned as the following process: top management asks each division of the company to calculate and submit an optimal production plan as though it were operating in isolation.[5] Once the plans are submitted, top management seeks to

[4] The decision to have only a single company constraint (1) was taken for simplicity in our illustrative calculations. However, it must be recognized that such a trivial case avoids most of the interesting problems of decentralization.

[5] A technical point must be mentioned here. When a problem such as that given in section 1 is decomposed it can easily happen that the feasible region for one or more divisions

TABLE 1

Objective function:	P				
Overall (corporate) constraints	A				$\leqq K$
Division a constraints	A_a				$\leqq K_a$
Division b constraints		A_b			$\leqq K_b$
	...	...	...	...	...
Division N constraints				A_N	$\leqq K_N$

modify these plans to suit the company's purposes. By successive reformulation of these divisional plans on the basis of marginal profit figures which are recomputed at each stage by top management and assigned by it to the divisions, an output plan which is optimal for the company as a whole is ultimately arrived at. This is the solution to the original programming problem which has been found by subdivision (decomposition).

Because the divisions' plans are designed without taking account of interdivisional interactions, at an intermediate stage of the calculation they will not be optimal (and perhaps not even feasible)[6] from the point of view of the company as a whole. In particular, if the production of some output by division k imposes burdens on other divisions by using up a scarce company resource, or by causing an upward shift in the cost functions pertaining to some other company operations, division k's calculation is likely to lead it to overproduce this item from the point of view of the company, because the costs to other divisions will not enter its accounts. This is the classical problem of external diseconomies. Similarly, if one of division k's outputs yields external economies, i.e., if a rise in its production increases the profitability of *other* divisions, division k may (considering just its own gains in its calculations) not produce enough of this product to maximize the profits of the firm.

This then, is the basic problem of decentralized decision making: to induce divisions to increase (by just the right amount) those activities which yield external economies and to decrease those which produce external diseconomies. The means whereby this can be accomplished is the addition to divisional earnings of a per unit subsidy or bonus of appropate magnitude for every external

is not bounded. This would occur, for example, if the inequality sign were reversed in constraint (3), for then there would be no upper bound to the outputs, Y_1, Y_2 and Y_3 which division 2 would consider itself able to produce. Note that this is possible even though the feasible region of the original problem is effectively bounded by the corporate constraints. As a practical matter this is not a serious problem either economically or for computation. No real division is likely to be without its own resource limitations, and in any case, a minor modification in the computational procedures has been designed to cope with this difficulty. See Dantzig and Wolfe [2], p. 105.

[6] I.e., at such an intermediate stage there is no guarantee that the divisional plans will satisfy the corporate constraints.

economy yielding output, and a per unit penalty[7] on those products which involve diseconomies.

The decomposition procedure then proceeds as follows:

1. Each division submits to the company a (suboptimal) plan based on a unit profit figure for each activity which has been assigned by the company.
2. The company calculates what burdens (or benefits) each such plan creates for all other divisions.
3. The company then tells the division manager that his unit return on output j is no longer the original unit profit, P_j. Instead, he is given a revised *net* profit figure composed of P_j plus or minus a per unit bonus or penalty equal to his division's marginal net contribution to or burden upon the profitability of other divisions.
4. The divisions submit new plans which are again designed to serve their own rather than total company interests, but recalculated in terms of the revised net profit figures.
5. The entire process is repeated (with recalculated net profit figures at each stage) as many times as necessary for an optimal set of decisions to be arrived at. Since there is only a finite number of options (divisional basic feasible solutions) to be tried, and since each step in the procedure is designed to increase the profits of the company, this calculation is guaranteed to arrive at an optimal solution after a finite number of such steps (see Dantzig and Wolfe, [2] for proof).

To understand the process (and, incidentally, to know when the computation terminates) it is necessary to see how the external economy bonuses and external diseconomy penalties are calculated. For this purpose we must digress to examine a more general class of the dual prices of linear programming than is usually discussed. The remarkable results which will be described are well known to specialists in the subject but they do not seem to be developed systematically anywhere in the published programming literature.[8]

3. Provisional Dual Prices[9]

We may designate *optimal* values of the ordinary or structural variables of the dual problem by $V_1, V_2, \cdots, V_m$ and the *optimal* values of the slack variables by $L_1, L_2, \cdots, L_n$. It is well known that for an optimal basic solution of the production problem the values of these variables may be interpreted as follows.

[7] That such bonuses and penalties can yield an overall optimum is of course not a new idea. It goes back at least to Marshall and Pigou ([10], pp. 164–165) and is discussed explicitly in terms of the firm in Hirshleifer [6], especially p. 99. Decomposition provides a systematic theoretical basis and an explicit method for computing the bonuses and the penalties.

[8] In our search for references we must acknowledge the help of Harold W. Kuhn and A. W. Tucker. The only case where the term "price" seems even to have been used in connection with these non-optimal but basic dual values occurs in Zoutendijk [13], p. 25 ff.

[9] For a more detailed discussion of duality theory, see, e.g., Dorfman, Samuelson and Solow [4], Chapters 3 and 7.

V_i is the shadow price or marginal profit value of input i and L_j is the opportunity cost (relative loss) involved in producing a unit of output j. That is, V_i tells the company how much its (gross) profit would increase if its investment in input i were increased by one unit[10] so that $V_i = \partial P/\partial C_i$ where, once again, P represents total profit and C_i represents the available amount (capacity) of input i. Similarly, L_j tells us how much company profits would be reduced if it undertook to produce one unit of some commodity, j, which is not in its optimal product line.

It is to be emphasized that the usual interpretation of these variables is confined to an optimal basic solution of the primal and dual problems. But it transpires that analogous figures, which we will call *provisional dual prices*, can be determined to correspond to any basic feasible solution of the primal (production) problem whether or not that solution is optimal. In this section the results will merely be described, with proofs left to the appendix of this paper, where a method of calculation of our provisional dual prices is also specified.

Let our provisional dual prices be designated by $\Pi_1, \cdots, \Pi_m, \Delta_1, \cdots, \Delta_n$. At the optimal solution these become the dual (shadow) prices and (dual slack) opportunity cost figures so well known in linear programming analysis. The Π_i, which are the provisional dual values of the company's scarce inputs, are called *simplex multipliers* and the Δ_j, which are the provisional opportunity costs of the outputs, are called the *simplex evaluators*.

More specifically, we have the following results:

1. Π_i is the marginal profitability of input i, so that $\Pi_i = \partial P/\partial C_i$. However, now this derivative represents the addition to profit, P, which could be earned by increasing the amount of input i *when the resource is used in the manner prescribed by the current basic feasible solution*, i.e., generally, when that resource is *not* employed optimally.
2. The Δ_j represents the opportunity loss incurred in introducing the production of a commodity less profitable than those currently employed in the basis, or *alternatively*—if it is negative, $-\Delta_k$ *can represent the net gain* (*the negative loss*) *obtained by introducing the production of a unit of output* k *if* k *is more profitable than any item currently in the basis*. For any item r currently in the basis, i.e., any output r which is produced in our feasible solution, we naturally have $\Delta_r = 0$.
3. Thus, unlike the *optimal* values of these dual variables which are all nonnegative, the provisional dual values, the Δ_j, may be negative, zero or positive. Similarly, there may be *negative* Π_i that represent resources which would be used in the manufacture of unprofitable items (!) if the current

[10] Throughout this paper degeneracy is assumed to be absent. Where degeneracy occurs this interpretation is apt to run into difficulties because it may not be possible to define a derivative (marginal profit figure). For proof and a more general theorem see Mills [9], pp. 186–193.

The marginal profitability figures, V_i, will usually be nonnegative, meaning that added (free) quantities of any input will not decrease profits. However, if the ith constraint in the primal problem is an equation rather than an inequality the non-negativity of V_i is no longer guaranteed.

basic solution were adopted.[11] For present purposes the possibility of negative Π_i and Δ_j is the only difference between the simplex multipliers and evaluators and the ordinary (optimal) dual prices.

4. In particular, we see that by introducing items, k, for which $-\Delta_k > 0$ we can obtain an improved (more profitable) basic feasible solution. Moreover, if and only if all $\Delta_j \geqq 0$ (so that the introduction of *any* item into the product line from outside the current basis involves a nonnegative opportunity loss) we will have arrived at an optimal solution. That is precisely why an optimal solution requires all $\Delta_j \geqq 0$.

4. Concepts for the Decomposition Procedure

It is convenient in the following discussion to employ terminology borrowed (and adapted for present purposes) from the language of business administration. The illustrations will be drawn from the small programming problem which appears at the beginning of this article.

A constraint such as (1) in which the outputs of several divisions are involved will be called a *corporate constraint*, while constraints like (2) which affect only the outputs of a single division (in this case, division 1) will be called *divisional constraints* (in this case, *division 1 constraints*).

A *solution to a division k programming problem* is an optimal solution to the programming subproblem constituted by the divisional constraints and some suitably chosen divisional objective function. For simplicity, our discussion will deal exclusively with a two division case[12] and we will denote these solutions by X_q^* and Y_r^* for divisions 1 and 2, respectively. Here X_q^* and Y_r^* are both solution vectors giving the magnitudes of the outputs of each of the (two) commodities produced by division 1 and each of the (three) items turned out by division 2. Since the divisions can submit a (finite) number of such proposed divisional solutions, $X_1^*, X_2^*, \cdots, X_q^*$ and $Y_1^*, Y_2^*, \cdots, Y_r^*$, the subscripts q and r are employed in order to indicate how many such proposed solutions have already been submitted by each division up to current stage of the calculation.

Corporate resources are the available amounts (such as C_1 in our example) of the inputs involved in the *corporate constraints*.

A *divisional resource* such as C_2, C_3 and C_4 is defined analogously.

Divisional profit coefficients are the coefficients of the objective functions of the divisional programming problems. Some or all of these profit figures are recomputed in each cycle.

The *executive program* is an apparently artificial programming calculation undertaken by company management to determine the appropriate values for the divisional profit coefficients at the current stage of the calculation. As we shall see, the executive program does take account of the corporate constraints. Its solution takes the form of a weighted average of the feasible solutions of the

[11] In other words, corresponding to a *non-optimal* basic solution of the primal problem we will (usually) have a *non-feasible* solution of the dual.

[12] This involves no real loss of generality and the reader can readily translate the discussion to the multi-divisional case.

divisional programs. The computation of the executive program consists of the calculation of the weight or proportion to be assigned to each divisional program in the solution of the entire problem. That is, if division 1 has so far submitted the solutions $X_1^*, X_2^*, \cdots, X_q^*$, the role of division 1 in the executive program solution will be assigned by a weighted average of these starred X's. However, during most of the calculation we are primarily concerned not with the solution of the executive program but with the corresponding values of the provisional dual prices which yield the divisional profit coefficients.

5. The Executive Program

Suppose the divisions have sent in, one at a time, proposed divisional solutions $X_1^*, \cdots, X_q^*; Y_1^*, \cdots, Y_r^*$ to the corporate accounting office. Here, if division 1 is involved in the production of n_1 items, then X_q^* is the vector $(X_{1q}, X_{2q}, \cdots, X_{n_1q})$ where X_{kq} represents the output of division 1's commodity k which is recommended in division 1's q^{th} solution proposal. Y_r^* is to be interpreted similarly. Note that here the X_{iq} and Y_{jr} are not variables—they represent specific numbers calculated by the divisions in the qth and r^{th} iterative solutions of the divisional programs and transmitted by them to the corporate accounting office.

When it receives the qth proposed solution from division 1 or the rth proposed solution from division 2 the corporate accounting office takes these and the corresponding data for previously proposed solutions and forms the following weighted average figures for each product X_i and Y_j, using the (as yet undetermined) weights $\mu_1, \cdots, \mu_q, \nu_1, \cdots, \nu_r$:

$$
(4) \qquad \begin{aligned} X_{iq}^a &= \mu_1 X_{i1} + \mu_2 X_{i2} + \cdots + \mu_q X_{iq} \\ Y_{jr}^a &= \nu_1 Y_{j1} + \nu_2 Y_{j2} + \cdots + \nu_r Y_{jr} . \end{aligned}
$$

Because they are weights, the μ_s and ν_t are required to satisfy

$$
(5) \qquad \begin{aligned} &\mu_1 + \mu_2 + \cdots + \mu_q = 1 \\ &\nu_1 + \nu_2 + \cdots + \nu_r = 1 \\ &\text{all } \mu_s \geqq 0, \qquad \text{all } \nu_t \geqq 0. \end{aligned}
$$

These weighted averages X_{iq}^a and Y_{jr}^a are then employed by corporate accounting as the variables of the executive program, which can now be described. The executive program has three components: an objective function which is based on the objective function of the original program, constraints which correspond to the corporate constraints, and constraints on the (unknown) weights (5), one constraint for each division.

Two characteristics of the executive program should be noted: a) the divisional constraints do not appear in the executive program, so that it usually contains many fewer constraints than the original problem and b) looking at the expressions (4) for the averaged variables X_{iq}^a and Y_{jr}^a of the executive program we see that they consist of two types of elements: the unknown weights, μ_i and ν_j, and the *given constants* such as X_{iq} and Y_{jr} which have been obtained from the proposed divisional solutions. It follows that the only true unknowns are the weights μ_s and ν_t and, as we shall see presently, by collecting terms, the master program is readily rewritten as an ordinary linear programming problem involving only these variables. Moreover, at any intermediate stage in the calculation, the object of the executive program may be described as the determination of an appropriate feasible (and basic) set of weights μ_s and ν_t associated with each divisional program so far proposed. These new weights are designed to yield a company profit figure greater than the returns corresponding to the preceding executive program calculation.

An example of the construction of an executive program should make these points clear. For simplicity, let us deal with the single corporate constraint case (1) with which this article started out. Suppose that the objective function and the corporate constraint are respectively

$$P = P_1X_1 + P_2X_2 + P_3Y_1 + P_4Y_2 + P_5Y_3 = X_1 + 2X_2 + 3Y_1 + Y_2 + 2Y_3$$

(6) and

$$a_{11}X_1 + a_{12}X_2 + a_{13}Y_1 + a_{14}Y_2 + a_{15}Y_3$$
$$= 4X_1 + X_2 + 2Y_1 - 5Y_2 + Y_3 \leqq C_1$$

Suppose, moreover, that three solutions have so far been proposed by division 1 and two solutions have been proposed by division 2 as follows:

(7)

Division 1 proposed solutions

1st proposal	2nd proposal	3rd proposal
$X_{11} = 7$	$X_{12} = 2$	$X_{13} = 6$
$X_{21} = 4$	$X_{22} = 0$	$X_{23} = 5$

Division 2 proposed solutions

1st proposal	2nd proposal
$Y_{11} = 0$	$Y_{12} = 0$
$Y_{21} = 12$	$Y_{22} = 0$
$Y_{31} = 0$	$Y_{32} = 9$

By direct substitution of values from the proposed divisional solutions (7) our weighted average variables (4) become (omitting their last subscript for simplicity)

$$(8)\quad \begin{cases} X_1^a = 7\mu_1 + 2\mu_2 + 6\mu_3 \\ X_2^a = 4\mu_1 \qquad\quad + 5\mu_3 \\ Y_1^a = 0 \\ Y_2^a = 12\nu_1 \\ Y_3^a = \qquad\quad 9\nu_2 \end{cases}$$

Now, our executive program is

$$\text{Maximize} \quad P = P_1X_1^a + P_2X_2^a + P_3Y_1^a + P_4Y_2^a + P_5Y_3^a$$

subject to

$$a_{11}X_1^a + a_{12}X_2^a + a_{13}Y_1^a + a_{14}Y_2^a + a_{15}Y_3^a \leqq C_1$$

$$\mu_1 + \mu_2 + \mu_3 = 1$$

$$\nu_1 + \nu_2 = 1$$

$$\text{all } \mu_s \geqq 0, \qquad \text{all } \nu_t \geqq 0.$$

Substituting in the values of the P_i and a_{1i} from (6) and the values of the X_i^a and Y_j^a from (8) the first two relationships become

$$P = (7\mu_1 + 2\mu_2 + 6\mu_3) + 2(4\mu_1 + 5\mu_3) + 12\nu_1 + 2(9\nu_2) = 15\mu_1 + 2\mu_2 + 16\mu_3 + 12\nu_1 + 18\nu_2$$

$$4(7\mu_1 + 2\mu_2 + 6\mu_3) + (4\mu_1 + 5\mu_3) - 5(12\nu_1) + 9\nu_2 = 32\mu_1 + 8\mu_2 + 29\mu_3 - 60\nu_1 + 9\nu_2 \leqq C_1 .$$

Hence, in final form, the executive program is[13]

$$\text{Maximize} \quad P = 15\mu_1 + 2\mu_2 + 16\mu_3 + 12\nu_1 + 18\nu_2$$

subject to

$$32\mu_1 + 8\mu_2 + 29\mu_3 - 60\nu_1 + 9\nu_2 \leqq C_1$$

$$\mu_1 + \mu_2 + \mu_3 = 1$$

$$\nu_1 + \nu_2 = 1$$

$$\mu_1 \geqq 0, \quad \mu_2 \geqq 0, \quad \mu_3 \geqq 0, \quad \nu_1 \geqq 0, \quad \nu_2 \geqq 0.$$

This has, indeed, changed from a problem in the variables X_i and Y_j into one for the determination of improved feasible weights μ_s and ν_t to be used in forming the average of the previously proposed divisional solutions.

It will be noted that the number of variables in the executive program increases as additional proposed divisional solutions are entered into the records. Whenever a division submits a new proposed solution and the corporate accounting office computes its resource use, another weight variable is added to the master program. Thus, when division 1 sends program X_{q+1}^* to the company accounting office, then μ_{q+1} will be added to the set of variables of the executive program.[14]

[13] Note that the coefficients of the divisional constraints play no direct role in the formulation of the executive program. This confirms our earlier assertion that decomposition requires no knowledge on the part of central management about the nature of the internal technological arrangements of the divisions. In this respect the procedure offers very real advantages of decentralized decision making.

[14] In practice, as a matter of computational convenience, at any stage of the calculation many of the previously proposed divisional solutions and the corresponding weight variables μ_s and ν_t may be disregarded in the executive program. The computation can be arranged so that at any stage a proposed solution which is given a zero weight by the executive program calculation is dropped from the next executive program calculation. I.e., if weight μ_i of divisional proposal X_i^* happens to be equal to zero at some stage, then X_i^* is dropped from the executive program before the following iteration.

6. Description of the Decomposition Procedure

Assume now that, up to this stage, division 1 has submitted $q - 1$ and division 2 has submitted $r - 1$ proposed solutions and the qth and r^{th} proposed solutions have now been received by the corporate accounting office.

Using the revised simplex method, by one pivot step of the simplex calculation an improved feasible solution for the executive problem is then found. However, the solution values of the variables in this program are disregarded until the final iteration which gives the optimal solution to the original (decomposed) programming problem.[15] Instead, the purpose of this computation is to determine the provisional dual prices (simplex multipliers), $\Pi = (\Pi_1, \cdots, \Pi_m, \bar{\Pi}_1, \bar{\Pi}_2)$, for each of the corporate resources. The last two of these dual prices, $\bar{\Pi}_1$ and $\bar{\Pi}_2$, correspond, respectively, to the constraints $\Sigma\mu_i = 1$ and $\Sigma\nu_j = 1$.

Using these provisional dual prices, revised divisional unit profit figures are then calculated for this q^{th} and r^{th} proposed divisional solution, in accord with the following expressions:

$$(9) \qquad \begin{aligned} R_{qi} &= P_i - (\Pi_1 a_{1i} + \Pi_2 a_{2i} + \cdots + \Pi_m a_{mi}) \quad \text{and} \\ S_{rj} &= P_j - (\Pi_1 a_{1j} + \Pi_2 a_{2j} + \cdots + \Pi_m a_{mj}). \end{aligned}$$

These divisional revised profit figures are to be employed in the next round of calculations as the coefficients of the divisions' objective functions

$$(10) \qquad R_q = \Sigma R_{qi} X_i \quad \text{and} \quad S_r = \Sigma S_{rj} Y_j .$$

Note that the last two entries in the Π vector, the $\bar{\Pi}_1$ and $\bar{\Pi}_2$, do not have any role in determining the revised profit figures. The revised profit figures (9) will presently be shown to differ from the ordinary profit coefficients, the P_i, by the addition of *bonuses* and *penalties* imposed upon activities for their use of company resources.

These revised divisional profit figures are sent to divisions 1 and 2 who then compute the optimal solution to the divisional linear programs which are composed of the objective functions (10) together with the divisional constraints.

The solutions are X_{q+1} and Y_{r+1}, i.e., they are the proposed divisional programs for the next iteration. As before, these solutions are then transferred to corporate accounting which computes the new weighted average solutions (4) to be used in the next executive program calculations.

The test for optimality may now be described. It is in this test that the last two shadow prices, $\bar{\Pi}_1$ and $\bar{\Pi}_2$, are employed. For this purpose the total revised profit contribution figures for the two divisions, R_q and S_r, as given by (10), are compared with $\bar{\Pi}_1$ and $\bar{\Pi}_2$, respectively. If either $R_q > \bar{\Pi}_1$ or $S_r > \bar{\Pi}_2$, or both, then the new divisional proposed solution improves the company's profit position. In this case the decomposition procedure introduces one of these solutions into

[15] As described in the preceding footnote, the solution of the executive program at any intermediate stage of the computations may also be used to determine which proposed divisional solution can be dropped from the next stage of the calculation. A proposed divisional solution whose weight, μ_i or ν_j, turns out to be zero will be omitted from the next executive program.

the executive program and goes on to the next iteration, repeating the calculations until an optimal solution is reached. On the other hand, if $R_q = \bar{\Pi}_1$ *and* $S_r = \bar{\Pi}_2$ then an optimal solution to the executive problem has been found. That is, the weights μ_i^* and ν_j^* determined by the executive program calculation of the previous iteration have now been shown to be optimal. The optimal solution to our original programming problem is given by the output levels X_i and Y_j which are obtained by the indicated averaging of the proposed divisional solutions:

$$X_i = \mu_i^* X_{i1} + \mu_2^* X_{i2} + \cdots + \mu_q^* X_{iq}\,; \qquad Y_j = \nu_1^* Y_{j1} + \nu_2^* Y_{j2} + \cdots + \nu_r^* Y_{jr}.$$

This then, in bare outline, is the essence of the decomposition procedure. Let us now try to see why it works.

7. Interpretation of the Executive Program

Let us next examine the artificial revised objective function which is assigned to division 1 by central management. At each stage, rather than maximizing $\Sigma P_i X_i$, the first division is told to maximize the revised objective function $\Sigma R_{qi} X_i = \Sigma_j (P_j - \Sigma_i \Pi_i a_{ij}) X_j$ which replaces the initial objective function

$$\Sigma_j P_j X_j\,.$$

The revised profit function differs from the original one by the amount

$$-\Sigma_i \Sigma_j \Pi_i a_{ij} X_j\,.$$

The economic meaning of this expression can readily be inferred when one recalls, that we interpret X_j as the quantity of output j, a_{ij} as the amount of input i needed to produce a unit of output j and Π_i as the value or marginal profitability (to the firm) of a unit of (corporate) input i. Thus $\Sigma_i \Pi_i a_{ij} X_j$ is the total value of all the inputs going into the production of output j and

$$-\Sigma_i \Sigma_j \Pi_i a_{ij} X_j$$

is the opportunity cost to the firm of all resources used by division 1 in producing all its outputs. In sum, at each iteration the division is told to maximize not its own profit, but rather *a net figure,* $\Sigma R_{qi} X_i$, *which subtracts from the profit figure the value to the rest of the firm of the scarce inputs that the division uses.*

Thus the division is, in effect, forced to pay a penalty for the external diseconomies which its outputs impose on the rest of the firm. It should be added that in those cases where a Π_k happens to be negative (indicating that at this iteration an input k involves a disutility to the rest of the firm), $-\Pi_k a_{kj} X_j$ will be positive, so that the division receives a bonus for using up this nuisance resource. That is, the division is compensated for any external economies which it brings about. We see, then, how the decomposition procedure provides each division with net profit figures which are designed to compensate for the external economies and diseconomies caused by its activities. This is the secret of the procedure, the means whereby it achieves results that are optimal for the operation as a whole, though decision making remains decentralized, at least in form.

Now let us look into the workings of the optimality test of the decomposition method. It will be recalled that in our two divisions case there are $m + 2$ constraints in the executive program. The first m of these correspond to the m scarce company input resources for whose use the two divisions of the company compete. Corresponding to these m scarce resources there are the m ordinary simplex multipliers $\Pi_1, \cdots, \Pi_m$. In addition, there are two constraints $\Sigma\mu_i = 1$ and $\Sigma\nu_j = 1$ which are associated with the multipliers $\bar{\Pi}_1$ and $\bar{\Pi}_2$.

The two last constraints serve to *require* us to select such weights that the X^a_{iq} and Y^a_{jr} variables (4) to be used in the master program are *true averages* of the divisions' proposed solutions. To see what this implies, suppose the constraint $\Sigma\mu_i = 1$ were replaced by $\Sigma\mu_i \geqq 1$. This would mean that the X^a_{iq} employed in the current solution of the executive program could exceed a weighted average of the previously proposed divisional programs for division one. $\bar{\Pi}_1$ may, now, be interpreted as the marginal profitability of a (unit) increase in the capacity figure (the C) associated with the corresponding constraint, $\Sigma\mu_i = 1$. But here the C is obviously equal to unity to begin with. Hence $\bar{\Pi}_1$ must be interpreted as the marginal profitability of letting the μ_i's add up to a total greater than unity. As we have just seen, this is tantamount to having division 1 increase its outputs beyond a weighted average of its previously proposed programs, as a result of which it must use up more of the company resources. In other words, $\bar{\Pi}_1$ *may be considered the relative marginal profitability of a transfer of some company resources to division 1*, and $\bar{\Pi}_2$ is the corresponding figure for division 2.[16]

We can now turn directly to the optimality test and the role of $\bar{\Pi}_1$ and $\bar{\Pi}_2$ in that criterion. Whenever the division completes another suboptimal calculation based on its revised objective function, it will have determined on a new proposed divisional solution $X_q = (X_{1q}, X_{2q}, \cdots, X_{n_1q})$. This proposed solution must next be compared in profitability to the company with the programs which the division had previously prepared. It will be remembered that, for this purpose, the division's revised profit figure

$$R_q(X_q) = \Sigma_j(P_j - \Sigma_i\Pi_i a_{ij})X_{jq} \tag{11}$$

which is yielded by the proposed program X_q, is compared with the value of $\bar{\Pi}_1$, the simplex multiplier associated with the master program constraint $\Sigma\mu_i = 1$. If $R_q = \bar{\Pi}_1$ (and if corresponding conditions are satisfied for each division) the current (preceding) solution of the executive program is judged to be optimal, whereas if $R_q > \bar{\Pi}_1$ a new improved executive program can be obtained by taking the most recently calculated divisional program X_q and averaging it in with divisional programs which had previously been proposed.

But we have seen in this section that the revised profit figure, $R_q(X_q)$, is a measure of the *net* profit contribution which division 1's proposed *new* solution

[16] More specifically $\bar{\Pi}_1$ is the profit to be earned from a 100 per cent increase in the company resources made available to division 1. For, starting with $\Sigma\mu_i = C = 1$, a unit increase in C gives us $\Sigma\mu_i = 2$. Thus, since in a linear programming problem returns do not diminish, $\bar{\Pi}_1$ is, in effect, the *total* profit contributed to the company by division 1 under the terms of the solution currently proposed by the executive program. Similar remarks, of course, apply to $\bar{\Pi}_2$.

X_q offers to the company, while $\bar{\Pi}_1$ is a measure of the profit contribution offered by the division's *previously* proposed solutions. Hence, the comparison of R_q with $\bar{\Pi}_1$ is simply an examination of the *net* profitability of the new proposed solution X_q in relation to the profits which are offered by the optimally weighted average of the previously proposed divisional solutions. If R_q exceeds $\bar{\Pi}_1$, the potential net gain from the introduction of the new solution, R_q, is greater than the marginal yield, $\bar{\Pi}_1$, of the assignment of additional company resources to division 1 to be used in accord with the averaged previous solutions. In other words, the new solution offers a higher *marginal* yield than the old, and the company will gain by taking some resources out of the use required by the previous solution and allocating them to the output pattern described by the new solution. In this case it pays to compute a new executive program which averages in (a more profitable manner) this new proposed solution along with those that preceded it, and to proceed with further iterations of the decomposition algorithm until the optimality criterion is finally satisfied.

One more observation may help to confirm our interpretation. Consider any division 1 proposal, X_p, which is currently being averaged with nonzero weight μ_p into the combined executive program solution X_q^a as given by (4). In other words, X_p is a previously proposed division 1 solution which has not been rejected by the master program (it has not been assigned a weight $\mu_p = 0$). Suppose, moreover, we were to use (11) to calculate a revised profit figure $R_q(X_p)$ for this old proposal X_p. It can be proved without too much difficulty (see e.g., Dantzig, [1]) that we must have $R_q(X_p) = \bar{\Pi}_1$. In other words, *every previous division 1 solution which has not been rejected by the executive program calculation must offer the same revised profit figure to the division and each such profit figure must be equal to the division 1 marginal yield,* $\bar{\Pi}_1$. We see at once that since the division's new proposal, X_q, has been calculated to maximize the revised revenue $R_q(X)$, we must have $R_q(X_q) \geqq R_q(X_p) = \bar{\Pi}_1$. Thus, the division's (optimal) new proposal must offer at least as high a revised revenue yield as its previous proposals, and only if it offers a higher return than the previous proposals, i.e., only if $R_q(X_q) > \bar{\Pi}_1$, will it pay to introduce the new proposal into the averaged company solution X_q^a as given by (4).

8. The Optimal Weighted Average Programs and Decentralization

Once the final stage of the calculation is reached, an optimal set of weights, μ_s^0 and ν_t^0 is calculated with the aid of the executive program. Substitution of these optimal weights into (4) yields the optimal weighted average divisional solutions. Those optimally averaged decisions constitute the solution which is most profitable for the company as a whole.

It is to be emphasized that now division managers *must be told by the company* what weights they are to employ, i.e., what combination of their proposals the company desires them to produce. There is no automatic motivation mechanism which will lead division managers to arrive at such a combination of outputs of their own volition. In this way, the decentralization permitted by decomposition breaks down completely at this point.

To understand the nature of the situation we can profitably examine the problem graphically. Figure 1 represents the feasible region of one of the divisions. Now, as is normal in linear programming, we look among the corners 0, A, B, C, D and E, for a program which is optimal from the point of view of the division. But there is no reason why the solution which is optimal for the *company* should occur at a corner of the *division's* feasible region. Indeed, usually the company's optimal solution point will occur at a non corner point (such as S) on the boundary of the divisional feasible region. That is precisely why a weighted average of several divisional proposals is required in this solution. In the present case the optimal point, S, is a weighted average of the solutions represented by points D and C.

Now, each revision of the divisional profit figures by the master program produces a shift in iso profit lines in the diagram. For example, at some stage in the calculations the revised profit function may be represented by the dotted parallel lines in Figure 1, so that the division's optimal program is point C. Subsequent calculations will twist these iso profit curves about. In particular, if the optimal solution lies at an interior point of the feasible region boundary, such as S, the terminal iso profit lines must be parallel to the boundary segment CD which contains S. We know that this must be so from our previous observation that *every* proposed divisional proposal, X_p, which is averaged into the final solution must yield the same revised profit figure $R_q(X_p) = \bar{\Pi}_1$. In the case shown in the diagram, since S is obtained as a weighted average of C and D, both solution point C and solution point D must yield a revised profit figure equal to $\bar{\Pi}_1$; i.e., C and D must lie on the same iso profit curve, $\bar{\Pi}\,\bar{\Pi}'$.

This tells us directly why the price system can not be relied on to induce the divisions of their own volition to produce the (company) optimal solution, S. Every point on boundary segment CD, including C, S and D must be equally profitable from the point of view of the division. In fact, since S is not a corner of the feasible region *no* set of fixed prices can make S the most profitable output for the division. For consider any straight iso profit line (such as PP') through S which does not also go through points C and D. Then either C or D must lie above PP', i.e., with the set of prices which yield profit line PP' either C or D must be more profitable than S.

We may conjecture that this difficulty is, in part, a consequence of the linearity of our problem. If the boundary of the division's (convex) feasible set of solutions were curved throughout, i.e., if diminishing returns (diminishing technical marginal rates of substitution) were everywhere present, this problem would sometimes disappear. This is illustrated in Figure 2 in which the feasible region is convex and its northeast boundary is curved throughout. If the optimal point is any point, such as S, on that boundary, there will always be an iso profit line TT', which is tangent to the boundary of the feasible region at the optimal point S, and which can therefore be used to determine prices appropriate for the guidance of divisional activities. It causes S to be the output combination which is most profitable for the division as well as for the company and so, with the prices corresponding to TT', the divisions can be left to make output decisions entirely by themselves.

Unfortunately, matters do not always work out in so straightforward a

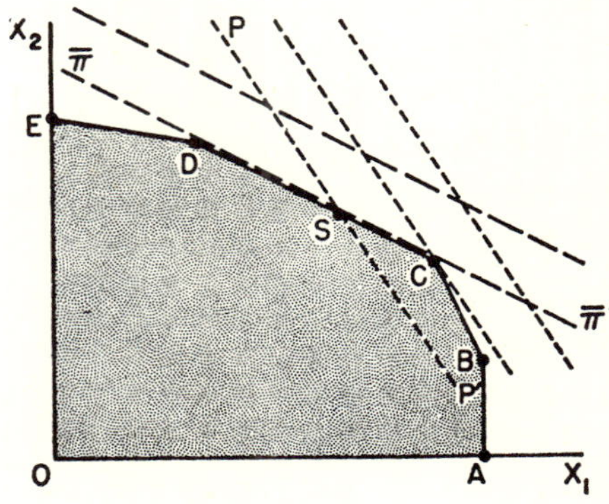

FIG. 1

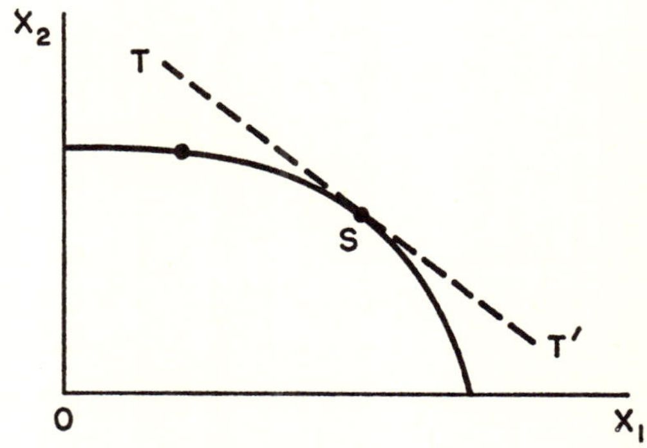

FIG. 2

manner. Both in the linear and in the nonlinear cases there may arise a more serious obstacle which precludes any set of fixed prices from inducing the divisions to make decisions which are optimal from the point of view of the company as a whole.

Throughout this discussion it was assumed that every point within the feasible region of divisional activity levels is also feasible for the company. This need not be the case. Indeed, corporate constraints may limit the solutions to a subregion of the divisional feasible region. The limitation might arise in two ways. First, the supply of some corporate resource might be insufficient to permit any division to produce some of the outputs which are not precluded by its own constraints, i.e., some output combinations which are division feasible may require more of a corporate resource than is available. Second, even though a corporate resource might be sufficient if it were used by one division alone, the solution process could allocate it in such a way that one or more divisions do not receive enough to render the entire divisional feasible regions feasible for the company as a whole. A simple linear case is shown in Figure 3 which is a reproduction of the feasible region of Figure 1 with two added constraints representing the limited corporate resources. Pairs of values of X_1 and X_2 falling within the lightly shaded area cannot be members of the company's set of optimal solutions.[17] The optimal

[17] Of course, no line on which point V lies in Figure 3 may happen to cut the divisional feasible region at two corner points. In such cases V will be expressed as the weighted

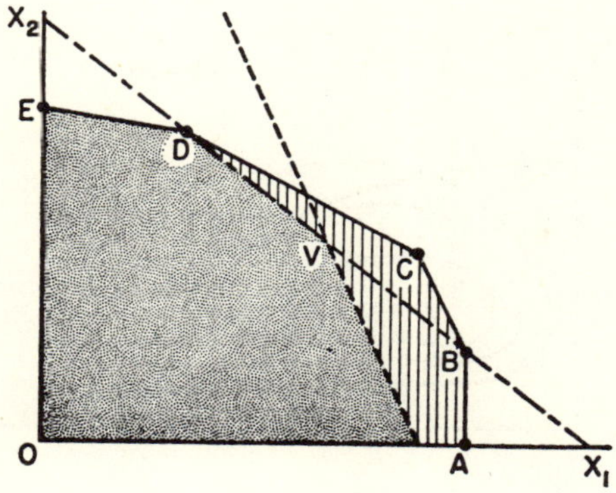

Fig. 3

solution can be, as before, a linear combination of two divisional extreme points, in this case *B* and *D*. For instance, with the corporate constraints as shown by the broken lines in Figure 3, the optimal solution might be the point *V*. But observe that this point is in the interior of the division's feasible region! In the previous cases, where the optimal solutions were points *C* or *S* (Figure 1) the corporate optimum corresponded to a divisional optimum, albeit, in point *S*, not a unique one. In the present case what is optimal for the company is not optimal for the division. We already observed that when the divisional solution is point *S* in Figure 1, no price system will guarantee that the division will automatically attain this point. This observation holds even more strongly for the case where the company optimum point is not a divisional optimum at the same time, i.e., when the company optimum corresponds to a point in the interior of a divisional feasible region. The division will then have to be instructed on either what weights to assign to the divisional extreme points, such as *B* and *D* in Figure 3, or, what might be just as easy, it must be told the optimal values of X_1 and X_2 at point *V*. These observations have an important bearing on decentralized decision making and the transfer price concept. This will be explored in a subsequent paper.

In the nonlinear case, even with the most desirable types of convexity (diminishing returns) conditions satisfied, interior optima and all their associated nasty pricing problems can arise another way. Even if the corporate constraints do not rule out any point in the divisional feasible region *the profit function* may reach a maximum at an interior point. In Figure 4 which is identical with Figure 2 except for the addition of a number of iso profit curves, we note that *W*, the point of maximum profit (the highest point on the profit hill) lies inside the division's feasible region.[18] There is obviously no iso profit line which goes only through point *W* and through no other point in the feasible region.

---

average of the values of X_1 and X_2 at more than two corner points of the divisional feasible set.

[18] One may conjecture that, in most long run economic problems, both diminishing returns and boundary solutions are likely to be the rule rather than the exception. After all, diminishing returns are part and parcel of the adaptation of facilities to varying situations, while an interior optimal solution means there must be excess capacities in the divisions which, in the long run, would surely be eliminated.

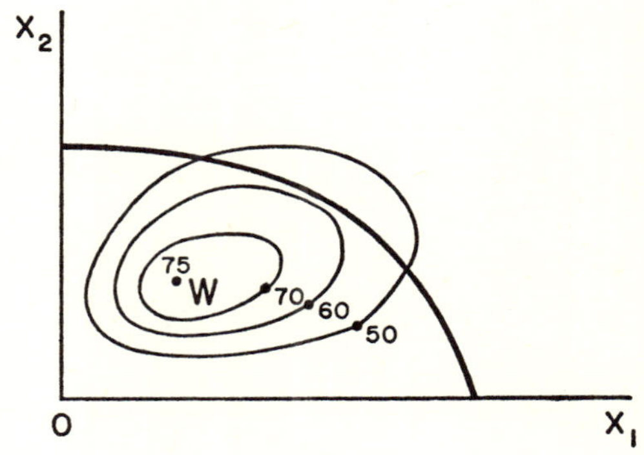

FIG. 4

While nonlinearity by itself does not solve our pricing problem, it is nevertheless fortunate that various types of nonlinearity can, in fact, be introduced into the problem without doing serious damage to the decomposition process.[19] We will see in the next section that this is extremely helpful for our economic interpretation.

9. Externalities and Nonlinear Divisional Constraints

It must be admitted that the linearity assumptions which have so far been employed in our model considerably restrict its domain of applicability. Especially the type of external economy (and to some degree, the type of external diseconomy) which occurs in the decomposition structure may well be considered a relatively bloodless member of the family. For it consists only of cases where one division's expanded activity directly reduces the availability of scarce resources to other economic subunits. This case is slightly more general than it may at first appear, for reduced availability of resources can affect the profitability of a division by forcing it to adopt a changed technology (the X_i's corresponding to outputs produced by some method A may be reduced to zero, and, instead, the outputs of some alternative process, B may be forced into the next proposed divisional solution as a result of changed input availabilities). Thus the externalities which arise in our linear model may not be so very different from the technological external economies or diseconomies of the literature of welfare economics. They are not just the pecuniary external diseconomies which arise when one producer's demand for an input bids up its price and thereby increases the costs of other producing units.[20]

Nevertheless, it is desirable to be able to deal with a far more general class of

[19] Of course, these nonlinearities must satisfy the appropriate convexity (diminishing returns) requirements. Moreover, nonlinearity means that we can never be sure a solution algorithm will arrive at the precise optimal solution in a finite number of steps. However, we can be assured of its convergence to the solution of the problem.

[20] This distinction which was first formulated by Viner [11] is of significance because pecuniary externalities are really part and parcel of the competitive process of allocation of resources, and, unlike technological externalities, they do not prevent a competitive general equilibrium from being Pareto optimal.

externalities, and, particularly in the presence of nonlinearities in the divisional constraints, it is easy to do so by means of a clever device which was first applied by Whinston to the problem of externalities (see [12] Chapter VI, pp. 36–49).

Suppose we have the following decomposable program:

$$(12)\quad \begin{cases} \text{Max } \Pi = P_1X_1 + \cdots + P_wX_w + P_{w+1}Y_1 + \cdots + P_{w+r}Y_r \\ \text{subject to the corporate constraints} \\ \quad a_{11}X_1 + \cdots + a_{1w}X_w + a_{1w+1}Y_1 + \cdots + a_{1w+r}Y_r \leqq C_1 \\ \quad \cdots\cdots\cdots\cdots\cdots\cdots\cdots\cdots\cdots\cdots \\ \quad a_{m1}X_1 + \cdots + a_{mw}X_w + a_{mw+1}Y_1 + \cdots + a_{mw+r}Y_r \leqq C_m \\ \text{and the (convex nonlinear) divisional constraints} \\ \quad f_1(X_1, \cdots, X_w) \leqq C_{m+1} \\ \quad \cdots\cdots\cdots\cdots \\ \quad f_s(X_1, \cdots, X_w) \leqq C_{m+s} \\ \qquad\qquad g_1(Y_1, \cdots, Y_r, X_k) \leqq C_{m+s+1} \\ \qquad\qquad \cdots\cdots\cdots\cdots \\ \qquad\qquad g_t(Y_1, \cdots, Y_r) \leqq C_{m+s+t}\,. \end{cases}$$

This differs from our earlier model in two significant respects:

1. the divisional constraints $f_i(X_1, \cdots, X_w) \leqq C_i$ and $g_j(Y_1, \cdots, Y_r) \leqq C_j$ are not necessarily linear, and
2. in the first constraint of division 2, $g_1(Y_1, \cdots, Y_r, X_k) \leqq C_{m+s+1}$, there is present a variable, X_k, representing a division 1 output.

Let us discuss the significance of these two characteristics. *The nonlinearities*, in fact, *make no essential difference to our decomposition procedure*; because all the special decomposition calculations, the executive program, the Π's, and the revised divisional profit functions, only involve the objective function and the corporate constraints. But both of these remain linear in (12). Hence, provided the divisional constraints yield bounded convex feasible regions so that the divisional programs possess unique optimal solutions which can be averaged together by the executive program, all remains essentially as it was in the linear case.

However, the presence of X_k in a division 2 constraint is of the utmost significance because it represents a perfectly general technological externality.[21] For it means that a division 1 output decision will produce a shift in one of division 2's technological relationships! This is precisely what we mean by a technological externality.[22]

[21] In the discussion which follows, for simplicity of exposition, we deal with only one division 1 output and one division 2 constraint but the argument can obviously be extended to as many such variables and constraints as desired, and to the case where division 2 variables also enter division 1 constraints.

[22] The significance of the nonlinearities for this discussion is that if the $g_1(Y_1, \cdots, Y_r, X_k)$ is a nonlinear function, a change in X_k can produce just about any type of shift in g,

But there is not the slightest difficulty in eliminating the X_k and reducing our problem to another form which appears to involve no externalities. That is, we can easily rephrase our problem in such a way that all our previous decomposition procedures remain completely applicable without further modification. To accomplish this we merely rename our externality variable X_k, writing $X_k = \lambda$. The first division 2 constraint now becomes $g_1(Y_1, \cdots, Y_r, \lambda) \leqq C_{m+s+1}$ and we add to our set of corporate constraints the *linear* definitional constraint $X_k - \lambda = 0$. We then end up with a new problem which is exactly the same as (12) except that it now contains one more linear corporate constraint. But in this rewritten version of our problem there is no variable which is common to a division 1 constraint and a division 2 constraint, as was true of X_k in (12). In other words, this simple transformation has taken a problem involving a completely general technological externality and transformed it into a standard decomposable problem (though into one which contains nonlinear divisional constraints).[23]

10. Concluding Comments

We have seen that the decomposition algorithm constitutes a decision mechanism for an entire decentralized but coordinated economic organization.[24] It can be taken to represent anything from a single firm to an entire economy. For the first time it offers a systematic approach to the planning problems resulting from the presence of external economies and diseconomies (or, in more general terms, divergence between private and social costs and benefits) and the consequent limitations which characterize suboptimal decisions made independently by subdivisions of the economic unit in question.

As has occurred on several other occasions in the history of our subject, the new analysis serves largely to confirm the economists' less rigorously derived conclusions. It reaffirms that the way to deal with externalities is to modify the pricing system, offering bonuses in the case of external economies and imposing penalties on the producers of external diseconomies. But the provisional dual price construction provides the first effective means whereby these penalties and bonuses can be calculated and imposed, and the decomposition algorithm offers a method for determining when the divisional programs have been properly

whereas in the linear case $g_1(Y_1, \cdots, Y_r, X_k) = b_1Y_1 + \cdots + b_rY_r + b_{r+1}X_k$ any change in the X_k must always cause a proportionate parallel shift in the division 2 constraint, and this is still a very restricted type of externality.

[23] The same argument also shows that nonlinearities in the corporate constraint which do not violate convexity, in principle, cause no problems for decomposition. For, formally, there is no difference between a corporate constraint and the division 2 constraint $g_1(Y_1, \cdots, Y_r, X_r) \leqq C_{m+s+1}$, which contains variables corresponding to outputs of both divisions! It appears that the decomposition procedure is in no fundamental way tied to the linearity assumption which is usually employed in its description.

[24] Of course, it is not suggested that this is how decentralized decisions are made in practice. Gale's model [5], pp. 85–93, comes off far better than the decomposition analysis as a representation of the decentralized decision making under competitive conditions. However, Gale does not provide a pricing and calculating mechanism.

coordinated to yield a solution that is optimal for the economic unit as a whole.

Appendix I: Derivation of the Provisional Dual Pricing Theorems[25]

Before turning to the derivation of the provisional dual pricing theorems it is convenient to deal with some preliminary matters, in particular, obtaining expressions for the values of our primal variables, and for the changes in these values when another item is introduced into the basis.

Suppose we are given the following general linear program (which is taken to include slack variables among the variables, X_j, so that all of the structural constraints are equations):

$$\text{(1)} \qquad \text{Max } P = P_1X_1 + \cdots + P_{m+n}X_{m+n}$$

subject to

$$\text{(2)} \qquad \begin{aligned} a_{11}X_1 + \cdots + a_{1m+n}X_{m+n} &= C_1 \\ \cdots\cdots\cdots\cdots\cdots\cdots & \\ a_{m1}X_1 + \cdots + a_{mm+n}X_{m+n} &= C_m \qquad \text{all } X_j \geqq 0. \end{aligned}$$

We may assume, without loss of generality, that in the current trial solution the basic (nonzero valued) variables are $X_1, \cdots, X_m$. Thus we have $X_1 > 0, \cdots, X_m > 0$, and $X_{m+1} = \cdots = X_{m+n} = 0$. Since terms with zeros in them drop out, our equations (2) reduce to

$$\begin{aligned} a_{11}X_1 + \cdots + a_{1m}X_m &= C_1 \\ \cdots\cdots\cdots\cdots\cdots\cdots & \\ a_{m1}X_1 + \cdots + a_{mm}X_m &= C_m . \end{aligned}$$

Using matrix notation, we can solve these equations for X, writing them as

$$\text{(3)} \qquad AX = C, \quad \text{i.e.,} \quad X = A^{-1}C,$$

where A is an $m \times m$ square matrix and X and C are m element column vectors.

Now suppose we were to introduce the production of one unit of commodity k whose output level was zero to begin with (i.e., X_k is a nonbasic variable at this stage). Our limited resources would then require that there be some reduction in the nonzero outputs, so that the output of (basic) commodity i would be changed, say, from X_i to $X_i - \Delta X_i$. In that case equations (2) become

$$\begin{aligned} a_{11}(X_1 - \Delta X_1) + \cdots + a_{1m}(X_m - \Delta X_m) + a_{1k} &= C_1 \\ \cdots\cdots\cdots\cdots\cdots\cdots\cdots\cdots\cdots & \\ a_{m1}(X_1 - \Delta X_1) + \cdots + a_{mm}(X_m - \Delta X_m) + a_{mk} &= C_m , \end{aligned}$$

[25] We emphasize again that there is nothing new or original in the materials which follow. This appendix is merely intended to supply materials which do not appear to have been developed systematically anywhere in the literature. The specialist reader will no doubt have the feeling that he has seen all of this before, but, apparently, the results have usually been absorbed and consolidated in his mind out of a variety of sources.

or in matrix terms, writing A_k for the vector of the kth column of coefficients in (2),

$$A(X - \Delta X) + A_k = C,$$

i.e.,

$$AX - A\Delta X + A_k = C$$

so that, subtracting (3), we obtain an expression for ΔX,

$$(4) \qquad -A\Delta X + A_k = 0, \quad \text{i.e.,} \quad \Delta X = A^{-1}A_k .$$

As a last preliminary matter let us write $\bar{P}$ for the row vector of the first m coefficients of the objective function (1), i.e., we set $\bar{P} = [P_1, P_2, \cdots, P_m]$. *This permits us to define*[26] *the provisional dual prices as the row vector* $\Pi = [\Pi_1, \Pi_2, \cdots, \Pi_m]$, *which is given by*

$$(5) \qquad \Pi = \bar{P}A^{-1}.$$

This last expression serves both as a definition and a calculation rule for our simplex multipliers (the provisional dual prices). We have yet to show that these Π_i have the required properties of dual prices. This will be demonstrated with the aid of the following three theorems whose implications for duality will only become clear in the discussion which follows their derivation:

Theorem 1: For any commodity k which is not in the current basis, Δ_k, the change in profit resulting from the introduction of a unit of output k into our basic solution, is given by

$$(6) \qquad \Delta_k = -\Pi A_k + P_k , \quad \text{i.e.,} \quad \Pi A_k + \Delta_k = P_k$$

Proof: From our profit function (1), the change in profit, Δ_k, resulting from the production of one unit of k, and the consequent changes, $\Delta_1, \Delta_2, \cdots, \Delta_m$, in the other outputs is

$$\Delta_k = -P_1\Delta X_1 - P_2\Delta X_2 - \cdots - P_m\Delta X_m + P_k ,$$

or, in matrix notation, $\Delta_k = -\bar{P}\Delta X + P_k$, so that from (4) and (5) $\Delta_k = -\bar{P}A^{-1}A_k + P_k = -\Pi A_k + P_k$. Q.E.D.

Theorem 2: For any commodity j in the current basis

$$\Pi A_j = P_j .$$

Proof: $\Pi A = \bar{P}A^{-1}A = \bar{P}$ or $\Pi A_j = P_j$. Q.E.D.

Theorem 3: $\Pi C = P.$

Proof: $\Pi C = \bar{P}A^{-1}C$ so that by (3) and the profit equation (1)

$$\Pi C = \bar{P}A^{-1}C = \bar{P}X = P. \qquad \text{Q.E.D.}$$

[26] We are here assuming that the first m variables, $X_1, X_2, \cdots, X_m$ are the currently basic variables, i.e., in the current basic solution these are the $X_i \neq 0$. This involves no loss of generality.

These three theorems imply the standard duality results:

i. Theorem 1 tells us at once that the Δ_k may be interpreted as the profit contributed by introduction of a unit of output k, i.e., it is the opportunity cost of not producing that item.[27]

ii. Equation (6) Theorem 1 may be written out as

$$a_{1k}\Pi_1 + \cdots + a_{mk}\Pi_m + \Delta k = P_k$$

which will be recognized as the kth constraint of the dual problem, so that the Π_i and the Δ_j satisfy these constraints, with the Δ_j playing the role of slack variables and the Π_i serving as the (provisional) dual variables.

iii. Written out, the equation of Theorem 3 is

$$P = C_1\Pi_1 + \cdots + C_m\Pi_m \tag{7}$$

which tells us that these dual prices are exactly large enough to impute all profits to the firm's scarce inputs, which is, of course, one of the basic theorems of duality theory.

iv. Comparison of Theorem 2 with Theorem 1 gives us $\Delta_j = 0$ for all j in the basis.

v. Our interpretation of the Π_i as marginal profit figures can be justified with the aid of Theorem 3 or equation (7) from which we infer by direct differentiation that $\Pi_i = \partial P/\partial C_i$, so that Π_i is, indeed, the marginal profitability of input i.[28]

vi. Another standard duality theorem which has not yet been discussed may be written as

$$Q_j\Delta_j = 0 \quad \text{for all } j \quad \text{and,} \tag{8}$$

$$\Pi_i U_i = 0 \quad \text{for all } i. \tag{9}$$

Here the U_i represent the slack variables of the primal problem and the Q_j are the remaining (structural) variables. The first of these equations tells us that any item which will be produced ($Q_j > 0$) must have a zero opportunity loss ($\Delta_j = 0$). The second equation states that any input with unused capacity ($U_i > 0$) must have a zero marginal profit value ($\Pi_i = 0$). The first of these

[27] There is a minor difficulty here about the sign of Δ_k. Usually in duality theory, it is customary to define the dual slack variable, L_k, as the opportunity cost of producing commodity k, whereas here we have found it convenient to interpret Δ_k as the opportunity cost of *not* producing k. Hence we would expect L_k and Δ_k to be equal and opposite in sign, and, indeed, the optimal value of $\Delta_k = -L_k$. Moreover, this observation explains why Δ_k does not appear with the minus sign usual for the slack variable in our dual constraint.

[28] The differentiation is permissible because, by (5), a *ceteris paribus* change in C_j will not affect the values of the Π's. It may be noted that, similarly, by (6), the Δ_k's will retain their values when the C's vary. Since, by assumption, we continue to employ the same basic solution throughout the calculation of our provisional dual prices only the magnitude of the nonzero X's (the basic primal variables) will change. As stated earlier, the differentiation process implicitly assumes the absence of degeneracy, for where degeneracy occurs $\partial P/\partial C_i$ may not even be defined.

relationships, (8), holds by iv, above, because for any $X_j = Q_j$ in the basis (i.e., for any $X_j > 0$), we have $\Delta_j = 0$, and for any other X, say X_k, we have $X_k = 0$ since X_k is not in the basis, so that in either case the equation is satisfied.

Equation (9) will also hold for our provisional dual variables. To see this, note first that the coefficient of any slack variable, U_i, in the objective function (its unit profit), P_i is zero. That is, excess capacity is assumed to produce neither profit nor loss for the firm. To prove that (9) is satisfied we observe that if $X_i = U_i$ is in the basis, so that $U_i > 0$, then by Theorem 2 $\Pi A_i = P_i = 0$ for our slack variable, as was just observed. But for such a slack variable A_i is the unit column vector $\{00 \cdots 010 \cdots 0\}$ with a unit in the ith location and zeros elsewhere. Hence we must have $\Pi A_i = \Pi_i$ and since we just saw that $\Pi A_i = 0$, our result follows; $\Pi_i = 0$. That is, for any $U_i > 0$ we must have $\Pi_i = 0$ so that (9) will hold.[29]

Appendix II: An Illustrative Problem

Statement of the Problem.

In this appendix the solution process for an extremely small scale numerical problem is described in detail to illustrate the computational procedure of the decomposition method. The problem is

$$
\text{(A.1)} \quad \begin{cases}
\text{Maximize} \quad P = X_1 + X_2 + 2Y_1 + Y_2 \\
\text{Subject to} \quad X_1 + 2X_2 + 2Y_1 + Y_2 \leqq 40 \\
\text{and} \\
X_1 + 3X_2 \leqq 30 \\
2X_1 + X_2 \leqq 20 \\
Y_1 \leqq 10 \\
Y_2 \leqq 10 \\
Y_1 + Y_2 \leqq 15
\end{cases}
$$

This simple problem has an obvious decomposable structure involving one corporate constraint and two divisions.

All basic feasible solutions to the divisional subproblems can easily be obtained

[29] However, it is easily shown by counterexample (and it also follows from the preceding argument) that if disposal activities are not free—say, if there is a cost to handling excess inputs, U_i, so that $P_i < 0$, then (9) will no longer be valid. In economic terms, of course, this is because in such a case excess inputs are no longer free goods—they carry with them a very real cost. We also may note that the argument used to prove (8) can be employed to show $X_j\Delta_j = 0$ for all j where the X_j represent both output variables (Q's) and slack variable (U's). This means that we can also determine simplex evaluators with the usual properties for the slack variables. The interpretation of such a slack variable evaluator Δ_i is straightforward. It is the opportunity gain (frequently negative) to be obtained by introducing the slack variable U_i into the basis; that is, the gain (loss) per unit involved in deciding to leave unused some amount of input i.

and, although one does not normally list these solutions in a routine procedure, it will be helpful in explaining the calculations, to have them on hand. Table A-1 gives all of these basic solutions. The solution value of all variables, including the slack variables, are listed.

By performing the calculations described in Section 5, a complete executive program can be derived. However, this is not necessary. Instead, the decomposition procedure obtains parts of the executive program by determining successive proposed divisional programs with the use of an iterative procedure.

The following description will show all computations required to obtain the optimal solution except the steps involving use of the simplex procedure to provide solutions to the divisional subproblems. Since the simplex method is so well known there is no need to describe it here.

First iteration.

Let us assume the divisions propose X_1^* and Y_1^* as their first tentative programs (see Table A-1.) Company accounting will then compute the associated profit figures and corporate resource usage in the manner shown in calculations (4) through (8) above. Since in the solutions proposed $X_1 = X_2 = Y_1 = Y_2 = 0$, at this stage of the iterative procedure the weighted averages will be

$$X_{11}^a = 0\cdot\mu_1 \qquad Y_{11}^a = 0\cdot\nu_1$$

$$X_{21}^a = 0\cdot\mu_1 \qquad Y_{21}^a = 0\cdot\nu_1 \,.$$

The slack variables X_{31}, X_{41}, Y_{31} and Y_{41} and their transformation into weighted averages can be neglected, since they pertain only to the divisions and do not enter the executive program.

We now form our executive program objective function

$$P = P_1X_{11}^a + P_2X_{21}^a + P_3Y_{11}^a + P_4Y_{21}^a$$
$$= 1\cdot(0\cdot\mu_1) + 1\cdot(0\cdot\mu_1) + 2\cdot(0\cdot\nu_1) + 1\cdot(0\cdot\nu_1),$$

TABLE A-1

Basic Solutions of the Subprograms

Division 1

		X_1^*	X_2^*	X_3^*	X_4^*
	X_{1q}	0	0	10	6
	X_{2q}	0	10	0	8
slack variables	X_{3q}	30	0	20	0
	X_{4q}	20	10	0	0

Division 2

		Y_1^*	Y_2^*	Y_3^*	Y_4^*	Y_5^*
	Y_{1r}	0	0	10	10	5
	Y_{2r}	0	10	0	5	10
slack variables	Y_{3r}	10	10	0	0	5
	Y_{4r}	10	0	10	5	0
	Y_{5r}	15	5	5	0	0

i.e.,

(A.2)

$$\boxed{P = 0\cdot\mu_1 + 0\cdot\nu_1}$$

Similarly our executive program (corporate) constraint is

$$1\cdot(0\cdot\mu_1) + 2\cdot(0\cdot\mu_1) + 2\cdot(0\cdot\nu_1) + 1\cdot(0\cdot\nu_1) = \boxed{0\cdot\mu_1 + 0\cdot\nu_1 \leqq 40}\,.$$

We next specify the constraints requiring the divisional weights to add to unity:

$$\boxed{\begin{aligned}\mu_1 \quad &= 1\\ \nu_1 &= 1\end{aligned}}$$

The statements in the three boxes together constitute the first executive program.

This problem is so simple that its solution and the solution to its dual can be obtained by inspection. The use of simplex procedures in dealing with the executive program is therefore postponed until our third iteration where our first really non-trivial executive program is encountered. The solution to our present executive program is:

$$\text{company profit} = 0, \qquad \mu_1 = 1, \qquad \nu_1 = 1, \qquad W = 40$$

(where W is the slack variable in the corporate constraint) and

$$\Pi = 0, \qquad \bar{\Pi}_1 = 0, \qquad \bar{\Pi}_2 = 0.$$

Clearly, the associated solution to the corporate problem (A.1) is feasible. It consists of 100 per cent of X_1^* (i.e., $\mu_1 = 1$) and 100 per cent of Y_1^* (i.e., $\nu_1 = 1$), making the values of the variables X_1, X_2, Y_1 and Y_2 equal to zero. Profit is zero. If we evaluate any other solution to the divisional problems in the profit function of (A.1), we immediately see that the current solution is not optimal. This will be indicated explicitly in the course of the next few steps of the decomposition algorithm.

By using the dual price, $\Pi = 0$, we calculate the revised unit profit of the divisional activities as in (9):

$$R_{11} = 1 - (1)\,\Pi = 1 \qquad S_{11} = 2 - (2)\,\Pi = 2$$

$$R_{12} = 1 - (2)\,\Pi = 1 \qquad S_{12} = 1 - (1)\,\Pi = 1.$$

Note that, since $\Pi = 0$, there is no change in the divisional profit figures at this stage. With these unit profit figures the two divisions compute optimal solutions to the following divisional programs:

Division 1:

Maximize

$$R_1 = R_{11}X_1 + R_{12}X_2 = X_1 + X_2$$

Division 2:

Maximize

$$S_1 = S_{11}Y_1 + S_{12}Y_2 = 2Y_1 + Y_2$$

Subject to

$$X_1 + 3X_2 \leqq 30$$
$$2X_1 + X_2 \leqq 20$$

Subject to

$$Y_1 \leqq 10$$
$$Y_2 \leqq 10$$
$$Y_1 + Y_2 \leqq 15.$$

The reader may use the simplex method or evaluate the basic solutions in Table A-1 to verify that the optimal solutions are $X_4^* = (6, 8, 0, 0)$ and $Y_4^* = (10, 5, 0, 5, 0)$.

Second iteration.

Since our initial divisional solutions X_1^* and Y_1^* did not constitute an optimal solution for the company, one of the two new proposed divisional solutions must also be employed in the next company calculation. We may select the program X_4^* of Division 1 for incorporation into the executive problem, since it satisfies our marginal profitability criterion, $R_1 > \bar{\Pi}_1$, i.e.,

$$R_1 = 6R_{11} + 8R_{12} = 14 > \bar{\Pi}_1 = 0.$$

Using the procedure described in the first iteration, we now compute the contribution of the X_4^* provisional program to corporate profit and also determine its corporate resource requirement. We find that the former is 14 and the latter is 22. Thus the new variable, μ_4 (corresponding to X_4^*), now enters the previous executive program (A.2) with the following vector of coefficients:

$$\begin{pmatrix} 14 \\ 22 \\ 1 \\ 0 \end{pmatrix}$$

The second executive program therefore becomes (with W again a slack variable)

$$\text{(A.3)} \quad \begin{cases} \text{Maximize} & (0\mu_1 + 14\mu_4 + 0\nu_1) \\ \text{Subject to} & 0\mu_1 + 22\mu_4 + 0\nu_1 + W = 40 \\ \text{and} & \mu_1 + \mu_4 = 1 \\ & \nu_1 = 1. \end{cases}$$

A new—and more profitable—solution can be determined from (A.3). The nonzero values of the primal variables are

$$\text{Company profit} = 14, \qquad \mu_4 = 1, \qquad \nu_1 = 1, \qquad W = 18$$

and the values of the dual variables become

$$\Pi = 0, \qquad \bar{\Pi}_1 = 14, \qquad \bar{\Pi}_2 = 0.$$

Since Π is still zero, the new profit figures for the divisional activities continue unchanged and so the proposed divisional programs remain X_4^* and Y_4^*.

Third iteration.

The proposed program of Division 1 no longer adds to company profits, since

$$R_2 = 6R_{21} + 8R_{22} = 14 = \bar{\Pi}_1 .$$

However, our problem is not yet solved. Further calculations must be undertaken to introduce the Division 2 proposal, Y_4^*, into the executive program because that proposal is shown to be profitable by

$$S_2 = 10S_{21} + 5S_{22} = 25 > \bar{\Pi}_2 = 0.$$

Thus, ν_4, the weight corresponding to Division 2's proposal, Y_4^*, will be the variable entering the executive program (A.3). Its coefficients in the profit function and in the corporate resource equation will both be 25 (see first iteration for the computing procedure.) The third executive program therefore becomes

$$\text{(A.4)} \quad \begin{cases} \text{Maximize} & 0\mu_1 + 14\mu_4 + 0\nu_1 + 25\nu_4 \\ \text{Subject to} & 0\mu_1 + 22\mu_4 + 0\nu_1 + 25\nu_4 + W = 40 \\ \text{and} & \mu_1 + \mu_4 = 1 \\ & \nu_1 + \nu_4 = 1. \end{cases}$$

We may now profitably examine the simplex procedure used to deal with an executive program such as (A.4).[30]

Since the last two constraints in (A.4) are equations, they contain no slack variables. However, we can arbitrarily treat μ_1 and ν_1 as the slack variables in these equations and obtain as our initial basic solution the one in which W, μ_1 and ν_1 constitute the basis, i.e., the solution in which both other variables, μ_4 and ν_4, are assigned the value zero. Our first simplex matrix then becomes:

			Primal nonbasic variables: μ_4	Primal nonbasic variables: ν_4		
	Profit	0	14	25		
Primal basic variables	$W =$	40	-22	-25	Π	Dual nonbasic variables
Primal basic variables	$\mu_1 =$	1	-1^*	0	$\bar{\Pi}_1$	Dual nonbasic variables
Primal basic variables	$\nu_1 =$	1	0	-1	$\bar{\Pi}_2$	Dual nonbasic variables
			$-\Delta_{14} =$	$-\Delta_{24} =$		
			Dual basic variables	Dual basic variables		

[30] In practice, at each iteration one simply incorporates the coefficients corresponding to the new proposed divisional program into the last executive simplex matrix obtained from the preceding iteration. It is the procedure of the so-called *revised simplex method*

This readily yields our first basic solution[31]

$$\text{Profit} = 0, \quad W = 40, \quad \mu = 1, \quad \nu_1 = 1,$$

$$\mu_4 = \nu_4 = \Pi = \bar{\Pi}_1 = \bar{\Pi}_2 = 0, \quad \Delta_{14} = -14, \quad \Delta_{24} = -25,$$

where Δ_{14} and Δ_{24} are, respectively, the first and second division dual slack variables (dual evaluators) corresponding, respectively, to μ_4 and ν_4.

Choosing pivot columns in the order in which they are presented by the divisions, our pivot column in the preceding matrix is chosen to be the starred -1 in column 2. This means that we replace μ_1 by μ_4 in the next basis. The next simplex matrix is then

		μ_1	ν_4	
Profit	14	-14	25	
$W =$	18	22	-25^*	Π
$\mu_4 =$	1	-1	0	Δ_{14}
$\nu_1 =$	1	0	-1	$\bar{\Pi}_2$
		$-\bar{\Pi}_1 =$	$-\Delta_{24} =$	

which yields our second basic solution[32]

$$\text{profit} = 14, \quad W = 18, \quad \mu_4 = 1, \quad \nu_1 = 1, \quad \bar{\Pi}_1 = 14, \quad \Delta_{24} = -25,$$

all other variable values zero.

Our third and last pivot step for the current executive program (A.4) takes as its pivot element the starred -25 in the last column, so that ν_4 now enters the basis in place of W. We then obtain the matrix

		μ_1	W	
Profit	32	8	-1	
$\nu_4 =$	18/25	22/25	$-1/25$	Δ_{24}
$\mu_4 =$	1	-1	0	Δ_{14}
$\nu_1 =$	7/25	$-22/25$	1/25	$\bar{\Pi}_2$
		$-\bar{\Pi}_1 =$	$-\Pi =$	

---

which permits this shortcut. But here it is convenient to proceed along the lines of the conventional simplex procedure except that pivot columns will be selected in the sequence presented by the divisions instead of the sequence that is customary when the simplex procedure is used.

[31] Note that this is, essentially, the solution previously obtained for our first executive program (A.2).

[32] Once again, this can be seen to be the same as the previously given solution to our second executive program (A.3).

This step finally gives us our current executive program solution:

$$\text{company profit} = 32, \quad \nu_4 = 18/25, \quad \mu_4 = 1, \quad \nu_1 = 7/25, \quad \bar{\Pi}_1 = -8, \quad \Pi = 1.$$

We observe that this is *not* an optimal solution to our program (A.4), since the second element in the first row of the matrix is positive.[33] Correspondingly, the dual variable $\bar{\Pi}_1 = -8$ so that the dual solution is nonfeasible, i.e., $\bar{\Pi}_1$ represents a *negative* marginal yield. Nevertheless, *for our purposes there is no need to go on to a fourth pivot step in the executive program calculation because company profits have already increased beyond what they were in the second decomposition iteration*, i.e., they have gone up from the 14 earned in the previous executive program (A.3) to the current profit level of 32.

Having gone as far as we need to in the solution of our current executive program, (A.4) let us return now to our discussion of the decomposition procedure proper.

Since our current solution involves $\Pi = 1$, the new unit profit figures for the divisional activities become:

$$R_{31} = 1 - (1)\,\Pi = 0 \qquad S_{31} = 2 - (2)\,\Pi = 0$$

$$R_{32} = 1 - (2)\,\Pi = -1 \qquad S_{32} = 1 - (1)\,\Pi = 0.$$

With these new profit figures, another simplex calculation shows that the new solution of the Division 1 program is X_1^* or X_3^*. We (arbitrarily) choose to introduce X_3^* into the executive program.[34]

Fourth iteration.

We observe that, since $X_3^* = (10, 0, 20, 0)$ by Table A-1, then

$$R_3 = 10R_{31} + 0R_{32} = 0 > \bar{\Pi}_1 = -8.$$

Therefore, X_3^* contributes to corporate profit in this iteration. The coefficient of the new variable, μ_3, in the profit function (which is obtained as in iteration 1) will be 10 and it will have the same coefficient in the corporate resource constraint.

The new executive program becomes (omitting the variable μ_1 in accord with footnote 14)

$$\begin{aligned} &\text{Maximize} && 10\mu_3 + 14\mu_4 + 0\nu_1 + 25\nu_4 \\ &\text{Subject to} && 10\mu_3 + 22\mu_4 + 0\nu_1 + 25\nu_4 \leqq 40 \\ &\text{and} && \mu_3 + \mu_4 = 1 \\ & && \nu_1 + \nu_4 = 1. \end{aligned}$$

[33] We could, of course, increase the number of pivot steps used in the executive program calculation and go on to compute the optimal solution of (A.4). This is, however, unnecessary, and there is no guarantee that it will reduce the number of decomposition iterations.

[34] It will be recalled that any one proposed divisional program can be incorporated into the next executive program provided that it satisfies the marginal profitability condition which is given next.

The new solution is obtained as before. It is

$$\text{company profit} = 110/3), \quad \mu_3 = 7/12, \quad \mu_4 = 5/12, \quad \nu_4 = 1$$
$$\Pi = 1/3, \quad \bar{\Pi}_1 = 20/3, \quad \bar{\Pi}_2 = 50/3.$$

The new unit profit figures become

$$R_{41} = 2/3 \qquad S_{41} = 4/3$$
$$R_{42} = 1/3 \qquad S_{42} = 2/3.$$

The optimal solutions to the divisional programs are, once again, X_3^* and[35] Y_4^* and the divisional contributions to profit corresponding to divisional proposals are

$$R_4 = 2/3(10) + 1/3(0) = 20/3 = \bar{\Pi}_1$$
$$S_4 = 4/3(10) + 2/3(5) = 50/3 = \bar{\Pi}_2 .$$

Thus the marginal net profit contributions of either divisional proposed program is now zero and additional iterations will not improve the solutions. We are at the optimum.[36]

The optimal averaged divisional programs therefore are:

Division 1 program: 7/12 of program 3 (since our last executive program calculation gave us $\mu_3 = 7/12$) and 5/12 of program 4 (since $\mu_4 = 5/12$).

Division 2 program: program 4 only. (since $\nu_4 = 1$, and all other $\nu_i = 0$).

The level of divisional activities and the divisional profit yields of the solution are left for the reader to compute. The reader may check his or her computational skills by solving the numerical problem employed in the body of the paper. The solutions are: $\mu_3 = 1$, $\nu_1 = .26$, $\nu_2 = .74$; $P = 32.5$.)

References

1. Dantzig, George B., *Linear Programming and Extensions*, Princeton University Press, Princeton, 1963, Ch. 23.
2. —— and Philip Wolfe, "Decomposition Principles for Linear Programs", *Operations Research*, Vol. 8, February, 1960.
3. —— and ——, "The Decomposition of Mathematical Programming Problems", The RAND Corporation, P-1818, 6 May, 1959.
4. Dorfman, Robert, Paul A. Samuelson and Robert Solow, *Linear Programming and Economic Analysis*, McGraw-Hill, New York, 1958.
5. Gale, David, *The Theory of Linear Economic Models*, McGraw-Hill, New York, 1960.
6. Hirshleifer, Jack, "Economics of the Divisionalized Firm", *Journal of Business*, Vol. XXX, April 1957.
7. Koopmans, Tjalling C., "Analysis of Production as an Efficient Combination of Activities", in T. C. Koopmans, ed., *Activity Analysis of Production and Allocation*, Cowles Commission Monograph 13, Wiley, New York, 1951.

[35] Actually X_4^* is also optimal and could have been used instead of X_3^*.

[36] At this point the simplex solution of our last executive program can be shown to be optimal, i.e., our final executive program pivot step must always satisfy the simplex optimality conditions.

8. ——, *Three Essays on the State of Economic Science*, McGraw-Hill, New York, 1957.
9. Mills, Harlan, "Marginal Values of Matrix Games and Linear Programs", in H. W. Kuhn and A. W. Tucker, eds. *Linear Inequalities and Related Systems*, Annals of Mathematics Study 38, Princeton University Press, Princeton, 1956.
10. Pigou, A. C., *Wealth and Welfare*, Macmillan, London, 1912.
11. Viner, Jacob, "Cost Curves and Supply Curves" *Zeitschrift für Nationalokonomie*, Vol Ill, 1931, Reproduced in G. J. Stigler and K. E. Boulding, eds, *Readings in Price Theory* Irwin, Chicago, 1952, and in Jacob Viner, *The Long View and the Short*, Free Press, Glencoe, Ill., 1958.
12. Whinston, Andrew, "Price Coordination in Decentralized Systems" (Unpublished Ph.D. dissertation) O.N.R. Research Memorandum No. 99 (Ditto), Carnegie Institute of Technology, Graduate School of Business Administration, Pittsburgh, June 1962.
13. Zoutendijk, G., *Methods of Feasible Directions*, Elsevier, Amsterdam, 1960.

[22]

ERROR PRODUCED BY LINEARIZATION IN MATHEMATICAL PROGRAMMING

BY W. J. BAUMOL AND R. C. BUSHNELL[1]

This paper offers a qualitative theoretical analysis of the error that may arise when a linear programming calculation is used to solve a problem involving some degree of nonlinearity. Six propositions are developed: (1) a linear approximation to a nonlinear program will not necessarily yield the true maximum; (2) it need not provide an answer better than a randomly chosen initial solution; (3) it may not even provide the best possible corner solution; (4) a reduction in the curvature of the profit surface does not always guarantee improvement in the accuracy of a linear approximation; (5) proximity of the initial point to the maximum need not increase the accuracy of the linear approximation; and (6) only if the objective function is monotone throughout can we be assured that a linear approximation will yield results which represent an improvement over the initial point. The paper also describes sampling experiments in which the correct solution of a quadratic programming problem subject to linear constraints was compared with the solution of a linear programming problem obtained by replacing the quadratic maximand by its tangent hyperplane at the initial point and by other linear approximations. In general, the linear programming calculations did not yield results very close to the true maximum nor did the approximation improve substantially as the curvature of the objective function was reduced.

1. THE CONSEQUENCES OF NONLINEARITY

IT SEEMS to be generally believed by economists and operations researchers that there exist wide classes of economic problems ranging from planning in underdeveloped areas to decisions within the individual business enterprise in which nonlinearities are sufficiently moderate to justify the employment of linear programming techniques in the analysis. However, the investigations reported in this paper suggest that even a very slight degree of nonlinearity (however this may be defined) can cause a linear programming calculation to yield answers which differ substantially from the true optimum and, while in some circumstances a reduction in the degree of nonlinearity may improve the linear approximation as intuition might lead one to expect, there are types of reduction in curvature that need not decrease the distortion in the calculated answer. Moreover, the linear programming calculation can easily produce a solution worse than that which serves as the initial point for the calculation. Specifically, this means that a decision maker who follows the advice

[1] The authors wish to acknowledge the very important contributions of Harold Kuhn and Richard Quandt who provided some basic suggestions for the paper, and to the National Science Foundation whose grant to their project, The Dynamics of the Firm, greatly facilitated the completion of this study. This work made use of computer facilities supported in part by National Science Foundation grant GP-579.

derived with the aid of a linear program is very apt to find himself further from his objective than if he had made no such calculation at all!

Of course the misspecification resulting from an inappropriate use of a linearity assumption can always lead to poor results. But we are suggesting that in a programming context the problem is peculiarly serious because for such problems there exist types of decrease in curvature that need not improve the quality of a linear approximation. A banal example should bring out the difference. In a price determination problem, if there is reason to believe that the curvature of the pertinent relationship is small, we need feel no qualms in using a straight line demand curve in our calculations. Thus, in Figure 1, suppose our experience only offers us indications about the location of two regions of the demand curve—as indicated by the two clusters of observed points, *A* and *B*. If the true demand curve happens to be relatively flat, as is *EE'*, a linear approximation will offer us fairly good predictions. It will tell us to expect that quantity *OU* will be demanded at price *OR*, while the true quantity will be *OT*. Only when the curvature of the demand relationship is fairly great, as when the true curve is *DD'*, will the linear approximation

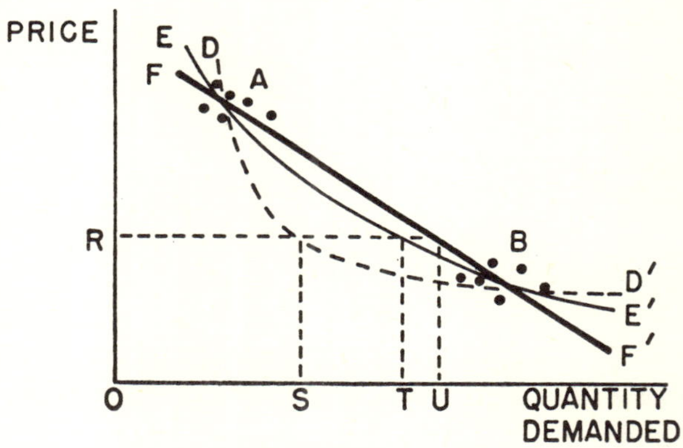

FIGURE 1

yield results which are seriously misleading. Though it may appear implausible at first, the same sort of behavior does not always characterize programming problems—the insignificance of the distortions caused by mild nonlinearities which experience and common sense would lead us to anticipate just does not hold in every case for programming.[2]

In this study we have approached the subject with the aid of two different methods: a graphic theoretical analysis and a sampling study utilizing several

[2] It is not difficult to document the general neglect of this problem. A careful review of the literature indicated that authors generally do not warn the reader that some degree of nonlinearity is probably present in the problem which their linear model is designed to describe. An occasional writer does mention that "linearity must be an acceptable approximation to reality" or that "the relations... could be expressed as linear relations without introducing serious error" (these are direct quotes) but "acceptable approximation" or "serious error" are not thereafter defined or quantified.

hundred randomly generated quadratic programs, whose true maxima were compared directly with the alleged maxima derived from linear calculations, starting from large numbers of randomly selected initial points. But before getting down to details, it seems desirable to offer the reader something of the flavor of the study's conclusions. It turned out that in over sixty six per cent of our sampled cases the linear programming calculation yielded less than fifty per cent of true maximum profits and that in fifty eight per cent of the cases it led to absolute losses. Moreover, in more than eighty eight per cent of our randomly selected examples the linear approximation gave results poorer than the randomly selected initial point! Since all of our problems are artificial, it is clear that no weight can be borne by these particular numbers, but they do suggest strongly that the use of linear methods should not be undertaken casually.

Before going further, some limitations of our analysis should be pointed out. In speaking of linear approximations we refer to linear programs in the strictest and simplest sense—we have excluded from our denotation all variants such as piecewise linear approximations, integer-linear calculations, etc. Thus, at several points in this paper, in order to remind the reader of our usage we have employed the expression "*strictly* linear approximations." Our emphasis on this extreme form of linearization is justified by the frequency with which it has been employed in empirical applications. While some industrial studies, for example, do utilize piecewise linear representations of their production relationships, they are the exception rather than the rule.[3]

Our analysis was also limited to problems involving nonlinear objective functions and linear constraints and left the investigation of the effects of nonlinearities in the constraints for the future.

2. NONLINEARITIES IN ECONOMIC PROGRAMMING PROBLEMS

Some degree of nonlinearity is the rule and not the exception in economic programming problems. For example, in the context of the diet problem, it is well established that there are foods which supplement or interfere with one another's usefulness,[4] and a more obvious nonlinearity arises when we try to take into

[3] An extensive search of the literature has revealed that of the published empirical programming applications, almost all employed strict linearity assumptions. Only two (both relating to petroleum) involved piecewise linear approximations and only seven really utilized nonlinear methods. We are told that there is a great deal of unpublished work using piecewise approximation and nonlinear programming in the planning work of the petroleum industry.

[4] See Victor E. Smith, *Electronic Computation of Human Diets*, Michigan State University Press, East Lansing, 1963, p. 11. This volume is an exhaustive report on the programming analysis of human diets. The first systematic formulation of the diet problem was produced by George Stigler, "The Cost of Subsistence," *Journal of Farm Economics*, Vol. 27, 1945. In that article there is an excellent discussion of the accuracy of the data and the reasonableness of the linearity assumption.

account the satisfaction derived from consuming the food, for it is by no means plausible that a doubling of the intake of a given food doubles the consumer's pleasure. So, as might be expected, the linear calculation yields a remarkably monotonous and unpalatable diet.[5] Similar observations apply to the media selection problem of advertising analysis.

But the main economic problem in whose analysis programming has been used both by economic planners and business consultants involves production and distribution planning. It should be obvious enough that technological diminishing and increasing returns sometimes arise in the production process and that the marketing process almost universally yields diminishing returns to scale—twice as much of a given output will provide disproportionately lower marginal returns because of the need to reduce price or increase selling efforts in order to move the increased output. It is ironic that large business firms, which long ago were shown by Dorfman to be characterized by nonlinear profit functions produced by rising marketing costs, are undoubtedly the prime users of applied linear programming calculations.

In sum, it is difficult to think of economic programming problems in which nonlinearities can confidently be ruled out. Some of these nonlinearities may be rather slight in magnitude. But it does not follow they are then insignificant. For it is here that the central contention of this paper enters—the assertion that in programming what appears to be a small nonlinearity may nevertheless produce serious errors in a linear approximation.

3. THE BASIC THEOREM AND THE DEPENDABILITY OF LINEAR APPROXIMATIONS

The discovery of the proposition usually called the "basic theorem of linear programming" was greeted with great enthusiasm by those concerned with calculation procedures, because by permitting them to ignore anything but corner points it makes life so much simpler. But the theorem should also have served as a warning to the economist. For, as we know, the basic theorem also tells us that there will be an optimal solution in which the number of nonzero valued activity variables cannot exceed the number of constraints; in economic terms this means that the number of commodities in a company's optimal product line will at most be equal to the number of scarce resources used by the firm in its production process—surely an artificial result with little general economic plausibility. We know very well that market conditions may make it desirable to turn out more than five items even in a firm with only five capacity constraints. Diminishing returns to the sale of any one item may make it profitable to introduce more items as the firm expands its scale of operations, and the nature of its customer's desires may force it to carry a fairly broad selection of items.

[5] Philip Wolfe has developed, somewhat facetiously, a quadratic program to deal with this sort of problem. See V. E. Smith, *ibid.*, pp. 29–31.

These observations suggest that there are, typically, very significant qualitative differences between the solutions to a linear and a nonlinear programming problem. We can judge something more about the magnitude of the quantitative differences that may arise from a simple solution space diagram.

Figures 2a and 2b represent two nonlinear programming problems in which the

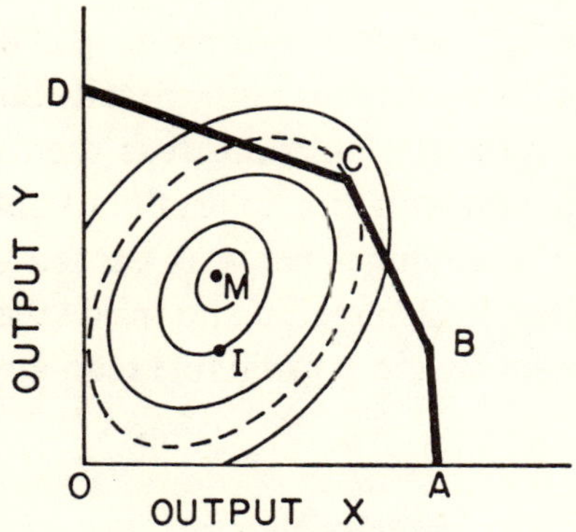

FIGURE 2a

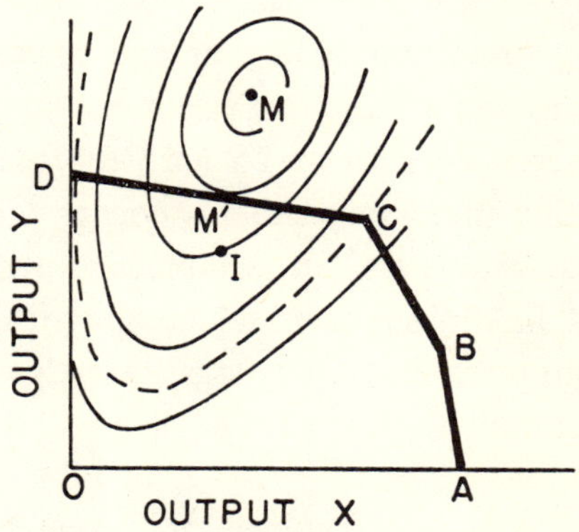

FIGURE 2b

isoprofit curves closer to point *M* represent higher profit levels. In Figure 2a the optimal point is *M* because it is both maximal and feasible. An approximating linear calculation substitutes some set of parallel straight line isoprofit lines for the isoprofit curves shown in the diagram. The basic theorem tells us that this substitution will ordinarily send us to some one of the diagram's corners, 0, *A*, *B*, *C*, or *D*, which will constitute the optimal point of the linear program. But observe in our diagram that *none* of these corner points is anywhere near the true optimum, *M*, and that in fact any one of these points yields profits which may well be considerably lower than those at *M*, depending on the rate of change of profits from one isoprofit curve to the next. We thus arrive at

PROPOSITION 1. *Given any linear program that is used to approximate a nonlinear program, the values of the variables $x'_1, x'_2, \ldots, x'_n$, which constitute the optimal solution of the former, can differ very substantially from the values $x_1, x_2, \ldots, x_n$, which are optimal for the latter. More important, the $x'_1, \ldots, x'_n$ may yield a much lower value of the true nonlinear objective function (much lower profits) than do the latter. Only if the true curvilinear maximum point happens to lie near a corner, or if the height of the profit surface near the corner points is not much lower than the true maximum, can the linear calculation yield results that are at all satisfactory, and only rarely if ever in an economic problem can we have any assurance in advance that these conditions will be satisfied.*

It may appear that this result is a consequence of the peculiar case dealt with in Figure 2a, in which the true maximum lies inside the feasible region so that there is nothing like the familiar solution involving tangency between the production possibility curve and an isoprofit curve. But Figure 2b shows at a glance that Proposition 1 holds also in such a case where the optimal tangency point, M′, may once again lie far from any corner.

One may be inclined, nevertheless, to argue that a linear calculation, even if it cannot always bring us to the best of all possible worlds, should be able to point the way to improvements. Linearization is still likely to be useful, since one should at least undertake whatever can make things better. Once more, the diagrams enable us to see that even this more qualified hypothesis is not generally borne out. In either Figure 2a or 2b let *I* represent the initial position. It is then clear on inspection that a move to any corner will cause a reduction in profit not only below the maximum, but in comparison with the amount that was earned initially. Indeed, any initial point which lies within the feasible region and inside the broken isoprofit curve in either diagram is also obviously more profitable than any corner solution. We then have

PROPOSITION 2. *A linear programming approximation may yield a solution less profitable than the initial position from which the calculation is undertaken, and there is no reason to assume that the loss in profits will be negligible.*

A linear programming calculation is not even guaranteed to select the best (most profitable) among the corner points. This is shown in Figure 3 where our initial point is taken to be *I*. Experience may have revealed the marginal rate of profit substitution of the two outputs at the initial point as indicated by the slope of the isoprofit curve at that point. One may suppose then (though this assumption does not really affect the argument)[6] that the approximating linear isoprofit curves are taken to have the same marginal rate of substitution, i.e., that they are all parallel to the tangent to the true isoprofit line at initial point *I*. Given this linear pseudo-profit function it follows that the calculated profit maximizing point is *D* since *D* lies on the highest attainable linear isoprofit curve. But this is surely not the best of the corner points, for point *C* is clearly more remunerative than *D*. We conclude

PROPOSITION 3. *A linear approximation may select an output combination which is not the most profitable corner point. (It follows, incidentally, that if the initial point*

[6] As a matter of fact, this is tantamount to the way in which the linear profit surface is frequently determined in practice. This linear function is normally found by examining the series of points which represents past experience, and fitting to it a plane which is taken as the linear objective function. We consider ourselves fortunate if this plane yields the same marginal returns figures as does the true curved objective function, i.e., if the two surfaces are tangent in the vicinity of the observed points. We are not suggesting that this is how such a plane ought to be fitted, but rather that this is how it is generally done in practice. The difficulties which are described in this paper, however, are in no way dependent on the method used to choose the approximating linear surface. Any linear approximation must give rise to the same sort of problems.

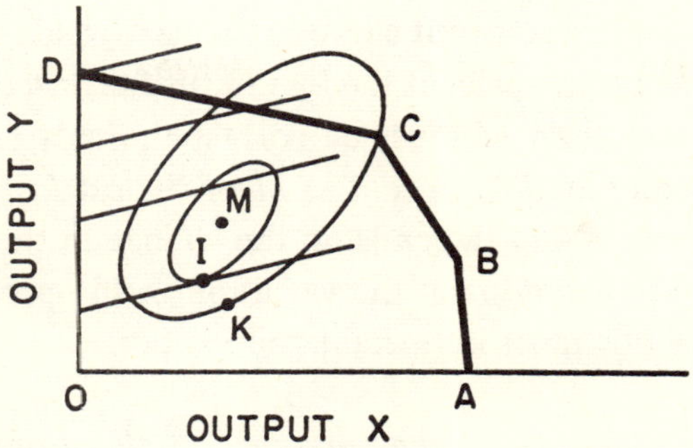

FIGURE 3

had been no more profitable or even less profitable than some of the corner points (e.g., if point K in Figure 3 *had been the initial point) the linear calculation could have caused a loss in profit.)*

Next, we come to the degree of nonlinearity and its consequences for the legitimacy of a linear approximation. Here our diagrams are helpful once again. They show at once that at least one type of flattening of the profit surface—that which results from a proportionate reduction in its slope at every point—will have absolutely no effect on the shapes of the countour (isoprofit) curves. Exactly the same isoprofit curves can be generated by a profit surface whose slopes curl precipitously downward from the maximal point, as a hill whose sides slope gently downward. This is the ordinality property of indifference curves so well known to economists. But if that is so, one must conclude that the preceding propositions, which depended essentially only on the shapes of the profit indifference curves, may hold equally for any degree of nonlinearity of the profit surface. Even if the profit hill corresponding to Figure 2a is almost flat, it remains true nevertheless that point M will be driven no closer to any of the corner points—as a matter of fact, the location of M will not be changed at all.

True, the flattening of the profit hill means, in absolute terms, that there is less at stake. The absolute loss in profits caused by a given miscalculation must be

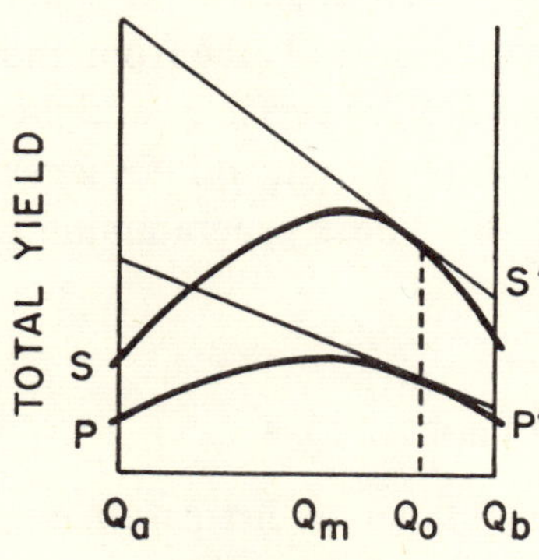

FIGURE 4a

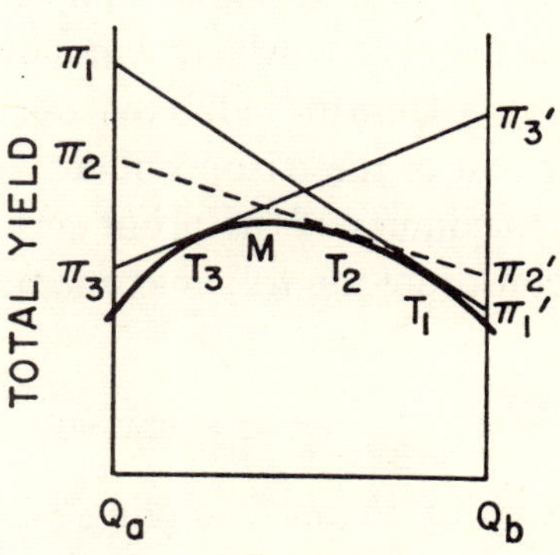

FIGURE 4b

smaller. If a move from one isoprofit curve to the next yields only a small change in profit (a relatively flat profit surface) the loss in profit consequent upon our choosing, say, point B rather than M must be correspondingly small. But the relative reduction in profitability at B from that at M or that at I need not be affected by reduction in curvature for that depends on the change in the height of points B, I, and M that happens to accompany the variation in the profit function. Thus we have what is perhaps our most important proposition,

PROPOSITION 4. *A reduction of the curvature of the profit surface does not by itself guarantee any improvement in the answers provided by a linear approximation. In particular, it may not reduce the percentage opportunity loss in profits incurred by the linear calculation.*

The role of curvature is perhaps brought out more clearly with the aid of Figure 4a in which there is only one independent variable, Q, and the curved lines are total yield (profit) functions $\pi = f(Q)$. We take Q to be constrained so that $Q_a < Q < Q_b$. In our strictly linear approximation let us take as our pseudo objective function a tangent to the true profit function at $Q = Q_0$. Then we see at once that the pseudo optimal solution value $Q = Q_a$ remains absolutely unchanged and moves no closer to the true maximum, Q_m, when the highly curved profit function SS' is replaced by the much flatter curve PP'. We must be careful to make clear just what is being asserted. We are merely saying that some types of flattening of the objective function offer no guarantee of improved results. In other words, we are warning the reader that flatness of the objective function by itself offers no grounds for complacency in the use of linear methods. Yet it should be clear that some types of flattening of the profit hypersurface will produce a straightening of the indifference curves. This would occur, for example, if the profit surface were a half sphere and its highest point were moved outward along a ray so that the isoprofit curves would be a family of concentric circles whose center was eventually moved very far from the origin. If the isoprofit curves become sufficiently straight it is plausible that the accuracy of the linear approximation will be improved. But even here there is no absolute guarantee as a simple example will show. Visualize a profit surface shaped like a peaked roof (one which slopes downward towards the front and the rear of the "building"). Here the indifference curves will all be perfectly straight and parallel but the furthest of these isoprofit curves from the origin will not generally correspond to a maximum of the profit surface—the linear programming solution still need not constitute the true maximum.

4. A FEW FURTHER PROPOSITIONS

Before turning to our sampling experiments let us list a few more pertinent observations that can be illustrated with the aid of our graphs.

In Figure 4b, which is constructed in a manner similar to 4a, our nonlinear objective function has the unique maximum M. If we take a linear pseudo-objective function to be tangent at a point T_1 which is fairly far to the right of M it will yield the corner point Q_a as the optimal solution to the linear program. But even if the tangent point is moved much closer to M, say to T_2, the solution will not vary one iota. Only the (false) profit prediction will decline from π_1 to π_2. However, once the point of tangency to which our objective function line is fitted moves to the other side of M, say to T_3, the computed maximum will jump abruptly to Q_b, our other corner point. We have

PROPOSITION 5. *In fitting a linear approximation to a nonlinear program a reduction in the distance between the observed points on which the fit is based and the true maximum need produce no improvement in the linear solution.*

This, of course, results from the fact that linear solutions change only by leaping from one corner to another, and generally will not respond at all to small changes in the parameters of the objective function.

Finally, we may note one condition that is clearly sufficient to guarantee the dependability of a linear approximation—monotonicity. A profit surface is flat enough to permit a linear approximation if it is monotonic in every direction everywhere in the feasible region; a requirement whose fulfillment we are likely to find hard to judge on the basis of our *a priori* information in any problem involving a substantial number of variables! Specifically, we may note that only if the slope of the profit surface along any straight line cross section never changes in sign (if any direction which starts off going uphill always continues to climb upward),[7] can one be sure that the linear programming calculation must actually effect an improvement as compared to the initial situation. This is illustrated in Figure 5 where it is clear that R''', the highest point on the tangent plane in the feasible region, $0ABC$, corresponds to a true profit level G which must be higher than that at the initial point T (though it is still unfortunately true even in this restrictive case that the calculated pseudo optimum, G, is not in fact the point of maximum profit, F). Thus we have arrived at the following result:

PROPOSITION 6. *If the portion of the objective function which lies in the feasible region behaves monotonically in every variable, an approximating linear program derived by fitting a tangent hyperplane should yield an improvement in the value of the objective function from that corresponding to the initial position.*

[7] In any programming problem with a substantial number of variables and constraints the number of corners and hence the number of pertinent directions will be astronomical so that it will not normally be possible to conclude in advance, without extensive investigation, that the monotonicity condition is satisfied.

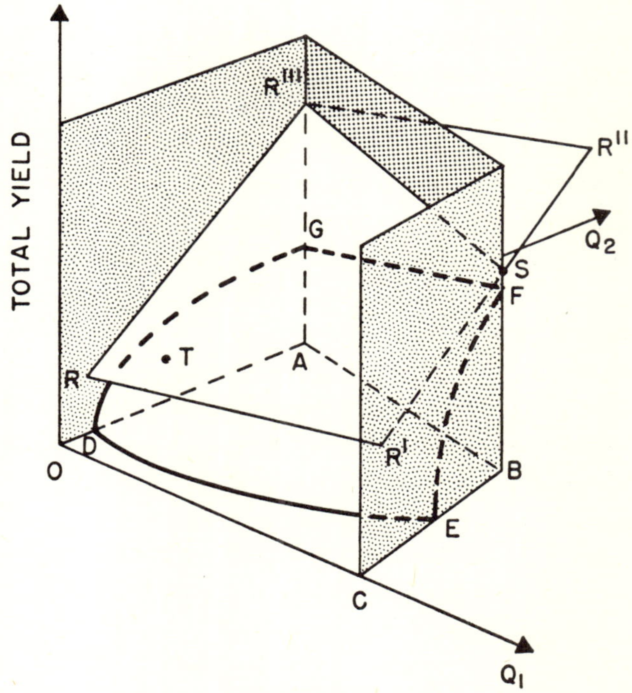

FIGURE 5

This observation leads to a hypothesis and a related rule of thumb procedure, both of which can be tested. It suggests that a linear programming calculation might usually be counted upon to produce an improvement in the value of the objective function if it is permitted only small changes in the values of the variables, that is, if to any approximating program we adjoin constraints that limit the magnitudes of variable changes. For example, the constraints might take the form[8] $x_{ki}+E \geqslant x_k \geqslant x_{ki}-E$ where x_{ki} is the initial value of the variable x_k, and E is some appropriately selected constant. For if E is chosen sufficiently small so that we are confined to a very limited neighborhood about the initial point, then within that small region the objective function is apt to behave monotonically—the sufficient condition of Proposition 6 for an approximating linear calculation to yield an improvement in comparison with the initial point.

5. ON SAMPLING EXPERIMENTS

Before describing the sampling experiments that were used to examine the workings of our propositions in some problems involving a large number of

[8] Perhaps a preferable type of constraint for this purpose might be $(1+\delta)x_{ki} \geqslant x_k \geqslant (1-\delta)x_{ki}$, which limits change to a specified proportion of our initial values. Note that any such additional constraints might also lead to a qualitative improvement in the answer in a diminishing returns case by increasing the upper bound on the number of nonzero valued variables in the optimal solution to the approximating linear program.

variables and constraints, it is essential that the fundamental limitations of such a procedure be spelled out very clearly. The generation of illustrative cases using random procedures for the selection of the parameter values does not avoid bias in the sample. The choice of frequency distribution used in generating the numbers utilized and the way in which the random numbers are used in constructing the pertinent functions must affect the outcome of the experiment and its results must therefore be loaded unintentionally or intentionally by the decisions made in constructing it.

Second, the underlying reality which the sampling experiments are designed to replicate may not really be composed of random phenomena or if random they may not have the same statistical characteristics as the models used in the experiment. Thus it might happen that a calculation procedure performs very badly in a set of problems randomly selected, but it may yet give very satisfactory results in reality because the world happens to produce cases of the type in which the method is at its best.

Thus the results of our calculations must be interpreted with care, always bearing in mind the fundamental limitations of the procedure.

6. SIMULATION PROCEDURES

In testing our propositions, over three hundred quadratic problems were constructed.

Experiment 1

Here 50 problems were generated. Each generation consisted of a randomly selected "true" quadratic program together with an approximating linear program. Each problem contained anything from two to twenty structural variables and from two to twenty constraints. Both of these had their parameters generated randomly and uniformly. The production matrix C in the constraint set $Cx \leqslant d$ consisted of elements generated uniformly between .01 and 1.00 with from ten to thirty per cent of such entries equal to zero. Each product was, in effect, assumed to have a straight line demand function of the type $p_j = a_j - b_j x_j$ (where p is price and

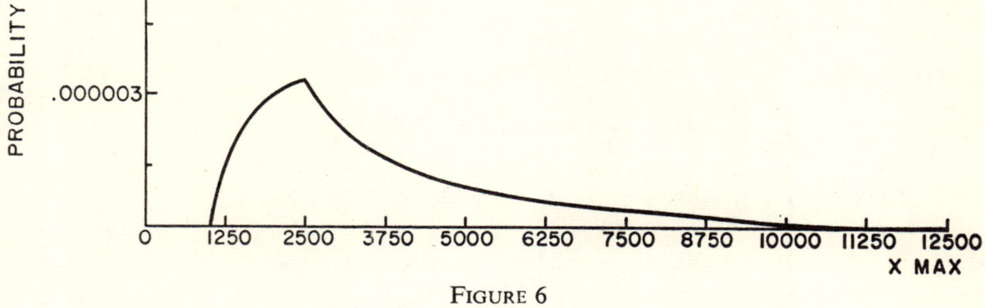

FIGURE 6

x is quantity). Our objective function, then, was the quadratic function[9] $\pi = \Sigma p_j x_j = \Sigma(a_j x_j - b_j x_j^2) + K$. The a coefficients were generated uniformly and randomly between one and five and the b coefficients between .002 and .010. The K, representing fixed cost, was generated uniformly between $-100n$ and zero where n is the number of structural variables. In the absence of constraints we would obtain the optimal quantity values $(x_{\max})_j = a_j/2b_j$. Thus $x_{\max}$ can be shown to be distributed as indicated in Figure 6.[10] The point at which these companies

[9] These functions were, then, orthogonal (no cross product terms) and concave.

[10] The graph is of the probability density of $x_{\max} = a/2b$ $(a > 0, b > 0)$. To see how this graph is derived, consider the probability density function of the quotient of two jointly continuous random variables as given in Parzen, Emanuel, *Modern Probability Theory and Its Applications* (Wiley, 1960), p. 318:

$$(1) \qquad f_{X/Y}(z) = \int_{-\infty}^{\infty} dx|x| f_{x,y}(xz, x)\,.$$

In particular for two uniformly distributed random variables whose density functions are $f_x = 1/(r-q)$ when $q \leqslant x \leqslant r$ and zero otherwise, and $f_y = 1/(t-s)$ when $s \leqslant y \leqslant t$ and zero otherwise, applying the formula (1) above yields $f_{X/Y}(z) = \int_{-\infty}^{\infty} (1/(r-q)(t-s))x dx$ within the domains $z, x > 0$, $z \leqslant zx \leqslant r$, and $s \leqslant x \leqslant t$, zero otherwise. Below we will write $(r-q)(t-s)$ as K in expressions such as $\int (1/K) x dx$. The variable z is the variable $x_{\max} = a/2b \equiv x/y$.

In the case at hand we are interested only in situations where $q/t > 0$ and thus also $z > 0$. Therefore we may say there are these conditions on x:

$$\frac{q}{z} \leqslant x \leqslant \frac{r}{z}; \qquad s \leqslant x \leqslant t; \qquad x > 0\,.$$

To meet all the requirements the domain of x may be given as

$$(2) \qquad \max\{q/z, s, 0\} \leqslant x \leqslant \min\{t, r/z\}\,.$$

It now only remains to break down the domain of z (which follows directly from the domains of x and y). This is $q/t \leqslant z \leqslant r/s$. To do this we must specify the relative magnitude of q/s and r/t.

CASE I: When $r/s > q/s$ then $q/t \leqslant q/s \leqslant r/t \leqslant r/s$. For each of these subdomains of z the permissible domain of x is calculated from relation (2). For example, for $q/t \leqslant z \leqslant q/s$, the domain of x is given by $\max\{q/z, s, 0\} = q/z$ and $\min\{t, r/z\} = t$. Therefore in the domain $q/t \leqslant z \leqslant q/s$: $f_{X/Y}(z) = (1/K)\int_{q/z}^{t} x dx = (1/2K)(t^2 - q^2/z^2)$. The complete specification for Case I $(r/t > q/s)$ is:

$$f_{X/Y}(z) = \begin{cases} \dfrac{1}{K}\displaystyle\int_{q/z}^{t} x dx = \dfrac{1}{2K}(t^2 - q^2/z^2), & q/t \leqslant z \leqslant q/s\,, \\ \dfrac{1}{K}\displaystyle\int_{s}^{t} x dx = \dfrac{1}{2K}(t^2 - s^2), & q/s \leqslant z \leqslant r/t\,, \\ \dfrac{1}{K}\displaystyle\int_{s}^{r/z} x dx = \dfrac{1}{2K}(r^2/z^2 - s^2), & r/t \leqslant z \leqslant r/s\,, \\ 0 & \text{otherwise.} \end{cases}$$

CASE II: Similarly when $q/s > r/t$ then $q/t \leqslant r/t \leqslant q/s \leqslant r/s$ and

$$f_{X/Y}(z) = \begin{cases} \dfrac{1}{K}\displaystyle\int_{q/z}^{t} x dx = \dfrac{1}{2K}(t^2 - q^2/z^2), & q/t \leqslant z \leqslant r/t\,, \\ \dfrac{1}{K}\displaystyle\int_{q/z}^{r/z} x dx = \dfrac{1}{2K}(r^2/z^2 - q^2/z^2), & r/t \leqslant z \leqslant q/s\,, \\ \dfrac{1}{K}\displaystyle\int_{s}^{r/z} x dx = \dfrac{1}{2K}(r^2/z^2 - s^2), & q/s \leqslant z \leqslant r/s\,, \\ 0 & \text{otherwise.} \end{cases}$$

were assumed to be operating initially was within one hundred units of $(x_{max})_k$; that is, the difference was generated uniformly over the range zero to one hundred. Last, the entries on the right hand side of the constraints (scarce resource availabilities) were generated to equal the input quantities required to produce the company's initial outputs plus a random number between zero and five multiplied by the number of products produced. The approximating linear program was the hyperplane tangent to the quadratic function at the assumed initial point.

Experiment 2

This was identical with Experiment 1 except that all initial points were taken to lie to the southwest of the true maximum so that each coefficient of the approximating linear profit function (the marginal profit yield of each output) was guaranteed to be positive. The logic of the experiment was this: It was assumed that experience would teach planners and businessmen to avoid levels at which any marginal profit return was negative and that they would certainly be unwilling to go along with a calculation which took any marginal yields to be negative. The purpose of the experiment, then, was to see whether such a restriction would produce any improvement in the quality of the results.

Experiment 3

It turned out that in most of the one hundred problems just described, the unconstrained maximum lay within the feasible region and the initial point was typically very close to the maximum point. To determine what would happen when the constrained quadratic maximum was different from the unconstrained maximum and the initial position was chosen to lie far from the quadratic maximum, fifty examples were generated precisely in the same manner as the first set but with the following critical differences in the objective function and the location of the initial point:

(a) The parameters were generated with *a* coefficients uniform and random between two and five and the *b* coefficients between .0002 and .0010. Thus $(x_{max})_j = a_j/2b_j$ was distributed as shown in Figure 7. We see by comparison with Figure 6

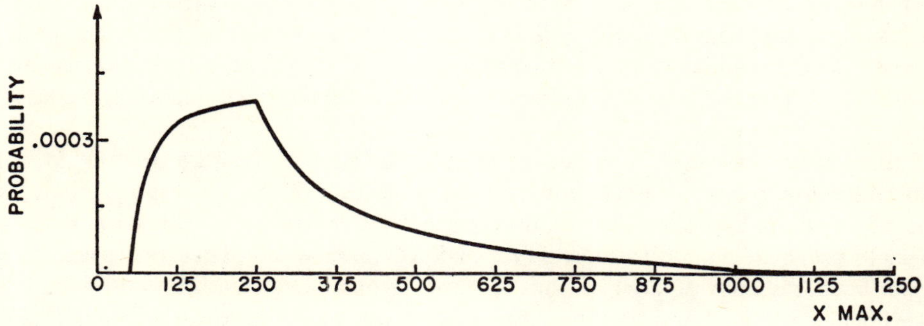

FIGURE 7

that the unconstrained maxima now typically involve much larger values of the variables than they did in our previous runs.

(b) The starting point is found by subtracting a number generated uniformly between eight hundred and one thousand from each x_{max} so that it involved values of the variables very much lower than their optimal values. Note that the generation of the coefficient matrix and the slack vector remains as in the first problems.

Experiments 4, 5, *and* 6

Another set of experiments reflected the observation that average data are apparently sometimes used instead of marginal figures in business practice. We therefore undertook to examine the effects of choosing the coefficients of the objective function on the basis of average rather than marginal revenues at the initial point.[11] Therefore each of the one hundred fifty problems already generated were rerun using average revenues in this way.

Experiment 7

This was a special set of experiments designed to test our conjecture (see Proposition 6) that by limiting the amounts by which the variables would be permitted to change one could increase the likelihood that a linear approximation would produce an improvement over the initial point. Some preliminary calculations showed that, in general, there was some validity to this conjecture, but it also indicated that there was wide variation, from problem to problem, in the point at which the permitted range of variation had been narrowed sufficiently to cause things to improve. Hence, it was impossible to develop an aggregative experiment in which for a substantial number of problems one could trace the typical improvement in linear calculation as the range of variation was reduced. We therefore decided to deal with this conjecture problem by problem. Ten quadratic programs were therefore investigated, each employing ten different values of the range where the range is defined as the proportion of the original feasible region within which variables are permitted to move.[12] Thus we have $0 \leqslant$ range $\leqslant 1$. The experiment was run twice. On the first run, the ten range values for each problem were chosen so

[11] That is, let $\pi = f(x_1, ..., x_n) + K$ be our true nonlinear objective function and let the approximating linear profit function be $\pi_L = C + \Sigma\alpha_k x_k$. In the marginal fitting approach we set $\alpha_k = \partial f/\partial x_k$ at the initial point $x_j = x_{ji}$ for all j, whereas in the average method we used $\alpha_k = \pi_i/x_{ki}$ where π_i is the initial value of π, and where we set C so that the initial values of π and π_L were equal.

[12] Thus, in effect, if range = .5 we replace the old feasible region with a new one in which each constraint hyperplane is parallel to the old, but now lies half way between the initial point and the old constraint hyperplane. Hence, the experiment is not completely equivalent to the one we originally proposed in our discussion of Proposition 6 where we talked of simply placing upper and lower bounds about the variables, thus in effect surrounding the initial point by small rectangular bounding regions. Instead it has proved more convenient to shrink the original feasible region proportionately about the initial point.

that one of them equalled 1.0 and the remaining nine values were chosen to fall randomly between .001 and 1.0. On the second run the range was simply forced to take the values 0.1, 0.2, ..., 0.9, 1.0. Five of the ten problems chose their initial points anywhere in the feasible region, while the remaining five took initial points at which all marginal products were positive (points on the uphill side of the profit function). In most cases the quadratic function had a maximum which violated some but not all of the constraints.

Since this matter is somewhat peripheral to our main inquiry it seems appropriate to summarize the results briefly at this point and get the subject out of the way. The results are best illustrated with the aid of Figure 8 which describes a typical case (the dots report actual data). The negatively sloping portion of the graph shows just what we had anticipated—the linear calculation does more poorly as the range of permitted variation is increased. However, the (rather small and unexpected) positively sloping segment of the curve shown in the highly enlarged inset to the figure is easily rationalized in retrospect. It shows that when the range of variation is restricted beyond the point where it excludes the true maximum, still further decreases in range must reduce attainable profits. Also noteworthy is the very large segment of the graph lying below the horizontal axis.

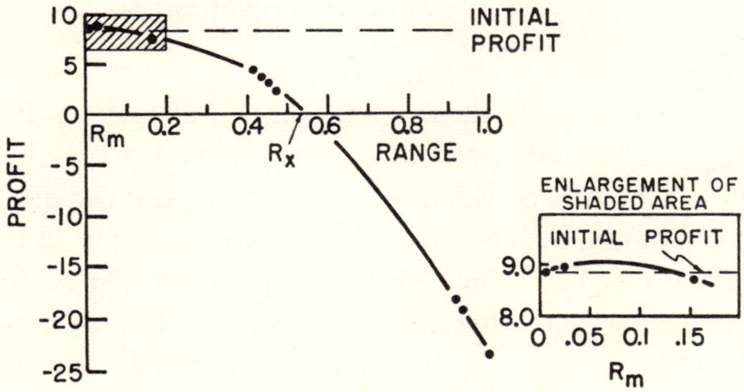

FIGURE 8

Though Figure 8 is fairly typical of our results in this experiment, there were wide variations from problem to problem in the location of the maximum point, R_m, and of the x intercept, R_x. In addition, the overall pattern is only valid for linear programming calculations in which the linear hyperplane objective function is taken to be tangent to the true objective hypersurface at the initial point. Clearly, if we use some other method to fit our plane there is no reason to expect that in a smaller region the slope of the surface will be better represented by the slope of the approximating plane. As a matter of fact, in one example where we fitted the plane to the "average yields" rather than the marginal yields of our variables (see footnote 11, above) the curve corresponding to that in Figure 8 had a positive slope throughout—the larger the permitted range of our variables the better was the linear approximation.

In general, we were disappointed by the performance of the variable range restriction device for which we originally had a great deal of hope as a practical expedient. It seems from our calculations that the range must be made very small before it can cause the linear calculation to yield profits greater than those at the initial position. Indeed, for three of the ten problems examined, *no* restriction of the range within our sample permitted the linear profit to exceed initial profits! For the other problems the largest range points in our random sample which gave the linear calculation an edge over the initial position were .02, .32, .26, .06, .001, .06, .05. This means, for example, that in the sample based on the first problem, the linear calculation improved the planner's decisions only when the constraints of the feasible region were moved to within two per cent of their original distance from the initial point. And in none of the ten cases was this procedure able to yield more than a one per cent improvement over the initial position even though in each case we chose the best values of the range—something which no policy maker could have done unless he had full information on the true nonlinear objective function, as we did. Thus at this point, this modified approach to linear approximation does not seem very promising.[13]

7. NOTATION TO DESCRIBE THE RESULTS

In our central experiments we employed a number of measures to evaluate the accuracy of the linear results. In the remainder of our dicussion it is convenient to use the following notation: $\pi_{\max}$ refers to true maximal profits; π_{lin} is the true (quadratic) value of the profits which would be obtained if the recommendations of the linear programming calculation were followed, i.e., if one utilized the values of the independent variables which the linear program alleged to be optimal; π_i refers to the profits earned at the initial point; x_{km} is the true maximal value of independent variable x_k, and x_{kL} is the pseudo-optimal value of variable x_k obtained from a linear calculation.

The following four measures were used to evaluate the results of the linear approximations in our experiments:

$\pi_{\text{lin}}/\pi_{\max}$ is the proportion of maximal profits yielded by a linear calculation.

$(\pi_{\text{lin}}-\pi_i)/\pi_i$ is the relative increase over initial profits produced by a linear calculation.

NE DIST is the normalized Euclidean distance

$$\frac{||x_m - x_L||}{||(x_m - x_L)/2||}\,.$$

[13] It is also interesting that most of the improvement observed as a result of reduction in the range was a consequence of the lower limits on the variable values—the fact that normally none of them was permitted to take a zero value in this experiment. A separate test in which we employed only the lower bounds under the variable values yielded almost as much of an increase in linear profits as did the full reduction in the permitted range of the variables.

Here $\|x_m - x_L\|$ represents the ordinary Euclidean distance $\sqrt{\Sigma(x_{km}-x_{kL})^2}$ from the initial point to the maximum point. It has been normalized by a factor $\|(x_m - x_L)/2\|$ which is the distance from the origin to a point midway between the linear and the optimal points. The purpose of this normalization is, roughly, to take account of the consideration that a given difference between the linear and the maximal point is relatively more serious the smaller the size of the feasible region.

ANGLE refers to the cosine of the angle between the ray from the origin to point $(x_{1L}, ..., x_{nL})$ and the ray from the origin to $(x_{1m}, ..., x_{nm})$.

The primary tests of goodness of fit must ultimately consider the value of the objective functions that is achieved, and that is what our first two (relative profit) indexes are designed to measure. There may also be some interest in how well a linear programming calculation does in estimating the values of the other variables —the x_k—and this is the purpose of the last two measures. The distance index, NE DIST, served as a measure of the overall closeness of the calculated optimal values of the independent variables to their true optimal values, and the cosine measure is an alternative index of the proximity of the two sets of independent variable values.

In our experiments four other measures played an important and fairly obvious role.

VA/CON is the ratio between number of variables and number of constraints.

$\text{DIST}_{\text{in-max}}$ is the Euclidean distance from the initial point to the true maximum point.

AVG CUR is an arithmetic average of the two dimensional curvatures of each of the cross sections through the initial point and parallel to one of the axis hyperplanes. Here two dimensional curvature is measured by the ratio of the angular distance per unit of distance along the curve. By convention, since our functions are concave these curvature figures are negative. Hence, a decreased value of this variable indicates increased curvature.

CURVE N is an n dimensional analogue of two dimensional curvature as described above.[14]

Before going on to describe our results it is desirable to present the results of one typical linear calculation in two types of problem (a "more variables than constraints" case and a "more constraints than variables" case) to provide the reader with some sense of the orders of magnitudes involved. Table I gives the initial, calculated and optimal values of the objective function, Π, the structural variables, Q_i, and the slack variables, U_j, in one ten-variable by twenty-constraints problem

[14] For the basic ideas see Coxeter, H. S. M., *Introduction to Geometry*, John Wiley and Sons, New York, 1961, pp. 345–353. Specifically, we define CURVE N as $K^{1/n}$ where n is the number of variables, $f(x_1, ..., x_n)$ is our function and

$$K = \left[\left| \frac{\partial^2 f}{\partial x_j \partial x_k} \right| \Big/ \left[1 + \Sigma \left(\frac{\partial f}{\partial x_j} \right)^2 \right]^{(n+2)/2} \right]_{x=x_{\text{initial}}}$$

TABLE I

CALCULATED VALUES FOR TWO QUADRATIC PROBLEMS

	Problem a				Problem b		
	10 Variables – 20 Constraints				20 Variables – 10 Constraints		
	Initial	Linear Calculation	True Maximum		Initial	Linear Calculation	True Maximum
π	5,957	−11,448*	6,148	π	6,881	−24,545**	7,320
Q_1	48	0	64	Q_1	61	0	109
Q_2	28	0	57	Q_2	368	0	351
Q_3	1,089	0	1,073	Q_3	95	0	164
Q_4	276	157	278	Q_4	180	1,349	274
Q_5	103	1,398	171	Q_5	76	0	97
Q_6	170	426	253	Q_6	331	0	346
Q_7	156	0	183	Q_7	229	877	295
Q_8	167	487	246	Q_8	233	0	275
Q_9	490	0	555	Q_9	198	0	199
Q_{10}	431	0	429	Q_{10}	155	0	151
U_1	0	0	32	Q_{11}	559	627	580
U_2	23	724	27	Q_{12}	253	367	255
U_3	35	1,375	94	Q_{13}	58	0	563
U_4	31	628	83	Q_{14}	178	0	199
U_5	7	631	39	Q_{15}	36	0	85
U_6	5	0	64	Q_{16}	336	0	393
U_7	9	482	34	Q_{17}	1	0	60
U_8	22	910	36	Q_{18}	243	0	318
U_9	39	866	128	Q_{19}	42	1,345	104
U_{10}	12	619	0	Q_{20}	330	0	347
U_{11}	16	1,261	56	U_1	47	0	145
U_{12}	10	0	149	U_2	53	0	0
U_{13}	19	520	143	U_3	8	0	138
U_{14}	39	331	118	U_4	41	638	72
U_{15}	34	779	84	U_5	7	0	48
U_{16}	2	614	6	U_6	24	463	79
U_{17}	38	0	107	U_7	51	192	0
U_{18}	14	482	1	U_8	52	998	89
U_{19}	17	566	61	U_9	66	0	99
U_{20}	7	1,040	44	U_{10}	15	680	0

Note: Q_i is the ith structural variable and U_j is the jth slack variable.
* The linear calculation alleges that $\pi_{cal} = 7{,}519$ but actually yields the figure shown.
** The linear calculation alleges that $\pi_{cal} = 10{,}091$ but actually yields the figure shown.

and one ten-constraints by twenty-variables problem. The results seem to us to be not unrepresentative of the two types of cases, though in both of them the initial point happens to have been chosen to lie close to the quadratic maximum. Note in particular the large number of zeros in each of the middle columns where the results of the linear calculations are presented. It is also interesting that in both problems the linear calculation alleges that it yields a profit that exceeds the true quadratic maximum (e.g., in the first problem the calculated linear maximum is 7,519 whereas the true maximum is 6,148) and that in both problems the linear calculation really leads to substantial losses not only in relation to the initial profits but also absolutely.

8. SUMMARY OF RESULTS

In general, the results of the experiments were all very similar. There was some improvement when we confined ourselves to an initial position at which the marginal yields (partial derivatives of the objective function) were all positive, and there was a further improvement when the initial point was far below the maximum and the unconstrained maximum lay outside the feasible region. Since we found few other significant differences, for purposes of brevity we will report only aggregated results or the results of those experiments which exhibit the best overall performance of the linear approximations.

Thus, Table II shows the mean, variance, and standard deviation of each of our measures of performance for the case where the constraints were effective (unconstrained maximum nonfeasible) and marginal rather than average methods of objective hyperplane fitting were employed. We see that, for example (second entry, first column) on the average linear profits were over 1,097 per cent below the initial values! (In one experiment the corresponding figure was 10,400 per cent.) Moreover, the corresponding standard deviation was nearly five times as large as the mean, in absolute value.

TABLE II

CHARACTERISTICS OF THE VARIABLES' DISTRIBUTIONS: EXPERIMENT 3

	Mean	Variance	Standard Deviation
$\pi_{\text{lin}}/\pi_{\text{max}}$	−9.7106	2261.1109	47.5511
$(\pi_{\text{lin}} - \pi_i)/\pi_i$	−10.9720	2365.1699	48.6330
NE DIST	0.6563	0.4269	0.6534
ANGLE	0.7795	0.0703	0.2651
VA/CON	1.2629	1.9700	1.4036
$\text{DIST}_{\text{in-max}}$	719.5543	491331.9375	700.9507
CURVE Ṅ	0.0002	0.0000	0.0001
AVG CUR	−0.0004	0.0000	0.0000

Table III reports coefficients of correlation between our various measures of goodness of fit and the variables, such as degree of curvature, which might have been expected to affect the results. The table deals with the same subset of experiments that was treated in the previous table, because it seems once again to constitute the example generally most favorable to the linear approximation.

TABLE III

CORRELATIONS BETWEEN VARIABLES: EXPERIMENT 3

	π_{lin}/π_{max}	$(\pi_{lin} - \pi_i)/\pi_i$	NE DIST	ANGLE
VA/CON	−0.5229	−0.5241	0.7988	−0.8361
$DIST_{in-max}$	−0.4348	−0.4357	0.8796	−0.8656
CURVE N	0.2566	0.2570	−0.6986	0.6405
AVG CUR	0.0316	0.0310	0.2356	−0.2263

Column two is perhaps the most interesting to us because it concerns the percentage increase in profit (positive or negative) over initial profit which is achieved by the linear approximation. It will be seen that the correlation coefficients in this column are extremely similar to those of column one that pertains to the ratio of the profits yielded by a linear calculation and true maximum profits. This similarity is hardly surprising and it permits us to comment on both columns simultaneously.

We observe, first, that the coefficients of correlation with our two measures of curvature are approximately 0.26 and 0.03—clearly not very impressive figures. In no experiment was either of the corresponding correlation figures significantly higher than these (in one case the 0.2566 was replaced by a 0.257). Moreover, the first of these correlations is of the wrong sign[15]—increased curvature seems to effect a slight improvement in the performance of the linear approximations!

There is one correlation coefficient in columns one and two which does seem worth emphasis. This is the first entry in each column (−0.5) which suggests that a large ratio between the number of variables and the number of constraints (in which case the basic theorem tells us there must be a large number of zeros in the linear solution) does tend to reduce the quality of the linear approximation, as might have been expected. In two of the experiments (those with interior maxima and positive marginal yields) these correlation coefficients were over 0.7 in absolute value.

Let us turn now to our measure of evaluation of the linear approximation's choice of values for the independent variables—the normalized Euclidean distance between the linear solution point and the true optimum point, and the angle between the rays from the origin through these two points. These are shown in the third and fourth columns of Table III and once again the extreme similarity between the figures in the two columns is striking.[16] In the table there are three rather high correlations—that with the ratio of number of variables to number of constraints, that with the distance of the initial point from the true maximum and that with

[15] The second correlation coefficient is not of the wrong sign because as we indicated when we gave its definition, average curvature is a negative number so that an increase in the value of this variable corresponds to a flattening of our objective function.

[16] They are opposite in sign because we measure our angle in terms of its cosine and the cosine of the angle varies inversely with the magnitude of the angle within the relevant range.

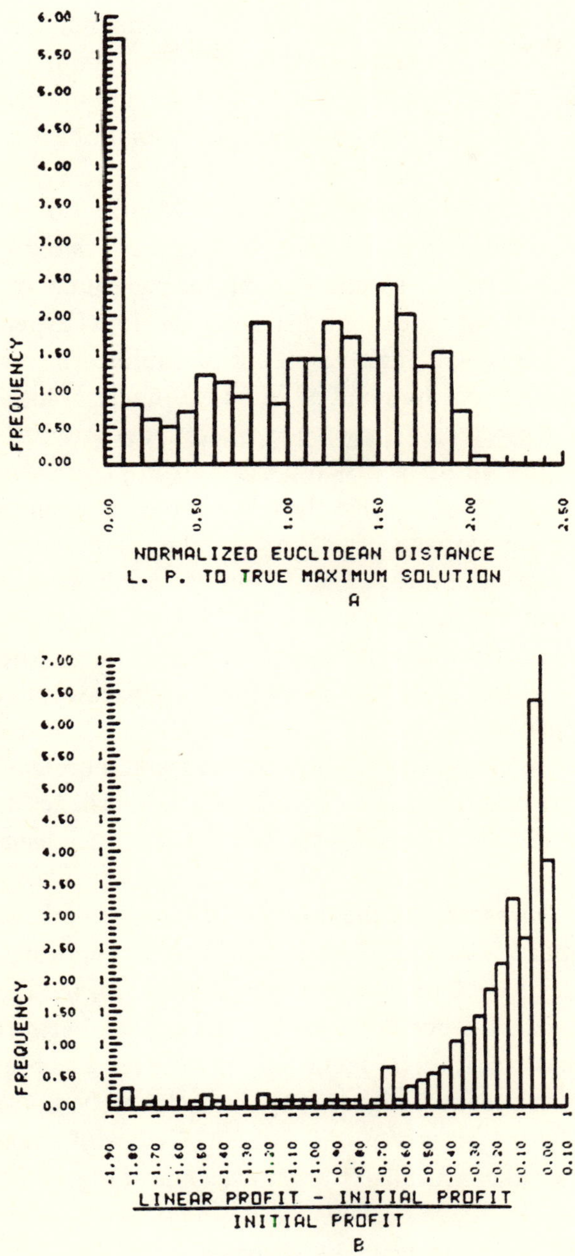

FIGURE 9

normalized curvature. Several of the corresponding correlation coefficients are considerably lower in a number of the other experiments. This time the curvature coefficients can both be considered to be of the wrong sign.[17] As curvature in-

[17] The corresponding coefficients in some of the other experiments are considerably lower—in one case the normalized curvature coefficient was approximately 0.32 and the average curvature figure was once — 0.04. But most of them are of the wrong sign.

creased the distance between the true and the calculated maximum actually tended to fall. Of course, this peculiar result may be explained very plausibly as a fortuitous consequence of the nature of our sample, but it certainly provides no ground for special confidence in the reliability of linear approximations when the curvature of the true underlying functions is small.

Figures 9a and 9b are histograms reporting the distribution of our linear results for all of our experiments combined.[18] Figure 9a describes the spread between the linear and the true maximal solution points as measured by the "normalized Euclidean distance" between the points in an *n* dimensional hyperspace representing the values of the independent variables in our programs. The bimodal distribution shows that in a substantial number of cases the linear solution does provide a relatively good fit. However, in those cases where it does not, the error is apt to be rather substantial. Figure 9b which reports on the percentage improvement of linear over initial profits, $(\pi_{\text{lin}} - \pi_i)/\pi_i$, brings out the problem even more sharply. Only the bar to the right of the vertical axis at the origin corresponds to cases in which the linear solution improved on the initial profit yield. In all other cases, representing nearly ninety per cent of our experiments, the linear calculation made things worse and, in a few cases, really spectacularly worse (the points far to the left of the origin)—in some cases involving opportunity losses equal to some 500,000 per cent of initial profit.

Finally, our last eight diagrams provide scatters representing the effects of changes in curvature and the values of other relevant variables on two measures of success of the linear calculations[19]—the normalized Euclidean distance and the $(\pi_{\text{lin}} - \pi_i)/\pi_i$.

Figures 10a and 10b show that the ratio of the number of variables to number of constraints does make a clear cut difference. As that ratio increases, so that the number of variables forced to take zero values goes up, the linear results clearly deteriorate, as might have been expected .The distance between the linear point and the true optimum increases (Figure 10a) and the relative profit contribution of the linear calculation declines (Figure 10b). Unfortunately, however, this does not entitle us to use linear approximations with any degree of equanimity even when the ratio of variables to constraints is very low. Thus in Figure 10a we see that even

[18] In Figures 9a and 9b, twenty two points are not shown because they lie outside the range of values reported. These are all to the left of the origin with values ranging from — 22 to — 4937. Figures 9–11 were all plotted directly by the Princeton 7094 using the graph package written by Professor Peter J. Warter, Jr. This program calibrates the axis scales in decimals between zero and unity with the appropriate exponent of the multiplying power of 10 printed to its right. Therefore, a number such as — 0.500 1 should be read as — 5.0 and a number such as 0.232 — 3 should be read as .000232.

[19] In these scatter diagrams, of the three hundred observation points, eight are not plotted in Figure 10a, twenty two in Figure 10b, sixteen in Figure 10c, thirty in Figure 10d, twelve in Figure 11a, six in Figure 11b, thirty four in Figure 11c, and twenty eight in Figure 11d because their values fall outside the ranges shown.

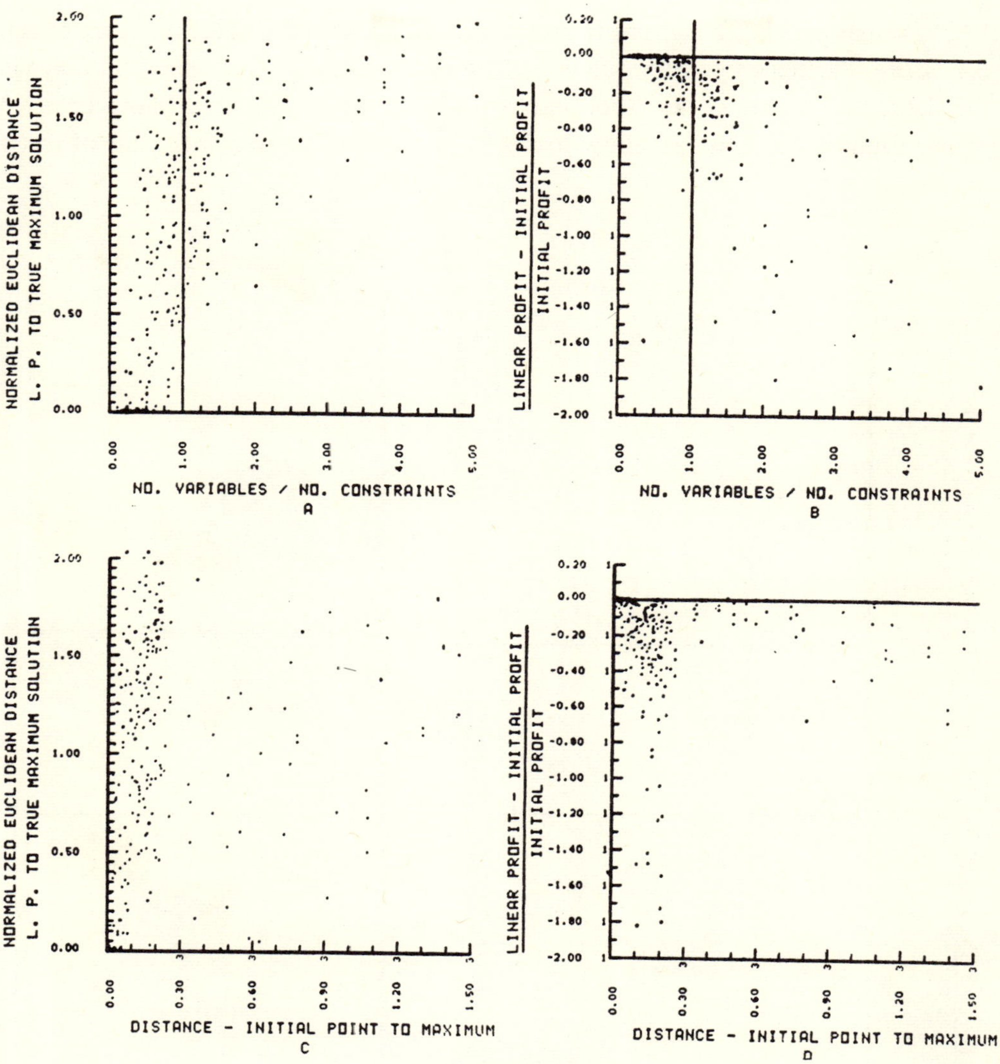

FIGURE 10

with that ratio as low as 0.5 the range of distances between the linear and true solution points is comparatively large. Or, looked at in profit terms (Figure 10b), with (number of variables/number of constraints) less than 0.5, the linear calculation can cause a 300 per cent reduction in profit from the randomly chosen initial point. With such a range of results we have no way of knowing for any given real problem whether it happens to be one of those felicitous cases where a linear calculation will do well for us.

Figures 10c and 10d show that the proximity of the initial point to the true maximum is even less dependable a measure of the reliability of a linear approximation. Since, in any event, in practice the programmer has no way of measuring this magnitude in advance, so that he cannot use it to help him decide whether to employ a linear calculation, it needs no further discussion.

The remaining four diagrams (Figures 11a–11d) report the effects of variations in curvature. Particularly noteworthy is the very wide range of goodness of fit when the degree of curvature was (deliberately) chosen to be very low (close to zero), where Figures 11c and 11d show losses of up to two hundred per cent of initial

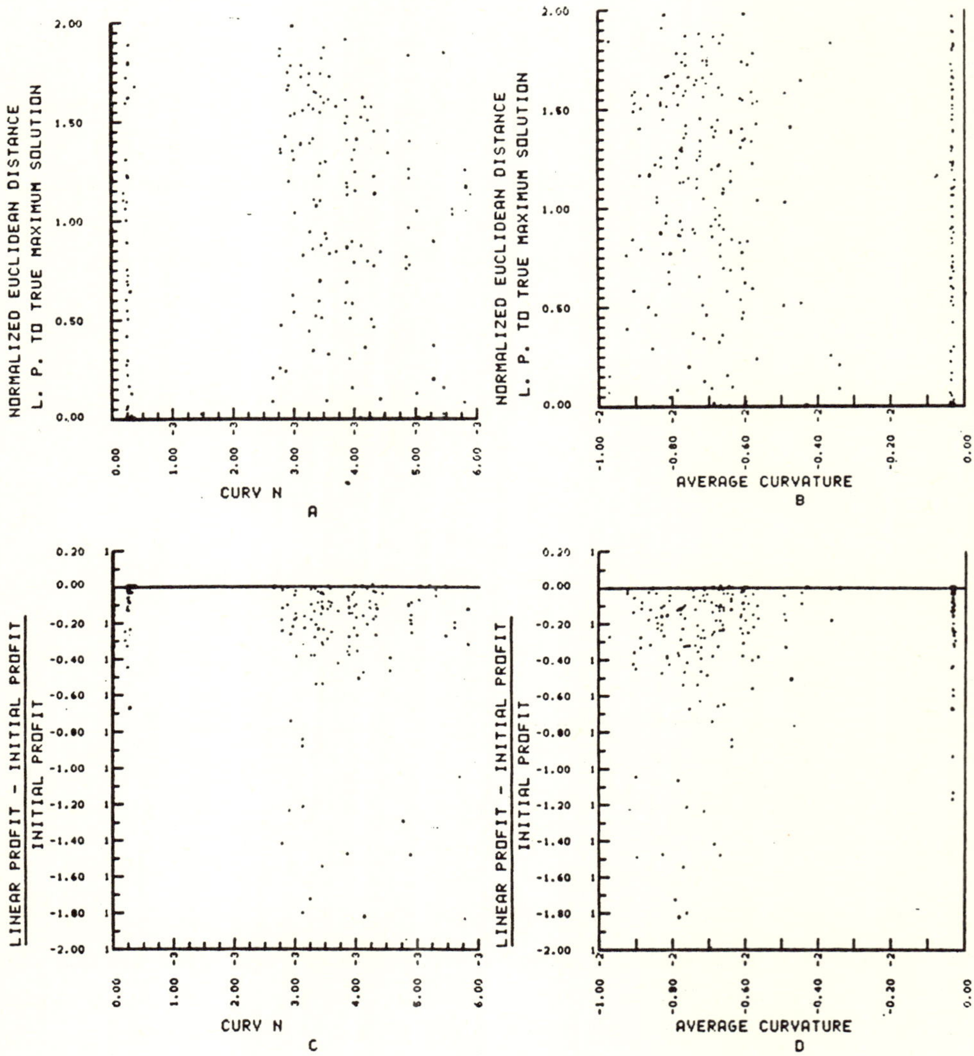

FIGURE 11

profits. Moreover, as already noted, among the (approximately thirty) points not plotted in the figure there occur far more substantial losses (in one case involving more than 490,000 per cent of initial profits).

Of course, these are all special and artificial cases and they offer no basis for generalization. Further experimentation, some of it already under way, may well show that other types of reduction in curvature do make a substantial difference.[20] But such results should not mislead the economic analyst whose only information about the overall shape of his objective function is that it is "reasonably flat." For unless he has investigated explicitly the dependability of a linear calculation in the context of his particular problem, it may still lead him into very serious error.

9. CONCLUDING COMMENT: IMPLICATIONS FOR THE USE OF PROGRAMMING

In concluding, let us comment briefly on the implications of the preceding discussion for the usefulness of programming in applied economics. The obvious moral is that in numerical calculations nonlinear programming methods must be employed more frequently, and that linear programming approximations should be used only with great precaution, and even then, only with considerable trepidation.

Unfortunately, in applied work it is the absence of adequate empirical information and not the lack of calculation techniques that is the most critical source of difficulty. The limitations of our data and of our econometric techniques are such that in many real economic problems we are unable to estimate effectively the characteristics of the pertinent nonlinear functions except, perhaps, for points very close to those where one has had recent experience. The whole of a plane can easily be deduced from its slopes at any point. But with an unspecified nonlinear function local information need only offer local implications. And if we do not know much about the nonlinear function in question we cannot very well make use of it in a nonlinear programming calculation.

Princeton University
and
Ohio State University

[20] For a very interesting recent study in which linear programming calculations are shown to provide good approximations to the solution of a nonlinear portfolio selection problem, see William F. Sharpe, "A Linear Programming Algorithm for Mutual Fund Portfolio Selection," *Management Science*, Vol. 13, March 1967.

[23]

Reprinted from THE REVIEW OF ECONOMIC STUDIES, Vol. XXXV (3), July 1968, M. L. BALINSKY AND W. J. BAUMAL, pp. 237-256.

The Dual in Nonlinear Programming and its Economic Interpretation [1]

The specification, interpretation and uses of the dual problem corresponding to any linear programme are well known and well documented in the literature. Among economists it is, however, not widely known that duals can be paired with *nonlinear* programming problems and that many of the duality relationships which hold in linear programming continue to hold for certain classes of nonlinear programmes. Specifically, if the entire primal problem is characterized by diminishing returns then many of the standard duality properties retain their validity, though certain symmetries of the linear case are lost.

Consider the general nonlinear programming problem:

$$\begin{aligned} &\text{Maximize} \quad \pi(x) = f(x_1, \ldots, x_n) \\ &\text{subject to} \quad g_1(x) \equiv g_1(x_1, \ldots, x_n) \leqq c_1 \\ &\qquad \vdots \\ &\qquad g_m(x) \equiv g_m(x_1, \ldots, x_n) \leqq c_m \\ &\qquad x_1 \geqq 0, \ldots, x_n \geqq 0 \end{aligned} \qquad \ldots(1)$$

where the objective function $\pi(x)$ and the constraint functions $g_i(x)$ are real valued in the real valued variables $x_1, \ldots, x_n$. Assuming these functions possess continuous first partial derivatives in each x_j, consider the programme (whose form is due to Wolfe [15]):

$$\text{Minimize} \quad \alpha(x, v) = f(x) + \Sigma v_i[c_i - g_i(x)] - \Sigma_j x_j(\partial f/\partial x_j - \Sigma_i v_i \partial g_i/\partial x_j) \text{ subject to}$$

$$\begin{aligned} &v_1 \partial g_1/\partial x_1 + \ldots + v_m \partial g_m/\partial x_1 \geqq \partial f/\partial x_1 \\ &\qquad \vdots \\ &v_1 \partial g_1/\partial x_n + \ldots + v_m \partial g_m/\partial x_n \geqq \partial f/\partial x_n \\ &v_1 \geqq 0, \ldots, v_m \geqq 0. \end{aligned} \qquad \ldots(2)$$

If f is concave and the g_i are convex functions[2] and, in addition, certain regularity conditions are satisfied, then (2) is taken to be the dual to the primal nonlinear programme (1) (see [15]). The important qualitative assumptions are that the constraint set of the primal problem be convex—interpreting feasible solutions x to be possible production levels, this means that given any two feasible levels x' and x'' then all " weighted average mixes " $\theta x' + (1-\theta)x''$, $0 \leqq \theta \leqq 1$, must also be feasible—and that the objective to be maximized be concave—interpreting $\pi(x)$ as profit, this means that marginal profit is nonincreasing. Mathematically these assumptions imply that if a feasible x is a local maximum for f then it is also a global maximum; alternatively, the " separating hyperplane " theorem applies. The same assumptions are important for the design of computational procedures; if these conditions hold, iterative algorithms with steps based on purely local information can be used to obtain global solutions.

[1] The work reported in this paper was supported by the Army Research Office, under Contract Number DA-31-124-ARO(D)-366, and by a grant of the National Science Foundation. It was suggested initially by a study carried out for MATHEMATICA.

[2] A function $h(x)$ is convex if $h(\theta x + (1-\theta)y) \leqq \theta h(x) + (1-\theta)h(y)$ for all x, y and $0 \leqq \theta \leqq 1$. Thus, linear interpolation overestimates the value of a convex function. $h(x)$ is concave if the reverse holds, i.e., if $-h(x)$ is convex.

This paper seeks to describe and interpret the duality theory relevant to the nonlinear programmes (1) and (2) and to supply, where possible, heuristic arguments supporting these assertions. It indicates why these relations fail to hold in the absence of the required concavity-convexity properties and, in the process, throws some light on the nature of duality in general. Finally, an economic interpretation of the dual (2) in terms of prices, marginal yields and rents is proposed.

1. REVIEW: THE KUHN-TUCKER THEOREM AND ITS ECONOMIC CONTENT

The Kuhn-Tucker propositions [7] are concerned, essentially, with the extension of the Lagrange multiplier approach to optimization over equality constraints to that of optimization over inequality constraints.[1] One manner of establishing a duality between problems (1) and (2) proceeds via the Kuhn-Tucker theory (see [5]), so it is appropriate to review the Kuhn-Tucker conditions before proceeding to examine the duality relationship.

Given a constrained maximization problem of form (1), define the function of Lagrangian type

$$L(x, v) \equiv f(x) + \Sigma v_i[c_i - g_i(x)]. \qquad \ldots(3)$$

The main " equivalence " theorem of the Kuhn-Tucker analysis states that if the convex constraint set S of (1) satisfies a qualification, then x^0 is an optimal solution to (1) if and only if there exists a $v^0 \geqq 0$ such that x^0, v^0 is a saddle point of the Lagrangian:[2]

$$L(x, v^0) \leqq L(x^0, v^0) \leqq L(x^0, v) \text{ all } x, v \geqq 0 \qquad \ldots(4)$$

i.e., x^0 maximizes $L(x, v^0)$ and v^0 minimizes $L(x,^0 v)$. Indeed, this saddle point theorem immediately brings to mind the minimax class of results of matrix games and linear programmes and identifies a symmetry if not a duality. This theorem thus permits us to solve the saddle value problem of finding an x^0, $v^0 (\geqq 0)$ to satisfy (4) instead of solving (1) directly.

But for x^0, v^0 to be a solution of the saddle value problem it is necessary, and sufficient, in view of the concavity-convexity assumptions, that the following " Kuhn-Tucker conditions " be satisfied (we take $\partial L^0/\partial x_j$ and $\partial L^0/\partial v_i$ etc., to mean the partials evaluated at x^0, v^0):

$$v_i^0 \geqq 0 \text{ and } \partial L^0/\partial v_i \geqq 0, \text{ that is, } v_i^0 \geqq 0 \text{ and } g_i(x^0) \leqq c_i,$$

and

$$v_i^0 \partial L^0/\partial v_i = 0, \text{ i.e., } v_i^0[c_i - g_i(x^0)] = 0; \; (i = 1, 2, \ldots, n) \qquad \ldots(5)$$

and

$$x_j^0 \geqq 0 \text{ and } \partial L^0/\partial x_j \leqq 0, \text{ that is, } x_j^0 \geqq 0 \text{ and } \Sigma_i v_i^0 \partial g_i^0/\partial x_j \geqq \partial f^0/\partial x_j,$$

1 It has recently been shown [1] that F. John's extension of the Lagrangian approach [6] can be used to deduce the Kuhn-Tucker conditions.

2 It is sufficient to assume as the constraint set qualification that if $v = (v_1, \ldots, v_m) \geqq 0$, $v \neq 0$, then there exists an $x \geqq 0$ such that $\Sigma_i v_i(c_i - g_i(x)) > 0$. The theorem is then quickly established. Suppose x^0, v^0 is a saddle point for L, so that $f(x) + \Sigma v_i{}^0(c_i - g_i(x)) \leqq f(x^0) + \Sigma v_i^0(c_i - g_i(x^0)) \leqq f(x^0) + \Sigma_i v_i(c_i - g_i(x^0))$ for all $x, v \geqq 0$. Then (since v could be 0) $\Sigma v_i^0(c_i - g_i(x^0)) = 0$ and (since v could be zero save for one component) $g_i(x^0) \leqq c_i$ all i. Thus $f(x) \leqq f(x) + \Sigma v_i{}^0(c_i - g_i(x)) \leqq f(x^0)$ for all feasible x. On the other hand, suppose x^0 is optimal for (1). Define $S_1 = \{z \mid z = (z_0, \ldots, z_m) \leqq [f(x), c_1 - g_1(x), \ldots, c_m - g_m(x)]$, some $x \geqq 0\}$ and $S_2 = \{y \mid (y_0, \ldots, y_m) > [f(x^0), 0, \ldots, 0]\}$. Then, by the concavity of f, and convexity of each g_i, S_1 and S_2 are convex sets, and are disjoint since x^0 maximizes f. Therefore, there exists a hyperplane separating them (" the separating hyperplane theorem "), i.e., there is a vector $u = (u_0, u_1, \ldots, u_m) \neq 0$ so that $uz \leqq uy$ for all $z \in S_1$, $y \in S_2$. But, then, $u \geqq 0$ for, otherwise, one could choose y's in S_2 to violate this inequality; also $u_0 > 0$, for otherwise $\Sigma u_i(c_i - g_i(x)) \leqq 0$ for any choice of $x \geqq 0$, contrary to the constraint set qualification. So, define $v^0 = 1/u_0(u_1, \ldots, u_m) \geqq 0$. We have $f(x) + \Sigma v_i{}^0(c_i - g_i(x)) \leqq f(x^0)$ for all $x \geqq 0$. Taking $x = x^0$ shows $\Sigma v_i^0(c_i - g_i(x^0)) \leqq 0$; but every term in this sum is nonnegative, so $\Sigma v_i^0(c_i - g_i(x^0)) = 0$. Therefore, the saddle point property is now established by the feasibility of x^0, since for any other nonnegative v we have $\Sigma v_i(c_i - g_i(x^0)) \geqq 0$ so that

$$f(x^0) + \Sigma v_i^0(c_i - g_i(x^0)) \leqq f(x^0) + \Sigma v_i(c_i - g_i(x^0)).$$

and

$$x_j^0 \partial L^0 / \partial x_j = 0, \text{ i.e., } x_j^0[\partial f^0/\partial x_j - \Sigma_i v_i^0 \partial g_i^0/\partial x_j] = 0, \ (j = 1, 2, ..., m). \qquad ...(6)$$

These conditions are clearly necessary; for example, (5) says nothing more than that if $v_i^0 > 0$ then $\partial L^0/\partial v_i = 0$, for otherwise an increase or a decrease in v_i could decrease the value of L, while if $v_i^0 = 0$ then $\partial L^0/\partial v_i \geqq 0$ for the same sort of reason. In other words, necessity is established by the obvious remark that x^0, v^0 must be a saddle point locally.[1]

It is readily seen that the inequalities preceding conditions (5) and (6) are simply the constraints found in the pair of dual nonlinear programmes (1) and (2). We will see presently that the equations (5) and (6) correspond to the well known complementary slackness conditions of the linear duality case, and can be given a similar economic interpretation.

Let us consider each of the conditions separately. Following our earlier view of (1) as the model for determining a product mix which maximizes profit, $g_i(x) \leqq c_i$ is the constraint which limits the use of resource i for production by the available quantity c_i, and $x_j \geqq 0$ the constraint which insures nonnegative production of item j. These are the direct analogues of the linear production model. Pursuing this parallelism, let us tentatively interpret $v = (v_1, ..., v_m)$ as the shadow prices or accounting values for the m scarce resources. Then the inequality $\Sigma_i v_i \partial g_i^0/\partial x_j \geqq \partial f^0/\partial x_j$ preceding (6) has a clear interpretation. $\partial g_i/\partial x_j$ is simply the marginal quantity of input i needed to produce another unit of output j. Consequently, $v_i \partial g_i/\partial x_j$ is the marginal (accounting) value of the amount of input i needed to produce an incremental unit of output j. Thus, the left side of this inequality is the sum of the values of all marginal (scarce) resources needed to produce an additional unit of output j. The right side, $\partial f/\partial x_j$, is the marginal profit yield of output j. Therefore the inequality requires the marginal accounting input cost of any output j never to fall short of its marginal profit yield.

Consider now condition (5) which asks that if $g_i(x) < c_i$ then $v_i = 0$ and if $v_i > 0$ then $g_i(x) = c_i$. In economic terms it means that if, in an optimal solution, there is an unused amount of input i then it must be a free resource, i.e., a resource with accounting value zero, while if the value of resource i is positive, then all of its available supply must be fully utilized by an optimal solution.

Finally, the symmetric conditions of (6) permit a completely analogous interpretation. They assert that if $x_j > 0$, so that product j is produced, then $\partial f/\partial x_j$, the marginal profit yield product of j, must equal the accounting value of its marginal input requirements, $\Sigma_i v_i \partial g_i/\partial x_i$, while if the marginal profit yield of j is less than the imputed accounting value of its inputs, then j will, optimally, not be produced, because it incurs an *opportunity* loss.

In summary, then, we see that these interpretations are the precise analogues of those for the constraints and variables of pairs of dual *linear* programmes. The only difference is that nonlinearity requires use of the marginal concept; in the linear case, marginal and average values are the same.

2. DUALITY

What does it mean to say that (2) is the dual programme to (1)? In order to pursue this question consider the (primal) *linear* programming problem:

Maximize $$\pi(x) \equiv f(x_1, ..., x_n) \equiv \Sigma p_j x_j \qquad ...(7)$$

[1] Sufficiency is also quickly provable. Note first that if a function h is concave and differentiable then $\Sigma(y_j - x_j)\partial h(x)/\partial x_j \geqq h(y) - h(x)$ for all x, y in the domain of h. This follows directly from the definition since $(1-\theta)h(x) + \theta h(y) \leqq h((1-\theta)x + \theta y)$ whence, for $0 < \theta \leqq 1$, $h(y) - h(x) \leqq (1/\theta)[h(x + \theta(y-x)) - h(x)]$ and, taking the limit as θ goes to zero, the statement holds, since this directional derivative is the differential with arguments $(y-x)$. The inequality is reversed if h is convex. $L(x, v)$ is convex (in fact linear) in v and concave in x, hence $L(x^0, v) - L(x^0, v^0) \geqq \Sigma(v_i - v_i^0)\partial L^0/\partial v_i = \Sigma v_i \partial L^0/\partial v_i \geqq 0$ by (5) and

$$L(x, v^0) - L(x^0, v^0) \leqq \Sigma(x_j - x_j^0)\partial L^0/\partial x_j = \Sigma x_j \partial L^0/\partial x_j \leqq 0 \text{ by (6).}$$

subject to $g_i(x) \equiv \Sigma_j a_{ij} x_j \leqq c_i,\ x_j \geqq 0.$

Taking (2) to be, by definition, the dual of (1), and noting $\partial f/\partial x_j = p_j,\ \partial g_i/\partial x_j = a_{ij}$, we obtain the " nonlinear " dual to (7):

Minimize $\alpha(x, v) = \Sigma_j p_j x_j + \Sigma_i v_i(c_i - \Sigma_j a_{ij} x_j) - \Sigma_j x_j [p_j - \Sigma v_i a_{ij}]$

which becomes, after cancelling terms

minimize $\alpha = \Sigma c_i v_i$

subject to $\Sigma_i v_i a_{ij} \geqq p_j,\ v_i \geqq 0,$ ...(8)

which is, of course, the ordinary dual problem of linear programming. Thus, our definition of dual programmes is not inconsistent with the standard definition of duality in the linear case. However, the reader may well feel that because of the relative complexity of the objective function in (2), the nonlinear dual is not the obvious extension of the dual linear programme (8). In particular, the reason that the terms in excess of $\Sigma c_i v_i$ appear in the dual objective (2) is not immediately clear. We will presently explain the necessity of these terms and the economic interpretations they impose. The reader will also note that in the nonlinear case the primal (1) is no longer the dual of the dual, that is, (1) is not the dual programme of its own dual (2); this is so because " dualization " increases the number of variables in the nonlinear case. Thus, an attractive symmetry of dual linear programmes (7), (8) is lost.[1]

What, then, might one mean by a dual problem? Basically, we conceive a dual in terms of its relationships to the primal and the properties or theorems which explain this connection. In linear programming a pertinent set of such properties is:

(*a*) one of the two problems, e.g., (7) is a constrained maximization problem, while the other, e.g., (8), is a constrained minimization problem.

(*b*) the value of the objective of the maximization problem π over feasible solutions (adopting our earlier notation) is never greater than the value of the objective α of the minimization problem, $\pi \leqq \alpha$.

(*c*) a pair of feasible solutions, one for each problem, constitutes optimal solutions to both programmes if and only if the objective values are equal, $\pi = \alpha$.

(*d*) there exists an optimal solution to one problem if and only if there exists an optimal solution to the other (and if one exists then, by (*c*), the objective values for optimal solutions are equal, $\pi = \alpha$).

(*e*) if one problem has feasible solutions but the other does not, then the first has a sequence of feasible solutions on which the objective has no finite bound in the desired direction.

(*f*) a pair of feasible solutions, one for each problem, constitutes optimal solutions to both programmes if and only if they satisfy complementary orthogonality or slackness conditions [(5) and (6)].

As noted above, all of these properties hold for pairs of dual linear programmes. Only some are true for nonlinear programmes (1) and (2). (*a*) obviously obtains. That (*b*) is valid is shown by the following argument.

Let $\hat{x}$ be feasible for (1) and (x, v) feasible for (2) and consider

$$\begin{aligned}\pi(\hat{x}) - \alpha(x, v) &= f(\hat{x}) - f(x) - \Sigma v_i[c_i - g_i(x)] + \Sigma x_j(\partial f(x)/\partial x_j - \Sigma v_i \partial g_i(x)/\partial x_j)\\ &= \{f(\hat{x}) - f(x) - \Sigma(\hat{x}_j - x_j)\partial f(x)/\partial x_j\} + \{\Sigma v_i[g_i(x) - g_i(\hat{x}) - \Sigma(x_j - \hat{x}_j)\partial g_i(x)/\partial x_j]\}\\ &\quad + \{\Sigma v_i[g_i(\hat{x}) - c_i]\} + \{\Sigma \hat{x}_j[\partial f(x)/\partial x_j - \Sigma v_i \partial g_i(x)/\partial x_j]\} \leqq 0.\end{aligned}$$

[1] Recent work of T. R. Rockafellar [9] [10] has extended earlier results, and a duality in conjugate functions, of the theory of Fenchel [4], which permits symmetric statements. These results can be used to deduce the duality of (1) and (2) and the Kuhn-Tucker work. Thus, there are underlying symmetries, but these are not readily apparent. Furthermore, a symmetric quadratic duality theory has been developed by Cottle [3].

The second equation results from the addition and subtraction of like terms and rearrangement of expressions. The final inequality follows because every term in curly brackets is nonpositive: the first because of the concavity[1] of $f(x)$, the second as a result of the convexity of each $g_i(x)$ and $v_i \geqq 0$, the third by the primal constraints and $v_i \geqq 0$, the last by the dual constraints and $x_j \geqq 0$.

Property (*c*) also holds, for if $\pi(\hat{x}) = \alpha(x, y)$ for feasible $\hat{x}$ and (x, v) then π has reached an upper and α a lower bound (by (*b*)) whence neither can be improved. On the other hand, if $\pi(\hat{x}) < \alpha(x, v)$ for feasible $\hat{x}$ and (x, v) then at least one of these is not optimal. For suppose $\hat{x}$ is optimal. Then, by the Kuhn-Tucker theory, there exists a $\hat{v}$ such that $(\hat{x}, \hat{v})$ satisfies the conditions (5), (6). But this means $(\hat{x}, \hat{v})$ is feasible for (2) and

$$\alpha(\hat{x}, \hat{v}) = \pi(\hat{x}) < \alpha(x, v),$$

so (x, v) cannot be an optimal solution.

Property (*d*) must be amended for our nonlinear case (see [3]). If the constraint qualification of Kuhn-Tucker is in force for (1) then if x^0 solves (1), there must exist a v^0 such that (x^0, v^0) solves (2). The converse portion of (*d*) needs an added assumption, for example, that employed in [5]: if (x^0, v^0) solves (2) and the matrix of second partial derivatives of $\alpha(x, v)$ with respect to x at (x^0, v^0) is nonsingular, then x^0 solves (1). Other more general converses using alternate assumptions have also been given (e.g., in [6]).

Property (*e*) does not hold except in some very restrictive circumstances.[2] Finally, property (*f*) holds for our pair of dual programmes. To simplify notation, let u_i and l_j represent the primal and dual slack variables, so that

$$u_i(x) = c_i - g_i(x) \quad \text{and} \quad l_j(x, v) = \Sigma_i v_i \partial g_i(x)/\partial x_j - \partial f(x)/\partial x_j.$$

Then we will say that a pair of feasible solutions, $\hat{x}$ for (1) and (x, v) for (2), satisfy the complementary slackness properties if $v_i u_i(\hat{x}) = 0$ for all i, and $x_j l_j(\hat{x}, v) = 0$ for all j. Suppose, first, that $\hat{x}$ and (x, v) satisfy this property. Then $\pi(\hat{x}) = \alpha(x, v)$, which by (*c*) shows these are optimal solutions. For the converse, suppose $\hat{x}$ and (x, v) are optimal solutions. Then $\pi(\hat{x}) = \alpha(x, v)$ by (*c*). Consider the string of relations used in proving property (*b*). Since $\pi(\hat{x}) - \alpha(x, v)$ is zero, every inequality is an equation and every term in curly brackets, since nonpositive, must be zero. This means $\Sigma v_i u_i(\hat{x}) = 0$ and

$$\Sigma \hat{x}_j l_j(x, v) = 0,$$

and, since every term in each sum is nonnegative, the complementary slackness property obtains.

Clearly, the duality theory of nonlinear programming is still in a somewhat confused state, although the conjugate function approach [10] lends hope for unification and, hence, clarification.

[1] See footnote 1, p. 239.

[2] The following example (for which we are indebted to a reader) shows that (*e*) does not hold: Let $f(x) = x_2$, $g_1(x) - c_1 = e^{-x_1} + x_2 - 1 \leqq 0$, $x_1, x_2 \geqq 0$ be the primal (1); then the dual constraints of (2) are $-ve^{-x_1} \geqq 0$ and $v \geqq 1$. The primal objective is bounded above by g_1, yet the dual constraint set is empty.

In general, if the constraints of (1) are linear and admit no feasible solutions, while the constraints of (2) admit feasible solutions, then the value of $\alpha(x, v)$ is unbounded from below (Theorem 3, [15]).

Further, it has been shown by Cottle [2, 3] that conditions (*a*) through (*e*) hold for the special case of symmetric dual quadratic programmes.

Lastly, one might consider replacing the conclusion of (*e*) by " at least one of the constraint sets of primal or dual is unbounded ". This is well known for linear programmes. It is also true for symmetric dual quadratic programmes [2].

3. ECONOMIC INTERPRETATION OF THE DUAL VARIABLES

The Kuhn-Tucker conditions suggested straightforward economic interpretations of the nonlinear dual constraints (2) which are direct generalizations of the interpretations of the constraints in the linear case. However, in that discussion, we took the v_i to be shadow prices or accounting values. In what sense is this valid? In general terms, this view of the v_i corresponds with that advanced by Samuelson (see [11] e.g., pp. 65-66) for, as we have seen, the v_i of the dual programme are the Lagrange multipliers which enter into the definition of $L(x, v)$. More exactly, one might wish that the v_k^0, the values of the dual variables at an optimum, correspond to the marginal values of the scarce inputs. To make this statement precise, consider the maximum profit to be a function of the available quantities of inputs, c_i:

$$\pi(c) = \pi(c_1, \ldots, c_m) = \max_x \{f(x) \mid g_i(x) \leqq c_i, x \geqq 0\}. \qquad \ldots(9)$$

The issue, then, is whether v_k^0 is equal to $\partial\pi(c)/\partial c_k$, i.e., whether the value of the kth dual variable is equal to the marginal profit of the kth input. Unfortunately, this asks a bit too much. Even in the linear programming case, for some changes in the values of the c_i, there will normally be points of discontinuity in the derivatives, points where there exist finite right and left hand partial derivatives, $\partial\pi(c)/\partial c_k \mid_+$ and $\partial\pi(c)/\partial c_k \mid_-$ but at which $\partial\pi(c)/\partial c_k$ itself is not defined. Exactly the same difficulty arises in the nonlinear programming case.

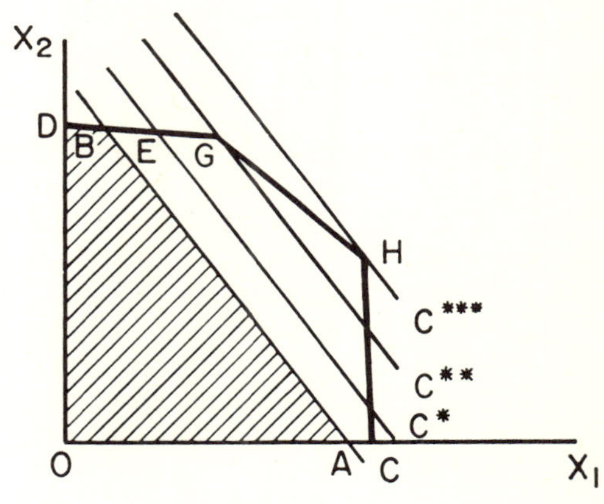

FIGURE 1*a*

The reason the problem occurs is easily shown with the aid of a simple diagram (Figure 1*a*).

Let the original feasible region for a linear programming problem be the shaded area *OABD*. Let the constraint line labelled *C* correspond to the *k*th scarce input. An increase in c_k, the available quantity of that resource, produces an outward shift in the constraint line, say to *C**. Suppose this changes the optimal point from *B* to *E*. It should be clear that in the linear case this will yield an increase in the value of the objective function proportionate to the distance through which the constraint line has shifted. Thus, over the range in question, $\partial\pi/\partial c_k$ will exhibit no discontinuities. However, once the level of resource *k* is increased up to the point where our constraint line is shifted to *C***, so that it goes through point *G*, the intersection of constraint lines *DG* and *GH*, a discontinuity occurs in the derivative. For the optimal point now moves along the more steeply sloping segment of the boundary, *GH*, so that a parallel shift in our constraint line of a given amount now produces a much greater move in the optimal point. Each time the optimal point passes through a corner of the feasible region there will thus be a discontinuity in $\partial\pi/\partial c_k$.

Trouble, therefore, arises whenever the shift in the constraint line produces a degeneracy in the programme—at an " overdetermined " corner point, where more than n hyperplanes in n dimensional space pass through a single point. The discontinuity is particularly dramatic when our constraint line shifts outward so far that it leaves the feasible region altogether (input k becomes redundant). This occurs in Figure 1*a* where our constraint becomes C^{***} and passes through corner point H. Any further outward shift in C will produce no change in the feasible region, and so it will yield no net increase in π. Thus, to the left of point H, we have $\partial\pi/\partial c_k = w>0$ where w does not approach zero as line C approaches C^{***}. Yet above and to the right of point H we have $\partial\pi/\partial c_k = 0$. This type of discontinuity in the value of $\partial\pi/\partial c_k$, then, can occur in both linear and nonlinear programmes. The linear case has been investigated thoroughly by Williams [14], who establishes necessary and sufficient conditions for the existence of a generalized notion of marginal values or derivatives due to Mills [8], in which all of the parameters of the linear programme are permitted to vary.

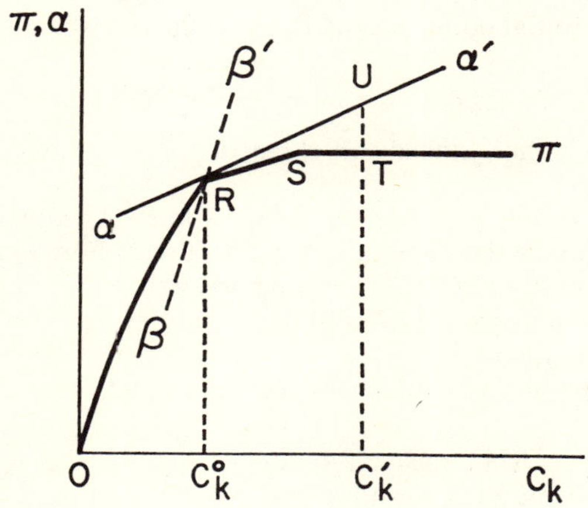

FIGURE 1*b*

Fortunately, however, there is a result (see, e.g., Uzawa [13]) which comes very close to our desired proposition that v_k^0 equals $\partial\pi/\partial c_k$. While the optimal value of the dual variable v_k^0 cannot always be interpreted as the marginal profit yield of the kth input, since the latter is not always defined, v_k^0 will invariably lie between the corresponding right and left hand partial derivatives which exist and are finite, given that the constraint qualification (see footnote 2, p. 238) holds. In symbols, we have $\partial\pi(c)/\partial c_k\,|_+ \leqq v_k^0 \leqq \partial\pi(c)/\partial c_k\,|_-$ for all k. It also follows at once that *at a value of c_k where the partial derivative is well defined so that the left and right hand derivatives are equal, then the optimal value of the corresponding dual variable v_k^0 must be precisely equal to that derivative, $\partial\pi(c)/\partial c_k$.*

Since the algebraic proof is rather lengthy, we first offer a shorter and more intuitive geometric argument, which is very much in the spirit of the more painstaking proof that follows. In Figure 1*b*, curve 0π records the changes in total maximal profit, π, that result from variations in c_k, the capacity changes that brought about the shifts in the constraint line shown in Figure 1*a*.

Since our programming problem is not necessarily linear, 0π need not consist of several connected line segments. However, it is apt to have kinks (points of discontinuity in the derivative) such as R and S, corresponding to values of c_k at which our shifting constraint line in Figure 1*a* passes through corner points such as G and H.

Now, consider the effects of the changes in the value of c_k on our dual programme (2). Suppose we begin with an optimal solution of our primal and dual and vary c_k from its initial value c_k^0 (which for illustrative purposes is taken to fall below a kink, R, in our profit function). Since c_k enters none of the constraints of the dual, the solution that was optimal at $c_k = c_k^0$ remains feasible for the dual programme given by any other value of c_k. Moreover, with only c_k varying, the dual objective function in (2) may be rewritten as the simple linear expression $c_k v_k + K$, since $c_k v_k$ is the only term in the dual objective function affected by the variations in c_k. This dual objective function is then represented by a straight line such as $\alpha\alpha'$ or $\beta\beta'$ in Figure 1*b*. Here, because at $c_k = c_k^0$ we have an optimal solution for both primal and dual, this line must coincide with the profit function. For, at an optimal solution, we always have $\pi = \alpha$, as we have seen. Moreover, at any other value of c_k, say $c_k = c_k'$, $\alpha\alpha'$ must not lie below 0π, for e.g., at c_k' points T and U are the values of α and π corresponding to feasible solution of the dual programmes with $c_k = c_k'$, and for any pair of feasible solutions $\alpha \geqq \pi$ as we have seen. We conclude that our dual cannot be represented by $\beta\beta'$ which cuts below 0π. Rather, it must be depicted by a line such as $\alpha\alpha'$ which goes through the initial optimal profit point R, and lies at or above 0π everywhere else. Our theorem now follows when we note that because $\alpha\alpha'$ is given by $v_k c_k + K$ its slope is v_k. Hence, at a kinked initial point such as R, by comparing the slopes of $\alpha\alpha'$ with that of 0π we have our result:

$$\partial\pi/\partial c_k \mid_+ \leqq v_k \leqq \partial\pi/\partial c_k \mid_- .$$

And at any point which is not kinked, all three of these variables are obviously equal in value.

We turn now to a rigorous proof of this proposition. As already noted, the validity of the theorem depends upon the constraint qualification. For, if the qualification does not hold, it is possible that $\partial\pi(c)/\partial c_k \mid_-$ does not exist. For example, if the optimal solution x^0 is the unique *feasible* solution and $g_k(x^0) = c_k$, then no feasible points exist with $g_i(x) \leqq c_i$, $i \neq k$ and $g_k(x) < c_k$.

We prove these statements and some supplementary facts concerning $\pi(c_k)$ in the next few paragraphs.

First, observe that $\pi(c_k)$ is a concave function of c_k. For, let c_k' and c_k'' be two input vectors admitting optimal solutions x' and x'' respectively. Then, for $0 \leqq \theta \leqq 1$

$$\pi(\theta c_k' + (1-\theta)c_k'') = \max_x \{f(x) \mid g_i(x) \leqq \theta c_k' + (1-\theta)c_k'',\ x > 0\}$$
$$\geqq f(\theta x' + (1-\theta)x'') \geqq \theta f(x') + (1-\theta)f(x'') = \theta\pi(c_k') + (1-\theta)\pi(c_k'').$$

The first relation holds by definition, the second since $\theta x' + (1-\theta)x'' \geqq 0$ is feasible for the problem with inputs $\theta c_k' + (1-\theta)c_k''$ by the convexity of the constraints, the third by the concavity of f and the last by definition.

Let us now confine our attention to $\pi(c_k)$ defined by

$$\pi(c_k) = \max_x \{f(x) \mid g_i(x) \leqq c_{i0},\ i \neq k,\ g_k(x) \leqq c_k,\ x \geqq 0\}, \qquad \text{...(10)}$$

that is, treat π as a function only of the input of type k, whose initial value is c_{ko}. $\pi(c_k)$ exists and is continuous for $c_{ko} - \delta < c_k < c_{ko} + \varepsilon$ for some $\varepsilon, \delta > 0$. First, $\pi(c_{ko} - \delta)$ must exist for some $\delta > 0$ because the constraint qualification implies the existence of a feasible point $\bar{x} \geqq 0$ with $g_i(\bar{x}) < c_{io}$ for all i, that is, the existence of an interior point. This is established as follows: suppose there is no $x \geqq 0$ such that $g_i(x) < c_{io}$ all i. Let

$$S = \{c = (c_1, \ldots, c_m) \mid g_i(x) < c_i + c_{io} \text{ for some } x \geqq 0\}.$$

S is a convex set which does not, by hypothesis, contain the origin. Therefore, by the separating hyperplane theorem, there exist $v = (v_1, \ldots, v_m) \geqq 0$, $v \neq 0$, so that $\Sigma v_i c_i \geqq 0$ for all $y \,\varepsilon\, S$. Suppose $x \geqq 0$ and let $\alpha_1, \ldots, \alpha_m$ be any positive numbers. Then c defined by $c_i = g_i(x) - c_{io} + \alpha_i$ must belong to S whence $\Sigma v_i(g_i(x) - c_{io}) + \Sigma v_i \alpha_i \geqq 0$ for all $\alpha_i > 0$. Therefore, $\Sigma v_i(g_i(x) - c_{io}) \geqq 0$ for all $x \geqq 0$ and the $v \geqq 0$ determined above, contrary to the constraint qualification. Therefore, the feasible set of the programme (10) with $c_k = c_{ko} - \delta$ must be nonempty for some $\delta > 0$, while the maximum value is bounded from above by $\pi(c_{ko}) = f(x^0)$. Second, $\pi(c_{ko} + \varepsilon)$ must exist for some $\varepsilon > 0$, because the feasible set is obviously nonempty with $c_k = c_{ko} + \varepsilon$, and the maximum value is bounded from above, as we will now see. Let x^ε be a feasible solution to (10) where $c_k = c_{ko} + \varepsilon$, $\varepsilon > 0$. Then, by the Kuhn-Tucker equivalence, with $L(x, v)$ the Lagrangian corresponding to the original constraint set in which $c_k = c_{ko}$, we have

$$L(x^\varepsilon, v^0) \leqq L(x^0, v^0) = f(x^0), \text{ or } f(x^\varepsilon) - f(x^0) - \Sigma v_i^0 (g_i(x^\varepsilon) - c_i) \leqq 0,$$

implying

$$f(x^\varepsilon) \leqq f(x^0) + \Sigma v_i^0 (g_i(x^\varepsilon) - c_i) \leqq f(x^0) + v_k^0 \varepsilon.$$

The preceding argument then establishes the existence of $\pi(c_k)$ for $c_{ko} - \delta < c_k < c_{ko} + \varepsilon$.

But we can say more. $\pi(c_k)$ is, as we saw before, concave; it is also continuous. For this purpose, define

$$L^\alpha(x, v) = f(x) + \sum_{i \neq k} v_i(c_{i0} - g_i(x)) + v_k(c_{k0} + \alpha - g_k(x)),$$

for $-\delta < \alpha < \varepsilon$ and let (x^α, v^α) be a saddle point. We have

$$L^0(x^\alpha, v^0) \leqq L^0(x^0, v^0) \leqq L^0(x^0, v^\alpha) \quad \text{and} \quad L^\alpha(x^0, v^\alpha) \leqq L^\alpha(x^\alpha, v^\alpha) \leqq L^\alpha(x^\alpha, v^0),$$

which implies

$$L^\alpha(x^0, v^\alpha) - L^0(x^0, v^\alpha) \leqq L^\alpha(x^\alpha, v^\alpha) - L^0(x^0, v^0) \leqq L^\alpha(x^\alpha, v^0) - L^0(x^\alpha, v^0)$$

or, what is the same thing since $\pi(c_{k0} + \alpha) = L^\alpha(x^\alpha, v^\alpha)$,

$$\alpha v_k^\alpha \leqq \pi(c_{k0} + \alpha) - \pi(c_{k0}) \leqq \alpha v_k^0, \quad -\delta < \alpha < \varepsilon. \qquad \ldots(11)$$

This establishes continuity. Recall that a concave function in one variable always possesses right and left hand derivatives. This is because the concavity of $\pi(t)$ implies

$$\{\pi(t_2) - \pi(t_1)\}/(t_2 - t_1) \geqq \{\pi(t_3) - \pi(t_1)\}/(t_3 - t_1) \text{ for } t_1 < t_2 < t_3,$$

(this is an immediate consequence of the basic definition). Therefore, $\frac{1}{\alpha}\{\pi(t+\alpha) - \pi(t)\}$ is monotone increasing as $\alpha \to 0$, $\alpha > 0$, implying the right hand derivative is either finite or infinite. But the infinite case is precluded by (11), showing the right hand derivative exists. The existence of the left hand derivative is shown in a similar manner, using the inequality $\{\pi(t_3) - \pi(t_1)\}/(t_3 - t_1) \geqq \{\pi(t_3) - \pi(t_2)\}/(t_3 - t_2)$, which is also implied by the concavity of $\pi(t)$. Consider, now, the right hand inequality of (11). If $\alpha > 0$

$$\frac{\pi(c_{k0} + \alpha) - \pi(c_{k0})}{\alpha} \leqq v_k^0 \text{ or } \left.\frac{\partial \pi(c_k)}{\partial c_k}\right|_+ = \lim_{\substack{\alpha \to 0 \\ \alpha > 0}} \frac{\pi(c_{k0} + \alpha) - \pi(c_{k0})}{\alpha} \leqq v_k^0,$$

while if $\alpha < 0$

$$\frac{\pi(c_{k0} + \alpha) - \pi(c_{k0})}{\alpha} \geqq v_k^0 \text{ or } \left.\frac{\partial \pi(c_k)}{\partial c_k}\right|_- = \lim_{\substack{\alpha \to 0 \\ \alpha > 0}} \frac{\pi(c_{k0} + \alpha) - \pi(c_{k0})}{\alpha} \geqq v_k^0.$$

This proves the basic proposition on the interpretation of the optimal value of the dual variable, v_k^0:

$$\partial \pi(c)/\partial c_k \,|_+ \leqq v_k^0 \leqq \partial \pi(c)/\partial c_k \,|_-, \text{ for all } k. \qquad \ldots(12)$$

4. INTERPRETATION OF THE OBJECTIVE FUNCTION

We turn, now, to the economic interpretation of the dual objective function. It is, itself, a function of Lagrangian type formed from *all* the constraints of (1), both the structural constraints, $g_i(x) \leqq c_i$, and the nonnegativity conditions, $x_i \geqq 0$.[1] Assume first, for simplicity, that the primal variables, $x_1, \ldots, x_n$, have been assigned their optimal values. Then the first term in the objective function, $f(x_1, \ldots, x_n)$, the maximal profit figure, can be treated as constant and so can be disregarded in discussing the minimization of the objective function as a whole.

In the second term of the objective function, $\Sigma_i v_i[c_i - g_i(x)]$, the item in square brackets $[c_i - g_i(x)]$ is the unused amount (capacity) of input i, while v_i is the unit accounting value of that unused item. Hence, minimization of this second term means minimization of the value of all unused inputs.

Finally, we come to the third term in the objective function, $\Sigma_j x_j[\partial f/\partial x_j - \Sigma_i v_i(\partial g_i/\partial x_j)]$. As we have seen, $\Sigma_i v_i \partial g_i/\partial x_j$ is the marginal input value of all resources going into output j. And, because $\partial f/\partial x_j$ is the marginal profit yield of output j, the term in square brackets (which by the dual constraints is always non-positive) may be described as the marginal opportunity loss incurred by an increment in output j. Multiplying by x_j, the magnitude of that output, and summing over all j, we obtain a weighted sum of the marginal opportunity losses of all outputs, where the weights are the magnitudes of the outputs (the x_j). Thus we may describe this last term of the objective function as the *marginal* opportunity cost of all outputs taken together. To summarize, then, minimization of the dual objective function is tantamount to the minimization of the value of unused inputs together with the marginal opportunity cost of total output.

A deeper and more interesting interpretation may be obtained by regrouping the terms of $\alpha(x, v)$ in the following way:

$$\alpha(x, v) = \Sigma c_i v_i + [f(x) - \Sigma v_i g_i(x)] - \Sigma_j x_j[\partial f/\partial x_j - \Sigma_i v_i \partial g_i/\partial x_j]. \qquad \ldots(13)$$

In (13), $\alpha(x, v)$ is described as the marginal evaluation of the firm's scarce resources, $\Sigma c_i v_i$, plus the sum of a number of other terms whose economic meaning may be explained in terms of the economic rents which accrue to the owner of the firm's production opportunities. Suppose that as a result of the holding of a patent, or scarce capital facility, or some other scarce resource, he is able to prevent the company from engaging in production. Then he can claim as economic rent the difference between the total yield that would accrue to the company were it to produce and the cost of the other inputs needed for production, evaluated by their marginal contributions. This is simply because no net return is possible without his consent. The economic rent is the difference between the firm's total return and the normal marginal productivity prices of the inputs; it is the net return yielded by the resources contributed by the individual who is in a position to collect the rent.

Economic rent, then, is the excess of the total profit yield, $f(x) = \pi$, over the payments given to the inputs actually used, $g_i(x)$, if each were paid v_i per unit, i.e., its marginal yield. Hence, the second term in (13) is the economic rent yielded by the firm. Thus, (again ignoring the last term in (13)), if in an optimal solution there is excess capacity in every input so that $g_i(x) < c_i$ all i and hence $v_i = 0$ all i, then the entire return becomes economic rent. Hence, as it does in the linear programming case, the objective function of the dual represents the payment which can be demanded by each contributor to the final output (including now the holder of the necessary patents or some other essential requisite for the

[1] For consider the corresponding Lagrangian $L'(x, v, l) = f(x) + \sum_1^m v_i[c_i - g_i(x)] + \sum_1^n l_j x_j$. We may identify the Lagrange multipliers, l_j, with $\Sigma v_i \partial g_i/\partial x_j - \partial f/\partial x_j$ so that l_j becomes the slack variable in the jth dual constraint, $\Sigma v_i \partial g_i/\partial x_j - l_j = \partial f/\partial x_j$. Writing $u_i = c_i - g_i(x)$ as the slack variable of the ith primal constraint, the dual objective function then takes the symmetric form $\alpha = \pi + \Sigma v_i u_i + \Sigma x_j l_j$.

output, whose payment takes the form of economic rent.) In the absence of increasing returns, the rent figure will be non-negative since, as will be shown presently, the marginal yield of an input i can be no greater than its " average yield ", in view of the convexity of the constraint $g_i(x)$.

The last term of (13) is not interpretable in quite as natural a manner. However, the same ideas can be carried over and we see that it can be translated as a deduction from rent resulting from an output k whose marginal yield is negative, $\partial f/\partial x_k < \Sigma v_i \partial g_i/\partial x_k$. Thus, total rent is total profit minus marginal value of inputs minus marginal profit loss of unprofitable outputs.

Why does the rent enter the nonlinear dual but not the linear dual? An explanation is found in the old " adding-up " discussion of distribution theory. Recall (see, e.g., [12]) that toward the end of the 19th century, a number of economists became very much concerned with the following question: if each input to a production process is paid the value of its marginal product, will the total factor payment exhaust the total profit, or will it leave over some unimputed profit, positive or negative? In terms of our present discussion, this is asking whether or not total profit at maximum $\pi(x)$, where $x = x^0$ is an optimal solution to (1), is equal to the total marginal value of inputs at an optimum, $\Sigma c_i v_i^0$ where (x^0, v^0) satisfies the constraints of (2). The answer proposed by some of the participants in the discussion was that this equality holds if the production function is linear and homogeneous. This is a direct consequence of Euler's Theorem which implies that if the profit function $\pi(c_1, \ldots, c_m)$, here viewed as a function of the available input quantities c_i, is a differentiable homogeneous function of degree one then $\pi = \Sigma c_i \partial\pi/\partial c_i = \Sigma c_i v_i$. This conclusion can be applied directly to the linear programming case which is, of course, characterized by constant returns to scale (linear homogeneity). In the linear programming case, the duality theorem confirms this result since $\pi(x) = \alpha = \Sigma c_i v_i$ at an optimum. At any rate, it is well known to economists that $\pi = \Sigma c_i v_i$ holds true only so long as there are constant returns to scale, at least locally.

But, in our nonlinear analysis, we are dealing with diminishing returns to scale (the concave objective function and convex constraint functions) and, in this case, an amount smaller than the total profit will normally be imputed to the factors. This is easily demonstrated. At an optimum, nonlinear duality establishes $\pi(x) = \alpha(x, v)$ or

$$\begin{aligned}\pi(x) - \Sigma c_i v_i &= f(x) - \Sigma_i v_i g_i(x) - \Sigma_j x_j[\partial f/\partial x_j - \Sigma_i v_i \partial g_i/\partial x_j] \\ &= \{f(x) - \Sigma_j x_j \partial f/\partial x_j\} - \{\Sigma_i v_i[g_i - \Sigma_j x_j \partial g_i/\partial x_j]\} \qquad \ldots(14)\end{aligned}$$

But, by footnote 1, p. 239, (taking $h = f$ and $y = 0$) since $f(x)$ is concave and the $g_i(x)$ are convex,

$$f - \Sigma x_j \partial f/\partial x_j \geqq f(0),$$

$$g_i - \Sigma_j x_j \partial g_i/\partial x_j \leqq g_i(0),$$

so that

$$\pi(x) - \Sigma c_i v_i \geqq f(0) - \Sigma_i v_i g_i(0),$$

which is nonnegative provided $f(0) \geqq 0$ and all $g_i(0) \leqq 0$, as was to be shown.

In economic terms this means that under diminishing returns, total rent, $\pi(x) - c_i v_i$, will be nonnegative, provided that we do not have either $f(0) < 0$ or any $g_i(0) > 0$. But the requirement $f(0) \geqq 0$ means that there are no fixed charges on the company which it cannot avoid by going out of business. If $f(0) < 0$ it means that by producing a zero output, the company will actually incur a loss. An example of such a situation is the case where the government assesses a tax of t dollars against the company so that $f(0) = -t$. The firm must pay the t dollars, whether or not it produces anything. It is obvious that if such a tax were set sufficiently high it could wipe out any rents which the company would otherwise be able to pay. That is why we can only be certain diminishing returns will yield positive rents if no such tax or any other such fixed charge is permitted.

The role of the requirement $g_i(0) \leqq 0$ is precisely the same. If $g_i(0)>0$ it means that the firm is committed to use up some of input i even at zero output levels, and, if the magnitude of this obligation were sufficiently large, then payment to these inputs of the value of their marginal yields, $v_i g_i(0)$, would offset any rent which the firm could otherwise afford.

But, in any other case, diminishing returns will lead to nonnegative (normally positive) rents, while, presumably, under increasing returns, rents will be nonpositive (normally negative), for in these circumstances marginal product values would impute to inputs more than the firm's total profits. (We say " presumably " since increasing returns violate the convexity conditions underlying the definition of the nonlinear dual). Roughly, this is all a reflection of the well-known observation that with falling average yields (diminishing returns) the marginal yield of an input will be less than its per unit yield, while, if the average yield is rising, the reverse will be true.

We can now see the role played in the nonlinear dual problem by the additional terms in its objective function—the elements which make no appearance in the linear dual problem. These can be ascribed to the requirement that $\pi(x) = \alpha(x, v)$ at an optimum. We have seen that with diminishing returns the expression $\Sigma c_i v_i^0$, is apt to take a value less than $\pi(x^0)$ and it is precisely this property which led to the conclusion that marginal product values can only impute to inputs an amount no greater than the total profit. The difference, if one exists, can, as we have seen, be described as economic rent.

5. GEOMETRY OF THE LINEAR DUAL

To understand more fully the nature of the relationship between the primal and the dual problems, and, in particular, to see the relevance of the convexity conditions for the existence of a dual problem, it is helpful to avail ourselves of a graphic interpretation of the two problems.

Unfortunately, the basic diagram is a bit difficult to describe without a somewhat involved three-dimensional graph; therefore, even in the linear case discussed in this section, we will have to proceed rather slowly. We begin with a graph of the primal linear problem into which we will presently incorporate the linear dual and, finally, we will adapt it to the nonlinear dual.

For expository convenience, we will take the primal problem to be the standard product line selection problem (7) in which only three products are taken to be under consideration ($n = 3$). The more usual geometric representation of a linear programming problem measures on its axes the output quantities, the x_j, i.e., it is depicted in what has been called " solutions space ". However, to make it possible for the dual to be incorporated into the diagram, we turn to the representation in " requirements space " in which the employed input quantities, $g_i(x)$, are measured along the axes. The reason for this is that, as we have seen, the dual linear problem may be interpreted, economically, as the determination of values (shadow prices) for the *inputs*. Hence, one cannot readily represent the dual problem in a diagram in which the inputs do not make some sort of explicit appearance.

Figure 2, which is included for purposes of review, and because it helps us to describe the somewhat more complex diagrams that follow, is the standard requirements space representation of our linear programme.

The quantities $OC_1 = c_1$ and $OC_2 = c_2$ measure the available amounts of our two inputs where g_1 and g_2 are the quantities of these inputs which are utilized. The ray OR_j represents the combination of input quantities needed to produce different specified quantities x_j of output j. Specifically, the point S_j represents the input combination needed to manufacture a single unit of output j.

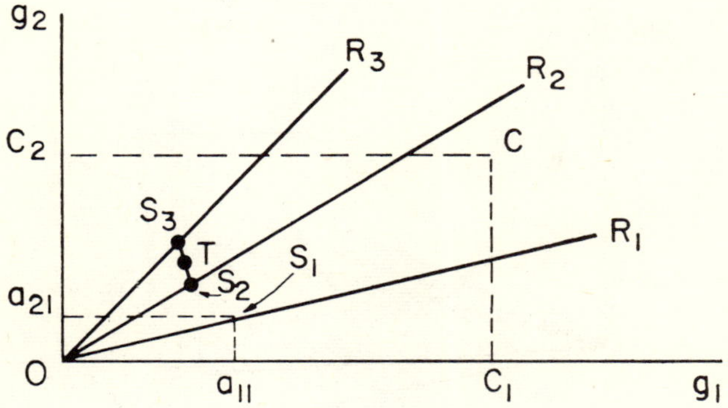

FIGURE 2

Next, in Figure 3, we add to this diagram a third axis representing the profits corresponding to the various input-output combinations in Figure 2. Let R_1P_1 be the total profit obtainable from the input combination represented by point R_1. Then, because of the linearity of our problem, and because, with zero inputs profits are zero, the total profit corresponding to any point on output ray OR_1 is given by the ray OP_1, which lies directly above OR_1.

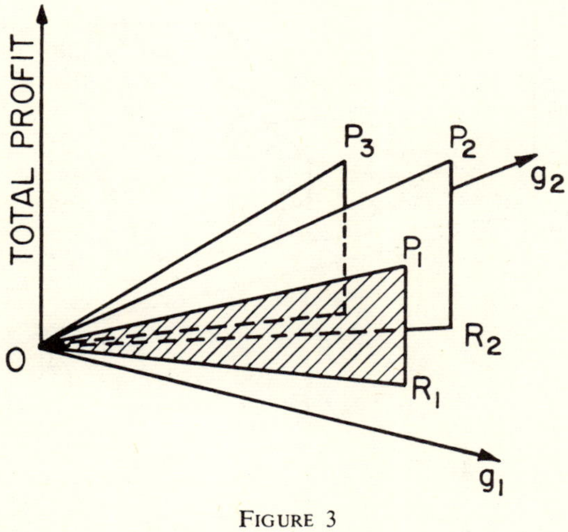

FIGURE 3

Similarly, we obtain the total profit rays OP_2 and OP_3 corresponding to output rays OR_2 and OR_3.

We now require a representation of the profits corresponding to combinations of outputs, i.e., to points lying between the individual output rays.[1] Because of the linearity of the problem, these profit figures are obtained by connecting OP_1 and OP_2 by means of a segment of a plane and by doing the same for OP_2 and OP_3. In other words, we obtain the remainder of the profit function by roofing in our figure where the triangles such as OR_1P_1 are treated as walls of the edifice. This is done in Figure 4.

[1] The reader will recall that point T in Figure 2, which is the midpoint of line segment S_2S_3, represents half the inputs of point S_2 plus half the inputs of point S_3. Hence, since S_2 corresponds to a unit of output 2 and S_3 to a unit of output 3, because of the linearity of our problem, point T gives the inputs needed to produce a half unit of output 2 and a half unit of output 3. Any interior point of the cone R_1OR_3 can be interpreted similarly as some combination of outputs 1, 2 and 3.

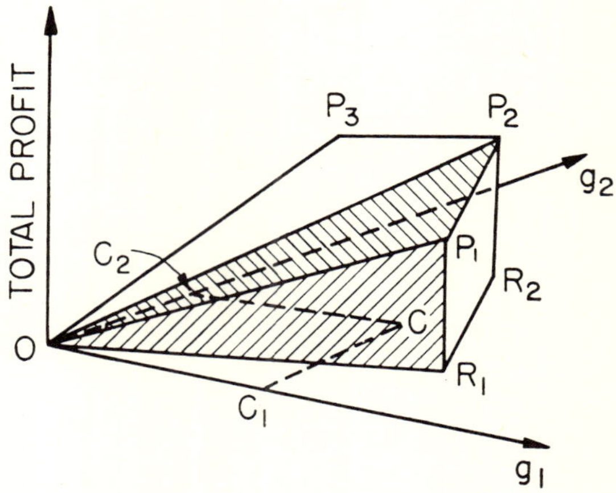

FIGURE 4

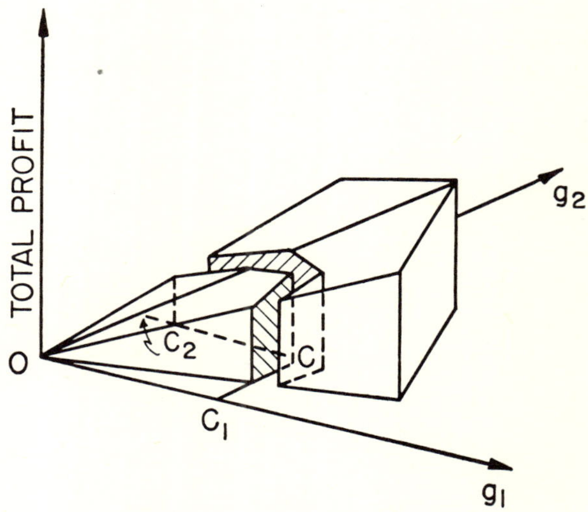

FIGURE 5

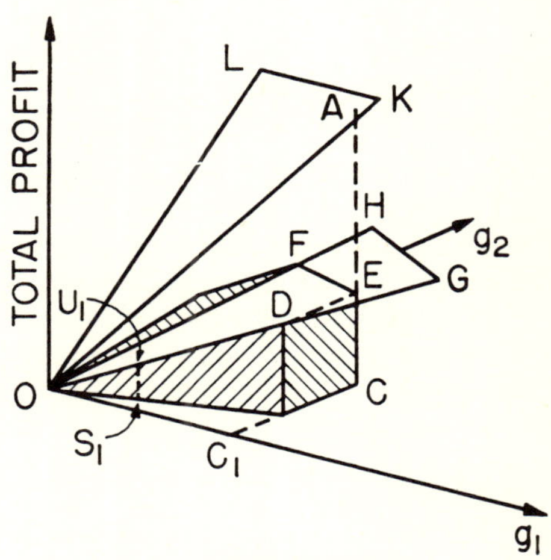

FIGURE 6

That same figure shows the available combinations of the inputs (the feasible region OC_1CC_2). The corresponding feasible portion of the profit surface may then be obtained by cutting away all of the profit function which lies outside the feasible region, as is shown in Figure 5, leaving the remaining relevant portion of the profit surface shown by the shaded form in our last graph for the linear case, Figure 6.

In that same diagram, we also represent the dual programme. Its objective function is shown with the aid of a plane, OKL, whose equation is $\alpha = v_1 g_1 + v_2 g_2$. In particular, for $g_1 = c_1$ and $g_2 = c_2$, this becomes $\alpha = v_1 c_1 + v_2 c_2$, the objective function of the dual problem. Geometrically, this value of α is represented by length CA from the capacity point C to the point A, which lies directly above it on the OKL plane.

Now, the objective of the dual problem is to minimize this value of α, i.e., to minimize length CA, subject to the constraints of the dual problem. We can now examine briefly the geometric representation of the first dual constraint,

$$a_{11}v_1 + a_{21}v_2 \geqq p_1.$$

p_1, the unit profit of product 1, is given by the length of the line S_1U_1, the height of the profit surface above the unit production point S_1 for output 1. Moreover, since (Figure 2) the coordinates of point S_1 are a_{11} and a_{21} (the quantities of the two inputs needed to produce a unit of output 1), the value of $a_{11}v_1 + a_{21}v_2$ is the height of the α plane above point S_1. In other words, geometrically, the first constraint states that the α plane must not pass below point U_1, the point on the profit surface directly above S_1, the unit production point for output 1.

Similarly, the second constraint tells us that the α plane must not pass below U_2 (not shown in the diagram), the corresponding unit profit point for output 2, etc.

We see then the geometric interpretation of the standard duality theorem $\alpha \geqq \pi$. For the primal constraints require that the plane be no lower than the profit surface. Moreover, the optimal (minimal) value is found just when the α plane is swung downward until it reaches position OGH where it coincides with a face, $ODEF$, of the profit surface. Thus, in such an optimal solution, $\alpha = \pi (= CE)$, as duality theory requires.

6. GEOMETRY OF THE NONLINEAR PRIMAL

The geometry of the nonlinear programming problem in many ways resembles that of the linear programming case, except that lines and hyperplanes are now replaced by curves and hypersurfaces with curvature. Consider, for example, the following illustrative case for which we provide both the dual and the solutions to both primal and dual.

Primal:

Maximize profit

$$\pi(x) = (268-10x_1)x_1 + (300-8x_2)x_2 + (248-6x_3)x_3$$

subject to

$$(x_1+x_2)^2 + 40x_3 \leqq 1284$$
$$6x_1 + (2x_2 - x_3)^2 \leqq 76$$
$$x_1, x_2, x_3 \geqq 0.$$

Dual:

$$\text{Min } \alpha(x, u, v) = \pi(x) + v_1(1284 - (x_1+x_2)^2 - 40x_3) + v_2(76 - 6x_1 - (2x_2 - x_3)^2) + l_1x_1 + l_2x_2 + l_3x_3$$

subject to

$$v_1(2(x_1+x_2)) + v_2(6) - l_1 = 268—20x_1$$
$$v_1(2(x_1+x_2)) + v_2(4(2x_2 - x_3)) - l_2 = 300 - 16x_2$$
$$v_1(40) + v_2(-2(2x_2 - x_3)) - l_3 = 248 - 12x_3.$$

Here, the $l_j = \partial f/\partial x_j - \Sigma_i v_i \partial g_i/\partial x_j$. are the dual slack variables. The unique optimal solution is $x_1 = 10$, $x_2 = 12$, $x_3 = 20$, and $v_1 = 1$, $v_2 = 4$, ($l_1 = l_2 = l_3 = 0$, i.e., the inequalities of the dual are satisfied as equations). Let us consider OR_1, the analogue to the linear process ray describing the input requirements of output x_1 when $x_2 = x_3 = 0$. The required quantities of the two inputs g_1 and g_2 are given by setting $x_2 = x_3 = 0$ in the two primal constraints, to yield

$$\begin{aligned} g_1 &= x_1^2 \leqq 1284 \\ g_2 &= 6x_1 \leqq 76 \end{aligned} \qquad \ldots(15)$$

and the corresponding profit relationship is

$$\pi(x_1, 0, 0) = (268 - 10x_1)x_1.$$

These are depicted in Figure 7, which corresponds to a portion of Figure 3 in the linear case.

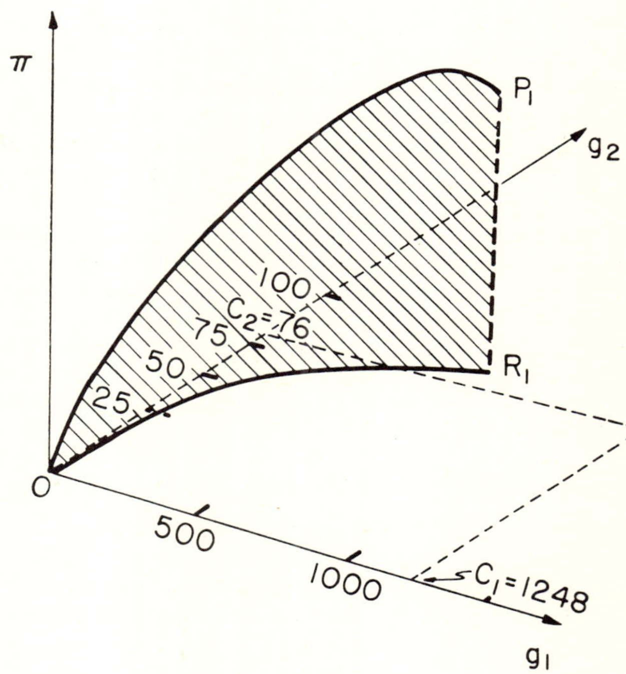

FIGURE 7

Here, as before, the feasible region is given by OC_1CC_2 where $OC_1 = c_1 = 1284$ and $OC_2 = c_2 = 76$. The equation of the input requirement curve OR_1 for output 1 is seen from equations (15) to be given by

$$g_2 = F(g_1) = 6\sqrt{g_1}.$$

Finally, the corresponding profit curve OP_1 is obtained from the profit function

$$\pi(x_1, 0, 0) = (268 - 10x_1)x_1$$

by substitution of the second constraint condition $g_2 = 6x_1$, to yield

$$\pi(x_1, 0, 0) = [268 - (10/6)g_2]g_2/6.$$

We see then (Figure 7) that the profit surface for the nonlinear primal will have an appearance not dissimilar to that in Figure 5, except that the surface will now be curved. Indeed, though this does not occur in the present case, the point of maximum profit can now lie inside the feasible region.

7. GEOMETRY OF THE NONLINEAR DUAL

The geometry of the nonlinear dual, however, is not so obvious an extension of the linear case. As a matter of fact, because its depiction is rather complicated, we will show its graph for an even more elementary illustration than that which has just been provided; a trivial one variable, one constraint case. For simplicity of exposition (though it does not affect the argument), we assume also that the primal constraint is the linear relationship $kx \leqq c$ so that the input use is proportionate to the output ($g = kx$) and, as a result, we can employ either g or x as the variable represented on the horizontal axis without changing the shape of our curves. We may then normalize without loss of generality by choosing our output unit so that $k = 1$, i.e., so that $g = x$. In Figure 8, we now show our profit function $\pi = f(x)$ (heavy line).

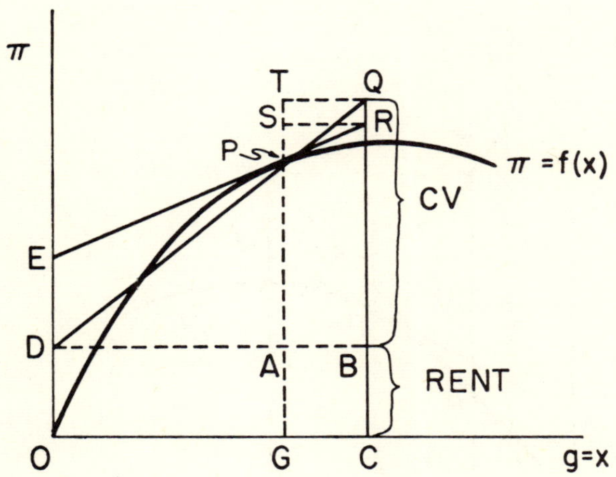

FIGURE 8

Let us now consider the value of the dual $\alpha(x, v)$ for a given value of x but with varying values of v. At any given x, call it x_1, the quantity of resources used is $g_1 = g(x_1)$ (which, in our simplified case, is equal to x_1 itself). This amount is represented on the horizontal axis by point G. Let P be the corresponding point on the profit surface. We have, by (2), since $\partial g/\partial x = 1$,

$$\alpha = \pi + (c-g)v + x(v - \partial f/\partial x).$$

Obviously, π is represented by line segment GP. Consider next cv and gv. Through point P draw a line segment DQ whose slope is v. Our dual constraint, $v \geqq \partial f/\partial x$, tells us that the slope of DQ through point P must be no less than the slope of $\pi = f(x)$ at P. Now since $g(x_1) = OG = DA$ and $v = AP/DA$, the value of the resources used

$$= g_1.v = DA(AP/DA) = AP.$$

Similarly, $c.v = BQ = AT$. Hence, $\pi + cv - gv$ is represented by $GP + AT - AP = GT$. We conclude $\alpha(x_1) = GT + x_1(v - \partial f/\partial x)$. Now, the objective of the dual is to select a value of v that minimizes α. But note that if we select a smaller value of v (a smaller slope for DQ), *both* terms on the right hand side of the preceding expression fall. Indeed, α clearly reaches its minimum when v attains the minimum value permitted by the dual constraint: when $v = \partial f/\partial x$, i.e., when the tangent ER is substituted for DQ. For, at that point, the term $x(v - \partial f/\partial x)$ drops out altogether, and PT, the excess of $c.v$ over $g.v$, is reduced to its lowest possible value, PS. Thus in our case, at any level of x, the α minimizing value of v is given by the slope of the profit function at that point.

Before going on to determine the effect of variation in the value of x, we may pause to note that at $g = x_1$ the magnitude GA is a measure of economic rent, for it is the difference between total profit, GP, and the marginal value of the input $AP = g.v$.

Figure 9 now shows how α varies with g. Point G is reproduced from Figure 8, and, as before, at that value of g we have $\alpha = GS$. At any other level of g, say OG', we obtain the corresponding value of α by drawing the tangent $E'R'$ to the profit function at that output level, since for that x the slope of this tangent is the α minimizing value of v. Then $G'S'$ will equal $\alpha = \pi + cv - gv$ for that output level. The locus of all points such as S and S', is then the representation of the dual, α, as a function of x or of input level g. Note that the lowest attainable value of α (i.e., the lowest α with $g \leqq c$) occurs at point $g = c$ where the available input is used up completely, and here we have $\alpha = \pi$, as required.

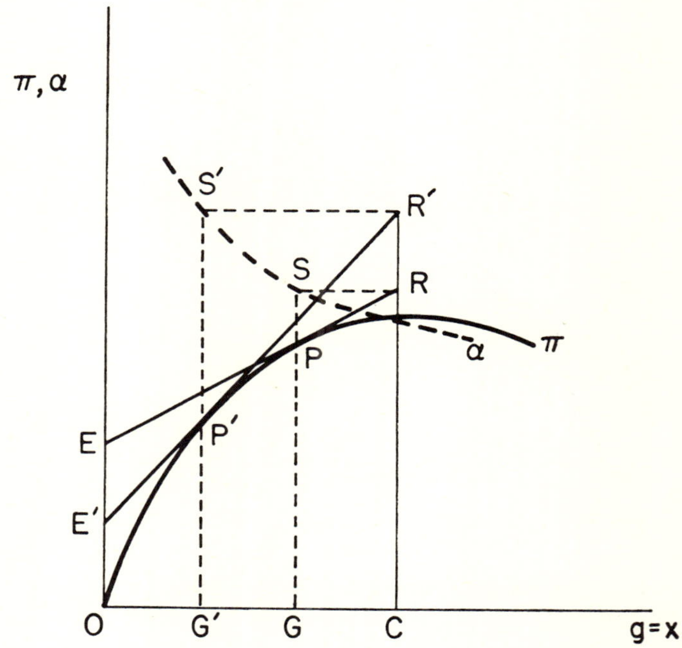

FIGURE 9

This diagrammatic construction can offer insight into two other matters: first, why the simpler objective function $\beta = cv$ works in the linear programming case, and, second, why the entire duality analysis breaks down in the event that the convexity conditions are not satisfied.

First, consider the linear programming case in Figure 10. $\beta(g) = vg$ is represented by a ray through the origin whose slope is v. We note that the linear profit function, π_{lin}, is also a ray through the origin. Thus, if v is reduced sufficiently so that the two rays coincide, we have $\beta(g) \geqq \pi$ throughout, and at the capacity figure $\beta(c) = cv = \pi$ as required. However, suppose the profit function had instead been characterized by diminishing returns to scale—instead of a straight line it were represented by π_d in Figure 10. Then we see that the requirement $\beta \geqq \pi$ for all $g(x)$ means that the tangent ray $0\beta_{\min}$ is the lowest admissible ray. But with this ray we must have $cv > \pi$ at $g = c$. That is, even though it is optimal to utilize the firm's resource fully, the value of this amount of resource, cv, exceeds the profits of the firm. We do not have β equals π and so we must substitute for β the more complex expression α in order to avoid over-accounting for the total profit—to satisfy the optimality requirement $\alpha = \pi$.

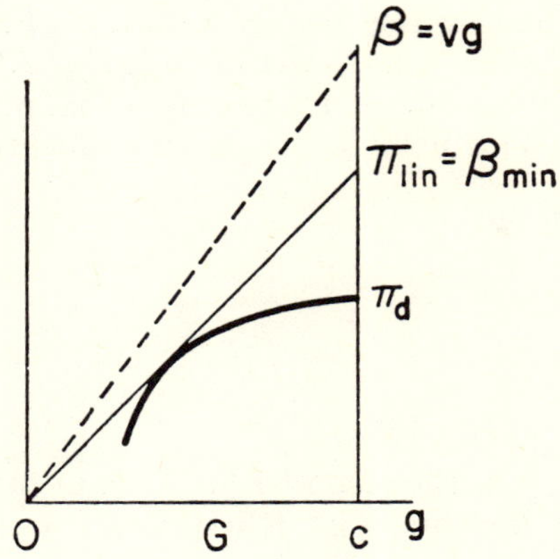

FIGURE 10

Finally, let us see some of the peculiarities which occur when the convexity conditions of duality theory are not satisfied. In our example this is the case of increasing returns to scale[1] so that the profit function would have the shape of $O\pi'$ in Fig ure 11—if differentiable

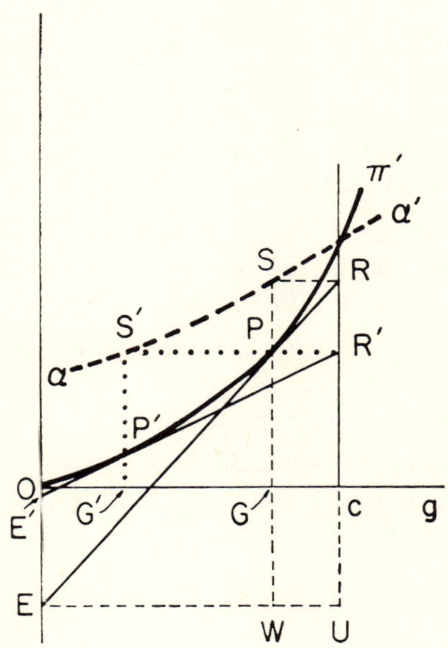

FIGURE 11

it would have a positive second derivative. Let us proceed, as before, to determine the shape of α as a function of g or x. At any $x = g$ we again let v be given by the slope of ER, which is tangent to the profit curve at P directly above G. Hence, since $\pi = GP$, $gv = WP$ and $cv = UR = WS$, we must have $\alpha = \pi + cv - gv = GS$. Thus S is the point on the α curve corresponding to $x = g$. Similarly, S' is the point on that curve corresponding to $x' = g'$, etc. Hence the α locus is the broken line $\alpha\alpha'$ shown in Figure 11. Now the reader can observe two peculiarities of this case:

[1] The convexity conditions would also be violated if the feasible region were nonconvex.

1. In the increasing returns case rent is *negative*. For example, at $x = OG$, the rent, $\pi(g) - gv$, is $GP - WP$ which is the negative quantity GW.

2. Though x is the point of maximum profits, at that point α also is at its *maximum* (for $g \leqq c$) rather than at its minimum as the ordinary duality theory requires.

City University of New York M. L. BALINSKI
Princeton University W. J. BAUMOL

REFERENCES

[1] Cottle, Richard W. " A Theorem of Fritz John in Mathematical Programming ", RAND Corporation, Memorandum, RM-3858-PR (October 1963).

[2] Cottle, R. W. Private communication (August 1966).

[3] Cottle, R. W. " Symmetric Dual Quadratic Programs ", *Quarterly of Applied Mathematics*, **21** (1963), 237-243.

[4] Fenchel, W. *Convex Cones, Sets, and Functions*, Lecture Notes (Princeton University, 1953).

[5] Huard, Pierre. " Dual Programs ", in *Recent Advances in Mathematical Programming* (McGraw-Hill Book Company, Inc., New York, 1963), pp. 55-62.

[6] John, F. " Extremum Problems with Inequalities as Subsidiary Conditions ", in *Studies and Essays*, Courant Anniversary Volume (Interscience, New York, 1948).

[7] Kuhn, H. W., and Tucker, A. W. " Nonlinear Programming ", in *Proceedings of the Second Berkeley Symposium on Mathematical Statistics and Probability* (University of California Press, Berkeley, 1951), pp. 481-492.

[8] Mills, Harlan D. " Marginal Values of Matrix Games and Linear Programs ", in H. W. Kuhn and A. W. Tucker, eds., *Linear Inequalities and Related Systems* (Princeton University Press, Princeton, 1956), pp. 183-193.

[9] Rockafellar, R. T. *Convex Analysis*, Lecture Notes (Princeton University, Spring, 1966).

[10] Rockafellar, R. T. " Extension of Fenchel's Duality Theorem for Convex Functions ", *Duke Mathematical Journal*, **33** (1966), 81-90.

[11] Samuelson, P. A. *Foundations of Economic Analysis* (Harvard University Press, Cambridge, Mass., 1948).

[12] Stigler, George J. *Production and Distribution Theories* (Macmillan, New York, 1946).

[13] Uzawa, Hirofumi. " A Note on the Menger-Wieser Theory of Imputation ", *Zeitschrift für Nationalökonomie*, **18** (August 1958).

[14] Williams, A. C. " Marginal Values in Linear Programming ", *Journal of the Society for Industrial and Applied Mathematics*, **11** (1963), 82-94.

[15] Wolfe, Philip. " A Duality Theorem for Nonlinear Programming ", *Quarterly of Applied Mathematics*, **19** (1961), 239-244.

PART FOUR

MONEY
AND FINANCE

[24]

THE TRANSACTIONS DEMAND FOR CASH: AN INVENTORY THEORETIC APPROACH

By William J. Baumol

A stock of cash is its holder's inventory of the medium of exchange, and like an inventory of a commodity, cash is held because it can be given up at the appropriate moment, serving then as its possessor's part of the bargain in an exchange. We might consequently expect that inventory theory and monetary theory can learn from one another. This note attempts to apply one well-known result in inventory control analysis to the theory of money.[1]

I. A Simple Model

We are now interested in analyzing the transactions demand for cash dictated by rational behavior, which for our purposes means the holding of those cash balances that can do the job at minimum cost. To abstract from precautionary and speculative demands let us consider a state in which transactions are perfectly foreseen and occur *in a steady stream.*

Suppose that in the course of a given period an individual will pay out T dollars in a steady stream. He obtains cash either by borrowing it, or by withdrawing it from an investment, and in either case his interest cost (or interest opportunity cost) is i dollars per dollar per period. Suppose finally that he withdraws cash in lots of C dollars spaced evenly throughout the year, and that each time he makes such a withdrawal he must pay a fixed "broker's fee" of b

1. T. M. Whitin informs me that the result in question goes back to the middle of the 1920's when it seems to have been arrived at independently by some half dozen writers. See, e.g., George F. Mellen, "Practical Lot Quantity Formula," *Management and Administration*, Vol. 10, September 1925. Its significant implications for the economic theory of inventory, particularly for business cycle theory, seem to have gone unrecognized until recently when Dr. Whitin analyzed them in his forthcoming *Inventory Control and Economic Theory* (Princeton University Press) which, incidentally, first suggested the subject of this note to me. See also, Dr. Whitin's "Inventory Control in Theory and Practice" (elsewhere in this issue, *supra*, p. 502), and Kenneth J. Arrow, Theodore Harris, and Jacob Marschak, "Optimal Inventory Policy," *Econometrica*, Vol. 19, July 1951, especially pp. 252–255. In addition to Dr. Whitin, I am heavily indebted to Professors Chandler, Coale, Gurley, Lutz, Mr. Turvey, and Professor Viner, and to the members of the graduate seminar at Harvard University, where much of this paper was first presented.

dollars.[2] Here T, the value of transactions, is predetermined, and i and b are assumed to be constant.

In this situation any value of C less than or equal to T will enable him to meet his payments equally well provided he withdraws the money often enough. For example, if T is \$100, he can meet his payments by withdrawing \$50 every six months or \$25 quarterly, etc.[3] Thus he will make $\frac{T}{C}$ withdrawals over the course of the year, at a total cost in "brokers' fees" given by $\frac{bT}{C}$.

In this case, since each time he withdraws C dollars he spends it in a steady stream and draws out a similar amount the moment it is gone, his average cash holding will be $\frac{C}{2}$ dollars. His annual interest cost of holding cash will then be $\frac{iC}{2}$.

The total amount the individual in question must pay for the use of the cash needed to meet his transaction when he borrows C dollars at intervals evenly spaced throughout the year will then be the sum of interest cost and "brokers' fees" and so will be given by

$$\frac{bT}{C} + \frac{iC}{2}. \tag{1}$$

2. The term "broker's fee" is not meant to be taken literally. It covers all non-interest costs of borrowing or making a cash withdrawal. These include opportunity losses which result from having to dispose of assets just at the moment the cash is needed, losses involved in the poor resale price which results from an asset becoming "secondhand" when purchased by a nonprofessional dealer, administrative costs, and psychic costs (the trouble involved in making a withdrawal) as well as payment to a middleman. So conceived it seems likely that the "broker's fee" will, in fact, vary considerably with the magnitude of the funds involved, contrary to assumption. However, *some* parts of this cost will not vary with the amount involved — e.g., postage cost, bookkeeping expense, and, possibly, the withdrawer's effort. It seems plausible that the "broker's fee" will be better approximated by a function like $b + kC$ (where b and k are constants), which indicates that there is a part of the "broker's fee" increasing in proportion with the amount withdrawn. As shown in a subsequent footnote, however, our formal result is completely unaffected by this amendment.

We must also extend the meaning of the interest rate to include the value of protection against loss by fire, theft, etc., which we obtain when someone borrows our cash. On the other hand, a premium for the risk of default on repayment must be deducted. This protection obtained by lending seems to be mentioned less frequently by theorists than the risk, yet how can we explain the existence of interest free demand deposits without the former?

3. In particular, if cash were perfectly divisible and no elapse of time were required from withdrawal through payment he could make his withdrawals in a steady stream. In this case he would never require any cash balances to meet his payments and C would be zero. However, as may be surmised, this would be prohibitive with any b greater than zero.

Since the manner in which he meets his payments is indifferent to him, his purpose only being to pay for his transactions, rationality requires that he do so at minimum cost, i.e., that he choose the most economical value of C. Setting the derivative of (1) with respect to C equal to zero we obtain[4]

$$-\frac{bT}{C^2}+\frac{i}{2}=0,$$

i.e.,

$$C=\sqrt{\frac{2bT}{i}}. \tag{2}$$

Thus, in the simple situation here considered, the rational individual will, given the price level,[5] demand cash in proportion to the square root of the value of his transactions.

Before examining the implications of this crude model we may note that, as it stands, it applies to two sorts of cases: that of the individual (or firm) obtaining cash from his invested capital and that of the individual (or firm) spending out of borrowing in anticipation of future receipts. Since our problem depends on non-coincidence of cash receipts and disbursements, and we have assumed that cash disbursements occur in a steady stream, one other case seems possible, that where receipts precede expenditures. This differs from the first case just mentioned (living off one's capital) in that the individual now has the option of withholding some or all of his receipts from investment and simply keeping the cash until it is needed. Once this withheld cash is used up the third case merges into the first: the individual must obtain cash from his invested capital until his next cash receipt occurs.

We can deal with this third case as follows. First, note that any receipts exceeding anticipated disbursements will be invested, since, eventually, interest earnings must exceed ("brokerage") cost of investment. Hence we need only deal with that part of the cash influx which is to be used in making payments during the period

4. This result is unchanged if there is a part of the "broker's fee" which varies in proportion with the quantity of cash handled. For in this case the "broker's fee" for each loan is given by $b + kC$. Total cost in "broker's fees" will then be

$$\frac{T}{C}\,(b+kC)=\frac{T}{C}b+kT.$$

Thus (1) will have the constant term, kT, added to it, which drops out in differentiation.

5. A doubling of *all* prices (including the "broker's fee") is like a change in the monetary unit, and may be expected to double the demand for cash balances.

between receipts. Let this amount, as before, be T dollars. Of this let I dollars be invested, and the remainder, R dollars, be withheld, where either of these sums may be zero. Again let i be the interest rate, and let the "broker's fee" for withdrawing cash be given by the linear expression $b_w + k_w C$, where C is the amount withdrawn. Finally, let there be a "broker's fee" for investing (depositing) cash given by $b_d + k_d I$ where the b's and the k's are constants.

Since the disbursements are continuous, the $R = T - I$ dollars withheld from investment will serve to meet payments for a fraction of the period between consecutive receipts given by $\frac{T-I}{T}$. Moreover, since the average cash holding for that time will be $\frac{T-I}{2}$, the interest cost of withholding that money will be $\frac{T-I}{T} i \frac{T-I}{2}$. Thus the total cost of withholding the R dollars and investing the I dollars will be

$$\frac{T-I}{2} i \frac{T-I}{T} + b_d + k_d I.$$

Analogously, the total cost of obtaining cash for the remainder of the period will be

$$\frac{C}{2} i \frac{I}{T} + (b_w + k_w C) \frac{I}{C}.$$

Thus the total cost of cash operations for the period will be given by the sum of the last two expressions, which when differentiated partially with respect to C and set equal to zero once again yields our square root formula, (2), with $b = b_w$.

Thus, in this case, the optimum cash balance after the initial cash holding is used up will again vary with the square root of the volume of transactions, as is to be expected by analogy with the "living off one's capital" case.

There remains the task of investigating $R/2$, the (optimum) average cash balance before drawing on invested receipts begins. We again differentiate our total cost of holding cash, this time partially with respect to I, and set it equal to zero, obtaining

$$-\frac{T-I}{T} i + k_d + \frac{Ci}{2T} + \frac{b_w}{C} + k_w = 0,$$

i.e.,

$$R = T - I = \frac{C}{2} + \frac{b_w T}{Ci} + \frac{T(k_d + k_w)}{i},$$

or since from the preceding result, $C^2 = 2Tb_w/i$, so that the second term on the right hand side equals $C^2/2C$,

$$R = C + T\left(\frac{k_w + k_d}{i}\right).$$

The first term in this result is to be expected, since if *everything* were deposited at once, C dollars would have to be withdrawn at that same moment to meet current expenses. On this amount two sets of "broker's fees" would have to be paid and no interest would be earned — a most unprofitable operation.[6]

Since C varies as the square root of T and the other term varies in proportion with T, R will increase less than in proportion with T, though more nearly in proportion than does C. The general nature of our results is thus unaffected.[7]

Note finally that the entire analysis applies at once to the case of continuous receipts and discontinuous payments, taking the period to be that between two payments, where the relevant decision is the frequency of investment rather than the frequency of withdrawal. Similarly, it applies to continuous receipts and payments where the two are not equal.

II. Some Consequences of the Analysis

I shall not labor the obvious implications for financial budgeting by the firm. Rather I shall discuss several arguments which have been presented by monetary theorists, to which our result is relevant.

The first is the view put forth by several economists,[8] that in a

6. Here the assumption of constant "brokerage fees" with $k_d = k_w = 0$ gets us into trouble. The amount withheld from investment then is never greater than C dollars only because a strictly constant "broker's fee" with no provision for a discontinuity at zero implies the payment of the fee even if nothing is withdrawn or deposited. In this case it becomes an overhead and it pays to invest for any interest earning greater than zero.

For a firm, *part* of the "broker's fee" may, in fact, be an overhead in this way. For example, failure to make an anticipated deposit will sometimes involve little or no reduction in the bookkeeping costs incurred in keeping track of such operations.

7. If we replace the linear functions representing the "broker's fees" with more general functions $f_w(C)$ and $f_d(I)$ which are only required to be differentiable, the expression obtained for R is changed merely by replacement of k_w, and k_d by the corresponding derivatives $f_w'(C)$ and $f_d'(I)$.

8. See, e.g., Frank H. Knight, *Risk, Uncertainty and Profit* (Preface to the Re-issue), No. 16 in the series of Reprints of Scarce Tracts in Economic and Political Science (London: The London School of Economics and Political Science, 1933), p. xxii; F. Divisia, *Économique Rationelle* (Paris: G. Doin, 1927), chap. XIX and the Appendix; and Don Patinkin, "Relative Prices, Say's Law and the Demand for Money," *Econometrica*, Vol. 16, April 1948, pp. 140–145. See also, P. N. Rosenstein-Rodan, "The Coordination of the General Theories of Money and Price," *Economica*, N. S., Vol. III, August 1936, Part II.

stationary state there will be no demand for cash balances since it will then be profitable to invest all earnings in assets with a positive yield in such a way that the required amount will be realized at the moment any payment is to be made. According to this view no one will want any cash in such a stationary world, and the value of money must fall to zero so that there can really be no such thing as a truly static monetary economy. Clearly this argument neglects the transactions costs involved in making and collecting such loans (the "broker's fee").[9] Our model is clearly compatible with a static world and (2) shows that it will generally pay to keep some cash. The analysis of a stationary monetary economy in which there is a meaningful (finite) price level does make sense.

Another view which can be reëxamined in light of our analysis is that the transactions demand for cash will vary approximately in proportion with the money value of transactions.[1] This may perhaps even be considered the tenor of quantity theory though there is no necessary connection, as Fisher's position indicates. If such a demand for cash balances is considered to result from rational behavior, then (2) suggests that the conclusion cannot have general validity. On the contrary, the square root formula implies that

9. It also neglects the fact that the transfer of cash takes time so that in reality we would have to hold cash at least for the short period between receiving it and passing it on again.

It is conceivable, it is true, that with perfect foresight the difference between money and securities might disappear since a perfectly safe loan could become universally acceptable. There would, however, remain the distinction between "real assets" and the "money-securities." Moreover, there would be a finite price for, and non-zero yield on the former, the yield arising because they (as opposed to certificates of their ownership) are not generally acceptable, and hence not perfectly liquid, since there is trouble and expense involved in carrying them.

1. Marshall's rather vague statements may perhaps be interpreted to support this view. See, e.g., Book I, chap. IV in *Money, Credit and Commerce* (London, 1923). Keynes clearly accepts this position. See *The General Theory of Employment, Interest and Money* (New York, 1936), p. 201. It is also accepted by Pigou: "As real income becomes larger, there is, prima facie, reason for thinking that, just as, up to a point, people like to invest a larger proportion of their real income, so also they like to hold real balances in the form of money equivalent to a larger proportion of it. On the other hand, as Professor Robertson has pointed out to me, the richer people are, the cleverer they are likely to become in finding a way to *economize* in real balances. On the whole then we may, I think, safely disregard this consideration . . . for a close approximation. . . . ." *Employment and Equilibrium*, 1st ed. (London, 1941), pp. 59–60. Fisher, however, argues: "It seems to be a fact that, at a given price level, the greater a man's expenditures the more rapid his turnover; that is, the rich have a higher rate of turnover than the poor. They spend money faster, not only absolutely but relatively to the money they keep on hand. . . . We may therefore infer that, if a nation grows richer per capita, the velocity of circulation of money will increase. This proposition, of course, has no reference to *nominal* increase of expenditure." *The Purchasing Power of Money* (New York, 1922), p. 167.

demand for cash rises less than in proportion with the volume of transactions, so that there are, in effect, economies of large scale in the use of cash.

The magnitude of this difference should not be exaggerated, however. The phrase "varying as the square" may suggest larger effects than are actually involved. Equation (2) requires that the average transactions velocity of circulation vary exactly in proportion with the quantity of cash, so that, for example, a doubling of the stock of cash will *ceteris paribus*, just double velocity.[2]

A third consequence of the square root formula is closely connected with the second. The effect on real income of an injection of cash into the system may have been underestimated. For suppose that (2) is a valid expression for the general demand for cash, that there is widespread unemployment, and that for this or other reasons prices do not rise with an injection of cash. Suppose, moreover, that the rate of interest is unaffected, i.e., that none of the new cash is used to buy securities. Then so long as transactions do not rise so as to maintain the same proportion with the square of the quantity of money, people will want to get rid of cash. They will use it to demand more goods and services, thereby forcing the volume of transactions to rise still further. For let ΔC be the quantity of cash injected. If a proportionality (constant velocity) assumption involves transactions rising by $k \Delta C$, it is easily shown that (2) involves transactions rising by more than twice as much, the magnitude of the excess increasing with the ratio of the injection to the initial stock of cash. More precisely, the rise in transactions would then be given by[3]

$$2 k \Delta C + \frac{k}{C} \Delta C^2.$$

Of course, the rate of interest would really tend to fall in such circumstances, and this would to some extent offset the effect of the influx of cash, as is readily seen when we rewrite (2) as

$$T = C^2 i/2b. \tag{3}$$

Moreover, prices will rise to some extent,[4] and, of course, (3) at best

2. Since velocity equals $\frac{T}{C} = \frac{i}{2b} C$ by (2).

3. This is obtained by setting $k = C i/2b$ in (3), below, and computing ΔT by substituting $C + \Delta C$ for C.

4. Even if (2) holds, the demand for cash may rise only in proportion with the money value of transactions when all prices rise exactly in proportion, the rate of interest and transactions remaining unchanged. For then a doubling of all prices and cash balances leaves the situation unchanged, and the received argument holds. The point is that b is then one of the prices which has risen.

is only an approximation. Nevertheless, it remains true that the effect of an injection of cash on, say, the level of employment, may often have been underestimated.[5] For whatever may be working to counteract it, the force making for increased employment is greater than if transactions tend, *ceteris paribus*, toward their original proportion to the quantity of cash.

Finally the square root formula lends support to the argument that wage cuts can help increase employment, since it follows that the Pigou effect and the related effects are stronger than they would be with a constant transactions velocity. Briefly the phenomenon which has come to be called the Pigou effect[6] may be summarized thus: General unemployment will result in reduction in the price level which must increase the purchasing power of the stock of cash provided the latter does not itself fall more than in proportion with prices.[7] This increased purchasing power will augment demand for commodities[8] or investment goods (either directly, or because it is used to buy securities and so forces down the rate of interest). In any case, this works for a reduction in unemployment.

Now the increase in the purchasing power of the stock of cash which results from fallen prices is equivalent to an injection of cash with constant prices. There is therefore exactly the same reason for suspecting the magnitude of the effect of the former on the volume of transactions has been underestimated, as in the case of the latter. Perhaps this can be of some little help in explaining why there has not been more chronic unemployment or runaway inflation in our economy.

III. The Simple Model and Reality

It is appropriate to comment on the validity of the jump from equation (2) to conclusions about the operation of the economy. At

5. But see the discussions of Potter and Law as summarized by Jacob Viner, *Studies in the Theory of International Trade* (New York, 1937), pp. 37–39.

6. See A. C. Pigou, "The Classical Stationary State," *Economic Journal*, Vol. LIII, December 1943.

7. Presumably the "broker's fee" will be one of the prices which falls, driven down by the existence of unemployed brokers. There is no analogous reason for the rate of interest to fall, though it will tend to respond thus to the increase in the "real stock of cash."

8. The term "Pigou effect" is usually confined to the effects on consumption demand while the effect on investment demand, and (in particular) on the rate of interest is ordinarily ascribed to Keynes. However, the entire argument appears to antedate Pigou's discussion (which, after all, was meant to be a reformulation of the classical position) and is closely related to what Mr. Becker and I have called the Say's Equation form of the Say's Law argument. See our article "The Classical Monetary Theory; the Outcome of the Discussion," *Economica*, November 1952.

best, (2) is only a suggestive oversimplification, if for no other reason, because of the rationality assumption employed in its derivation. In addition the model is static. It takes the distribution of the firm's disbursements over time to be fixed, though it is to a large extent in the hands of the entrepreneur how he will time his expenditures. It assumes that there is one constant relevant rate of interest and that the "broker's fee" is constant or varies linearly with the magnitude of the sum involved. It posits a steady stream of payments and the absence of cash receipts during the relevant period. It deals only with the cash demand of a single economic unit and neglects interactions of the various demands for cash in the economy.[9] It neglects the precautionary and speculative demands for cash.

These are serious lacunae, and without a thorough investigation we have no assurance that our results amount to much more than an analytical curiosum. Nevertheless I offer only a few comments in lieu of analysis, and hope that others will find the subject worth further examination.

1. It is no doubt true that a majority of the public will find it impractical and perhaps pointless to effect every possible economy in the use of cash. Indeed the possibility may never occur to most people. Nevertheless, we may employ the standard argument that the largest cash users may more plausibly be expected to learn when it is profitable to reduce cash balances relative to transactions. The demand for cash by the community as a whole may then be affected similarly and by a significant amount. Moreover, it is possible that even small cash holders will sometimes institute some cash economies instinctively or by a process of trial and error not explicitly planned or analyzed.

2. With variable b and i the validity of our two basic results — the non-zero rational transactions demand for cash, and the less than proportionate rise in the rational demand for cash with the real volume of transactions, clearly depends on the nature of the responsiveness of the "brokerage fee" and the interest rate to the quantity of cash involved. The first conclusion will hold generally provided the "broker's fee" never falls below some preassigned level, e.g., it never falls below one mill per transaction, and provided the interest rate, its rate of change with C and the rate of change of the "broker's fee" all (similarly) have some upper bound, however large, at least when C is small.

9. I refer here particularly to considerations analogous to those emphasized by Duesenberry in his discussion of the relation between the consumption functions of the individual and the economy as a whole in his *Income, Saving and the Theory of Consumer Behavior* (Cambridge, Mass., 1950).

The second conclusion will not be violated persistently unless the "brokerage fee" tends to vary almost exactly in proportion with C (and it pays to hold zero cash balances) except for what may roughly be described as a limited range of values of C. Of course, it is always possible that this "exceptional range" will be the one relevant in practice. Variations in the interest rate will tend to strengthen our conclusion provided the interest rate never decreases with the quantity of cash borrowed or invested.[1]

It would perhaps not be surprising if these sufficient conditions for the more general validity of our results were usually satisfied in practice.

3. If payments are lumpy but foreseen, cash may perhaps be employed even more economically. For then it may well pay to obtain cash just before large payments fall due with little or no added cost in "brokers' fees" and considerable savings in interest payments. The extreme case would be that of a single payment during the year

1. For people to want to hold a positive amount of cash, the cost of cash holding must be decreasing after $C = 0$. Let b in (1) be a differentiable function of C for $C > 0$ (it will generally be discontinuous and equal to zero at $C = 0$). Then we require that the limit of the derivative of (1) be negative as C approaches zero from above, where this derivative is given by

$$\text{(i)}\ -b\frac{T}{C^2} + \frac{T}{C}b' + \frac{i + i'C}{2}.$$

Clearly this will become negative as C approaches zero provided b is bounded from below and b', i, and i' are all bounded from above.

The second conclusion, the less than proportionate rise in minimum cost cash holdings with the volume of transactions, can be shown, with only b not constant, to hold if and only if $b - b'C + b''C^2$ is positive. This result is obtained by solving the first order minimum condition (obtained by setting (i), with the i' term omitted, equal to zero) for $\frac{T}{C}$ and noting that our conclusion is equivalent to the derivative of this ratio with respect to C being positive.

Now successive differentiation of (i) with the i' term omitted yields as our second order minimum condition $2(b - b'C) + b''C^2 > 0$ (note the resemblance to the preceding condition). Thus if our result is to be violated we must have

$$\text{(ii)}\ b - Cb' \leqq -b''C^2 < 2(b - Cb'),$$

which at once yields $b'' \leq 0$. Thus if b' is not to become negative (a decreasing *total* payment as the size of the withdrawal increases!) b'' must usually lie within a small neighborhood of zero, i.e., b must be approximately linear. However we know that in this case the square root formula will be (approximately) valid except in the case $b = kC$ when it will always (by (i)) pay to hold zero cash balances. Note incidentally that (ii) also yields $b - Cb' \geq 0$ which means that our result must hold if ever the "brokerage fee" increases more than in proportion with C.

Note, finally, that if i varies with C the first order condition becomes a cubic and, provided $\infty > i' > 0$, our conclusion is strengthened, since T now tends to increase as C^3.

which would call for a zero cash balance provided the cash could be loaned out profitably at all. Cash receipts during the relevant period may have similar effects, since they can be used to make payments which happen to be due at the moment the receipts arrive. Here the extreme case involves receipts and payments always coinciding in time and amounts in which case, again, zero cash balances would be called for. Thus lumpy payments and receipts of cash, with sufficient foresight, can make for economies in the use of cash, i.e., higher velocity. This may not affect the rate of increase in transactions velocity with the level of transactions, but may nevertheless serve further to increase the effect of an injection of cash and of a cut in wages and prices. With imperfect foresight, however, the expectation that payments may be lumpy may increase the precautionary demand for cash. Moreover, the existence of a "broker's fee" which must be paid on lending or investing cash received during the period is an added inducement to keep receipts until payments fall due rather than investing, and so may further increase the demand for cash.

4. The economy in a single person's use of cash resulting from an increase in the volume of his transactions may or may not have its analogue for the economy as a whole. "External economies" may well be present if one businessman learns cash-economizing techniques from the experiences of another when both increase their transactions. On the diseconomies side it is barely conceivable that an infectious liquidity fetishism will permit a few individuals reluctant to take advantage of cash saving opportunities to block these savings for the bulk of the community. Nevertheless, at least two such possible offsets come to mind: (a) The rise in the demand for brokerage services resulting from a general increase in transactions may bring about a rise in the "brokerage fee" and thus work for an increase in average cash balances (a decreased number of visits to brokers). If cash supplies are sticky this will tend to be offset by rises in the rate of interest resulting from a rising total demand for cash, which serve to make cash more expensive to hold. (b) Widespread cash economizing might require an increase in precautionary cash holdings because in an emergency one could rely less on the ability of friends to help or creditors to be patient. This could weaken but not offset the relative reduction in cash holdings entirely, since the increase in precautionary demand is contingent on there being some relative decrease in cash holdings.

5. A priori analysis of the precautionary and the speculative demands for cash is more difficult. In particular, there seems to be

little we can say about the latter, important though it may be, except that it seems unlikely that it will work consistently in any special direction. In dealing with the precautionary demand, assumptions about probability distributions and expectations must be made.[2] It seems plausible offhand, that an increase in the volume of transactions will make for economies in the use of cash for precautionary as well as transactions purposes by permitting increased recourse to insurance principles.

Indeed, here we have a rather old argument in banking theory which does not seem to be widely known. Edgeworth,[3] and Wicksell[4] following him, suggested that a bank's precautionary cash requirements might also grow as the square root of the volume of its transactions (!). They maintained that cash demands on a bank tend to be normally distributed.[5] In this event, if it is desired to maintain a fixed probability of not running out of funds, precautionary cash requirements will be met by keeping on hand a constant multiple of the standard deviation (above the mean). But then the precautionary cash requirement of ten identical banks (with independent demands) together will be the same as that for any one of them multiplied by the square root of ten. For it is a well-known result that the standard deviation of a random sample from an infinite population increases as the square root of the size of the sample.

William J. Baumol.

Princeton University

2. See Arrow, Harris and Marschak, *op. cit.* for a good example of what has been done along these lines in inventory control analysis.

3. F. Y. Edgeworth, "The Mathematical Theory of Banking," *Journal of the Royal Statistical Society*, Vol. LI (1888), especially pp. 123–127. Fisher (*loc. cit.*) points out the relevance of this result for the analysis of the cash needs of the public as a whole. The result was independently rediscovered by Dr. Whitin (*op. cit.*) who seems to have been the first to combine it and (2) in inventory analysis.

4. K. Wicksell, *Interest and Prices* (London, 1936), p. 67.

5. The distribution would generally be approximately normal if its depositors were large in number, their cash demands independent and not very dissimilarly distributed. The independence assumption, of course, rules out runs on banks.

[25]

STOCKS, FLOWS AND MONETARY THEORY*

By WILLIAM J. BAUMOL

I. THE DOUBLE (STOCK-FLOW) EQUILIBRIUM CONDITION

Bushaw and Clower[1] seem to have been the first to point out that general equilibrium theory should employ (at least) two equations to represent the equilibrium conditions for each commodity. One of these equations states that the supply of and demand for the *flow* of that commodity must be equal, and the second equation is the corresponding *stock* equilibrium condition.

More specifically, let us classify flows into three types: production, consumption, and net addition to stocks. Since we will be dealing only with competitive markets, these, in turn, can be combined into two excess demand functions: the excess consumption demand (consumption demand, D_c, minus production supply, S_p) and the excess inventory investment demand (demand for goods to be added to stocks, D_I, minus supply of goods out of current stocks, S_I). The marketing of flows will be defined to be in equilibrium when the sum of these two excess demands is zero, i.e., when total demand for flows equals their total supply. This may be written symbolically as

$$ED_f = D_c - S_p + D_I - S_I = 0. \tag{1}$$

There are obvious analogues in stock concepts: the definition of the excess demand function for stocks (inventories) and of equilibrium in the marketing of stocks. Thus we obtain the stock equilibrium requirement[2]

$$ED_s = D_I - S_I = 0. \tag{2}$$

* The author would like to acknowledge his gratitude to the Ford Foundation whose grant to the Department of Economics of Princeton University helped in the completion of this paper.

1. See especially D. W. Bushaw and R. W. Clower, *Introduction to Mathematical Economics* (Homewood, Illinois: Irwin, 1957).

2. See the Appendix for a further discussion of this relationship.

Note that this double condition involves something more profound than just a classificatory breaking up of the excess demand for a commodity into two segments (stocks and flows) to permit us to discuss them one at a time. For example, if we were to try to proceed, analogously, to divide the excess demand for citrus fruits into Californian and non-Californian excess demands we would find a permanent excess supply in the former and an excess demand in the latter. Thus, even long-run equilibrium in the citrus market can prevail despite the fact that there is zero excess demand in neither sector. Clearly, two zero excess demand equations are not legitimate here.

However, when we consider the Bushaw-Clower division of a market into the consumption and investment sectors, we see that excess supplies and demands cannot cancel out between them for an unlimited period of time. It is true that in the short run an excess supply out of stocks can just offset an excess consumption demand for any commodity. But as stock levels adjust to their desired magnitudes (or after they drop to zero) the excess supply of stocks will cease. Excess consumption demands must then go unsatisfied and the short-run flow equilibrium must break down. Thus long-run equilibrium requires that the excess demands for stocks and flows *both* be zero, as Bushaw and Clower assert.

This paper will discuss some implications of this double condition for several matters of monetary theory.

II. On the Patinkin Dichotomization Argument

As we all know, Professor Patinkin has argued that it is illegitimate to split the economy completely into a real and monetary sector with relative prices determined entirely in the one and price level in the other. For, by Walras' law, if some set of relative prices can produce (flow) equilibrium for every commodity but money, then the *flow* demand for and supply of money must automatically also be equal, no matter what the price level, and there then remains no other equilibrium equation which can determine the level of absolute prices.

Ever since the beginning of the discussion there seems to have hung over it an obscurely expressed view that Patinkin's argument is inconclusive because there are really *two* monetary equations to be satisfied — both a stock and a flow equilibrium condition. Thus, it would appear to have been argued, even if Walras' law takes the flow equilibrium condition out of the running as a price level determinant, there remains the stock equilibrium condition to do the job.[3]

As we have seen, the Bushaw-Clower stock-flow analysis does indeed require two equilibrium equations for each commodity. But while this can be of considerable significance for other aspects of monetary theory, I will show now that it really is irrelevant for the Patinkin problem.

In most discussions of monetary theory the stock of money is taken to be fixed exogenously so that the public can neither "consume" money nor in any way influence the volume of its production. Now this is clearly economic nonsense, particularly when bank deposits are included in the money supply;[4] and even the treasury is far from immune from the effects of the behavior of the private sector — e.g., an inflationary increase in private outlays will have some more or less predictable effects on governmental monetary policies, at least as far as the direction of change is concerned.[5]

But suppose, first, for the sake of argument, that the money supply is fixed so that its (net) production, $D_c - S_p$, is zero. Our analysis shows that, in such a case, the two-equation problem disappears because the stock and flow equilibrium conditions collapse into one. For in this situation the flow equilibrium relationship (1) reduces to the stock equilibrium condition (2). That is, then, all there is to the matter.[6]

But if we accept the Pigouvian view that the money supply can be treated as an endogenous variable in a general equilibrium system the matter becomes slightly more interesting. Let us see how it might work out in a simplified concrete situation. Suppose, for example,

3. Thus see, e.g., W. Braddock Hickman, "The Determinacy of Absolute Prices in Classical Economic Theory," *Econometrica*, Vol. 18 (Jan. 1950), esp. pp. 13 and 15. See also S. Valavanis, "A Denial of Patinkin's Contradiction," *Kyklos*, VIII, 1955 (though Professor Patinkin interprets both of Valavanis' monetary equations as flow conditions).

4. Though, of course, they are likely to play little part in the real balance effect since bank deposits represent a debt, and, as has often been pointed out, a change in price level will have opposite, and possibly offsetting effects on the real value of the relevant assets of a creditor and a debtor.

5. As far as I know, the only formal model which builds governmental and banking system monetary responses explicitly into its machinery is to be found in Pigou's last major work, *Employment and Equilibrium* (London: Macmillan, 1941), pp. 60–63. Any gold standard model must also treat production of money as an endogenous variable.

6. This result holds whether we accept the Patinkin argument that this stock and flow excess demand must be identical, or the more moderate Bushaw-Clower position as described in the Appendix to this paper, for even on the latter view the excess demand for investment flow will normally be zero when and only when the excess demand for monetary stocks is zero as well.

that the economy has just experienced a rise in price level, that all prices have adjusted so that every commodity market is in equilibrium and that sufficient time has elapsed for any desired transfer of monetary stocks to take place. In this intermediate short-run period there may still be a difference between long-run desired production and "consumption" of money. Specifically, it may mean that the machinery of governmental monetary policy is slowly creaking into motion. We might, for example, expect some action to reduce the money supply as a means for countering the price rise. As the net production of money thus declined, cash stocks would decline also, the excess demand curve would shift rightward and the price level (the reciprocal of the "real price of money") would have to adjust downward accordingly. This, then, is the interpretation of the other monetary equilibrium equation — it represents the response of monetary production — the reactions of the monetary authorities and banking system — to changes in the values of the system's variables, and it can be a critical feature of the theory of monetary policy, particularly if that theory has any pretension to explaining actual historical phenomena.

So much for what the second (production equilibrium) equation does. But perhaps it is more interesting for our purposes to see what it *cannot* do. It is easy to show now that this condition cannot rescue an economic model from the Patinkin problem. For our additional equation brings with it an additional variable — the total stock of money. Hence it cannot serve to determine the price level if the system is incapable of determining the price level without it.[7]

III. . . . And Liquidity Preference vs. Loanable Funds

Occasionally there is still a revival of the rather tired liquidity preference loanable funds discussion.

In a recent note[8] Cliff L. Lloyd suggests that the double equilibrium condition for each commodity causes difficulties for the

7. It is true that any sensible monetary production equation will save the situation by forcing the introduction of nonhomogeneity into the model. That is, it will not usually be consistent with the assertion that all supplies and demands are independent of the price level. But this merely means that the addition of the equation has reminded us how to construct a more sensible model.

8. "The Equivalence of the Liquidity Preference and Loanable Funds Theories and the New Stock-Flow Analysis," *Review of Economic Studies*, XXVII (June, 1960). See also S. C. Tsiang, "Liquidity Preference and Loanable Funds Theories, Multiplier and Velocity Analyses: A Synthesis," *American Economic Review*, XLVI (Sept. 1956) and the comment by G. Ackley and reply by Tsiang in the same journal, XLVII (Sept. 1957).

Hicksian argument[9] which is designed to demonstrate the equivalence of the two theories. It will be recalled that Hicks asserts that this equivalence follows from the redundancy of an equation in the Walrasian system, since we can with equal justice drop the money equation (thus allegedly leaving us with a loanable funds system) or we can omit the bond (loans) equation and obtain what can be described as a liquidity preference model. But, since in our Bushaw-Clower general equilibrium system there are now *two* equations for each item, we cannot, by dropping a single redundant equation, eliminate both monetary equilibrium equations or both bond market equilibrium equations. Thus we are not left with a pure system of either variety.

If this is enough to destroy the Hicksian argument I fear it is not much of a loss. As Patinkin has maintained, the classification implicit in the argument has little economic content. It is true that Walras' law does tell us that nothing of substance is left out of consideration when we ignore any one excess demand equation, be it the bond, the money or Lerner's peanut equation. But this means that the Hicksian analysis amounts, in effect, to saying the same thing twice, calling the first round liquidity preference, the second loanable funds, and then asking us to express surprise at the similarity in content of the two statements!

In an unpublished paper Professor E. O. Edwards has, I believe, directed us to the right place to look for differences in the alternative theories of the determination of "the" rate of interest. He has pointed out once again that, under conditions of full equilibrium, the interest rate must be considered a *general* equilibrium phenomenon and it is meaningless to single out money or bonds as "most" relevant in its determination. Thus the distinction among liquidity preference, loanable funds, and real theories must in these conditions be relatively pointless. Only under conditions of partial *dis*equilibrium is it apt to be helpful to assign any ranking to the theories in terms of their ability to explain the facts. That is, only when some markets are not in equilibrium is it legitimate even to contend that the money market, or the bond market, or the combined labor and goods markets, is by itself the primary determinant of the rate of interest. And in such circumstances, which (if any) of these markets holds this critical status is, as Edwards concludes, an empirical question.

I do believe, however, that with the aid of the Bushaw-Clower stock-flow discussion it is possible to go one stage further in this

9. See *Value and Capital* (2d ed.; New York: Oxford University Press, 1946), pp. 158–62.

investigation, even with our limited store of empirical information. Our knowledge of the structure of these markets and their time rate of response to exogenous events is highly relevant. For if one market, A, responds and returns to (partial) equilibrium much more quickly than does another, B, we can argue that in that short run the rate of interest must satisfy the equilibrium requirements for market A, but not those for B. We may then say with some justice that in such a period the rate of interest is for practical purposes determined in market A.

To be more specific, let us divide the economy into four markets, the bond (securities) market, the commodity market, the labor market, and the money market; and let us exercise our option to treat the latter as residual because I think it is easier to rank the remaining three markets in terms of speed of response.

I shall not attempt to get out of the voluminous and confused literature the "correct" definitions of liquidity preference and loanable funds. Rather, I have set up the following operational definitions which have a very tenuous relationship with their predecessors:

(a) Loanable funds: in the short run the rate of interest must satisfy the bond *flow* equilibrium condition.

(b) Liquidity preference: in the short run the rate of interest must satisfy the money *stock* equilibrium condition.

(c) Real theories: in the short run the rate of interest must satisfy both the goods market and labor market flow equilibrium conditions (the latter, full employment, condition being an integral part of the classical interest rate adjustment mechanism).[1]

(a) *The Short Short Run*

It seems clear that, of the three markets, the securities market will normally be by far the quickest to achieve some sort of equilibrium. Indeed, with the securities markets as centralized and as efficiently organized as they are, short-run (Marshallian) equilibrium will ordinarily be attained in no more than a matter of minutes. If there is an excess demand for a heavily traded security, its price will rise at once until its supply and demand are equated. In particular, this will be true in the bond market so that the prices of bonds, and hence their rates of interest, must almost always satisfy the exchange equilibrium requirements.

1. Cf. the related approaches of Mr. Hahn ("The Rate of Interest and General Equilibrium Analysis," *Economic Journal*, LXV, March 1955) and Professor Harry Johnson ("The *General Theory* after Twenty-Five Years," *American Economic Review*, LI, May 1961).

This result then states that, even in the very short run, the rate of interest will satisfy the conditions that the public will voluntarily hold the available stocks of loan market assets. It must not, however, be read to state that the loanable funds theory is the more valid short-run interest analysis. For the argument only states that, in the very short run, interest rate determination will satisfy the stock but *not* the flow equilibrium condition for the bond market. That is, it states that interest rates must be at such levels that everyone who wishes to acquire (sell) securities which are already extant will be able to do so. It is, in effect, a security inventory exchange equilibrium assertion, not a security "production" equilibrium hypothesis. This, by itself, does not imply that the liquidity preference analysis is invalid in such a very short period. The supply of and demand for exchanges of existing securities may be a direct reflection of the excess demand (positive or negative) for cash, so that, when the bond market is in short-run equilibrium, the money market may be in equilibrium, too. However, we may expect that this will frequently not be the case. If, e.g., we start off with a situation of general excess supply, even when the bond market makes its initial adjustment (zero excess demand for securities) there will normally continue to be excess supplies of both goods and labor so that, by Walras' law, there must be an excess demand for cash, as we would normally expect in a depression period. Note that, in such a situation, the real interest theories do not hold either since there will be excess supplies of goods (*ex ante* saving exceeds investment).

(b) *The Intermediate Short Run*

I have implied that, in the short short run, interest rates may, for example, be so low that there will be an excess flow demand for loanable funds until firms have had time to complete arrangements for the flotation of new issues. Over a somewhat longer period, say over a period of months, the supply of securities can also normally be adjusted, so that, in such an intermediate short run, the rates of interest will have to meet the loanable funds (security *flow*) equilibrium conditions. But, by then, equilibrating forces will also have been at work in other markets as well.

At least the more competitive sectors of the commodity market may also be expected to have eliminated excess stock and flow demands over such a period. In the excess supply case a sufficient reduction in outputs can achieve this result, while in the case of excess demand a rise in prices can do the trick if expectations are inelastic. Thus, for example, a depression period does not witness the limitless accumulation of inventories (a chronic excess supply of commodity flow). If nothing else, total cessation of production can prevent commodity stocks from rising further. Both the security and commodity markets will then have attained an unhappy sort of equilibrium. The labor market, and therefore (under the rules of Walras' law), the money market,[2] will be left to bear the brunt of the disequilibrium in that there will remain an excess supply of labor and an excess (flow) demand for money.[3] These, then, are the conditions that the interest rates and other variables of the system will have to satisfy in the intermediate short run.

Such a state may well endure for a matter of years. Indeed, we have no assurance that any period is sufficiently long to guarantee the working of an automatic mechanism which eliminates excess supply on the labor market. Certainly the real balance effect (the Pigou effect) offers us, at best, rather feeble reassurance.

To sum up, it appears that, starting from a position of disequilibrium, in the short run something related to, but not the same as the loanable funds mechanism may be expected to determine interest rates. In an intermediate period, when the full loanable funds mechanism comes into play, interest rates will also have to satisfy the condition that excess flow and stock demand for commodities be zero. The position of liquidity preference remains quite ambiguous — our analysis is simply not powerful enough to offer us a priori information on the validity of that theory. However, it does indicate that the neoclassical "real" theories will hold only when full general equilibrium is achieved so that all of the interest theories are equally valid (and equally one sided).

Appendix: The Excess Demand for Stocks

Our equation (2), the equilibrium condition for stocks, asserts that the excess demand for stocks is equal to $D_I - S_I$, the difference between the demand for and supply of inventory investment. This

2. What this means is that workers are offering their services in exchange for money (the excess demand for money) and finding no takers. In an ultimate sense we might rather say that workers are demanding commodities (not money) in exchange for their services so that it is the goods market and not the money market in which there is an excess demand. This is a matter of interpretation but note that the goods market is shielded from the pressures of these demands by workers' inability to lay their hands on the money. Incidentally, these workers may also be considered a source of excess supply of "bonds" if they can find no takers for their I.O.U.'s.

3. This involves no obvious implication about the validity of our version of liquidity preference which only calls for a zero excess demand for money *stocks*, and which is perfectly compatible with an excess demand for money flows.

statement presents some problems, specifically, because it apparently measures stock and flow magnitudes in similar units.

Now, it is surely plausible that there will be some relationship between the excess demand for stocks, ED_s, and the excess (flow) demand for inventory investment, $D_I - S_I$. One would expect, for example, that an undersupply of inventory would lead to an excess demand for flows into inventory (investment in stocks). Bushaw and Clower have a very lucid exposition of this point:

> . . . if unsatisfied demands for stock holdings of a commodity vary, every-day experience indicates that current market purchases of the commodity will vary in the same direction. Also, if unsatisfied demands to hold stocks are non-zero, it is certainly true in practice that some individuals will attempt to increase (or decrease) stock holdings by making current purchases (sales) in the market. That such purchases (sales) will not occur if unsatisfied demands are zero is a more dubious proposition, but common sense suggests that it may be true in some circumstances. With these considerations in mind, therefore, we shall assume that [excess inventory investment demand] is an increasing function of [the excess demand for stocks] . . . and that [the excess demand for investment will be zero whenever the excess demand for stocks is zero].[1]

This means that if we take supplies and demands to be functions of current price,[2] we will have two relevant supply-demand diagrams: one for inventory investment flow and one for stocks. The shapes of the stock and flow excess demand curves will have a considerable degree of independence of one another, but their intersection points with the Y-axis (zero excess demand) will necessarily occur at the same height, i.e., the price which equates stock supply and demand will also bring net investment demand to zero. And on this view, as Bushaw and Clower emphasize " . . . there is in general no necessity for the investment [flow] demand curve to have the same form as the stock demand curve except that both must be upward or downward sloping for any given value of the price variables."[3]

In an unpublished paper, I had independently made a similar assertion. However, the argument was questioned by Patinkin who had maintained in an earlier article[4] that the excess demand for stocks and that for investment flows must not just behave similarly —

1. *Op. cit.*, p. 16.

2. Clearly expected future prices must also affect stock demands and supplies, but for simplicity of exposition I have taken these as given, or at least I have assumed that expectations are inelastic, so that only current price changes need be considered explicitly.

3. *Op. cit.*, p. 17. Normally, this requirement would specify simply that both excess demand curves must have a negative slope as well as an identical Y intercept.

4. "The Indeterminacy of Absolute Prices in Classical Economic Theory," *Econometrica*, Vol. 17 (Jan. 1949), p. 8.

they must be identical. I responded that his argument has to be illegitimate since stocks and flows are measured in different units, specifically, since flows are measured in time units while stocks are not. Thus, I asked whether an excess demand amounting to, say, $12 billion of cash (stocks) should be equated with a net flow demand of $12 billion per month or $12 billion per year ($1 billion per month) or to still another rate of flow. Surely any assertion that these stock and flow demands are necessarily identical must have sneaked into the argument some arbitrary choice of time period for the measurement of the flow.

Patinkin responded as follows:

There is a time period implicit in my *Econometrica* argument, though I quite agree that it should have been made explicit. If I may restate this argument, it is as follows:

1. Stock analysis, as well as flow analysis, presumes a period of time. In the case of the former, this is the period at the end of which the desired stock is to be held. This period may, of course, be an instantaneous one.

2. If the periods presumed by the analyses are the same, the excess-demand function of the stock analysis is identical with that of the flow analysis.

And to this I would now add:

3. Conversely, if the periods are *not* the same, then these excess-demand functions will *not* be identical *and in particular there is no necessity for their zero points to coincide. . . .*

In other words, your analysis implicitly assumes that if at the end of n periods the public wishes to change its stock of money by the quantity X, then it will want to make this change at the rate of $\frac{1}{n}X$ per period — so that if X is zero, the net inflow per period is also zero (i.e., both sets of curves intersect at the same rate of interest). But why assume that the time path of adjustment is necessarily linearly homogeneous in this way? Surely the general situation with respect to anticipated income for future periods is such that the adjustment path for these periods can assume a much more general form. Correspondingly, there is no reason why the rate of interest [or price] which equates stocks demanded and supplied n periods hence should also equate the inflow and outflow of each and every period before that. Indeed, we should generally expect this not to be the case.[5]

Thus, for example, if people want to get rid of $12 billion of stocks over the next year they might very well choose (in anticipation of rising prices for the item) to build inventory up over the course of the next few months and then dispose of it all toward the end of the year. In that case there is an excess stock *supply* (for the next year) but an excess *demand* for investment flow for the next few months!

5. Letter dated March 3, 1957. A similar point of view was later expressed in his "Liquidity Preference and Loanable Funds: Stock and Flow Analysis," *Economica*, XXV (Nov. 1958).

Only if the same reference period is chosen for the two is there any necessary correspondence, and then they have to be identical — if over the next year we want to dispose of $12 billion in stocks we must necessarily want a $12 billion net outflow over that period.

This is an extremely persuasive argument, and as a matter of fact, I am now pretty much convinced that Patinkin's position is the relevant one. We are interested in stocks here because of the disturbing effects which stock disequilibrium will have on prices, and this effect can only manifest itself in the market through the flows by means of which the public adjusts its inventory holdings. It is in this way that I end up with our second (stock) excess demand equilibrium condition

$$ED_s = D_I - S_I = 0.$$

Thus, since D_I and S_I refer to flows, in effect I have simply dropped the idea of obtaining a stock equilibrium condition and substituted for it the inventory investment *flow* equilibrium condition

$$ED_{fI} = D_I - S_I = 0.$$

Perhaps, therefore, it is more honest and straightforward to state that the system involves two flow equilibrium conditions, not one stock condition and one flow condition.[6]

6. Professor Hurwicz suggested in conversation that there is an alternative and meaningful way to define the excess demand for stocks as "how much more inventory would I have arranged to hold today if I had it to do all over again?" This concept restores our faith in the view that stock measurements can be undertaken without specifying any time period. However, I think we agree that an excess demand for stocks on this Hurwicz definition may or may not lead the consumer to do anything about it on the market, and so it is not the relevant concept for our purposes: the explanation of price and inventory level determination.

Note the relationship of the entire discussion to the Lernerian distinction between the marginal efficiency of capital and the marginal efficiency of investment (*Economics of Control;* New York: Macmillan, 1944, pp. 334–37).

PRINCETON UNIVERSITY

[26]

MANAGEMENT SCIENCE
Vol. 10, No. 1, October, 1963
Printed in U.S.A.

AN EXPECTED GAIN-CONFIDENCE LIMIT CRITERION FOR PORTFOLIO SELECTION*[1]

WILLIAM J. BAUMOL

Princeton University, Princeton, New Jersey

A new efficiency criterion is proposed for the Markowitz portfolio selection approach. It is shown that the use of standard deviation as a measure of risk in the original Markowitz analysis and elsewhere in economic theory is sometimes unreasonable. An Investment with a relatively high standard deviation (σ) will be relatively safe if its expected value (E) is sufficiently high. For the net result may be a high expected floor, $E - K\sigma$, beneath the future value of the investment (where K is some constant). The revised efficient set is shown to eliminate paradoxical cases arising from the Markowitz calculation. It also simplifies the task left to the investor. For it yields a smaller efficient set (which is a subset of the Markowitz efficient set) and therefore reduces the range of alternatives from among which the investor must still select his portfolio. The proposed criterion may also be somewhat more easily understood by the nonprofessional.

The economic literature has frequently sought to explain[2] and set up norms[3] for the selection of portfolios of stocks, bonds and other securities in terms of two standard statistical concepts which are taken to indicate the value of the portfolio to the investor. These variables are the expected return, E, representing the most likely net yield of the investment, and the standard deviation of that return, σ, representing, in some sense, the degree of undependability of the yield. The greater the standard deviation of the return the more risky the portfolio is generally assumed to be and, consequently, the less desirable from the investor's viewpoint.[4] This premise has led to the argument that, given the value of E, any *ceteris paribus* increase in σ is undesirable.

* Received March 1963.

[1] The author is grateful for their helpful comments to E. J. Kane, B. K. Malkiel and Harry Markowitz, to E. Zinbarg of the Prudential Insurance Company for first calling the problem to his attention, and to the National Science Foundation whose grant was so helpful in completion of this paper.

[2] See, e.g., Tobin [8] p. 71 ff. and Lintner [2] pp. 254–261 and 264–266. Both of these authors use variance rather than standard deviation, but the latter concept is more convenient for present purposes.

[3] See Markowitz [4] and [5].

[4] Because of the observed rate of increases of sample variances with the size of sample, and on a number of other statistical and heuristic grounds, some of the students of the data have recently come to feel that many economic series, and particularly security yield and price statistics, are drawn from a sample of infinite variance. If this is so, the standard deviation of a sample, while necessarily finite, is not very meaningful and is certainly a poor measure of risk. This criticism is equally applicable to the Markowitz construction and to the alternative which is proposed in this paper. For a detailed discussion of the implications for economics of distributions with nonfinite variances by the leading investigator of the subject, see Mandelbrot [3].

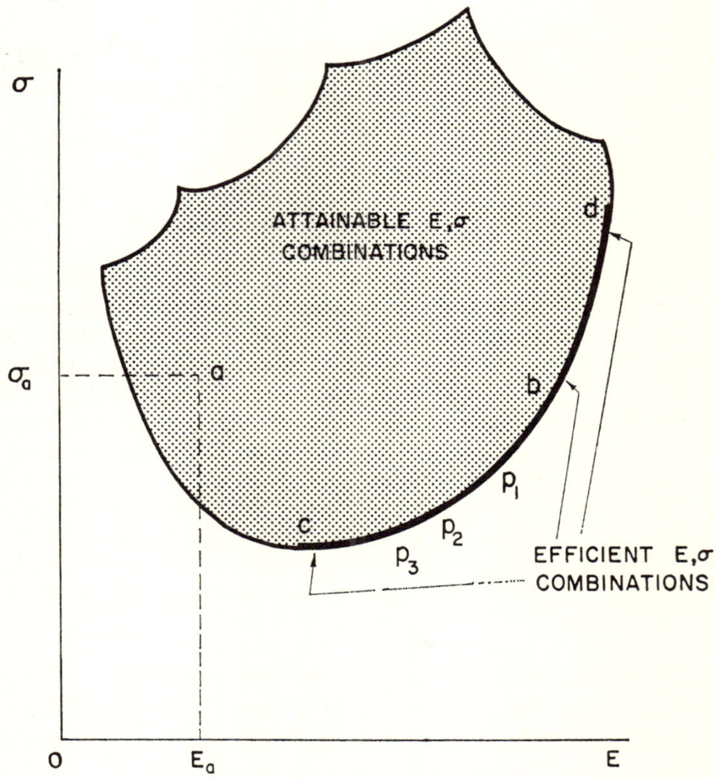

FIGURE 1

More specifically, in his pathbreaking work on Portfolio Selection, Markowitz has on this basis defined a portfolio to be *efficient* if ". . . it is impossible to obtain a greater average [expected] return without incurring greater standard deviation; it is impossible to obtain smaller standard deviation without giving up return on the average." ([5] p. 22.) He goes on to imply that, in the absence of specific knowledge of the investor's preference structure one cannot say that one efficient portfolio is better than another. Only "judgment" can be "employed in choosing one of the set of all efficient portfolios" (*loc. cit.*)

Markowitz uses a diagram similar to Figure 1 to illustrate the point.

Suppose some portfolio, A, offers an expected return E_a and a standard deviation σ_a. Then this portfolio can be represented by point a in the diagram. Assume all portfolios available with a fixed amount of money to be invested have been represented similarly and that the dots describing them constitute the shaded region in the figure. We see then that A is not an efficient portfolio because c which lies below and to the right of a offers a higher expected yield and a lower standard deviation. The locus of all efficient portfolios is the lower right hand segment of the boundary of the shaded region because these points represent all lowest σ-highest E combinations. This locus is the heavy arc *cbd*.[5]

[5] Markowitz points out ([5] pp. 152–3) that the efficient locus, cbd, will, in fact, be made up of arcs of hyperbolas.

Now I shall argue that this efficient set is very likely to contain portfolios which, many investors would agree, should be rejected out of hand. I shall suggest that the expected yield-standard deviation investment criterion [henceforth referred to as the (E, σ) criterion] does not accomplish quite what it is designed to do, and should be replaced by another closely related standard.[6] Fortunately, the criterion I shall propose calls for no extensive modifications of the arguments of the current literature. Indeed, all of the standard Markowitz analysis remains equally applicable, except that some unacceptable portfolios which do not satisfy the criterion have to be culled out of the Markowitz (E, σ) efficient set.

Before going further I must emphasize that my criticism of Markowitz's work is in no way meant to detract from his very significant contribution. Rather, I intend it to be regarded as an amendment which adds somewhat to the applicability of his approach, and which calls for no major change in his analytic and computational machinery.

1. Unacceptable (E, σ) Efficient Portfolios

Consider two portfolios A and B which have the expected values and standard deviations shown in Table 1. Note that A and B may both be efficient—neither "dominates" the other because B has the better expected return but the poorer standard deviation. Yet we see that if we take $E + \sigma$ and $E - \sigma$ as a sort of upper and lower confidence limit, that is, if $E - \sigma$ is considered the (equally likely) lowest plausible outcome for each investment and $E + \sigma$ is the highest plausible outcome for each investment it may well be questioned whether anyone in his right mind would ever choose portfolio A. For the worst anticipated outcome associated with B, $E_b - \sigma_b = 11$ is better than the highest plausible outcome for $A = E_a + \sigma_a = 10$!

What has gone wrong here? The difficulty is that the investor is not interested in σ per se. He would prefer the danger of coming out \$10 short on a \$100 expected return as against an \$8 shortfall below a \$50 expected return. That is, while *for a given value of* E $\sigma = \$10$ is always worse than $\sigma = \$8$ this need no longer be the case when the value of E varies.

2. An Alternative Efficient Portfolio Criterion

What alternative measure, then, should be employed to represent the investor's risk? One possibility is suggested by standard probability theory which tells us the following: If our basic random variable (the return on our investment) is normally distributed,[7] then there is only about a 16 percent probability

[6] It should be mentioned that Markowitz does consider several other criteria. See, e.g., [5], pp. 15 and 187. However, he does not seem to think highly of them and does not pursue their analysis very deeply.

[7] Markowitz ([5], p. 51–52) does consider some alternative efficiency concepts and recognizes their relationship in the normal distribution case. However, (though his concept is not clearly defined) he seems to be in error in arguing that a portfolio is (E, σ) efficient *if* and

TABLE 1

	A	B
E	8	15
σ	2	4
$E + \sigma$	10	19
$E - \sigma$	6	11

that the realized return will ever fall below $E - \sigma$, there is only a 2 percent probability that it will ever be lower than $E - 2\sigma$, no more than a 0.1 percent probability that it will fall below $E - 3\sigma$, etc. Thus we may say that the risk involved in a given portfolio is represented by $E - K\sigma$ for some appropriately chosen value of K. Here $E - K\sigma$ may be considered the lower confidence limit for the investor's return.[8]

The situation may perhaps be made clearer with the aid of the following diagram (Figure 2). On the horizontal axis we represent the expected values, E, of various efficient portfolios and on the vertical axis we represent the values of $E + K\sigma$, E and $E - K\sigma$ corresponding to these same portfolios.[9] Here the 45° line, as usual, describes the identity $E \equiv E$ so by adding or subtracting $K\sigma$ from the 45° line we obtain, respectively, the $E + K\sigma$ and $E - K\sigma$ curves.

Now, even though these portfolios are all efficient on the Markowitz (E, σ) criterion it is easy to see that the investor may readily reject some of them. For example, he will generally prefer portfolio A to portfolio C because $E_a > E_c$ and $E_a - K\sigma_a > E_c - K\sigma_c$. That is, Portfolio A offers both a higher expected return and a higher floor on earnings $(E - K\sigma)$. This is so because our $E - K\sigma$ curve has a positive slope between E_c and E_a—over this range of the curve portfolios with higher expected returns are also safer! Only to the right of point M, where the $E - K\sigma$ curve begins to turn down, do we get to portfolios which are efficient in terms of our alternative (E, L) criterion (where for brevity I write $L = E - K\sigma$ to designate the *lower* confidence limit). For only in this negatively sloping segment does the investor have to make up his mind in trading off greater expected return against reduced safety.[10]

only if it is what he calls "mean-probability of loss efficient". The "only if" is valid, but the "if" is not, if I interpret him correctly.

[8] For a somewhat similar approach to utility theory, see Quandt [6]. Cf. also Roy [7]. The reader may prefer a decision theoretic approach to the matter in which the value of K is determined in terms of the *cost* of an erroneous choice, but this would complicate matters excessively for present purposes. Note also that this confidence limit approach, by ignoring all contingencies more remote than K standard deviations from the expected value, implicitly assumes a rather simple minded investor utility function.

[9] That is, the (E, σ) efficient locus cbd in Figure 1 may be described by the equation $\sigma = f(E)$. The equation for the upper curve in Figure 2 is then $L = E + kf(E)$, where E is the abscissa of any point on the curve and L is its ordinate. A similar equation, equation (1) below, holds for the lower curve in the figure.

[10] Of course, I am defining a portfolio to be (E, L) efficient if there exists no other portfolio which offers a higher value of E without any reduction in L.

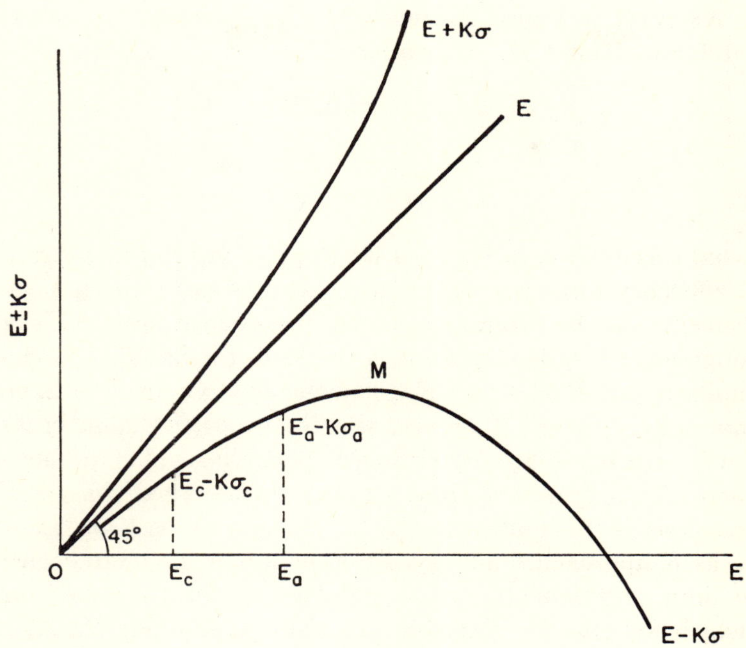

FIGURE 2

3. Relationship Between (*E*, *L*) Efficiency and (*E*, σ) Efficiency

Let us see now how the set of (*E*, *L*) efficient portfolios is related to the Markowitz (*E*, σ) efficient set. It is easy to argue that *the former is a subset of the latter*.[11] That is, no portfolio can be (*E*, *L*) efficient without being (*E*, σ) efficient. For suppose portfolio A were not (*E*, σ) efficient because it is "(*E*, σ) dominated" by portfolio *B*, that is, because $E_b \geq E_a$ and $\sigma_b \leq \sigma_a$. Then we must have for our *L* figures $L_b \geq L_a$ since $L_b = E_b - K\sigma_b \geq E_b - K\sigma_a \geq E_a - K\sigma_a = L_a$. Hence (*E*, σ) inefficient portfolio *A* cannot be (*E*, *L*) efficient either, because as compared with *B* it involves both a lower expected return, *E*, and a smaller lower confidence limit, *L*.

We can go further and determine what portion of the (*E*, σ) efficient set *cbd* in figure 1 is also (*E*, *L*) efficient. For this purpose let the equation of the curve *cbd* be represented by $\sigma = f(E)$. then we have

$$L = E - K\sigma = E - Kf(E). \tag{1}$$

But we have seen that for (*E*, *L*) efficient portfolios, portfolios offering larger expected values of *E* must be characterized by less high values of *L*, i.e., such efficient portfolios are represented by the negatively sloping segment of the

[11] Indeed, one may helpfully describe the (*E*, *L*) investment procedure as follows: the investor chooses on the basis of *E* and σ, but from his calculated (*E*, σ) efficient points he excludes from consideration all portfolios dominated in the (*E*, *L*) plane, i.e., he excludes all portfolios like portfolio *A* in Table 1.

$L = E - K\sigma$ curve in Figure 2. Hence, (E, L) efficiency requires $dL/dE < 0$, so that, differentiating (1), we obtain

$$dL/dE = 1 - Kf'(E) < 0$$

or

$$f'(E) > 1/K. \tag{2}$$

To see what this implies, in Figure 1 let P_1, P_2, and P_3 represent the points on the (E, σ) efficiency locus *cbd* where the curve has slope unity, $\frac{1}{2}$ and $\frac{1}{3}$ respectively. Then since as the diagram is drawn, the slope of arc P_1bd is greater than unity throughout, (2) tells us that it is the locus of the (E, L) efficient set for $K = 1$. Similarly, arc P_2bd is the (E, L) efficiency locus for $K = 2$, etc. Thus we see that, normally,[12] *the* (E, L) *efficient set will be a proper subset of the* (E, σ) *set*, i.e., there will be many Markowitz efficient portfolios which are not efficient on the proposed (E, L) criterion. However, it is to be noted that the Markowitz (E, σ) efficient set is the limit of the (E, L) efficient set as K becomes larger and larger, i.e., as K approaches infinity. In other words the more conservative our confidence limit criterion—the more standard deviations below our expected outcome which we consider plausible, the more closely our (E, L) efficient set will approximate the Markowitz (E, σ) set.

This result is really not difficult to explain. The basic objection to the Markowitz criterion is that in the expression $L = E - K\sigma$ an increasing E may more than counterbalance an increase in σ, so that despite greater variability in the return from the portfolio with the larger E, it may be considered relatively safe because the lower confidence limit L is relatively high. But the larger the value of K in $E - K\sigma$ the more of a rise in E it will take to compensate[13] for a given fall in σ. When K is very large the $K\sigma$ becomes the overwhelmingly important term in $L = E - K\sigma$ and so the behavior of L will be almost perfectly correlated with that of σ. Hence an (E, L) criterion will then not differ significantly from an (E, σ) criterion.[14]

4. The (*E*, *L*) Criterion in Applied Portfolio Selection

It can be claimed for the (E, L) criterion that it is a somewhat more easily interpreted measure of risk than is (E, σ). In fact, it is possible with the former to

[12] The only exception occurs if arc cbd in Figure 1 is of slope greater than, say, unity throughout its length, with a kink at point *c*. In that case the (E, L) efficiency locus for $K > 1$ will also be cbd so that it will coincide with the (E, σ) efficient set.

[13] For example, in the case shown in Table 1, with a sufficiently large K investment B would yield a smaller value of L than does investment A. The borderline occurs where $K = 3.5$, at which $L_a = L_b = 1$.

[14] An alternative way of looking at the entire matter is to say that the choice of K depends on the investor's attitude toward risk, and that this psychological element determines the region within which one can expect to find points of tangency between the investor's indifference curves and the (E, σ) efficiency locus. The smaller the value of K the greater, *ceteris paribus*, will be the slopes of the indifference curves and, therefore, the further to the right on arc cbd must the possible tangency points lie.

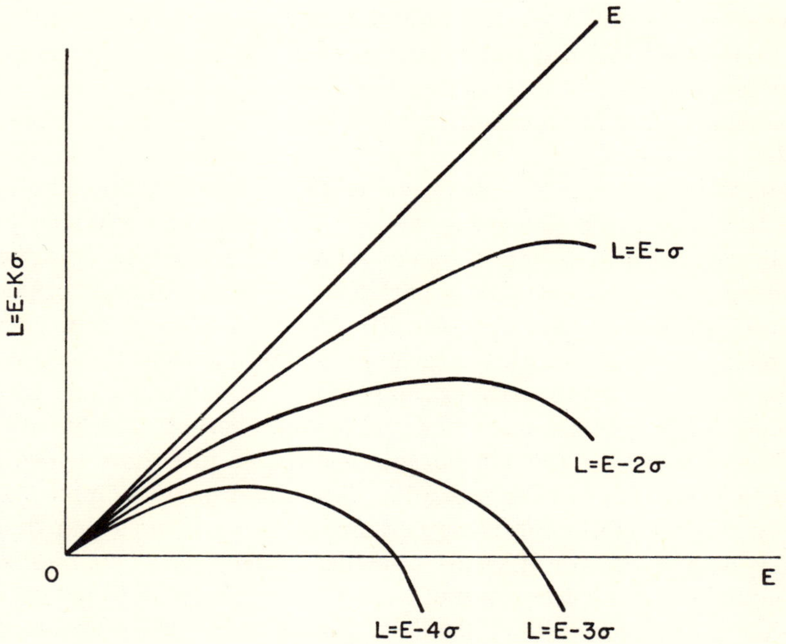

FIGURE 3

take explicit account of differing atitudes toward risk and to examine their consequences. Figure 3 shows a family of different $L = E - K\sigma$ curves for different values of K, and indicates the alternative (E, L) combinations which are available with different selections of the value of K. The higher the value of K chosen by the investor, the more conservative he must be considered since he must then be taking into account far less likely possibilities of loss. As is to be expected, Figure 3 shows that an investor whose K is 4, and who must surely be considered extremely conservative on almost any standards, may plausibly be expected to accept relatively low values of E. For his is the lowest curve shown in the figure, and the points where it turns down and crosses the E axis are well to the left of the corresponding points on the other curves shown in the diagram. This relationship is mentioned merely to illustrate the ready interpretability of our diagram.[15]

One disadvantage of the (E, L) approach is that is imposes on the user of the analysis yet another explicit judgment which takes a form to which he is little habituated.[16] For, to employ the method, the investor must first express his risk

[15] Another example of the interpretation which may be given Figure 3 follows from our observation that (E, L) efficient points must lie on negatively sloping segments of our curves. We see in the diagram that, as K increases, the positively sloping (inefficient) segment of the curve grows shorter and shorter so that the efficient set grows more and more extensive, as we have already seen. In the limit, as K approaches infinity, the slope of the corresponding curve will be negative even at the origin, and every point on the curve will be (E, L) efficient.

[16] Here it may be appropriate to remark briefly on Markowitz' apparent reluctance to use historical data as a basis for estimation of the E and σ values needed in his calculation. No doubt it is true that extrapolation of these values from past history is a risky business

preferences by choosing a specific value for K. But even where the distribution cannot be assumed to be approximately normal this requirement is not totally unreasonable, because, with the aid of Chebyshev's inequality[17] any value of K can be assigned an interpretation in terms of the likelihood that observations will fall beyond $E \pm K\sigma$.

The preceding remarks are somewhat peripheral to the basic question of application to which this section is addressed. The purpose of the Markowitz analysis may be described in general terms as a procedure whereby, from among the astronomical number[18] of candidate portfolios, the vast majority of possibilities can be ruled out because they are not worth the investor's consideration (they are not in the efficient set). The goal of the approach is to present the investor (or his counsellor) with a much smaller and more tractable list of alternatives from among which he must still make up his mind, perhaps partly with the help of the E, σ data used in the calculation. The (E, L) procedure which has been proposed in this note, besides providing data which may be more meaningful intuitively and ruling out confusing paradoxical cases such as that described in Table 1, is helpful because it yields a smaller efficient set. This means that far fewer (and only more clearly relevant) alternatives are likely to be offered to the investor for comparison in the difficult and complex selection process. In effect, then, the proposed (E, L) approach may add efficacy to the pruning procedure which is the basic application of the Markowitz analysis.

References

1. Feller, William, *An Introduction to Probability Theory and Its Applications*, Vol. I, Wiley, New York, 1950.

---

and when there is specific information indicating changes in the operations of a particular company or in the performance of the economy as a whole, this should clearly be taken into account. But, particularly because investment management is not habituated to translating its experience into the language of expected values, variances, and covariances required for the computation, there is surely much to be said for providing these measures routinely by more or less mechanical statistical calculation, *but then having them examined and modified by the professional investors before they are used in the portfolio selection procedure.*

For this purpose it is probably not desirable to proceed as Markowitz does in his illustrative calculations ([5] Chapter 2) by dealing with a time series of annual returns data. This implies that investors are typically concerned with a one year experience and perhaps even that portfolios will characteristically be held for one year periods. Since securities will be held for varying lengths of time, it may well be preferable to collect data for much shorter time periods (say monthly) and then select a sample of time periods for the calculation of mean variances and covariances with the aid of a table of random numbers. That is, if one employs data about a security extending over a 36 month period, this approach might, for example, have us dealing with the return from month 3 to month 12, the return from month 8 to month 24, etc. Such a random sample of possible investor experience in holding the security in question may well be helpful to a potential purchaser who does not know in advance for how long a period he will keep it in his portfolio.

[17] Chebyshev's inequality (whose proof is quite elementary) states that for *any* distribution with given mean and variance, the probability of observations outside the range $E \pm K\sigma$ will be no greater than $1/K^2$! See, e.g., Feller [1], pp. 183–4.

[18] I assume here that expenditures on any security can be made only in discrete amounts so that the number of possible portfolios will be finite.

2. LINTNER, JOHN, "Dividends, Earnings, Leverage, Stock Prices and the Supply of Capital to Corporations," *Review of Economics and Statistics*, Vol. XLIV, August, 1962.
3. MANDELBROT, BENOIT, "The Variation of Certain Speculative Prices," I.B.M. Research Note NC-87, March 26, 1962.
4. MARKOWITZ, HARRY, "Portfolio Selection," *Journal of Finance*, Vol. VII, March, 1952.
5. ——, *Portfolio Selection*, Cowles Foundation Monograph 16, Wiley, New York, 1959.
6. QUANDT, RICHARD E., "A Contribution to the Pathology of Gambling," *Zeitschrift Für Nationalökonomie*, Vol. XX, 1960.
7. ROY, A. D., "Safety First and the Holding of Assets," *Econometrica*, Vol. 20, July, 1952.
8. TOBIN, JAMES, "Liquidity Preference as Behavior Toward Risk," *Review of Economic Studies*, Vol. XXV, February, 1958.

[27]

INVESTMENT AND DISCOUNT RATES UNDER CAPITAL RATIONING—A PROGRAMMING APPROACH [1]

Although the capital rationing case may have an appearance of artificiality, investment decisions made under conditions which closely approximate to capital rationing are frequently encountered in practice. The investment decisions of government agencies and many company divisions are circumscribed by budgets whose magnitudes are largely beyond their control. Some companies seek to operate without recourse to the capital market, and indeed, corporate funds are often obtained preponderantly from internal sources. In times of tight money some companies are perhaps likely to find that their capital is effectively rationed by the funds market, which apparently contracts its operations by rejecting applications for funds rather than just by increasing interest rates. Capital rationing is also of considerable interest to theorists, both because it serves as a limiting case to the diverging borrowing and lending-rate problems which have recently received so much attention in the literature and because capital rationing plays an important role in a number of theoretical constructs such as Hayek's "Ricardo Effect."

This paper uses the tools of mathematical programming to explore the choice of optimal investment project combinations and shows how a number of problems left unsolved in the previous literature can be handled. In doing so, it brings together two strands of economic literature: The neoclassical theory of capital and the mathematical analysis of capital budgeting.

I. The Fisher Solution

The capital-rationing case poses peculiar analytical and computational difficulties which have long been recognised in the literature. Irving Fisher is justly credited with the crucial theoretical contribution. He showed (see [3], pp. 266–9) that equilibrium under capital rationing requires the investor's subjective discount rate between two periods to be equal to the marginal rate of transformation between outputs in those two periods; that is, the discount rate must equal the ratio of the marginal yields (products) of the investor's resources in those periods. This result, as Fisher showed, is

[1] We want to express our gratitude to the National Science Foundation whose grant to our project on the dynamics of the firm permitted the completion of this paper. We must also thank Harold W. Kuhn, Burton G. Malkiel, Edward S. Pearsall and Douglas Keare for their extremely helpful comments.

simply the now commonplace requirement that in equilibrium there be tangency between the production (profit) possibility curve and an investor's indifference curve.[1]

Unfortunately, this solution, while correct, nevertheless cannot cope with a number of difficult problems:

1. The equilibrium conditions themselves give us no clue as to how an optimal capital budgeting decision can be made. If budgets are fixed and the firm has under consideration a sizeable set of investment projects the number of combinations which the company can afford, and should therefore examine, is likely to be astronomical.[2] Fisher's production possibility curve cannot even be constructed until all combinations are investigated to determine which of them are "profit efficient," meaning that they constitute the north-east boundary of the graph showing their returns in the various periods.

2. The position of Fisher's production possibility curve, which is to be used in determining the discount rate, is itself affected by the magnitude of the discount rate. Fisher recognised this point, remarking that, "Of course the [production possibility] line cannot be drawn without the aid of valuations which involve the market principles and so involve the rate of interest. . . . Thus, strictly speaking [the production possibility] line is not to be pictured as immovable like a rock, but as subject to some slight change with every change in the [discount rate]" ([3], 278–9). But it was left to Hirshleifer to show the difficulty which that causes: "The discount rate to be used for calculating present values . . . is the rate given by the slope. . . . But this rate cannot be discovered until the solution is attained, and so is of no assistance in reaching the solution" ([4], Section D). We will see later the specific form which this difficulty assumes in a programming analysis.

3. Strictly speaking, the Fisher solution applies only to interior maxima, *i.e.*, to cases where investment occurs in every period and where no type of investment is totally rejected. If, for example, there is no investment in period t the ratio of the marginal product of investment in period t to that in $t - 1$ may be less than the corresponding discount rate. Though the equilibrium condition is easily amended to take this (corner maximum) possibility into account, it gives rise to fundamental computational difficulties with which only programming calculations can cope.

[1] Here the "production possibility curve" refers to the locus relating the yields from investment in two years, t and t'. For each possible return in year t the curve shows the maximum yield which the company can obtain in the year t' from the investment opportunities which it has available to it. Thus, it is the ordinary transformation locus between yields in periods t and t'.

[2] If, for example, it is considering some twenty projects and can finance only five of them the arithmetic of permutations and combinations tells us that 15,504 investment project combinations must be examined by the investor in order to find the most profitable among them.

II. Investment Selection Models

Quite independently of the Fisher–Hirschleifer approach to the problem there has developed a parallel line of analysis, which was better adapted to the computations necessary for the selection of investment projects. This type of investigation makes no use of the production possibility locus, and begins instead on a more fundamental level with the individual candidate investment projects and their expected streams of returns. Perhaps the first analysis in this category which makes allowance for capital constraints in more than one future period was developed by one of the present authors (see [1]). However, that study employed the Lagrange multiplier methods of the differential calculus. It was therefore unable to deal with the important corner maximum problem which has already been discussed.

Soon after that paper appeared, Lorie and Savage addressed themselves to the project selection problem in a classic article [5]. They succeeded in indicating very clearly the complexities which beset optimal decision making in the area, but their proposed selection criteria were later shown to suffer from several critical defects.[1]

Since then a number of mathematical programming models have been designed for investment project selection.[2] These have proved to be extremely powerful analytic instruments. But as we shall see, their authors have left serious gaps in these structures in failing to come to grips with the discount-rate problem. Happily, as this paper will show, it is possible to determine an appropriate set of discount rates, rates which rely heavily on the shadow prices of the dual programmes. Moreover, as has so often occurred in programming studies of other subjects, the dual programme will turn out to agree with the classical theory. The Fisher analysis will be shown to come once again into its own, and the Hirschleifer paradox, too, will fall into place.

III. Programming Models for Investment Decisions

The basic approach taken by the programming models of investment project selection under capital rationing involves maximisation of an objective function expressing the discounted present value of the (positive and negative) future cash flows corresponding to any combination of investment projects selected. This maximisation is carried out under the limitations imposed by a number of constraints. At least some of them are budget constraints which represent the distribution of the monies among competing uses available during each period in which the supply of cash is expected to be limited.

[1] For a discussion, see Weingartner [6].

[2] See Charnes, Cooper and Miller [2] and Weingartner [6].

A simple form which might be assumed by a model of the sort we are discussing is the following:

Maximise

$$\Pi = \sum_{j=1}^{n} \sum_{t=0}^{h} [a_{jt}/(1+i)^t]x_j \quad . \quad . \quad . \quad . \quad . \quad . \quad (1)$$

subject to [1]

$$\sum_{j=1}^{n} b_{jt}x_j \leqslant M_t \qquad (t = 0, 1, \ldots, h)$$

$$\text{all } x_j \geqslant 0 \quad . \quad . \quad . \quad . \quad . \quad . \quad . \quad . \quad (2)$$

Here i represents the rate of interest;

a_{jt} represents the net cash flow obtained from a unit of project j during period t;

b_{jt} is the net amount of cash used up by a unit of project j during period t;

x_j is the number of units of project j constructed; and

M_t is the amount of cash made available from outside sources during t;

so that $\sum_{t=0}^{n} a_{jt}/(1+i)^t$ is the discounted present value of the earnings of project j.

It is difficult to overstate the power and flexibility of models of this type. Their versatility is easily indicated by the following illustrative situations which, as will be indicated, are readily handled as special cases of the general programming model:

1. Cases where the funds $M_0, M_1, \ldots$, invested in the various periods must eventually be repaid can easily be handled in the constraints by taking the M values on the required repayment dates to be negative. For example, if all borrowings are to be paid with interest during the horizon period, h, and if the sum to be repaid is K dollars, we need merely set $M_h = -K$ and the model will then automatically cope with the repayment requirement.

2. Some investment project, s, may involve expenditures beginning only at some future date. Thus, suppose s represents a decision today to purchase a lathe 5 periods hence. Then to adapt the model we need merely specify $b_{0s} = b_{1s} = \ldots = b_{4s} = 0$, *i.e.*, that the net outlays associated with project s during its first 5 periods are equal to zero. Thus, in this model, X_s may represent the number of lathes purchased during period 5 while $X_{s'}$ may represent the number of lathes bought during some other period.

3. If some project, k, is indivisible, so that X_k, the number of units of project k, cannot contain a fraction, we require as part of the programming analysis that the value of X_k be an integer. We then must employ

[1] Unfortunately, the literature offers no satisfactory method for selection of the horizon period, h, and this paper has nothing to contribute on the subject.

the methods of integer programming in our calculation, but the analysis is otherwise unchanged.[1]

4. Two investment projects, *a* and *b*, may be indivisible and mutually exclusive. That is, *a* and *b* may be two alternative models of a machine so that if the investor undertakes *a* he will not want *b* and vice-versa. The analysis can take care of this specification by requiring $X_a + X_b \leq 1$. For then, since both X's will be non-negative, if project *a* is adopted, so that $X_a = 1$, then necessarily $X_b = 0$, *i.e.*, project *b* must certainly be rejected.

IV. Limitations of the Preceding Model

A number of problems arise out of this formulation, and it is to these that this paper is addressed. Some of them are relatively minor and can be solved in straightforward fashion. One problem, however, involves difficulties so serious that the attempt to overcome them actually leads to a fairly basic reformulation of the simple model. One might say that the difficulties inherent in the simple model lead to the formulation of the " right " model.

First we may list several minor problems which can easily be taken care of: (1) there exists the possibility that funds may also be used for investment outside the firm or for personal consumption by the capitalist (the stockholder) and the model described in the preceding section has made no explicit allowance for these alternatives; (2) funds unused during period t can normally be retained for use during later periods and the model should provide for this possibility; (3) there is apparently some relationship between a_{tt} and b_{tt}, since whenever an investment yields a positive (or negative) cash flow it should add to (or reduce) the amount of money available during that period for use in other investments. This relationship must be discussed before we can proceed.

The M_t's are, by definition, autonomously given amounts of money which are disbursable in each period; hence the constraints are meaningful only if b_{jt} is interpreted as the net input of cash needed by project j in period t. That is, if R_{jt} and C_{jt} are defined as the total revenue generated and total cost incurred by project j in period t, $b_{jt} = C_{jt} - R_{jt}$. But the maximand is the discounted value of the net cash inflows $R_{jt} - C_{jt}$; hence [2]

$$a_{jt} = -b_{jt} \quad . \quad . \quad . \quad . \quad . \quad . \quad . \quad (3)$$

[1] This and the following cases are systematically described by Weingartner [6] who also indicates a number of special applications.

[2] Note that characteristically some of the a_{jt} will be positive and some negative, because the typical investment project will require net expenditures during some portions of its life and yield net returns during other periods. If it never involved positive net costs the project would require no financing and the corresponding programming problem—in our later formulations—will turn out to be unbounded, whereas if it never yielded positive net returns no one would be willing to undertake it. There are other cases in which the feasible region is unbounded, for example, where in each period some project yields enough returns to finance the others. The problem of boundedness of the feasible region is, however, no different from that arising in any other programming problem.

It is left as a trivial exercise for the reader to show that (3) remains valid if there are lags in the system; *e.g.*, if the revenue earned in period $t - 1$ becomes available only in period t.

V. The Discount Rate in the Programming Capital Rationing Model

The most serious difficulty of all lies in the assumption that we are given an appropriate discount rate $1/(1 + i)$. So long as the firm can lend or borrow in unlimited amounts at a fixed rate of interest, i, and provided that this is the only way in which it can acquire funds, clearly $1/(1 + i)$ is the correct discount rate. But the very nature of our model rules out these borrowing and lending possibilities. If during period t capital is in short supply and is effectively limited to the amount M_t, then, obviously, the firm cannot borrow in unlimited amounts. The firm is thereby necessarily cut off from the capital market and, as a consequence, from any external discounting criteria.

The manner in which the literature has dealt with the determination of the discount rate for such a model must be considered casual and unsatisfactory. Three of the most prominent authors in the area, Lorie and Savage and Weingartner, simply state that future earnings are discounted " . . . at the company's cost of capital." These authors are, of course, well aware that the cost of capital is an ill-defined concept which has been the subject of a great deal of controversy in the literature. Moreover, such definitions of the cost of capital as have been proposed have all been based on various market related phenomena, such as interest rates, prices at which the company can sell additional shares, etc., all of which are irrelevant for our pure capital rationing model. Thus Weingartner states that: " The choice of the appropriate rate by which future flows are to be discounted is not our primary concern. As mentioned, Lorie and Savage take this to be the cost of capital, although how this concept is to be measured is not discussed by them, and will not be discussed by us " ([6], p. 8, footnote). Clearly, this fails to meet the issue. Still less satisfactory is the statement by Miller, Charnes and Cooper that in their model future earnings are simply added together without discounting, for as they indicate, " This assumption can be interpreted as implying that an ' adequate ' allotment of funds has been granted to the manager . . . " ([2], footnote 5), and indeed, it implies that the company has no other use for money (including even the purchase of government securities as a means of earning interest). But if this is so, the money constraints in the model cannot inhibit company operations, and they must be totally irrelevant for the analysis.

An alternative approach which was once employed by one of the present authors (see [1]) uses at least part of Fisher's approach and argues that in the absence of any external discounting criterion the appropriate discount rate must be determined subjectively by the decision maker in a manner which is consistent with his utility function. Although there is no logical objection to this method of resolution, care must be exercised in employing it for two reasons: (1) since no way of determining the appropriate utility function has been suggested, the proposed method of resolution may not be operational; (2) if utility is what the decision maker seeks to maximise, then the objective function will normally not take the same form as (1). Rather the objective function must be the (unspecified) utility function $U = f(x_1, \ldots, x_n)$. Since this is equivalent to abandoning the present value approach, one ought to be convinced that the latter method cannot make a contribution here. Eventually we shall see that we are driven to a compromise which utilises both explicit discount rates and subjective utilities and which is fully consistent with Fisher's solution.

VI. Dual Values and Implicit Discount Rates

We shall now develop a preliminary pure discount rate model. However, it will turn out that this model runs foul of Hirschleifer's problem—the difficulty of determining a discount rate when that rate is needed to construct the very model which will be used in its calculation. Our preliminary model will therefore turn out badly, but in an instructive manner which leads to a more satisfactory solution. We therefore ask for the reader's indulgence as we describe our first construct.

To determine the nature of the appropriate discount rate we must look back to the basic rationale of the discounting process. Suppose we are given either S_0 dollars at present or S_1 dollars one period hence. *If* we are indifferent between S_0 and S_1 and if $S_0 = kS_1$, then k is defined as the discount rate. In our model when will such an indifference relationship be satisfied? The present value of S_0 is the present value of the stream of earnings which it makes possible. But if the firm has available an additional dollar in period zero (if units are sufficiently small) this will add $d\Pi/dM_0$ to the capitalised present value of its earnings stream, and so the contribution of S_0 dollars must be approximately $S_0 d\Pi/dM_0$. Similarly, the present value of having S_1 dollars available one period from now is $S_1 \dfrac{d\Pi}{dM_1}$.

Since indifference between S_0 and S_1 requires that these two expressions be equal, we have

$$S_0 d\Pi/dM_0 = S_1 d\Pi/dM_1$$

or

$$S_0 = \left(\frac{d\Pi}{dM_1} \Big/ \frac{d\Pi}{dM_0}\right) S_1 \quad . \quad . \quad . \quad . \quad (4)$$

Therefore the expression in parentheses is the (marginal) discount rate, *i.e.*, it is the rate corresponding to the opportunity cost of postponement of receipt of a "*small*" amount of money. Now it is well known that $d\Pi/dM_t$ is equal to the dual price corresponding to the tth constraint, *i.e.*, to the value of the tth variable in the problem which is the dual of our linear programme. Let us designate this value by ρ_t, so that (4) becomes $S_0 = (\rho_1/\rho_0)S_1$.

By a similar argument, it can be shown that a sum S_t in period t will have the same value (during period $t - 1$) as a sum S_{t-1} available during the previous period if

$$S_{t-1} = (\rho_t/\rho_{t-1})S_t.$$

Thus, writing D_t for the corresponding (one period) discount rate, we have $D_t = \rho_t/\rho_{t-1}$, and then the present value of S_t (discounting for all t periods up to the present) is

$$S_0 = D_0 D_1 \ldots D_t S_t = (\rho_t/\rho_0)S_t.$$

This suggests immediately that the correct form of the objective function in our problem is not (1), but is rather

$$\Pi = \sum_{j=1}^{n} \sum_{t=0}^{h} (a_{jt}\rho_t/\rho_0)x_j = (1/\rho_0)\Sigma\Sigma a_{jt}\rho_t x_j \quad . \quad . \quad (5)$$

Several peculiarities of this objective function and the corresponding discount rate can be observed immediately.

(*a*) The discount rate ρ_t/ρ_0 is independent of monetary phenomena outside the firm, as it must be in this model. It is, however, not a subjective discount rate, that is, it is an entirely objective discount rate representing the opportunity cost of postponed receipts, *i.e.*, the marginal profit or loss incurred by postponing the receipt of money to some future date.

(*b*) Unlike the usual situation, there is nothing in the model as specified so far to preclude $(\rho_t/\rho_0) > 1$, *i.e.*, one cannot rule out a case in which money in the future is *more* valuable than money to-day. This odd characteristic arises out of the fact that our initial model does not permit the transfer of any funds from one period to another. Hence money during period t may have a scarcity value considerably higher than money during some earlier period. However, it will be shown later that if money can be saved from one period to the next, then for any t we must have $\rho_t \leq \rho_{t-1}$, so that discount rates must, as we normally expect, take on values below unity. The reason saving restores this normal property of the discount rate is, of course, that if we were to have, say, $(\rho_{t+1}/\rho_t) > 1$, then it would pay to transfer money from period t to period $t + 1$ until the discount rate was depressed below unity by raising the marginal productivity of money in $t + 1$ and reducing its marginal yield in period t.[1]

(*c*) A final peculiarity of our objective function is that it cannot even be formulated until the dual problem has been solved. Since, however, the dual cannot be solved (or even specified) unless the primal problem is known,

[1] A special problem arises if some of the coefficients of the period t constraint are non-positive, so that it might be possible to withdraw all funds from period t without reducing the value of ρ_{t+1}/ρ_t below unity. Otherwise such a corner maximum is precluded because if all money is withdrawn from period t we must necessarily have $x_1 = x_2 = \ldots = x_n = 0$, in accord with the tth period constraint $\Sigma b_{jt}x_j < M_t$.

it would appear that some sort of simultaneous solution is required. We shall see presently that matters are even more difficult than this seems to suggest. Nevertheless, we may note in economic terms why the problem arises at all. The trouble simply is that in the circumstances under consideration we cannot determine a discount rate until we can calculate a marginal profit opportunity cost of postponement; but we cannot calculate profit until we have obtained our discount rate.

VII. The Dual Problem

To summarise, we may now rewrite the primal problem as follows:

Maximise
$$\frac{1}{\rho_0}\sum_j\sum_t a_{jt}p_t x_j$$
subject to
$$-\sum_j a_{jt}x_j \leq M_t \qquad t = 0,1, \ldots, h$$
$$x_j \geqq 0$$

Unfortunately, as we shall now see, this reformulated model collapses in our hands. The typical constraint of the corresponding dual problem is

$$-\sum_t a_{jt}p_t \geqq \frac{1}{\rho_0}\sum_t a_{jt}p_t$$

that is,

$$\left(-1 - \frac{1}{\rho_0}\right)\sum_t a_{jt}p_t \geqq 0$$

Since the dual variables are also constrained to be non-negative, this implies

$$\sum_t a_{jt}p_t \leqslant 0 \text{ for all } j$$

Because this means that the coefficients of x_j in the primal objective function must also all be non-positive, it follows that the primal objective function has an upper bound of zero which is in fact attained when $x_1 = \ldots = x_n = 0$. But even this trivial optimal solution turns out to be illusory, for it implies by virtue of the requirement that we minimise the dual objective function, $\sum_t M_t p_t$, where $M_t > 0$, that $\rho_0 = \ldots = \rho_t = 0$. Since ρ_0 is in the denominator of the primal objective function, that objective function is indeterminate and, in fact, no optimum exists!

What has gone wrong? It seems that our carefully laid plans to provide a genuine internal discount rate have gone seriously astray. The trouble is that there is nothing in the model to prevent the marginal contribution of an extra dollar of spendable resources in the zeroth period (ρ_0) from being arbitrarily close to zero; since discount rates are ratios of ρ's they may become indefinitely large. It seems then that we have reached an impasse: if there is capital rationing and external rates of interest are irrelevant we cannot simultaneously insist on a present value formulation of the objective function and have the relevant discount rates determined internally by our problem.[1]

Fortunately this does not mean that the capital budgeting problem cannot be formulated in a meaningful manner. This will be the task of the remaining section.

VIII. A Utility Formulation and the Dual Discount Rate

In order to arrive at a more satisfactory formulation we have to return to an argument employing a utility function. The reason for this is that for the model to possess any rationale it must yield some sort of gain to the investor. He then must be taken to wish ultimately to maximise—in some sense—his ability to consume, that is, to maximise the stream of purchasing power provided by his bundle of investments. But maximisation of ability to consume directly requires us to use a utility approach as a means for evaluating the stream of earnings.

Assume for simplicity that utility is linear in money.[2] The entrepreneur plans to withdraw in the tth period ($t = 0, \ldots, h$) a sum W_t to be used for consumption.[3] In order to maximise the value to the entrepreneur of withdrawing W_0 in the zeroth period, W_1 in the next period, etc., we

maximise $$\sum_t U_t W_t$$

subject to $$-\sum_j a_{jt} x_j + W_t \leq M_t$$

$$x_j \geq 0$$

$$W_t \geq 0$$

where U_t is the (fixed) utility of a dollar in period t. This is now an ordinary linear programming problem and has the dual[4]

minimise $$\sum_t p_t M_t$$

subject to $$-\sum_t a_{jt} p_t \geq 0$$

$$p_t \geq U_t$$

This shows almost immediately that our intuition was not entirely wrong in suggesting the formulation discussed in the previous sections. For consider

[1] This conclusion is, of course, closely related to Hirshleifer's observation which was cited above.

[2] The argument could have been made to appear far more esoteric and profound by dealing with non-linear utility functions, bringing in concave programming, the Kuhn–Tucker theorem and all the associated paraphernalia. However, as a later footnote shows, this would have added nothing to the argument.

[3] Consumption is here defined in a very broad sense; thus W_p, the withdrawal in the last period, may represent the inheritance he will leave his heirs.

[4] If instead of the linear utility function we had employed the more general (concave) function $U = f(W_0, W_1, \ldots, W_h)$ the Kuhn–Tucker conditions would make the last set of constraints in the dual problem $p_t \geqslant \partial f / \partial W_t$ which has the same economic implications as the linear model. See *e.g.*, Wolfe [5].

an optimal solution and assume that W_t and $W_{t'}$ are positive in the optimal solution. Then by the duality theorems we have

$$\rho_t = U_t$$

$$\rho_{t'} = U_{t'}$$

so that

$$\frac{U_t}{U_{t'}} = \frac{\rho_t}{\rho_{t'}} \quad \ldots\ldots\ldots \quad (6)$$

Equation (6) states that the marginal rate of substitution between withdrawals in the two periods equals the discount rate at the optimum if funds are withdrawn during both period t and period t'. On the other hand, suppose money is not withdrawn during t but it is withdrawn during t'. In that case (6) becomes

$$\frac{U_t}{U_{t'}} \leq \frac{\rho_t}{\rho_{t'}}$$

Thus the relative subjective discount (valuation) rate for period t, $U_t/U_{t'}$, must be no greater than what we might call the production opportunity discount ratio, $\rho_t/\rho_{t'}$, *i.e.*, the rate of exchange permitted by the available investment opportunities. That is exactly what Irving Fisher's analysis would have led us to expect. It is precisely in such circumstances that it does not pay to make withdrawals during t.[1] The marriage between Fisher's analysis of the discount rate under capital rationing and the programming approach is thus complete.

The reader may feel that the discounted present value of withdrawals approach which has been employed in our last model is a rather special case and that many alternative objective functions may sometimes be more relevant. However, a little thought indicates that our objective function is really of remarkably wide applicability. For example, if instead of regular withdrawals management is interested only in the terminal (horizon) value of its investment, W_h, we need merely adjust our discount coefficients to reflect this goal. We do this by setting $U_0 = U_1 = \ldots = U_{h-1} = 0$ and $U_h = 1$ (or some other positive constant). Similarly, if the entrepreneur desires to maximise the value of the firm's earned net income, our objective function can continue to serve. For we have, by straightforward subtraction,[2] $W_t = M_t + \sum_j a_{jt}x_j$, so that our objective function can be rewritten as

$$\sum_t U_t W_t = \sum_t U_t(M_t + \sum_j a_{jt}x_j)$$

But the discounted present value of the firm's net income is clearly $\sum_t \sum_j U_t a_{jt} x_j$,

[1] The distinction between the subjective and the production opportunity discount rate throws some light on the reason for the breakdown of our preliminary model of Section IV. Only at the optimal point should these two marginal rates be equal.

[2] If $U_t > 0$ then the constraint $\sum - a_{jt}x_t + W_t \leq M_t$ must always be satisfied as an equation in an optimal solution. For then the withdrawal of any unused cash must always increase the investor's total utility.

which differs only by the constant amount $\sum U_t M_t$ from the discounted present value of withdrawals, $\sum U_t W_t$.

IX. The Carry Over of Funds

As a final extension of our model we can amend it slightly to show how one can handle the more plausible case where funds can be carried over from one period to the next. Let the amount carried from period t to $t + 1$ be denoted by C_t. Then C_t may be interpreted as the slack variable [1] for the period t constraint and our problem becomes [2]

$$\begin{array}{ll} \text{maximise} & \sum U_t W_t \\ \text{subject to} & -\Sigma a_{jt} x_j + W_t + C_t - C_{t-1} \leq M_t \\ & x_j \geq 0 \\ & W_t \geq 0 \\ & C_t \geq 0 \end{array}$$

with the additional requirement that $C_0 = 0$.

It is now easy to show, as was asserted earlier, that with carry over permitted, every discount rate ρ_t/ρ_0 must be no greater than unity. To prove this we need merely formulate our dual problem:

$$\begin{array}{ll} \text{minimise} & \sum \rho_t M_t \\ \text{subject to} & -\sum a_{jt}\rho_t \geq 0 \\ & \rho_t \geq U_t \\ & \rho_0 - \rho_1 \geq 0 \\ & \rho_1 - \rho_2 \geq 0 \\ & \vdots \\ & \rho_{t-1} - \rho_t \geq 0 \\ & \rho_t \geq 0 \end{array}$$

The last constraints show at once that the discount rates, ρ_t/ρ_0, will all necessarily be less than (or equal to) unity as was asserted.

X. Conclusions

We have constructed a model for the capital rationing case which, while it makes use of a subjective utility index, for the first time also provides an

[1] The reader will doubtless have observed the peculiarly incestuous flavour of our models, with dual prices appearing in primal objective functions consisting of linear sums of the coefficients of the constraints, and slack variables being carried over to subsequent constraints.

[2] Though we have written our structural constraints as inequalities they must again necessarily hold as equations in an optimal solution because it will never pay to leave money unused. So long as the utility of money is positive in the current period or any future period, any funds otherwise unused will be withdrawn at once or held for future use or future withdrawal.

objective measure of the discount rate. We have thus made the distinction between a subjective discount rate U_t/U_0 and the objective internal production opportunity rate ρ_t/ρ_0, which is the ratio of the dual prices corresponding to the budget constraints for periods t and 0. The entire construct seems to accord fully with what economic analysis has told us about the subject and brings together the programming and the indifference curve approaches to the problem. It is also cast in a form which is usable directly in the computations required for optimal investment project selections.

The analysis may be of wider applicability than at first appears to be the case. As was indicated toward the beginning of this paper, government agencies, company divisions and a variety of other organisations operate on fixed budgets set for them by others. For such groups the choice of discount rate for investment project selection is a very real and a very practical problem toward whose solution this analysis may perhaps provide some contribution.

WILLIAM J. BAUMOL
RICHARD E. QUANDT

Princeton University.

REFERENCES

[1] Baumol, W. J. " Income Effect, Substitution Effect, Ricardo Effect," in Helen Makower and W. J. Baumol, " The Analogy Between Producer and Consumer Equilibrium Analysis," *Economica*, N.S. Vol. XVII, February 1950.

[2] Charnes, A., W. W. Cooper and M. H. Miller, " Application of Linear Programming to Financial Budgeting and the Costing of Funds," *Journal of Business*, Vol. XXXII, January 1959, reproduced in Ezra Solomon, editor, *The Management of Corporate Capital* (Glencoe, Ill.: The Free Press, 1959).

[3] Fisher, Irving, *The Theory of Interest* (New York: Macmillan, 1930). (Reprinted by Augustus M. Kelley, New York, 1961.)

[4] Hirshleifer, J., " On the Theory of Optimal Investment Decision," *Journal of Political Economy*, August 1958, reproduced in Ezra Solomon, *op. cit.*

[5] Lorie, J. H., and L. J. Savage, " Three Problems in Rationing Capital," *Journal of Business*, Vol. XXVIII, October 1955, reproduced in Ezra Solomon, *op. cit.*

[6] Weingartner, H. Martin, *Mathematical Programming and the Analysis of Capital Budgeting Problems* (Englewood Cliffs: Prentice-Hall, 1963).

[7] Wolfe, Philip, "A Duality Theorem for Nonlinear Programming," *Quarterly of Applied Mathematics*, Vol. XIX, No. 3, 1961.

[28]
THE
QUARTERLY JOURNAL
OF ECONOMICS

Vol. LXXXI November, 1967 No. 4

THE FIRM'S OPTIMAL DEBT-EQUITY COMBINATION AND THE COST OF CAPITAL *

William J. Baumol and Burton G. Malkiel

I. The Problem

To the management of most corporations the selection of a ratio of debt to equity in the firm's capital structure and the decision between retention of earnings or the issue of some type of security as a means of raising additional funds are matters of high corporate policy. But, by and large, the literature seems to have offered little formal analysis that would shed light on *optimal* decisionmaking in these matters. In fact, the already classic contribution of Modigliani and Miller [1] deals primarily with a simplified world in which the authors are able to show that the financing decision makes absolutely no difference at all — where one combination of means of financing is just as good for the company as any other so that *any* decision is necessarily optimal! Of course, these authors are careful to point out that considerations such as the differential tax

* This paper was completed at the Princeton University Financial Research Center. The authors wish to thank Nevins D. Baxter, Merton H. Miller and Ezra Solomon for extremely helpful comments. They are also grateful to the National Science Foundation and the Ford Foundation whose grants greatly facilitated our study.

1. Franco Modigliani and Merton H. Miller, "The Cost of Capital, Corporation Finance, and the Theory of Investment," *American Economic Review*, XLVIII (June 1958), 261–97.

treatment of the earnings associated with different sources of finance require us to modify their results, but they give little systematic guidance on the application of their analysis to optimal financial policy.

This paper undertakes to provide a model that at least offers an approach to an optimality analysis. In this construct transactions costs and risk will turn out to play important roles just as they do in the theory of money, where, without them, it is difficult to see why anyone would want to hold any money at all. In addition, corporation and personal income taxes will be integrated explicitly into the analysis. It will be seen that the Modigliani-Miller result is an artifact (albeit a highly instructive one) of their frictionless world, in which we should never be surprised to encounter behavior about as peculiar as the permanent flight of a ball that is thrown in a frictionless physical universe. It should be made clear, however, that this paper is not intended in any way to be critical of Modigliani and Miller (henceforward M and M). On the contrary, it will rely very heavily on their pathbreaking work.

In addition to its attempt to provide a formal optimality analysis this paper undertakes several other tasks. It describes exactly what is involved in the Modigliani-Miller "homemade leverage" process, which the individual investor utilizes to provide for himself whatever degree of risk he wishes to undertake when investing in a company. We show exactly what the investor must buy or sell to achieve any specified degree of leverage and the extent to which specific institutional obstacles impede this process. We describe also how the formal analysis of corporation finance fits in with the standard value theory of economic analysis and, in the process, reconcile some apparent inconsistencies between the two, particularly in the definition and measurement of the "cost of capital."

II. Cost of Capital: Whose Opportunity Cost?

Before turning to the main burden of our discussion, it seems appropriate to consider briefly some questions that might be raised about the foundations of much of the analytic work in the area, the contents of this article included. The financing decision is very closely dependent on the opportunity cost of funds derived from various sources. But once opportunity cost enters the matter, one must decide whose opportunity should concern us. The obvious answer, and, that ordinarily accepted without question, is "the stockholders'," on the usual assumption that the corporation is or should be run primarily for the well-being of those who hold its shares. Even if one agrees with this answer it must be recognized that it is not without its problems. The body of stockholders is a heterogeneous group composed of persons pursuing different financial strategies, in different tax brackets, and with different alternative investment opportunities open to them. It follows that the opportunity cost of a given decision to stockholder A is not necessarily the same as that imposed on B and a very real aggregation problem is therefore implicit in the concept of stockholder opportunity cost.

In addition, one should not reject out of hand the unorthodox view that the stockholders' ownership of the company is something of a legal fiction. It can be argued that the firm raises money more effectively by differentiating its securities just as it may sell its output better by differentiating its final product. On that interpretation the stockholder is, in a sense, a lender who prefers a gamble greater than that offered to him by a bond, and he is in reality no more an owner of the firm than is the holder of a debenture.

Such a position would lead one to conclude that while the stockholder's interests do enter into what may be considered the objectives of the firm, the company's goals also encompass an inseparable compound of the interests of the managerial group, perhaps the employees and even the general public welfare. For example, company gifts to universities or to orchestras or hospitals are not always just a matter of public relations and sometimes reflect management's notions of its public responsibilities, quite apart from any stockholder interests. It may even be that a management's view of the compensation of the stockholder is not very different from its attitude toward its obligation to the bondholder. It may feel that the owners of stocks should simply receive an "adequate" return on their investments — something more akin to "satisficing" than to maximization of stockholder returns. Stockholders would then be expected to receive a normal rate of return on their investment, including a payment for risk, a compensation a bit like the interest payment on a bond but a little higher, on the average, and a little less certain.

III. A Few Formal Relationships

Having raised some basic questions about analytic framework we shall proceed to ignore them in what follows. In order to get on with the substance of the analysis we will assume throughout that the goal of the firm is maximization of the wealth of its stockholders. We begin by providing a few simple and fairly well-known relationships that will prove useful in the discussion that follows. By definition, earnings per dollar of equity are given by

(1) $i = (X - rD)/S$

where

i = earnings (after interest payments) per dollar of equity
X = total company earnings before deduction of interest payments
S = total equity at current market value
D = total debt at current market value and
r = the effective rate of interest payments on company debt (D).

Given the prospective earnings of the firm and the riskiness of its operations, then, according to M and M the market values D and S, its debt and equity, will satisfy the relationship

(2) $S + D = V$ (constant).

The surprising feature of this proposition is its implication that the market value of the firm, $S + D$, is totally independent of the firm's capital structure — the ratio between its debt and equity. No matter whether the company's indebtedness is heavy or light, given the expected value and the other moments of its anticipated earnings stream, $S + D$ will remain equal to V. The reason this is so in their analysis is that if a company's leverage, its debt/equity ratio, D/S, is not at the level desired by some particular stockholder, he can utilize a process which M and M call "homemade leverage" to rearrange his own holdings in a way that achieves for him exactly the financial returns that would flow from his preferred value of D/S. Suppose for simplicity that the individual holds some stocks and some bonds in our company and that he wishes the company would increase its leverage (increase its expected return per share even though this increases his risk). He can achieve the same effect by selling some of his bonds and using the money to purchase more of the company's stocks, thus increasing his expected overall rate of return as well as its variance. Even after he has sold all of his bonds he can increase the leverage of his personal portfolio further by borrowing money (in effect selling his personal bond) and using it to purchase still more stock. In this way he can offset completely any leverage decision by the company management. As a result, to each and every stockholder, any financial structure for the company will be just as good as any other and so equation (2) must hold regardless of the ratio between D and S. Even if substantial leverage is desired by most investors, levered companies cannot command a premium in the market, as was held by traditional financial analysts, because "homemade leverage" is a perfect substitute for company leverage.

It is moderately easy to prove rigorously the assertions of the last few paragraphs and to show precisely what steps the individual must undertake to achieve any specific degree of leverage he desires. For this purpose we must conduct a conceptual experiment in which our firm considers several alternative leverage ratio decisions and their consequences, all other things remaining equal. For purposes of exposition it is a little easier to do this by considering two companies, i and k, whose respective amounts of debt and equity outstanding are D_i, S_i, D_k and S_k and which are in all other respects identical. Suppose our investor would have been content to invest the P dollars of his principal in the stock of his ideal company, i. This would earn for him $P(X - rD_i)/S_i$. But, in the absence of taxes, transactions costs and differences in the lending and borrowing rates that apply to himself and the company, he could (with a total investment outlay for the moment unspecified) earn exactly the same total amount by investing in company k, purchasing

$$(3) \qquad PS_k/S_i$$

dollars of its stocks and

$$(4) \qquad P(D_k - D_i)/S_i$$

of its bonds, for the total earnings of this combination are

$$(5) \qquad \frac{PS_k}{S_i}\,\frac{(X - rD_k)}{S_k} + \frac{rP}{S_i}(D_k - D_i) \equiv \frac{P(X - rD_i)}{S_i},$$

i.e., they are identical with the earnings obtainable by investing P dollars in ideal company i. Notice that this result is completely independent of the value of X—both sets of securities will yield exactly the same returns whether the two companies' earnings are high or low. Hence, *no matter how risk is defined*, the two purchases must be identical *both in risk and expected earnings*. Our individual has been able to duplicate for himself, in company k, the leverage of his ideal company i.

This result also leads at once to the M and M theorem that, in equilibrium the market value of a company is totally unaffected by its leverage arrangements: $S + D = V$ (equation (2) above). Since our two investment alternatives yield exactly the same returns it follows that they must have the same market value for otherwise money would flow from the more expensive to the cheaper alternative until the two prices were brought into line. Hence the P dollar investment in company i must equal the dollar value of the equivalent stock and bond investment in company k as given by equations (3) and (4), so that we must have

(6) $$P = PS_k/S_i + P(D_k - D_i)/S_i.$$

Thus, $S_i = S_k + D_k - D_i$, i.e., $S_i + D_i = S_k + D_k$ — whatever the difference in their leverage the market values of the two companies must be equal.[2]

Let us see next how transactions costs, which have so far been assumed to be zero, affect the M and M results. First, we note that their presence is likely to lead to a violation of equation (2) — the proposition that $S + D$, the market value of the firm, is unaffected by the degree of the firm's leverage. For if homemade leverage does involve a net addition to transactions costs, then the purchases of company k's stocks and bonds specified in (3) and (4) would return less than P dollars of company i's stocks, the difference being equal to the amount of the transactions costs. Hence our individual would be indifferent between the two sets of securities only if the specified set of company k securities cost him less than the company i stocks, i.e., if equation (6) were replaced by the inequality

$$P > PS_k/S_i + P(D_k - D_i)/S_i.$$

In such circumstances it follows that if many security purchasers held similar views about the degrees of leverage adopted by the two companies, then we must have $S_i + D_i > S_k + D_k$, i.e., the value of company i will exceed that of k.

IV. A Diagrammatic Approach to Cost of Capital

To examine further the effects of transactions costs it becomes convenient to utilize a graphic procedure including an indifference

2. We can employ relationships (3) and (4) to make up an illustrative homemaker's guide. The table below assumes that the company has a 20 per cent debt/equity ratio and that \$100 is to be invested by an individual so that $P = 100$, $D_k = 20$ and $S_k = 80$. The reader may verify that the table shows the amounts of personal debt and stockholdings that will enable the individual to produce some alternative degrees of leverage he may desire.

Homemade Leverage Guide: Company with 20 Per Cent Debt/Equity Ratio

Desired Proportion of Debt	Value of Individual Stock Purchases ($100\ S_k/S_i$)	Value of Individual Bond Purchases ($100\ (D_k - D_i)/S_i$)
0	\$ 80	\$ 20
0.2	100	0
0.4	133	− 33*
0.6	200	−100*

* Net borrowing

curve representation of investor attitudes on risk and expected earnings.

In Figure I let CC' represent the opportunity locus or transformation curve giving the combinations of expected earnings on equity and safety levels corresponding to different leverage

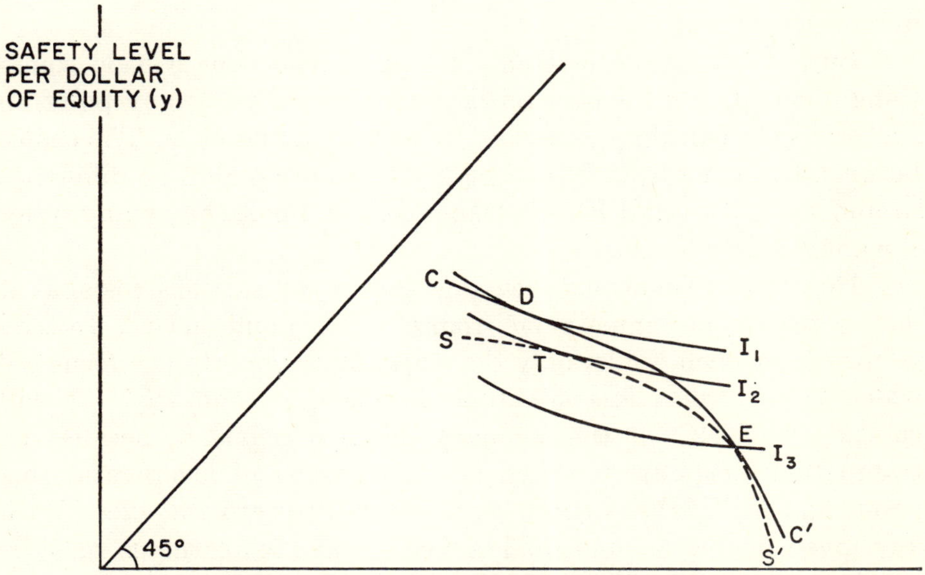

FIGURE I

ratios. On the horizontal axis we measure expected earnings per dollar of equity and on the vertical axis we have some sort of index of "safety" — a magnitude that varies inversely with some measure of risk, however selected.[3]

3. The construction of an opportunity locus using concrete numbers is illustrated below in Appendix A. The equation for the opportunity locus is $y = f(\bar{\imath})$, where y represents safety level and $\bar{\imath}$ represents expected earnings. The definition of safety level is not obvious and a number of alternatives are possible. Among the more intuitively attractive are a measure which takes the safety level to be some fixed number of standard deviations below expected earnings:

$$y_1 = \bar{\imath} - k\sigma.$$

Alternatively, we may assume that there is some plausible range of earnings such that earnings outside this range are so improbable that they can be neglected. Let $i_{min} = X_{min} - rD$ be the lower bound of this range. Then a second possible definition of safety level is

$$y_2 = X_{min} - rD.$$

It is shown in Appendix B that, under fairly attractive but oversimple assumptions, either of the preceding definitions of safety level requires the company opportunity locus CC' to be linear. That is, its equation $y = f(\bar{\imath})$ will be linear. Nevertheless, for reasons which will be given presently, the facts of the matter seem to suggest that CC' will normally have a shape similar to that shown in Figure I. The reader will see later that this shape makes

Now from the point of view of the stockholder the optimal financial arrangement is given by the point of tangency, D, between one of his indifference curves,[4] I_1, and the opportunity locus CC'. Suppose instead that management decides on the leverage ratio corresponding to some other point, say E. In that case, if the investor can do nothing about it, he will simply end up on a lower indifference curve I_3.

But, if homemade leverage is free, the investor can do something about it. On his own initiative he can move to any point on CC' and so he can simply proceed to his optimal point D. The choice between financing by debt and equity therefore makes no difference to him and all capital has the same cost as far as he or any other stockholder is concerned.

However, if homemade leverage incurs transactions costs, as it does in reality, he cannot move from E to any point on CC'. Instead he may have open to him only the stockholder opportunity locus SS' which is somewhat less advantageous to him than CC'. It will coincide with CC' at the company decision point, E, because no transactions costs are incurred in homemaking of leverage at this point, and will perhaps curve more sharply toward the axes. With any given degree of homemade leverage, his net earnings may be less than if the company itself had chosen that leverage ratio, since the stockholder's expected stream of net earnings will be reduced by a stream of payments equal in present value to his transactions-cost outlay. We will see later that in practice the relative shapes of SS' and CC' are not exactly as they are shown here, but for our present discussion that does not matter. What is important here is that the investor will end up at a second-best point of tangency, point T on SS'. This will get him onto an indifference curve I_2, better than that through the company decision point E but not so good as that at the optimum point D.

We see then that, once transactions costs enter, the financial structure of the company is not irrelevant to the stockholder, and from his point of view there is an optimal point, D, because any other point must land him on a lower indifference curve.

little difference to the discussion in this and the immediately following sections though it will prove very important at a later point, where its significance will be indicated explicitly.

It will be noted that the opportunity loci lie entirely below and to the right of a 45 degree line through the origin because y, the safety level, will always be lower than the expected earnings, the value of the abscissa, except if there is no risk, in which case they will both be equal.

4. For the moment we ignore the complications introduced by differences in the indifference maps of the various stockholders. We will see later that their consequences are not so serious as they appear to be at this point.

V. Transactions Costs and Taxes in Practice

We will now try to specify the transactions expenses and other costs involved in homemade leverage in real capital markets.[5] We will first discuss matters in general terms and after examining specific illustrations in which the numbers are chosen to be representative of those encountered in practice, we will show how the geometry of the analysis can be used to determine the optimal financial structure.

First consider the case where the company's leverage is lower than that desired by the investor (he wishes to move toward the right in Figure I). To increase his earnings and his risk, the investor must simultaneously purchase stocks and borrow money. Normally he will do this by buying stocks on margin. His brokerage costs will be greater than would otherwise have been the case simply because he must purchase a larger volume of securities than he would if the firm had provided the degree of leverage he desired. In addition, our investor must pay the interest on his loan, the real interest rate being significantly higher than that which is normally paid by the corporation.[6] Once the individual has taken full ad-

5. In a long-run comparative statics analysis it is not legitimate to include the readjustment costs of current stockholders who are induced to change their portfolios when the company varies the composition of its funds. In our analysis we must consider different company leverage ratios as alternative long-run choices, and the transactions cost incurred in the homemade leverage process must be that of the investor who is switching his holdings from cash to securities, given whatever leverage ratio happens to have been selected by the firm. It should also be noted that we are not the first to introduce taxes and transactions costs into a discussion of financial decision-making. For example, John Lintner has previously examined the effects of transactions costs and taxes on optimal financial policy in a somewhat different context. See his "Dividends, Earnings, Leverage, Stock Prices and the Supply of Capital to Corporations," *Review of Economics and Statistics*, XLIV (Aug. 1962), 243–69.

6. Here we must be careful in comparing the two rates of interest — the individual borrower's liability is unlimited, unlike that of the corporation. This means that, all other things being equal, the individual borrower undertakes a greater risk than does the corporate debtor. Hence, even if the two nominal borrowing rates were equal, the individual's real cost of borrowing would be the higher. Since the individual's nominal borrowing rate is normally above that of the firm, this suggests that the true disparity is even greater.

Merton Miller has suggested to us that the difference between individual and corporate borrowing rates does not seem quite so arbitrary a phenomenon when one recognizes that it is closely tied up with the kinds of economies of scale that give rise to the corporation in the first place. Empirical evidence on the transactions costs associated with corporate borrowing indicates that such costs, expressed as a per cent of the amount borrowed, decline with the size of the issue. See *Costs of Flotation of Corporate Securities, 1951–1955* (Washington: U.S. Government Printing Office, June 1957). This suggests that a large part of the transactions charges associated with the borrowings of corporations and individuals is of the fixed-cost variety. The lower average transactions costs for the corporation may largely be explained by the ob-

vantage of the margin permitted him by law he can borrow from other sources, but, since he cannot legally use his stocks as security for the loan, his borrowing rate is now likely to rise substantially. All of this means that if the stockholder wishes to move toward the right of the company's decision point (point E in Figure I), as he must do if he wishes to increase the leverage in his holdings (higher expected earnings but a lower safety level), he will find a difference between his opportunity locus SS' and the company locus CC', and the distance between them will normally increase considerably the further one gets from E. For some (e.g., institutional) investors whose borrowing for this purpose is limited by law or tradition, the individual opportunity loci SS' may simply fall vertically, at least after a point, i.e., there will for them be an absolute limit to the extent to which they can increase the leverage of their holdings via the homemade leverage process.

Consider next what happens if the investor feels the company's stock is overlevered, i.e., he wishes to move to the left of the company decisions point E. Now he will find (again neglecting tax considerations for the moment) that *homemade leverage imposes on him virtually no added transactions costs.* The investor simply purchases a combination of stocks and bonds rather than stocks alone, and, since this does not affect the total volume of his security purchases, he can do it with little change in brokerage cost. Indeed, the transactions charges for dealing in bonds are often slightly smaller than those applicable to common stocks. Moreover, the cost of this process is not changed by the extent to which he uses it because when he lends, the relevant rate of interest will not vary with the magnitude of his bond purchases — unlike the case where he borrows to increase leverage, when the rate of interest is likely to go up with the volume of his borrowing. Thus, to the left of the company decision point, E, the company locus CC' and the individual locus SS' will correspond for a stretch. The investor who buys a combination of stocks and bonds can receive precisely his pro rata share of the interest payments and earnings made by the corporation, and the brokerage cost in purchasing a bond is not materially different from that on a stock. This is made more precise in the discussion of our numerical example in Appendix B.

Thus the individual opportunity locus takes the general form

servation that the fixed costs for a single new borrowing of \$10 million are less than the sum of the fixed costs incurred by a thousand individuals each borrowing \$10 thousand. One would have to turn to legal and conventional constraints on financial institutions, however, to explain why "arbitraging" operations are not conducted by levered investment trusts that presumably could borrow on the same terms as corporations.

shown by SS' in Figure II. We note also that the individual locus extends leftward for a considerable stretch SC beyond the end of the company locus. This additional segment of the individual locus in-

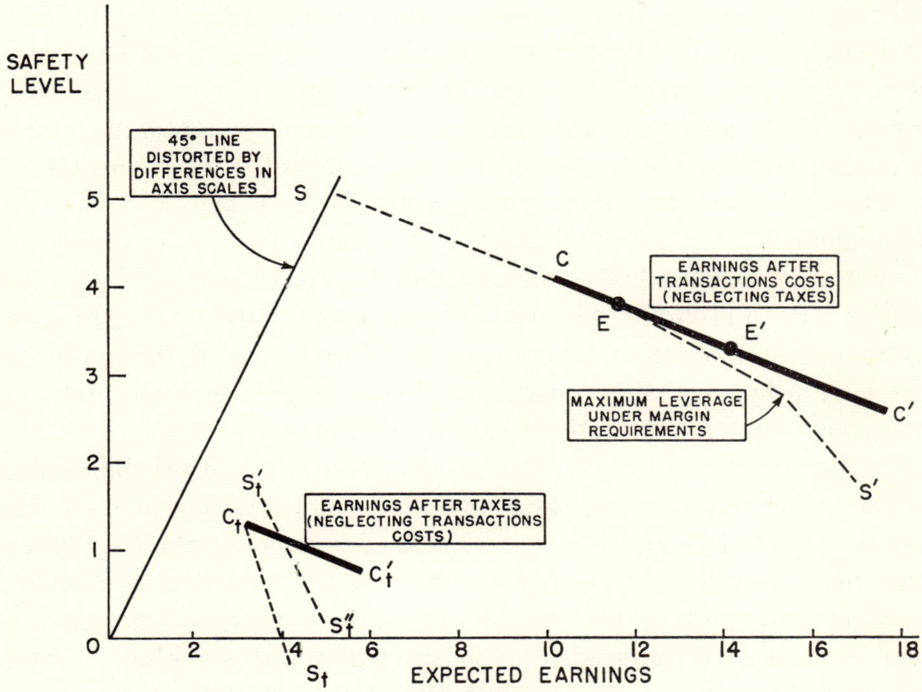

FIGURE II

volves what might be considered homemade negative leverage — a proportion of bonds in the individual portfolio so great that its safety is greater than that which would be provided by an unlevered equity stream, i.e., by company stocks in the case where the company's debt was zero (point C). The left-hand end, point S, of the individual's opportunity locus corresponds to a portfolio consisting exclusively of bonds.

Next we consider the role of taxes and the fact that interest payments, unlike dividends, are not subject to the corporate income tax. The first effect of corporate income taxes is to reduce proportionately both the expected earnings and the safety level of the shareholder.[7] More important, the difference in tax treatment of debt and equity will tend to increase substantially the divergence

7. This is so because the safety level itself is a potential level of corporate income — one that is relatively low and so it is also reduced in proportion to the tax rate. Of course, if the safety level corresponded to corporate earnings less than $25,000 per year, or if it involved a loss, a lower tax rate (or even a rebate) would apply to the safety level and the conclusion in the text would have to be modified.

between the company opportunity locus CC' and the stockholder opportunity locus SS', because the stockholder is not able through the homemade leverage process to duplicate the tax advantages available to the corporation. This is so because the corporation, by shifting from equity to debt, can actually increase the total amount of interest plus dividend payments that can be distributed to its security holders. It is as if the company provided by itself each dollar of dividend payments made, but received a matching grant from the government of one dollar for each dollar of interest distributed. In fact (as is shown in Appendixes A and B), this tax arrangement can cause the two opportunity loci to intersect as they do in the lower left-hand corner of Figure II (curves $C_tC'_t$ and $S'_tS''_t$). The individual who wants little leverage may actually gain by investing in a highly levered company that obtains the maximal tax advantage, and then purchasing bonds in sufficient quantity to undo the leverage to whatever extent he desires.[8]

One other related observation completes our a priori discussion of the influences affecting the shape of the opportunity loci. If the firm is subject to a rising marginal cost of borrowing, the CC' curve may begin to fall more steeply at its lower end (it will curve downward toward the right) [9] and the degree of divergence between the two loci may be reduced (since the individual stockholder who wishes to increase leverage for himself may be able to escape some of the rising interest costs that the company must pay). Moreover, the introduction of a risk concept more general than the "safety level," that has been used here for illustrative purposes only, would provide additional reasons to expect that the company opportunity locus would be nonlinear. For example, consider the inclusion of the risk of insolvency. Even if insolvency did not lead to the ulti-

8. The tax advantage of capital gains can produce an offsetting divergence between the individual and the company opportunity locus. The individual who unlevers his holdings, in effect, accepts a contract to receive part of his payments in the form of interest on which he must pay his marginal personal income tax rate, and none of which will be plowed back to receive favorable tax treatment at the lower capital gains rate. On the other hand, the individual who buys stocks on margin can receive part of his income in favorably taxed capital gains and can deduct the interest he pays on his personal debt at ordinary marginal income tax rates. For individuals to whom this can make a very significant difference, then, the relation between individual and company opportunity loci may be a bit closer to that shown in Figure I. However, it should be recognized that some very large security holders are nonprofit institutions — foundations, universities, etc. Capital gains clearly offer them no tax advantage.

9. If the cost of borrowing rises far enough, the lower end of the CC' curve may even begin to bend backwards — further borrowing will not only increase risk — it will also reduce the expected earnings per dollar of equity. This will occur if r exceeds $\overline{X}/(S+D)$.

mate ruin of the stockholders through the liquidation of the assets of the company at forced-sale prices, it entails, at least, a costly reorganization and disruptive effects on company operations that would impair the expected earnings stream. It is reasonable to suppose that, after a maximal "safe level" of debt has been reached, perceived risk increases sharply with any increase in leverage.

VI. A Few Comments on the Opportunity Loci

It should be made clear to the reader that the curves in Figure II have not been drawn in an arbitrary manner. Rather, as shown in Appendix A, they have been based on rather careful calculations intended to constitute realistic numerical examples. Thus, the curves *CC′* and *SS′* which take into account transactions costs but not taxes, are based on the following assumptions whose empirical basis is described in the Appendix: That there is a 1 per cent commission on the purchase of stocks and a ¾ per cent commission on the purchase of bonds, and that an individual can borrow on margin at a rate of 5½ per cent while the corporation's borrowing rate is 5 per cent. Similarly, the lower curves in the figure are based on a 50 per cent corporate tax rate and on the premise that the stock purchaser is in the 50 per cent marginal tax bracket so that his capital gains are taxed at 25 per cent.

The striking conclusion demonstrated by the graph is that, even in the absence of transactions costs, homemade leverage is not an effective substitute for company leverage. Despite the fact that we have allowed for a tax advantage to the individual who buys common shares (some of the return is taxed at preferential capital gains rates), the individual cannot homemake the same menu of returns and safety levels that firms can produce by alternative leverage ratios. In the lower portion of Figure II, we can see clearly the asymmetric effects that result when an individual rolls his own leverage and unmakes company leverage. If the company chooses a levered capital structure, the individual who desires no leverage is actually better off than he would be buying unlevered common shares directly — the relevant portion of the individual opportunity locus $S'_t S''_t$ actually lies well above the company locus. Only when the individual makes more leverage than the company has chosen, is he in a worse position than he would be if he bought common shares in a company that had itself made use of the desired amount of debt in its capital structure.[1]

1. This suggests that in practice (in contrast with a pure M and M world) the dividend payout ratio is not irrelevant to the stockholder. For

It can also be shown that the shape of the curves shown in Figure II is not a fortuitous matter of the numbers chosen in our calculation. As is demonstrated in Appendix B, these curves will all have the general characteristics displayed in the diagrams since they share the following properties (see Figure III).

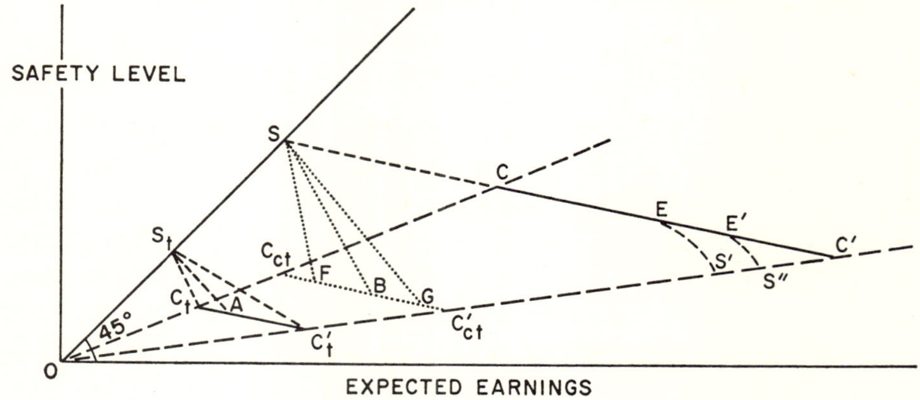

FIGURE III

(a) Corporate profits and individual income taxes at a fixed rate will reduce both earnings and safety levels (on equity) proportionately. Consequently, the relation between the before-tax and after-tax company opportunity loci, CC' and $C_tC'_t$, is that points C and C_t will lie on one straight line through the origin and points C' and C'_t will lie on another such a line, with $OC/OC_t = OC'/OC'_t$, i.e., the slopes of the company loci before and after taxes will be the same.

(b) The portions of the individual opportunity loci to the left of the company decision points (see, for example, SE, S_tC_t, S_tA and $S_tC'_t$) are necessarily linear. For what is involved is the reallocation of a fixed amount of investor money between bonds and stocks at prices which are not affected by the individual's purchase decisions.

(c) If we were to consider only the corporation income tax, then the company opportunity locus would shift toward the origin by an amount proportionate to the corporate tax, as shown by $C_{ct}C'_{ct}$. If we were to assume further that interest on bonds is certain (riskless), then *all* of the individual opportunity loci would have to start from the same point, S, a point on the 45 degree line given by $y = \bar{\imath} = r$. (See, for example, SF, SB and SG.) This is the same point from

example, if the degree of leverage that currently characterizes the firm is below the optimal level, then stockholders would be better off if dividends were increased and, instead, more debt were used to finance the company's investment plans.

which the no-tax opportunity locus, SE, also starts. For S is the point of minimal stockholder risk — the point where all of his fixed stock of investment dollars is spent on bonds, whose returns are not subject to the corporate income tax. With a given bond price, a given amount of money will purchase a fixed number of bonds and a fixed expected return.[2] And, since it is assumed to be completely certain, this expected return is also the minimum return (the safety level) and, hence, S must lie on the 45 degree line.

(d) If we take into account the personal income tax, the after-tax S point will be moved downward along the 45 degree line because interest income is reduced by the income tax. This is shown by the position of point S_t in Figure III which lies much closer to the origin than point S corresponding to a zero personal tax rate.[3]

All of these general properties of our opportunity loci play some role in the discussion that follows.

VII. Characteristics of an Optimal Financial Structure

We can now discuss the implications of our analysis for the nature of the firm's optimal financial decision. It will be recalled that if we ignore taxes, the company and individual opportunity loci will be as shown in the upper part of Figure III. This suggests that it will be advantageous to stockholders for the company to move as far to the right on CC' (to borrow as much) as is consistent with prudence and legal and institutional limitations.[4] For, consider the zero tax case, for simplicity, and suppose E is the company's decision point whereas some investor would prefer E'. Homemade leverage will not permit him to reach this point because his opportunity locus $SCES'$ lies well below it. Suppose next that positions are reversed: that the stockholder wants to get to E but the company decision point is E'. Any individual opportunity locus must go through the company's decision point since the stockholder always has the option of holding a portfolio consisting exclusively of company stocks. Hence, with the company decision point moved

2. When general equilibrium considerations are taken into account, the S point after corporate taxes will, in fact, be lower than the pretax S point because, when the corporation income tax reduces the effective return on stocks throughout the economy, one would expect a transfer of funds out of stocks and into bonds and so the market rate of interest on bonds would fall.

3. The unchanged slopes of the company opportunity loci are, of course, a result of the assumption of constant tax rates. Were we, for example, to allow personal tax rates to vary with the income and safety level produced by the company, then the slope of $C_tC'_t$ would not necessarily remain the same.

4. A similar conclusion is reached by Solomon. See Ezra Solomon, *The Theory of Financial Management* (New York: Columbia University Press, 1963), p. 103.

to E' the individual opportunity locus must shift to $SCE'S''$, which it will be observed, enables the stockholder to arrange to get back to E if he wishes. As we have seen (lower curves in Figure III) tax considerations may well make these relationships even stronger. A highly levered company may as a result offer both higher earnings and greater safety even to the investor who desires little or no leverage in his personal portfolio.

It follows that, for such a company, failure to finance enough of its investment by borrowing may indeed cause a reduction in its market value. Particularly institutional investors, whose holdings of risky high-return securities is severely circumscribed by law, may bid up the shares of more highly levered companies relative to those of our firm so that, for the two companies, the ratio between earnings and $S + D$ will no longer be equal.

Yet, there are limits of prudence to company borrowing: When borrowing reaches a point where insolvency becomes a real possibility, the self-interest of management as well as the interests of the stockholders may restrain the firm from going further in this direction.[5] Probably a more tangible and much more immediate consideration in practice is the customary limit to the amount which sources of debt capital permit the firm to borrow. If, for example, banks refuse to lend to companies who have issued too many bonds, the company may wish to stop well before the rightmost point on the company locus that this permits them, in order to leave open the possibility of short-term borrowing in case of unforeseen contingencies.

We are now in a position to be far more specific and indicate exactly how an optimal financial structure can be determined in a wide variety of cases. Even if there were no institutional impediments circumscribing the borrowing of the firm, the risk incurred by excessive company debt would still limit the amount of debt which the firm should undertake in an optimal financial arrangement. In Figure IV the company opportunity locus, CC', is shown to curl downward as it approaches point C'. For as the firm increases its borrowings (moves toward the right) its risk of insolvency and the interest rate on its loans will rise and will ultimately rise sharply. Thus, earnings will be lower and risk greater than they would be under the assumptions that call for a linear company opportunity locus.

5. See Solomon, *op. cit.*, p. 117. In "Leverage, Risk of Ruin and Cost of Capital," forthcoming in the *Journal of Finance*, Nevins D. Baxter has considered in detail the experiences of several bankrupt corporations, thereby illustrating the heavy costs to the firm of undergoing bankruptcy proceedings.

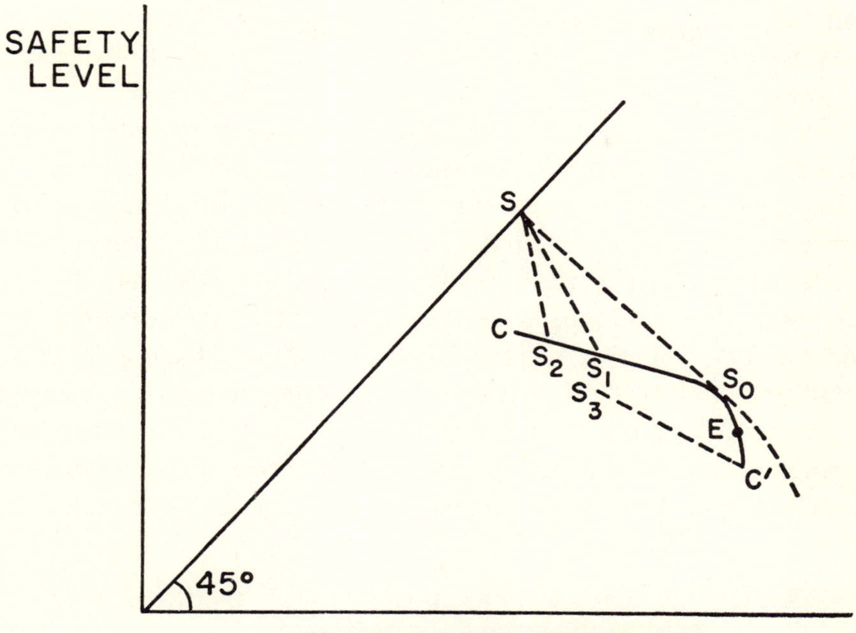

FIGURE IV

Now consider the linear segments such as SS_0, SS_1, and SS_2 of the various individual opportunity loci corresponding to the different decision points (S_0, S_1, S_2, etc.), the segments lying to the left of these decision points. These are the line segments connecting the various points on CC' with a fixed point[6] S on the 45 degree line where S lies above and to the left of CC'. Hence it is to be expected that one of these, SS_0, will be a segment of a line tangent to CC'. Point S_0, the point of tangency, will for a considerable portion of its stockholders normally represent the company's optimal financial structure. For SS'_0 will then be the highest opportunity locus available to any individual investor who does not have so strong a desire to speculate that he wishes to be at a point to the right of S_0. Thus, only from point S_0 can any such stockholder reach his highest attainable indifference curve. This conclusion then has the remarkable property that it may be *independent of the shape and position of most stockholders' indifference curves*. This is so because any other

6. Strictly speaking, S will not be fixed for company decision points lying sufficiently far to the right. When company debt grows sufficiently great, the rate of return on debt can no longer be considered riskless. Hence a given number of bonds might now offer a lower expected return and certainly a lower minimal return. Thus, for example, the individual opportunity locus through point C' might look like S_3C' which lies entirely below the company locus. However, this observation does not appear to affect the conclusions of the text.

company decision offers poorer opportunities (higher risks and lower earnings) to *all* stockholders who do not wish to bear extremely great risks.

In fact, it is possible that in a wide variety of cases point S_0 will be optimal for all potential stockholders — including those who prefer even greater leverage. For as Figure II indicates, in practice, transactions costs at first only cause a very gradual displacement from linearity of the *individual* opportunity locus. On the other hand, once the firm exceeds conventional standards of prudent leverage, the *company* opportunity locus may curve sharply downward because normal debt sources will be unwilling to provide additional debt to the firm. In that case the individual locus (SS_0 and its rightward extension in Figure IV) would not lie below the company curve CC' at any point.[7]

VIII. The Real Marginal Cost of Debt and Equity

The preceding materials have immediate implications about the cost of various sources of capital from the point of view of our stockholder.

To get at the *cost* of an increment in company funds we must avoid any confusion that would result if one were to introduce into the discussion the revenues that will be produced by the investment financed with these moneys. In Figure V we therefore show what would happen to the company opportunity locus $C_1C'_1$ if it were to raise some additional funds and simply keep them idle. That is, the figure takes into account only the costs of these additional funds and abstracts from any yield they may subsequently produce.

Suppose first that the firm were initially at its all equity point C_1 (with a high safety level and relatively low expected earnings) and that it increased its capital by the raising of new equity. Since we are deliberately ignoring any revenues that could be obtained with the aid of these funds, the added equity must cause a reduction in the expected earnings per dollar of equity (along BC_1) because earnings must now be spread over a larger amount of equity. Some change [8] in the safety level (C_2B) is also likely to result, so that we

7. Still, it is conceivable, even in such a case, that a "nonoptimal" locus will for some interval lie above the "optimal" locus (SS_0 extended) at the extreme right of the diagram, and in such a case, SS_0 extended might not be preferred by all investors.

8. The increase in equity will certainly reduce both i and σ by (9) and (10) (Appendix B) so that it may or may not change safety level, $i - k\sigma$. On the other hand, if we define the safety level as $(X_{min} - rD)/S$ (see fn. 3,

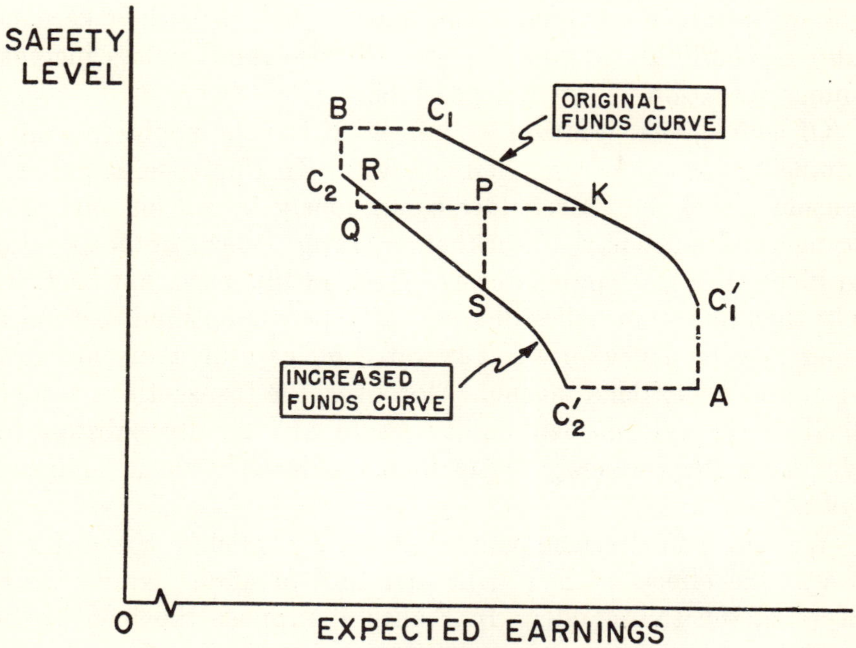

FIGURE V

will be brought to some new point such as C_2. Similarly, were we to start out from a highly levered position, C'_1, and just issue new bonds, this would reduce the safety level and reduce earnings per share (after the increased interest payments) and so it would land us at a point such as C'_2. There would then be some curve $C_2C'_2$ that connects these extreme points and represents the locus opportunities corresponding to different debt-to-equity ratios in the additional funds.

The difference between retained earnings and a new stock issue as means for increasing equity can readily be described in terms of our diagram. Consider, for example, the case of a company whose shareholders have no need to consume the income from their holdings. The flotation of securities usually involves very heavy transactions costs which would be escaped by retention.[9] Since these transactions costs can be translated into an equivalent stream of payments, they are tantamount to a long-term reduction in earnings. Hence the CC' curve corresponding to a new issue of stock will, other things being equal, lie below and to the left of the curve

p. 553), the increase in S holding D constant must certainly reduce the safety level.

9. In addition many of these shareholders are in high marginal tax brackets and therefore receive after-tax dividend returns far smaller than the actual number of dollars paid. This provides an additional reason for them to prefer having new equity capital raised through retained earnings. Retention allows them to realize their returns through favorably taxed capital gains.

involving retained earnings. This means that in such a case new equity is simply an uneconomic way to raise funds unless increased earnings retention is just not possible.

Of course, the situation is changed if the shareholders want to consume the income from their holdings. In this case, a policy of retention forces the shareholder continuously to sell off part of his holdings and so it is the stockholder, rather than the corporation, who incurs the transactions costs. Even in this case, however, it is likely that retention will still frequently be the optimal method for raising new equity capital. Tax rates on capital gains are lower than those on dividend income. Moreover, the transactions costs involved in the sale of new equity issues are usually substantially larger than the brokerage costs involved in the sale of shares by small stockholders.[1]

We can also describe somewhat more explicitly the difference between the effects of new debt and that of added equity on the welfare of the shareholder. In Figure V suppose the firm's initial financial position had corresponded to point K. If it were now to increase its debt, this would reduce expected earnings by some amount KP, and it would also reduce the safety level by an amount PS, thus moving us to a point S on the lower opportunity locus $C_2C'_2$. The *nominal* incremental cost of the added debt is simply KP, the amount of interest required by the funds in question, which causes a corresponding reduction in expected equity earnings. But we see that the *real* marginal cost of the debt is greater than KP since the indifference curve through the debt point, S, will lie below the indifference curve through the nominal-debt-cost point, P.

Similarly, if from K the company were to move to $C_2C'_2$ with the help of new equity, expected earnings per dollar of equity would be decreased by some larger amount, KQ, than it would with the issue of debt. But because the leverage ratio would thereby be reduced, the variance of earnings per share would fall (see equation (9) Appendix B) and there might even be an increase in safety level,[2] QR, so that the real marginal cost of equity would then be lower than its nominal amount, QK.

An analogous distinction between real and nominal costs applies

1. For new security issues over $1 million in size, total transactions costs for equities registered with the Securities and Exchange Commission, as a percentage of proceeds, have been between 4.66 per cent and 13.58 per cent, depending on the size of the issue. See *Costs of Flotation of Corporate Securities, 1951–1955, op. cit.* Unless the shareholder literally sells off his shares one at a time, it is therefore unlikely that his percentage brokerage charges will exceed corporate transactions costs.

2. See footnote 8, p. 564.

with equal force to other outlays by the firm, though its revelance seems to have been overlooked in the bulk of value theory. A three-year contract with a labor union, which specifies a minimum number of persons to be employed, is a commitment perfectly analogous with that imposed by a three-year bond. Compare this with the noncontractual purchase of a raw material whose quantity is settled transaction by transaction. Clearly, the former exposes the stockholder to far greater risk than does the latter. From the point of view of the stockholder it is no more legitimate to add the number of dollars tied up in the labor contract to the number of dollars spent on raw materials than it is to add the nominal cost of debt and equity. The outlay on labor also incurs a cost of commitment that increases its real cost over its nominal value, and this may be just as pertinent in a production decision as it is for the choice of capital structure.

IX. A Measure of the Cost of Capital

We may now develop an explicit measure of cost of capital and see the effect of homemade leverage upon its magnitude. In Figure VI we add three stockholder indifference curves to our previous diagram. The first, I_1, is tangent to the old opportunity locus at initial point K, which for simplicity is assumed to have been optimal. The second indifference curve is that tangent to the new lower op-

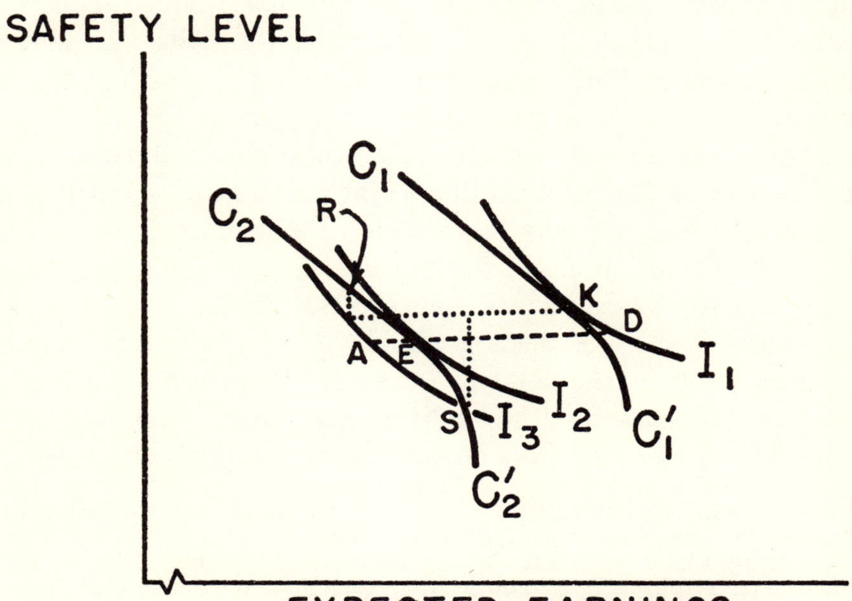

Figure VI

portunity locus, with optimal point E. Finally, the third indifference curve is that through point S, the increased debt point.

Let us define as an index of the marginal cost of capital the increase in expected earnings per dollar of equity necessary to get the stockholder back to his initial level of satisfaction after the change in financing. Again, for the moment, assume taxes and transactions costs to be zero. Let us (in analogy with the Fisher-Hirshleifer construct [3]) consider the investor to undergo a two-step adjustment process. First the added debt moves him from K to S. Then he may use homemade leverage to move himself along $C_2C'_2$ to his optimal point E. If he does so, it is clear that from point E an annual cash payment equivalent to an increase in expected earnings ED will move him back to his initial level of utility. This, then, is the incremental cost of debt capital to him. However, had homemade leverage or even a partial adjustment been ruled out for any reason, so that he would have been forced to remain at point S, then he would have been on a lower indifference curve and the real incremental cost of capital (the compensating variation in earnings) would have been the larger amount, AD.[4]

It is easy to see that had we drawn another indifference curve through point R (the new equity point), then we could have produced a precisely analogous representation of the marginal cost of equity both with and without homemade leverage. With no transactions costs and taxes it is clear that the stockholder can get to optimal point E just as easily from R as he can from S. Thus with homemade leverage his cost of equity would also be ED, and we have the M and M result: with homemade leverage costless, the real marginal costs of debt and equity are always equal.

Figure VII now shows the effects of taxes and transactions costs. If the new financial decision point is P on $C_2C'_2$ and P is not the optimal point, S'_0, the stockholder opportunity locus will be $S_1S'_1$, which lies below $C_2C'_2$ to the right of point P. Again, taking the investor to undergo a two-step process, having been moved to point P, the best adjustment available to him involves a further move along $S_1S'_1$ to the point of tangency, R, with his indifference curve I_1. This is a second-best adjustment which leaves him better off than he was at P, but does not get him to his optimal indifference

3. See Jack Hirshleifer, "On the Theory of Optimal Investment Decision," *Journal of Political Economy*, LXVI (Aug. 1958).

4. Clearly this measure suffers from the same ambiguities as the measures of consumers' surplus. The compensating variation, the horizontal distance between two indifference curves, varies with the height at which this distance is measured. See J. R. Hicks, *Value and Capital*, (New York: Oxford University Press, 1939), Chap. 2, Appendix.

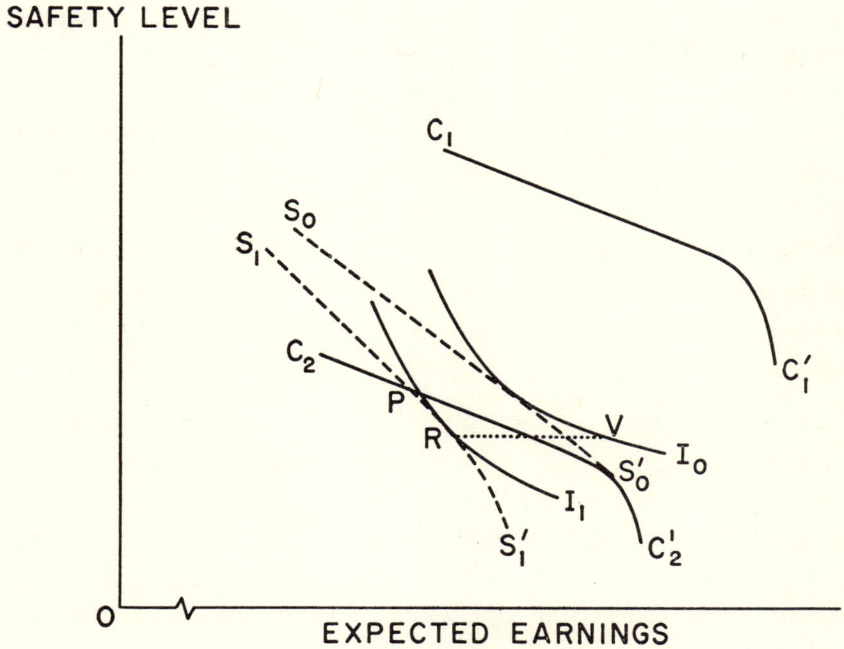

FIGURE VII

level, I_0, the level he could attain if the company were to make an optimal financial choice (point S'_0) from which opportunity locus $S_0S'_0$ becomes available to the stockholder. Thus there is an added real cost to the acquisition of capital by a nonoptimal method as compared with the zero-tax, zero-transaction-cost case, a cost which may be represented by distance RV. Note that, since the magnitude of RV varies with the location of point P, the marginal real costs of debt and equity need no longer be equal.[5]

X. Capital as a Weighted Average

Our analysis can perhaps help to clear up a point which, as it now stands in the literature, appears to constitute a cleavage between the logic of financial theory and ordinary economic analysis. In standard economic theory, when a *homogeneous* resource can be obtained from any of several different sources, the real cost of that resource is always taken to be the price charged by its cheapest supplier. For there is no motivation for the purchaser of that item

5. If we were to plot a graph representing RV plus an appropriate constant K, as a function of the leverage ratio, D/S, we would have a curve showing how the *total* cost of capital varies with the debt/equity ratio. For if K were chosen to be the cost of capital at the optimal debt/equity ratio (however defined), $K + RV$ would represent that cost at nonoptimal points because RV is by definition the excess of the cost of capital at any arbitrarily chosen point P over the cost at the optimal point.

even to consider any other source since it would be irrational for him to buy any of this item from anyone else.

But in the theory of corporation finance there is a standard proposition which would appear to conflict with that result. It states that the cost of capital is a weighted *average* of the costs of capital from the alternative sources available. Indeed, this result follows directly from equation (11) (Appendix B) once we accept the M and M argument that $\bar{X}/V$ is the cost of capital.[6] For we then have, solving (11) for the value of $\bar{X}/V$,

$$\bar{X}/V = (\bar{\imath}S + rD)/(S + D). \quad (7)$$

Since r is the rate of interest on debt, and $\bar{\imath}$ is the corresponding rate of return on equity, $\bar{X}/V$ is clearly the average of the two, weighted respectively by the values of debt and equity.

However, the two propositions refer to different matters and there is therefore no real conflict. The point is that both r and $\bar{\imath}$ are only *nominal* costs and constitute neither the real cost of debt nor that of equity. This is most obvious in the case of r, the interest rate on debt, which as we have seen, understates the true cost of debt because it makes no allowance for the leverage risk incurred by additional borrowing. Similarly, $\bar{\imath}$ fails to take into account the risk reduction that results from the decreased leverage ratio when there is a *ceteris paribus* increase in the amount of equity. Thus (7) is merely a computational device that permits us to translate the nominal costs of funds into their real magnitude. Whether in the presence of taxes and transactions costs this calculation still provides a valid approximation to the true cost of capital is a matter that requires further investigation.

So much for the nominal costs of debt and equity. It remains for us to see that their real costs accord with the standard economic proposition that one borrows only from the cheapest sources. As M and M show, when both debt and equity are employed their real marginal costs are *both* given by $\bar{X}/V$. Thus, when both sources are utilized neither has a lower real marginal cost, just as standard economic analysis requires. But we have seen that, because of taxes and transactions costs, the marginal cost of *new* shares may, in practice, be greater than $\bar{X}/V$. In such a situation new equity is more expensive than added debt or retained earnings and it will not pay to issue additional shares. Our optimal solution will then be a corner solution in which the amount of funds derived from the

6. See Modigliani and Miller, *op. cit.*, Sec. IIA.

issue of new stocks is zero, and the marginal cost of new shares will not affect the real marginal cost of capital to the firm.

XI. Conclusion

The main purpose of this article has been to show that there is no basic conflict between the conclusions that emerge from the new theory of corporation finance and much of what one observes in company behavior, and that these two in turn are consistent with the precepts of received economic theory. It has been shown that in practice there *is* an optimal capital structure for the firm, and that its existence really follows from the logic of the M and M analysis supplemented only by a few simple institutional observations.[7] In general, the tax advantages of bond financing and the near zero transactions costs incurred in *un*doing leverage make it desirable for the firm to employ as much debt as is consistent with considerations of financial prudence. It turns out that, despite differences in preferences, the financial decision toward which this result points will, in fact, be preferable for wide classes of stockholders. The prescriptions for optimal financial policy that emerge seem to be consistent with general company practice, where capital structure is considered a matter that requires highly careful decisionmaking and where management seems characteristically to turn to the issue of new stocks only as a last resort when all other reasonable sources of funds have been utilized.

Appendix A. Some Reasonably Realistic Opportunity Loci

In discussions of relatively abstract concepts such as the company and the individual opportunity loci, it is useful to determine with some care the shapes they are likely to assume in practice. Only in that way can one hope to evaluate the importance of the

7. There is, however, one unfortunate consequence of the softening of some of the more paradoxical M and M conclusions. It means that it may be even more difficult than has been thought to test empirically the relative merits of the M and M analysis as against the more traditional views on the consequences of different degrees of leverage for the value of a company's securities. For it follows from our discussion that even in an M and M world, but one in which transactions costs are present, a curve representing the value of $S + D$ as a function of the leverage ratio D/S is likely to have a maximum point rather than being a horizontal line as it would be in a pure M and M model. Thus the predictions of the M and M analysis and of the traditional approach are not easily distinguished in statistical terms. Empirical testing would require some sort of a priori specification of the degree of curvature in the $S + D$ functions predicted by the alternative models, and since we really know very little about the shapes of the curved portions of the opportunity loci this may well be a very formidable task.

various elements that enter the analysis, and to avoid being misled by curves whose shape is determined by an arbitrary drawing process. As a matter of fact, the theoretical discussion of this paper was heavily influenced by the numerical calculations described in this appendix.

In our example, we employ the following assumptions: that X/V, the capitalization (discounting) rate for unlevered streams in companies like ours, equals 10 per cent; that r, the interest rate on borrowing, is 5 per cent; that $\overline{X}$, the expected value of future earnings for our company, is $1,000 per year; and that $X_{\min}$, the lower bound to anticipated future earnings, is $400 per year. Table I describes the relevant company transformation schedule, i.e., it tabulates the various earnings rates and safety levels which the company can manufacture by altering its debt/equity ratio.

We note first that the entries in columns 1 and 2 for each row sum to $10,000. This reflects M and M's Proposition One, which states that, given the vector of expected earnings for the company, the debt/equity ratio (i.e., the manner in which earnings are packaged for distribution) cannot affect the total value of the company. Columns 3 and 4 calculate the expected earnings per dollar of equity ($\bar{i}_c$) and safety level (y_c) via (1) and the expressions for y given in footnote 3, p. 553. As noted earlier, the company opportunity locus drawn on these assumptions is linear.

TABLE I

Company Transformation Schedule

(1) Company Debt Outstanding (D_c)	(2) Value of Company's Equity (S_c)	(3) Expected Earnings per Dollar of Equity ($\bar{i}_c$) $\bar{i}_c = \frac{\overline{X} - r_c D_c}{S_c}$	(4) Safety Level (y) $y_c = \frac{X_{\min} - r_c D_c}{S_c}$
0	$10,000	10.0%	4.0%
$2,000	8,000	11.3	3.8
3,000	7,000	12.1	3.6
4,000	6,000	13.3	3.3
6,000	4,000	17.5	2.5

1. *The Effect of Transactions Costs*

We now introduce transactions costs into the analysis. We employ three additional assumptions: (1) the investor pays a brokerage commission of 1 per cent of the dollar value of all equities purchased.[1] (2) Brokerage charges of ¾ of 1 per cent must be paid on the market value of all bonds purchased.[2] (3) Individuals

1. One per cent represents the standard brokerage charge per round lot for a stock selling at $40 per share.

2. The standard brokerage charge per $1000 bond is $2.50. Moreover, a typical spread in the over-the-counter market between bid and asked prices is approximately $5.00 per bond. The total transactions cost is taken to be

can borrow on margin accounts at 5½ per cent while corporations can borrow at 5 per cent.[3]

Table II presents the relevant transformation schedules after transactions costs. In Columns 2 and 3 the company transformation schedule from Table I has been adjusted to reflect our assumption that each individual who buys common shares must pay a 1 per cent brokerage charge. Consequently, the entries in Table II are 1 per cent lower than the corresponding entries in Table I. In Columns 4 and 5 the individual's transformation schedule is presented. It has been calculated with the aid of relationship (5) on the basis of the three assumptions just given. It assumes that the company has chosen a debt/equity ratio of three to seven and that the stockholder holds his securities for one year.[4]

Turning to an examination of the table itself, we note that the first three rows of Table II show that the company and individual transformation schedules are identical. Homemade leverage is a perfect substitute for company leverage. Without additional transaction costs, the individual is always able to undo any leverage that the company has produced. As we move to more levered positions, however, the individual and company transformations schedules begin to diverge. This is so because of the greater total transactions

the sum of the brokerage cost plus the bid — asked spread, \$7.50 per \$1000 bond or ¾ of 1 per cent.

3. These figures are representative of the actual bond yields and interest costs charged margin traders during January 1966.

4. Two illustrations will clarify the calculation procedure: Assume first that the investor wishes to have the equivalent of a pure equity portfolio (row 1 of Table II) and, consequently, to undo the company's leverage he buys \$70 of common stock and \$30 of bonds (1 per cent of the stocks and bonds of the company). He will receive the following dollar return,

$$\$70/\$7{,}000\ [\$1{,}000 - .05(\$3{,}000)] + \$30/\$3{,}000\ [.05(\$3{,}000)] = \$10.00.$$

His total cost will be \$70.00 + \$0.70 (the appropriate brokerage charge applicable to the common shares) plus \$30.00 + \$0.225 (the relevant brokerage cost for the bonds) or \$100.925. His overall rate of return will equal

$$\$10.00/\$100.925 = 0.099.$$

Our second illustration will treat a more complicated case. Assume the investor desires a $D/(D + S)$ ratio of 0.6 (row 6) and has funds $P = \$70$. Using relationships (3) and (4) we find that if the investor purchases \$122.50 of common while borrowing \$52.50, he will have "homemade" the appropriate degree of leverage. We may write his dollar return from his equity holdings as:

$$\$122.50/\$7{,}000\ [\$1{,}000 - .05(\$3{,}000)] = \$14.875.$$

From this we must subtract the investor's interest cost. Under a 70 per cent margin requirement, he is permitted to borrow only \$30 at the assumed 5½ per cent rate for brokers' loans. We assume that the additional borrowing of \$22.50 can be undertaken only at a 6½ per cent penalty rate, bringing the investor's total interest obligation to \$3.1125. Thus, the investor's total dollar return is \$11.7625. The last step of the calculation requires that we find the investor's equity commitment (plus transactions costs) so that we may compute his return on investment. The investor puts up \$70.000 + \$1.225, the brokerage cost required to buy \$122.50 of equity. His return on investment is, therefore,

$$\$11.7625/\$71.225 = 0.165.$$

If the securities were held for a longer period the brokerage and other transactions costs per annum would, clearly, be correspondingly lower. Nevertheless, since the difference in interest cost for personal and corporate borrowing (the major impediment to arbitrage) does continue each year, the choice of a one-year horizon does not have a very great effect on our results.

costs undertaken when the individual buys a larger quantity of stock and because the interest rate on personal borrowing is assumed to exceed the rate on corporate borrowing. After the maximum leverage has been obtained (see row 5) the curve diverges more sharply since it is assumed that additional borrowing can only be undertaken at a 6½ per cent penalty rate. These relationships are illustrated in Figure II where the numerical data of Table II are plotted as the company locus CC' and the individual locus SS' (the upper curves).

TABLE II

COMPANY AND INDIVIDUAL TRANSFORMATION SCHEDULES AFTER TRANSACTIONS COSTS

$D/D+S$ Ratio	Company Transformation Schedule (Less 1 per cent transactions cost)		Individual Transformation Schedule (If company chooses $D/D+S$ = 0.3)	
	$\bar{i}_c$	y_c	$\bar{i}_p$	y_p
0	9.9%	3.96%	9.9%	3.96%
0.2	11.2	3.71	11.2	3.71
0.3	12.0	3.54	12.0	3.54
0.4	13.2	3.27	13.1	3.21
			14.8*	2.71*
0.6	17.3	2.48	16.5	1.77

* point of maximum leverage under 70 per cent margin requirements.

2. *The Role of Taxes*

We now introduce corporate and personal income taxes into the previous example. We continue to assume that the expected value of future company earnings is 10 per cent of the funds provided the company by the stock and bondholders and that the safety level is 4 per cent. In the presence of corporate income taxes the returns to the shareholders become

$$(8) \qquad \bar{i} = (\bar{X} - rD)(1 - t_c) / S$$

where t_c, the corporate tax rate for our calculations will be assumed to be 50 per cent, roughly the present rate.

Next we allow for the effects of personal income taxes. For the sake of illustration, we assume that the stockholders receive half their income as dividends and the other half as capital gains. Income from dividends and bond interest will be taxed at a constant rate t_p, assumed to be 50 per cent, and capital gains at a rate ½ t_p. These assumptions represent roughly the present investment environment for an individual in the 50 per cent marginal tax bracket. Experience over twenty-five years of market history indicates that investors in common shares have received more than half of their return in the form of preferentially taxed capital gains.[5] The present

5. See J. Lorie and L. Fischer, "Rates of Return on Investments in Common Stocks," *Journal of Business*, XXXVII (Jan. 1964), 1–17.

tax rate on capital gains is one half that on regular income for investors whose marginal tax rates are no greater than 50 per cent and proportionately less for higher-income investors.

Under these assumptions, the stockholder's after-tax dollar return is

$$\tfrac{1}{2}k[\bar{X} - rD](1 - t_c)(1 - t_p) +$$
$$\tfrac{1}{2}k[\bar{X} - rD](1 - t_c)(1 - \tfrac{1}{2}t_p)$$

where k represents the percentage of the company's stocks (or bonds) he owns. The bondholder's after-tax income from bonds becomes

$$krD\ (1 - t_p).$$

Of course, if the individual buys stocks on margin his bond interest is deductible dollar for dollar against ordinary income.

Utilizing these relationships, we may now calculate company and individual transformation schedules accounting for the effects of corporate and personal income taxes. In Columns 2 and 3 of Table III we first present points on the company after-tax transformation schedule ($C_tC'_t$ in Figure II). It shows the net return and safety level that would be earned by shareholders in companies that had the capital structures listed in Column 1. In Columns 4 and 5 we show points on an individual transformation schedule on the assumption that the company has no debt (curve C_tS_t in Figure II). It is assumed that the individual creates homemade leverage sufficient to achieve the alternative debt/equity ratios we described earlier.

TABLE III

Company and Individual Transformation Schedules After Corporate and Personal Taxes

$\frac{D}{D+S}$	Company Transformation Schedule		Individual Transformation Schedule: Company with No Debt		Individual Transformation Schedule: Company with 30/70 Debt/Equity Ratio	
	Expected Earnings	Safety Level	Expected Earnings	Safety Level	Expected Earnings	Safety Level
(1)	(2)	(3)	(4)	(5)	(6)	(7)
0	3.125%	1.250%	3.125%	1.250%	3.406%	1.532%
0.2	3.516	1.172	3.281	.938	3.633	1.290
0.3	3.795	1.117	3.393	.714	3.795	1.117
0.4	4.167	1.042	3.542	.417	4.010	.887
0.6	5.469	.781	4.063	−.625	4.766	.080

Appendix B. Properties of the Opportunity Loci

1. *Some Basic Relationships*

Before determining the nature of the opportunity loci themselves it is necessary to review a few basic mathematical relationships which, incidentally, show the advantages and disadvantages offered to the stockholder by increases in the company's financial leverage.

If we take total company earnings, X, to be a random variable, the variance of earnings per dollar of equity, i, is by definition (see (1)), given by

$$(9)\qquad \sigma^2 = \frac{1}{N}\Sigma\,(i-\bar{\imath})^2 = \frac{1}{N}\Sigma\left(\frac{X-rD}{S} - \frac{\bar{X}-rD}{S}\right)^2 = \frac{1}{N}\Sigma\left(\frac{\bar{X}-X}{S}\right)^2$$

that is, it is given by the variance in earnings (before interest payments) per dollar of equity.

We see that since a rise in S (a decrease in D) will leave both X and $\bar{X}$ unaffected, by (9) it must cause a reduction in the variance of i. Moreover, a rise in S (a reduction in D) will decrease the probability that the earnings per share will be negative since the probability of loss, $P[(X - rD) \leq 0]$, clearly increases with the value of D. This result follows no matter what the probability distribution of X. Thus an increase in debt increases the risk of the stockholder on both counts. Let us next examine what he receives by way of compensation. Assume we are in a M and M world in which the firm is considering alternative proportions of debt and equity, all other things remaining equal. In that case equation (2), $D + S = V$ (constant), must hold, and substitution of this into the expression for expected earnings per dollar invested in equity (1) yields

$$(10)\qquad \bar{\imath} = (\bar{X} - rV + rS)/S = [(\bar{X} - rV)/S] + r.$$

This tells us that provided $(\bar{X} - rV)$ is positive[6], $\bar{\imath}$ will decrease with S (it will increase with the magnitude of D).[7]

2. *Linearity of the Company Opportunity Locus*

We have utilized two illustrative definitions of safety level: $y = \bar{\imath} - k\sigma$ and $y = i_{\min}$ where i represents earnings per share and σ is their standard deviation.

It is easy to show that if we employ either of these definitions and the M and M proposition $S + D = V$ (constant), then the

6. This requires $r < \bar{X}/V$ (the earnings rate on assets be greater than the rate of interest) — debt must be "sufficiently cheap" for its use to offer an advantage to the stockholder.

7. We can express this result in a somewhat different way by writing $\bar{\imath}$ not as a function of S alone, but instead as a function of the debt/equity ratio, D/S. To do this we obtain from (2)

$V/S = D/S + 1$ so that $1/S = D/SV + 1/V$, i.e.,

$$\frac{\bar{X}}{S} = \frac{\bar{X}}{V} + \frac{\bar{X}}{V}\frac{D}{S}.$$

Substituting this last expression into (1) we have

$$(11)\qquad \bar{\imath} = \frac{\bar{X}}{S} - r\frac{D}{S} = \frac{\bar{X}}{V} + \frac{\bar{X}}{V}\frac{D}{S} - r\frac{D}{S} = \frac{\bar{X}}{V} + \left(\frac{\bar{X}}{V} - r\right)\frac{D}{S},$$

an expression that clearly increases linearly with the debt/equity ratio, D/S. This is the Modigliani-Miller Proposition II. *Op. cit.* Eq. (8).

company opportunity locus, $y = f(\bar{\imath})$, will be a straight line. For example, taking $y = \bar{\imath} - k\sigma$, we have from (9) $\sigma = (1/S)\ (\Sigma(\bar{X} - X)^2/N^2)^{1/2}$ and from (10) $1/S = (\bar{\imath} - r)/(\bar{X} - rV)$ so that $y = \bar{\imath} - k\sigma = \bar{\imath}(1 - k(\Sigma\ (\bar{X} - X)^2/N^2)^{1/2}/(\bar{X} - rV)) +$ a constant, which is clearly linear in $\bar{\imath}$.

Similarly, if we take $y = (X_{\min} - rD)/S$ then from $V = S + D$, $y = [(X_{\min} - rV)/S] + r$. Dividing $y - r$ by $\bar{\imath} - r$, as given by (10), we obtain $(y - r)/(\bar{\imath} - r) = (X_{\min} - rV)\ (\bar{X} - rV)$ so that the equation for our opportunity locus is $y = \bar{\imath}(X_{\min} - rV)/(\bar{X} - rV) +$ a constant. This is again linear in $\bar{\imath}$ and has a negative slope if and only if $\bar{X} > rV > X_{\min}$. Of course, considerations such as rising borrowing costs can introduce nonlinearities into the relationships, and the preceding calculations take no account of risk phenomena such as increasing danger of insolvency as leverage grows.

3. *The Corporate Income Tax and the Company Locus*

We have seen by equation (8) that, in the presence of a corporate income tax at the rate t_c, the expected return to the individual who invests one dollar in the stock of the company will be

$$(12) \qquad \bar{\imath}_t = \frac{\bar{X} - rD}{S}(1 - t_c) = (1 - t_c)\bar{\imath}.$$

A similar relationship holds for the safety level, y, if the latter is defined by the substitution of $X_{\min}$ for $\bar{X}$ in (12). Moreover, by (9) and (12) the standard deviation before taxes, σ, will be related to the standard deviation after taxes, σ_t, by the equation $\sigma_t = \sigma(1 - t_c)$. Hence, on either definition of safety level, $y = i_{\min}$ or $y = \bar{\imath} - k\sigma$, the ratio $\bar{\imath}/y$ will be unaffected by the value of the tax rate t_c, since both the numerator and denominator will be multiplied by $(1 - t_c)$. Whether the tax rate is zero or nonzero, the expected return-safety level ratio for the shareholder will be the same. Hence we conclude:

The imposition of a corporate tax at a fixed rate will transform any point on the company opportunity locus $y = f(\bar{\imath})$ into a point closer to the origin, where both the original and the new point will lie on the same ray through the origin. A given tax rate will reduce the coordinates of the two points on the original locus by exactly the same proportion, t_c.

4. *Homemade Reductions in Leverage*

Given the financial structure chosen by the company, let the expected earnings and safety level be given by $\bar{\imath}_k$ and y_k respectively. If the individual j decides to unlever his holdings to some extent, he will divide each dollar of his investment in the company between purchases of its stocks in amount S_j and purchases of its bonds in an amount D_j, so that $S_j + D_j = 1$. The corresponding expected earnings of his dollar are then (since $D_j = 1 - S_j$)

$$(13) \qquad \bar{\imath}_j = S_j\bar{\imath}_k + rD_j = S_j(\bar{\imath}_k - r) + r.$$

If we consider the definition of safety level, $y = i_{\min}$, we have for y_j, the safety level of individual j's portfolio,

(14) $\quad y_j = S_j i_{k\min} + rD_j = S_j(y_k - r) + r.$

In the case of the other definition of the safety level an expression for y_j is only slightly more difficult to determine. By direct substitution of (13) into (9), we may write the variance of the mixed portfolio as

$$\sigma^2{}_j = \frac{1}{N} \Sigma\ (S_j i_k + rD_j - S_j \bar{i}_k - \bar{r}D_j)^2.$$

Since $r = \bar{r}$ (by assumption, debt payments are expected with certainty), this may be rewritten as $\sigma^2{}_j = \frac{1}{N} \Sigma\ (S_j i_k - S_j \bar{i}_k)^2$. Direct comparison with (9) indicates that $\sigma_j = S_j\sigma$. Thus the alternative safety level equation is

$$y_j = \bar{i}_j - k\sigma_j = S_j(\bar{i}_k - r - k\sigma) + r = S_j(y_k - r) + r,$$

giving us the same final expression for y_j as we obtained in (14). Now, eliminating S_j between (13) and (14), the equations for $\bar{i}_j$ and y_j we obtain

(15) $\quad (y_j - r)/(\bar{i}_j - r) = (y_k - r)/(\bar{i}_k - r),$

which in turn gives as the equation of the relevant segment of the individual opportunity locus $y_j = F(\bar{i}_j)$,

(16) $\quad y_j = \bar{i}_j(y_k - r)/(\bar{i}_k - r) + r[1 - (y_k - r)/(\bar{i}_k - r)],$

an equation which is obviously linear in its variables, y_j and $\bar{i}_j$, the individual's safety level and expected earnings. If the investor holds no bonds, so that $\bar{i}_j = \bar{i}_k$, we obtain $y_j = y_k$ (as is seen readily from equation (15)), that is, the individual opportunity locus $y_j = F(\bar{i}_j)$ passes through the company decision point $(y_k, \bar{i}_k)$ as is required. And if the individual holds nothing but bonds so that $\bar{i}_j = r$ we obtain directly by subtraction in (16), $y_j = r$. Hence we conclude:

The portion of the individual decision locus to the left of the company decision point (i.e., along which the investor holds some company stocks and some company bonds) is a straight line segment with the company decision point $(y_k, \bar{i}_k)$ as one of its end points, and the other end point given by $(y_j = r, \bar{i}_j = r)$, a point that lies on the 45 degree line through the origin.

PRINCETON UNIVERSITY

PART FIVE

BUSINESS BEHAVIOR

[29]

The Analogy Between Producer and Consumer Equilibrium Analysis

Income Effect, Substitution Effect, Ricardo Effect[1]

By William J. Baumol

I

In the detailed algebraic micro-analysis of the firm it is usually assumed that competition is perfect, and that as a result the firm can purchase inputs without limit (for practical purposes) at a fixed price.[2] Cash (the loan of purchasing power) is usually included among the inputs that can be obtained thus. Now, as a matter of fact I think it is considerably more realistic to assume that firms are limited in purchasing power, either in the sense that increased credit can, after a point, be obtained only at increasing cost, or that it cannot be obtained at any price because at any moment the firm can only borrow up to a level determined by the trust with which the money market regards it. Largely because of analytic difficulties analogous to those leading to the adoption of the premise of perfect competition in most such discussions, I adopt the latter, absolute money capital limit, assumption.

With the aid of this premise, several interesting conclusions can be deduced. For one thing, it is usually argued that an increase in the price of one input alone will *always* result in a reduction in the quantity of the item employed. But this is because it is taken that there are no limits to the firm's resources (purchasing power), and so the untoward income effect of the theory of the consumer is not present here to provide the basis for a " Giffen Paradox ". However, with limitation of money capital to the firm, in the sense that the firm's expenditure on at least some of its resources is effectively subject to some limit, so that it must budget

[1] The basic idea of the first part of this paper is entirely Dr. Makower's. Professor Hayek has been exceedingly kind and helpful in the work on the Ricardo effect. I am also indebted to Mr. Graaff for his invaluable advice given while he was himself working on a similar problem, and much of the argument of Part II is based on his suggestions.

[2] True, it is sometimes specified that there is some "factor" limited in quantity to prevent the production function being effectively linear and homogeneous in the inputs so that the diminishing returns required for the second-order maximum conditions may be obtained. *See*, e.g., J. R. Hicks: *Value and Capital*, p. 322. Here I prefer to follow Samuelson in ignoring " factors " of this sort, whose quantity is not generally measurable (*The Foundations of Economic Analysis*, pp. 84–5). Cf. Professor Chamberlin's " Proportionality, Divisibility and Economies of Scale ", *Quarterly Journal of Economics*, February 1948, and the discussion in the same journal, February 1949.

its payments, the income effect returns again, as I shall now attempt to show.

In the argument I shall employ three basic assumptions :

1. That aside from (effective) limitation of money capital competition is in every sense perfect.
2. That the entrepreneur's sales, price and other expectations are unique and definite (although they may be represented by figures which have been discounted for risk) and
3. That the entrepreneur seeks to maximise something which we shall call his utility, and which is about to be described.

It is usually assumed that the entrepreneur seeks to maximise the capitalised present value of the stream of his expected profits (surpluses). This is a usable concept when money can be borrowed and loaned in indefinitely large quantities at a fixed rate of interest, for then the opportunity cost of receiving a unit of money at some future date rather than in the present is the interest lost by not having the amount now. We can therefore evaluate the present value of expected future returns and sum them (having thus rendered money receivable at different dates comparable) to obtain the capital value of the stream of expected profits.

With effective rationing of capital, however, the rate of interest paid on the money borrowed does not measure the firm's loss in postponement of receipts, since the firm cannot borrow as much as it wants and its loss in not having more cash now must be greater than the interest cost of borrowing. Thus there arises a difficulty in measuring the capitalised present value of the stream of expected profits.

It might at first seem that the solution is to calculate the loss in profits resulting from the postponement of the opportunity to invest a unit of currency which is received later rather than now, and to base our discount on this loss. That this solution is spurious can, however, be seen when we consider that the profit opportunity loss must be defined as the most valuable of the streams of surpluses which could have been obtained had the unit of currency been available now, and the value of these streams can only be computed, and (in general) compared *after* the appropriate discount factors have been found.

The solution must then be a recourse to the entrepreneur's scale of preferences, his ordinal utility function U, arbitrary up to any monotone transformation. We thus assume that the entrepreneur acts so as to maximise his utility.

Here, there arises another problem. We may consider that the entrepreneur seeks to maximise the utility of his stream of surpluses, or we may consider him as a consumer and assume that he maximises the utility of the goods which he buys for his personal use. In a formal sense, the latter is more general since we may visualise the entrepreneur spending everything on the single commodity (money), and then the analysis following from the use of the former assumption can readily be made into a special case of the discussion employing the latter.

Let us now write $X_{ti} = \leqslant O$ and P_{ti}, respectively, for the quantity and price of *input* i in period t, if $i = 1, 2, \ldots . s$. Also let these represent the quantity and price of the ith good *purchased by the entrepreneur for his own consumption* during that period when $i = s + 1,\ s + 2, \ldots, m$. Finally let X_{ti} and P_{ti} represent the quantity and price of the ith *output* during period t if $i = m + 1$, $m + 2, \ldots, n$.

Note that one of the items in question may be money, and that physically similar goods may appear simultaneously as inputs, consumers' goods and outputs.

We now assume that the entrepreneur maximises his utility,[1]

$$(1) \qquad U = U(X_{01}, \ldots\ldots, X_{hn}),$$

subject to the limitations imposed on him by the transformation function and his money capital limitations given by conditions (2) and (3) below. Here h is the economic horizon, i.e., the number of periods ahead for which the entrepreneur makes his plan.[2]

[1] Strictly speaking, (1) should perhaps be written
$U = U(X_{os+1}, \ldots . X_{hm})$ (entrepreneurial utility depends *only* on his consumption) but for symmetry and simplicity of notation I write it as above, where we may take it that $\dfrac{\partial U}{\partial X_i} \equiv 0$ for $i = 1, 2, \ldots\ldots, s, m + 1, m + 2, \ldots n$. I employ a similar notational device for the transformation function.

[2] Of course, everything left at the end of period h must be considered as part of the entrepreneur's personal consumption.

The transformation function is given by

(2) $$T(X_{01}, \ldots\ldots, X_{hn}) = 0.$$

Cash or other highly durable goods held are of course transformed into the same quantities of the same items in the next period.

The money capital limitations of the firm are given by

(3) $$\sum_{i=1}^{n} X_{ti}P_{ti} = R_t, \qquad t = 0, 1, \ldots, h,$$

when R_t is the net borrowing permitted the firm during period t. We may prefer, as a special case, to take $R_t = 0$ for $t \neq 0$ so that the borrowing of the firm all takes place initially. Condition (3) of course states that the excess of payments for purchases of inputs and consumers' goods (including cash) over receipts from the sale of outputs (including sales to himself) must be equal to borrowing during any period.[1]

Now the first-order conditions for maximisation of (1) subject to (2) and (3) are given by (2), (3) and

(4) $$U_{ti} + AT_{ti} + k_tP_{ti} = 0, \qquad i = 1, 2, \ldots n; \quad t=0, 1, \ldots h,$$

where we write

$$U_{ti} = \frac{\partial U}{\partial X_{ti}}, \quad U_{tisj} = \frac{\partial^2 U}{\partial X_{ti}\partial X_{sj}},$$

$$T_{ti} = \frac{\partial T}{\partial X_{ti}} \text{ and } T_{tisj} = \frac{\partial^2 T}{\partial X_{ti}\partial X_{sj}},$$

and where A and k_t are Lagrange multipliers. Now to find the effect of change in one of the prices or expected prices, or in the entrepreneur's money resources, R_t, during any period t we differentiate (4), (2) and (3) totally, in that order and get

(5) $$\sum_{s,j}[U_{tisj} + AT_{tisj}]\,dX_{sj} + T_{ti}dA + P_{ti}dk_t = -k_t dP_{ti},$$
$$i = 1, \ldots, n; \quad t = 0, 1, \ldots\ldots, h,$$

[1] Mr. Graaff has drawn my attention to the danger that in certain circumstances (3) will not provide true budget restraints. Thus, if inputs in a given period affect only output in the same period (zero turnover period), output is so to speak, self-financing, and the firms' operations are not limited by money borrowing limitations. Moreover, the form of the restraint by itself suggests that output may effectively be financed by negative consumption in some periods, and clearly the utility function must be made such as to preclude this possibility. We do not, of course, preclude the possibility that some inputs have a negligible turnover period and so are not effectively limited to the firm. The restraint (3) may also easily be modified to cover the case where money capital for investment in some assets, e.g., especially liquid assets, is not effectively limited for the firm, so long as there is a group of inputs for which the firm has not all the purchasing power it would like.

$$(6) \qquad \sum_{t,i} T_{ti} dX_{ti} = 0, \text{ and}$$

$$(7) \qquad \sum_i P_{ti} dX_{ti} = dR_t - \sum_i X_{ti} dP_{ti}, \qquad t = 0, 1, \ldots h.$$

Here (5), (6) and (7) are $nh + 1 + h$ linear equations in the same number of variables dX_{ti}, dk_t and dA. Write D for the determinant of the system and $D_{(ti)(sk)}$ for the cofactor of the element in its $(ti)^{\text{th}}$ row and $(sj)^{\text{th}}$ column, where items are ordered lexicographically,[1] e.g., if $h = 1$ and $n = 3$ the X_{ti}'s are arranged in the order X_{01}, X_{02}, X_{03}, X_{11}, X_{12}, X_{13} and $D_{(02)(11)}$ is the cofactor of the element in the s econd row and fourth column of D. For the cofactor of the element in the *eighth* row (note that D is a 9th order determinant) and *fourth* column, we write in this case $D_{(8)(11)}$.

The solution of the system then gives, by Cramer's Rule,

$$(8) \qquad dX_{sj} = \frac{-\sum_{t,i} k_t dP_{ti} D_{(ti)(sj)} + [dR_t - \sum_i X_{ti} dP_{ti}] D_{((h+1)n+1+t)(sj)}}{D},$$

so that

$$(9) \qquad \frac{\partial X_{sj}}{\partial P_{ti}} = -k_t \frac{D_{(ti)(sj)}}{D} - X_{ti} \frac{D_{((h+1)n+1+t)(sj)}}{D},$$

and in particular

$$(10) \qquad \frac{\partial X_{ti}}{\partial P_{ti}} = -k_t \frac{D_{(ti)(ti)}}{D} - X_{ti} \frac{D_{((h+1)n+1+t)(ti)}}{D}$$

and

$$(11) \qquad \frac{\partial X_{sj}}{\partial R_t} = \frac{D_{((h+1)n+1+t)(sj)}}{D}.$$

Thus the second term on the right-hand side of (9) and (10) represents the *ceteris paribus* change in expendable money resources in period t resulting from the increase in P_{ti}, and might by analogy with the income effect in the theory of consumer's behaviour be termed the resources effect. In general there is nothing we can say about its sign.

The first terms on the right of (9) and (10) are then the substitution effects, and these are, as we might expect, well behaved in sign ; that is to say the first term in (10) is always negative, so that a rise in its price always makes for a reduction in the purchase of an input or consumers' good, or an

[1] See, e.g., A. C. Aitken : *Determinants and Matrices*, p. 90.

increase in the quantity of an output (for which, of course, X_{ti} is defined to be negative).[1]

This can be seen as follows. The second order conditions for maximisation of U subject to (2) and (3) require[2]

$$(12) \qquad \frac{D_{(ti)\,(ti)}}{D} < 0.$$

Moreover, $-k_t$ may be interpreted to be the marginal utility of money capital in period t, i.e., $\frac{dU}{dR_t}$. For we have

$$(13) \qquad \frac{dU}{dR_t} = \sum_{s,j} U_{sj} \frac{\partial X_{sj}}{\partial R_t} = \sum_{s,j} U_{sj} \frac{D_{((h+1)n+1+t)\,(sj)}}{D}$$

by (11). Then by (4)

$$(14) \qquad \frac{dU}{dR_t} = -A \sum_{s,j} T_{sj} \frac{D_{((h+1)n-1-t)\,(sj)}}{D} - \sum_s k_s \sum_j P_{sj} \frac{D_{((h+1)n+1+t)\,(sj)}}{D}.$$

Comparison with (7) in its relation to D shows that all of the terms on the right-hand side of (14) except

$$(15) \qquad -k_t \sum_j P_{tj} \frac{D_{((h+1)n+1+t)}}{D} = -k_t \frac{D}{D} = -k_t$$

are zero since they represent expansions of D by false cofactors, i.e., by multiplying the elements of some other row by the cofactors of the corresponding elements of the $(h+1)n+1+t^{\text{th}}$ row. This and substitution from (15) into (14) gives

$$(16) \qquad \frac{\partial U}{\partial R_t} = -k_t > 0$$

if the firm is taken (as it must be with effective limitation of money capital) to prefer a *ceteris paribus* increase in the money capital available to it in period t. Thus (16) together

[1] Actually, these results are not completely general. Where the price whose change we consider is that of a product, i, transformed (used as a raw material or produced) by our entrepreneur and this is at the same time a good, j, consumed by him (so that $P_i \equiv P_j$), we get a different result. Then the substitution term in $\frac{\partial X_k}{\partial P_i} = \frac{\partial X_k}{\partial P_j}$ becomes the sum of the terms representing the substitution of k for i and that representing the substitution of k for j. The reader should have no difficulty in showing that this substitution term will no longer be symmetrical, as is the case with the ordinary substitution term. That is, this term in $\frac{\partial X_k}{\partial P_i}$ will not be the same as the substitution term in $\frac{\partial X_i}{\partial P_k}$. Furthermore, the sign of the substitution term in (10) becomes ambiguous. Some exceedingly interesting implications of such a result have been most elegantly indicated by Mr. Graaff in an unpublished paper.

[2] See, e.g., Samuelson: *Foundations of Economic Analysis*, Appendix A.

with (12) make the first term on the right-hand side of (10) negative, giving the well behaved substitution term we require.

Our substitution term may readily be shown to have all the standard properties of the substitution term in the ordinary theory of consumer behaviour. Moreover, if we write for the substitution term

$$S_{(ti)(sj)} = -k_t \frac{D_{(ti)(sj)}}{D},$$

then in addition to, but similar to Mosak's[1] condition (4), i.e.,

$$\sum_{t,i} P_{ti} S_{(ti)(sj)} = 0,$$

we easily obtain (by Mosak's argument) the $h+1$ conditions

$$(17) \qquad \sum_{i} P_{ti} S_{(ti)(sj)} = 0, \qquad t = 0, 1, \ldots, h.$$

Similarly, in addition to Mosak's condition (5), i.e.,

$$\sum_{(ti) \neq (sj)} P_{ti} S_{(ti)(sj)} > 0$$

we have

$$(18) \qquad \sum_{i \neq j} P_{si} S_{(si)(sj)} > 0.$$

This arises, of course, because of the multiplicity of side conditions (3) relevant to the theory of the firm, and which are substituted for the one budget restriction in the theory of consumer behaviour. The strict analogues of Mosak's (4) and (5) clearly follow from (17) and (18) by summation. There is no point in repeating the oft discussed interpretation of these properties here. We may merely note that (18) states that there must be a certain amount of substitutability among the relevant items (inputs, outputs and consumer's goods) not just over the plan as a whole, but also in any one period.

II

An extension of the preceding analysis appears capable of providing a test of the Ricardo effect. Indeed it seems strange that the extensive discussion of this effect[2] consists largely of a dispute as to the realism of the assumptions which it was suspected would lead to the results. Little

[1] J. Mosak: *General Equilibrium Theory in International Trade*, pp. 23–6.

[2] See F. A. Hayek: *Individualism and Economic Order*, Ch. XI for references on this topic and for an exposition of Professor Hayek's thesis.

formal analysis seems to have been attempted to see whether the conclusions do indeed follow from the premises in question, this despite the obvious importance of the hypothesis to business cycle analysis.

First, what is the Ricardo effect? Originally employed by Professor Hayek to explain the fall in the demand for capital goods at the end of a boom, it is argued that in certain circumstances a *ceteris paribus* rise in output prices will lead firms to decrease their demands for more durable (more capital-like) inputs relative to their demand for less durable inputs, i.e., it will induce them to make their production less capital-intensive. Now it is generally acknowledged that such a result may sometimes follow with inelastic price expectations, for then an output price rise must mean a relative rise in present as compared to expected future output prices, and so a relative fall in the demand for those inputs (i.e., capital goods) tending more than others to augment future outputs.

But the essence of the Ricardo effect is that it is supposed to work independently of expectations. The basic premise is that the money capital of firms is limited, and it is argued that a rise in output prices should serve as an inducement for increasing the turnover of the effectively limited money capital and thus lead to a lower capital-intensive investment.

Now a complete non-mathematical analysis of this proposition seems exceedingly difficult, if not, in practice, impossible. For, as we have seen, the firm's money capital limitations require recourse to such complications as an entrepreneurial utility function rather than now generally inapplicable constant rates of discount. Moreover, an argument in terms of the situation in a single period is necessarily inadequate to take care of such essential features of the problem as rates of turnover. Nor can we assume with any sort of generality that outputs, inputs, etc., will continue at a constant per period rate and so confine ourselves to the analysis of the events of one of these identical periods. The possibility that the firm will be unable to increase its borrowing after the initial period or that it may accumulate some money thereafter, precludes this approach. Thus a mathematical analysis appears to be essential.

A completely general proof might still be rather nasty. However, it turns out that a moderately simplified model suffices to show that there appears to be little reason, in general, to expect the Ricardo effect to work as described.

In our model we assume an $h\,(h > 3)$ period horizon as before. There is one (composite) entrepreneurial consumer good of which M_t is consumed in period t. There is one output produced in quantity Z_t in that period, and a non-durable (labour) input bought in quantity L_t in period t for $t \neq h$, which affects output only in the period after the one in which it is purchased.[1] Since the entrepreneur must be taken to treat assets remaining at the horizon as part of his consumption, any investment in labour in period h may be included in M_h. There is also a durable capital good bought in quantity C_t in period $t\,(t < h - 1)$ and which affects outputs in periods $t + 1$ and $t + 2$. Since any of this input bought in period $h - 1$ affects output in only one period before the horizon it must be treated as a non-durable input and included in $L_h - 1$. Any of its usufruct remaining in period h, as well as any capital purchase in period h, must, like a labour good purchase in that period, be treated as entrepreneurial consumption, and included in M_h after suitable choice of units.

For notational convenience the units of our inputs and consumption good are so chosen in each period that their unit price is equal to unity, and the units of the output are chosen so that its initial unit price is P in all periods considered. Since in examining the Ricardo effect we take all prices other than output prices to remain fixed, and (to prevent a pseudo-Ricardo effect arising via inelastic expectations) we take present and all expected future output prices to vary in proportion (unit elasticity), this choice of units involves no loss of generality.

Our system is then given by the entrepreneur's utility function

$$(1) \qquad U(M_0, \ldots\ldots, M_h) = U,$$

and one production function for each period

$$(2) \qquad Z_t = {}_tT(L_{t-1}, C_{t-1}, C_{t-2}) \qquad t = 0, 1, \ldots\ldots h$$

where it should be understood that $L_h = C_h = C_{h-1} = 0$ and L_{-1}, C_{-1}, and C_{-2} are all constants determined by

[1] We may assume the output to be perishable to prevent the labour factor affecting output (sales) in the more distant future.

past decisions, so that Z_0 is also a constant similarly determined. We also have the firm's budget restraints

(3) $R_t + PZ_t = M_t + L_t + C_t,$

where R_t is the firm's borrowing in period t.

We could proceed to operate with this system directly, but it is convenient first to eliminate the Z_t's by substituting from (2) into (3) to obtain the restraints

(4) $$R_t + (P)_t T(L_{t-1}, C_{t-1}, C_{t-2}) = M_t + L_t + C_t, \quad t = 0, 1, \ldots, h.$$

We then assume that the entrepreneur seeks to maximise his utility subject to (4). The first-order conditions are given by (4),

(5) $$U_t - k_t = 0, \qquad t = 0, 1, \ldots\ldots h,$$

(6) $$k_t(P)_t T_L - k_{t-1} = 0,$$

and

(7) $$k_{t+1}(P)_{t+1} T_D + k_t(P)_t T_C - k_{t-1} = 0,$$

where the k_t's are Lagrange multipliers, and we use the notation

$$\frac{\partial U}{\partial M_t} \equiv U_t,\ \frac{\partial_t T}{\partial L_{t-1}} = {}_tT_L,\ \frac{\partial_t T}{\partial C_{t-1}} = {}_tT_C \text{ and } \frac{\partial_t T}{\partial C_{t-2}} = {}_tT_D$$

as well as $\dfrac{\partial U}{\partial M_s \partial M_t} = U_{st},\ \dfrac{\partial_t T}{\partial L_{t-1}\partial C_{t-1}} = {}_tT_{LC}$, etc.

Total differentiation of (5), (6), (7) and (4) gives

(5a) $$\sum_s U_{ts} dMs - dk_t = 0,$$

(6a) $$k_t P[{}_tT_{LL}dL_{t-1} + {}_tT_{LC}dC_{t-1} + {}_tT_{LD}dC_{t-2}] + {}_tT_L P dk_t - dk_{t-1} = -{}_tT_L k_t dP,$$

(7a) $$\begin{aligned} k_{t+1}P[{}_{t+1}T_{DL}dL_t + {}_{t+1}T_{DD}dC_{t-1} + {}_{t+1}T_{DC}dC_t] \\ + k_t P[{}_tT_{CL}dL_{t-1} + {}_tT_{CD}dC_{t-2} + {}_tT_{CC}dC_{t-1}] \\ + {}_{t+1}T_D P dk_{t+1} + {}_tT_C P dk_t - dk_{t-1} \\ = -[{}_{t+1}T_D k_{t+1} + {}_tT_C k_t]dP \end{aligned}$$

and

(4a) $$\begin{aligned} -dM_t + (P)_t T_L dL_{t-1} - dL_t + (P)_t T_D dC_{t-2} \\ + (P)_t T_C dC_{t-1} - dC_t \\ = -dR_t - {}_tT dP \end{aligned}$$

From which we get by Cramer's rule (where D is the determinant of the system)

$$(8)\qquad \frac{\partial L_s}{\partial P} = -\sum_t\Big[{}_t\mathcal{T}_L k_t \frac{D_{h+2+t,\ h+2+s}}{D} + ({}_{t+1}\mathcal{T}_D k_{t+1} + {}_t\mathcal{T}_C k_t)\frac{D_{2h+3+t,\ h+2+s}}{D} + {}_t\mathcal{T}\frac{D_{3h+4+t,\ h+2+s}}{D}$$

The expression for $\frac{\partial C_s}{\partial P}$ is clearly identical with the R.H.S. of (8) except that $D_{t,\ 2h+s+3}$ is substituted for $D_{t,\ h+s+2}$ throughout.

Now the Ricardo effect is the assertion that $\partial\left(\frac{C_s}{L_s}\right)\Big/\partial P$, i.e., that

$$(9)\qquad L_s\frac{\partial C_s}{\partial P} - C_s\frac{\partial L_s}{\partial P},\qquad 1 < S < h-1$$

is negative (capital intensity of input rises with price). If we substitute into (9) from (8) and the analagous expression for $\frac{\partial C_s}{\partial P}$ we obtain a linear homogeneous expression in some of the $\frac{D_{ij}}{D}$ with coefficients

$$-L_s\,{}_t\mathcal{T}_L k_t,\quad -L_s[{}_{t+1}\mathcal{T}_D k_{t+1} + {}_t\mathcal{T}n_C k_t],\qquad -L_s\,{}_t\mathcal{T},$$
$$C_s\,{}_t\mathcal{T}_L k_t,\quad C_s[{}_{t+1}\mathcal{T}_D k_{t+1} + {}_t\mathcal{T}_C k_t]\qquad \text{and } C_s\,{}_t\mathcal{T}.$$

Now we assume, on economic grounds, that L_s, the input of labour in period, s, C_s, the input of capital in that period, ${}_t\mathcal{T}_L$, the marginal product of labour in period t, ${}_t\mathcal{T}_C$, the marginal product of new capital in that period, ${}_{t+1}\mathcal{T}_D$, the marginal product of old capital in the next period, ${}_t\mathcal{T}$, output in period $\mathcal{T}$, and k_t, the marginal utility of consumption in period t (by (5)), are all positive. Hence the first three coefficients listed are negative, the other three positive, and *all of them unrestricted in magnitude*.[1] But among the $\frac{D_{ij}}{D}$ which appear in (9) there are $\frac{D_{h+s+2,\ h+s+2}}{D}$ and $\frac{D_{2h+s+3,\ 2h+s+3}}{D}$, both of which must be negative if the

[1] Indeed, it is clear that the relative and absolute values of these items, e.g., the marginal products and inputs of labour and capital and the marginal utility of capitalists' consumption will vary immensely from industry to industry and from firm to firm.

second-order maximum conditions are to be satisfied. Hence the terms in which these appear, i.e.,

$$C_{s\ s}T_L k_s \frac{D_{h+s+2,\,h+s+2}}{D}, \text{ and}$$

$$-L_s[{}_{s+1}T_D k_{s+1} + {}_s T_C k_s] \frac{D_{2h+s+3,\,2h+s+3}}{D}$$

must be respectively negative and positive, and unrestricted in magnitude. It follows that so long as the second-order maximum conditions hold, the sign of (9) is ambiguous, no matter what the type of utility or production functions.[1]

Princeton University.

[1] In models involving a small number of periods it is not difficult to prove the other terms ambiguous in sign, without recourse to second order maximum conditions. The argument is, however, tedious and seems unnecessary.

[30]

CHAPTER 14

The Ricardo Effect in the Point Input–Point Output Case

By WILLIAM J. BAUMOL*

I have argued elsewhere[1] that in the general case, the Ricardo effect does not follow from the assumptions which are alleged to lead to that result. In this note I hope to demonstrate that even where the firm's capital is effectively rationed and it is operating in a point input–point output situation, the Ricardo effect need not follow, though it will necessarily hold in two subcases often encountered in the literature.

The Ricardo effect amounts to the following assertion: In the firm whose capital is effectively rationed, an increase in the price of its output, all input prices remaining unchanged, will make profitable a decrease in the roundaboutness (or capital intensity or average period of investment) of the productive process. This is certainly plausible for the case where the entrepreneur has inelastic expectations, for then a rise in current output price will lead to a less than proportionate rise in the future prices expected by him. Hence it will be profitable for him to decrease his employment of durable inputs, i.e., inputs which are relatively future-output producing. However, the Ricardo effect is supposed to hold also for unit, and even somewhat more elastic expectations. In this paper I shall concentrate on the case of unit elasticity of expectations, relying on a continuity assumption to carry the result over to situations involving more elastic expectations.

The point input–point output case is very convenient for the analysis of our problem, for in this circumstance and in no other, there is a well-defined turnover period given by the amount of time the input is permitted to "ripen." In this situation we may then define the Ricardo effect as follows: With a *ceteris paribus* increase in output prices, even with elasticity of expectations equal to or slightly greater than unity, it will pay the firm with rationed capital to reduce its turnover period.

I employ the Hicksian device which treats outputs of the same commodity at different dates as outputs of different goods. This is particularly convenient here since a lengthening of the turnover period may affect the quality as well as the quantity of the product; i.e., it may give us a "better" (or after a while a "worse") tree and not just "more" tree and, even more obviously, better wine rather than more wine. This device also permits us to measure the output of the same good in different units at different dates,

* Princeton University.

[1] "The Analogy Between Producer and Consumer Equilibrium Analysis," *Economica*, Vol. XVII (n.s.), February 1950, pp. 75–80.

and I shall then be able without loss of generality to choose the unit of output at every date to be such that its initial price is exactly p.[2]

1. THE ZERO TIME DISCOUNT CASE

The case considered by Professor Hayek[3] to argue the plausibility of his hypothesis assumes that a return of six per cent in six months is worth the same as twelve per cent in one year. This procedure dodges the difficult problem of comparing a dollar now with a dollar in six months, for with capital rationing there is no interest rate with which to discount returns expected in the future.[4] We can only allow for the opportunity cost of not having future profits to invest now and for psychic time preference cost. Hayek's approach seems to imply that the entrepreneur is determined not to invest profits since otherwise there would be profit on the reinvested profit, making the total return on two consecutive investments more than twice that on the first investment alone. The Hayekian "simple interest case" is thus a peculiar case to include under the head of effective capital rationing when resources will surely not be kept idle, and I discuss it only because the analysis here is so simple and because it has been used in the literature.

Let $f(I, T)$ represent the maximum output obtainable in a period, with I the money value of input, and T the number of turnover periods in a year, which is assumed to be an integer throughout the paper ($1/T$ is the length of one turnover period). Then Hayek's approach involves an examination of the effect of maximization of what we may call the annual equivalent of the returns on each turnover, that is to say, the return on each turnover multiplied by the number of turnover periods in a year. Thus, since the return on each turnover is the total revenue $pf(I, T)$ minus total cost I, the annual equivalent net return is

$$T[pf(I, T) - I] \tag{1}$$

which is to be maximized by an appropriate choice of length of turnover period subject to the constant value of I imposed by capital rationing. In the differentiable case, if this is to be a true maximum, the second derivative of (1) with respect to T must be negative, i.e., we must have

$$2pf' + Tpf'' < 0. \tag{2}$$

[2] I am assuming that the output resulting at any given date from our single initial input is homogeneous.

[3] See *Profits Interest and Investment* (London: Routledge, 1939), p. 9, and Section 2 of "The Ricardo Effect," *Economica*, Vol. IX (N.S.), May 1942, reprinted in *Individualism and Economic Order* (London: Routledge, 1949).

[4] So, strictly speaking, it is not correct to refer to Professor Hayek's procedure as the neglect of compound interest, as does Professor Haberler in *Prosperity and Depression* (New York: United Nations, 1946), p. 485.

Maximization of (1) also requires

$$pf + Tpf' - I = 0. \tag{3}$$

We can now investigate the Ricardo effect in this case by seeing how the system adjusts to a change in price p. If (3) is to continue to hold when price changes, we must have (by total differentiation)

$$[2pf' + Tpf''] \, dT + [f + Tf'] \, dp = 0$$

or

$$dT/dp = -[f + Tf']/[2pf' + Tpf''] \tag{4}$$

where the denominator of the right-hand side is negative, by (2), and the numerator will normally be positive since it is equal to I/p, by (3). Thus dT/pd will be positive, so that the number of turnover periods in a year will increase in response to a *ceteris paribus* rise in output price; i.e., we will have a Ricardo effect.

2. REINVESTMENT IN THE FIRM: PRODUCTION FUNCTION LINEAR IN *I*

Let us now leave the simple Hayekian "non-compounding" case. Effective capital rationing would, more plausibly, call for reinvestment of revenues, living costs of the entrepreneur being treated as costs in the same way, say, as payments to workers. Here period analysis is called for and we get the first-order difference equation

$$I(t) = pf[I(t-1), T] \tag{5}$$

relating investment $I(t)$ in the tth turnover period to that in the preceding period, where $f[I(t-1), T]$ is the output in period $t-1$ resulting from an investment of $I(t-1)$ and a turnover period T. The equation merely states that gross returns in each period will be invested in the next period. The object is again to examine the effects of maximization of annual returns, i.e., maximization of

$$I(T) = pf[I(t-1), T], \tag{6}$$

where the magnitude of $I(0)$, that is, the initial investment, is the quantity of capital rationed to the firm.

In the special case where the production function is linear and homogeneous in I alone we obtain

$$f[I, T] \equiv a(T)I$$

where $a(T)$ is independent of the value of I. In this case, (5) becomes the first-order homogeneous linear difference equation with constant coefficients

$$I(t) = Pa(T)I(t-1).$$

This, as is well known, has the solution

$$I(t) = [Pa(T)]^t I(0),$$

i.e., investment will increase geometrically from its initial level, $I(0)$. We are interested in the amount accumulated at the end of the first year, i.e., after the passage of T periods. Thus substituting $t = T$ in the last equation we obtain

$$I(T) = [pa(T)]^T I(0) \tag{7}$$

and we desire to choose that turnover period T that makes this quantity as large as possible. Expression (7) will be at a maximum only where

$$\log I(T) = T \log p + T \log a(T) + \log I(0) \tag{8}$$

is. But this in turn requires

$$-\log p = d[T \log a(T)]/dT \tag{9}$$

which differentiated totally yields

$$-dp/p = [d^2 T \log a(T)/dT^2]\, dT$$

where the bracketed expression is the second derivative of (8) and so must be negative for a true maximum. This at once gives the required result: $dT/dp > 0$. The Ricardo effect holds here.

3. REINVESTMENT IN THE FIRM: PRODUCTION FUNCTION NON-LINEAR IN I

Where the production function is not linear in I the Ricardo effect need not follow. In particular if the production function corresponding to processes involving longer turnover periods yields relatively sharply increasing returns to I, or if the production function corresponding to processes involving shorter turnover periods yields relatively sharply diminishing returns to I, an increase in output price may increase annual profits on long-turnover-period processes more than in proportion to the increase in short-turnover-period profits. This is, of course, the reverse of the Ricardo effect.

To prove this consider the following two counterexamples:

EXAMPLE 1 (Sharply increasing returns on the more roundabout process).

Let $f[I(t-1), 2]$ (the two-turnover period per year, i.e., the 6-month turnover production function) be $[I(t-1)]^3$. Then successive substitution into (5) gives the firm's assets at the end of the year as $p^4 I(0)^9$. Similarly, let $f[I(t-1), 3]$ (the four-month turnover production function) be, say, $3I(t-1)$. Then with this process the firm's year-end assets will be $27p^3 I(0)$. Clearly, a rise in p will raise profits on the six-month turnover period more than in proportion to that on the four-month process, contrary to the Ricardo effect assertion.

EXAMPLE 2 (Sharply diminishing returns on the less roundabout process). Here it is convenient to employ $S(t)$ to denote investment in the tth period in a (shorter) four-month process ($T = 3$), and $L(t)$ to denote the corresponding item for a (longer) six-month process ($T = 2$). Now let $f[L(t-1), 2]$ be $30L(t-1)$ and let $f[S(t-1), 3]$ be given by $10S(t-1)$ for $0 \leq S \leq 100$, and by $1000 + 1.1[S(t-1) - 100]$ for $S > 100$. This is a kinked but continuous function giving positive marginal profits throughout, despite the sharp decrease in marginal returns to investment S after $S = 100$.

Assume that price is initially equal to unity and the firm considers employing a unit of investment on one of these processes for one year. The six-month process would yield by successive substitution into (5), $L(1) = 30$ and $L(2) = 900$, the firm's assets at the end of the year. The four-month process offers $S(1) = 10$, $S(2) = 100$, and $S(3) = 1000$. Suppose now that the unit product price goes up to two. Then we obtain the figures $L(1) = 60$, $L(2) = 3600$, $S(1) = 20$, $S(2) = 400$, and $S(3) = 2660$. Clearly the annual gross returns on the longer process will have increased fourfold (from 900 to 3600) in response to the price rise, whereas the returns to the shorter process will have been multiplied by only 2.66 (having risen from 1000 to 2660). Indeed, the rise in final product price will make it profitable to substitute the longer process for the shorter, which is the reverse of what the Ricardo effect would have us expect.

4. INTERPRETATION

It may be helpful to offer an intuitively plausible explanation for the efficacy of the Ricardo effect in the more simple cases and its breakdown in the presence of certain types of non-proportional returns.

If we examine the expressions (1) and (7), which represent the end-of-year yield in the two cases where the effect holds, it is not too difficult to see what is going on. In the compounding linear homogeneous production function case (7), the most simple-minded view of the matter turns out to be valid. In (7) price has been raised to the Tth power, meaning that it has had T periods to be reinvested and compound itself as a yield to the firm. Hence a given price rise will add more to profits the greater the value of T, the exponent of p^T. That is, a rise in price will be more lucrative to management if its investment is turned over more times in a year.

A somewhat similar though less obvious explanation applies to (1). Roughly speaking, a process with more turnover periods gives a specified price increase more turns to add up during the course of a year. More specifically, let us divide the net yield of the process $pTf - IT$ into its total revenue pTf and its total investment cost IT. Then a rise in p will increase both the total revenue and the marginal revenue, $dpTf/dT = p(f + Tf')$ of an increase in the number of turnover periods. However, the price rise will leave the total and marginal investment cost (I) unchanged. Hence,[5] with an increased marginal yield to T and an unchanged marginal cost, it will pay to employ a larger value of T.

But why can relatively increasing returns to capital intensive (long-turnover-period) processes cause trouble in the compounding case? The answer is fairly straightforward. A rise in price increases the scale of the entire operation after the first period; i.e., it offers the firm more capital to invest in subsequent periods. Hence, a process which offers greater returns to large-scale operation is given an advantage. If this advantage goes to the long-turnover-period process, it can, if it is of sufficient magnitude, overcome the fact that this process does not give the price rise as many opportunities to compound as does one with a more frequent turnover.

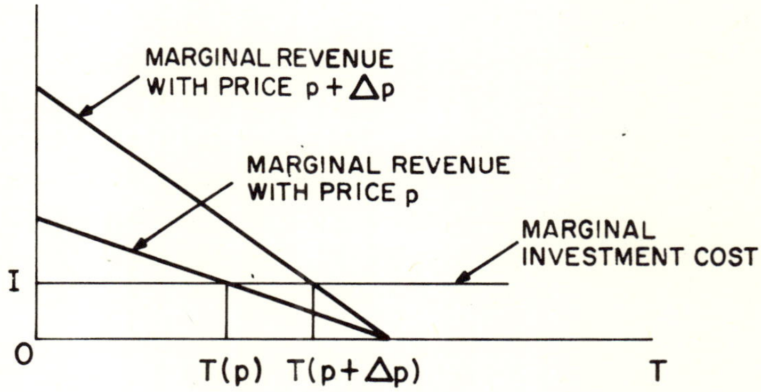

FIGURE 1

[5] More precisely, we will have the situation shown in Figure 1 where the marginal investment cost curve and the marginal revenue curves before and after a price rise are depicted. In the linear case, when price increases from p to $p + \Delta p$, the marginal revenue curve is rotated upward about its old intersection with the T axis. That is because marginal revenue is multiplied throughout by the same constant factor $(p + \Delta p)/p$, i.e., it goes up from $p(f + Tf')$ to $(p + \Delta p)(f + Tf')$. Since the marginal investment cost curve is a horizontal line and the marginal revenue curve must cut it from above (it must have a negative slope) by the second-order maximum conditions, the optimal number of turnovers will *increase* from $T(p)$ to $T(p + \Delta p)$.

[31]

VARIETY IN RETAILING*

WILLIAM J. BAUMOL AND EDWARD A. IDE

Princeton University and Alderson and Sessions

Many marketing problems which promise to be amenable to the techniques of operations research have apparently not been subjected to systematic analysis. This article is a first attempt at an analysis of one such area—the number of items stocked by a retailer and its relation to his sales, his costs, and his profits.

The analysis of the relations among these variables permits the development of criteria for an optimal variety of items; that is, of expressions which can indicate to the retailer whether an increase or a reduction in the number of commodities, styles and brands which he offers for sale will enhance his profits. The discussion also throws some light on a number of well-known retailing phenomena like the growth of suburban shopping centers and supermarkets. By and large, these results are reassuring rather than startling.

The tentative nature of the model cannot be overemphasized. Its structure has purposely been greatly simplified. In particular, linearity has been assumed wherever it does not seem to conflict directly with the properties which the expressions are intended to describe. It is, therefore, noteworthy how often non-linearities have imposed themselves on the model or have arisen out of the mathematical manipulations.

I. Equilibrium of the Consumer

1. *The gains from increased variety*

A shopper does not know in advance (with certainty) whether he will obtain what he wants by entering a particular shop, i.e. whether it does or does not carry some of the items he desires. Generally, there will be one or several alternative sets of items, the availability at acceptable prices of any one of which will make the shopping trip successful in the consumer's view. The greater the number of items carried by the store he enters, the greater, ordinarily, is the consumer's reason for expecting that the shopping trip will in this sense be successful. Of course, this is only true so long as any additional items carried are not known to exclude all commodities desired by the consumer. For example, a known addition to a store's line of paints will not help attract necktie shoppers.

This can readily be translated into probabilistic terms. Let N be the number of different items, i.e., the number of varieties, sold by the retailer. Then we

* This article is a product of the empirical and theoretical investigations carried out in connection with the Alderson & Sessions Basic Research Program. For a description of the other aspects of the program see: COST AND PROFIT OUTLOOK, Vol. IX, No. 2, February, 1956. COST AND PROFIT OUTLOOK, Vol. IX, No. 3, March, 1956. PRINTERS' INK, January 20, 1956, p. 25. BUSINESS WEEK, November 12, 1955, p. 58.

may write

(1) $$p(N)$$

for the probability that the consumer will find some set of items in the store which will make his trip successful. On the usual convention, we have $0 \leqq p(N) \leqq 1$ where, for example, $p(N) = 1$ means certain foreknowledge of success. In the absence of specific customer information about the nature of the items carried in the store, $p(N)$ will be close to unity only if the customer is easily satisfied or if N is very large.

Since an increase in the number of items stocked is taken to increase the probability of success in shopping, we also have $dp/dN \geqq 0$.

It must be emphasized that since we are here not primarily interested in the influence of prices and advertising, they are both assumed to remain unchanged throughout. In particular, they are taken to be unaffected by the number of items stocked by the retailer. Of course, this is not likely to occur in practice. The influence of both these variables is clear. When there is a decrease in prices or an increase in informative advertising, there will be an increase in the probability of successful shopping trips, for consumers are then more likely to know which store carries the items they want and are more likely to find them offered for sale at acceptable prices.

2. *The costs of shopping*

In going to some particular store the customer incurs some costs. Some of these represent the cost and trouble of transportation. If the distance of the consumer from the store is D, we assume that for him these costs are strictly proportionate to D and are given by c_dD where c_d is a constant.

Moreover, the difficulty of shopping increases with the number of items stocked by the store—the more items stocked the further we must walk to get to the spot where some items are kept. Roughly speaking, the average distance walked to an item may be expected to increase as the square root of the number of items carried by the store if it is all located on one story since area increases as the square of the radius of a circle or the length of the sides of a rectangle. For similar reasons, if the store operates with a multi-story building we might expect these costs to vary as the cube root of the number of items offered for sale. For our purposes, we shall assume that these costs are directly proportionate with the square root of the number of items stocked, and are given by $c_n\sqrt{N}$.

Finally, there are costs which do not vary with the number of items sold or the consumers' distance from the store. Simply taking the initiative to shop involves time and effort as well as opportunity costs, including other shopping opportunities foregone. For example, a shopper knows that by spending the day shopping, she may be giving up a chance to catch up with her darning or to spend a quiet evening at home. For some who enjoy shopping this cost, c_i, (and perhaps c_n) may be negative. It should be emphasized that c_i is defined as a total, not an average cost, and includes the opportunity cost of foregoing other alternative shopping trips.

Thus the costs of shopping to the consumer are assumed to be given by the sum of these three classes of cost, i.e., by

$$c_dD + c_n\sqrt{N} + c_i . \tag{2}$$

3. *The demand function*

Presumably the decision to shop or not to shop at a given retail outlet will result from a weighing of the probability of success as given by (1) against the costs of shopping (2). We assume that the typical consumer does this simply by assigning unconsciously subjective weights w and v (both of which are taken to be positive) to the two components and then seeing which is the larger. The constants v and w are viewed as being invariant over a collection of stores offering similar types of assortments. Here the relevant probability function $p(N)$ is presumably subjective and its relation to the objective probability function is a matter for empirical investigation.

Thus the consumer will not shop at this store unless for him

$$f(N, D) = wp(N) - v(c_dD + c_n\sqrt{N} + c_i) \tag{3}$$

is positive.[1] The function $f(N, D)$ is a measure of the consumer's expected net benefit from entering the store in question and shows how this will vary with D, his distance from the store, and N, the number of items offered for sale there.

We can now examine the effect of variation in the number of items carried. An increase in the variety of items handled by the store will involve an increase in the probability of success but it will also increase shopping costs. We must see how $f(N, D)$ will vary with N. Direct observation yields the following results:

a) When the number of items stocked is small the function will be negative. Specifically, $f(0, D) < 0$ since, when nothing is stocked by the store, the probability of success $p(0) = 0$; and hence the term of which w is the coefficient, and which is ordinarily the only non-negative term in (3), becomes zero. This point amounts to the trivial observation that it does not pay to shop in an empty store.

b) For very large values of N, f will also be negative since the first term in (3) can never[2] exceed w while $vC_n\sqrt{N}$ grows indefinitely large.

c) For intermediate values of N and small values of D, f will be positive if w is sufficiently large relative to v, i.e. if the probability of finding what he wants is weighted sufficiently highly by the customer relative to shopping cost.

d) In this case if the expression is assumed to be continuous throughout, i.e., if $p(N)$ is continuous, f must attain at least one maximum in the intermediate range.

e) After f has passed its maximum, the term $-vC_n\sqrt{N}$ will ultimately domi-

[1] Since c_i takes account of foregone opportunities to shop elsewhere (i.e., $f(N, D)$ is a measure of *net* benefits), the value of f will be negative for any store which does not offer the consumer maximum expected gross benefit.

[2] Of course, this is really only an artifact resulting from the linearity of the expression and the constancy of the model's coefficients but it seems also to be rather reasonable, especially in view of what follows.

nate the expression. Since this term decreases at a decreasing rate (positive second partial derivative with respect to N), this must eventually also be characteristic of f.

f) Marginal and average values of f will be negative for low values of N. They will subsequently become positive and finally decline to a negative value again after reaching a maximum.

4. *Economic implications*

These conclusions have several rather common sense economic implications:

a) Increased variety is an advantage to a consumer only up to a point. Ultimately a store may stock so large a variety of items that shopping costs become prohibitive. This suggests why Sears Roebuck might find it profitable to catalogue many lines which Macy's will not carry. By issuing separate catalogues for different lines some mail order houses have been able to reduce e_n further and thereby have made an even larger N feasible.

b) The minimum number of items necessary to induce a consumer to shop at a given store will increase with D, his distance from that store. This is simply the plausible assertion that the high shopping costs of a distant consumer can only be overcome by a high probability of a successful shopping trip.

c) The optimum variety from the consumer's point of view, i.e., that value of N for which $f(N, D)$ is a maximum, is independent of his distance from the retailer. This was assumed directly in the form postulated for the function f. For the term in $f(N, D)$ which contains D does not contain N. This term will therefore drop out when we solve for the optimum N by setting $\delta f/\delta N = 0$.

d) For every value of N, there will be a maximum consumer distance from the store beyond which it will not pay this consumer to purchase from this shop. The net benefit is a function also of the place of residence of the consumer. Thus about each store and for a particular net benefit, i.e., for a particular value of $f(N, D)$, we may conceive of a contour line or indifference curve associated with a locus of residence about the store. The maximum shopping distance is given by the equation of the indifference curve which offers the consumer zero net benefit from shopping at this store. This maximum distance is obtained by setting $f(N, D) = 0$ (zero net benefit) and solving for D to yield

$$D_m = \frac{w}{vc_d}\, p(N) - \frac{1}{c_d}\,(c_n\sqrt{N} + c_i). \tag{4}$$

More economic implications of our model will be indicated in the next section.

II. The Retailer's Demand Situation

1. *The aggregate demand function*

From the point of view of the retailer, a function very much like $f(N, D)$ may be taken to determine the proportion of the population which shops at his establishment. This may be related directly to sales in the following manner: Suppose, once a customer decides to shop at this particular store, the number of items he buys is independent of the number of items available. This assumption is clearly false and we shall modify it later. This premise implies that the volume of a store's sales will depend directly on the number of individuals who can be induced to shop there, i.e., on a relationship like (3). At any distance from the retailer, sales will, in the simplest circumstances, vary directly with the proportion of the population which decides to shop at this outlet. This is strictly in accord with our decision to employ linear assumptions wherever possible. In this case, the proportion of the population residing at a distance D from the store which will decide to shop at this store is given by a function similar in form to $f(N, D)$. Let us take capital letters to indicate the parameters in the new function analogous to those represented by lower case letters in f. The new function may then be written

$$(5) \quad F(N, D) = WP(N) - V(C_dD + C_n\sqrt{N} + C_i) \equiv A(N) - VC_dD,$$

where $A(N) = WP(N) - V(C_n\sqrt{N} + C_i)$. It should be noted that since VC_dD does not vary with N both $F(N, D)$ and $A(N)$ will be similarly affected by changes in the value of N. It should also be observed that while f and F are similar in form the latter should be derived independently from the data rather than from some process of aggregation of the f's of different shoppers.

To determine the volume of Sales, we must also know something about the density of population in the area surrounding the store; that is, the distribution of population within the area whose boundaries are given by the relationship gotten by substituting the parameters of F for those of f in (4) and which lie within a distance D_m from the store. We discuss only two very simple possibilities in line with our determination to simplify the model to the utmost:

case i. population per square mile is everywhere given by the constant K so that Population within an area of Radius D_a is $K\pi D_a^2$.

case ii. the store is located at the point of greatest population concentration, and population density, K/D varies inversely with the distance from the retailer. The area lying within a distance D_a from the store is πD_a^2. The population within the circular area of radius D_a is given by

$$\int_0^{\pi D_a^2} \frac{K}{D}\, d\text{ Area} = \int_0^{D_a} \frac{K}{D}\, 2\pi D\, dD = 2\pi K D_a.$$

First consider case i. Here

$$\begin{aligned} \text{Sales} &= \int_0^{D_m} F(N, D)d \text{ Population} \\ &= \int_0^{D_m} [A(N) - VC_d D] 2\pi K D\, dD \\ &= 2\pi K \left[A(N)\frac{D^2}{2} - VC_d \frac{D^3}{3} \right]_0^{D_m} \\ &= 2\pi K D_m^2 \left(\frac{A(N)}{2} - VC_d \frac{D_m}{3} \right). \end{aligned}$$

Now from (4) and (5)

$$D_m = \frac{A(N)}{VC_d}.$$

Substituting this in our results yields[3]

$$\text{(6)} \qquad \text{Sales} = \frac{2\pi K}{V^2 C_d^2} A(N)^3(\tfrac{1}{2} - \tfrac{1}{3}) = \frac{1}{3}\frac{\pi K}{V^2 C_d^2} A(N)^3 = \tfrac{1}{3} VC_d \pi K D_m^3.$$

Turning now to case ii,

$$\text{Sales} = \int_0^{D_m} [A(N) - VC_d D] 2\pi K \, dD$$

$$= 2\pi K \left[A(N)D - \frac{VC_d D^2}{2} \right]_0^{D_m}.$$

Thus[4]

$$\text{(7)} \qquad \text{Sales} = 2\pi K D_m \left[A(N) - \frac{VC_d D_m}{2} \right] = \frac{\pi K}{VC_d} A(N)^2 = VC_d \pi K D_m^2.$$

In both cases sales will vary directly with the maximum customer distance, in one case as the cube of that distance and in the other as the square of that distance.

2. *Economic implications*

These results also enable us to discuss the relationship between the expected sales of the retailer and the number of lines he offers for sale directly in terms of $A(N)$. This, as can be seen from (5) will vary with N as does $F(N, D)$ or, by analogy, $f(N, D)$ whose shape we have already analyzed. We are thereby led to a number of economic conclusions.

a) An increased number of items will at first yield increasing average returns, then decreasing marginal and average returns. Finally, it will yield negative marginal returns.

b) This means that, even neglecting considerations of retailer costs, it will

[3] This result can be made intuitively plausible as follows: $A(N)$ is an index of any one customer's inducement to purchase when he is located near the store. It also determines the maximum shopping distance—i.e. the radius D_m is proportionate to $A(N)$—specifically $D_m = A(N)/VC_d$ by (4). Because population is taken to be uniformly distributed, the number of persons in the area will be proportionate to πD_m^2. Since total sales equals sales per person times the number of persons, they will be given by a constant multiplied by $A(N)\pi D_m^2 = A(N)^3 \pi/(VC_d)^2$ which is essentially our result.

[4] This implies that sales would be positive for very large or small values of N when $A(N)$ is negative, which is clearly nonsense. This peculiarity arises because $A(N)$, sales per customer would supposedly have negative values at these values of N whereas in fact sales can never be less than zero. It would be more appropriate (though the complication is not worth it) to employ instead of $A(N)$ the function with discontinuous derivative given by $A(N)$ for intermediate values of N but which is zero elsewhere.

not pay a store to proliferate limitlessly the variety of items it carries. There will be some maximum value of sales which can be found by setting the derivatives of (6) and (7) with respect to N equal to zero.

c) The existence of a range of rising average sales deserves attention. This conclusion asserts that not only will total sales be increased up to a point by an increase in the variety stocked but the sales *per item carried* will also rise. Increased variety will then be attracting a disproportionate number of additional customers.

d) Our results are obviously in line with the common sense explanation of the reason why large retailers tend to locate at metropolitan centers since high population density means a large value of K.

e) The results are consistent with the recent increase in emphasis on decentralized retailing and large suburban shopping centers. In terms of our model this can be accounted for in two ways—the increased movement of population toward the suburbs which involves a rise in the K pertaining to the suburban relative to the metropolitan dealers, and the increasing difficulty of driving into and parking in cities which in our model involves increases in C_d and C_i for the metropolitan dealers. This suggests that C_d and C_i are themselves functions of population density.

f) The analysis also fits in with the supermarket phenomenon in grocery retailing. The size of these giant stores can partly be explained by their relatively low C_n—the relative ease with which a consumer can get at additional items which results from the layout permitted by their spaciousness and from their self-service arrangements. Parking lots offer a relatively low C_i. The supermarkets' methods of handling and prepackaging also reduces their inventory and handling costs, and this, as shall be seen in the next section, tends to make for a high value of N, the number of items stocked.

Supermarkets are still increasing the number of items they handle and going into the sale of toiletries, housewares, clothing and appliances. However, it is our impression that no very great further increase in the number of items carried is to be expected in the absence of a marked autonomous or induced change in the value of the coefficients.

3. *Purchases per customer and the number of items stocked*

So far, we have retained the false assumption that purchases per consumer are independent of the number of items stocked by a retailer. Yet up to a point the more items stocked the more likely is a consumer to run into things he had not been planning to buy on this trip but which on being observed become irresistible. This may well serve as a partial offset to the ultimately diminishing returns to an increased number of items carried. But there would appear to be limits to this offset. The customer may not be able to look over more items in a very large store than in a moderately large store simply because of time limitations. After some point, further increases in N may then yield no further increases in sales per customer, though it is conceivable that this value of N is well beyond the relevant range.

III. The Profit Maximizing Variety

1. *The retailers' costs*

To determine an optimum variety from the point of view of the retailers' profits we must include in our model a discussion of the effects of changes in variety on his costs. These effects will primarily involve inventory and handling costs.

In inventory theory, it is customary, as first approximation, to deal with inventory costs as follows:[5] Let E be the mean expected sales volume of all commodities per period, r be the handling, clerical and other related costs of each reordering, T be the warehousing costs per item per period and I the quantity ordered for inventory each time stocks are replaced. Suppose, moreover, that inventory is replaced when, and only when, stocks on hand fall to level R. Then inventory costs per commodity are, on these simplest assumptions, given by

$$\frac{E}{I}r + \left(\frac{I}{2} + R\right)T. \tag{8}$$

The first term represents the cost of keeping the inventory replenished, for E/I is the number of times during a period that inventory will be depleted if sales go on at a steady rate. Since r is the cost of reordering once, then total reordering cost will be r multiplied by E/I, the number of times reordering will take place. The second term in (8) represents warehousing cost since the quantity of the commodity held in stock will vary between $I + R$ and R so that the average level of inventory will be approximately $(I/2) + R$.

Costs can be minimized by picking an appropriate level of I. Setting the first derivative of (8) equal to zero yields the well known result $I = \sqrt{2Er/T}$. Substituting this in (8) gives minimum

$$\text{cost per item} = \frac{Er}{\sqrt{\dfrac{2Er}{T}}} + \frac{1}{2}T\sqrt{\frac{2Er}{T}} + RT$$
$$= \sqrt{2rTE} + RT.$$

In the simplest circumstances, the total cost of carrying N items will be equal to fixed costs, Q plus N times the cost of handling one item plus the additional costs resulting from the increased complexity of handling a variety of items. We may then take this cost to be given by

$$Q + N\sqrt{2rTE} + NRT + a\sqrt{N} \tag{9}$$

where the last term is again given a square root form on the argument that the average distance to any one item will increase as the square root of the number of items so long as all handling takes place in a one-story building.

We can combine (9) with our previous expression for E, the expected mean

[5] See, e.g., T. M. Whitin, *The Theory of Inventory Management*, Princeton, 1953, pp. 31–33.

sales per commodity to obtain an expression for minimum retailing costs. Using (7) rather than (6), for illustrative purposes, total sales are $\pi K/VC_d A(N)^2$ so that average sales will be this expression divided by N.

Substituting this for E in (9) and writing $b = \sqrt{2\pi KrT/VC_d}$ yields as the expression for minimum retailing cost

$$(10) \qquad Q + b\sqrt{N}A(N) + NRT + a\sqrt{N}.$$

2. *The retailer's profits*

We may now obtain an expression for the retailer's total profits by subtracting his total costs (10) from his total revenues which can be obtained by multiplying the sales volume (7) by an appropriate price index. Let $s = (\pi K/VC_d)p^*$ where p^* is the price index; then

$$\text{Profits} = sA(N)^2 - Q - \sqrt{N}[bA(N) + a] - NRT.$$

As we have seen, we may expect $A(N)$ to have two positive roots at which points nothing will be sold and so profit will be negative. In between we may expect for reasonable values of the coefficients that the expression for profits will somewhere rise to a maximum which we can find by setting the first derivative equal to zero. This will indicate the optimum variety in his merchandise from the point of view of the retailer.

In particular, it is easy to see that the higher the handling and inventory costs, i.e., the higher a, r and T (and hence, the higher the value of b) the lower will be the optimal value of N, i.e. the smaller the variety it will pay to stock.

As in many operations research analyses the results have been formulated in terms for which there is no simply obtained quantitative empirical counterpart. In applying results like these, improvisation and ingenuity will no doubt be required to obtain even approximations to the true parameters. Moreover, this very preliminary model will no doubt have to be modified and tailored case by case to fit the facts of the situation, and even then computed results will have to be interpreted and employed only with extreme caution.

On the Theory of Oligopoly[1]

By William J. Baumol

The oligopoly model which is described in this paper does not pretend to generality. It is meant only to describe approximately the current behaviour of a class of firms and there is no doubt that in other times and circumstances the analysis may become totally inapplicable. Nor does it say anything about the strategic give and take which plays so important a part in the theory of games. And in some respects it breaks sharply with received oligopoly theory. But the model seems to accord fairly well with my own rather spotty observation of the behaviour of a number of American business firms. Moreover, it seems to explain several well known features of business behaviour which have been puzzling, and to carry some concrete implications for welfare economics, taxation theory, development theory and the theory of monetary and fiscal policy in which the place of oligopoly has been somewhat obscure. A few of these applications are described below.

1. The Sales Maximisation Hypothesis

On grounds which I shall only hint at here, I believe that the typical large corporation in the United States seeks to maximise not its profits but its total revenues which the businessman calls his sales. That is, *once his profits exceed some vaguely defined minimum level*, he is prepared to sacrifice further increases in profits if he can thereby obtain larger revenues. This is suggested by his readiness to use sales as a criterion of the state of his enterprise (e.g. familiar statements such as " Business is good—sales are increasing "). More important, it is confirmed by a number of cases where businessmen have rejected opportunities (pointed out to them by consultants) to increase their profits at the expense of sales. If they accepted the consultants' analysis of the facts of the situation, as appears to have been the case, this is the acid test. For them the additional profits (and they were not just short-run profits) were not worth the loss in sales.

My hypothesis, then, is that oligopolists typically seek to maximise their *sales* subject to a minimum profit constraint. The determination of the minimum just acceptable profit level[2] is a major analytical

[1] This paper is taken from a forthcoming book tentatively entitled *Business Behavior, Value and Growth* (to be published by the Macmillan Company in New York). I must express my gratitude to the Guggenheim Foundation for the generous grant which enabled me to complete the manuscript. The paper was delivered as a public lecture at the London School of Economics.

[2] More often the profit constraint probably specifies a minimum rate of return on sales or on investment rather than a minimum total profit level. However, it is easily shown that these alternative forms of the profit constraint make no difference to any of the conclusions which follow.

problem and I shall only suggest here that it is determined by long-run considerations. Profits must be high enough to provide the retained earnings needed to finance current expansion plans and dividends sufficient to make future issues of stocks attractive to potential purchasers. In other words, the firm will aim for that stream of profits which allows for the financing of maximum long-run sales. The business jargon for this is that management seeks to retain earnings in sufficient magnitude to take advantage of all reasonably safe opportunities for growth and to provide a fair return to stockholders.

Let us see how the businessman, as a good marginalist, will proceed to set his price and hence his output in order to maximise his sales under the profit constraint.

2. Price-Output Determination: Partial Analysis

Sales maximisation under a profit constraint does not mean an attempt to obtain the largest possible physical volume (which is hardly easy to define in the modern multi-product firm). Rather it refers to maximisation of total revenue (dollar sales) which, to the businessman, is the obvious measure of the amount he has sold.[1] Maximum sales in this sense need not require very large physical outputs. To take an extreme case, at a zero price physical volume may be high but dollar sales volume will be zero. There will normally be a well determined output level which maximises dollar sales. This level can ordinarily be fixed with the aid of the well known rule that maximum revenue will be attained only at an output at which the elasticity of demand is unity, i.e. at which marginal revenue is zero.

But this rule does not take into account the profit constraint. That is, if at the revenue maximising output the firm does in fact earn enough or more than enough profits to meet the competitive requirements, then it will want to produce the sales maximising quantity. But if at this output profits are too low the firm's output must be changed to a level which, though it fails to maximise sales, does meet the profit requirement.

We see, then, that two types of equilibria appear to be possible: one in which the profit constraint provides no effective barrier to sales maximisation and one in which it does. This is illustrated in Fig. 1, which shows the firm's total revenue, cost and profit curves as indicated.

The profit and sales maximising outputs are, respectively, OQ_p and OQ_s. Now if, for example, the minimum required profit level is OP_1 then the sales maximising output OQ_s will provide plenty of profit and that is the amount it will pay the sales maximiser to produce. His selling price will then be set at Q_sR_s/OQ_s. But if the producer's required profit level is OP_2, output OQ_s which yields only profit Q_sP_s clearly will not do. Instead, his output will be reduced to level OQ_c which is just compatible with his profit constraint.

[1] We may be tempted to say then that he suffers from money illusion. But this can hardly be taken as a criticism of his rationality—his objectives simply are what they are and there is nothing inherently rational or irrational about them.

I shall argue presently that in fact only equilibrium points in which the constraint is effective (OQ_c rather than OQ_s) can normally be expected to occur when other decisions of the firm are taken into account.

FIG. 1

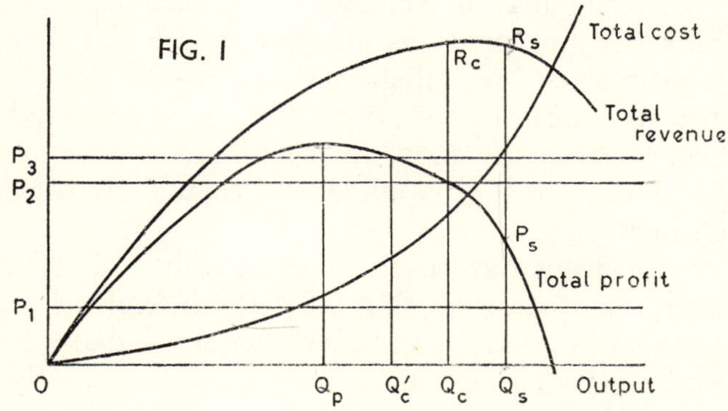

The profit maximising output OQ_p will usually be smaller than the one which yields either type of sales maximum OQ_s or OQ_c. For if at the point of maximum profit the firm's marginal costs are positive an increase in output will increase total sales revenue since marginal revenue must at that point be equal to marginal cost and hence it too must be positive. Therefore, if at the point of maximum profit the firm earns more profit than the required minimum,[1] it will pay the sales maximiser to lower his price and increase his physical output.

Suppose now that the total profit curve has a single peak, as in Fig. 1, rather than being composed of several hills and valleys. Then a rise in required minimum profits, if it affects output at all, will cause a rise in price and a decrease in the quantity produced. For starting from a sales maximising output of either variety, an output level which was just shown to be larger than the profit maximising quantity, any increase in output will only lower profits. Hence if the required minimum profit rises, say from OP_2 to OP_3, so that at the initial output OQ_c the profit level is no longer acceptable, the higher required profit level can only be attained by a cut in physical sales (to OQ'_c), i.e., by a rise in price.

3. Choice of Input and Output Combinations

The typical oligopolistic firm is a multi-product enterprise (frequently the number of distinct items runs easily into the hundreds) and, of course, it employs a large variety of inputs. In this section I examine briefly the effect of sales (rather than profit) maximisation on the amounts and allocation of the firm's various inputs and outputs.

We obtain the following result which may at first appear rather surprising: given the level of expenditure the sales maximising firm

[1] If it earns less than the required minimum at this output there is obviously no output which will satisfy the profit constraint.

will produce the same quantity of each output, and market it in the same ways as does the profit maximiser. Similarly, given the level of their total revenues, the two types of firm will optimally use the same inputs in identical quantities and will allocate them in exactly the same way. This result may be somewhat implausible because one is tempted to think of some products or some markets as higher profit-lower revenue producers than others and one would expect the profit maximising firm to concentrate more on the one variety and the sales maximising firm to specialise more in the other. But we shall see in a moment why this is not so, though later I shall show that this view contains an element of truth.

It is easy to illustrate our result geometrically. In Fig. 2 let x and y represent the quantities sold of two different products (or sales of one product in two different markets) or the quantities bought of two different inputs. The curves labelled R_1, R_2, etc. are iso revenue curves, i.e. any such curve is the locus of all combinations of x and y yielding some fixed amount of revenue. Where x and y represent quantities sold if their prices were fixed the R curves would be ordinary straight price lines. Their convexity to the origin represents the diminishing marginal revenues from the sale of x and y as their quantities increase which is the result of their falling prices (negatively sloping demand curves).[1] Similarly, curve CC' represents all combinations of x and y which can be produced with a fixed outlay (total cost). The standard analysis tells us that the point of tangency T, between CC'

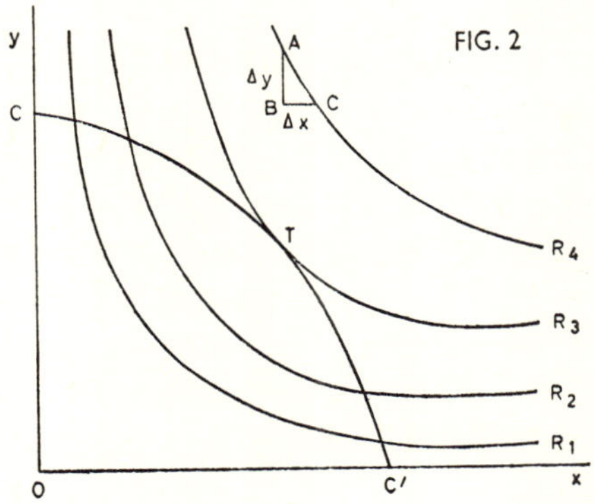

FIG. 2

and one of the R curves is the point of profit maximisation. But it is also the point of revenue maximisation because it lies on the highest revenue curve attainable with this outlay. This demonstrates our result.

A little reflection should now render the result quite plausible. The point is simply that, *given the level of costs*, since profit equals revenue

[1] The absolute value of the slope of such a line equals the ratio of the marginal revenue of x to that of y. For points A and C represent the same total revenue. Hence the move from A to B represents a loss in revenue $\triangle R$ equal to the gain from moving from B to C. I.e. we have $\triangle R = \triangle y$. marginal revenue of y=the marginal revenue of x. $\triangle x$ (approximately) so that $\triangle y / \triangle x = MRx/MRy$. Therefore the falling slope of an R curve as x increases implies a falling marginal revenue of x relative to that of y. A similar discussion applies to the input analysis.

minus costs, whatever maximises profits must maximise revenues. Hence differences between the profit and the sales maximiser's output composition or resource allocation must be attributed not to a reallocation of a given level of costs (or revenues) but to the larger outputs (and hence total costs and revenues) which, we have seen, are to be expected to accompany sales maximisation.[1]

Explained in the way we have just done our theorem is completely trivial. But when the sales maximiser's profit constraint is taken into account a more interesting but closely related conclusion can be drawn.

We may view the difference between maximum attainable profits and the minimum profit level expected by the sales maximiser as a fund of sacrificeable profits which is to be devoted to increasing revenues as much as possible.[2] Since each output is produced beyond the point of maximum profits its marginal profit yield will, of course, be negative. In other words, each time it increases the output of some product in order to increase its total revenue the firm must use up more of its fund of sacrificeable profits. This fund of sacrificeable profits must be allocated among the different outputs, markets, inputs, etc. in a way which maximises total dollar sales. The usual reasoning indicates that this requires the marginal revenue yield of a dollar of profit sacrificed, e.g. by product x, to be the same as that obtained from a dollar of profit lost to any other product, y. In other words, we must have

$$\frac{\text{Marginal revenue product of } x}{\text{Marginal profit yield of } x} = \frac{\text{Marginal revenue product of } y}{\text{Marginal profit yield of } y}$$

This relationship indicates that, even in the sales maximising firm, relatively unprofitable inputs and outputs are to be avoided, whatever the level of outlay and total revenue.

4. Advertising and Service Competition

As Professors Chamberlin and Brems have emphasised, firms characteristically compete not only in terms of price. In fact, more typically the oligopolist's competitive strategy is planned in terms of advertising outlay, product modification and special services offered to the buyer. The decision as to how far to carry each of these activities can be influenced profoundly by the firm's choice of objectives—whether it chooses to maximise sales or profits.

I shall discuss explicitly only the decision on the magnitude of the advertising budget because it is so easily quantifiable. However,

[1] We conclude that when the operations researcher encounters the problem of allocating optimally some *fixed* quantity of a firm's resources, the values of all other decision variables being given, his answer will be exactly the same whether he is dealing with a sales or a profit maximising firm.

[2] Provided that sales maximisation does not permit a surplus of profits over the required minimum as would be the case (Fig. 1) when required minimum profit is OP_1 so that the sales maximising output OQ_s is optimal. But as already noted, I shall argue in a later section that this will not normally occur, i.e. that the profit constraint will ordinarily be effective.

the analogy with service and product characteristic planning is fairly clear and certainly suggestive.

The relevant diagram for the advertising decision is completely elementary. On the horizontal axis in Fig. 3, I represent the magnitude of advertising expenditure and on the vertical axis total sales (revenue) and total profit. In drawing the total revenue curve I assume, as most businessmen seem to do, that increased advertising expenditure can

FIG. 3

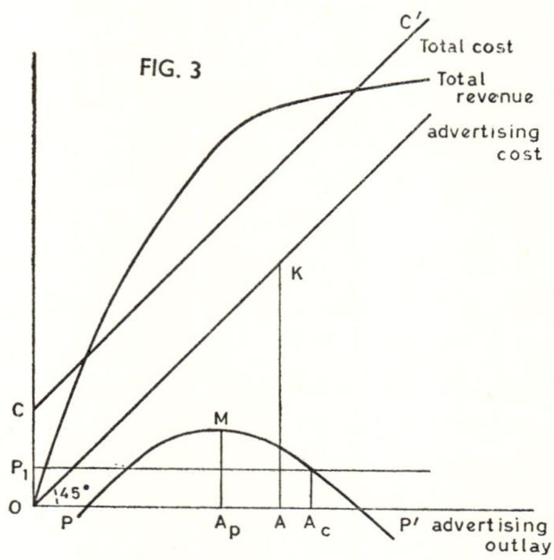

always increase physical volume, though after a point sharply diminishing returns may be expected to set in.[1] This means that total revenue must vary with advertising expenditure in precisely the same manner. For unlike a price reduction a *ceteris paribus* rise in advertising expenditure involves no change in the market value of the items sold. Hence, while an increase in physical volume produced by a price reduction may or may not increase dollar sales, depending on whether demand is elastic or inelastic, an increase in volume brought about by added advertising outlay must always be accompanied by a proportionate increase in total revenue.

The 45° line, as usual, is able to transfer data on advertising expenditure from the horizontal to the vertical axis—i.e. advertising outlay OA is equal to AK. The other costs of the firm (OC) are taken to be independent of the level of advertisement, since it simplifies but does not affect the argument.[2] If these other costs are added (vertically) to the advertising cost curve (45° line) we obtain the line which depicts the firm's total (production, distribution and selling) costs as a function of advertising outlay. Finally, subtracting these total costs from the level of dollar sales at each level of advertising outlay we obtain a total profits curve PP'.

[1] Of course this is not necessarily true—potential customers may perhaps be repelled by excessive advertising.

[2] In fact, this assumption is virtually certain to be false for if advertising increases physical sales volume it must surely increase total production and distribution costs. We may prefer to interpret the diagram as a cross section of three-dimensional revenue and cost functions taken perpendicular to the output axis so that advertising is permitted to increase revenue only by allowing a rise in the price at which the given output is sold.

We see that the profit maximising expenditure is OA_p at which PP' attains its maximum, M. If, on the other hand, the sales maximiser's minimum acceptable profit level is OP_1 the constrained sales maximising advertising budget level is OA_c. It is to be noted that there is no possibility of an unconstrained sales maximum which is analogous to output OQ_s in Fig. 1. For, by assumption, unlike a price reduction, increased advertising always increases total revenue. As a result it will always pay the sales maximiser to increase his advertising outlay until he is stopped by the profit constraint—until profits have been reduced to the minimum acceptable level. This means that sales maximisers will normally advertise no less than, and usually more than, do profit maximisers. For unless the maximum profit level A_pM is no greater than the required minimum OP_1, it will be possible to increase advertising somewhat beyond the profit maximising level OA_p without violating the profit constraint. Moreover, this increase will be desired since, by assumption, it will increase physical sales, and with them, dollar sales will rise proportionately.

5. Determination of Prices and Outputs: Multivariable Analysis

The inter-relationship between output and advertising decisions now permits us to see the reason for my earlier assertion that an unconstrained sales maximising output OQ_s (Fig. 1) will ordinarily not occur. For if price is set at a level which yields such an output profits will be above their minimum level and it will pay to increase sales by raising expenditure on advertising, service or product specifications. This is an immediate implication of the theorem that there will ordinarily be no unconstrained sales maximising advertising level. Since its marginal revenue is always positive advertising can always be used to increase sales up to a point where profits are driven to their minimum level.

In fact we can strengthen this result and rule out even the possibility that by coincidence the profit constraint will happen to be satisfied exactly at the point of maximum revenue OQ_s so that this point will coincide with OQ_c. For at the point of maximum total revenue the marginal revenue of each output must be zero. On the other hand, the marginal revenue of advertising expenditure is presumably positive. Hence the equilibrium condition (analogous with that of section 3, above)

$$\frac{\text{Marginal revenue of product } x}{\text{Marginal profit yield of product } x} = \frac{\text{Marginal revenue of advertising}}{\text{Marginal profit yield (cost) of advertising}}$$

can never be satisfied at such a point since the *marginal* profit yield of (or loss from) advertising is always finite.

Examining further the multivariable (many products, many types of advertising expenditure) case we shall see that some overall validity remains to two basic results of the earlier part of this article: that the sales maximising outputs will exceed those which maximise profits and that a reduction in the minimum acceptable profit level will increase both outputs and advertising expenditures. However, these conclusions do require some modification in detail—for there may be some exceptional products or types of advertising expenditure for which they do not hold.

To see the sense in which the results retain their overall validity we note that as the profit requirement is reduced, production, distribution and selling expenditure must be increased in total, so that at least some outputs or some types of advertising activity must have risen. The reason these costs must grow is almost a matter of arithmetic—as the profit constraint is weakened total revenue is permitted to increase. But if revenue grows and profits fall it follows by subtraction that total costs must become larger.[1]

But while there is necessarily an inverse relationship between the minimum profit requirement and the overall levels of output and advertising this need not be true of every type of product and promotion outlay. For it can be shown that there may be some commodities which are fairly profitable but are inferior revenue producers. These play a role completely analogous with that of inferior goods in the theory of consumer behaviour. When revenues and overall outputs are reduced by stricter profit requirements these inferior outputs and perhaps the funds to be spent advertising them will rise.

6. Some Applications: Pricing and Changes in Overhead Costs

The foregoing analysis has a number of implications for various areas in economic theory, most of which I did not foresee when I first began to work with the sales maximisation hypothesis. First, I shall argue that it can be used to explain some types of business behaviour which have often been observed in practice but which are difficult to rationalise in terms of a profit maximisation objective.

Students consistently find one of the most surprising conclusions of the theory of the firm to be the assertion that overhead costs do not matter. So long as these costs really do not vary with the level of output, and provided that it does not lead the firm to close down altogether, no change in the level of its overhead costs should lead the

[1] In particular we can conclude that there will be an overall growth in output and advertising in a move from profit to (unconstrained) sales maximisation. For profit maximisation is equivalent to constrained sales maximisation where nothing less than maximum profit is acceptable while pure sales maximisation is tantamount to an appropriately low (possibly negative) profit requirement. Of course there may be no finite amount of advertisement which yields (unconstrained) maximum sales although here we must probably give up our assumption that advertisement always yields positive marginal revenues. A simple alternative form of the argument employs the notation $P\max = Rp - Cp$ for the profit maximiser's total profits, revenues and costs and $Ps = R\max - Cs$ for those of the sales maximiser. Since $P\max \geq Ps$ and $R\max \geq Rp$, then $Cs = R\max - Ps \geq Rp - P\max = Cp$ so that the sales maximiser's production and advertising outlays will never fall short of those of the profit maximiser.

profit maximising firm to change either its prices or its outputs. This piece of received doctrine is certainly at variance with business practice where an increase in fixed costs[1] is usually the occasion for serious consideration of a price increase.

It is easy to show, however, that this is precisely the sort of response one would expect of the firm which seeks to maximise sales and treats its profits as a constraint rather than as an ultimate objective. For if, in equilibrium, the firm always earns only enough to satisfy its profit constraint, as I argued in the previous section, then a rise in overhead cost must mean that earnings fall below the acceptable

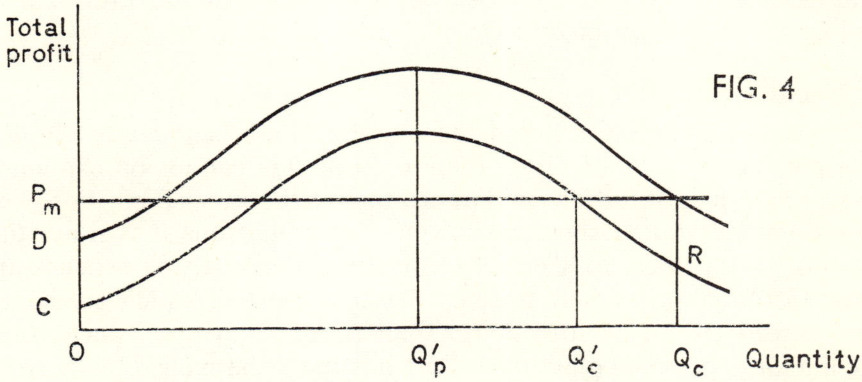

FIG. 4

minimum. The result is precisely the same as that of an increase in the minimum profit level; outputs and/or advertising expenditures must be reduced in order to make up the required profits. The purpose of any such decrease in production is, of course, to permit an increase in selling price.

This is very easily restated in terms of Fig. 4. An increase in overhead costs means, geometrically, a uniform downward shift in the total profit curve by the amount of the overhead expenses. Hence if overheads rise by amount CD output will fall from OQ_c to OQ'_c, for at OQ_c profits will now be Q_cR which is less than the minimum acceptable level OP_m. By contrast, the change in overhead costs will leave the profit maximising output unchanged at OQ_p.

Again, inferior outputs and types of advertising constitute an exception. Sales of these relatively ineffective revenue earners will be increased when increased overheads force the firm to husband its profits more carefully. However, I doubt whether this exception is likely to be very important. Certainly, one would not expect it to loom large in the actual behaviour of business firms whose rough and ready decision-making processes are likely to by-pass the more subtle adjustments called for by optimisation analysis.

In line with this last remark I do not wish to go too far in rationalising the businessman's behaviour with respect to overhead costs. Doubtless, prices are sometimes raised in response to an increase in fixed cost

[1] I use the terms " fixed costs " and " overheads " loosely, treating them as synonyms, although this is not standard practice.

simply because executives are making their pricing decisions in accord with a crude average cost pricing rule of thumb—if costs rise so must prices. And doubtless average cost pricing is sometimes misused to serve the businessman's interests badly. High prices are charged because costs are high at current low output levels—without consideration of the possibility that lower prices can increase volume and so may reduce unit costs. I have come across several such cases. But we must be careful not to sell the businessman short—he is often shrewd and well educated by experience. I really believe that it is not much of an exaggeration to say that the constrained sales maximum hypothesis often is a fairly close approximation to the rationale of the businessman's use of average cost pricing.

7. Non-Price Competition

Economists have often noted the oligopolist's reluctance to employ price cutting as a competitive weapon. But this cannot be explained entirely as a manifestation of a desire to live the quiet life. For even when competitive activity does become more vigorous it is notorious that this is very likely to take the form of more advertising expenditure or the introduction of new product features some of which are sometimes considered to be little more than frills. It would appear then that the large firm's competitive effort has been channelled away from price policy and into advertising, service and product characteristic modification.

This phenomenon is not a necessary consequence of sales maximisation any more than of profit maximisation. But the sales maximisation hypothesis can certainly help to account for the psychology behind these practices.

To see why this is so we must remember that to the businessman " sales " mean total revenue, not physical volume. Now a dollar spent on advertising, if it increases physical volume, must necessarily increase total revenue. But a price reduction is a double-edged sword which, while it serves as an influence to increase total revenue in that it usually adds to the number of units which can be sold, simultaneously works in the opposite direction by reducing the revenue on each unit sold. In other words, as the economist knows so well, depending on whether demand is or is not elastic, price cutting is an uncertain means for increasing dollar sales.

True, price cutting is equally undependable as a method of increasing profits—indeed more so, for if it fails to increase total revenue it must almost certainly reduce profits because the resulting increase in outputs must also add to total costs. But, on the other hand, the effect of advertising, improved service, etc. on sales is fairly sure while, very often, their profitability may be quite doubtful. Thus sales maximisation makes far greater the presumption that the business man will consider non price competition to be the more advantageous alternative.

8. Implications for Ideal Output Analysis

Because of the theorist's failure to formulate a well defined theory of oligopoly pricing (even the kinked demand curve analysis indicates why price may tend to stay what it is, and not how it was set in the first place) oligopolistic output has never been subjected to much explicit analysis by welfare economists in their discussions of ideal output. One comes away only with a rather vague general feeling that after all the oligopolist is practically a monopolist and so he is very likely to fall under the same cloud as an output restricter. One suspects that his outputs are smaller than they would be under the full reign of consumer (or rather, public) sovereignty.

The sales maximisation hypothesis does provide us with an analysis of oligopolistic pricing and output determination. Unfortunately it does not seem to open the way to any firm and simple welfare judgments (though what market form *can* be evaluated categorically ?). However, some impressionistic conclusions can be drawn.

We recall first that under sales maximisation outputs will tend to be larger, overall, than they would be under profit maximisation. Nevertheless, they may be smaller than those which would result in zero profits, i.e. smaller than the output levels which are often misleadingly called competitive. This means that in a world where competition was everywhere else perfect, the allocation of resources to an oligopolistic industry would probably be too small—though less so than one would expect of a profit maximisation hypothesis.

But approximations to perfect competition are rare and marginal cost pricing, if it is to be found at all, is the exception rather than the rule even in governmentally operated enterprises. Even this weak condemnation of the oligopolistic resource allocation must therefore be considered suspect. Since other industries also fail to bid for resources with energy as great as that which is to be expected of perfect competition, there is no reason to feel that the oligopolistic firm gets less than its appropriate share. Indeed, if it is true (as is suggested in my book) that competition sets the level of the minimum profit rate so that in all firms costs bear a somewhat similar relation to prices we may surmise that some sort of rough parity is established and that oligopolistic pricing leads to an allocation of resources which is as close to the optimum as can reasonably be expected.[1] That is, the distortions may tend roughly to cancel out.[2]

So much for the judgment of oligopoly in a static context. When we include in our evaluation the contribution of oligopoly to economic

[1] We must be careful, however, and heed Professor McKenzie's warning that *proportionality* of prices and marginal costs will not ordinarily produce an optimal resource allocation. This accounts, in part, for the vague terms in which my present discussion is couched. See Lionel McKenzie, " Ideal Output and the Interdependence of Firms ", *Economic Journal*, Vol. LXI, December 1951.

[2] In fact, it is tempting to argue that if oligopolistic profits are kept just high enough to yield a normal return on stockholders' investment these firms will actually produce competitive outputs.

growth it will be even clearer that the sales maximisation hypothesis sheds a favourable light on the effects of oligopolistic organisations on the social welfare. Lest this be taken as apologetics pure and simple, let me add that the discussion provides no grounds for us to dispense with the services of a vigorous authority charged with enforcement of the anti-trust laws in order to prevent the corruption and abuse which can be and often have been, the fruits of great concentration of economic power.

The sales maximisation hypothesis has another, rather disturbing, implication for welfare theory. It means that prefixed lump sum (" poll ") taxes must lose their convenience for discussions of income redistribution. For even these taxes, like other overheads, can and will be shifted, and their imposition will affect incentives and the allocation of resources. They will be shifted because, when they are levied on him, the oligopolist will raise his prices and reduce his selling costs to a point where his profit constraint is once again satisfied. The explanation of the shiftability of this apparently unshiftable tax is simple—the profit non maximiser has a reserve of unclaimed profits to fall back on when he is driven to do so by what he considers to be an unsupportable increase in his costs, though he can do so only at the sacrifice of sales which mean so much to him. Since no one seems to deny that businessmen do in fact often raise prices when their overheads increase, this point must be accepted even by someone who questions the sales maximisation hypothesis.

. . . .

In describing the workings and implications of the sales maximisation hypothesis I have given only the barest indications of the grounds on which it is advanced. At best it is just an approximation to a set of complex and variegated facts and there seems to be no way for it to be tested by statistical or other standard techniques of empirical investigation. Nevertheless on the basis of careful examination of a number of cases it appears to represent the facts somewhat better than do some of the more usual models. In addition, as I have just shown, it helps to explain a number of otherwise puzzling features of oligopolistic behaviour. These are surely standard grounds of scientific method for permitting tentatively one hypothesis to supersede another.

Princeton University.

[33]

CHAPTER 10

Growth in the activity of the firm*

From our static model of decision-making by the economy's larger firms we turn now to the structure of the company's growth decision process. We will consider on what basis management determines how rapidly to expand its outputs and its activities generally. In the course of the discussion we shall see how a conventional profit maximization approach can serve as the basis for a growth equilibrium decision model and how one can extend the static model of the firm to deal with problems of considerable importance to management. We will also examine what differences may be produced by management's choice of objectives. The discussion undertakes to shed some light on the origin and determination of the profit constraint that plays so important a role in the sales maximization model of Chapter 7. But, above all, the chapter is designed to argue that the extraordinary long-term growth record of the Western capitalist economies can to a considerable extent be ascribed to the motivation for growth in the business firm. It will be shown that any of a variety of plausible company objectives can call for a considerable rate of business expansion, either as an end in itself or as an essential instrument for the achievement of the goals of the firm. This is the primary purpose of the growth-equilibrium model to which we now turn.

1. A profit-maximizing–growth-equilibrium model

In the ordinary static model of the firm, once the optimal or profit maximizing output level has been determined, the firm will be motivated to continue to produce this quantity in perpetuity. The level of output

*I must express my thanks for permission to reproduce in this chapter portions of two articles: to the editors of the *American Economic Review* for passages from my "The Theory of Expansion of the Firm," which appeared in Vol. LII, December 1962, pp. 1078–87; and to Richard D. Irwin, Inc., for a passage from my chapter entitled "Company Goals, Growth, and the Multiproduct Firm," in Reavis Cox, Wroe Alderson, and Stanley J. Shapiro, eds., *Theory in Marketing*, Second Series, Homewood, Ill., Richard D. Irwin, Inc., for the American Marketing Association, 1964.

will not change until some fortuitous circumstance causes a shift in consumer attitudes or in technology that modifies the cost or demand structure and makes some alternative production level more profitable. Thus, once the equilibrium level of output is found, the operation of the firm can be considered a routine exercise. There is no really essential decision-making role to be performed by management so long as market conditions and technology remain the same.

However, economists who have spent time observing the operations of business enterprises come away impressed with the extent of management's preoccupation with growth. Expansion is a theme that (with some variations) is dinned into the ears of stockholders and is constantly reported in the financial pages and the journals devoted to business affairs. Indeed, in talking to business executives one may easily come to believe that the growth of the firm is the main preoccupation of top management. A stationary optimum would doubtless be abhorrent to the captains of industry, whose main concern is surely not at what size their enterprises should finally settle down (except where sheer size endangers their standing with the administrators of the antitrust laws) but rather how rapidly to grow.

Although the static theory of the firm is a helpful snapshot description of a system in motion,[1] it is useful also to have an alternative construction of the kind described in this chapter—another equilibrium analysis in which the *rate of growth* of output, rather than its *level*, is the variable whose value is determined by optimality considerations.

For simplicity, our first growth model is confined to a case in which input and output prices are fixed (pure competition) and where the production function is linear and homogeneous. With constant returns to scale and constant prices there would seem to be no economic bounds to the firm's output. If production level Q is profitable, output kQ must be k times as profitable because costs and revenues each must have risen exactly k times. This would seem to force us to the ludicrous conclusion that management should in these circumstances expand its output without limit and that it should presumably do so immediately.[2]

[1]Thus, I am emphatically *not* proposing that the conventional theory of the firm be relegated to the garbage heap or the museum of curious antiquities. Static analysis of a nonstationary phenomenon can be immensely illuminating, and the received theory of the firm contains many very helpful results, both from the point of view of the understanding of the workings of the economy and the applied work of the operations researcher. It would be folly to deny ourselves the use of this body of analysis just because its domain of applicability is somewhat limited.

[2]This is closely related to a well-known argument of Kaldor's. See N. Kaldor, "The Equilibrium of the Firm," *Economic Journal*, Vol. XLIV, March 1934, reprinted in N. Kaldor, *Essays in Value and Distribution*, Glencoe, The Free Press, 1961.

There are several fairly obvious reasons why things do not work out this way in practice.

First, sheer construction costs involved in providing physical facilities increase disproportionately as expansion is accelerated. If it normally takes two years to complete the erection of a certain type of factory, a crash program to get it finished in one year is likely to be far more expensive, and any attempt to build many factories of the same sort at once is very likely to strain the capacity of those who construct them and so may add substantially to costs.

A second reason for increasing costs of expansion is financial. The capital market that faces any one company is usually far from perfect. As the company's demand for funds increases, it is likely to find that the cost it must pay for them goes up. The amount of expansion that can be financed out of retained earnings is limited. Too large an issue of new stocks or bonds will drive down the price significantly, and financial institutions may place absolute limits on the amounts they are willing to lend or will increase their lending only if they are offered extremely attractive terms.

Third, there is an internal limitation to expansion: the fact that administrative and organizational costs are almost certain to rise disproportionately with the rate of expansion of the firm. As the growth of the company increases, managerial capacity must also expand. Members must be added to the executive group, and there must be time for their training and opportunities for them to acquire experience.[3]

Fourth, investment in expansion is an inherently risky proposition—a venture into markets whose potential is never fully known. The cost of this risk will tend to rise with the proportion of the company's funds committed to growth. All of this means that costs are virtually certain to be a function, and a sharply rising function, of the firm's rate of growth. This is illustrated in Figure 10.1, where the total cost curve

Here the author reminded us that equilibrium of the competitive firm requires some sort of increasing costs to make it unprofitable for the company to expand indefinitely. But under pure competition there seems to be no obvious source of diminishing returns and, hence, little reason for *any* scale of operations of the competitive firm to constitute a long-run stationary equilibrium situation.

[3]"In numerous companies . . . the volume of new profitable investment opportunities being turned up is substantially larger than can be handled with the company's management organization and staff. Too rapid growth has proved embarrassing in the past, as a result of excessive strain on other parts of the organization, or because of loss of customer good will or other unhappy developments attributable to undigestable rates of expansion." Lintner, "Effect of Corporate Taxation . . . ," *op. cit.* p. 528. *Cf.* also S. Melman, "The Rise of Administrative Overhead in the Manufacturing Industries of the United States 1899–1947," *Oxford Economic Papers*, Vol. III, February 1951, and E. Penrose, "Limits to the Growth and Size of Firms," *American Economic Review*, Vol. XLV, May 1955.

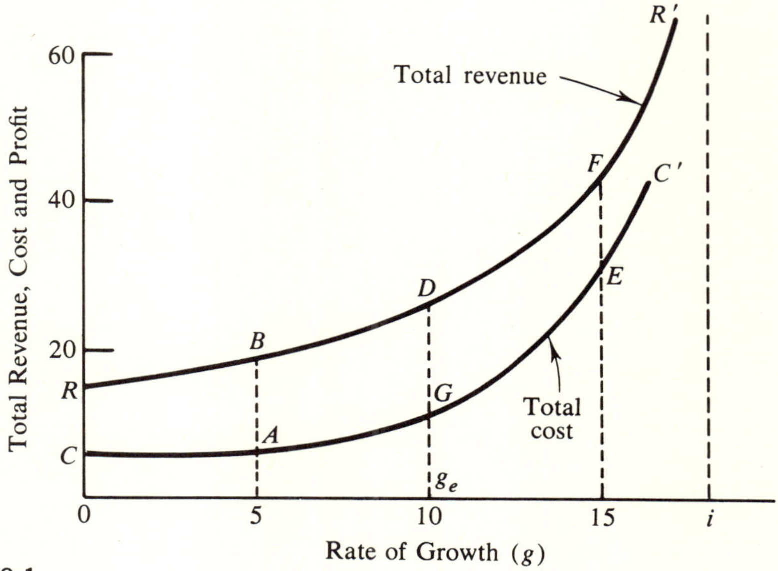

FIG. 10.1

rises more rapidly as we move from left to right. That is, as the firm considers a rate of growth of 5 or 10 or 15 percent, management is confronted with the fact that its total costs at a 15 percent rate of growth will be far higher than those that would apply if a 10 percent rate of growth were decided upon.

Total revenue, which may be defined as the discounted present value of the future stream of returns, is also a rising function of rate of growth. That is, a company that selects a more rapid rate of growth over its lifetime may expect higher receipts than one which chooses to expand more slowly.

Now it will be observed in Figure 10.1 that total profits first increase and then decrease as we move toward the right. That is, *GD* is larger than *AB* but *EF* is smaller than *GD*. This means that there will be an optimal (profit-maximizing) rate of growth for the firm described in this diagram. But it is the *rate of expansion* of the firm's output rather than the *level* of its production that is to be determined by this equilibrium analysis. Each company will find it unprofitable to expand either too slowly or too quickly, and there will be a rate of expansion (in the case of the diagram, 10 percent) that makes a maximal contribution to the company's long-run profits.

Thus, in the model described in Figure 10.1, firms grow not *despite* the effect of expansion on profits but *because* such growth makes the firm more profitable. Growth occurs and continues out of the very logic of the analysis and not as a result of some appendages subsequently imposed upon the model.

2. Formalization of the growth-equilibrium model

This model employs several specific assumptions: first, that management considers only a very simple growth pattern—a fixed percentage rate of growth, to be continued into the indefinite future. This heroic assumption is adopted to permit a simple characterization of the optimal growth path by means of a single variable, the permanent percentage rate of growth, g.[4] Second, it is also assumed, at least for the moment, that the company's objective (which determines the optimal rate of growth of its output) is conventional profit maximization. Finally, it is posited that costs can be divided into two categories: ordinary production and operating costs and costs that arise only as a result of the expansion process. Any costs that would be associated with a given level of output if the output rate were not changing may be classed under output costs; any additional outlays above and beyond the output costs are called expansion costs. Output costs will only be taken into account implicitly, in the net revenue figures. That is, in discussing revenues, net revenue figures from which output costs have already been deducted will be employed.

Let R represent the initial net revenue of our firm, g be the rate of growth (which is to be determined), and i be the rate of interest relevant in discounting future revenues. Thus, i is the company's "cost of capital"—which is likely to be considerably higher than any more or less pure interest rate such as the rate on any class of government bonds. Then, because of the constancy of the prices of all of the firm's inputs and outputs and the linear homogeneity of the production function, net revenues will grow precisely in the same proportion as inputs. In t periods, the firm's net revenue will be $R(1+g)^t$, and the discounted present value of that net revenue will be $R[(1+g)/(1+i)]^t$. The present value of the expected stream of revenues therefore will be:

$$P = \sum_{t=0}^{\infty} R\left(\frac{1+g}{1+i}\right)^t$$

$$= R\frac{1}{1-[(1+g)/(1+i)]} = R\frac{1+i}{i-g} \tag{10.1}$$

provided only[5] that $g < i$, so that $(1+g)/(1+i) < 1$, as is required for convergence of the geometric series (10.1).

[4] If this premise is not employed and the optimal rate of growth at every future moment of time is left to be determined, we are forced into the morass of the theory of functionals, and we cannot escape without at least some recourse to the calculus of variations.

[5] The problems caused for such a model if the rate of growth exceeds the rate of interest are well known. Specifically, the geometric series (10.1) will then not converge

It is perfectly obvious in this situation that we have

$$(10.2) \qquad \frac{\partial P}{\partial g} > 0,$$

that is, the present value of the net revenue stream will grow indefinitely with the rate of expansion g. In fact, P will grow at an increasing rate with g, and its value will exceed any preassigned number as g approaches i, as is shown in the net revenue curve, RR', in Figure 10.1. There is nothing here, then, to place a limit on the rate of expansion of the firm.

As we have just seen, the firm will be constrained from accelerating its activities without limit by its expansion costs, the present value of which we designate $C(g)$. It may be expected that after some point the resulting increases in costs will catch up with the marginal revenues derived from more rapid expansion.[6] That is, it may be assumed that the slope of the cost curve CC', which is the graph of the function $C(g)$, will normally be less than that of RR' near the horizontal axis, but that eventually the slope of the former will catch up with and finally exceed that of the latter. (It may be, however, that in some cases the slope of the cost curve will exceed that of the revenue curve throughout the

---

and the present value of the firm's profit stream will no longer be finite. See, e.g., D. Durand, "Growth Stocks and the Petersburgh Paradox," *Journal of Finance*, Vol. XII, September 1957. However, as Miller and Modigliani have shown, the case $g > i$ is not a serious possibility. They write: "Although the case of (perpetual) growth rates greater than the discount factor is the much-discussed 'growth stock paradox' . . . it has no real economic significance . . . . This will be apparent when one recalls that the discount rate . . . though treated as a constant in partial equilibrium (relative price) analysis of the kind presented here, is actually a variable from the standpoint of the system as a whole. That is, if the assumption of finite value for all shares did not hold, because for some shares g was (perpetually) greater than i, then i would necessarily rise until an over-all equilibrium in the capital markets had been restored." M. H. Miller and F. Modigliani, "Dividend Policy, Growth and the Valuation of Shares," *Journal of Business*, Vol. XXXIV, October 1961, fn. 14. (The notation has been changed from the original to that employed here.)

An alternative way of avoiding this problem is to drop the (unrealistic) premise that the horizon is infinite. However, a finite horizon (say, one involving five periods) will yield an expression for total revenue that is somewhat more messy than (10.1). Though it will be a fifth-degree polynomial, it will have only positive coefficients, and so any equilibrium still will be unique. Indeed, the results of the infinite horizon model all seem to continue to hold in the finite horizon case.

[6]This view of the shape of the cost function can also be defended with the aid of the usual (somewhat shaky) appeal to the second-order maximum conditions, for given the shape of our revenue function, the cost curve must behave in the manner shown in Fig. 10.1 or there would be no profit-maximizing growth rate.

Note also that C is likely to be a function of other variables in addition to g, i.e., it is apt to depend on the initial absolute level of output. A small firm will perhaps find it less costly to expand at a rate of 10 percent than will a large company.

positive quadrant so that the optimal growth rate will be zero or negative.)

Specifically, we obtain the growth-profit function:

$$(10.3) \qquad \Pi = P - C(g) = R\frac{1+i}{i-g} - C(g).$$

The profit-maximizing conditions are then (using the notation Π_g for $\partial\Pi/\partial g$, etc.)

$$(10.4) \qquad \Pi_g = P_g - C'(g) = R\frac{1+i}{(i-g)^2} - C'(g) = 0,$$

(the first-order marginal revenue equals marginal cost condition) and

$$(10.5) \qquad \Pi_{gg} = 2R\frac{1+i}{(i-g)^3} - C''(g) < 0$$

(the second-order condition).

Graphically, the equilibrium rate of growth is given by Og_e in Figure 10.1, the value at which the slope of the expansion cost curve CC' and that of RR' are equal.[7]

3. Digression: comparative statics in the analysis of the model[8]

This simple growth model can easily be made to yield some results in terms of comparative statics. While some of these results are not particularly surprising, they may offer some reassurance that the model does not possess particularly perverse properties and that it can serve as an instrument of analysis much like the standard stationary equilibrium model.

First, a rise in the interest rate will reduce the present value of the stream of expected revenues, for we have[9] by (10.1)

$$(10.6) \qquad P_i = R\frac{(i-g)-(1+i)}{(i-g)^2} = -R\frac{1+g}{(i-g)^2} < 0.$$

[7]We might even envision a long-run zero-profit competitive growth equilibrium in which entry has caused shifting of the RR' and CC' curves and produced a zero-profit tangency position at which growth rate has settled. There is some question in my mind whether, in a growth model such as this, much relevance can be ascribed to that type of long-run adjustment.

[8]Because the mathematics employed in this section are a bit more demanding than those used in the remainder of the book and, because in any event the content of the section is not directly relevant to the main theme of the volume, some readers may prefer to omit it.

[9]A complication is introduced by the fact that interest payments are among the output costs which have been subtracted from our net revenue figure R, so that R should no longer be treated as a constant when differentiating with respect to i. This

Moreover, a rise in the interest rate will reduce the *marginal* revenue yield of increased economic growth, P_g, for we have, differentiating (10.6) partially with respect to g,

$$(10.7) \qquad P_{ig} = P_{gi} = -R\frac{(i-g)^2 + 2(i-g)(1+g)}{(i-g)^4} < 0$$

by our basic assumption $g < i$.

It is now rather simple to prove that (at least in a perfect capital market where some market rate of interest determines the relevant discount factor) a rise in the interest rate will reduce the equilibrium rate of growth of the firm. Differentiating the first-order maximum condition (10.4) totally and setting $d\Pi_g = 0$ (so that the equilibrium condition continues to hold) we obtain:

$$d\Pi_g = P_{gi}di + \Pi_{gg}\,dg = 0$$

or

$$(10.8) \qquad \frac{dg}{di} = -\frac{P_{gi}}{\Pi_{gg}} < 0$$

by (10.5) and (10.7).

Geometrically, this obvious result is a consequence of the fact that a rise in i reduces the slope of the RR' curve in Figure 10.1 throughout its length, as indicated by (10.7), so that the equilibrium growth level, Og_e, must move to the left.

A somewhat more interesting application arises out of some recent proposals to stimulate business growth by means of appropriate government subsidies.[10] Suppose one is considering two alternative subsidy plans for this purpose. The first plan involves payments (S_{1t}) proportionate with the percentage rate of the increase of the firm's output:

$$S_{1t} = s_1 g_t = s_1 g.$$

The present value of all such expected future subsidy payments is

$$(10.9) \qquad S_1 = s_1 g \sum_{t=0}^{\infty}\left(\frac{1}{1+i}\right)^t = s_1 g\left(1 + \frac{1}{i}\right).$$

can be taken care of by noting that our assumptions of linear homogeneity and constant price imply that the quantity of money capital employed by the firm should be strictly proportionate with $R(1+g)^t$. Say it will equal $kR(1+g)^t$ and therefore incur an annual interest payment $ikR(1+g)^t$. In that case we need merely write $R = R^*(1-ik)$ and make this substitution in our revenue function (10.1). It may then easily be verified by direct differentiation that the resulting expression for P_i will be slightly more complicated than (10.6) but that it will still be negative. A similar remark holds for (10.7) and (10.8).

[10] For example, in the Kennedy Administration 1961 investment credit proposals. See also Canadian House of Commons, *Proceedings*, April 10, 1962, and Ch. 15 in this book.

The alternative plan proposes to offer a stream of subsidies (S_{2t}) proportional to the absolute rate of increase of output:

$$S_{2t} = s_2[R(1+g)^t - R(1+g)^{t-1}] = s_2 gR(1+g)^{t-1}$$

whose capitalized present value is:

$$S_2 = \frac{s_2 gR}{1+g}\sum_{t=1}^{\infty}\left(\frac{1+g}{1+i}\right)^t = \frac{s_2 gR}{1+g}\left\{\left[\sum_{t=0}^{\infty}\left(\frac{1+g}{1+i}\right)^t\right] - 1\right\}$$

$$= \frac{s_2 gR}{1+g}\left(\frac{1+i}{i-g} - 1\right) = \frac{s_2 gR}{1+g}\cdot\frac{1+g}{i-g}$$

or

$$(10.10)\quad S_2 = \frac{s_2 gR}{i-g}.$$

Adding, in turn, the subsidy expressions (10.9) and (10.10) to our basic profit function (10.3) we obtain the two new profit expressions:

$$(10.11)\quad \Pi^* = R\frac{1+i}{i-g} - C(g) + s_1 g\left(1 + \frac{1}{i}\right)$$

and

$$(10.12)\quad \Pi^{**} = R\frac{1+i}{i-g} - C(g) + \frac{s_2 gR}{i-g}.$$

By the same procedure as was employed when the effect of an interest rate change was examined, we arrive at the respective comparative statics results:

$$(10.13)\quad \frac{dg}{ds_1} = -\frac{1+1/i}{\Pi^*_{gg}} > 0$$

and

$$(10.14)\quad \frac{dg}{ds_2} = -\frac{iR}{\Pi^{**}_{gg}(i-g)^2} > 0$$

if the second-order conditions $\Pi^*_{gg} < 0$ and $\Pi^{**}_{gg} < 0$ both hold. Thus, both types of subsidy indeed would stimulate the growth of the profit-maximizing firm.

We can go beyond this somewhat uninteresting conclusion by asking which of these two types of subsidy will yield more growth per dollar of government outlay. For this purpose we must deal not with s_1 and s_2, the subsidy rates, but with the total subsidy outlays, S_1 and S_2, as given by (10.9) and (10.10). From these we obtain:

$$(10.15) \quad \frac{ds_1}{dS_1} = \frac{1}{g(1 + 1/i)}$$

and

$$(10.16) \quad \frac{ds_2}{dS_2} = \frac{i - g}{Rg}.$$

Multiplying (10.13) by (10.15) and (10.14) by (10.16) and writing out the expressions for Π^*_{gg} and Π^{**}_{gg} we obtain:

$$(10.17) \quad \frac{dg}{dS_1} = -\frac{1}{g\Pi^*_{gg}} = -\frac{1}{g\{2R[(1 + i)/(i - g)^3] - C''(g)\}}$$

and

(10.18)

$$\frac{dg}{dS_2} = -\frac{i}{g(i - g)\Pi^{**}_{gg}}$$

$$= -\frac{i}{g\{2R(1 + i)/(i - g)^3 - C''(g) + [2is_2R/(i - g)^3]\}(i - g)}.$$

Hence, subsidy S_2 will yield higher marginal returns than subsidy S_1 if and only if expression (10.18) exceeds expression (10.17), that is, if and only if

$$-\frac{1}{g\Pi^*_{gg}} < -\frac{i}{g(i - g)\,\{\Pi^*_{gg} + [2is_2R/(i - g)^3]\}}.$$

This requires

$$(i - g)\left[\Pi^*_{gg} + \frac{2is_2R}{(i - g)^3}\right] > i\Pi^*_{gg}$$

or

$$-g\Pi^*_{gg} + (i - g)\,\frac{2is_2R}{(i - g)^3} > 0$$

and (because $\Pi^*_{gg} < 0$ by the second-order condition) since both terms in this last expression are positive, this requirement will always be satisfied. We conclude, then, that in our model a subsidy of the second type will always yield higher marginal growth returns than a subsidy of the first type.

It is also noteworthy that a net investment tax credit of the sort originally proposed is essentially equivalent in our model to a growth subsidy proposal of type two, for the investment credit is a subsidy proportionate to the level of net investment. With our linear homogeneous production function, and with constant input prices, the capital-output ratio will be constant, so that a subsidy proportionate to investment automatically will be proportional to the absolute rate of increase in output.

Because so many other considerations must enter any decision among alternative growth stimulation methods, there is no point in laboring this discussion further. The case serves, however, to illustrate how meaningful theorems can be derived from the growth-equilibrium model of the firm.

4. Alternative company objectives[11]

The discussion so far has been confined to the case of pure competition and has assumed that the firm's objective is to maximize profit. But larger *oligopolistic* firms may well have a different set of objectives. Specifically, I have suggested earlier in this book that management's goal may well be to maximize sales (total revenue) subject to a profit constraint. Though I remain firmly convinced of the merit of the hypothesis as a static characterization of the current facts of oligopolistic business operation, in the present context—a growth equilibrium analysis—it is desirable to modify the hypothesis in two respects.

First, maximization of *rate of growth* of sales revenue seems a somewhat better approximation to the goals of many management groups in large firms than is maximization of the current *level* of sales. For example, most company publicity materials seem to emphasize the extent to which the firm has "progressed" rather than the sheer magnitude of its current operations. In my earlier static model I was forced to employ a sales-level objective as an approximation to a measure of the rate of growth of the firm's scale of operations. A growth-equilibrium model now frees me from this necessity.

The second modification deals with the nature of the profit constraint, which in a static model may have seemed to be arbitrarily imposed from the outside—perhaps even a device to avoid explaining what had to be explained, very much like the fixed mark-up of doubtful origin which lies at the heart of the full-cost pricing discussions. A multiperiod analysis in which growth is taken into account enables me to give an explanation of the profit constraint which, I hope, is somewhat less superficial and rather more convincing.

From a long-run point of view, profit no longer acts as a constraint in the calculations of the sales maximizer or the growth maximizer. Rather, it is an instrumental variable—a means whereby management

[11]For a different view on some of the discussion that follows see J. Williamson, "Profit, Growth, and Sales Maximization," *Economica*, Vol. XXXIII, New Series, February 1966.

works toward its goals. Specifically, profits are a means for obtaining capital needed to finance expansion plans. Capital is raised both by direct retention of profits and by the payment of dividends to induce outside investors to provide funds to the company. But, beyond some point, profits compete with sales. The lower prices and higher marketing outlays necessary to promote sales also cut into net earnings. Hence, too high a level of profits will reduce the magnitude of the firm's current operations, while too low a profit level will prevent future growth. The optimal profit stream will be that intermediate stream consistent with the largest flow of output (or rate of growth of output) over the firm's lifetime.

Because I have no desire to argue that all firms are united in their choice of objective or to deny that the goals of management are subject to change with the passage of time, it seems desirable to consider a variety of possible company objectives rather than just sales growth maximization. For this purpose one may utilize a set of relationships such as the following:

$$(10.19) \quad \Pi = f(R, g, i)$$

$$(10.20) \quad S = \Sigma_t R\left(\frac{1+g}{1+i}\right)^t = R\left(\frac{1+i}{i-g}\right) \qquad \text{[by (10.1)]}$$

$$(10.21) \quad g = G(I, R)$$

$$(10.22) \quad I \leqq F(\Pi)$$

where Π is the present value of the stream of total company profits, S is the present value of the stream of expected sales (here we drop our earlier assumption that these are net of output costs), R is the initial level of sales, i is the company's discount rate, assumed to be a known constant, g is the rate of growth of company output, and I is the present value of investment, that is, the *total* money capital invested by the firm.

Equation (10.19) shows the dependence of profits on the growth rate and the initial sales level. It is the same as Equation (10.3) but utilizes slightly more general notation. Specifically, the function f in (10.19) behaves in the manner illustrated in Figure 10.1, so that at sufficiently large values of g profits may be expected to decline.

Equation (10.20) simply defines S as the discounted present value of long-run sales. Equation (10.21) describes the dependence of growth rate on the firm's level of investment, including research outlays as well as expenditures on capital utilizing current technology. It also takes into account the investment outlay required for current sales, R, thus expressing the competition of R and g for company funds. Finally, inequality (10.22) is a financial constraint indicating that the amount of money available to the firm is dependent on its expected profits.[12]

The firm may now be taken alternatively to maximize Π, g, S, or R or perhaps some combination (say, some sort of weighted average) of their values, with some or all of the other relationships serving as constraints. Profit maximization, for example, would take (10.19) as its objective function with (10.21) and (10.22) serving as constraints, whereas growth maximization would take (10.21) as its maximum with (10.19) and (10.22) as its constraints.

A diagrammatic depiction of this model perhaps can make clearer the nature of the relationships. It can also suggest the qualitative consequences of pursuit of alternative objectives. In particular, it will indicate that the goals are inherently independent—that attainment of any one of the four objectives does not imply that any of the others need simultaneously be achieved.

Figure 10.2 is a three-dimensional diagram representing (10.19), (10.21), and (10.22), with the axes indicating values of g, R, and Π. The domelike shaded figure is the profit function (10.19), whose location and shape will vary with the value of i. We have already seen why after some point Π will begin to decline with further increases in g. Similarly, in accord with the standard assumptions of static theory we would expect that profit would ultimately begin to decline with excessive current sales, that is, with increases in R. Equations (10.21) and (10.22) have been combined to yield a relationship $\Pi \geqq \phi(g, R)$ indicating the minimal profit level necessary to provide the finance requisite for any given combination of g and R. For simplicity this finance requirement is represented in the diagram by a plane $I'I''I'''I$ that slopes upward as we move away from the origin, thus implying that more financing is needed to attain larger values of g and R. As drawn, the plane does not go through the origin, indicating that some funds are needed even by a firm that is not expanding. We note that the only feasible g and R combinations are those corresponding to points inside the intersection of this plane with the profit surface, that is, points lying inside the curve labeled "growth possibility boundary." For only at such points are company profits at least as high as the amount needed to finance the g, R combination represented; that is, everywhere else the profit surface lies below the finance requirement locus.

[12]The precise form of the relationship does not matter for present purposes, though I take the available I to be an increasing function of Π. This certainly seems to accord with the conclusions of both the theoretical and the descriptive literature of corporation finance.

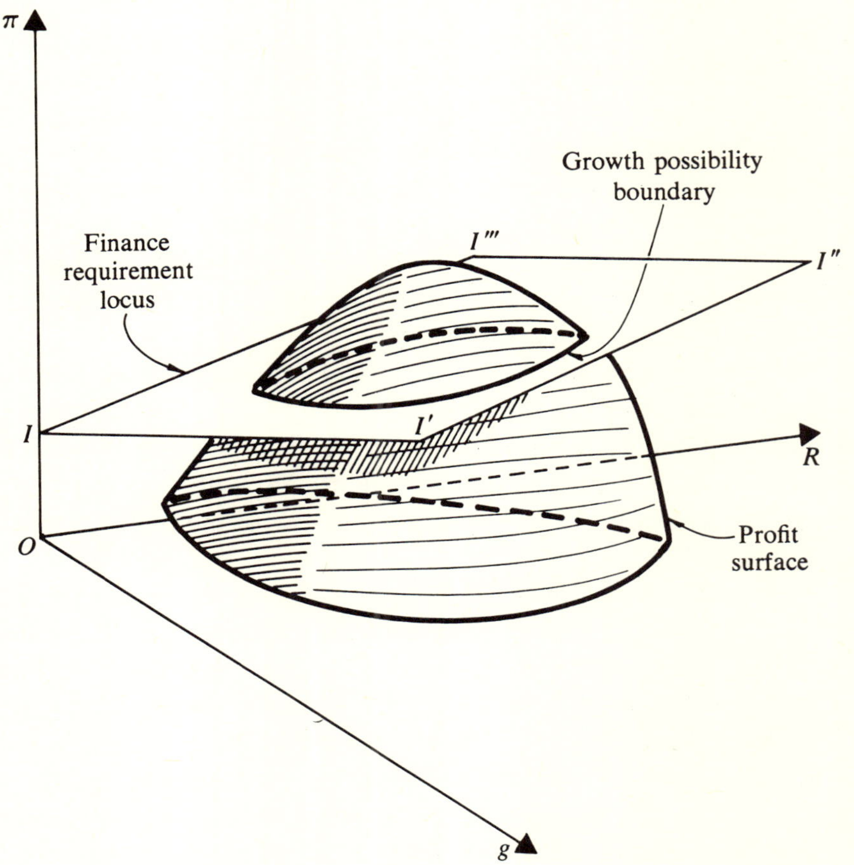

FIG. 10.2

Contour lines are used to collapse Figure 10.2 into a two-dimensional diagram in Figure 10.3. This figure shows the growth possibility boundary crossing the R axis but not the g axis. This means that the firm can survive financially with zero growth but not with zero sales. This latter graph also shows the set of (long-run) iso-sales loci obtained from (10.20) by setting $R(1 + i)/(i - g) = k$ (constant). These are the linear relations $R = -kg/(1 + i) + ki/(1 + i)$ whose slope is clearly negative and all of which have the g intercept $g = i$.

In this diagram only profit maximization occurs in the interior of the feasible region, at the point $\Pi_{\max}$. Growth maximization occurs at the most rightward point on the growth possibility boundary; the $R_{\max}$ point occupies the highest point on the boundary, while $S_{\max}$ is given by the point of tangency between the boundary and an iso-sales line. The figure shows at once that $S_{\max}$ is not generally consistent with $R_{\max}$ or $g_{\max}$, as some of my correspondents have suggested. Indeed, it

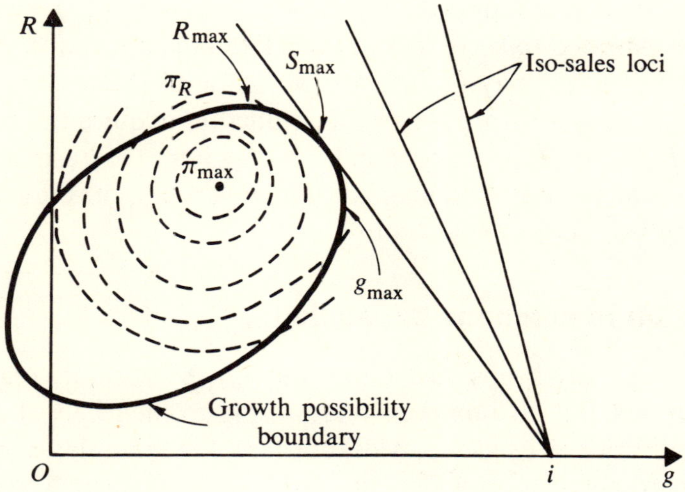

FIG. 10.3

is seen that all the objectives we have considered can be mutually inconsistent.

Figure 10.3 also shows more clearly the nature of the profit constraint and the dependence of the minimal acceptable profit level upon the choice of a long-run company objective. To illustrate the point, if the company desires to achieve maximal R, this yields for the static model a profit constraint of the form $\Pi \geqq \Pi_R$ in accord with the iso-profit curve, Π_R passing through point R_{max}. To maximize current R one is forced to choose values of g and hence Π that provide the finance necessary to achieve R_{max}.

Finally, and for our purposes most important, we consider the value of g corresponding to each of our four objectives.[13] In each case we see that a very substantial rate of growth may be required even if growth is not among the company's objectives. Though the company may seek ultimately to maximize sales volume, current or future, or may be

[13]If we write g_Π, g_R, g_S, and g_g for the rates of growth corresponding to maximal Π, R, S, and g respectively, it is obvious that g_g must always be greater than or equal to any of the others. We will also have $g_S \geqq g_\Pi$ because by (10.3) and (10.20) $\Pi = S - C(g) - \phi(S)$, where $\phi(S)$ is the ordinary production cost associated with sales volume S. But S increases with g for any level of i and R, so that we would expect both $\phi(S)$ and $C(g)$, the expansion cost, to increase monotonically with g, and the result follows. Similarly, we must have $g_S \geqq g_R$ because by (10.20) for any given R, $\partial S/\partial g > 0$. This can also be seen from Figure 10.3 where R_{max} will always occur at the maximal point where the growth possibility boundary is horizontal, while S_{max} will occur at a point on the northeastern portion of the boundary where its slope is negative (since the iso-sales locus to which it is tangent must be of negative slope). There seems, however, to be no necessary relationship between the magnitudes of g_Π and g_R.

interested primarily in profits, a considerable rate of growth may plausibly be expected to serve its interests. Even maximization of R, the *current* value of sales, may require a sizable rate of expansion, for that helps to provide the prospective profits needed to acquire the financing utilized by R_{max}. Thus, in an economy such as ours the business firm is seen to be a source and, it seems plausible, a very important source, of the economy's drive for expansion.

5. Contagion in company expansion

Management usually keeps its eye not only on the absolute magnitude of its operations, but also on their relationship to the levels of achievement of other firms in its group. Market share, for example, seems to be one of the barometers most widely utilized by businessmen. The result is that one firm's growth begets another's.

In fact, management is not ordinarily content to play a passive role in the growth process; that is, it is not prepared to wait for fortuitous events to impose growth upon it. The businessman understands thoroughly the nature of the battle for market share. He realizes that sooner or later someone will grow and he will then be forced to fight to maintain his firm's relative position. How much more satisfactory it is to grow first, especially because it is then possible to choose one's own timing strategy. Rather than waiting passively for someone to make a first move, anticipation leads firms to undertake active programs of expansion, and the desire to maintain market share renders these programs contagious.[14]

6. Motivation for "orderly" growth

Because the typical oligopolistic firm is a conglomeration of heterogeneous enterprises, it can offset their risks against one another on the familiar insurance principle. This means that the oligopolist can better afford to go where the competitor must fear to tread. He is well equipped to undertake the innovation and investment that produce economic growth.

However, there is another side to this picture. With the development of the corporate form of organization the vast body of stockholders

[14]". . . in progressive industries, vigorous competitors will be basing their judgement on what they think (or what they are afraid) other leading firms are (or may be) going to do—not simply on what they have already done except insofar as a vigorous, progressive past is properly extrapolated to the future. One or a few firms 'hell-bent for progress' can so stack the cards in the competitive game that others must follow suit or lose out . . . ." J. Lintner, "Effect of Corporate Taxation on Real Investment," *American Economic Review*, Vol. XLIV, May 1954, p. 524.

have lost effective control over the organizations of which they are the legal proprietors. As has often been observed, absentee ownership increases management's reluctance to undertake risks. Reasons are not hard to find.

The remuneration of the top executive is fairly sticky. If his gamble turns out well the executive is likely to receive little permanent addition to his income stream, though profit-sharing schemes may result in his getting something out of it. Failure, on the other hand, can have serious consequences. At best, it is only embarrassing. At worst, the management group will be turned out of office.

Moreover, the executive who gambles successfully may find that his reward is worse than meager—sometimes he will suffer an indirect penalty. In fact, extraordinary but unrepeatable success may cost him almost as dear as failure. If in one year his efforts have brought in 20 percent returns, the next year he can expect to be asked why if only 12 percent was earned. As a result, businessmen may even be tempted to avoid extraordinary profits. I have been told of one large enterprise whose management realized a few weeks before the preparation of its annual report that it was likely to show spectacular profits. An energetic expenditure program (involving office modernization and other legitimate but somewhat optional purchases) was launched at once and achieved its objective—to bring the year's earnings into line and avoid spoiling the stockholders.[15]

Absentee ownership, then, means that management must curb, somewhat, its spirit of adventure because gambling comes close to being a "heads you win, tails I lose" affair. Even relatively riskless but extraordinary and temporary profit possibilities can be unattractive. It is clear that, as a result, some opportunities for innovation and expansion will be foregone. To this extent the separation of ownership from management may act as a drag on economic growth.

But just staying out of trouble will not usually keep stockholders satisfied. Management must try to keep the firm growing with little interruption. Certainly sales must not be permitted to fall or the market

[15]In objecting to the cessation of unusually high profit rates, the stockholder need not be wholly irrational. Extraordinary earnings, if the public does not know when they will cease, may be capitalized by the market on the assumption that they will continue for a substantial period. The value of the shares of the firm will rise so as to reduce relatively these earnings to a percentage rate comparable with the returns being paid out by other firms. If, subsequently, the earnings of this enterprise fall back to their previous level, the recent stock buyer will in fact have cause for complaint. He will have suffered a capital loss or, what amounts to the same thing, he will have to be content with extraordinarily low yields on the money which he has paid for the stocks.

share to decline. Expansion should be conservative and steady, and bursts of innovation and expansion are undesirable. In this, too, management in nonowner-operated firms will seek to avoid alike risk and brilliant accomplishments that raise expectations for its future conduct too high.

Therefore, when the firm in which management is separated from ownership comes across a number of expansion opportunities, if some of them can be deferred, it may pay management to keep a few of these opportunities unused and in reserve and to take advantage of them gradually. In prosperous periods this influence may even decrease total investment. On the other hand, when expansion opportunities are scarce, management may nevertheless feel itself under stockholder pressure to show some results by way of increased sales. The executive may decide, for reasons of internal politics, to expand at a modest pace even when the profitability of growth is somewhat questionable, provided only that it is not likely to be disastrous. If this happens in many firms at once, the investments can for this very reason turn out to be profitable.

In this way the separation of ownership from management can reduce the amplitude of fluctuations in investment expenditure by reducing both peaks and troughs. If all of the investment expenditure occurred during boom periods, it might, because of resource limitations, have served only to increase prices and to change the composition of investment, rather than to increase its total. Thus, this policy of constant but limited investment makes for a larger national capital stock and a greater national product.

The character of the innovation process is also affected by the separation of ownership from management. Erratic invention and discovery is no longer good enough, and research, too, must be put on a businesslike basis. I believe the huge current industrial expenditures on research can partly be explained by management's demand for a dependable flow of new ideas that have been thoroughly pretested to reduce their risk to a minimum. National economic growth is thereby likely to be stimulated.

7. Concluding comment

In this chapter I have argued that the institutionalized structure and psychology of our business enterprise provides a powerful and sustained force making for the expansion of the economy. The businessman's concern with his market share, the large firm's ability to spread its risk, and the desire to promote profitability all make for expansion.

Even the conservatism that seems to result from nonowner management may serve to put expansion on a less haphazard basis and can thereby increase growth on balance. I do not maintain that these are the only expansionary influences in the economy, but I insist that an economy that lacks such forces must acquire some substitutes or find itself lagging ever further behind.

[34]

RULES OF THUMB AND OPTIMALLY IMPERFECT DECISIONS

By William J. Baumol and Richard E. Quandt*

It is easy to jump to the conclusion that the widespread use of rules of thumb is good evidence of sloppy workmanship on the part of business management. We shall argue in this paper that, on the contrary, rules of thumb are among the more efficient pieces of equipment of optimal decision-making. We shall therefore investigate in fairly general terms how "good" rules of thumb can be designed and evaluated. The paper also reports on an illustrative application of the analysis. A simulation procedure is used to determine the relevant properties of a number of alternative pricing rules of thumb and to compare their performance as guides to decision-making in a single-product monopolistic firm.

I. *Optimally Imperfect Decisions*

The more refined the decision-making process, the more expensive it is likely to be, and therefore, especially where a decision is not of crucial importance, no more than an approximate solution may be justified. Since all real decisions are made under conditions of imperfect information, calculation down to the last decimal place is pointless in any event. One can easily formulate the appropriate (though not very helpful) marginal condition for what one may call an *optimally imperfect decision*, which requires that the marginal cost of additional information gathering or more refined calculation be equal to its marginal (expected) gross yield. The expenditure of any further effort in this direction can be ascribed only to miscalculation of its returns or its costs or to what one economist has happily described as "an irrational passion for dispassionate rationality."

There seems to be a close affinity between this position and Professor Simon's view that the businessman's goal can be better described as "satisficing" than as some sort of maximization. Simon appears to be asserting, in effect, that businessmen usually do not even attempt to

* The authors are, respectively, professor and associate professor of economics at Princeton University. They would like to acknowledge their gratitude to the National Science Foundation, whose grant to their study on the dynamics of the firm enabled them to complete this paper. They are also indebted to Professor H. W. Kuhn and Messrs. H. Shapiro and L. Sydor for their very constructive advice and to Mr. F. Foulkes for assistance with the computation. Most of the calculations were performed on a CDC-1604 Computer.

find maximal solutions[1] precisely because they recognize the limited accuracy of their information and excessive costs of persnickety calculation, and that, instead, they are well satisfied with viable solutions to their problems.[2]

For the purposes of this paper we define a rule of thumb to be a set of rules describing a decision procedure with the following characteristics:

(a) The variables which are employed in the decision criteria are objectively measurable.

(b) The decision criteria are objectively communicable, and decisions do not depend on the judgment of individual decision-makers.

(c) As a corollary to (b), every logically possible configuration of variables corresponds to a (usually unique) determinate decision.

(d) The calculation of the appropriate decision is simple, inexpensive, and well suited for frequent repetition and for spot checking by managment in higher echelons.

A decision process with these characteristics seems to be designed as the instrument par excellence of optimally imperfect decision-making for routine and recurrent problems.[3]

II. *Optimal Rules of Thumb: Definitional Problems*

Even conceptually, the ranking of rules of thumb is not as easy as one might think because problems of multidimensionality are inherently involved.

It may at first glance seem sufficient to say that, of two rules which are equally costly to operate, the one which yields the closer *average* approximation to the true maximum is to be preferred. But some measure of the dispersion of the results is, surely, also of comparable relevance. In fact, all the characteristics of the frequency distribution of errors are significant. The "best" rule of thumb can only be determined by taking all of these characteristics into account and assigning appropriate weights to them.[4]

[1] For our purposes it is convenient to distinguish between a *maximal* and an *optimal* solution. The former term shall be used throughout this paper to connote the exact solution which would be obtained if there were no data limitations or calculation costs, while the term "optimal solution" refers to the ideal approximation to the maximal solution.

[2] See e.g., Herbert Simon [5]. Simon is, of course, saying considerably more than this—he is proposing the hypothesis that businessmen, at least implicitly, set up a number of criteria of satisfactory performance and are willing to accept any decision that passes these tests. It is, as it were, constrained maximization with only constraints and no maximization!

[3] Note that the operations researcher's strategy is usually to replace his client's current rules with some others which he considers more satisfactory, *but which remain rules of thumb nevertheless*.

Moreover, even in computer simulation models, where the world is considerably simplified, and information gathering and refined calculations are relatively cheap and easy, it has in many cases proved impossible even for the sophisticated designers of the models to have their "firms" operate by means other than rules of thumb.

[4] The assignment of weights is, of course, equivalent to determination of an appropriate utility function.

It would appear to follow that there is no cut and dried mechanical way of determining which of two rules is the more satisfactory unless one of them is what might be called "Pareto preferable," that is, it is not inferior in any of its relevant characteristics and superior at least in some.[5]

Another difficult problem, intrinsic to the search for an optimal rule of thumb, arises out of the need to specify the range of alternatives to be tested. In other types of decision this task is sometimes fairly simple, as in a decision problem consisting in a choice of the (numerical) value of a variable, where one need at most specify the end points of the range to be considered.

But in selecting a rule of thumb we are to choose not a number but a functional relationship. For example, inventory might be regulated either by a usual business rule of thumb, $I=kS$, or by the simplest inventory theoretic rule, $I=\sqrt{aS}$ (where I is the level of inventory, S is sales volume per unit of time, and k and a are constants), or it can be determined by any of a variety of alternative simple expressions. Unfortunately, there is no obvious way to supply a reasonably representative list, let alone an exhaustive list of such possibilities.[6]

III. *Calculation Problems*

A crucial step in the determination of an optimal rule of thumb is the calculation of the expected consequences of the adoption of any particular rule of thumb. Ideally, this step should produce a frequency function of the errors to be expected of any such rule of thumb in its approximation to true maximal solutions.

In principle, it may be possible to determine these frequency functions analytically if the structure of the system and the probability distributions of the structural variables are known. However, in practice, such a procedure is almost always impossible. First, an a priori specification of probability distributions for the structural variables usually represents most heroic assumptions that rarely stand up under comparison with the facts. Secondly, even under these conditions, analytic methods of determination of the expected effects of a rule of thumb are likely to be prohibitively difficult.

This means that one must turn to some alternative methods of testing and calculation. The methods of simulation using artificial data and of "dry run" testing on the basis of past history seem well suited to

[5] It is worth noting that the possibility of intransitivity is one of the unpleasant consequences of the multidimensional character of the comparison of several rules of thumb. This is entirely analogous with the paradox of voting, and can arise whenever the choice of rule of thumb is decided by determining which of the candidate rules has a majority of preferred characteristics. For a discussion of the paradox of voting see Arrow [1, pp. 2–3].

[6] This observation also indicates a difficulty inherent in the optimality calculation. Because, in selecting a rule of thumb, one chooses a function rather than a value of a variable, the problem falls within the difficult territory of the theory of functionals.

the problem. By considering a sufficient number of simulated cases the analyst may be able to come away with a fair idea of the rule's likely performance. Unfortunately, invented case histories are apt to be very poor approximations to reality or they may constitute a biased selection out of the set of possibilities. Moreover, to test how well the rule of thumb performs, one must be able to compare it with the true maximal solution in the selected cases. In models that are somewhat complicated this is not always possible.

The alternative to simulation is a procedure for testing the rule with the aid of a number of cases appropriately selected from actual past experience. This procedure reduces the danger of selection of artificial and excessively simple or unrepresentative test cases, but it is perhaps even more likely than is a simulation to result in difficulties in computing the true maximum.[7]

IV. *Approaches to an Optimality Analysis*

Though, as emphasized in Section II, there exists no systematic method for specifying all the rules of thumb which should be tested in any particular case, the matter is not completely hopeless. Many functions can be approximated fairly well, at least for limited ranges of the independent variables, by one of a small set of simple algebraic functions, such as equations of the conic sections, polynomials of reasonably low degree, logarithmic functions, and so on.

This approach, combined with a simulation or a statistical estimation and testing procedure, can sometimes be used to generate rules of thumb that may plausibly be expected to yield a fair degree of approximation to the true maximum. That is the basic method employed in this paper.[8]

Before turning to our application of this method, it is appropriate to mention an alternative and promising approach to the selection of rules of thumb which is based on the use of axiomatic methods.[9] In effect, this procedure gives up the search for a truly maximal solution. Rather, it specifies sets of acceptability conditions, in the form of axioms, which serve as constraints capable of narrowing down the range of possible

[7] Fortunately, these problems are not always very serious. For example, in one statistical study based on actual records of approximative rules for transportation-routing decision-making the calculations were relatively straightforward, and rather definitive conclusions were obtained as to which of the proposed rules gave the best performance. See Kuhn and Baumol [3].

[8] We have also used it in other connections. For example, in one unpublished inventory investigation, numerical methods were employed to determine the least-cost inventory levels for a number of alternative sales levels. It was then found that the exponential expression $I=cS^b$ provided a very good fit to the results but for a value of b considerably different from the 0.5 exponent of the standard simplified inventory theory relationship $I=\sqrt{aS}$.

[9] Thus it is possible to interpret the Chernoff or the Milnor approaches to the decision problem as illustrations of rule-of-thumb selection. See Chernoff [2] and Milnor [4].

solutions.[10] For example, in setting up a reasonably simple decision rule of thumb it may be proposed that any such rule which does not yield a transitive relationship is completely unacceptable. By a sufficiently skillful selection of such a set of requirements it is sometimes even possible to arrive at a unique solution, which, if it is simple enough in form, may then be adopted as the desired rule of thumb.

V. *Designing a Price-Setting Rule*

Let us turn now to an illustrative application of our proposed procedure, to one of the microeconomist's favorite subjects—the price setting of a retail firm. The performance of a number of alternative pricing rules of thumb was tested by a simulation process employing a considerable number of artificial randomly generated demand and cost functions.

In planning the analysis several alternative types of pricing rules were considered for testing:

(a) *Markup rules* which set price by means of a more or less fixed markup over wholesale cost, as is apparently done in a variety of retailing establishments.

(b) *Imitative rules* in which each firm seeks to keep its price at the level set by its competitor. Such rules would fit in with the standard kinked-demand-curve analysis and are compatible with such observed retailing institutions as comparison shopping.

(c) *Learning rules* whereby, if a firm raises its price and then finds its profits have increased, it raises price again; while, if its profits have fallen, in the next period it lowers its price.

(d) *Pseudo maximizing rules* in which simple demand and cost curves are crudely fitted by quick and inexpensive methods to recently observed data and, from these simple curves, an approximative profit function is derived and used to determine the price formula (rule of thumb) which maximizes the value of that approximative function.

Our analysis was confined to the last of these four categories, the pseudo maximizing rules of thumb. Our approach proved to be totally unsuited to analysis of the first two types of rule. Testing of fixed markup rules requires some knowledge of the relationship between wholesale cost (which is the basis for the markup price) and the operating costs of the retailer (which must affect the profit-maximizing price). If the two types of cost bear only a random relationship to one another,

[10] Note the resemblance of the entire approach to Simon's satisficing hypothesis (see [5]). Sometimes the acceptability constraints are so demanding that they eliminate the feasible region altogether, so that no solution can possibly satisfy the acceptability conditions. An excellent illustration is the Arrow possibility theorem [1, Ch. 5]. In other cases the acceptability conditions will not be sufficiently strong to reduce the set of possibilities to a single choice. In that case the axiomatic approach may still have to be supplemented by some sort of optimality calculation which chooses among the remaining possibilities.

it is clear that a fixed markup price would be randomly related to the maximizing price.[11] In reality, the two types of cost are, no doubt, closely interconnected, but there seems to be no way in which this relationship can be captured by the random-number cost-generating mechanism.

We did not study pricing rules of type b (imitative pricing) for similar reasons. Imitation implies the presence of someone to imitate, and since we were generating data for only one firm, and not dealing with any sort of explicit oligopoly relationships, there was no way in which such rules could be investigated.

Rules of type c (the learning rules) could have been tested. We did not investigate these by simulation techniques because we felt the calculations had already gone far enough for our present purpose—illustration of a method of approach. However, a few observations on the properties and testing of such learning rules are offered in Appendix A.

The last type of rule of thumb, the type discussed in the remainder of this paper, is what we have called the pseudo maximizing rule. Details of each rule depend on the character of the functions used as estimates of the cost and demand functions. We considered four possible sorts of approximating function: linear, quadratic, logarithmic, and exponential. Of course, various combinations are possible—the demand curve can be linear and the cost curve logarithmic, etc. Thus 16 possible combinations were examined (and a few others in addition). Most of these were quickly abandoned because they required computations too complex to permit them to qualify as rules of thumb, and we emerged with four possibilities to use in our test.[12] Two other rather arbitrary "naïve" pricing rules were set up as standards of minimal performance.

We imposed one rather strong condition on the construction of our rules in order to assure that they were sufficiently simple to qualify as rules of thumb: in no case was the decision-maker asked to take account of more than two points on his demand curve and two points on his cost curve in his calculations. Very clearly this (intentionally) restricted us to

[11] Thus, it may be argued that the randomly chosen price rule of thumb (Rule 2) which we did test is the best approximation to a fixed markup rule that our analysis can achieve! The reason for our inability to test a markup rule can be made clearer in the simple case where marginal and average cost are constant and hence equal to one another. By the standard marginal revenue expression, $MR=p(1-1/e)$ where e is the elasticity of demand. Hence, if price, p, is optimal so that $MR=MC=AC$, we must have $p(1-1/e)=AC$. The optimal markup over average cost is thus $1/(1-1/e)-1=1/(e-1)$. This well-known result shows that the optimal markup is constant only if e is constant. Moreover, a fixed markup price will have a random relationship to an optimal price so long as e is a random number. Similar arguments hold when MC is not equal to AC.

[12] Several other cases might have qualified. For example, the linear cost function $D+Eq$ and the demand function $p=A-Bq^{k-1}$ can readily be shown to yield the maximum pricing rule $p=(kA-A+E)/k$.

the crudest sort of approximation procedures, for we wanted to see how far one can get with such extremely imperfect tools.

VI. *Description of the Experiments: the Cost and Demand Functions*

Before describing the details of our experiments, it is convenient to summarize the basic methods that were used. First, a demand (average revenue) curve facing the entrepreneur and his total cost curve are generated by a random process. The resulting pair of demand and cost curves are regarded as the "true" curves, describing correctly the actual state of affairs. The entrepreneur is assumed to know only two points on each of these curves. He uses some rule of thumb to calculate from these two pairs of points the price he is to charge in the market. We can determine from the true demand and cost curves the profit-maximizing price and the maximum amount of profit as well as the entrepreneur's actual profit resulting from his rule-of-thumb price. The comparison of actual and maximum profit provides an estimate of the efficiency of the rule of thumb.

The detailed discussion of our basic experiments can conveniently be divided into three parts: (1) the methods that were used to generate demand and cost functions, (2) the rules of thumb that were employed, (3) the method that was used to obtain estimates of the performances of various rules of thumb.

1. *The demand (average revenue) function.* The hypothetical product we deal with is assumed to be such that the quantity demanded is zero when the price, p, is greater than or equal to 21. The demand function (as well as the cost function) is discrete. The quantity demanded is defined only for integral values of p. The demand function was obtained by requiring the graph to start off at the point with coordinates $p=21$, $q=0$ and then calculating *increments* in the quantity demanded corresponding to successive unit reductions in the price. The increments were selected in one of two ways:[13] (i) in Runs 1, 2, 3, 4, and 5 the increments are uniformly distributed over the integers 1, $\cdots$, 64; (ii) in Run 6 the tth increment is X_t+2t where X_t is uniformly distributed over the integers 1, $\cdots$, 64. Note that the total revenue function need not be concave everywhere, and that a finite amount is demanded when the price is zero.

[13] These two methods generate demand functions whose expected values are, respectively, linear and quadratic. That is, in Runs 1–5, with each unit increase in price the expected (average) decrease in demand is $(1+2+\cdots+64)/64=32.5$. Hence the expected dq/dp is constant and the expected demand curve is linear. In Run 6 the expected sales increment when price is $p=21-t$ is $\Delta q=32.5+2t$, so that we can take $\Delta q/\Delta p=-32.5-2t$ (approx.), and hence the expected demand function generated in Run 6 is quasiquadratic. Similar interpretations hold for the cost functions that were used in the various runs. More information about the nature of these functions is given in Appendix B.

2. *The total cost function.* The demand function was obtained by associating with each price, p, a quantity $q=f(p)$. The cost function associates with each of these q's a total cost figure $C=g(q)$. With zero output we associate a cost figure which is chosen from the uniform distribution over the integers $1, \cdots, 64$. Each successive cost figure (associated with the successively higher output levels) is obtained from the immediately preceding one by the addition of an increment. Depending on the run, the tth increment is (i) chosen from the same distribution, (ii) a multiple of an increment chosen from the same distribution, or (iii) expressible as Y_t+8t where Y_t is chosen from the same distribution.

It is obvious that maximum profit and the optimal price are easily determined from these functions, simply by examining in turn, each of the 22 possible price levels ($p=0$ to $p=21$) and calculating, in each case, the associated profit figure. The six experiments are summarized in the table below, showing the manner in which the tth increments for the demand and cost functions were generated. Letting X_t and Y_t be random variables distributed uniformly over the integers $1, \cdots, 64$, we have:

	Demand function increment	Cost function increment
Run 1	X_t	Y_t
2	X_t	$4Y_t$
3	X_t	$8Y_t$
4	X_t	Y_t+8t
5	X_t	$4Y_t+8t$
6	X_t+2t	Y_t

3. *Entrepreneurial estimates of the demand and cost functions.* For the purpose of calculating rule-of-thumb solutions to the profit-maximization problem we assumed that, on the basis of recent experience, the entrepreneur knew exactly two points on his demand function and two points (with the same abscissae as the points on the demand function) on his cost function. The entrepreneur was then assumed to calculate his pseudo optimal price on the basis of the information contained in these four points. It is to be noted that if the pseudo optimal price, p, turned out to be fractional, it was rounded to the smallest integer greater than p. The profit accruing to the entrepreneur under a particular rule of thumb was then calculated from the true demand and cost functions.

It is clear that the entrepreneurial estimates of the demand and cost functions will depend, in general, upon which two of many possible points on the demand and cost functions the entrepreneur is assumed to know. In order to evaluate the *average or expected* effectiveness of a rule of thumb statistically, the experimenter must therefore present the entrepreneur, seriatim, with various alternative pairs of points and observe his behavior in each of these possible cases. The manner in which such pairs of points were selected for the purposes of the experiment is described in Section VIII.

VII. *The Rules of Thumb*

The six rules of thumb which were investigated were chosen essentially on the basis of their (relative) simplicity. No attempt was made a priori to choose rules which would in some sense be highly reasonable. In particular, the first two of the rules which are about to be described may be considered totally arbitrary and unreasonable. These "naïve rules" were designed only to provide minimum standards of performance, in that any rule which does not provide results better than those offered by our naïve rules should, doubtless, be rejected out of hand.

(Naïve) Rule 1. Fixed price. Irrespective of the location of the two known points on the demand function and the cost function, charge a price $p=11$, which is the midpoint of the range of relevant positive prices. Strictly speaking, this is not even a rule of thumb under our definition because no decision machinery is provided whereby the decision-maker can actually select his unvarying price on the basis of objectively measurable data.

(Naïve) Rule 2. Random price. Choose a price from the uniform distribution over the integers $3, \cdots, 17$, irrespective of the two known points from the demand and cost functions.

Rule 3. Linear demand, linear cost. Fit to the two known points on the demand function the linear relation $p=a-bq$, and to the two points on the total cost function the linear relation $c=d+eq$. If the two pairs of points are given by (p_1, q_1), (p_2, q_2) and by (c_1, q_1), (c_2, q_2), estimates of a, b, d, and e are obtained from the expressions

$$\hat{b} = \frac{p_1 - p_2}{q_2 - q_1}$$

$$\hat{a} = p_1 + \hat{b}q_1$$

$$\hat{e} = \frac{c_1 - c_2}{q_1 - q_2}$$

$$\hat{d} = c_1 - \hat{e}q_1.$$

Here, for example, the expressions for $\hat{b}$ and $\hat{a}$ are obtained directly by elimination from the two equations $p_1=\hat{a}-\hat{b}q_1$ and $\hat{p}_2=\hat{a}-\hat{b}q_2$. The entrepreneur is then assumed to calculate his pseudo optimal price by maximizing profit on the basis of the estimated demand and cost functions. Profit is

$$\pi = aq - bq^2 - d - eq,$$

and maximizing,

$$\frac{d\pi}{dq} = a - 2bq - e = 0$$

so that

$$q = \frac{a - e}{2b}$$

and, from our demand equation,[14]

$$p = a - b\left(\frac{a - e}{2b}\right) = \frac{a + e}{2} \cdot$$

By virtue of the method by which the true demand function is generated, $b > 0$ and the second-order condition for a maximum is always satisfied.

Rule 4. Linear demand, quadratic cost. In Rule 4 the demand function was estimated in the same manner as in Rule 3. The cost relationship fitted was the quadratic function $c = dq + eq^2$. The coefficient estimates were given by

$$\hat{e} = \frac{c_1 q_2 - c_2 q_1}{q_1 q_2 (q_1 - q_2)}$$

$$\hat{d} = \frac{1}{q_1}\left[c_1 - \hat{e} q_1^2\right].$$

Maximizing profit

$$\pi = aq - bq^2 - dq - eq^2$$

yields the first-order condition

$$\frac{d\pi}{dq} = a - 2bq - d - 2eq = 0$$

[14] The clerk who actually makes the rule-of-thumb calculation does not have to make an explicit estimate of the demand and cost equations to determine price. From our next equation we have $p = (a+e)/2$ and so, substituting the preceding estimating expressions for a and e, we obtain $p = (p_1 q_2 - p_2 q_1 + c_2 - c_1)/2(q_2 - q_1)$. This equation permits calculation of price directly in terms of the observed prices, cost and sales levels. A similar observation applies to our other rules.

whereby

$$q = \frac{a-d}{2(b+e)}, \quad \text{and} \quad p = a - b\left(\frac{a-d}{2(b+e)}\right).$$

The second-order condition is

$$2(b+e) > 0.$$

We observed the following conventions:

(a) Where the second-order condition failed (which can happen since e may be negative), a price $p=21$ was charged.[15]

(b) If the calculated optimal quantity was nonpositive, a price $p=21$ was charged.

(c) Marginal cost was constrained to be positive for the entire relevant range of outputs.

Rule 5. Linear demand, logarithmic cost. In Rule 5 the demand curve was obtained as before. But this time the cost function was

$$c = dq + e \log(q+1).$$

From the two given points on the cost function, the coefficients d and e were estimated by

$$\hat{e} = \frac{c_1 q_2 - c_2 q_1}{q_2 \log(q_1+1) - q_1 \log(q_2+1)}$$

$$\hat{d} = \frac{1}{q_1}\left[c_1 - \hat{e}\log(q_1+1)\right].$$

Maximization of the profit function

$$\pi = aq - bq^2 - dq - e\log(q+1)$$

yields the first-order condition

$$\frac{d\pi}{dq} = a - 2bq - d - \frac{e}{q+1} = 0,$$

whence

$$q = \frac{(a-d-2b) \pm \sqrt{(a-d-2b)^2 + 8b(a-d-e)}}{4b}.$$

[15] This convention and the corresponding conventions for Rules 5 and 6 may plausibly be considered to have introduced some bias against these rules in our final evaluation. For with $p=21$, sales are zero and profits negative; presumably in cases where a rule breaks down in so obvious a manner even a moderately intelligent clerk could often do better than that, so that it is probably unfair to credit these rules with no more than a zero profit contribution in these cases.

The second-order condition is

$$-2b + \frac{e}{(q+1)^2} < 0.$$

Various problem possibilities arise in this calculation, and they were handled by the conventions indicated below:

(a) Double roots. If the single distinct q was negative, a price of 21 was charged. If the single distinct root was positive but the second-order condition was not satisfied, a price of 21 was charged, yielding zero sales.

(b) If roots were complex, a price of 21 was charged.

(c) If the roots were real and distinct, a price of 21 was charged either if both roots were negative or if the single positive root corresponded to a minimum.

If a positive q^*, corresponding to a maximum of the profit function, existed, the entrepreneur charged the price $p = a - bq^*$.

Rule 6. Hyperbolic demand, quadratic cost. In Rule 6 the demand function is approximated by $p = a - b/q$, and its coefficients were estimated from the two "observed" points by

$$\hat{b} = -\frac{p_1 - p_2}{q_2 - q_1} q_1 q_2$$

and

$$\hat{a} = p_1 + \frac{\hat{b}}{q_1}.$$

The cost function was estimated as under Rule 4.

The profit function now is

$$\pi = aq - b - dq - eq^2$$

and, maximizing, we obtain

$$\frac{d\pi}{dq} = a - d - 2eq = 0,$$

yielding

$$q = \frac{a - d}{2e},$$

and the second-order condition is now

$$e > 0.$$

If either the second-order condition was violated or the pseudo optimal q was nonpositive, the pseudo optimal price $p=21$ was chosen. Otherwise the entrepreneur was taken to charge

$$p = a - b\left(\frac{2e}{a-d}\right).$$

VIII. *Methods of Testing*

As indicated earlier, Rules 1 and 2 yield results which are independent of the particular information assumed to be immediately available to the entrepreneur. Therefore one and only one rule-of-thumb solution is provided by each of these two rules for any given randomly generated demand function-cost function pair.

This is not the case with Rules 3, 4, 5, and 6. The particular solution obtained from these rules depends on which two out of the possible 22 points on the demand and cost functions are used in fitting the demand and cost functions.

We have assumed that a zero output or an output salable only at a zero price is never used by the entrepreneur in this calculation. Hence 20 points remain, out of which "nature" was taken to choose two for the entrepreneur to observe. In order to evaluate the performance of a rule of thumb we calculated its solution for each possible pair of points chosen out of the total of 20. There are 190 such pairs and therefore 190 profit figures corresponding to a single "true" demand function-cost function combination, i.e., to a single rule of thumb. For each particular true demand function-cost function combination we thus obtained the profit accruing under Rules 1 and 2, and each of these was compared with the *average* profit figure accruing under Rules 3, 4, 5, and 6.

Altogether, 24 different true demand function-cost function combinations were generated for each run.

IX. *Results of the Calculations*

Table 1 contains a summary of the results of the calculations. The table is divided into six sets of rows, each set corresponding to one of the six runs, and seven columns, corresponding to true profit maximization and the six rules of thumb. In each set of rows corresponding to a particular run the first row contains the mean profit (for the 24 cases) under true profit maximization and the various rules of thumb; the second row records mean profit as a percentage of maximum profit; the third row contains the standard deviations of the profit expectations for the 24 cases; the fourth row reports the standard deviation divided by the mean; the fifth row contains the standard deviation over the 24 cases of the difference between maximum profit and mean profit achieved (a measure of *dependability* of the rule in approximating the

TABLE 1—SUMMARY OF RESULTS

	Max. Profit	Rule 1	Rule 2	Rule 3	Rule 4	Rule 5	Rule 6
RUN 1							
Mean Profit	3,398.2	3,204.7	2,350.8	2,980.9	2,971.8	2,985.0	223.5
Mean Profit/Maximum Profit	1.000	.943	.692	.877	.875	.878	.066
Standard Deviation	535.4	500.7	803.6	459.6	458.6	459.0	290.7
Standard Deviation/Mean Profit	.158	.156	.342	.154	.154	.154	.130
Standard Deviation of (Mean Profit − Maximum Profit)		190.3	890.5	168.0	152.0	169.4	441.8
Lowest Profit		2,016.0	483.0	1,925.6	1,951.6	1,928.5	−55.0
RUN 2							
Mean Profit	2,446.5	2,091.1	991.3	1,934.4	1,898.6	1,947.1	− .9
Mean Profit/Maximum Profit	1.000	.855	.405	.791	.776	.796	—
Standard Deviation	614.2	554.8	1,151.4	516.8	565.9	521.4	220.8
Standard Deviation/Mean Profit	.251	.265	1,161	.267	.298	.268	.237.46
Standard Deviation of (Mean Profit − Maximum Profit)		321.4	1,271.1	212.4	220.5	202.6	481.7
Lowest Profit		870.0	−1,770.0	1,001.5	1,118.1	1,040.9	−220.0
RUN 3							
Mean Profit	1,340.8	606.2	−821.3	741.3	650.2	770.7	−181.7
Mean Profit/Maximum Profit	1.000	.452	—	.553	.485	.576	—

TABLE 1—(*Continued*)

	Max. Profit	Rule 1	Rule 2	Rule 3	Rule 4	Rule 5	Rule 6
Standard Deviation	720.2	717.6	1,747.1	618.8	752.8	587.3	205.8
Standard Deviation/Mean Profit	.537	1.184	2.127	.835	1.158	7.62	1.133
Standard Deviation of (Mean Profit−Maximum Profit)		489.7	1,849.8	273.4	340.1	259.3	601.7
Lowest Profit		−658.0	−4,774.0	118.8	−658.7	129.0	−440.0
RUN 4							
Mean Profit	3,048.9	2,764.7	1,617.5	2,519.9	2,608.4	2,541.0	522.5
Mean Profit/Maximum Profit	1,000	.907	.531	.826	.856	.833	.171
Standard Deviation	550.9	500.7	1,168.1	450.0	471.4	451.9	251.4
Standard Deviation/Mean Profit	.181	.181	.722	.179	.181	.178	.481
Standard Deviation of (Mean Profit−Maximum Profit)		277.3	1,275.7	212.8	169.4	204.2	428.6
Lowest Profit		1,576.0	−1,037.0	1,661.7	1,708.9	1,673.2	−25.7
RUN 5							
Mean Profit	2,186.3	1,651.1	258.0	1,574.7	1,639.7	1,608.0	26.7
Mean Profit/Maximum Profit	1.000	.755	.118	.720	.750	.736	.012
Standard Deviation	610.1	554.8	1,567.5	472.3	561.4	480.0	205.9

TABLE 1—(*Continued*)

	Max. Profit	Rule 1	Rule 2	Rule 3	Rule 4	Rule 5	Rule 6
Standard Deviation/Mean Profit	.279	.336	6.076	.300	.342	.298	7.867
Standard Deviation of (Mean Profit−Maximum Profit)		380.3	1,688.3	272.9	226.0	257.6	469.6
Lowest Profit		430.0	−3,290.0	913.7	791.5	983.3	−220.0
RUN 6							
Mean Profit	4,337.8	4,194.7	3,287.1	4,152.3	4,104.0	4,155.0	311.1
Mean Profit/Maximum Profit	1.000	.967	.758	.957	.946	.958	.072
Standard Deviation	517.1	500.5	883.2	485.6	487.6	487.6	498.4
Standard Deviation/Mean Profit	.119	.119	.269	.117	.119	.117	1.602
Standard Deviation of (Mean Profit−Maximum Profit)		125.0	853.4	73.0	126.0	73.6	614.3
Lowest Profit		3,006.0	1,167.0	2,969.2	2,958.5	2,967.2	−32.6

maximum), and, finally, the last row indicates the least profit encountered in the 24 cases.

The figures in Table 1 suggest that Rules 2 and 6 can be eliminated immediately on the basis of their poor performance. Rule 2 does not perform badly in Run 1 but tends to be much worse in most later runs. The reason is that, because of the upward shift in the cost function in Runs 2–5, the average optimal price is higher in these runs; hence the average deviation (average mistake) involved in using Rule 2, which uses random price setting, tends to increase in the later runs. The hyperbolic demand function involved in Rule 6 is bad because the true demand function is pseudo linear (except in Run 6) in the sense that if, in generating the demand function, we replace the random element by its expected value, we would indeed obtain a set of points lying on a straight line. In fact, the various actual demand functions generated can be judged visually to be linear to a reasonable level of approximation. Fitting a hyperbolic function to a linear set of points (particularly on the basis of two points only!) is likely to lead to poor results.

The relatively good performance of naïve Rule 1 (especially in Run 1) is not as inexplicable as it may appear. It is largely an artifact of the nature of our simulated cost and demand functions, as is shown in Appendix B. Indeed, it was the surprising profitability of Rule 1 which indicated some of the biases of our simulation model and led to the analysis in the Appendix.

Rules 3, 4, and 5 involve linear demand functions and linear, quadratic, and logarithmic cost functions, respectively. Since the total cost function is generated in essentially the same way as the demand function, it is pseudo linear (except in Runs 4 and 5 where it is pseudo quadratic) and we would, on the basis of previous arguments, expect Rule 3 to perform best in Runs 1, 2, 3, and 6. In terms of mean profit this is not quite the case but, on any criterion, the performance of Rule 3 is difficult to distinguish from that of Rule 5. All three of these rules yield high average profits, Rules 3 and 5 providing the largest returns in Runs 1, 2, 3, and 6. In Runs 4 and 5 the cost function is pseudo quadratic, and Rule 4 performs best in terms of mean profit, as indeed it should. On the basis of other criteria they do quite well too. With the exception of Rule 6, profits under Rules 3, 4, and 5 exhibit the smallest standard deviations, indeed in most cases *smaller than the standard deviation of the true optimal profit figures*. In most cases (except Run 3, Rule 4) the standard deviation as a fraction of mean profit is of the same order of magnitude for Rules 3, 4, and 5 as for maximum profits. The standard deviation of the difference between mean and maximum profit is lowest (except for one minor exception) for Rules 3, 4, and 5 and varies from run to run in such a manner as to preclude an unambiguous ranking of these three rules. The lowest profit figures produced by Rules 3, 4, and 5 are also relatively high, easily beating the alternative rules of thumb except in a few cases.

Thus Rules 3, 4, and 5 seem to be the best of our rules of thumb, whether judged on variability of profit yield or on the basis of the maximum criterion. On the grounds of simplicity and lowest cost of computation, Rule 3 comes out ahead because it uses only linear functions. It is noteworthy that the simplest rule is also among the best as judged by the other criteria.

It may be noted in conclusion that the performance of these rules of thumb in terms of mean profit is indeed remarkable in view of the fact that the profit calculations were based on demand and cost functions fitted only to *pairs* of points on the two functions. Since the demand and cost functions are pseudo linear or pseudo quadratic in the sense described, we would expect reasonably good estimates of the true functions when the estimation procedure involves a pair of points lying relatively far from one another. However, we would expect rather poor estimates of the functions when the points upon which they are based are close together. On the whole, therefore, the mean profit results (which are averages of "good" and "bad" estimates) are surprisingly good, even those of Run 3. Although, when taken as per cent of maximum profit, the yields of the rules fell considerably in Run 3 (e.g., in that run Rule 3 earned only 55.3 per cent of maximum profit on the average), the absolute discrepancy between maximum profit and mean profit remained substantially unchanged through the three runs, the difference between maximum profits and Rule 3 profits being 417.31 in Run 1, 512.09 in Run 2, and 599.70 in Run 3.

X. *Concluding Comments*

The primary goal of this paper has been to open up a new area of investigation rather than to produce any final conclusions. We have discussed the general considerations which must be involved in the choice of effective rules of thumb. The difficulties inherent in the problem, both practical and analytical, were examined in some detail. Because of these problems, and the relative crudeness which characterizes portions of our investigation, even its limited results should, perhaps, be considered rather remarkable. The tests utilized in the analysis seem to have shown themselves capable of producing an effective ranking of alternative rules of thumb.

We are well aware that our results are highly dependent on the nature of the frequency distribution implicit in our random-number generators, on the set of rules which were chosen for testing, and on our methods of construction of the cost and demand functions. Future experimenters might well try a number of alternatives, including demand and cost data involving random errors of observation and shifting cost and demand functions. The learning rules described in Appendix A would appear to merit further examination, and alternatives to the simulation methods employed in this paper should be considered. Empirical evaluation studies of rules of thumb used in industry might also be undertaken. It is obvious, then, that our main result is a set of suggestions for further research and some degree of assurance that this line of investigation is capable of yielding meaningful conclusions.

There still remains the question, how can the results of such a study be used? Surely, on the basis of our artificial and fragmentary experimentation no serious recommendation can be offered to anyone who is responsible for pricing decisions in practice. One path which may be more promising would require a far larger number and more diversified set of simulation calculations. It might then be possible for any given rule of thumb to characterize the types of situation in which it can be expected to perform relatively well. If this is done with sufficient care and the characterizations are carefully designed to be operational, it may even be possible to apply these conclusions to real decision problems.

At any rate, we have tried to illustrate the surprisingly difficult nature of a problem which, though often mentioned obliquely, seems never before to have been subjected to systematic attack. We must leave it to the reader to judge whether these initial results can be considered encouraging.

Appendix A: Learning Rules of Thumb

We undertook no simulation study of rules of thumb in which the profit-maker attempts by trial and error to grope his way toward an optimum. Part of the reason is that the simulation model used by us would not have constituted an adequate trial of such a learning rule. With no shifts in the profit function, a well-designed learning rule can usually be relied on to converge toward the optimum as will be illustrated presently. Indeed, experience with analogous mathematical procedures such as Newton's method for approximating the roots of an equation suggests that they will often converge in fairly short order. Only in a model with frequent and unpredictable shifts in the cost and profit function is a learning rule put to the acid test, for only then can we see whether its convergence towards an optimum proceeds more quickly than the obsolescence of the past information which has been used in constructing it. With a fixed-profit function a good learning rule must almost certainly perform more satisfactorily in the long run than any other type of rule of thumb, but whether it will do so in practice depends entirely on the volatility of the relevant functions.

The learning-model pricing procedures can usually be represented by difference equations. However, these equations must be at least of second order.[16] Such a rule states that the change from the price of this period to the next depends on the preceding price change and the resulting change in profit. Symbolically, we then have $p_{t+1}-p_t=f(p_t-p_{t-1}, \pi_t-\pi_{t-1})$ where p_t and π_t, respectively, represent price and profit in period t, and where we can eliminate the profit figure from the equation by substituting in the profit function, $\pi=g(p_t)$.

This difference equation will normally be nonlinear because the profit function is normally nonlinear; indeed, it must be so if (in the absence of constraints) there is to be any profit-maximizing price.

In addition, a nonlinearity will be imparted by the fact that the sign of next period's price change depends both on the sign of last period's price change and on the sign of last period's profit change. More specifically, we require that if profits have gone up, next period's price change will be of the same sign as that of last period. But if profits have fallen, next period's price change will be of sign opposite from that of the preceding period.

One simple relationship which meets this requirement is

$$p_{t+1} - p_t = k\,\frac{\pi_t - \pi_{t-1}}{p_t - p_{t-1}}$$

if $p_t \neq p_{t-1}$ and $p_{t+1}-p_t=0$ otherwise, where k is a speed-of-adjustment parameter. But this is only one of many possible equations which will satisfy our learning rule-of-thumb requirements. A simulation approach did not seem necessary since the consequences of such a learning rule can be ascertained analytically in at least some cases, as will now be shown.

(i) *A discrete model with quadratic profit function.* Define Δp_t as p_t-p_{t-1} and let the profit function be

$$\pi_t = ap_t - bp_t^2$$

where it may reasonably be assumed that $a\geqq 0$ and $b\geqq 0$. The learning rule then gives

$$\Delta p_{t+1} = k\,\frac{a(p_{t-1} + \Delta p_t) - b(p_{t-1} + \Delta p_t)^2 - ap_{t-1} + bp_{t-1}^2}{\Delta p_t},$$

which simplifies to

$$p_{t+1} - (1 - b')p_t + b'p_{t-1} = a' \tag{1}$$

[16] A Newton's-method type of learning rule must be of third order. For to find the point of maximum π it seeks a value of p at which $\Delta\pi/\Delta p$ approximates zero. This it does by taking two successive values $(\Delta\pi/\Delta p)_t$ and $(\Delta\pi/\Delta p)_{t-1}$ and fitting a linear relationship $(\Delta\pi/\Delta p)=a+bp$ to these observations. The value of p which satisfies $a+bp=0$ is the first approximation to the optimal price, and the corresponding marginal profit figure is taken as $(\Delta\pi/\Delta p)_{t+1}$ for the next iteration. Hence we have a second-order relationship in the $\Delta\pi/\Delta p$, which we may write $(\Delta\pi/\Delta p)_{t+1}=f[(\Delta\pi/\Delta p)_t, (\Delta\pi/\Delta p)_{t-1}]$. But since $(\Delta\pi/\Delta p)_t=(\pi_{t+1}-\pi_t)/(p_{t+1}-p_t)$, this relationship is of third order in our initial variables π_t and p_t. In other words, each iteration of such a Newton's-method rule requires *three* profit and price observations, π_{t-1}, π_t, π_{t+1}, p_{t-1}, p_t and p_{t+1}.

where $b' = kb$ and $a' = ka$. It is readily shown that the second-order linear difference equation given by (1) converges to the equilibrium solution $a/2b$ if and only if $0 < b' < 1$. That is to say, the solution converges if (a) the speed of reaction, k, is sufficiently small or (*b*) for given value of k, if the demand function and the marginal cost function are both relatively steeply inclined. For any given value of b it is then possible to construct a convergent learning rule by selecting $k < 1/b$, i.e., by employing a sufficiently moderate speed of reaction.

(ii) *A continuous model.* The learning model can be reformulated as follows:

$$\text{(2)} \qquad \dot{p} = k\frac{\dot{\pi}}{\dot{p}} \quad \text{if } \dot{p} \neq 0$$

$$\dot{p} = 0 \qquad \text{otherwise}$$

where the dot denotes differentiation with respect to time and k is positive. Equation (2) is the continuous analogue of the discrete model discussed earlier.

Assume now that the profit function is a concave, differentiable function of p, that is

$$\pi = f(p)$$

and

$$f''(p) < 0.$$

Equation (2) then becomes

$$\text{(3)} \qquad \dot{p} = k\frac{f'(p)\dot{p}}{\dot{p}} = kf'(p).$$

The stability of (3) is now examined from the global point of view. A system is globally stable if it converges to equilibrium irrespective of the initial condition of the system. Stability can be established by showing that the distance between the solution of (3) and equilibrium declines monotonically with time.[17]

Since equilibrium is given by $\dot{p}_t = 0$, we choose as our distance function the Euclidean norm

$$\text{(4)} \qquad V(t) = \tfrac{1}{2}(\dot{p} - 0)^2$$

$V(t) \geqq 0$ for all t. If, then, we show that $\dot{V}(t) < 0$ for all t, we will have proved global stability.

Differentiating (4) we obtain

$$\dot{V}(t) = k^2 f'(p) f''(p) \dot{p}$$

[17] See Struble [6].

and, since $kf'(p)=\dot{p}$, we have $\dot{V}(t) = kf''(p)\dot{p}^2 < 0$ by the concavity of the profit function, and the system is globally stable.

Appendix B: Properties of the Simulated Profit Function

We are fortunate that the distribution of the random variables on which our simulation is based is sufficiently simple to be amenable to direct analysis, and that, on this basis, the performance of Rule 1 can be predicted. For by comparing observed results with those derived from analytic calculations, one can obtain an estimate of the degree of reliability of the simulation approach employed.

Let x_i and y_i be random variables distributed uniformly over the integers $1, \cdots, 64$. The x_i are the variables which (together) constitute the demand figure, whereas the y_i add up to the cost figure at any level of price. Let t be a new variable defined by $t=21-p$ where p is the price. It is then easy to verify that the method of generating the demand and cost functions yields the profit function:

$$\pi_t = (21 - t) \sum_{i=1}^{t} (x_i + 2ai) - \sum_{i=0}^{t} (by_i - 8ci)$$

where the values of a, b and c in the six runs are as follows:

	Run 1	Run 2	Run 3	Run 4	Run 5	Run 6
a	0	0	0	0	0	1
b	1	4	8	1	4	1
c	0	0	0	1	1	0

Since[18] $E(x_i)=E(y_i)=32.5$ and[19] $\sigma^2(x_i)=\sigma^2(y_i)=341.25$, the expected profit and variance can be expressed as

$$E(\pi_t) = (21 - t)(32.5t + at(t + 1)) - b(32.5(t + 1)) - 4ct(t + 1)$$

and

$$\sigma^2(\pi_t) = (21 - t)^2 t\sigma^2(x_i) + b^2(t + 1)\sigma^2(y_i)$$

yielding, for $p=11$, the following figures:

	Run 1	Run 2	Run 3	Run 4	Run 5	Run 6
$E(\pi_t)$	3,217.5	2,145.0	715.0	2,777.5	1,705.0	4,428.0
$\sigma(\pi_t)$	645.4	687.7	808.1	645.4	687.8	645.4
$\sigma(\bar{\pi}_t)$	132.0	140.6	165.3	132.0	140.6	132.0

[18] $E(x_i) = E(y_i) = \frac{1}{64} \sum_{i=1}^{64} i = 32.5.$

[19] $\sigma^2(x_i) = \sigma^2(y_i) = \frac{1}{64} \sum_{i=1}^{64} (i - 32.5)^2 = 341.25.$

The observed mean profit under Rule 1 approximates well the theoretical mean in all runs, although all observed means are greater than the corresponding theoretical quantities. The observed standard deviations tend to be lower than the theoretical ones but, using the test quantity ns^2/σ^2 distributed as χ^2, we cannot reject the hypothesis on the .10 significance level that the observed distributions are generated by theoretical distributions with the stated means and standard deviations. Whatever relatively bad agreement exists between some of the observed and theoretical quantities must be attributed to the random-number generator.

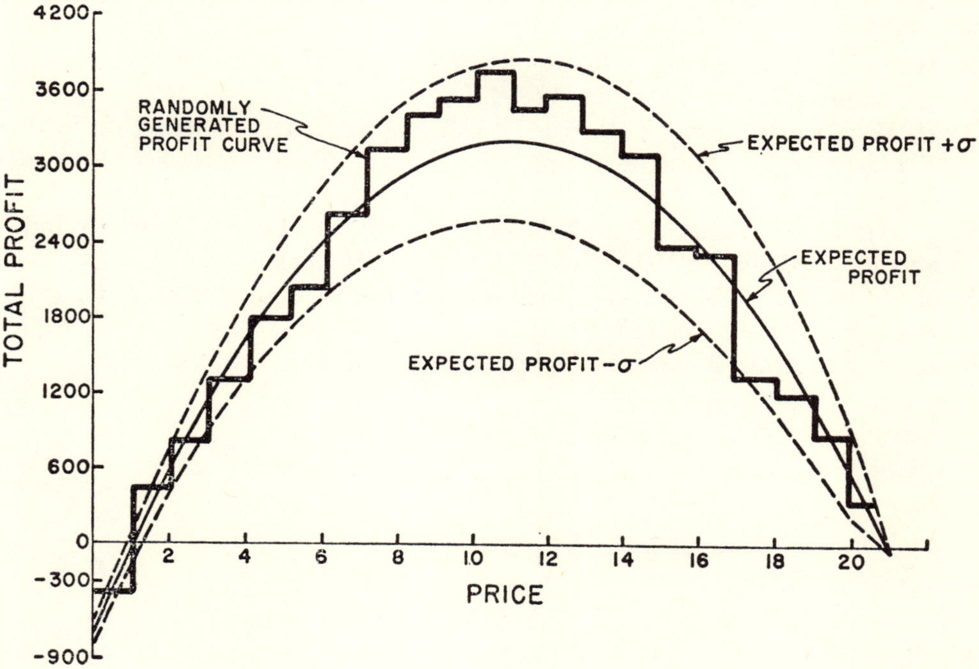

FIGURE 1

The relative goodness of Rule 1, particularly in Runs 1 and 6, becomes understandable in view of the fact that the expected profit function is fairly flat in the neighborhood of $p=11$: for example, for a price of $14 expected profit diminishes in Run 1 from 3217.5 to 2925.0, less than 10 per cent. The situation can be made clearer with the aid of a graph. Figure 1 represents our simulated profit function. For Run 1 the expected profit function is a parabola with its maximum at $p=11$. If we draw dotted curves one standard deviation above and below the expected profit curve, we obtain a band between these lines that is rather narrow near the tails of the parabola but widens considerably in the neighborhood of the maximum point. This means that the simulated profit figures almost certainly must rise just to the right of the origin and that they almost certainly must fall as the expected profit graph approaches the horizontal axis. However, in the middle range, the stochastic curve can be relatively flat. This means that even when the peak of the expected profit curve is shifted to the right (as it was in Runs 2 and 3) a fixed price $p = 11$ may still yield a total profit figure very close to the maximum profit level. It also becomes clear why Rule 1 does not do so well in Runs 2 and 3: the expected profit functions corresponding to these runs achieve their maxima at higher and higher prices. As a matter of fact, the observed mean optimal price was 10.25 in Run 1, 13.42 in Run 2, 14.58 in Run 3, 13.00 in Run 4, 13.83 in Run 5, and 10.88 in Run 6.

References

1. Kenneth J. Arrow, *Social Choice and Individual Values.* New York 1951.
2. Herman Chernoff, "Rational Selection of Decision Functions," *Econometrica*, Oct. 1954, *22*, 422–43.
3. H. W. Kuhn and W. J. Baumol, "An Approximative Algorithm for the Fixed-Charges Transportation Problem," *Naval Research Logistics Quart.*, March 1962, *9*, 1–15.
4. J. Milnor, "Games Against Nature," in R. M. Thrall, C. H. Coombs, and R. G. Davis ed., *Decision Processes*, New York 1955.
5. H. A. Simon, "Theories of Decision-Making in Economics," *Am. Econ. Rev.*, June 1959, *49*, 253–83.
6. R. A. Struble, *Nonlinear Differential Equations.* New York 1962.

[35]

CALCULATION OF OPTIMAL PRODUCT AND RETAILER CHARACTERISTICS: THE ABSTRACT PRODUCT APPROACH

WILLIAM J. BAUMOL*
Princeton University

In an unpublished paper Professor A. R. Oxenfeldt (1966) has recently called to our attention the fact that the standard models of the firm do not treat some of the most critical decision problems that arise under monopolistic competition. These models do not tell us how sellers deal with the diversity of consumer tastes that characterize most real markets and how, consequently, the firm decides on a competitive strategy that encompasses the specifications of its products and the "marketing mix" that constitutes the distinctive personality of its selling effort. It has long been recognized that these are issues that loom very large in the mind of management—often much more so than the routine pricing decisions that are the focus of most standard models. Yet it has often been felt that they are too amorphous and too difficult to define for their effective incorporation in a model that is analytically tractable.[1]

Utilizing a relatively new analytic framework which I call the "abstract product approach," this paper provides a model that undertakes to describe the calculation of an optimal selling posture: the choice of product characteristics and retailer stance that respond most effectively to diverse consumer tastes and the characteristics of products and firms that are already in the market. It illustrates in a small-scale case how the calculation can actually be conducted and describes a programing formulation that can be used in the general case. The computation does require data on consumers' tastes and costs of alternative strategies that are not always readily available. Yet reasonable approximations to the requisite data are potentially obtainable by standard means such as the market survey. And the required information is far more accessible than are the figures needed in areas of analysis considered to be on the verge of becoming operational. Here I have in mind, for example, investment decision models, many of which call for relatively firm notions on the future stream of returns that is offered by each candidate investment project.

The objective of the model provided here, then, is rather ambitious. It seeks to analyze in theoretical terms some of the most fundamental decision problems that arise out of monopolistic competi-

* The author wishes to thank the National Science Foundation and the Ford Foundation, whose grants greatly facilitated the completion of this paper. Since its completion there has appeared a pathbreaking new analysis by Kelvin Lancaster (1966) applying a similar point of view to a closely related area. The author also wishes to thank Michel Balinski and Henry Grabowski for their extremely helpful comments and suggestions. For a discussion of some of the other benefits offered by the abstract product approach and an application, see R. E. Quandt and W. J. Baumol (1966).

[1] There have, however, been a number of interesting writings on the subject. See, for example, Hans Brems (1951) and Lawrence Abbott (1955). See also Harold Hotelling (1929). A highly suggestive game-theoretic analysis has been provided by Robert Reichardt (1962).

tion and the diversity of buyers, products, and competitive strategies. In addition, it points the way to an approach to the matter that is tractable computationally and that offers some hope for eventual application.

However, the analysis evades completely one important aspect of the problem—the effects of oligopolistic interdependence. As is the case with so many models of the firm that seek to show how optimal decisions are arrived at, my construct simply ignores this vital issue and quite illegitimately assumes away the countermeasures to which our company's competitors are likely to be led by its decisions.[2]

I. CHARACTERIZATION OF CONSUMER AND SELLER DIVERSITY

Though it is obvious that there is diversity in the tastes of consumers, the manner in which these differences are sometimes characterized is most inconvenient for analytic purposes. One consumer may be extremely price conscious, while another may assign a good deal of weight to the courteous and considerate service provided by a retailer. Yet these differences are not absolute, as some descriptions might seem to suggest. For example, it is plausible that the first of the preceding customers would ignore minimal price differences if service in the slightly more expensive shop were also vastly better.

Willingness to substitute one desired attribute for another, provided the exchange rate is right, is of course representable with the aid of the individual's indifference map, and we shall use this device here. For simplicity of exposition it will be assumed that (in the two variable cases) each person's indifference curves are a set of parallel straight lines, so that the marginal rates of substitution among store or product attributes will be taken to be constant, at least over the relevant range. Hence, any individual's indifference map can be characterized completely with the aid of a single parameter: the slope of any one of his indifference curves. When the analysis is generalized to deal with n attributes of a product or store, the straight-line indifference curves must clearly be replaced by families of parallel $n - 1$ dimensional hyperplanes which are then determined uniquely by the values of their $n - 1$ partial derivatives. In the n-attribute discussion this linearity assumption will enable the analysis to remain within the realm of *linear* integer programing, and so it will play a role considerably more significant that mere expository convenience.

Though in Section V we will turn to an n-attribute analysis, the discussion of the next few sections will deal with the two-dimensional diagram—the two-attribute case. In Figure 1 we have such a diagram, and along its axes we measure two illustrative attribute variables for a retailing establishment: expenditure (per customer) on store renovation and maintenance and expenditure (per customer) on sales force, each of which is assumed to improve the desirability of the store to the shopper. A noteworthy example of other attribute measures we might have used instead of the preceding is the variable $1/p$, where p is some index of the store's price level, so that a *ceteris paribus* rise in $1/p$, that is, a fall in p, will be

[2] For a treatment of the subject of oligopolistic interdependence in product design, see Reichardt (1962). See also Martin Shubik (1959, pp. 295–308). One reader suggested an approach to this matter in which each firm solves its own problem, uses the same reasoning to calculate the responses of competitors, on this basis recalculates its own decision, etc. I have no idea whether these calculations by different firms would yield consistent results or whether the process would be convergent.

desired by the customer who does not judge quality by price and is not taken by snob appeal.

II. EQUILIBRIUM OF THE CONSUMER

ABSTRACT COMMODITIES AND RETAILERS

For our analysis it is convenient to describe a store or a product entirely as an abstract bundle of attributes such as those which have just been discussed. This is the essence of the abstract product approach, which ignores the explicit identity of any item that it is analyzing and considers it only as an attribute bundle. Thus in Figure 1 a store or a product is characterized *completely* by a point in the diagram (which we may call its "strategy point"). Point R_1, for example, represents a retailer whose strategy consists of the expenditure of OM_1 dollars on maintenance and OR_0 dollars on his sales force. The diagram also shows two other retailer or commodity strategy points, R_2 and R_3, representing two other selling outlets or two other goods. The parallel lines labeled I_1, I_1', and I_1'' are indifference curves of one customer, while those marked I_2, I_2', and I_2'' are indifference curves of another.

Since the absolute slope of the I_1 lines is less than that of R_1R_2, the straight line connecting points R_1 and R_2, customer 1 will attain maximal satisfaction by shopping at store 1. For this customer points R_2 and R_3 lie on lower indifference curves than does R_1. Similarly, because the slope of consumer 2's indifference curves is between that of R_1R_2 and that of R_2R_3, customer 2 will, if he is rational, shop at store 2. No one will shop at a "dominated" store such as k, whose attributes place it at a point R_k below and to the left of any point on the line segment (R_1R_2) connecting two other store points, because any consumer can reach a higher level of satisfaction by shopping at one or the other of the stores (1 or 2) represented by the end points of that line segment.

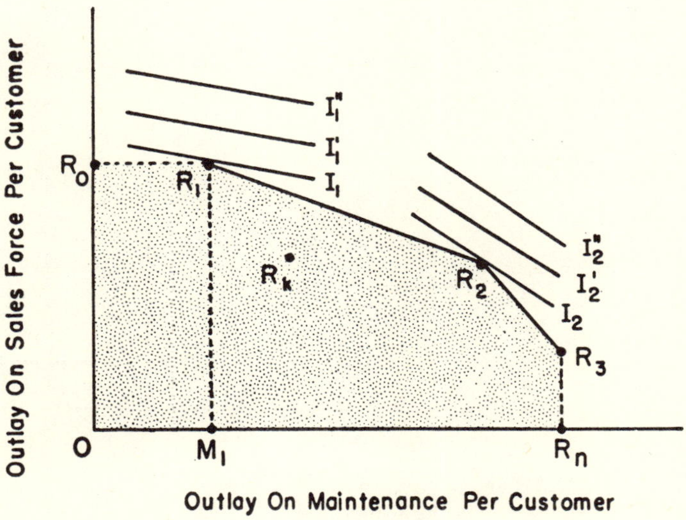

Fig. 1

This, in essence, describes the determination of the equilibrium of the consumer. We can summarize its properties with the aid of the following conventions:

Exclude from consideration dominated store points such as R_k at which no one will shop, and number the remaining store strategy points in order from left to right, $R_1, R_2, \ldots, R_{n-1}$. Let R_0 and R_n be fictitious "dummy" store points, where R_0 is the point on the vertical axis directly to the left of R_1 and R_n is the point on the horizontal axis directly below the rightmost store point, R_{n-1}

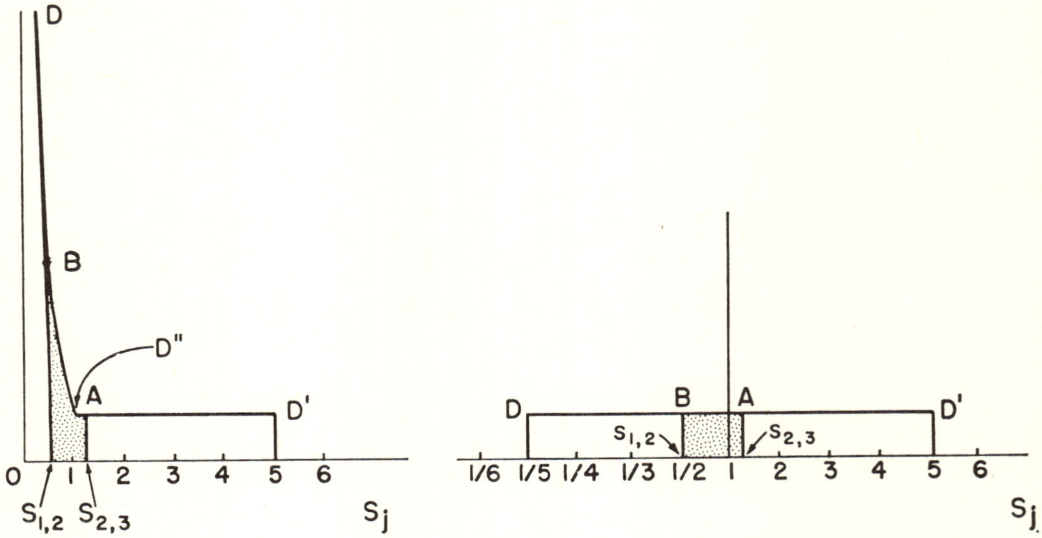

FIG. 2

(which is R_3 in the diagram). Note first that, together with the axes, R_0, R_1, $R_2, \ldots, R_n$ must constitute the boundary of a convex region. Let S_j be the (absolute) slope of one of individual j's indifference curves, and let $S_{i,i+1}$ be the (absolute) slope of the line segment R_iR_{i+1}. Then we have the following result that completely characterizes the equilibrium of the consumer:

Theorem 1.—Sufficient condition: A rational consumer j will always shop at store i if $S_{i-1,i} < S_j < S_{i,i+1}$. Necessary condition: j will not shop at store i unless $S_{i-1,i} \leq S_j \leq S_{i,i+1}$.

The rationale of this result should be obvious on examination of the diagram.

III. TOTAL DEMAND FOR A PRODUCT OR A STORE

It is now simple, in principle, to determine the demand which will be attracted by a store's or a product's characteristics. It is convenient—though, as we will see, not necessary—to assume that a customer's total demand for the items in question is relatively fixed—he is merely concerned with the choice of store in which to purchase or the choice among the competing products meeting his general specifications. Then we may consider a customer who is willing to purchase $2k$ units as the equivalent of two customers, with the same indifference-curve slopes, each one purchasing k units, and, correspondingly, an increase in demand by any one customer may be translated as a rise in the number of buyers present in the market. Utilizing this definition of "a customer," one can construct a diagram showing the distribution of customers as a function of the slope of their indifference curves (Fig. 2, *left*). This distribution is represented by DD', whose peculiar shape will be explained presently. The area under the curve between any two points S_a and S_b on the S_j (horizontal) axis represents the total number of customers (total sales to customers) whose indifference-curve slopes lie in the interval $S_a \leq S_j \leq S_b$.

In the diagram we show specifically the points $S_{1,2}$ and $S_{2,3}$ corresponding, respectively, to the slopes of line segments R_1R_2 and R_2R_3 in Figure 1. Since, by theorem 1, all individuals whose indifference curves have slopes falling in this interval will shop at store 2, we see that the sales volume of this store will be given by shaded area $S_{1,2}S_{2,3}AB$. Similarly, store 1 will obtain all customers corresponding to the available area to the left of point $S_{1,2}$, and store 3 will obtain the demand given by the area under the DD' curve to the right of point $S_{2,3}$.

This is all there is to say on the determination of demand for each store. A word should be said, however, about the peculiar distribution function DD' utilized in Figure 2, *left*, because this provides some illumination on the nature of the relevant demand function. I have as-

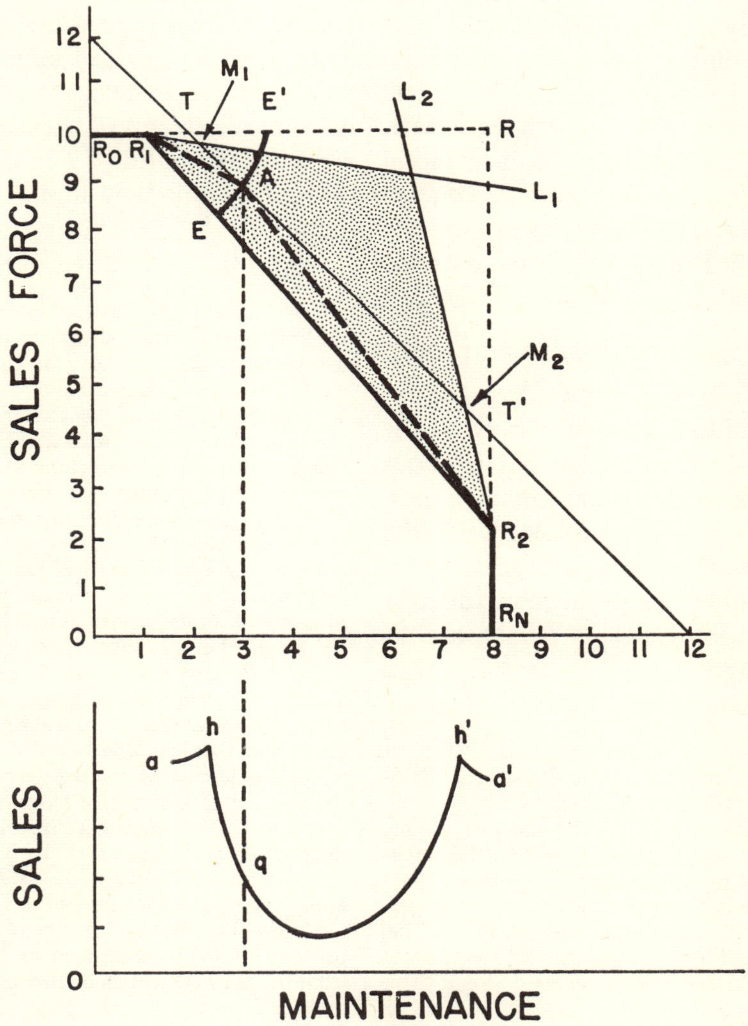

Fig. 3

sumed here as a standard of reference that the slopes of customers' indifference curves are in a sense uniformly distributed between, say, $S_j = \frac{1}{5}$ and $S_j = 5$. However, in our standard-of-reference case it seems appropriate to suppose that customers' preferences are more or less symmetrically distributed between the two attributes represented by the axes in Figure 1. That is, there should be about as many indifference maps with slopes less than unity as there are with slopes greater than unity. Thus, to show a uniform distribution in the usual way, one would have to distort the horizontal axis by extending the portion of that axis lying to the left of point $S_j = 1$, in the manner shown in Figure 2, *right*. If one then transforms the diagram back to a normal axis, the DD' curve is distorted in the manner shown in Figure 2, *left*, because the area under the curve to the left of point $S_j = 1$ must be the same as the corresponding area in Figure 2, *right*.[3]

IV. THE OPTIMAL COMPETITIVE STANCE OF A BUSINESS FIRM

We can address ourselves now to the optimal strategy of a firm that is about to open a new store or launch a new product. For reasons explained in note 4, we assume that there are initially (at least) two other competitors in the area and that their strategy points are as shown in Figure 3 by R_1 and R_2. It is clear that our store's optimal strategy point cannot lie beneath and to the left of the boundary line $R_0R_1R_2R_n$. Moreover, there is no motivation for management to spend the money necessary to take it beyond point R, which lies directly to the right of R_1 and directly above R_2. For at R our company dominates both its competitors, and, if they undertook no countermoves, he could take away all their customers. Thus all the relevant strategy points for our company must lie in the triangular region R_1RR_2.

Let TT' be a locus of all strategy points in the relevant triangular region involving a constant total expenditure on maintenance (M) and sales force (F). In our case, since we are measuring these variables in terms of the expenditure devoted to them, line TT' has the equation $M + F =$ constant, and it has a slope of minus one.[4]

One can then, as will be shown pres-

[3] The equation for the portion of the DD' curve in Figure 2, *left*, that lies to the left of point D'' is $y = f(S_j) = k/S_j^2$.

Proof.—Write $S_j = q$ for the abscissa of any point to the left of $S_j = 1$ and $S_j = p$ for the abscissas of any point to the right of this. Moreover, let k be the ordinate of any point on the horizontal segment of DD'. We require the area under DD' between $S_j = q$ and $S_j = 1$ to be the same as the area between $S_j = 1$ and $S_j = p$, where $p = 1/q$. This requires for all q that $-f(q)dq = f(p)dp$, for $p = 1/q$, $q \leq 1$. Since $f(p) = k$, this means $f(q) = -kdp/dq = k/q^2$, which is our result.

[4] We can see now why our analysis assumes that (at least) two firms are already in the market before our company starts to plan its entry. In terms of our model there is no optimal strategy for a monopoly firm. For with total demand given it would capture the entire market with any sort of reasonable facilities or product characteristics. It would, however, find it profitable to make itself sufficiently attractive to discourage the entry of new competitors. This would mean that its strategy point, R_1, would have to be at a considerable distance from the origin. Fear of retaliation aside, it would pay a second firm to locate its strategy point just above or just to the right of R_1. Thus, in Figure 3, consider any strategy point A for our second firm on iso expediture line TT'. By theorem 1, this company will capture more of the market the smaller the absolute slope of R_1A, for it will then get the business of all customers whose indifference curves are steeper than this. But the slope of R_1A decreases monotonically as A approaches T. Note that this result is independent of the position of R_1. One concludes that there are only two motivations for our second seller to differentiate himself from seller 1: first, he may want to avoid retaliation by seller 1, and, second, he may want to prevent a third entering firm from cutting him off from the market, just as he had previously done to seller 1. If he had picked a point just to the right of R_1, he would have been as vulnerable to this sort of move as seller 1 was initially.

ently, determine what point on TT' yields a maximal sales volume to our firm. Suppose this optimal point is A, which therefore represents the optimal strategic stance for our company given the constant level of expenditure specified by TT'. If one next considers the various other possible expenditure levels (various shifts in TT'), the set of corresponding optimal points such as A forms a locus EE'. This is the company's expansion path, describing the variation in its optimal strategic stance for different expenditure levels.

Let us now examine a simple though rather artificial example to describe the numerical computations involved in the determination of the optimal points. The main purpose of the derivation, of course, is to illustrate the nature of the calculation, not to obtain a result that pretends to be representative. Some readers may prefer to skim over its details or to proceed directly to the generalized n-attribute formulation in programming terms that is provided in the next section.

In Figure 3 the x and y co-ordinates of points R_1, A, and R_2 are shown in the following table:

	R_1	A	R_2
y	10	9	2
x	1	3	8

Thus, we have as the absolute slopes S_{1a} and S_{a2} for line segments R_1A and AR_2, respectively, $S_{1a} = (10 - 9)/(3 - 1) = \frac{1}{2}$ and $S_{a2} = \frac{7}{5}$. With a rectangular distribution of the sort represented in Figure 2, we consider first the area under the curve DD' between points $S_j = 1$ and $S_j' = S_{a2} = \frac{7}{5}$, which is clearly $k(S_j' - S_j) = k(\frac{7}{5} - 1) = \frac{2}{5}k$. Similarly, the area under the curve to the left of $S_j = 1$ will be $k[(1/S_{1a}) - 1] = k(2 - 1) = k$. Hence at point A total demand will be the sum of these two areas $= k + \frac{2}{5}k = \frac{7}{5}k$. This is represented by point q on the sales curve aa' shown toward the bottom of Figure 3.

From this observation we can proceed to the derivation of the entire demand relationship. Let P be any point on TT', and let its co-ordinates be (x, y). Then the absolute slopes of R_1P and PR_2 are, respectively,

$$(1) \quad S_{1P} = \frac{10 - y}{x - 1} \quad \text{and} \quad S_{P2} = \frac{y - 2}{8 - x}.$$

Since for any point on TT' we have $y = 12 - x$, these slopes become by substitution

$$(2) \quad S_{1P} = \frac{x - 2}{x - 1} \quad \text{and} \quad S_{P2} = \frac{10 - x}{8 - x}.$$

Now as point P moves toward the right along the iso expenditure curve TT', both of the preceding slopes will obviously increase in absolute value. The rise in S_{1P} will result in a loss in customers by theorem 1, for any customer j whose indifference curves have the slope S_j will cease shopping at our store once S_{1P} exceeds S_j. However, while the rise in S_{1P} loses customers whose S_j is small, the simultaneous rise in S_{P2} brings in new customers whose S_j is large; that is, it attracts customers whose S_j was formerly greater than S_{P2} in absolute value. Thus, every rightward move of point P has two counteracting effects on demand: It brings in some new customers, and it loses some old ones. This is only to be expected, for as a store changes its attributes it will attract those customers who value highly its new characteristics and will drive away the purchasers who preferred the alternative store image.

However, the peculiarity of our assumed demand distribution places a limit on this balancing process. For our illustrative premise is that $\frac{1}{5} \leq |S_j| \leq 5$ (see Fig. 2). Hence, once point P moves so far to the right that $S_{2P} = 5$, any further rightward move will yield no new customers—it will only drive away old ones. This will occur[5] where the abscissa of point P is 7.5 (point M_2 in Fig. 3). Hence the firm will never move to any point on TT' to the right of M_2. More generally, if we consider iso expenditure curves other than TT', it will never pay the company to move to any point outside the relevant shaded region that lies to the left of line segment[6] R_2L_2, for any such point P will involve a slope $S_{P2} > 5$. Similarly, the company will never consider any point P on TT' to the left of M_1 where $x = 2.25$, or any point P on any iso expenditure curve that lies above line segment R_1L_1, for at any such point the slope S_{1P} would be less than $\frac{1}{5}$ in absolute value, and so an upward move from line M_1L_1 to such a P would bring in no new customers, since, by Figure 2, there are no potential purchasers with a marginal rate of substitution lower than this.[7]

We may now examine the shape of the demand curve corresponding to M_1M_2, the relevant segment of TT'. By theorem 1, demand (D) at any point P can be obtained with the aid of (2) by considering separately the areas (in Fig. 2) to the left and to the right of the unit slope point, $S_j = 1$. This gives us

$$D = k\left(\frac{1}{S_{1P}} - 1 + S_{P2} - 1\right)$$

$$(3) \qquad = k\left(\frac{x-1}{x-2} - 1 + \frac{10-x}{8-x} - 1\right)$$

$$= \frac{k}{x-2} + \frac{2k}{8-x}.$$

This is our desired demand function. To determine some of its properties we differentiate it to obtain

$$\frac{dD}{dx} = \frac{2k}{(8-x)^2} - \frac{k}{(x-2)^2}.$$

Hence, by inspection, we see that the second derivative must be positive[8] when $2 < x < 8$, since any increase in x increases the positive term and reduces the negative term in dD/dx. Thus the portion of the demand curve corresponding to points on M_1M_2 will have the form shown by hh' in Figure 3 and will have only an interior minimum.[9] This result is totally independent of the particular values chosen for the co-ordinates of the competitive points R_1 and R_2. The entire demand curve will have the shape given by aa', and the optimal point will clearly be one of the two peaks h or h' (in this case it will be point h).[10]

[5] For by (2) this is the point where $5 = S_{P2} = (10 - x)/(8 - x)$, so that $40 - 5x = 10 - x$, that is, $x = 7.5$.

[6] By (1) the equation of R_2L_2 is given by $S_{P2} = (y - 2)/(8 - x) = 5$ so that $y = 42 - 5x$.

[7] By (1) the equation of R_1L_1 is $S_{1P} = (10 - y)/(x - 1) = \frac{1}{5}$. By (2), point M_1 is the point on this line at which $x + y = 12$, so that $(x - 2)/(x - 1) = \frac{1}{5}$, that is, $5x - 10 = x - 1$, and so $x = 2.25$.

[8] More formally, $d^2D/dx^2 = 4k/(8 - x)^3 + 2k/(x - 2)^3 > 0$ for $8 > x > 2$.

[9] Note the relationship to the conclusion by Hotelling (1929) that in spatial competition in a linear world competitors would tend to select adjacent positions in the center of the line. Abbott (1955, p. 184) points out that this sort of conclusion is "apparently the result of the highly artificial assumption that demand terminates abruptly at each end of the line, rather than tapering off at the outer fringes," and of the "assumption that an increase in the distance between buyer and seller does not diminish the quantity bought."

[10] For points to the left of h the equation for the demand curve is obtained by substituting $\frac{1}{5}$ for S_{1P} in equation (3), while the equation for $h'a'$ is ob-

V. EXTENSION TO AN n-ATTRIBUTE CALCULATION

We turn now to the generalization of our analysis to the n-attribute case. The form of our approach suggests that the firm's optimality calculation can be transformed into a linear- or non-linear-programing computation. The boundary $R_0R_1R_2 \ldots R_n$ in Figure 1 looks just like that of the feasible region in a linear-programing calculation, and the imbedded maximization calculations of the individual consumers at once suggest the decentralized-decision approach of decomposition theory. It turns out that a programing approach to the matter does work, though it is not precisely what seems to be suggested by our figures. In mathematical terms our n-attribute problem may be described as follows:

Let x_{ij} represent the proportion of consumer i's shopping done at store j (or for product j), so that we would expect $\Sigma_j x_{ij} = 1$ for any consumer i ($i = 1, 2, \ldots, m$), ($j = 0, 1, 2, \ldots, n$); let a_{jk} be the value of attribute k provided at store j or by product j ($k = 1, 2, \ldots, r$); finally, let u_{ki} be the marginal utility[11] of attribute k to consumer i. In order to permit *linear*-programing methods to be used in the following discussion, these marginal utilities are assumed to be constant, so that customers' indifference maps are again taken to be composed of families of parallel hyperplane indifference surfaces.

The objective of our store, say, store zero, is to choose values of the a_{0k} which will

$$(4)\quad \begin{cases} \text{maximize} \quad \Sigma_i x_{i0} \\ \text{subject to the budget constraint} \\ \qquad g_0(a_{01}, \ldots, a_{0r}) \leq B_0 \\ \text{and the non-negativity requirement} \\ \qquad \text{all } a_{0k} \geq 0\,. \end{cases}$$

The x_{ij}, the demands by the various customers i for the product of store j, are determined by the m subsidiary maximization calculations:[12]

$$(5)\quad \begin{cases} \text{maximize the utility of customer } i\text{:} \\ \qquad \Sigma_j\Sigma_k a_{jk}u_{ki}x_{ij} \quad (i = 1, 2, \ldots, m) \\ \text{subject to}^{13} \\ \qquad \Sigma_j x_{ij} \leq 1 \quad \text{and all} \quad x_{ij} \geq 0\,. \end{cases}$$

The solution of the consumer's decision problem (5) is trivial, for it is a

tained by substitution of 5 for S_{P2} in equation (1). The values of quantity of demands at the two candidate maxima, h and h', are determined by substitution of their x values into (3) to obtain

$$D_h = k(1/0.25 + 2/5.75) = 4\tfrac{8}{23}k\,;$$
$$D_{h'} = k(1/5.5 + 2/0.5) = 4\tfrac{2}{11}k\,.$$

[11] This can be expressed as a ratio to u_{si}, the marginal utility of any arbitrarily chosen standard attribute s. Then we need deal only with ordinal utility and marginal rates of substitution, which, as in the earlier portion of the paper, are constant as a result of the assumed constancy of the u_{si}.

[12] In this calculation the values of all competitors' attribute variables, $a_{jk}(j \neq 1)$, are taken to be given in advance. Thus we once again evade the issues raised by oligopolistic interdependence.

[13] The inequality in the constraint $\Sigma x_{ij} \leq 1$ makes it possible for the consumer to end up at any point inside the feasible region. This already provides some degree of flexibility to consumer demand. In any event, it should be observed that the analysis does *not* require total demand either of the individual consumer or of the market as a whole to be fixed and predetermined. Variability of demand can be introduced by means of two simple devices: (*a*) an increase of demand by any one consumer (say a trebling of his demand) may be described as the entry into the market of two additional consumers with similar utility functions; (*b*) new customers may be taken to flow in from store n, which is a fictitious retailing establishment offering zero prices and zero outlays on other attributes. That is, retailer n becomes the location of all potential customers who do not initially shop at any real store in the analysis but who might be induced to shop at our store (zero) if it makes itself sufficiently attractive.

single-constraint linear-programing problem in the variables x_{ij}. Since the constraint coefficients are all equal to unity, if there is a unique maximum we must have the following solution:

$$x_{iw} = 1 \quad \text{for}$$
$$\Sigma_k a_{wk} u_{ki} = \max (\Sigma_k a_{jk} u_{ki}) ;$$
$$x_{ij} = 0 \quad \text{for} \quad j \neq w .$$

The seller's decision problem (4) is not so easily solved, however, since it involves some relatively difficult combinatorial allocation problems. In effect, each time management reallocates its resources to cater to the tastes of one set of consumers, it is likely to alienate some other set of its clientele. The problem is to find some way to balance these gains and losses and thus to design a systematic procedure which leads to an optimal solution.[14] Several simplifications can help us to make the problem more tractable. First, we redefine the a_{jk} to represent the amount of *money* spent by firm j on attribute k. Then the budget constraint takes the simple linear form

$$\Sigma_k a_{0k} \leq B_0 . \tag{6}$$

Second, as a matter of convenience in application it is helpful to divide the set of consumers into subsets such that any two consumers in the same subset have reasonably similar utility functions. We will let y_{ij} be a variable whose value is unity if customers in set i find it advantageous to shop in store j and whose value is zero otherwise, and let s_i be the number of dollars to be spent by this customer set per unit of time. As a final preliminary we observe that customers in set i will purchase from our store (zero) if[15]

$$\Sigma_k a_{0k} u_{ki} \geq \max_{j \neq 0} (\Sigma_k a_{jk} u_{ki}) ,$$

that is, if store zero offers consumers i greater utility than is made available by any other retailer, j. However, all values on the right of the inequality are known in advance, since both the utility coefficients, u_{ki}, and the competitors' attributes, a_{jk}, are given. Hence we can write $\text{Max}_{j \neq 0}(\Sigma_k a_{jk} u_{ki}) = K_i$ for the utility of the best alternative offered to consumers in set i by store zero's competitors. The condition under which these customers will shop at store zero thus becomes

$$\Sigma_k a_{0k} u_{ki} \geq K_i . \tag{7}$$

It is now possible to combine the maximization problem of our seller with those of each customer set into a single mixed-integer program:[16]

Maximize $\Sigma s_i y_{i0}$ subject to

$$\Sigma a_{k0} \leq B_0 ,$$
$$y_{i0} \leq 1 ,$$

[14] Note the structural resemblance of our problem to the Colonel Blotto game in which a player can capture a chunk of territory or an installation by assigning to it more of his pieces than his opponent has placed there. Our calculation problem is rendered somewhat more difficult, since in it the weight (utility) assigned to different pieces (dollars of attribute expenditure) varies from territory to territory (consumer to consumer), and one piece (attribute expenditure) can simultaneously serve several consumers. On the other hand, the Blotto game takes into account the full problem of competitive strategy, while our discussion assumes all rivals' decisions (product designs and retailing characteristics) to be determined in advance. On the Blotto problem see D. W. Blackett (1954, pp. 55–60).

[15] This inequality disposes of the possibility of ties by assuming arbitrarily that if a customer is indifferent between store zero and another retailer he will shop at the former. The economics of the situation really offers us no information which enables us to deal with the problem more reasonably. A variety of conventions can be used to dispose of ties—for example, we can assume that if w stores each offer the same utility to customers in subset i, then $1/w$ of these customers will go to each of those retailers.

[16] I am indebted to M. Balinski for suggesting this approach to the problem.

$$\Sigma_k a_{0k} u_{ki} \geq y_{i0} K_i ,$$
$$\text{all } a_{0k} \geq 0 , \qquad y_{i0} \geq 0 ,$$
$$y_{i0} \text{ integer} .$$

Here the first constraint is company zero's budget constraint, (6), and the three constraints $y_{i0} \leq 1$, $y_{i0} \geq 0$, and y_{i0} integer guarantee that this variable can take only one of two values: either zero or one. However, it is the third constraint which constitutes the heart of the translation into a single program. It (together with the objective function) serves to guarantee that $y_{i0} = 1$ if condition (7) is satisfied and that $y_{i0} = 0$ otherwise. The reason this constraint has that effect is easily explained. The objective function guarantees that $y_{i0} = 1$ will always be chosen instead of $y_{i0} = 0$ if the former value does not violate the constraints of the problem. But if $y_{i0} = 1$, the right-hand term in our third constraint, $y_{i0}K_i$, simply becomes K_i, and this constraint is then identical with requirement (7). Hence we will have $y_{i0} = 1$ if and only if (7) is satisfied. If, however, (7) is not satisfied, so that $y_{i0} = 1$ is not feasible, then $y_{i0} = 0$ is the only possible alternative. In that case the third constraint is, in effect, annulled by being transformed into the trivial requirement[17] $\Sigma a_{0k} u_{ki} \geq 0$. We see, then, that the form of the third constraint is such that it is changed into (7) if $y_{i0} = 1$, while the constraint, for all practical purposes, becomes inoperative if $y_{i0} = 0$, exactly as the analysis requires.

[17] If some of the u_{ki} are negative, for example, if store expenditure on "background music" offends some customers, even this last weak requirement may not automatically be satisfied. In that event the constraint $\Sigma a_{0k} u_{ki} \geq y_{i0} K_i$ can be replaced by the more general form $\Sigma a_{0k} u_{ki} \geq K_i - M(1 - y_{i0})$ with M sufficiently greater than K_i. Obviously if $y_{i0} = 1$ this again reduces to (7), while if $y_{i0} = 0$ the right-hand side of the inequality reduces to $K_i - M$, so that $\Sigma a_{0k} u_{ki}$ is constrained only to exceed this negative number.

Computational approaches to this sort of mixed-integer-programing problem have recently been developed. In particular, a partitioning approach invented by Benders seems to be a promising way to deal with the matter (see J. F. Benders, 1962, and M. L. Balinski, 1965, esp. pp. 271–74 and 268–90). The procedure has the advantage that, should the calculation prove too long and expensive, it can be stopped at an intermediate step to obtain an approximating feasible solution along with an estimate of its distance from the optimum.

VI. CONCLUDING COMMENTS

We have developed a model that constitutes an approach to the analysis of the optimal strategy of product design and retailer-characteristic determination. These decisions are, of course, at the heart of product differentiation and are among the most crucial issues faced by company managements.

The analysis has drawn its methods from several lines of analysis, perhaps the most important being the abstract product approach (in which goods and retail establishments become just bundles of attributes). This is the very fruitful method that was first contributed by Kelvin Lancaster (1966) and independently arrived at by R. E. Quandt and the present author (Quandt and Baumol, 1966). The source of the problem studied in this paper is to be found in Oxenfeldt's more empirical view of the firm (1966), and for its calculations our investigation turned to the methods of integer programing. Thus from this variety of strands there emerges what may be a promising approach to a problem that seems previously to have appeared to be intractable, so that despite its obvious importance it has heretofore produced a comparatively scanty literature.

REFERENCES

Abbott, L. *Quality and Competition*. New York: Columbia Univ. Press, 1955.

Balinski, M. L. "Integer Programming: Methods, Uses, Computation," *Management Sci.*, XII (November, 1965), 253–313.

Benders, J. F. "Partitioning Procedures for Solving Mixed-Variables Programming Problems," *Numerische Math.*, IV (1962), 238–52.

Blackett, D. W. "Some Blotto Games," *Naval Res. Logistics Q.*, I (March, 1954), 55–60.

Brems, H. J. *Product Equilibrium under Monopolistic Competition*. Cambridge, Mass.: Harvard Univ. Press, 1951.

Hotelling, H. "Stability in Competition," *Econ. J.*, XXXIX (March, 1929), 41–57.

Lancaster, K. J. "A New Approach to Consumer Theory," *J.P.E.*, LXXIV, No. 2 (April, 1966), 132–57.

Oxenfeldt, A. R. "Broad Outlines of a New Model of Markets: Buyer and Seller Diversity." New York: Columbia Univ., March, 1966 (mimeographed).

Quandt, R. E., and Baumol, W. J. "The Demand for Abstract Transport Modes: Theory and Measurement," *J. Regional Sci.*, VI, No. 2 (1966), 13–26.

Reichardt, R. "Competition through the Introduction of New Products," *Zeitschrift Nationalökon.*, XXII (1962), 41–84.

Shubik, M. *Strategy and Market Structure*. New York: John Wiley & Sons, 1959.

[36]

CHAPTER EIGHT

REASONABLE RULES FOR RATE REGULATION: PLAUSIBLE POLICIES FOR AN IMPERFECT WORLD*

by William J. Baumol

Sub-second-best Proposals for Public Policy

A considerable proportion of the goods and services supplied by the public utilities (broadly defined) have long been provided under conditions of natural monopoly. Because effective competition in the production of at least some of the firm's products is not a reasonable alternative in most of these cases, the necessity of public regulation of rates and of other aspects of the operation of these firms is widely accepted. Yet despite extensive experience, the regulatory principles that have emerged still seem far from perfect. This paper undertakes the formulation of a set of procedures which have a somewhat firmer foundation in economic analysis. These procedures are designed to deal with the problems which may potentially arise from the monopolistic nature of the firms in question. But it should be recognized that some of the problems discussed may in practice turn out to be unimportant, or they may arise only infrequently. And, because the discussion ignores completely the existing legal framework and regulatory traditions, some of the proposals discussed are of doubtful practical import, but they should at least be of some interest in bringing out the relevant issues.

Economists complain with some reason that the criteria employed by regulatory agencies find little justification in economic analysis. Yet a regulatory commissioner can reply with at least equal justice that the economic literature offers little help to those who must decide on policy in our imperfect world. For the economists' tests, in all their subtlety and sophistication, break down completely when arrangements in the remainder of the economy do not accord with the underlying premises of his models. Welfare economics tells us that there is much to be said for a system of pricing in which *every* rate in the economy is equal to the marginal cost incurred in supplying the service. And from this a number of investigators have jumped to the conclusion that the resulting rule is a good guide for pricing in a nationalized industry. Presumably such an approach has not been advocated widely for public utilities operated as private enterprises only because of the financial loss which it would in many cases impose and

* I am very much indebted to Ralph Turvey and James C. Bonbright for their helpful suggestions and to the National Science Foundation and the Ford Foundation, whose grants greatly facilitated the completion of this paper.

the political problems that must inevitably accompany such deficits. Yet it does not require the mathematical elaboration of the Lipsey–Lancaster second-best theorem for us to see that if other products in the economy are not priced at marginal cost, the use of marginal-cost pricing by a few nationalized firms can easily lead to a misallocation of resources. By making relatively cheap the few services supplied by these firms demand is apt to be distorted and activity in the nationalized sector overexpanded.

The theory of the second best tells us, in principle, how such a situation should be dealt with. In formal terms it goes through the mathematical calculations that determine the best that can be done under these conditions. But no one, least of all the authors of the theorem, has ever pretended that this is a practical alternative. To carry out such a procedure one must be able to specify explicitly all the economy's imperfections, employing them as constraints in the optimality calculations. This and the other information requirements of such a procedure place it well beyond the realm of practicality.

What then is the alternative? Two approaches seem possible, each of which is used at some points in this paper. First, one can simply proceed on grounds of plausibility: one can describe a set of procedures which, taking into account all that economic analysis has told us, seem likely as a matter of subjective judgment to lead to results that promote the public welfare as well as might reasonably be expected in the circumstances. Second, one can formulate a set of desiderata—a set of minimal objectives which we feel a public policy must accomplish before it is considered acceptable. Thereupon one can proceed to design policies that satisfy these minimal acceptability criteria.[1]

What this paper attempts, then, is to provide a set of basic rules for the regulation of public utility rates, principles which seem to accord roughly with the spirit of the results derived by more rigorous analysis for the idealized circumstances that are analytically tractable. In doing so the discussion takes no account of any existing procedures and traditions of regulatory policy. It assumes, in effect, that it is possible to clean the slate and start all over again.

Some Desiderata of Utility Rate Regulation

To the economist two goals of regulatory policy are obvious: first while one wishes to permit the firm to earn a reasonable rate of return, pure

[1] This approach has honorable antecedents in economic theory: it is, for example, the basis of Kenneth Arrow's analysis in his *Social Choice and Individual Values* (New York: 1951). Note also the relationship to Herbert Simon's satisficing concept: the regulatory agency that employs the approach under discussion satisfices (it makes sure that its policies meet the minimum conditions required for them to be considered satisfactory) but gives up any pretense of *maximizing* the social welfare.

monopoly profits, however defined, should be prevented. Second, one desires to minimize the misallocation of input that results because prices do not generally reflect the real resources used up in supplying a unit of output to a consumer. However, there are a number of other desiderata which are somewhat less obvious, some of which arise out of the nature of the regulatory approach normally employed.

A sensible procedure for the prevention of monopoly profits, and one that is widely utilized, imposes some sort of ceiling on over-all company earnings, a ceiling normally expressed as a maximal rate of return on investment (the "rate base"). But, while treating one problem, this arrangement creates a host of other difficulties. Where, as seems frequently to be the case, the demand for some services of a public utility is inelastic over the relevant range, the maximal permitted earnings rate and the actual rate of return are most unlikely to diverge substantially. For if the company's returns threaten to fall short of the ceiling, it need merely raise its rates for its inelastic demand services by a suitable amount, and the short-fall will be eliminated. This means that with any reasonable degree of efficiency and in the absence of any serious shortage in demand, such a company is virtually guaranteed its permitted earnings level. However, there is only one way open to the company for increasing its total earnings: an expansion of its rate base.

Several unfortunate consequences may then follow, consequences whose prevention may reasonably be considered an appropriate objective of public policy.

1. The company may lose much or all of its incentive for operating efficiency and innovation. For if the firm is virtually certain of earning x dollars, no more and no less, whatever its cost outlays—if it can make up for any rise in cost by a suitable increase in rates for its inelastic demand services, there is little motivation to keep down expenditures. Waste becomes costless to the company, and if management's motivation includes empire building as an objective in addition to profitability,[2] it may not resist the temptation to hire unnecessary staff and to increase salary rates beyond the levels they would ordinarily attain. What is really remarkable, then, is the rather high degree of efficiency that seems to characterize the operations of many public utilities in practice.

2. The obvious avenue for an increase in rate base is an investment outlay. And for our regulated company the usual profitability criteria for an investment decision do not automatically apply. If an increase in investment means that the firm is permitted a corresponding rise in its over-all earnings *which can, if need be, be obtained by raising rates on*

[2] See, e.g., O. E. Williamson, *The Economics of Discretionary Behavior* (Englewood Cliffs, N. J.: 1964).

inelastic demand services, the new investment will necessarily produce the usual rate of profit, whether or not it is utilized effectively and serves an economic purpose.

3. Investment, whether useless or useful, is not the only way to augment the rate base. If the rate base is evaluated in terms of replacement or reproduction cost, it is even profitable to have suppliers of the company's equipment raise their prices! A 10 per cent increase in the price of a new machine causes the company no loss in profits (for it will still obtain its permitted r per cent rate of return) and in addition *its older machines may then automatically be revalued* at their increased replacement cost so that the corresponding portion of the rate base will go up 10 per cent![3]

4. Destructive pricing may be defined as the temporary lowering of rates in order to drive out a competitor and thus clear the field for monopoly pricing and monopoly profits. While the typical public utility supplies some of its services under monopoly conditions, often it faces competitors in the market for a number of its other products. Regulatory agencies have for a considerable time sought to prevent destructive pricing in these markets. But with limitation of rate of return, the deliberate elimination of a competitor may serve yet another purpose: it may clear the way for expansion of the offending firm, as a means to increase its investment and hence its rate base.[4]

Most of the practices that have just been described (some of which are perhaps hypothetical) would involve the misuse of society's resources through the promotion of relatively useless investment, inefficient operation, etc., and might clearly have adverse effects on the company's competitors. It is only a little less obvious that the interests of one other class of individuals are likely to be served badly. For the cost of any type of inefficiency in the production of an item, particularly one whose demand is elastic, may well fall on the consumer of some other service or services of the firm. If inefficiencies are paid for by increases in the prices of items whose demand is inelastic, the cost will be shifted directly to the purchasers of these other services.

In sum, attempts to regulate away one sort of problem are all too likely to give rise to other difficulties. It is this list of difficulties which this paper takes to constitute the basic assignment of the regulatory agency. A good program of regulation of utility rates, then, is required to accomplish at least the following:

1. The prevention of monopoly profits without at the same time precluding the profitable operation of the company.

[3] This possibility was apparently first pointed out by Westfield. See F. M. Westfield, "Regulation and Conspiracy," *American Economic Review,* Vol. 55, (June 1965).

[4] See H. Averch and L. L. Johnson, "Behavior of the Firm under Regulatory Constraint," *American Economic Review,* Vol. 52, (Dec. 1962), pp. 1057-1059.

2. The reduction as far as can reasonably be expected of the misallocation of resources and the distortion of demand patterns resulting from the administratively determined rates for the various company services.
3. The provision of some strong motivation for operating efficiency and innovation.
4. The prevention of predatory competition in those product lines which are not provided under monopolistic conditions.
5. The protection of the consumers of company services whose demands are inelastic from the burden of inefficiencies in other portions of the company's operations.
6. The elimination of the motivation for uneconomic investment as a means of expanding the rate base.
7. The preclusion of the use of other socially undesirable means to expand the rate base—of methods such as the encouragement of price rises by equipment suppliers and the elimination of competitors as means of providing new investment opportunities.

The remainder of this paper, then, undertakes to describe some regulatory policies which are responsive to these criteria. It is to be emphasized that since they are all untested, any one of these measures may well lead to unanticipated side effects that are undesirable in themselves, or produce some unforeseen consequences that are politically unpalatable. In any event, there is no reason to believe that this is the only set of measures capable of doing the job, or that it will do the job more effectively than any substitute proposal. I suggest only that these policies seem to meet the minimum conditions of acceptability which have just been set out. It must also be emphasized that if some of the regulatory problems that have just been listed turn out to be unimportant in practice, prudence and economy may recommend that the corresponding regulatory proposals be dropped from consideration. If it can be shown that some anticipated problem is virtually nonexistent, it would be folly to devote effort and resources to its prevention.

Profit Ceilings and the Encouragement of Operating Efficiency

Short of providing some effective competitors—a possibility which in most cases is patently ludicrous—there unfortunately appears to be no substitute for a ceiling over company earnings as a means to prevent monopoly profit. Moreover, it makes economic sense to proportion these permitted earnings to the company's level of investment, in effect producing a limit, not to total earnings, but on rate of return for investment.

Though it is likely to rub an economist the wrong way, there is also some rough justice in the contention that the rate base—the calculated volume of investment to which the ceiling rate of return on investment is applied—should be based on historical or sunk costs rather than on reproduction or replacement cost. The economist, who is normally concerned with efficiency rather than with considerations of justice, usually wishes to determine the consequences of a course of action currently under consideration. And for this purpose, sunk cost is a piece of ancient history over which no one any longer has any influence. But where equity is involved one may argue persuasively that matters go the other way. A ceiling on earnings precludes for the investor any windfall gains. It seems only fair that as compensation he should also be provided some protection against windfall losses. This means that the earnings he is offered ought not to depend on the valuation which subsequent fortuitous events have imposed on his investment. Rather, it should be based on the investment outlays he actually incurred in the past. On this line of reasoning, original cost data require only depreciation and price-level corrections in the calculation of the value of the rate base. Price-change adjustments are appropriate, for without them, in a world of secular inflation, the investor is not protected effectively from windfall loss. The *r* per cent earnings permitted to him he will receive in relatively debased dollars in compensation for an investment which was paid for in far more valuable monetary units. This suggests that an appropriate price index for this purpose might be the consumer price index or some other index in the family which measures changes in the purchasing power of the security-holder's funds. However, as usual there is no unique index for the job.

There is another reason that favors an original cost evaluation of the investment base, corrected only for price-level changes and depreciation. For this arrangement eliminates any possibility of tacit or explicit conspiracy between a utility and its equipment-suppliers to increase the utility's rate base through a rise in the price of new equipment. If the rate base is evaluated in terms of original equipment outlays, a change in replacement cost simply will leave the rate base unaffected and so the utility will have no motivation to encourage such price moves.

It is appropriate to include a few comments on the choice of the number that is to constitute the *r* per cent rate of return permitted to the company. Ideally this should be what in the literature of corporation finance is called the cost of capital for the company's risk class. Roughly, it is the rate of earnings on capital (current market value of total company equity and debt) which is presently received by other firms whose stockholders are subject to comparable risks. A company which is not permitted such a rate of earnings will have difficulty in obtaining the funds required for its growth, since it will find itself at a direct disadvantage in comparison with the other firms with which it competes for financing.

The cost-of-capital figure to which the company's rate of return should be equated is not the same as the rate of interest which the company pays for its borrowings. As is clear from the literature of corporation finance, the company's bond interest rate is merely a nominal capital cost which fails to take into account the risk that added debt imposes on the stockholder.[5] It is to be expected, then, that the cost of capital will be higher, and typically substantially higher, than the interest return on company debt.

With such an earnings ceiling, how can one motivate the firm to watch its outlays, to combat waste, and to seek actively to institute cost-saving innovations? The answer is to be found in the workings of the competitive process for which the regulatory mechanism is presumably intended to serve as a substitute. As Schumpeter showed many years ago,[6] while competition tends to eliminate "above-normal" profits in the long run, the excess profits which it permits in the short run are essential for economic progress. The motivation for a firm to innovate is the unusual but temporary profits which the innovation permits. Of course, once competitors learn about the new idea and its effectiveness they will be led to imitate it, and so the profits will ultimately disappear. But in the meantime these profits will have done their job—they will have induced management to adopt the innovation, a process which will not subsequently be reversed when earnings have returned to their normal level.

This immediately suggests an analogous arrangement for the regulation of returns to a utility. Suppose rates are subject to regulatory reexamination only at periodic intervals; as an illustration, say that they are reconsidered every 3 years. At such a reexamination date these rates could be set to provide the company currently no more than the *r* per cent rate of return on historical investment that is considered justified. Suppose, however, that the company is permitted to retain all the earnings it makes during the three-year interval before the next review date, *whatever the level of these earnings*. In doing so the company would be permitted to lower its rates wherever it chose to do so subject only to the several proposed rate-reduction regulations which will be described presently. However, it would not

[5] See, e.g., E. Solomon, *The Theory of Financial Management* (New York: 1963), pp. 71-88. The main argument in the Averch and Johnson article (n. 4, p. 111) seems to rest on a confusion between the interest cost of borrowing and the cost of capital. These authors argue, correctly, that if the regulatory ceiling on company earnings were higher than its cost of capital the company would be led to overexpansion and to an inefficiently large utilization of capital as a substitute for other inputs. However, they seem clearly wrong in contending that the difference between the permitted rate of return and the interest cost of borrowed funds indicates the presence of this problem.

[6] J. A. Schumpeter, *The Theory of Economic Development*, translated by R. Opie (Cambridge, Mass.: 1936).

be allowed any interim rate raises except under most unusual circumstances.[7]

This proposal is thus designed to permit the company to retain the fruits of its cost-saving efforts. It would find it profitable to save money because cost reductions would then lead directly to corresponding though temporary increases in profits.

It is said that in a rough and ready manner such a procedure is already employed, albeit unintentionally, by many regulatory commissions. Because it is simply not practical to review and revise rates constantly, there is usually a regulatory hiatus and a lag in price adjustment which permits the company to increase its profits somewhat when it manages to effect a decline in cost. It is not clear whether more general and more even application of such an approach and the explicit dissemination of information on its workings would yield increases in efficiency sufficient to justify the required upheaval in the mode of operation of the regulatory agencies.

Protecting the Consumer of Services with Inelastic Demands: Tests of Compensatory Operation

Much of the complexity of the regulatory problem arises from the ability of the regulated firm to shift any relative losses incurred by inefficient portions of its operations onto consumers of services whose demand is inelastic. But once the problem is stated so explicitly, economic analysis readily provides a solution which is straightforward in its outlines, even if its details do involve a number of complications.

[7] Thus, if there were an unanticipated inflationary upsurge in prices generally a review by the regulatory commission at the request of the company might determine that some increase in rates is required for the viability of company operations.

It may be objected that the proposed regulatory principle would in practice give most companies more than the r per cent return that is considered socially desirable. But experience should soon permit regulation to prevent excessive profits from this source. The initially permitted r per cent rate of return would just have to be adjusted downward sufficiently. If it were found that rates initially yielding r per cent typically yielded kr per cent over the three-year period, only an initial rate of return of r/k per cent might be allowed, so that in fact an average utility or a given firm would over the long run average r per cent on its investment and only companies whose efficiency rose to an unusual extent would do better than this. Note also, in accord with the comment of the preceding paragraph, that in an inflationary period k might prove to be less than unity (actual earnings tending to less than r per cent) so that the adjusted initial return, r/k, would exceed r.

Professor Bonbright has suggested that a 3-year review period (which is used in this paper merely as an illustrative figure) is a very short interval for the purpose. But he also notes that managements might be tempted to bunch their price-reducing inducements right after each rate-setting period. For just this reason a short review period (or a review period of random length) may have something to be said for it.

Incidentally, Professor Bonbright credits public yardstick rates and cost comparisons among private companies as effective influences toward efficiency in public utilities.

A service can be defined as compensatory (its provision under current arrangements is justified by economic considerations) if its availability affects adversely neither the interests of the stockholders nor the consumers of alternative company services. In most cases we would of course expect somewhat more than this—the provision of a service on terms that are compensatory should in fact normally provide real benefits to at least one of these groups. In other words, given its current mode of operation, a service is compensatory if its elimination would redound to the net disadvantage of stockholders or of the consumers of other company output.

The nature of the appropriate criterion of compensatory operation should now be obvious: a service is compensatory if its revenues exceed what Professor Lewis terms its "escapable costs"[8]—the costs that would in the long run be avoided if the company were to terminate the provision of the service in question. For if this condition is met, without an effective ceiling on profits, stockholders are clearly better off with the provision of the service than without it. On the other hand, if because of regulatory restrictions the rate of return would remain the same whether or not the service were available, provision of a service that is compensatory must reduce the amount of profit obtained from the consumers of other company services—with services whose demand is inelastic this would necessarily require lower rates than those which would prevail in the absence of our compensatory service.

It follows that many of the problems of rate regulation could be solved by requiring regulated companies to submit evidence (either periodically or on request) showing that each of their services is supplied on a compensatory basis, and by requiring them to make corrective adjustments whenever this test is not passed. The nature of the appropriate corrective adjustments is not always obvious, but it raises no serious problems in principle. It may, of course, involve an increase in rates for a service that is noncompensatory. But if demand for the service is highly elastic a decrease in rates may be what is needed to put the service on a compensatory basis. It is also conceivable that no adjustment will prove capable of rendering the service compensatory. In that case, in the absence of marked external benefits sufficient to justify a public subsidy, provision of the service should be discontinued altogether.

In principle, then, the test of compensation can prevent 3 of the major difficulties of utility rate regulation: the exploitation of the consumers of other company services, the recourse to uneconomic investments undertaken only as a means to expand the rate base, and, in particular, the attempt to

[8] W. A. Lewis, *Overhead Costs* (London: 1949), pp. 9ff. Sometimes it is not obvious how a particular service should be defined. For example, in supplying gas, is the commercial supply to be considered different from the domestic supply even though they employ common distribution mains? In principle *any* service or combination of services, however defined, should be subject to a test of compensatory operation, but, of course, simpler rules of reason would have to be used in practice.

eliminate competitors as a means to clear the way for expansion of the rate base. Of course, it might still be possible for our company to outcompete a rival firm by providing a service more cheaply. But if the service is supplied on a compensatory basis, economic efficiency is clearly served by competition of this variety. Even if the competitor is unable to survive, he will have been driven from the field only by his inability to supply his output without an excessive use of resources. It may be that our regulated company is the more efficient supplier of the service only because he can provide it jointly with some other services, which together offer substantial economies of scale. But this is still a matter of real economic efficiency—it makes the firm that has been driven from the field no less a casualty of economic progress. Its exit is the normal price exacted for growth in economic productivity, the elimination of the inefficient suppliers.

While the test of compensatory operation promises to help considerably with the regulatory problems, its appropriate utilization does involve several complicating caveats:

a. The pertinent information is that reporting *long-run* escapable costs. That is, it must include the present value of all future outlays required to keep the service in operation (unless the company plans to terminate provision of the service in the foreseeable future).[9] For a service is not compensatory if the present value of the stream of its expected revenues falls short of the discounted stream of costs to which it commits the company.

b. The test of compensatory operation does not tell us whether the terms on which the service is provided are optimal either from the point of view of the company or from that of society. Thus a company may wish to change the price or the rate of growth of supply of even a compensatory service. But then the test must be administered anew; indeed, it may be desirable that this be done frequently when market conditions or the nature of company operations change. For the fact that an activity is compensatory under one set of circumstances does not guarantee that it will be so under other conditions.

c. If the rate base is calculated in terms of historical "imbedded" cost of the company's capital, then, strictly speaking, a double test of compensatory operation is called for. First one must see whether escapable cost is covered, evaluating equipment in terms of its prospective replacement costs and its current opportunity value, in the manner already described. In addition, however, it is necessary to determine whether the service yields at least the *r* per cent return legally permitted the company on the portion of the historical rate base which could be eliminated under current legal and accounting

[9] Of course, to this figure one must add the value of the firm's current equipment and inventory in their best alternative use, for if the service were discontinued, its assets would presumably be transferred to the most profitable employment open to them. Thus such opportunity costs would then also be avoided.

practices by sale or scrapping of equipment or any other appropriate means if the service were discontinued. Suppose the company were permitted r per cent earnings on its rate base and, if the service were eliminated, the resulting reduction in rate base and expected net revenues were ΔB and ΔR respectively. Then if $(\Delta R/\Delta B) < r$, consumers of the company's other services would not have to provide so large a contribution as before to yield the r per cent rate of return on the remainder of the rate base.[10] Thus provision of the service must in these circumstances impose a burden on the consumers of other company services, i.e., provision of our service would not be compensatory in the sense we have defined it. However, this is a matter of the conventions of the rate-base calculation and there are no purely economic criteria to determine the rules of this second test of compensatory operation.

d. In all this it should be remembered that statistical calculation of escapable costs runs into the many difficulties that beset the determination of marginal cost figures, so that one can expect to obtain no more than approximate but defensible escapable cost figures, and these are likely to require substantial outlays for data gathering.

Prevention of Destructive Pricing

Destructive pricing may be described as the temporary reduction of rates undertaken to eliminate competitors in order to clear the way for monopoly prices in the future. The regulatory program which has so far been outlined goes at least part of the way toward meeting this danger. For the effective way to prevent destructive pricing is to eliminate its profit yield. If the firm is limited in its over-all rate of return, it cannot at a later date expect arbitrarily to raise its rates unless there is a simultaneous increase in the company's rate base. The proposals of the following section, if adopted, would also appear to eliminate any danger of destructive pricing, as will be shown presently.

However, an alternative or perhaps a supplementary provision would operate by putting firms on notice that once they lower rates they will not be permitted to raise them again after competition has been eliminated, unless the firm can show that some unexpected and unavoidable increase in costs has subsequently occurred. The fact that the service has been sup-

---

[10] Let $B + \Delta B$ and $R + \Delta R$ be the total initial rate base and the total initial net revenues respectively, where

$$(R + \Delta R)/(B + \Delta B) = r.$$

Let R' be the revenue required to yield an over-all r per cent return to the company after elimination of the service, so that

$$(R'/B) = r.$$

Since $(\Delta R/\Delta B) < r$ it follows that $R/B > r$ and so $R' < R$, as asserted in the text. Note, incidentally, that the legal and accounting conventions might sometimes prevent any reduction in the rate base on elimination of a service, i.e., we would have $\Delta B = 0$ so that our second test would automatically be passed.

plied at a certain price while competition was present would constitute prima facie evidence that the company can afford to supply at that price when it no longer has rivals to contend with. And, if technological progress makes for a secular decline in the company's costs, it might in the future even be appropriate to require it to reduce its rates correspondingly.

It may be felt that the sort of guarantees which have just been described constitute a desirable supplement to the ceiling on a company's over-all rate of return, because it is always possible that a firm will wish to eliminate a competitor not in order to raise its rates immediately but as a matter of insurance—as a means to shift a service from the elastic to the inelastic demand categories so that if at some future date the company falls on harder times, it will have another string to its bow—it will have another service which can be used to provide the profits it is legally permitted. With the restriction on future rate increases just described, the elimination of competitors would no longer offer this attraction.

However, the proposals discussed in the following section would also serve this purpose, in addition to the objective they are primarily designed to achieve.

Relative Pricing and Improved Resource Allocation

We come finally to what may well be the most questionable among the set of proposals offered in this paper: the rules suggested for the determination of relative rates for different company services. Two systematic approaches have been proposed elsewhere for the purpose: (1) "full cost pricing" and (2) a mixed arrangement in which prices for services whose demands are elastic are set so as to maximize the net profits flowing from each such service, and in which the remaining rates are determined residually by these profit flows and the ceiling on over-all company earnings imposed by regulation. There is no need to recapitulate in detail the economist's objection to "full-cost pricing"—its arbitrary allocation of joint costs, the likelihood that it will yield results deleterious to the general welfare by discouraging the consumption of decreasing-cost output, etc. Surely our profession should be able to design a pricing arrangement which is at least superior to that based on a "fully allocated cost" calculation.

The second approach, while somewhat more attractive, itself differs in two respects from an abstract ideal. First, there is no basis in terms of the perfect competition model which we use as a criterion in much of our pure theory for such a differentiated treatment of inelastic and elastic demand commodities. The only justification usually offered for the distinction accorded the two classes of output is the fact that the profit-maximizing price is likely to be more or less reasonable where demand is elastic, while with inelastic demand the sky is the limit—the higher the price the greater the profit. In addition, this approach leaves some degree of ambiguity in the calculation. If a company provides only one service whose demand is inelastic, the r per cent limitation on over-all company earnings does automatically fix its price. Since the profits of this service rise monotonically with its price, there will be exactly one price at which total company profits (including the maximal yields from the elastic demand services) add up to r per cent of the rate base. However, if the company offers m different inelastic demand services, this rule can only be used to determine some sort of average price. It will not select the m individual prices. It offers us only one equation to determine m variable values. Given the prices of the elastic demand output, if total profits are represented by $T = f(p_1, \ldots, p_m)$ where p_i is the price of the ith inelastic demand service, then the condition

$$f(p_1, \ldots, p_m) = rB \text{ (B = rate base)}$$

is obviously insufficient to determine the values of $p_1, p_2, \ldots, p_m$.

The literature does suggest that, where two such services are substitutes, there is something to be said for setting their relative prices equal to the ratio of the marginal costs, for the consumer is likely to compare directly their advantages and disadvantages in choosing between two substitutable goods, and a price reflecting their relative resources cost will guide the consumer to allocate resources optimally between them.[11]

But precisely the same considerations would seem to suggest that it would be desirable for *all* public utility prices to be set so that they are proportional to marginal costs. Since utilities are typically decreasing-cost operations, obtaining the legally permitted rate of return on the rate base would normally require all rates to exceed marginal costs. However, under this proposal they would all exceed marginal costs by the same percentage.[12]

[11] It has also been suggested that in some cases it is instead desirable to set prices so that the difference in the prices of the two services is equal to the difference between their marginal costs. Suppose, for example, that one service is the same as another except that the former contains some supplementary features (e.g., a newspaper provided at a newstand *vs.* a newspaper delivered to one's door, or a trip on a train with a dining car *vs.* a trip on a train without one). Then it has been proposed that the choice between acceptance and rejection of the supplementary service feature is least distorted by a price that is actually equal to the marginal cost incurred in its provision. In that case the difference between the prices of, e.g., a delivered and an undelivered newspaper would be the marginal home delivery cost.

[12] It has been known for some time that such an arrangement will not lead to an optimal allocation of resources, even if *every* seller priced at the same percentage mark-up over marginal cost. For example, McKenzie has pointed out that if a commodity serves both as a consumer's good and as input to another process (coal), a k per cent mark-up on that good will result in a more than k per cent mark-up on resources cost for the commodity that utilizes our good as input. For in the process a second k per cent will be added on the coal—the coal-mining firm will have added k per cent in extracting the coal, and the steel firm that uses the coal will apply k per cent to its own input costs, which include the coal purchase price. See L. McKenzie, "Ideal Output and the Interdependence of Firms," *Economic Journal,* Vol. 61, (Dec. 1951). Since in our world it is not even true that all firms apply the same mark-up to marginal costs, one is left with very little presumption that the proposal will lead to an optimal allocation of resources or even to a second-best allocation.

Under this arrangement, then, in a rough and ready way the consumer would at least receive the right relative price (cost) signals for a rational choice among the alternatives provided by the company. Prices would, in principal, be perfectly determinate, subject only to the obvious difficulties involved in calculating marginal costs *not as fixed scalars but as functions of the quantities supplied.* For the choice of prices will surely affect quantities purchased and hence marginal costs. Thus, if we write the marginal cost function for commodity i as $mc_i = g_i(p_1, \ldots, p_n)$ the prices of the company's n services (this time including both the items whose demands are elastic and those which are inelastic) would normally be determined by the $n - 1$ relative price conditions,

$$p_i / p_n = g_i(p_1, \ldots, p_n) / g_n(p_1, \ldots, p_n)$$

and the total profit constraint $f(p_1, \ldots, p_n) = rB$. If, as seems plausible, these equations are consistent and independent, the prices of all items of company output would be uniquely specified.

As a practical matter, of course, this proposal is even less straightforward then it may seem at first glance. It would certainly not be easy to keep the calculation up to date. And while it is hard enough to obtain current marginal-cost figures, even these are not the data that the computation requires. For the relevant marginal costs to which prices should be proportioned are the hypothetical marginal costs which would apply after the change in output and demand caused by the required price revisions—marginal-costs figures whose calculation would require us to know in some detail the demand functions for each item of the company's output!

It might, moreover, be necessary to make a few modifications in the prices of some of the elastic demand services. For it is possible that prices set in accord with the principles just described would result in noncompensatory operation of a number of company services. In such a case, readjustment of the corresponding prices would be required, but in every case the price modification permitted should be as small as possible—the price should vary from proportionality with marginal cost by the minimal amount needed to permit the service to pass our tests of compensatory operation.

The justification for such "discriminatory pricing" is the fact that a good sold on compensatory terms must yield a positive consumers' surplus. For if at some price consumers in total are willing to pay for a service an amount greater than its real escapable cost, provision of the service must by definition yield a positive net benefit to society.

Since the price of each service presumably affects the revenues obtainable from the others, instead of minimizing the adjustments in the prices of the services one item at a time, it might be more desirable to minimize some sort of weighted-average-price adjustment. In that case prices would be determined as follows:

Let $p_1^*, \ldots, p_n^*$ be the prices satisfying $p_i^*/p_n^* = mc_i/mc_n$, $i = 1, \ldots, n-1$ and $f(p_1^*, \ldots, p_n^*) = rB$. Then the final prices p_i might be those which minimize the variance of prices (the weighted average of their squared deviations from the prices that are proportional to the marginal costs). That is, letting Q_i be the quantity sold of item i and $E_i(p_1, \ldots, p_n)$ be the escapable cost incurred by service i, the p_i would be those that minimize.

$$\Sigma_i Q_i (p_i - p_i^*)^2 / \Sigma Q_i$$

subject to

$$f(p_1, \ldots, p_n) = rB \text{ (the legal profit ceiling)}$$

and which pass the test of compensatory operation:

$$p_i Q_i \geq E_i(p_1, \ldots p_n)$$

and where, of course, all $Q_i \geq 0$.

Of course this calculation probably involves refinements too far beyond what can be achieved in practice. It does offer the advantage, perhaps not always negligible, of precluding destructive pricing. For under the suggested pricing rules the discretion required in order to price destructively—the ability to cut prices temporarily as a means to drive out a competitor and then to raise price again—would simply be denied to the firm.

However, we can achieve this result and determine prices in a manner more firmly based in economic analysis with the aid of a theorem originally derived by Manne and subsequently rediscovered by Flemming, Boiteux and others.** The theorem asserts the following: Suppose a firm is required to meet some prestated profit requirement, e.g., it is required to cover all of its costs including its cost of capital. If this result is not attained by prices equal to marginal costs, then consumers' surplus from the consumption of the outputs in question will be maximized if, for any two of the firm's outputs i and j, prices are set so that the ratio between $(p_i - mc_i)/p_i$ and $(p_j - mc_j)/p_j$ is equal to the inverse ratio of the elasticities of demand of the two items.

This theorem is particularly interesting because it takes into account not only costs but also consumers' relative preference patterns. Moreover, it is not simply a plausible rule of thumb, but it derived from explicit consideration of consumers' surplus (or Hicksian compensating variation) so that it does in fact arise out of an analysis of the requisites of welfare maximization. Moreover, the theorem, whose logic may at first seem obscure, has a

** See Alan S. Manne, "Multiple-Purpose Public Enterprises—Criteria for Pricing," *Economica,* N. S. Vol. 19, August 1952, pp. 322-326. See also Marcus Flemming, "Optimal Production with Fixed Profits," *Economica,* N. S. Vol. 20, August 1953, pp. 215-236; and Marcel Boiteux, "Sur la gestion des Monopoles Publics astreints à l'équilibre bugétaire," *Econometrica,* Vol. 24, No. 1, January 1956, pp. 22-40. For simple proofs of the theorem see Manne and Boiteux. Professor Bradford and the present author have extended the result to cover the influence of cross elasticities and to derive the result in terms of the concept of compensating variation. This and other related results will be published elsewhere.

simple intuitive explanation. For if we consider as a distortion in demand any departure in demand patterns from those that result from prices set at marginal costs then, if it is necessary in order to meet a revenue requirement to vary prices from marginal costs, the least distortion will be caused if the largest price changes fall on those items whose demand is inelastic, i.e., those items whose demand will not change markedly in response to a departure from marginal cost pricing.

Concluding Comment

By and large the proposals presented in this paper are in line with the precepts of economic analysis and seem to be the logical means to deal with the issues that have been posed. They would provide for compensatory operation of the firm, motivation for efficiency and innovation, and should serve effectively to discourage deliberate rate-base inflation and destructive competition. It would be visionary to expect that regulatory procedures will march abruptly in the directions that have been outlined. The main practical impact of the discussion is perhaps its systematic account of the shortcomings of current regulatory practice. Yet there are some indications, just barely discernible, suggesting that regulatory procedures are beginning to move slowly toward some of the broader patterns suggested by the paper.

[37]

ENTREPRENEURSHIP IN ECONOMIC THEORY*

By WILLIAM J. BAUMOL
Princeton University

The entrepreneur is at the same time one of the most intriguing and one of the most elusive characters in the cast that constitutes the subject of economic analysis. He has long been recognized as the apex of the hierarchy that determines the behavior of the firm and thereby bears a heavy responsibility for the vitality of the free enterprise society. In the writings of the classical economist his appearance was frequent, though he remained a shadowy entity without clearly defined form and function. Only Schumpeter and, to some degree, Professor Knight succeeded in infusing him with life and in assigning to him a specific area of activity to any extent commensurate with his acknowledged importance.

In more recent years, while the facts have apparently underscored the significance of his role, he has at the same time virtually disappeared from the theoretical literature. And, as we will see, while some recent theoretical writings seem at first glance to offer a convenient place for an analysis of his activities, closer inspection indicates that on this score matters have not really improved substantially.

This paper will undertake to examine three major matters. First, I will review briefly the grounds on which entrepreneurship should concern us. Second, I will seek to explain why economic theory has failed to develop an illuminating formal analysis of entrepreneurship and I shall conclude that it is unlikely to do so for the foreseeable future. Finally, I shall argue that theory can say a great deal that is highly relevant to the subject of entrepreneurship even if it fails to provide a rigorous analysis of the behavior of the entrepreneur or of the supply of entrepreneurship.

Before proceeding with the discussion I would like to make a distinction that is somewhat artificial but nevertheless important. It is necessary for us to differentiate between the entrepreneurial and the managerial functions. We may define the manager to be the individual who oversees the ongoing efficiency of continuing processes. It is his task to see that available processes and techniques are combined in proportions appropriate for current output levels and for the future outputs that are already in prospect. He sees to it that inputs are not wasted, that

* The author would like very much to thank his colleague W. A. Lewis, whose comments were used liberally in the revision of this paper. He must also thank the National Science Foundation whose grant greatly facilitated the completion of this paper.

schedules and contracts are met, he makes routine pricing and advertising outlay decisions, etc., etc. In sum, he takes charge of the activities and decisions encompassed in our traditional models.

The preceding description is not intended to denigrate the importance of managerial activity or to imply that it is without significant difficulties. Carl Kaysen has remarked that in practice most firms no doubt find themselves in a position well inside their production possibility loci and one of their most challenging tasks is to find ways of approaching those loci more closely; i.e., of increasing their efficiency even within the limits of known technology. This is presumably part of the job of the manager who is constantly on the lookout for means to save a little here and to squeeze a bit more there. But for many purposes the standard models would appear to provide an adequate description of the functions of the manager. Given an arrangement which calculation, experience, or judgment indicate to constitute a reasonable approximation to the current optimum, it is the manager's task to see that this arrangement is in fact instituted to a reasonable degree of approximation.

The entrepreneur (whether or not he in fact also doubles as a manager) has a different function. It is his job to locate new ideas and to put them into effect. He must lead, perhaps even inspire; he cannot allow things to get into a rut and for him today's practice is never good enough for tomorrow. In short, he is the Schumpeterian innovator and some more. He is the individual who exercises what in the business literature is called "leadership." And it is he who is virtually absent from the received theory of the firm.

I. *On the Significance of the Entrepreneur*

If we are interested in explaining what Haavelmo has described as the "really big dissimilarities in economic life," we must be prepared to concern ourselves with entrepreneurship. For the really big differences are most usually those that correspond to historical developments over long periods of time or to the comparative states of various economies, notably those of the developed and the underdeveloped areas.

It has long been recognized that the entrepreneurial function is a vital component in the process of economic growth. Recent empirical evidence and the lessons of experience both seem to confirm this view. For example, some empirical studies on the nature of the production function have concluded that capital accumulation and expansion of the labor force leave unexplained a very substantial proportion of the historical growth of the nation's output. Thus, in a well-known paper, Solow [6, p. 320] has suggested on the basis of American data for the period 1909–49 that "gross output per man-hour doubled over the interval, with $87\frac{1}{2}$ percent of the increase attributable to technical change and the remaining $12\frac{1}{2}$ percent to increase in the use of capital."[1] But any such innovation, whether it is purely technological or it consists in a modification in the way in which an industry is organized, will require entrepreneurial initiative in its introduction. Thus we are led to suspect that by ignoring the entrepreneur we are prevented from accounting fully for a very substantial proportion of our historic growth.

Those who have concerned themselves with development policy have apparently been driven to similar conclusions. If we seek to explain the success of those economies which have managed to grow significantly with those that have remained relatively stagnant, we find it difficult to do so without taking into consideration differences in the availability of entrepreneurial talent and in the motivational mechanism which drives them on. A substantial proportion of the energies of those who design plans to stimulate development has been devoted to the provision of means whereby entrepreneurs can be trained and encouraged.

The entrepreneur is present in institutional and applied discussions of a number of other economic areas. For example, his absence is sometimes cited as a significant source of the difficulties of a declining industry, and a balance-of-payments crisis is sometimes discussed in similar terms. Thus both macro problems and micro problems offer a substantial place for him in their analysis. Whether or not he is assigned the starring role he would appear in practice to be no minor character.

II. *The Entrepreneur in Formal Models*

Contrast all this with the entrepreneur's place in the formal theory. Look for him in the index of some of the most noted of recent writings on value theory, in neoclassical[2] or activity analysis models of the firm. The references are scanty and more often they are totally absent. The theoretical firm is entrepreneurless—the Prince of Denmark has been expunged from the discussion of *Hamlet.*

It is not difficult to explain his absence. Consider the nature of the model of the firm. In its simplest form (and in this respect we shall see that the more complex and more sophisticated models are no better) the theoretical firm must choose among alternative values for a small number of rather well-defined variables: price, output, perhaps adver-

[1] Solow's result and other similar conclusions have recently been challenged in an article by Jorgenson and Griliches [3]. However, their contention does not necessarily imply any denigration of the role of the entrepreneur. They argue merely that entrepreneurship and innovation have achieved growth in outputs only with the aid of corresponding increases in input quantities.

[2] There is one residual and rather curious role left to the entrepreneur in the neoclassical model. He is the indivisible and non-replicable input that accounts for the U-shaped cost curve of a firm whose production function is linear and homogeneous. How the mighty have fallen!

tising outlay. In making this choice management is taken to consider the costs and revenues associated with each candidate set of values, as described by the relevant functional relationships, equations, and inequalities. Explicitly or implicitly the firm is then taken to perform a mathematical calculation which yields optimal (i.e., profit maximizing) values for all of its decision variables and it is these values which the theory assumes to be chosen—which are taken to constitute the business decision. There matters rest, forever or until exogenous forces lead to an autonomous change in the environment. Until there is such a shift in one of the relationships that define the problem, the firm is taken to replicate precisely its previous decisions, day after day, year after year.

Obviously, the entrepreneur has been read out of the model. There is no room for enterprise or initiative. The management group becomes a passive calculator that reacts mechanically to changes imposed on it by fortuitous external developments over which it does not exert, and does not even attempt to exert, any influence. One hears of no clever ruses, ingenious schemes, brilliant innovations, of no charisma or of any of the other stuff of which outstanding entrepreneurship is made; one does not hear of them because there is no way in which they can fit into the model.[3]

It must be understood clearly that what I have been saying constitutes no criticism, not even an attempt to reprove mildly the neoclassical model of the firm. I think that model does what it was designed to do and does it well. Like any respectable analysis, one hopes that it will be modified, amended, and improved with time. But not because it cannot handle an issue for which it is irrelevant. The model is essentially an instrument of optimality analysis of well-defined problems, and it is precisely such (very real and important) problems which need no entrepreneur for their solution.

Some readers may suspect that I am subtly putting forward as more appropriate candidates for the job some alternative models of the firm with which I have to some degree been associated. But this is certainly not my intention, because it seems clear to me that these models are

[3] The problem was recognized long ago by Thorstein Veblen. One may recall the characteristic passage in which he described the economic man as "a lightning calculator of pleasures and pains, who oscillates like a homogeneous globule of desire of happiness under the impulse of stimuli that shift him about the area, but leave him intact. He has neither antecedent nor consequent. He is an isolated, definitive human datum, in stable equilibrium except for the buffets of impinging forces that displace him in one direction or another. Self-imposed in elemental space, he spins symmetrically about his own spiritual axis until the parallelogram of forces bears down upon him, whereupon he follows the line of the resultant. When the force of the impact is spent, he comes to rest, a self-contained globule of desire as before. . . . [he] is not a prime mover. He is not the seat of a process of living, except in the sense that he is subject to a series of permutations enforced upon him by circumstances external and alien to him" [7, pp. 73–74].

no better for the purpose than the most hidebound of conventional constructs. For example, consider what Oliver Williamson has described as the "managerial discretion models," in which the businessman is taken to maximize the number of persons he employs, or sales, or still another objective distinct from profits. True, this businessman has (somewhere outside the confines of the model) made a choice which was no mere matter of calculation. He has decided, in at least some sense, to assign priority to some goal other than profit. But having made this choice he becomes, no less than the profit maximizer, a calculating robot, a programmed mechanical component in the automatic system that constitutes the firm. He makes and enforces the maximizing decision and in this the choice of maximand makes no difference.

Nor can the "practical pertinence" of the decision variables make the difference in carving out a place for the entrepreneur. Maximization models have recently been developed in which, instead of prices and outputs, the decision variables are the firm's real investment program, or its financial mix (the proportion of equity and debt in its funding), or the attributes of a new product to be launched by the company. These decisions seem to smell more of the ingredients of entrepreneurship. But though the models may be powerful and serve their objective well, they take us not a whit further in the analysis of entrepreneurship, for their calculations are again mechanistic and automatic and call for no display of entrepreneurial initiative.

Finally, it must be understood that the timeless nature of these models has nothing to do with the problem. Professor Evans [2] long ago developed a model in which the firm considered the consequence of its decisions for the time path of prices and where the calculus of variations served as his instrument of analysis. In one of my own models the firm was taken to choose not a stationary, once-and-for-all output level, but selected instead an optimal growth rate. None of these alternatives helps matters. In all these models, automaton maximizers the businessmen are and automaton maximizers they remain.

And this shows us why our body of theory, as it has developed, offers us no promise of being able to deal effectively with a description and analysis of the entrepreneurial function. For maximization and minimization have constituted the foundation of our theory, and as a result of this very fact the theory is deprived of the ability to provide an analysis of entrepreneurship. The terminology of game theory has been extremely suggestive; the willingness of the behaviorists to break away from traditional formulations has been encouraging; but I see no real breakthroughs in this area even on the distant horizon. At most I hope for more brilliant observations and descriptive insights such as those provided by Schumpeter and more recently by Leibenstein, but I foresee for the immediate future no more formal, manipulatable engine of calculation and analysis.[4]

III. *On the Supply of Entrepreneurship*

There is yet another reason why a marriage between theory and policy is not easily arranged in this area. In its discussions of inputs our formal analysis deals, by and large, with the way in which these inputs are used, and tells us relatively little about where they come from. In our growth models, for example, the behavior of the labor supply exerts a critical influence on the economy's expansion path. But the determination of the growth of the labor force itself is generally taken to be an exogenous matter. Similarly, in a neoclassical or a programming analysis of production one investigates how inputs should be used in the production process, but one assumes that their supply is somehow determined outside the system. Thus even if we were to develop a model which were successful in advancing the theory of entrepreneurship to the level of sophistication of our treatment of other inputs, we would have defined more effectively the entrepreneurial role, but we would have added relatively little to our understanding of the determinants of the level of output of entrepreneurship.

From the point of view of policy, however, the priorities would seem to be reversed. The first order of business in an economy which exhibits very little business drive is presumably to induce the appearance of increased supplies of entrepreneurial skills which would then be let loose upon the area's industry. The policy-maker thus is interested primarily in what determines the supply of entrepreneurship and in the means that can be used to expand it.

But there is reason to suppose that these issues are to a very considerable extent matters of social psychology, of social arrangements, of cultural developments and the like. And perhaps this is why many of the recent discussions of the theory of entrepreneurship have been contributed by the sociologists and the psychologists.[5] This may then be no

[4] My colleague, Professor Lewis, has adduced yet another reason why the current theory does not help us to understand the entrepreneur. He remarks in a note to me that "the entrepreneur is doing something new and is therefore to some extent a monopolist. . . . We have no good theory of entrepreneurship because we have no good theory of monopoly. Our theory that monopolists [act] to maximize profit is obviously absurd, given the low elasticity of demand of most monopolized products." I agree that this observation points to a most fundamental gap in the theory of the firm.

[5] For a remarkable study of entrepreneurship by a social psychologist, see McClelland [4]. While the book is not free of somewhat distracting jargon, and is naïve in spots, particularly in its literal interpretation of the role of the profit motive in economic analysis, it does offer a number of extremely interesting hypotheses and provides in their support quantities of psychological test results relating to a great variety of cultures. In what is perhaps the most interesting part of his discussion from our point of view, the author claims to show that entrepreneurs are motivated by n-achievement (the need for achievement) and not by desire for money (pp. 233–37). In his tests, people with high levels of n-achievement do no better when offered larger

fortuitous development. The very nature of the more pressing issues relating to entrepreneurship may invite more directly the attention of the practitioners of disciplines other than theoretical economics.

IV. *A Place for Theory and Entrepreneurship*

Given these difficulties besetting any attempt to construct a relevant economic theory in the area, I can offer only one suggestion for a theoretical approach to entrepreneurship, but one which I think is not without promise. We may not be able to analyze in detail the supply of entrepreneurship, the entrepreneur's strategy choices, his attitudes to risk, or the sources of his ideas. But one can hope to examine fruitfully what can be done to encourage his activity. Here an analogy is illuminating. The Keynesian analysis really bypasses the issue of expectations which is surely at the heart of the investment decision and yet the model succeeds in coming to grips with some means that can stimulate investment. In the same way one can undertake to grapple, assisted by theoretical instruments, with the policies that encourage entrepreneurship.

This can be done by considering not the means which the entrepreneur employs or the process whereby he arrives at his decisions but by examining instead the determinants of the payoff to his activity.[6] In his operations he must bear risks, never mind just how he does this, but let the theory consider how the marginal costs of his risk bearing can be reduced. He employs the results of work in research and development; very well, let us investigate what means make it easier, economically, to undertake R and D. Theoretical analysis of the effects of alternative tax arrangements, for example, should shed some light on these matters. The role of the structure of interest rates is no doubt also pertinent and we do have a powerful body of literature which treats of

amounts of money for success, whereas people with low *n*-achievement scores do much better when offered money. However, it should be noted that while a rise in absolute income levels does not seem to stimulate *n*-achievers, a rise in marginal returns does seem likely to spur them on, according to the author because it provides a clearer measure of accomplishment. (The economist would no doubt propose a different explanation.) He also claims to show that *n*-achievers choose smaller risks than the average man: they are not gamblers, but are calculators and planners. The entrepreneur is not essentially a man who chooses to bear risks—that is the speculator, a man with quite a different personality (pp. 210–25). Another interesting McClelland claim is that the *n*-achiever is not an individualist and does not depend for his success on private enterprise (pp. 292–300). He gets just as much satisfaction from the manipulation of a committee, or from working for a government, since his interest is in results rather than in these other considerations. This is perhaps the reason huge committee-run corporations can be successful.

[6] I believe the key element of Schumpeter's contribution to the theory of entrepreneurship is precisely of this variety. In its discussion of the functions of the entrepreneur, *The Theory of Economic Development* [5] offers us little more than a taxonomy. But enormous illumination is provided by Schumpeter's analysis of the process whereby the rewards of innovation are only gradually eroded by the competitive process and the corollary observation that some imperfection in the market mechanism is essential to permit some financial reward for innovation.

these matters. On all of these fronts analysis is well advanced and it is no heroic exercise to imagine rather complex and probing theoretical formulations capable of shedding light upon them.

It should be recognized, moreover, that such a theoretical analysis can be of enormous significance for policy. In a growth-conscious world I remain convinced that encouragement of the entrepreneur is the key to the stimulation of growth. The view that this must await the slow and undependable process of change in social and psychological climate is a counsel of despair for which there is little justification. Such a conclusion is analogous to an argument that all we can do to reduce spending in an inflationary period is to hope for a revival of the Prostestant ethic and the attendant acceptance by the general public of the virtues of thrift! Surely we have learned to do better than that, in effect by producing a movement along the relevant functional paths rather than undertaking the more heroic task involved in shifting the relationships. This is precisely why I have just advocated more careful study of the rewards of entrepreneurship. Without awaiting a change in the entrepreneurial drive exhibited in our society, we can try to learn how one can stimulate the volume and intensity of entrepreneurial activity, thus making the most of what is permitted by current mores and attitudes. If the theory succeeds in no more than showing us something about how that can be done,[7] it will have accomplished very much indeed.

[7] For a crude attempt at such an analysis, see the last chapter of [1].

REFERENCES

1. W. J. Baumol, *Business Behavior, Value and Growth* (revised ed., Harcourt, Brace and World, 1967).
2. G. C. Evans, "The Dynamics of Monopoly," *Amer. Math. Monthly*, Feb., 1924, pp. 77–83.
3. D. W. Jorgenson and Z. Griliches, "The Explanation of Productivity Change," *Rev. of Econ. Studies*, July, 1967, pp. 249–83.
4. D. C. McClelland, *The Achieving Society* (Princeton, 1961).
5. J. A. Schumpeter, *The Theory of Economic Development* (Cambridge, Mass., 1936).
6. R. M. Solow, "Technical Change and the Aggregate Production Function," *Rev. of Econ. and Statis.*, Aug., 1957, pp. 312–20.
7. T. B. Veblen, "Economics and Evolution," *The Place of Science in Modern Civilization* (New York, 1919).

[38]

Input choices and rate-of-return regulation: an overview of the discussion

William J. Baumol
Professor of Economics
Princeton University

and

Alvin K. Klevorick
Associate Professor of Economics
Yale University

This article reviews the substance of the literature stemming from the Averch-Johnson model of the firm under rate-of-return regulation. It examines a number of propositions, among them the following: (1) The profit-maximizing firm under rate-of-return regulation will tend to use a capital-labor ratio greater than that which minimizes cost for its output level; (2) The profit-maximizing firm under regulatory constraint will use a capital-labor ratio and produce an output greater than it would in the absence of regulation; (3) The closer the "fair rate of return" is to the true cost of capital, the greater the quantity of capital the firm will want to use; and (4) The sales (total revenue)-maximizing firm under regulatory constraint will use a labor-capital ratio greater than it would when unconstrained. The second of these propositions, which has been widely taken to have been proved by Averch and Johnson, is shown to be false. The paradoxical assertion in the third proposition is explained and its regulatory implications discussed. Two models involving regulatory lag are described along with their implications for policy. Finally, some evaluative comments are offered on the entire issue of what has come to be known as the "A-J effect" and its importance in regulatory economics.

■ The imposition of an artificial constraint on a decision process that would otherwise be optimal will certainly lead to no improvement in outcome and will generally make things worse. In particular, a regulatory constraint on the firm's rate of return, if it affects input proportions at all, may be expected to reduce their efficiency. This issue was explored explicitly by Harvey Averch and L. L. Johnson

Dr. Baumol has taught at Princeton University since 1949. He was appointed Professor in 1954. He holds the B.S.S. degree from the City College of New York (1942) and the Ph.D. degree from the University of London (1949). Dr. Baumol has published extensively on subjects ranging from the theory of the firm to the economics of the performing arts and has frequently been involved in proceedings relating to public utility regulation.

Dr. Klevorick has been with Yale University since 1967, where he is Associate Professor and a member of the Cowles Foundation. He was a Lecturer in Economics at Princeton in 1966–67. He holds the B. A. degree from Amherst College (1963), and the M. A. and Ph.D. degrees from Princeton (1965 and 1967, respectively). Dr. Klevorick is currently on leave-of-absence at the London School of Economics.

The authors are grateful to the National Science Foundation and the Ford Foundation for support while this paper was being completed. Dr. Klevorick held an Air Force Office of Scientific Research–National Research Council fellowship which also facilitated this work. The authors are also grateful to Mrs. E. E. Bailey for invaluable criticisms and bibliographical assistance and to Dr. E. E. Zajac for helpful comments.

in a pathbreaking article in 1962 [1], using a model similar to one constructed almost simultaneously in a paper written independently by S. H. Wellisz[1] [11]. These authors showed within a static equilibrium framework that, given a number of conditions to be discussed presently, rate-of-return regulation will indeed modify the capital-labor ratio utilized by the profit-maximizing firm. Specifically, their model led to a demonstration that under the conditions postulated the firm will find it profitable to employ more capital relative to labor than is consistent with minimization of cost for the quantity of output produced.

These results have led to a considerable discussion, technical and informal, in terms of abstract general principles and concrete policy implications. The writings on the subject have disputed the rigor of the original proofs and supplied alternative derivations; they have raised questions about the assumptions and expressed doubts about the applicability or the importance of the results in practice.

Without surveying the literature item by item, this paper seeks to review the substance of the discussion. It first restates the relevant theorems and assertions and provides informal and formal proofs. It then turns to some related propositions that have been developed and discusses some work currently in progress in the area. Finally, it offers, for whatever they may be worth, our views of the upshot of the discussion. In sum, we conclude that the analytical approach employed by the original authors is a very fruitful one. Indeed, their piece represents a breakthrough in the theory of regulation, constituting a major contribution to the rigorous analysis of the principles of regulation of industry, a field which has recently blossomed. Moreover we agree that there are dangers to economic efficiency in the rate-of-return approach to rate regulation. Nevertheless, we will suggest that the phenomenon that emerges from the A-J theorem may not be of very great significance in practice. It is at least plausible that other potential sources of difficulty in the regulatory process dwarf the consequences of the distortion in the capital-labor ratio that the model predicts.

1. The A-J model of the regulatory process

■ The original Averch-Johnson analysis provides a simple and comprehensible depiction of a regulatory process and its relation to the behavior of the firm. The company is taken to produce one output and to use two inputs, labor and capital, each of which is available to it in unlimited quantities at a fixed price per unit. The firm's decisions are affected by the regulator in only one way: it is permitted to earn no more than some fixed proportion of the value of its capital—the regulatory "fair rate of return" on its rate base. In all other respects management is permitted to pursue its objective, maximization of profit, exactly as it could in the absence of regulation. Finally, it is assumed that the rate of return permitted to the firm by regulation is less than the return it would obtain if it were able to maximize its profits, but is at least as great as the rate of return on capital. These assumptions can be brought out more

[1] While the Wellisz model deals with the same sort of regulated firm, it concerns itself primarily with the effects of regulation on peak-load pricing rather than on input usage. The Wellisz discussion will, therefore, not be examined in this article.

explicitly with the aid of mathematical notation, which largely follows that in the original A-J article.

Let

π = the firm's total profit,
z = the physical quantity of the firm's output,
x_1 = the quantity of capital in the firm's rate base,[2]
x_2 = the quantity of labor input,
r_1 = the unit cost of capital = the opportunity cost of resources tied up in plant and equipment,
r_2 = the unit cost of labor,
$s = r_1 + v$ be the rate of return permitted by regulation, $v \geq 0$,
$z = z(x_1, x_2)$ = the production function, $\partial z/\partial x_1 > 0$, $\partial z/\partial x_2 > 0$ and $z(0, x_2) = z(x_1, 0) = 0$,
$p = p(z)$ = the inverse demand function.

Then the company is assumed to select the values of z, x_1 and x_2 that maximize total profit

$$\pi = pz - r_1x_1 - r_2x_2 \tag{1}$$

subject to the regulatory constraint

$$\frac{pz - r_2x_2}{x_1} \leq r_1 + v = s\,. \tag{2}$$

Specifically, since $r_1 + v$ is taken to be less than the profit-maximizing rate of return, it is assumed by A & J that the constraint (2) is an equation rather than an inequality.[3]

Notice the very rudimentary regulatory process that is encompassed in this model. First, it is assumed that the firm can decide for itself on any price-output combination it wishes, so long as the rate-of-return constraint is satisfied. Second, it will be assumed at least for part of the discussion (following most of the literature) that the rate-of-return constraint is satisfied as an equality at all times and that there is no regulatory lag. If the regulatory commission decrees that net returns will not exceed s percent of the rate base, then they will equal s percent precisely, no more and no less, even as a temporary matter. Clearly, this is not quite the way the regulatory process works, though the model's simplification of the facts is not unreasonable as a first approximation. We shall see later what analytical difficulties one gets into in seeking to represent the regulatory process more closely.

The firm in this model is also rather rudimentary, its production process involving only two inputs and one output, and its objective being total profit maximization pure and simple. However, the choice of objective aside, no one seems to have suggested that any significant loss of generality results. The analysis also adopts several common assumptions as a matter of mathematical convenience: all relevant functions are assumed twice differentiable, and the appro-

[2] Because of depreciation the value of such resources will normally be less than the acquisition cost of these capital assets. For simplicity we will follow Averch and Johnson in assuming depreciation to be zero and the acquisition cost of capital to be unity.

[3] If capital were to depreciate, the rate of return in equation (2) would have to be expressed, not in terms of the acquisition cost of the capital, but in terms of its depreciated value. That is, x_1 would have to be the depreciated value of the company's capital, and current depreciation would appear as an operating cost. As just stated, it is convenient to assume this complication away.

priate second-order maximum (concavity-convexity) conditions are taken to hold throughout. Some of these will be discussed explicitly later.

2. The A-J theorems

■ Under the circumstances postulated it is easy to prove that the capital-labor ratio chosen by the firm will, in general, be different from the one that minimizes the cost of whatever output is decided upon. It is only slightly more difficult to show that the resulting input proportions will be more capital-intensive than efficiency requires. There has been some discussion of the validity of the argument used by A & J in arriving at this second result. As a matter of fact, as we shall see presently, it may not even be the result they had in mind when they wrote their paper. For such reasons, we find it useful to divide the hypotheses explicit and implicit in the discussion into several different propositions. We begin with

PROPOSITION 1. *The firm described in the model (1) and (2) will adopt input proportions different from those that minimize the cost of the final output level,* z^*.

PROOF: Minimization of the cost of the output selected requires minimization of $r_1x_1 + r_2x_2$ subject to $z(x_1, x_2) = z^*$, which yields the Lagrangian

$$r_1x_1 + r_2x_2 + \mu[z^* - z(x_1, x_2)]$$

and this leads to the first-order conditions

$$r_1 - \mu z_1 = 0\,, \quad r_2 - \mu z_2 = 0$$

where z_i denotes $\partial z/\partial x_i$, the marginal product of $x_i (i = 1, 2)$ or

$$r_1/r_2 = z_1/z_2\,. \tag{3}$$

Turning next to the regulated firm, its Lagrangian is, by (1) and (2) (treating the latter as an equality until otherwise noted),

$$L = pz - r_1x_1 - r_2x_2 - \lambda(pz - sx_1 - r_2x_2)\,. \tag{4}$$

We now obtain the first-order conditions[4]

$$(1 - \lambda)MR_zz_1 - r_1 = -\lambda s, \text{ i.e., } (1 - \lambda)MR_zz_1 - (1 - \lambda)r_1 = \lambda(r_1 - s) \tag{5a}$$

$$(1 - \lambda)MR_zz_2 - (1 - \lambda)r_2 = 0 \tag{5b}$$

where

$$MR_z = \frac{dpz}{dz} \text{ (marginal revenue of output)}.$$

We will follow the literature in assuming through most of the discussion that

$$s > r_1 \tag{6}$$

(the "fair rate of return" exceeds the cost of capital). It then follows

[4] Averch and Johnson utilize the Kuhn-Tucker conditions at this point because the regulatory constraint (2) is an inequality. However, they always assume this constraint is effective, so that they treat it as an equation throughout their discussion. As Takayama [10] points out, it is consequently unnecessary to use the Kuhn-Tucker conditions.

from (5a) that $\lambda \neq 1$. For if $\lambda = 1$ (5a) becomes simply $r_1 = s$, thereby contradicting (6). Thus we may divide equation (5a) by (5b), obtaining, after some rearrangement,

$$z_1/z_2 = r_1/r_2 - \lambda(s - r_1)/(1 - \lambda)r_2 \,. \tag{7}$$

Thus, if we can show that the last term in (7) is not equal to zero, it will follow that requirement (3) for the least-cost input combination is violated by our regulated firm. Because we have $s > r_1$ and $\lambda \neq 1$ as was just shown, we need only to show that $\lambda \neq 0$. This follows from comparison of the Lagrangian (4) with the original objective function (1). For if $\lambda = 0$ the two expressions are identical, so that the constrained maximization problem will yield a profit level identical with that which can be achieved by a firm unconstrained by regulation. Since we have assumed that the rate-of-return constraint does reduce company profits, it follows that we cannot have $\lambda = 0$. This completes the proof of the first A-J theorem.

A number of the published discussions leap from this result to one of the following two conclusions:

(ALLEGED) PROPOSITION 2. *The capital-labor ratio of the regulated firm will be larger than that of the unconstrained profit-maximizing monopolist.*

PROPOSITION 3. *The capital-labor ratio of the regulated firm will be larger than the one that minimizes costs for the output level that it elects to produce.*

It is not quite clear which of these A & J had in mind when they wrote their article. Certainly their discussion on this point is ambiguous (compare their Figure 1 with their discussion on p. 1053, top, and 1056, bottom).

As we shall see, proposition 2 is simply false, as a generalization, while proposition 3 is correct under the circumstances postulated although details of the proof require some care. We shall, in section 6, provide a counterexample to proposition 2 and discuss its problems in general terms. For the moment we shall confine our discussion to proposition 3, which is the more significant of the two from the point of view of efficiency of resource utilization. We will therefore present in detail a proof of the result. A critical step in the argument is the following lemma, which we will also utilize later in this article.

LEMMA. *If the firm maximizes its total profit (1) subject to the regulatory (inequality) constraint (2), in which $s > r_1$, and if, in addition, the regulatory constraint is binding and $x_1 > 0$ and $x_2 > 0$, then we must have $0 < \lambda < 1$.*

Since the discussion of this lemma in the literature is somewhat disjointed and impressionistic (see Takayama's criticism of A & J on this score), a more systematic derivation seems appropriate. Maximization of (1) subject to (2) yields as its first-order (Kuhn-Tucker) conditions with $x_1 > 0$, $x_2 > 0$, equations (5a), (5b), and

$$pz - sx_1 - r_2x_2 \leq 0 \tag{5c}$$

$$\lambda(pz - sx_1 - r_2x_2) = 0 \tag{5d}$$

$$\lambda \geq 0\,. \tag{5e}$$

Writing R_1 as an abbreviation for $MR_z z_1$, the marginal revenue product of x_1, and using similar notation for x_2, we obtain by solving[5] (5a) for λ,

$$\lambda = (r_1 - R_1)/(s - R_1)\,. \tag{8}$$

The unconstrained profit maximum is given by the values of x_1, x_2 satisfying

$$R_1 = r_1\,, \quad R_2 = r_2\,.$$

By (5b), the second of these conditions is satisfied also by the regulated firm. Hence, since the regulatory constraint is assumed to be effective, i.e., it prevents the firm from maximizing profits, we must have

$$R_1 \neq r_1$$

and consequently, by (8), $\lambda \neq 0$. Therefore by (5e)

$$\lambda > 0\,.$$

We have already seen, in the discussion immediately following (6), that $\lambda \neq 1$. To prove that $\lambda < 1$ we utilize the second-order conditions for the constrained profit maximum, which require a positive value for the bordered Hessian, i.e.,

$$H = \begin{vmatrix} (1-\lambda)R_{11} & (1-\lambda)R_{12} & s - R_1 \\ (1-\lambda)R_{21} & (1-\lambda)R_{22} & r_2 - R_2 \\ s - R_1 & r_2 - R_2 & 0 \end{vmatrix} > 0$$

where R_{ij} denotes $\partial^2 pz/\partial x_i \partial x_j$. However, by (5b) $r_2 - R_2 = 0$. Therefore the preceding condition becomes (on expanding the determinant in terms of its last column),

$$H = -\,(s - R_1)^2(1 - \lambda)R_{22} > 0\,.$$

Diminishing revenue returns to labor [concavity of $R(x_1, x_2)$] gives us $R_{22} < 0$ so that we obtain immediately

$$(1 - \lambda) > 0$$

as was to be shown.

It follows, incidentally, that $R_1 < r_1 < s$, i.e., that for the regulated firm in equilibrium the marginal revenue product of capital will be less than r_1, the cost of capital. This follows from (8), which indicates that if $r_1 < R_1 < s$ then $\lambda < 0$, while if $r_1 < s < R_1$ then $\lambda > 1$.

We now return to the main algebraic argument adduced in support of proposition 3. We see at once from the preceding lemma that the last term in (7) must be negative since $0 < \lambda < 1$ and since, by (6), $s > r_1$. From this one obtains the required result. Having shown by (7) that

$$z_1/z_2 < r_1/r_2\,, \tag{9}$$

comparison with (3) demonstrates that the relative use of capital must, under (9), exceed the ideal proportion corresponding to (3). For z_1/z_2, the marginal rate of substitution of capital for labor, is now below the ratio of input prices r_1/r_2. With diminishing marginal

[5] The division by $s - R_1$ is legitimate because if $s = R_1 \equiv MR_z z_1$, we must have, by (5a), $s = r_1$, and this is ruled out by (6).

rate of substitution of capital for labor for a fixed output level, this can occur only as the result of a relative increase in the use of capital.

We deal next with the remaining contention of the A-J paper:

(ALLEGED) PROPOSITION 4. *The regulated firm will produce an output larger than that which maximizes profits.*

Strangely, one looks in vain for any attempt at a formal proof of this assertion. A & J seem to arrive at their result through a simple heuristic argument: From (5a) or (9) they conclude that the regulated firm will purchase more capital than the amount that maximizes profit [actually this does not follow directly from the equations cited, though, as will be shown later (proposition 5), the assertion about the capital stock *is* correct]. Similarly, equation (5b) can be rewritten simply as $MR_z z_2 = r_2$, asserting that the marginal revenue product of labor (x_2) will be equal to the wage level (r_2). This seems to have suggested that the profit-maximizing quantity of labor will be hired. With that quantity of labor and with the quantity of capital greater than the amount that maximizes profit, it follows that output must be greater than the profit-maximizing value of z.

As already noted, it is not clear that this is the argument that leads A & J to their allegation about the firm's output level. In any event, the argument is simply incorrect. Condition (5b) does *not* require the quantity of labor hired by the regulated firm to be the same as the amount that would be employed under pure profit maximization. The quantity of labor employed by the firm will still depend on the quantity of capital it uses and the nature of the production function. As Takayama [10] shows, rate-of-return regulation can in fact lead to a decrease in the quantity of labor hired by the firm, a point to which we will return presently. Indeed we will show later that, as a generalization, proposition 4 simply is not valid.

The invalidity of proposition 4 may perhaps be considered unfortunate. If it were true it might have been claimed as a virtue of the regulatory process. For generally the monopolistic firm's output is taken to be smaller than the level that is socially optimal. If regulation of rate of return were to guarantee an increase in output above the monopolistic level it might have been considered to be most desirable. Indeed, some authors have defended fair-rate-of-return regulation on the ground that it will have a beneficial effect on output. For example, Alfred E. Kahn [6] recognizes explicitly the input inefficiency such regulation can engender. But, he argues, by inducing the regulated firm to overinvest in capacity and hence to *increase its output*, fair-rate-of-return regulation helps to reduce—if not overcome—the monopolist's tendency to underinvest and restrict output. The fact that proposition 4 is not valid as a general statement weakens somewhat the case of Kahn and others who take a similar position.

3. The geometry of the A-J propositions

■ As it turns out, a good deal of illumination can be contributed by translation of the model's relationships into geometric terms. Two closely related graphic interpretations have been provided independently by Zajac [14] and by Klevorick and Baumol [8]. The discussion here will employ elements of both analyses.

FIGURE 1

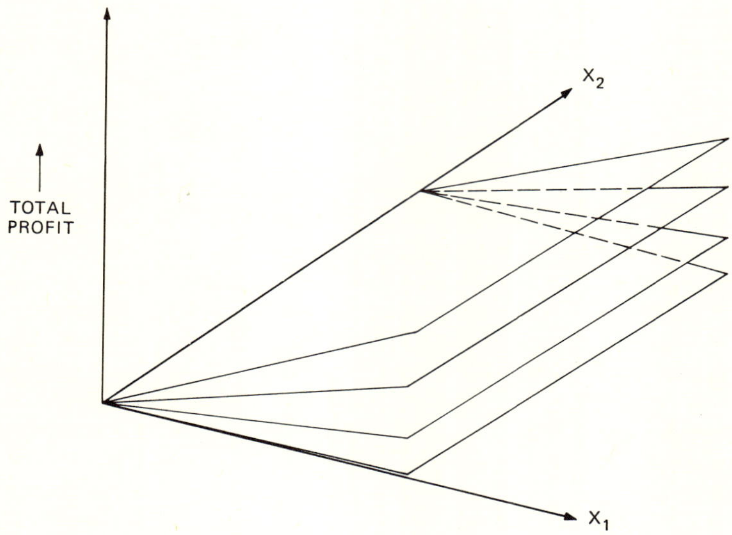

Figure 1 is a three-dimensional diagram depicting on its axes the values of x_1, x_2, and total profit. It also shows several planes, all of them hinged on the x_2 axis and hence satisfying the equation

$$\pi = vx_1 \tag{10}$$

for different values of v. Any such plane represents the rate-of-return constraint (2) for a particular value of v. The interpretation of the left-hand side of (10) as a profit function follows directly from (1) and (2). Rewriting our regulatory constraint (2) as an equality, as we are now treating it, and substituting this into the original profit function (1) we obtain at once

$$\pi = (pz - r_2x_2) - r_1x_1 = sx_1 - r_1x_1 = vx_1\,, \tag{11}$$

FIGURE 2

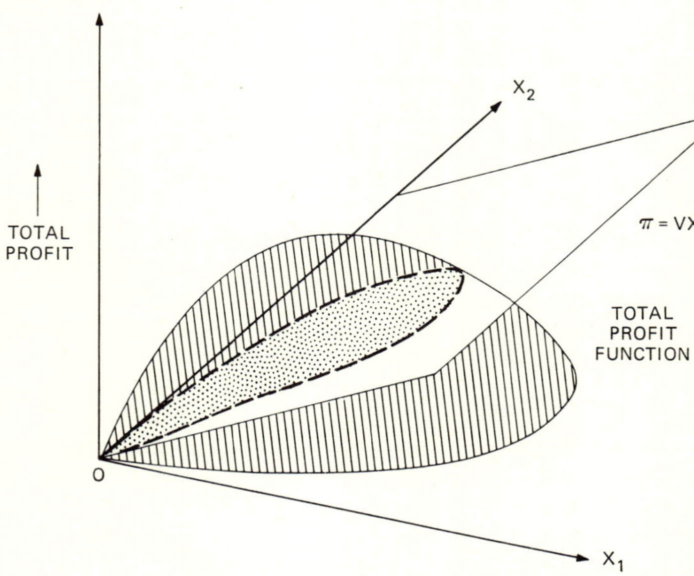

FIGURE 3

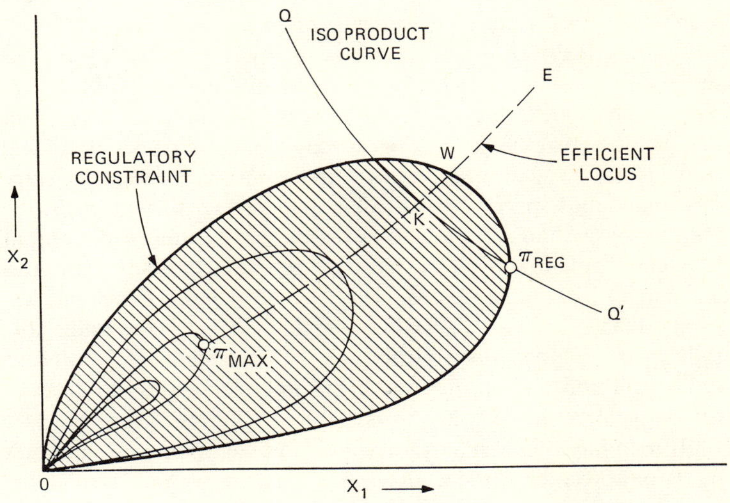

which is an expanded restatement of (10). We see from (11) that the slope of any of the cross sections of a constraint plane taken parallel to the (x_1, π) plane represents $s - r_1$, the excess of the regulatory "fair rate of return" over the cost of capital.

In Figure 2 the firm's profit function has been included in the diagram as the shaded hill-shaped figure. The heavy broken curve is the intersection of the profit surface and the regulatory constraint plane. Its projection on the x_1x_2 plane represents all combinations of the two inputs which just satisfy the rate-of-return constraint requirement. The heavy curve in Figure 3 depicts that projection on the x_1x_2 plane. The shaded region inside the constraint curve (the maximal-rate-of-return curve) corresponds to input combinations that yield rates of return higher than the maximum permitted by regulation. The heavy constraint curve is an iso-rate-of-return locus; i.e., points on that curve represent input combinations all offering the same rate of return on capital. Three other iso-rate-of-return loci, all of them offering higher rates of return than permitted by the constraint, are also shown. Point π_{max} corresponds to the highest point on the profit surface: it is the point the profit-maximizing firm would select in the absence of regulation.[6] The point π_{reg} is the input combination that maximizes profit given the regulatory constraint.[7] A moment's thought shows that π_{reg} must be the rightmost point on the regulatory constraint curve since this gets the firm to the highest total profit point on the constraint plane in Figure 2. Looked at another way, the rightmost point maximizes *total* profit consistent with the constraint because all points on the constraint curve yield the same net *rate* of return, v, and the rightmost point involves the largest rate base, x_1, and hence the largest value of $\pi = vx_1$.

[6] Note that point π_{max} which yields maximum total profits does not offer the maximal rate of return. For, as the diagram shows, there are iso-rate-of-return loci inside the curve through π_{max}, whose rates of return are higher than that through π_{max}.

[7] While in this diagram the output at π_{reg} is greater than that at π_{max} as proposition 4 claims is generally true, we shall show presently that this result does not always hold.

The broken curve in Figure 3 is the locus of efficient combinations of labor and capital. For any given output level the least-cost input combination will be given by some point on this curve, $\pi_{\max}E$.

Proposition 3 corresponds to the assertion that the constrained maximum point lies below (to the right of) the efficient locus, $\pi_{\max}E$. For if this is true then QQ', the iso-product curve through point π_{reg}, will cross the efficiency locus at some point K that lies above and to the left of π_{reg} (since iso-product curves must have a negative slope in capital-labor space). K is, by definition of the efficient locus, the least expensive input combination for the production of the output level corresponding to QQ'. That is, K produces the same output as π_{reg} but at lower cost, and K clearly involves more labor and less capital than π_{reg}. Thus, if we can prove that π_{reg} lies below and to the right of the efficiency locus, it follows that the regulated firm in our model will utilize an inefficiently high capital-labor ratio to produce the output level it selects, as proposition 3 requires.

It therefore only remains for us to show that point π_{reg} does not lie on or above the efficiency locus $\pi_{\max}E$. To prove this, assume the contrary, as in the case depicted in Figure 4, where π_{reg} lies above the efficient locus. Let point A be the intersection point of the efficient curve with QQ', the iso-product locus through π_{reg}, and let B be the intersection of the efficient locus with the constraint curve.

Obviously, A is more profitable than π_{reg} since it yields the same output at a lower production cost. Moreover, by the concavity conditions implicit in the argument, profit increases monotonically as one moves along the efficiency locus toward $\pi_{\max}$. Thus B must be at least as profitable as A. Hence B must be more profitable than π_{reg}, contradicting the definition of π_{reg} as the most profitable point on the constraint locus.

This completes the Zajac proof of proposition 3.

There is an alternative geometric derivation of the A-J result that is also illuminating. Figure 5a depicts the firm's iso-profit curves—curves of constant *total profit*, the contour lines for the total profit surface that was represented in Figure 2. The concavity of the profit

FIGURE 4

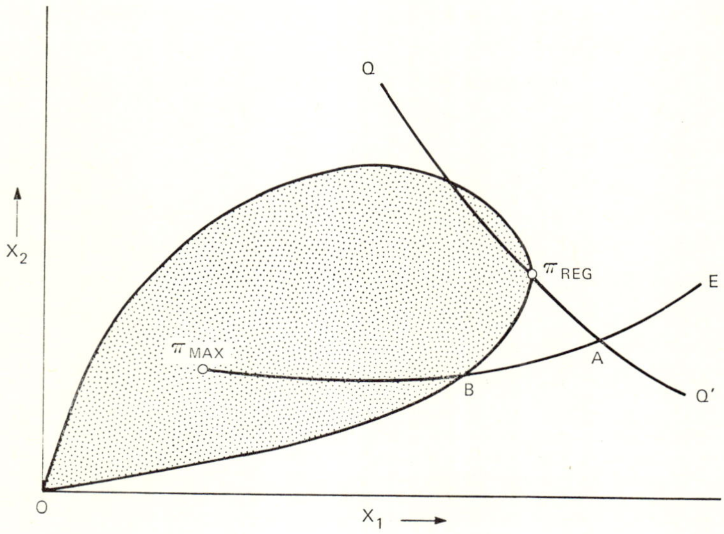

FIGURE 5

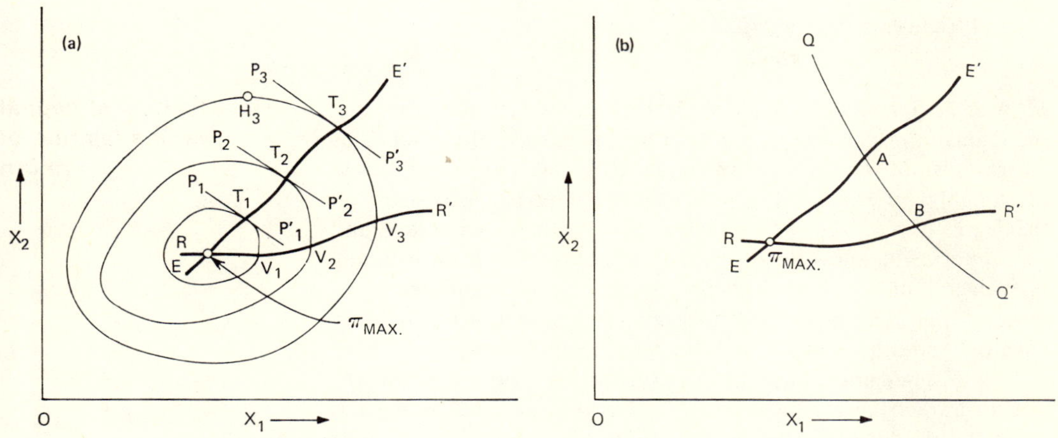

surface assures us that each such curve is the boundary of a convex region.

We shall use this diagram to describe explicitly the location of the firm's efficient locus, EE', and of its expansion path RR', showing the combinations of inputs that will be hired by the regulated firm with different values of s, the permitted rate of return. That is, RR' is the locus of all equilibrium points, π_{reg}, for our firm. If we can show that everywhere to the right[8] of the maximum profit point, π_{max}, the locus RR' lies below and to the right of the efficient locus, as it does in Figures 5a and 5b, then the A-J result must follow. That is, under rate-of-return regulation, in producing a given quantity of output the firm must utilize a capital-labor ratio larger than that required for maximal efficiency. For since (Figure 5b) the iso-product curve QQ' has a negative slope, its intersection point, B, with the lower expansion path locus, RR, must lie below and to the right of A, the efficient point for that output.

We prove our assertion about the relative positions of RR' and EE' as follows: Curve EE' is the locus of tangency points,[9] T_i, between the iso-profit curves and the parallel negatively sloped price lines P_iP_i'. Hence curve EE' must intersect the iso-profit curves in their negatively sloping segments such as H_3V_3 in Figure 5a.

However, the expansion path, RR', is the locus of right-hand vertical points on the iso-profit curves.[10] Our result follows at once from the convexity properties of these curves: A tangency point, T_i

---

[8] As is shown in proposition 5, below, when the rate of return constraint is effective, the firm will always use a quantity of capital greater than that at π_{max}. Hence, any solution point must lie to the right of π_{max} in the diagram. This also follows directly from Figure 3 where we see that π_{reg}, the constrained maximum point, must always lie to the right of π_{max} since π_{reg} is the rightmost point on the constraint curve.

[9] The slope of the price lines is, of course, equal in absolute value to the ratio of input prices, r_1/r_2. The slope of an iso-profit curve (see the following note) is $-\pi_1/\pi_2$ where $\pi_i = \partial\pi/\partial x_i$. Hence, tangency between an iso-profit curve and a price line requires

$$r_1/r_2 = \pi_1/\pi_2 = (MR_z z_1 - r_1)/(MR_z z_2 - r_2) \quad \text{or} \quad r_1 MR_z z_2 - r_1 r_2 = r_2 MR_z z_1 - r_1 r_2,$$

i.e., $r_1 z_2 = r_2 z_1$, which is the same as the necessary condition for efficiency (3).

[10] *Proof:* The iso-profit curve is given by π = constant, from which we deduce $\pi_1 dx_1 + \pi_2 dx_2 = 0$, that is, the slope of the iso-profit curves is $dx_2/dx_1 = -\pi_1/\pi_2$. But from (5b) we obtain $\pi_2 = MR_z z_2 - r_2 = 0$. Hence, equilibrium of the regulated firm thus requires the iso-profit curve to be vertical.

An argument that is more geometric in spirit is also possible. We have already noted that equilibrium of the regulated firm requires it to be on the vertical (right-hand) point of an iso *rate-of-return* curve π/x_1 = constant, since at this point x_1, and hence π, will be at a maximum. The slope on the negatively sloping portion of any one of these curves on its rightmost end must lie above and to the left of the corresponding vertical (right-hand) point, V_i.

4. The cost of capital vs. the fair rate of return

■ A & J emphasize that their results depend on the assumption that the regulatory "fair rate of return" exceeds the cost of capital. This assertion is not very easy to test empirically, since the cost of capital presumably varies from firm to firm, depending at least in part on the degree of risk incurred by anyone who provides capital to it, and we do not really know how to measure that cost of capital with any high degree of precision. The proceedings of the regulatory commissions that determine the firm's fair rates of return certainly do have the appearance of a search for a figure approximating the cost of capital. They argue in terms of the return necessary to enable the firm to attract the capital it needs, and that is presumably what is meant by the (opportunity) cost of capital. In other words, it is at least arguable that the regulator often attempts to set the "fair rate of return" at a level as close to the cost of capital as he can determine.

For this reason, if not as a purely analytic matter, it is of interest to examine what happens to the A-J propositions as the regulated rate of return, s, approaches the cost of capital, r_1, and what occurs when the two coincide. As already implied, A & J themselves point out that their result breaks down when $s = r_1$. However the nature of this breakdown is a bit surprising. Our intuition might suggest that once capital no longer receives a return that may be termed "excessive," the firm will find it unprofitable to use an inefficiently large quantity of capital and it will therefore be motivated to utilize the efficient capital-labor ratio. As a matter of fact, when $s = r_1$ the firm has no motivation to select this ratio or any other particular ratio. *Any* capital-labor ratio becomes as profitable to the regulated firm as any other.

This result can be demonstrated with the aid of the first-order maximum conditions (2), (5a), and (5b). When $r_1 = s$ we see that $\lambda = 1$ satisfies (5a) and (5b). But when $\lambda = 1$ the firm's capital-labor ratio is indeterminate because the only first-order condition that continues to be effective is the original profit constraint (2). Any values of x_1 and x_2 that satisfy the regulatory constraint must, therefore, satisfy all of the first-order maximum conditions, and any such pair of values is as profitable to the regulated firm as any other.

Geometrically we can see more clearly why the A-J results collapse in this peculiar way. Returning to Figure 1, we recall from (10) and (11) that the slope of one of the constraint planes taken parallel to the x_1, π plane is $v = s - r_1$. Hence when $s = r_1$ the plane is flat—regulation offers the firm no opportunity to increase its total profit either through an increase or a decrease in the quantity of x_1. The constraint plane is now perfectly horizontal and, in fact, it coincides with the floor of the diagram—the x_1x_2 plane. Regulation

of the iso-rate-of-return curve is obtained by total differentiation thus:

$$d(\pi/x_1) = \left(\frac{\pi_1}{x_1} - \frac{\pi}{x_1^2}\right) dx_1 + \left(\frac{\pi_2}{x_1}\right) dx_2 = 0$$

so that

$$dx_2/dx_1 = -(\pi_1 - \pi/x_1)/\pi_2 .$$

At a vertical point on this curve we must therefore have $\pi_2 = 0$, which is precisely the condition for the iso *total* profit curve to be vertical since, as we have just seen, its slope is $dx_2/dx_1 = -\pi_1/\pi_2$.

now guarantees that the firm receives for its capital exactly what has to be paid for it, no more and no less. That is, profits will equal zero after payment of the "normal" return to capital, r_1. In this circumstance the firm has no particular motivation to employ an efficient quantity of capital, nor any motivation to avoid doing so. Entrepreneurial choice in this matter just has no effect on its total profits.

However, it is implausible that in such circumstances management will not adopt some other objective, one which is perhaps secondary but which, if profit is not affected, will be used as a basis for company decisions. It can then be shown that if $s = r_1$ and the firm seeks to maximize either total physical volume[11] or sales (total revenue), pz, it is likely to be driven to the ideal input combination point for the corresponding constraint locus, point W in Figure 3. That is, a regulatory restriction on rate of return with $s = r_1$, together with a company goal of sales or output maximization, will yield both ideal output and efficiency in use of resources!

The reason this is so is that maximization of pz or z does require the firm to be on the efficiency locus,[12] and the firm will therefore be forced to W, the only such point on our constraint curve.

Once we leave the case where r_1 and s coincide, matters seem to follow more closely the course one might expect. As A & J point out, if $s < r_1$ the firm loses money and it must, in the long run, go out of business. If, on the other hand, $s > r_1$, propositions 1 and 3, the basic results, follow directly. But even here things do not behave quite as one might at first anticipate.

It may seem plausible that the degree of inefficiency in the capital-labor ratio will decline as s is driven closer to r_1. That is, it may appear that the more closely the regulator succeeds in pushing the regulatory ceiling return, s, to the cost of capital, the less motivation the firm will have to use inefficiently large quantities of capital. In fact, this turns out to be false. On the contrary, one can show that, at least for some classes of production function, as s approaches r_1 the capital-labor ratio will depart further and further from its efficient value! More generally, one can show, following a conjecture of F. M. Scherer, that as s approaches r_1 the constrained profit-maximizing quantity of capital will *always increase*.

This result was proven geometrically by Fred M. Westfield,[13] but it was left to Takayama to provide the first rigorous mathematical derivation of the proposition. Curiously though, neither Westfield nor Takayama quite realized the importance of the proposition for regulatory policy. We shall return to its implications after the proof is completed.

Takayama's argument proceeds as follows. Let r_m be the rate of return on capital obtained at the (unconstrained) profit-maximizing

---

[11] The idea of maximization of physical volume was suggested to us by Milton Kafoglis.

[12] This can be shown as follows. Since the firm cannot survive with negative profits, the regulatory constraint *must* be in our present case satisfied as an equality, i.e., we must have $\pi = pz - r_1x_1 - r_2x_2 = 0$. Maximizing z subject to this constraint we obtain the Lagrangian conditions

$$z_1 + \lambda MR_z z_1 - \lambda r_1 = 0\,, \quad \text{i.e.,} \quad z_1(1 + \lambda MR_z) = \lambda r_1$$
$$z_2 + \lambda MR_z z_2 - \lambda r_2 = 0\,, \quad \text{i.e.,} \quad z_2(1 + \lambda MR_z) = \lambda r_2\,,$$

and straightforward division of one relationship by the other shows that the efficiency condition $z_1/z_2 = r_1/r_2$ must be satisfied. The proof for the sales maximization case where the maximand is pz rather than z follows the same argument step by step.

[13] In [12], Westfield's argument employed a geometric apparatus totally different from the one presented in section 3. For example, his diagram is drawn in capital-profits space rather than capital-labor space. See [12], pp. 429–32.

input-output combination. Then we have $r_m > s > r_1$. For this range of values of s we can conduct a comparative statics analysis of the value of dx_1/ds. We will prove

PROPOSITION 5. *For the firm that seeks to maximize total profit (1) subject to the regulatory constraint (2) we have* $dx_1/ds < 0$ *for* $r_1 < s < r_m$.

In other words, the greater the difference between the regulatory fair rate of return and the cost of capital (since we are increasing s holding r_1 constant), the *smaller* will be the value of x_1, the firm's use of capital!

This result is surely counterintuitive, at least at first blush.

The proof is not difficult. It follows from total differentiation of the first-order conditions (5a), (5b), and (2), utilizing the standard comparative statics procedure to determine how the values of x_1 and x_2 respond to a change in the value of s, holding r_1 constant. For simplicity, let us again rewrite total revenue pz as $R(x_1, x_2)$ so that, e.g., $R_1 = \partial R/\partial x_1$ represents the marginal revenue product of x_1. Then the first-order conditions (5a), (5b) and (2) become (treating the regulatory constraint as an equality)[14]:

$$R_1 - r_1 = (r_1 - s)\lambda/(1 - \lambda) \tag{12}$$

$$\begin{aligned} R_2 - r_2 &= 0 \\ R - r_2x_2 &= sx_1 \,. \end{aligned} \tag{13}$$

Differentiating the last of these conditions totally, one obtains

$$(R_1 - s)dx_1 + (R_2 - r_2)dx_2 = x_1 ds \,. \tag{14}$$

By (13) the second term in this equation is zero. Moreover, by (12)

$$R_1 - s = r_1 - s + (r_1 - s)\lambda/(1 - \lambda) = (r_1 - s)/(1 - \lambda) \,. \tag{15}$$

Thus, substituting this relationship into (14) and after dropping its second term by (13) we have

$$dx_1/ds = (1 - \lambda)x_1/(r_1 - s) < 0 \,. \tag{16}$$

This is negative since the lemma of Section 2 gave us $0 < \lambda < 1$ and since $r_1 < s$ by assumption. Q.E.D.

It is worth examining this result somewhat more carefully. As already indicated, Takayama asserts that this is an alternative proof of the A-J theorem, but that is simply incorrect. Neither proposition 2 nor 3 follows from his argument. True, he has shown that the imposition of the constraint, as it reduces the rate of return from the profit-maximizing level r_m to the legal ceiling s, does increase the firm's use of x_1. But provided that the firm simultaneously expands its use of x_2 sufficiently, there is no need for the resulting capital-labor ratio to be inefficient. Indeed, as the value of s decreases we would normally expect an *efficient* value of x_1 satisfying the regulatory constraint to increase as well. For by increasing x_1 and x_2 sufficiently along the efficient path, profit can be driven down to the level required by a lower value of s. In terms of Figure 3, a lower rate-of-return ceiling moves the constraint curve further away from π_{max}, and therefore it moves the profit-maximizing point, π_{reg}, the vertical

[14] Recall that since $r_1 < s$ we know that $\lambda < 1$ and since $s < r_m$ we have $\lambda > 0$ (the Lemma of section 2).

point on the constraint curve, further to the right. That is precisely why a decrease in the permitted rate of return necessarily increases x_1, the quantity of capital that will be used by the firm. However, the reduction in value of s also leads the efficient point, W, on that curve to move further to the right, meaning that a larger use of capital is also required to maintain efficiency. In sum, there is no necessity of inefficiency implicit in the result that the value of x_1 is increased by regulation.

This moderately painstaking discussion of the Takayama result was undertaken primarily because of the importance of the proposition for regulatory policy. For proposition 5 at least yields the disquieting result that a better job of setting the fair rate of return close to the cost of capital will not reduce the *absolute* capital bias and that it need not reduce the inefficiency in the input proportions shown by proposition 3. On the contrary, the result of better estimation of the cost of capital by the regulator may simply be to aggravate that inefficiency if the rise in the use of capital is not matched by an appropriate increase in the quantity of labor utilized.

A concrete example will demonstrate that this can in fact happen, i.e., that as s approaches r_1 not only will x_1 increase but there can also be an increase in the difference between the profit-maximizing capital-labor ratio x_1/x_2 and the efficient value of that ratio.

For this purpose let the total revenue function be

$$R(x_1, x_2) = a \ln x_1 + b \ln x_2$$

where $a > 0$, $b > 0$ so that $R(x_1, x_2)$ is strictly concave. Then as our marginal revenue products we have

$$R_1 = a/x_1 \quad R_2 = b/x_2 .$$

By (3) the efficient path is given by $R_1/R_2 = r_1/r_2$, i.e., by

$$r_1 b x_1 = r_2 a x_2 ,$$

which is clearly a straight line through the origin in (x_1, x_2) space. Thus, in this case the efficient path involves a constant capital-labor ratio.

On the other hand, we know by (16) that $dx_1/ds < 0$ while, as we will see presently, from (18), dx_2/ds must in this case equal zero since $R_{21} = 0$. Thus we see that as s moves closer and closer to r_1 the constrained profit-maximizing x_1/x_2 ratio must always increase, and hence it must constantly depart farther from the constant proportion between x_1 and x_2 that is required for efficiency.[15]

5. The demand for labor and the profit-maximizing output level[16]

■ One may be tempted to infer, carelessly, that since by (5b) $R_2 = r_2$, the regulated firm will employ the optimal quantity of labor. In fact, this conclusion is simply incorrect. A glance at Figure 3 readily confirms that the firm in the model will employ an inefficiently small quantity of labor for whatever level of output it chooses to produce. The reason, of course, is that the condition $R_2 = r_2$ is

[15] A more "realistic" example is provided by the revenue function $R(x_1, x_2) = 2ax_1^{\frac{1}{2}} + 4bx_1^{\frac{1}{4}}x_2^{\frac{1}{4}} + 2cx_2^{\frac{1}{2}}$, $a > 0, b > 0, c > 0$. The argument is similar to that just given.

[16] After the paper was completed it came to our attention that Westfield had, in fact, presented results essentially the same as those derived in this section. (See [12], p. 430.) His verbal statements involve some slight imprecision, and there appears to be an error—probably typographical—in the footnote where he demonstrates the effect of regulation on the profit-maximizing output level. However, there is no doubt that he had arrived correctly at the relevant conclusions.

consistent with the efficiency requirement $R_1/R_2 = r_1/r_2$ if and only if $R_1 = r_1$, which will occur only at the unconstrained profit-maximizing point.

Consequently, one may wish to inquire further into the effect of the regulatory constraint upon the firm's use of labor. Does the firm's employment of labor necessarily increase (or necessarily decrease) when a regulatory revenue constraint is imposed? As is the case in its use of capital, is there necessarily a monotonic relationship between the quantity of labor hired and the gap between s and r_1? It can be shown that no such generalization is possible. Depending on the marginal rate of substitution between x_1 and x_2, the employment of labor may either increase or decrease as s gets closer to r_1. If labor and capital are complementary in the gross revenue function, then as the quantity of capital used by the firm increases its use of labor will also rise. But if capital is a substitute for labor in producing revenue, then x_1 and x_2 will move in opposite directions in the A-J model.

The proof follows the comparative-statics procedure utilized in deriving the Takayama result. However, the proof will be indicated only implicitly as part of our discussion of another issue—the effects of the regulatory constraint on the firm's output level. It will be recalled that the A-J allegation on this subject, designated proposition 4 above, asserts that effective rate-of-return regulation will lead the firm to increase its output level. Let us now see under what circumstances this is true.

Using the production function $z = z(x_1, x_2)$, one obviously has

$$\frac{dz}{ds} = z_1 \frac{dx_1}{ds} + z_2 \frac{dx_2}{ds} \tag{17}$$

where z_1 and z_2 are, respectively, the marginal products of capital and labor. To determine the sign of dz/ds it is necessary to evaluate dx_1/ds and dx_2/ds. Total differentiation of (13) yields

$$R_{21}dx_1 + R_{22}dx_2 = 0 \quad \text{or} \quad dx_2 = -(R_{21}/R_{22})dx_1 . \tag{18}$$

Since $R_{22} < 0$ by the strict concavity of R or simply by diminishing (marginal revenue) returns to labor, it follows immediately that the change in the employment of labor, dx_2, must have the same sign as the change in the use of capital, dx_1, if and only if capital and labor are complements in the production of revenue, $R_{21} > 0$. If they are substitutes in revenue production, their employment levels must change in opposite directions.

Substituting from (18) for dx_2 into (17), one obtains

$$\frac{dz}{ds} = \left(z_1 - z_2 \frac{R_{21}}{R_{22}}\right)\frac{dx_1}{ds} = \frac{z_1R_{22} - z_2R_{21}}{R_{22}}\frac{dx_1}{ds} . \tag{19}$$

We want to evaluate $z_1R_{22} - z_2R_{21}$ in (19). For this purpose we note that since R = total revenue = pz,

$$R_2 = (p + p'z)z_2$$
$$R_{22} = (p + p'z)z_{22} + (2p' + p''z)z_2^2$$
$$R_{21} = (p + p'z)z_{21} + (2p' + p''z)z_1z_2 .$$

Consequently,

$$z_1R_{22} - z_2R_{21} = (p + p'z)z_1z_{22} + (2p' + p''z)z_2^2z_1 - (p + p'z)z_2z_{21} - (2p' + p''z)z_2^2z_1$$

or

$$z_1R_{22} - z_2R_{21} = (p + p'z)(z_1z_{22} - z_2z_{21})\,. \tag{20}$$

Now, $(p + p'z)$ is simply MR_z, the marginal revenue of z, and is usually assumed to be positive (though with a constraint on rate of return this, clearly, need not be so). We may also assume $R_{22} < 0$ (diminishing marginal revenue returns to labor—which follows from the strict concavity of R). As a result, by (20) and (19) dz/ds must have the same sign as dx_1/ds (i.e., they must both be negative) if and only if

$$z_1z_{22} - z_2z_{21} < 0\,. \tag{21}$$

There is, however, no basis on which to prejudge the sign of z_{21} since capital and labor can be either complements or substitutes in producing output. Therefore, we simply cannot conclude that the A-J proposition 4 is always valid.

Yet there is a plausibility argument in its favor. Since we do expect $z_1 > 0$ and $z_2 > 0$ (positive marginal productivity of each input) we can write (21) as

$$\frac{z_{22}}{z_2} < \frac{z_{21}}{z_1}\,.$$

But this requires that the proportional change in the marginal physical product of labor which results from an increase in labor *alone* is *algebraically smaller* than the proportional change in the marginal physical product of capital which results from the same increase in labor alone. The condition is met if $z_{21} > 0$ so that capital and labor are complements in production. If, on the other hand, $z_{21} < 0$ so that capital and labor are substitutes, then it is met if the proportional decrease in marginal physical products as a result of a labor increase is greater for labor than for capital. In sum, the expression $z_1z_{22} - z_2z_{21}$ can be said to be negative so long as labor is a better substitute for labor than it is for capital.[17]

Alternatively, by differentiating totally the equilibrium conditions for an unconstrained profit-maximizer, that is, (5a) and (5b) with $\lambda = 0$, and the production function for the firm, all with respect to a change in the market cost of capital, r_1, one can easily show that the key expression in (19), $z_1R_{22} - z_2R_{21}$, will be positive if and only if x_1 (capital) is a "regressive" input—i.e., an input such that a *rise* in its price leads the firm, *ceteris paribus*, to *increase* the output of the final product. In short, if marginal revenue is positive and if labor is a better substitute for labor than it is for capital—or equivalently, if capital is *not* a regressive factor—then $dz/ds < 0$ so that output will indeed increase as the regulatory constraint becomes tighter (s decreases) as is required for the validity of the A-J conjecture (proposition 4 above).

17 If both terms in (21) are multiplied by x_2, the expression takes the form of a comparison of elasticities of marginal products with respect to changes in x_2 and it is then units free.

6. The capital-labor ratio with and without regulation

■ Finally, we are now in a position to deal with (alleged) proposition 2, which claims that the profit-maximizing firm subject to an effective rate-of-return constraint will necessarily employ a capital-labor ratio higher than that of an unconstrained enterprise.

We will first show in general terms why this need not be true and then we will offer a specific counterexample.

Proposition 2 asserts that

$$\frac{d(x_1/x_2)}{ds} < 0\,,$$

that is, by (16)

$$\text{sign}\,\frac{d(x_1/x_2)}{ds} = \text{sign}\,\frac{dx_1}{ds}\,. \tag{22}$$

Since we care only about signs we can look at the *proportional* change in x_1/x_2 when s decreases (i.e., when regulation is tightened). We have as this proportional change

$$\frac{d(x_1/x_2)}{x_1/x_2} = \left(\frac{dx_1}{x_2} - \frac{x_1}{x_2^2}dx_2\right)\frac{x_2}{x_1} = \frac{dx_1}{x_1} - \frac{dx_2}{x_2}\,.$$

But from (18) we know that

$$dx_2 = -\,(R_{12}/R_{22})dx_1\,.$$

Therefore

$$\frac{d(x_1/x_2)}{x_1/x_2} = \frac{dx_1}{x_1} + \frac{R_{12}}{R_{22}}\frac{dx_1}{x_2} = dx_1\left(\frac{1}{x_1} + \frac{1}{x_2}\frac{R_{12}}{R_{22}}\right).$$

Thus (22) holds if and only if

$$\left(\frac{1}{x_1} + \frac{1}{x_2}\frac{R_{12}}{R_{22}}\right) > 0\,, \quad \text{i.e.,} \quad \frac{x_2}{x_1} > -\frac{R_{12}}{R_{22}}\,.$$

Now this is surely true if $R_{12} < 0$, i.e., if capital and labor are substitutes in the production of revenue, because then we have $R_{22} < 0$, $R_{12} < 0$.

But suppose $R_{12} > 0$. Then the preceding condition becomes

$$\frac{x_2}{x_1} > \frac{R_{12}}{R_{22}} = \frac{|R_{12}|}{|R_{22}|} \quad \text{or} \quad \frac{|R_{22}|}{x_1} > \frac{R_{12}}{x_2}$$

which is obviously not necessarily true, nor is it even easily interpretable.

We now provide a simple counterexample to the allegation of proposition 2. Let us suppose the firm's revenue function is

$$R(x_1, x_2) = ax_1^2/2 + bx_1x_2 + cx_2^2/2$$

where

$$a < 0\,, \quad c < 0 \quad \text{and} \quad ac - b^2 > 0$$

so that $R(x_1, x_2)$ is strictly concave. By (5b) our constrained profit maximizer will satisfy $R_2 = r_2$, i.e.,

$$bx_1 + cx_2 = r_2 \quad \text{or} \quad x_2/x_1 = r_2/cx_1 - b/c$$

which increases as x_1 increases since $r_2 > 0$, $c < 0$. But by proposition 5 x_1 will be larger for the constrained than for the unconstrained firm, so that in this case the labor-capital ratio will be *increased* by the regulatory constraint, contrary to the assertion of proposition 2.

7. The revenue-maximizing firm under regulation

■ We have now completed our discussion of the basic A-J propositions and their formal validity. We turn now to some related theoretical results that have developed from the model.[18] One line of investigation which has grown out of the A-J analysis has examined the effects of the regulatory constraint (2) upon the firm that seeks to maximize total revenue or some other maximand instead of total profits. Such models have been studied by Bailey and Malone [3], Kafoglis [5], and Zajac [14]. Among the maximands that have been suggested by these authors are total revenue (sales), pz, physical volume, z, and rate of return, π/x_1. In each case the analysis proceeds exactly as before, only with the substitution of one of the preceding maximands for the total profit function (1). There is no need to go through the details of the analyses.

Not surprisingly, Zajac concludes that for a regulated firm maximizing its rate of return, the capital-labor ratio becomes indeterminate. Any point on the constraint curve in Figure 3 becomes as good as any other. The firm will simply select *any* capital-labor combination that enables it to attain that iso-rate-of-return curve, since it will then have achieved the greatest rate of return permitted by regulation.

Bailey and Malone, however, following the A-J procedures find that under sales (i.e., total revenue) maximization the nature of the inefficiency discussed by Averch and Johnson appears to reverse itself. Assuming that the firm's production function is quasiconcave so that the iso-product curves are convex to the origin, they prove:

PROPOSITION 6. *The sales-maximizing firm under rate-of-return regulation is motivated to use a labor-capital ratio greater than that which minimizes cost for the output level it chooses to produce.*

To prove proposition 6 we note that to obtain the new maximand, total revenue, we simply drop the terms $-r_1x_1$ and $-r_2x_2$ from the profit function (1) so that (5a) and (5b) become respectively

$$(1-\lambda)MR_z z_1 = -\lambda r_1 - \lambda(s - r_1)$$
$$(1-\lambda)MR_z z_2 = -\lambda r_2\,.$$

Dividing the first equation by the second we have

$$z_1/z_2 = r_1/r_2 + (s - r_1)/r_2 \tag{23}$$

where the last term is obviously positive. Comparison with (7) shows that, unlike the profit-maximizing case, this time z_1/z_2 exceeds r_1/r_2 which, given the convexity assumption for the iso-product curve, can only occur at a point where the labor-capital ratio exceeds its efficient value.

[18] We had intended to include in this paper a discussion of Klevorick's graduated fair return proposal [7]. However, C. R. Wichers [13] has found a significant error in the original formulation and it has therefore been thought advisable to postpone the discussion until the matter has been resolved.

This is shown explicitly in Figure 3. Suppose the firm's output corresponds to iso-product locus QQ'. At every point on that locus, since output is fixed, the price of the company's product is the same. Hence at any point on QQ' the value of z_1/z_2 is given by the slope of this curve. At the efficient point, K, this slope is equal to r_1/r_2, the slope of the budget line. Only at points on QQ' above and to the left of efficient point K will z_1/z_2, the slope of QQ', exceed r_1/r_2. But at these higher points on QQ' the labor-capital ratio exceeds its efficient value.

To compare geometrically the sales-maximizing firm's behavior with that of the profit-maximizing firm, assume that demand is elastic over the relevant range. In this case the firm will move to the highest iso-product (iso-revenue)[19] locus attainable on the constraint locus.

Usually in sales (total revenue) maximization models the firm is taken to maximize its total revenue function $R(x_1, x_2)$ subject to some sort of profit constraint such as $\pi(x_1, x_2) \geq mx_1$, which guarantees that the firm take advantage of opportunities to earn enough profit to satisfy its stockholders. The discussion implicitly assumes that the profit constraint (2) of the regulatory model also serves, with the inequality reversed, as the *minimum* profit requirement for the sales-maximization hypothesis. If the regulatory constraint permitted the firm to earn more than the profit needed to satisfy stockholders, revenue maximization would require it to move to an iso-rate-of-return curve lying entirely outside the shaded region in Figure 3, where the shaded region represents the input combinations prohibited by the fair rate of return ceiling.

Since the firm wishes, therefore, to move to the highest iso-revenue locus on the constraint curve, it will go to the locus *tangent* to the constraint curve. And since any iso-revenue (iso-product) curve is negatively sloped, the input point chosen by the regulated sales maximizer will therefore occur on a negatively sloping portion of the constraint curve. It must then involve a labor-capital ratio higher than that selected by the profit-maximizing regulated firm which, as we have seen, corresponds to the rightmost (vertical) point on the constraint curve (point π_{reg} in Figure 3).

The preceding result, since its conclusion is precisely the opposite of that of proposition 3, may be considered one of a number of attempts to show that the A-J conclusions lack general validity.

A rather informal argument by Zajac with a somewhat similar objective may be mentioned in passing. This discussion raises no questions about the formal validity of the deductions from the theoretical model but does indicate doubts about the model's applicability. Zajac suggests that the firm in reality knows its cost relationships far better than its demand function. As a result it may find it far easier to locate points on its efficient locus than to approximate its constrained profit maximum point, π_{reg} in Figure 3. Zajac suggests that the firm may perhaps attempt to work towards π_{reg} by any of a large number of alternate trial-and-error procedures. He chooses to focus on two of these possible series of moves. In the first set the firm follows along the regulatory constraint curve, while in the other

[19] Since we take $p = p(z)$, for any fixed value of z we must also have a constant value of p. Consequently, a locus along which z is fixed (an iso-product locus) must also involve a fixed total revenue (pz).

the firm, knowing no better, proceeds to the point of minimum cost for whatever output it happens to be producing initially (a point on the efficient path) and then moves roughly along the efficient path toward the most profitable point on that path, the point where it intersects the constraint curve. Which of these strategies, *if either*, the firm is in fact likely to adopt we cannot say. Zajac points out, though, that depending on the relative speed of the two trial-and-error processes, it is perfectly possible that the efficient-path strategy will actually prove more profitable for the firm, despite its relative unprofitability in static equilibrium with full information. Clearly, if this is the course selected by management, the conclusion of proposition 3 simply does not hold. Of course, the Zajac argument shows only that with imperfection of information of the sort that may plausibly be expected in this area it is virtually impossible to predict what will happen. Things may turn out either better or worse than the A-J model suggests. But that is just the point that Zajac wishes to make.

8. Regulatory lag

■ In practice the rate-of-return constraint is not enforced continually. Rather, the regulator restudies the company's prices and profits from time to time and decrees, if necessary, that these be readjusted so as to yield for the firm the fair rate of return. Regulatory lag means, for example, that the firm will often be able to earn profits greater than those considered appropriate by the regulator, as judged by the permitted rate of return, for limited periods of time. We will argue later that this lag is potentially of very great significance for economic efficiency in general. In the present context one might surmise that it serves to weaken the A-J input-proportion effect, at least to some extent.

Bailey and Coleman [2] have undertaken to investigate formally some of the implications of regulatory lag for the A-J model. They discuss two possible courses of events, one in which the firm simply acquires inefficiently large quantities of capital and holds them idle until the regulator, by changing the price the firm can charge, readjusts the total return the firm is permitted to earn, and the second in which the company makes the best possible use of that capital even though the quantity is inefficiently large for the output being produced. Since the former case, though the less realistic, is considerably easier to describe, and since it enables us to characterize the essence of the Bailey-Coleman argument, we will use it as the basis of our discussion. Moreover, although Bailey and Coleman considered the case of a firm with a finite horizon as well as the case of a firm with an infinite horizon, we shall restrict our discussion to the latter as it serves to bring out the basic point of their argument.

The course of events envisioned in the Bailey-Coleman article is roughly the following: capital can be acquired easily, but the regulator does not adjust the company's prices immediately after the acquisition of new capital. The firm must therefore consider the advisability of obtaining an inefficiently large quantity of capital à la A-J, knowing that the new capital will reduce profits until the price adjustment and increase profits thereafter. While management does not know the length of the time it takes for the regulator to react by making a price adjustment, it does have an estimate of its expected value, believing this to be n periods in the future.

Utilizing the same notation as before, if the excess capital is acquired at once, the company will immediately incur a cost of $r_1\Delta x_1$ dollars per period, where Δx_1 is the quantity of capital in question. Once the regulatory readjustment takes place the company will add to its total earnings $s\Delta x_1$ dollars per period but will continue to have to pay $r_1\Delta x_i$ dollars per period for the privilege.

Letting D be the appropriate discount factor, the net effect upon the profits of the firm will therefore be

$$\Delta\Pi = - r_1\Delta x_1 \sum_{t=0}^{n-1} D^t + (s - r_1)\Delta x_1 \sum_{t=n}^{\infty} D^t .$$

This will be positive, (i.e., the investment will be profitable) if and only if

$$- r_1 \sum_{t=0}^{n-1} D^t + (s - r_1) \sum_{t=n}^{\infty} D^t > 0 , \text{ i.e.,}$$

$$- r_1(1 - D^n)/(1 - D) + (s - r_1)D^n/(1 - D) > 0 ,$$

or

$$- r_1 + sD^n > 0 .$$

Since $D < 1$, the last inequality shows that if the length of the lag is sufficiently great relative to $(s - r_1)$ it will not pay to overinvest by the postulated amount Δx_1. Increased regulatory lag will therefore decrease the likelihood in this model that the firm will want to acquire an excessive quantity of capital in the manner suggested by A & J.

In this simple and unrealistic case, the one in which the excess capital is held idle, the amount of excess capital is not well defined because there are no diminishing returns to excess capital. The limit to the amount that will be acquired is presumably imposed by an influence that does not appear in the model explicitly. If the elasticity of demand for its product limits the amount that the company can, in fact, earn to less than the amount permitted by an expanded rate base, there simply will be no point in acquiring additional capital. The value of Δx_1 that enables the firm to reach the point of maximum profits under the fair rate of return constraint (π_{reg} in Figure 3) will then be the amount, Δx_1^*, that it pays the company to obtain. If n is sufficiently small to make it profitable to acquire any excess capital at all, it will pay to obtain this full amount, Δx_1^*.

Bailey and Coleman show, however, that this all-or-none result is an artifact of the simplifying premise that the excess capital is retained unused. They argue that it will, in fact, always pay to use the capital to replace some of the company's labor, rather than keeping it idle. In that case we may expect a diminishing profit yield to increased quantities of capital as a consequence of the diminishing marginal rate of substitution of capital for labor. Bailey and Coleman show that in their model it will always pay the firm to acquire *some* excess capital, but that the amount it is profitable to obtain will vary inversely with the length of the regulatory lag. The reason is simple. In their world the excess capital always faces a period in which it is expected to incur a net loss. The sooner it can begin to earn a net profit as a result of regulatory price readjustment, the more capital it will pay the firm to acquire for the purpose.

The authors of this paper have also constructed and examined a number of models of regulatory lag. The regulatory process and its effects as depicted in our model are, however, somewhat more complex than in most of the other models that have been described, in accord with our view of the nature of the regulatory process in reality. In our model the time sequence of profits and losses is reversed from that in the Bailey-Coleman model. While Bailey and Coleman regard the period before a regulatory review as the time when the firm suffers a loss because it is carrying an excessive amount of capital, now the period between reviews is regarded as the time when the firm has the possibility of earning a profit rate exceeding that specified by the constraint. When the regulatory review occurs, this excess is eliminated by the regulators' adjustment of the prices the firm can charge. In contrast, in the Bailey-Coleman model it is the review point which enables the firm to gain at last the benefits of the excess capital it has purchased earlier.

As we see it, regulation proceeds, roughly, by taking the latest information available on company costs and demands, and resetting prices so that the firm's *current* rate of return—based on its current capital stock, technology, demand conditions, and so forth—is reduced to the "fair" rate level. The firm is required to leave those prices unchanged until another regulatory review takes place either at the behest of the company or some other interested party. Thus, unlike the company in the A-J model, the firm in this analysis cannot simply select an output level and charge for it the corresponding price as indicated by the demand curve. On the contrary, the price is set by the regulators and the company, as a public utility, is then required to supply whatever volume of output happens to be demanded at that price.

How then can any excess profits be earned? Leaving aside any demand shifts the firm may be able to induce with the aid of advertising and the like, the answer is that by research and innovation the company can hope to reduce its costs below those that prevailed when prices were last set by the regulators. So long as the initial output and input prices prevail, it will be able to retain for its stockholders whatever savings the innovation makes possible. But this additional earnings flow is only a temporary benefit. At the next regulatory review, prices will be readjusted once again to take into account the firm's improved technology and the process begins all over again.

In the analysis of this process the firm is taken to utilize (at least) three inputs: labor, capital, and knowledge. Labor is a non-durable input, and the amount employed is determined anew at each of the firm's decision points. Each instant's net investment, however, constitutes an addition to the firm's total stock of capital, and, similarly, each period's research adds to the firm's accumulated stock of knowledge. The issues, then, are: first, whether or not in this model the regulated firm will be motivated to employ an efficient combination of the three inputs; second, whether the degree of input inefficiency, if there is any, varies with the length of the regulatory period; and third, how the equilibrium stock of knowledge is affected by the length of time between regulatory reviews.

This last issue is potentially of great importance. If one can demonstrate a functional relationship between the length of time between regulatory reviews and the long-run equilibrium stock of knowledge, it would suggest that regulators have at their disposal an instrument, regulatory lag, of which they have not made much conscious use. Suppose, for example, that the regulated firm faces a static demand curve—i.e., one which does not shift with time. Now, the long-run goal of regulation is surely related to the net flow of benefits to consumers and to the producer (the total producer's plus consumers' surplus produced by the regulated firm) *and* the distribution of those benefits between producer and consumers. Other things being equal, the total net benefits generated by the regulated firm will be increased by downward shifts in the firm's long-run marginal cost curve produced by improvements in its technology—i.e., by increases in the long-run equilibrium stock of knowledge.

Suppose the equilibrium stock of knowledge increases with the length of the regulatory lag, because the firm undertakes more research the longer are the periods during which it enjoys the temporary benefit of an excess earnings flow. Then the total discounted present value of the benefits generated by the regulated firm will rise when the length of the regulatory lag increases. For example, with instantaneous regulation—a lag of length zero—and technical progress which increased the productivity of capital and labor proportionately, one would expect the firm to undertake no research outlays since it could never reap any benefits from such an expenditure, while with no regulatory review—a lag of infinite length—one would expect the firm to accumulate a maximal stock of knowledge since it reaps the benefits of its research work forever.

While one might consequently expect the length of the lag to be positively related to the *total* discounted present value of producer's plus consumers' benefits, it is clear that a smaller *proportion* of these benefits will be distributed to the firm the shorter is the lag. That is, the shorter the periods during which the firm can earn "excess" profits and retain them for itself, the greater is the portion of the accumulated surplus which is taken from the firm and given to consumers.

To each length of regulatory lag, then, there corresponds a discounted present value of total gains and a proportion of these gains which accrues to the consuming public. The latter decreases as the lag increases, while one would expect the former to increase as the lag increases. In the simplest case, society faces an opportunity locus of the type shown in Figure 6, where total surplus (benefit) is measured on the vertical axis and the proportion of the total gains accruing to consumers is measured on the horizontal axis. Point A corresponds to instantaneous regulatory adjustment, while point B corresponds to an infinitely long period between rate reviews. Society—or the regulators—may then be assumed to choose among the points on this locus with the aid of a social welfare function defined on the two arguments—total net benefits, and their distribution—and to maximize the social welfare function subject to the opportunities-locus constraint. In the simplest case, the optimal point selected in this way will correspond to a unique length of the regulatory lag. In any event, the regulators can then choose a length for the period between reviews which will attain the social optimum with respect to the amount and distribution of producer's plus consumers' surplus. If regulatory agencies have chosen the time period between

FIGURE 6

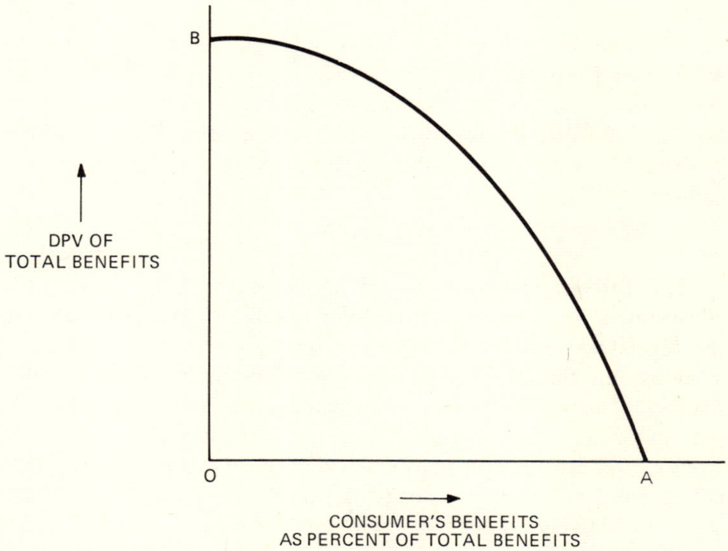

reviews in some more or less *ad hoc* fashion, this model would suggest that they have neglected a potentially valuable instrument of control.

With the aid of some additional notation, it is easy to describe one of the formal models used to investigate this issue of regulatory lag and research. Let

$$\left.\begin{aligned} z &= \text{the flow of output} \\ x_1 &= \text{the stock of capital} \\ x_2 &= \text{the quantity of labor used} \\ x_3 &= \text{the stock of knowledge} \\ \dot{x}_1 &= \text{the flow of investment} \\ \dot{x}_3 &= \text{the flow of research activity,} \end{aligned}\right\} \text{all at time } t,$$

p_i = the price the firm is allowed to charge in the ith regulatory period: p_1 is exogenously given while for $i \geqq 2$, p_i emerges as the adjusted price after the $(i-1)^{st}$ regulatory review,

$z = F(x_1, x_2, x_3)$ is the production function,

r_2 is the wage rate,

$g(\dot{x}_1)$ is the (total) cost of investment,

$h(\dot{x}_3)$ is the (total) cost of research and,

v is the discount rate.

Assume that the length of time between regulatory reviews, i.e., the length of the regulatory lag, is T.

The discounted present value of the firm's profits is then

$$\Pi = \sum_{i=1}^{\infty} \int_{(i-1)T}^{iT} [p_i F(x_1, x_2, x_3) - r_2 x_2 - g(\dot{x}_1) - h(\dot{x}_3)] e^{-vt} dt \,. \quad (24)$$

The firm's goal is to maximize the discounted present value of profits subject to the transition equations (25) and (26) for capital and the stock of knowledge:

$$\frac{dx_1}{dt} = \dot{x}_1 \quad (25)$$

$$\frac{dx_3}{dt} = \dot{x}_3 \geq 0. \tag{26}$$

As is clear from (25) and (26), we assume that there is no capital depreciation and no decay of knowledge through time. Finally, the firm must operate subject to the transition equation for price which is dictated by the price-adjustment procedure of the regulators, namely,

$$p_i(z_i)F\{x_1[(i-1)T], x_2, x_3[(i-1)T]\} - r_2x_2 = sx_1[(i-1)T]. \tag{27}$$

This price-transition equation represents the fair-rate-of-return constraint in our model incorporating regulatory lag. It states that the regulators proceed as follows in setting the price for period i. They assume that the firm does no research and no investing after the end of period $i - 1$, so that its capital stock and stock of knowledge in period i are assumed to be $x_1[(i-1)T]$ and $x_3[(i-1)T]$, respectively. Then, the regulators calculate what price will just yield to the firm the fair rate of return in period i on its assumed capital stock for that period. In fact, equation (27) may be regarded as an implicit equation for x_2 since $x_1[(i-1)T]$, $x_3[(i-1)T]$, s and r_2 are all given at the beginning of period i. When the solution value for x_2 is obtained, p_i, the price the firm is allowed to charge in period i, follows from the inverse demand function, $p = p[F(x_1, x_2, x_3)]$.

We are still investigating the implications of this model, and others similar to it, for the issues described earlier. The methods of analysis used to examine these questions are, primarily, the standard tools the economist employs in studying problems involving optimization over time: optimal control theory, dynamic programming, and nonlinear programming. In our case, we use these techniques to characterize the optimal path for the firm maximizing the discounted present value of profit subject to the particular formulation of the regulatory constraint. For example, in the model just presented, we use these methods to study the optimal path for the firm maximizing (24) subject to (25)-(27). Then one examines the conditions characterizing this path to see whether or not the firm's use of inputs along its optimal trajectory is efficient. In particular, the efficiency or inefficiency characterizing the equilibrium point to which the firm's optimal path leads it is also examined. To investigate the effect of the length of the regulatory lag on the firm's behavior, an experiment in comparative dynamics is then performed. The parameter representing the regulators' speed of response—in the model just presented, this parameter is T—is varied, and one observes the effect of this variation on the path chosen by the firm. In particular, one performs a special comparative-statics experiment at the firm's equilibrium point to determine the effect of the change in the regulatory lag on the equilibrium stock of knowledge.

The main reason for presenting the model here is that it appears, despite its oversimplification, to be a closer representation of the regulatory process than has been available before and because it encompasses the important policy issues that were just discussed. While results are still being derived for this and similar models, it would be fair to say that the general impression suggested by the conclusions already obtained is that there is a definite role for regulatory lag to play in inducing regulated firms to undertake research, *but* that the exact relationship—even the direction of the relationship—between the length of the lag and the equilibrium stock of knowledge depends critically on the nature of the production function $F(x_1, x_2, x_3)$ and, particularly, on the way the stock of knowledge enters that function. A similar remark applies to the effects of regulatory lag on the A-J conclusions. In some models, notably the Bailey-Coleman model, the inefficiency in the capital-labor ratio declines as the lag increases. But here too there is a great deal yet to be done.

9. Evaluative comments

■ As a contribution to the theory of regulation the work of Averch and Johnson represents a significant landmark. It shows how rigorous methods can be used to draw illuminating conclusions in an area in which historical description and impressionistic discussion has until recently played a preponderant role in the literature. This is clearly to the good, and it is hard to see how this accomplishment can be questioned.

This still leaves open, however, the issue of the significance of the A-J results for policymaking. And here, it seems to us, the conclusion we should draw is rather mixed. The analysis is certainly pertinent in pointing out that rate-of-return regulation can impose its social costs in the form of input inefficiency. Unfortunately, no one has yet found a good substitute for limitation on rate of return as a device to prevent the earning of monopoly profits by public utility firms, an objective that few persons probably would be willing to abandon. Yet any constraint on the decision process which is not designed explicitly to avoid undesired interference with the allocation of resources is likely to produce distortions in their usage. Most taxes have such effects, and it is hardly surprising that a fair-rate-of-return constraint will have such consequences.

The next step, then, is to determine the most important of these undesirable effects and to consider what can be done about them. The A-J effect certainly seems to be a candidate, although we have seen that in any particular model it may or may not be present, depending on the behavioral assumptions employed. Thus, for example, in the case where the firm is a sales maximizer we have seen that excessive labor rather than capital intensiveness follows from the premises. But even in a world populated by profit-maximizers we cannot be sure that the consequences for public welfare of the A-J effect are likely to be very serious. Harberger, in a well-known article [4] has estimated, on the basis of a calculation that was admittedly crude, that the social loss through misallocation resulting from monopoly and elements related to it is surprisingly small—a rather negligible proportion of the GNP. Leibenstein [9] following this line of thought has suggested that a far more serious source of welfare loss is what he calls "X inefficiency"—cases where management, characteristically as a result of imperfect knowledge, has simply failed to organize the firm's operations in a highly efficient manner.

Regulation seems to provide particularly apt examples of this distinction. The A-J overcapitalization is an example of the inefficiencies emphasized in the more conventional analyses. But even if it occurs in practice it does not seem likely to produce effects that are very serious. This seems so, if for no other reason, because, as we have already observed, firms may have neither the extensive information nor the refined decision processes necessary to lead unerringly to the A-J input distortions.

Of course, even if the A-J overcapitalization effect is not widespread, it does not follow that rate-of-return regulation is without its dangers.[20] It has been suggested that it has sometimes been used by regulators as a means to keep inefficient firms in business, shoring them up by preventing their rivals from passing their lower costs on to the consumers. The regulator's apparent distaste for the demise of any business firm no matter how tenuous its economic justification may well contribute in no small measure to X inefficiency.

Moreover, a rate-of-return ceiling by its very nature tends to contribute another X-inefficient influence. By ruling out all profits in excess of some predetermined rate as potential fruits of monopoly, a rate-of-return constraint also precludes extraordinary rewards for extraordinary entrepreneurial accomplishment. Indeed, if such a constraint were applied with complete inflexibility it might well eliminate altogether any financial reward for efficiency and innovation. If the firm cannot hope to earn more than the ceiling, *even temporarily*, and if the demands for its products are inelastic so that it can reasonably count on that profit rate in any event, what can management hope to gain by working for increased efficiency in its operations? Fortunately, as we have indicated, regulatory lag, like the Schumpeterian innovation process, by permitting temporary rewards for efficiency can perhaps provide just the necessary incentives. This is not the place to pursue the issue further. The point is simply that while regulation may well be suspected of being the source of some non-negligible inefficiencies in the economy, it is not clear that the phenomenon encompassed by A-J analysis is the most disquieting of these.

References

1. Averch, H. and Johnson, L. L. "Behavior of the Firm Under Regulatory Constraint," *American Economic Review*, Vol. 52 (December 1962), pp. 1053–69.
2. Bailey, E. E. and Coleman, R. D. "A Mathematical Model for Regulatory Lag," unpublished memorandum, Bell Telephone Laboratories, October 1969.
3. Bailey, E. E. and Malone, J. C. "Resource Allocation and the Regulated Firm," *Bell Journal of Economics and Management Science*, Vol. 1, No. 1 (Spring 1970), pp. 129–142.
4. Harberger, A. C. "Using the Resources at Hand More Effectively," *American Economic Review*, Vol. 49 (May 1959), pp. 134–47.
5. Kafoglis, M. Z. "Output of the Restrained Firm," *American Economic Review*, Vol. 59 (September 1969), pp. 583–89.
6. Kahn, A. E. "The Graduated Fair Return: Comment," *American Economic Review*, Vol. 58 (March 1968), pp. 170–73.
7. Klevorick, A. K. "The Graduated Fair Return: A Regulatory Proposal," *American Economic Review*, Vol. 56 (June 1966), pp. 577–84.

[20] On this issue see also the alternative theoretical analyses of some other problems of rate-of-return regulation in Wellisz and in Westfield.

8. ——— and BAUMOL, W. J. "Regulation of Public Utility Profits and Operating Efficiency," unpublished manuscript, 1968.

9. LEIBENSTEIN, H. "Allocative Efficiency vs. 'X Efficiency,'" *American Economic Review*, Vol. 56 (June 1966), pp. 392–415.

10. TAKAYAMA, A. "Behavior of the Firm Under Regulatory Constraint," *American Economic Review*, Vol. 59 (June 1969), pp. 255–60.

11. WELLISZ, S. H. "Regulation of Natural Gas Pipeline Companies: An Economic Analysis," *Journal of Political Economy*, Vol. 71 (February 1963), pp. 30–43.

12. WESTFIELD, F. M. "Regulation and Conspiracy," *American Economic Review*, Vol. 55 (June 1965), pp. 424–43.

13. WICHERS, C. R. "A Note on Klevorick's Regulatory Proposal," unpublished memorandum, Bell Telephone Laboratories, 1970.

14. ZAJAC, E. E. "A Geometric Treatment of Averch-Johnson's Behavior of the Firm Model," *American Economic Review*, Vol. 60 (March 1970), pp. 117–125.

PART SIX

DOCTRINAL HISTORY

31.

[39]

GARY S. BECKER
Columbia University

WILLIAM J. BAUMOL
Princeton University

The Classical Monetary Theory: The Outcome of the Discussion[1]

I. INTRODUCTORY

Recently a number of economists have shown a revived interest in the monetary theory of the classicists and of the members of the Lausanne School and their successors.[2] It has been maintained that all of these authors held basically common views which have been called "the classical system". Moreover, it has been argued that this system suffers from serious formal shortcomings, in particular that either it is inconsistent or it must leave the absolute price level indeterminate.

We believe a summary of the results of the discussion is now appropriate, and that the conflicting views can be evaluated and to some extent reconciled. Moreover, the arguments can be stated rigorously without recourse to the mathematical apparatus which has been employed. A detailed restatement is therefore included in the belief that the discussion will become available to many who did not follow it before.

For our purposes we may consider the attack on the earlier writers to have been opened by Lange [13], although the discussion, as is indicated below, goes back much further. However, the immediate centre of conten-

Reprinted from *Economica*, n.s. XIX (November 1952), 355–76, considerably modified and enlarged, by permission of the authors and the publisher.

tion is Patinkin's restatement and refinement of the Lange position. We shall therefore describe the Lange-Patinkin version of the classical system and the difficulties which they have shown to be inherent in it. A more satisfactory structure which Patinkin has called "the modified classical system" will then be outlined. Finally, it will be argued through re-examination of some of the classical writings that most of the group probably never held views like those ascribed to them. Indeed, it will appear that "the modified classical system" is a considerably closer approximation to their analysis. No doubt it is true that "the classics", particularly as the term has been used in the discussion, denotes too heterogeneous a group to permit wholesale judgement to be passed on the basis of selections from several members alleged to be representative. Nevertheless, many of the members of that group, among them some of those specifically accused, have passages in their writings which explicitly contradict the charges against them. We do not mean that none of these writers ever expressed himself incorrectly or in a misleading manner on this subject, or that they were all in possession of a full analysis of the logical structure of the problem. It does, however, seem that in most cases where the problem was considered *explicitly,* it was analysed in a manner which is at least formally valid.

II. A MODERN VERSION OF THE CLASSICAL SYSTEM

Consider an exchange economy using (say) paper money as a medium of exchange. An individual who demands (supplies) a commodity gives up (receives) an equal value of the medium of exchange. If we call paper money a good and sum over all individuals, then by definition the total value of *goods*[3] (including money flow) demanded in this economy is identically equal to the total value of goods (including money flow) supplied. In other words, any offer to supply ten dollars worth of goods is made only in expectation of receiving an equivalent value in payment, and this supply therefore also constitutes a demand for ten dollars (either in cash or securities or other commodities). Thus every x dollar supply is automatically also an x dollar demand, and similarly, every demand for y dollars worth of goods must be backed up by an offer to supply in exchange something worth y dollars. Since this is true for *every* supply and *every* demand the total value of all goods (and money) effectively demanded must always be exactly equal to the total value of all goods (and money) effectively supplied — a conclusion which represents little more than an accounting identity. This result, which Lange calls Walras' Law,[4] has nothing whatsoever to do with equilibrium in the various markets, and holds for *all* price configurations.

Suppose that at *any* given set of prices people will supply commodities when and only when they use (and intend to use) the money received to demand other commodities "immediately", i.e., during the period under consideration. Again, by summing over all individuals, we see that at any set of prices the total money demand for *commodities* will be equal to the total money value of the quantity supplied of all *commodities.* It is to be noted that (unlike the case of Walras' Law) demands for and supplies of *money* do not enter into this total which implies that if people sell hats for money they only do so *not* because they want to hold the money, but because they intend to run right down to the corner shoe store to trade that money in for footwear. Thus the result states that commodities in general (and no matter what their prices) will never lack customers, because vendors will *always* want to buy from one another as much (in value terms) as they offer for sale. It is this which Lange and Patinkin have identified with Say's Law. Because it is taken to hold no matter what the price structure and to distinguish it from other versions of the "Law" we shall refer to it as Say's Identity.

Patinkin in discussing his version of the classical system indicates[5] one particular set of circumstances which involves Say's Identity. He states that the classics, particularly the members of the Lausanne School, believed that money has no utility of its own, taking this to imply that in the static classical world there is no reason for any individual to desire any cash balances. Anyone who receives cash will try to exchange all his (useless) money for goods which have utility, so that, if there is a non-zero money supply, prices will rise indefinitely and the money market will be in equilibrium only with infinite prices.[6] Patinkin concludes that a classical economy can operate only if there are no stocks of money, and presents the paradox that this sort of "monetary" economy must in effect be a barter economy with a non-existent money acting only as a unit of account! Moreover, if people have no money stocks and never add, or want to add, to them, Say's Identity clearly holds, as it must in a barter economy, since commodities will be demanded at once in any exchange.

An immediate implication of Say's Identity, or rather an equivalent way of stating it, is that the quantity of money demanded, considered either as a stock or a flow, is independent of the price structure and is always equal to the quantity of money supplied. For at any set of prices, the value of the total quantity of commodities supplied is equal to the total (non-reservation or flow) demand for money. Likewise the value of the total commodity demand is the quantity of money flow supplied. Let us restate this argument in three somewhat oversimplified steps: (i) Say's Identity states that the total demand for commodities x is always the same as the value of commodities supplied (i.e. its supply must also equal x dollars); (ii) but (Walras' Law) x dollars are always supplied to back up a demand for x dollars worth of commodities, and (iii) x dollars are always demanded in return for a supply of x dollars worth of commodities. Therefore, (iv) when supply of commodities equals demand for commodities equals x dollars, it must also be true that supply of money (flow) equals demand for money flow equals x dollars. Clearly the converse must also be true. Thus with Say's Identity the quantity of money flow demanded must always equal the quantity supplied.

But when will the demand for and supply of money flow be equal as Say's Identity requires? This equality would appear to hold if and only if the quantity of money *stock* supplied (the total of the economy's cash balances) is equal to the quantity demanded, because if there is, e.g., an excess supply of cash, people will want to get rid of more money flow than is demanded. Thus, Say's Identity holds if and only if the quantity of money stock demanded is always equal to the quantity supplied.[7]

In our Say's Identity economy, let the money price of all commodities double (the quantity of money remaining unchanged or varying in an arbitrary manner). Since the relative prices of all commodities have remained the same we cannot expect buyers or sellers to make any substitutions among commodities. Only a substitution of money for commodities (an excess supply of commodities) is indicated, commodity prices having risen. But Say's Identity clearly precludes this too. Thus nothing will change with the change in price level.

It follows that the quantity demanded of each commodity will depend only on relative commodity prices. This is what is meant by the Leontief ([15])-Lange-Patinkin contention that the classical supply and demand (excess demand) functions are homogeneous of degree zero *in prices alone*. This rather ponderous nomenclature means only that the quantity of any commodity demanded or supplied is unaffected by a proportional change in prices no matter what is happening to the stock of cash – even if the stock of cash remains constant. It also requires that quantities demanded or supplied and relative prices of commodities, can never, even momentarily, be affected by the quantity of money. In other words, if, *whenever* all prices increase by exactly 12.63 per cent (so that the relative prices of, say, bananas and applejack are unchanged), people do not change any of their demands or supplies, we say that demands and supplies are *homogeneous of degree zero in prices alone*. This is what classical economists have been alleged to have assumed.

The condition that equilibrium exists in all commodity markets can be sufficient at most to determine relative commodity prices. To determine absolute prices we must look at the remaining market – the money market. But the money market is *always* in equilibrium, no matter what the levels of the various prices. Hence, the condition that it be in equilibrium cannot be used to *determine* absolute prices. We conclude that in a Say's Identity economy, relative commodity prices are determinate, commodity quantities demanded and supplied depend only on relative commodity prices, and absolute (money) prices are indeterminate. Money is a "veil" since a good can have importance in the determination of equilibrium in the various markets of an economy only if the market for this good can conceivably be *out* of equilibrium.

In this version of the classical system the analysis of price determination is thus necessarily incomplete as it cannot specify (equilibrium) absolute prices.[8] According to Lange and Patinkin, the classics nevertheless sought to dichotomize the pricing process by determining relative prices in the "real sector" of the economy and absolute prices by introducing an additional relationship – the so-called Cambridge equation or its equivalent in a cash balance or other form of the quantity theory of money. This relates the quantity of money which people wish to hold to the price level by postulating that the quantity of cash the public demands will rise with absolute prices. Thus there would, *ceteris paribus,* be one and only one equilibrium price level corresponding to every level of the supply of cash – that at which people were willing to hold the amount of cash supplied. Clearly this contradicts Say's Identity which, as we have seen, requires that the quantity of cash demanded equal the supply *no matter what the price structure.*[9]

Thus, with the addition of a quantity theory or any other explanation of the absolute price level, this version of the classical system becomes self-contradictory. Without any such addition the system is incomplete in its explanation of the behaviour of the economy.

III. "THE MODIFIED CLASSICAL SYSTEM"

The system just considered may be modified in a simple manner to eliminate the difficulties discussed. Patinkin[10] has called this revised model "the modified classical system". To accomplish this we need merely drop the obviously unrealistic assumption that the quantity of cash demanded is independent of the price structure. We may assume that the quantity of cash demanded will increase with the money value of transactions.

Suppose then that the prices of all commodities double, and that as a result, the quantity of money demanded increases. Since the relative prices of commodities have remained unchanged, there will not be any substitution among commodities. People *will,* however, seek to increase their cash holdings by giving up commodities, i.e., by increasing the quantities of commodities (in money terms) they supply or decreasing the quantities they demand. We can conclude that when there is a significant money market, the demand for commodities cannot depend merely on relative commodity prices, but must also depend on absolute money prices. Thus, any attempt to dichotomize the pricing process by determining relative commodity prices in the commodity markets alone, is impossible (except in a very special sense indicated below) once a significant money market exists. Thus, if any equilibrium is possible, a Cambridge equation, or anything else implying that the quantities of money demanded and supplied are not equal at all price levels, requires that quantities of commodities supplied and demanded must be unaffected by changes in prices alone. This can also be seen as follows: suppose prices, originally in equilibrium, are doubled, the stock of cash remaining constant, and that the quantities of cash stocks and flows demanded now (say) exceed the supply. By Walras' Law the quantity of some commodity supplied must exceed the demand. The demand for or the supply of that commodity must then have changed as a result of the change in price level alone, in violation of homogeneity. Hence, Hickman's system ([8]) which involves both a Cambridge equation and the assumption that the quantities demanded and supplied of all commodities are homogeneous of degree zero in prices alone, must be in error. What he has done, in effect, is assume that the quantity of cash stock demanded can differ from the supply (the Cambridge equation) whereas at the same time (Say's Identity) the quantity of cash flow demanded is identically equal to its supply, so that there are two separate conditions giving equilibrium in the monetary sector of the economy. Brunner has pointed out to us that this last sentence is not quite accurate – Say's Identity is not directly involved in Hickman's argument. However it comes close enough to the source of his difficulty for present purposes.

This argument also indicates that the difficulty in the system attributed by Lange and Patinkin to the classics arises out of the homogeneity assumption, since this precludes inequality in money supply and demand. Say's Identity, since it implies homogeneity, provides a special case of this difficulty. Patinkin seems to have been the first to observe this point.

The situation we are now considering is thus clearly inconsistent with Say's Identity – supply of all commodities does not necessarily equal total demand for all commodities. In particular, these will not be equal if the price structure is such as to cause the quantity of cash demanded to differ from the supply. Nevertheless, the present authors would like to point out that the ambiguous proposition called Say's Law can be interpreted in a way which makes it compatible with an economy in which the absolute price level does matter. This form of Say's Law, which we will call Say's Equality, states in effect that "supply will create its own demand," not despite the behaviour of the price level but because of it. The comparative statics argument is that an excess supply of goods, obtained by disturbing a market equilibrium situation by a cash reduction, will cause the price level to fall to just that point where the excess demand for money is eliminated, since the price level will fall so long as and only so long as there is an excess demand for (insufficient supply of) cash. The foregoing is, in effect, the reasoning behind the cash balance forms of the quantity theory of money and, incidentally, the Pigou effect.

The Cambridge equation implies that for every relative price structure there exists a unique absolute price level at which the money market will be in equilibrium (Say's Equality). This is equivalent to stating that for every set of relative prices there exists a price level which brings about *over-all* equilibrium in the commodity markets, i.e., the total quantity of money offered for commodities is equal to the total value of commodities supplied. Thus it is clear that this version of Say's Law is compatible with determinacy of an absolute price level.

Now assume that we start from a position of equilibrium in all markets. When all commodity prices and every stock of money doubles, the equilibrium is unaffected.[11] No substitutions take place since a proportionate change of commodity prices precludes substitution among commodities, and a substitution between commodities and money is rendered unnecessary, the doubled demand for money being satisfied by the augmented supply. This invariance is to be expected since in the models considered so far a doubling of the stock of money and all prices is strictly equivalent to a change in the unit of account (the "let's call fifty cents a dollar case") and, in effect, involves only a change in the name given the monetary unit.

If we assume that there never exists more than one set of prices compatible with equilibrium (the dangerous uniqueness assumption so often implicitly employed in comparative statics arguments) we arrive at the following comparative statics result: a doubling of the stock of cash *will* double equilibrium prices. Once again money is merely a veil. The phrase is, however, now used in the following comparative statics sense: the quantity of money in circulation affects only the equilibrium price level *and has no effect at all on equilibrium relative commodity prices,* and hence involves no inter-commodity substitution once a new equilibrium is attained. Thus the price system can legitimately be dichotomized into a "real" sector and a monetary sector, but only in a discussion of *equilibrium* relative prices.[12]

IV. THE POSITION OF "THE CLASSICS"[13]

We may sum up the allegations which have been made against the classics in the following three charges:

1. that they believed that cash has no utility of its own in the extreme sense that, in the static model which the classics (meaning in particular the members of the Lausanne School [cf. fn. 2 of this paper]) are alleged to have employed in their monetary analysis, people should, if consistently pursuing their own desires, seek to get rid of all their money as soon as possible;

2. that the classics believed that supplies of and demands for all commodities are homogeneous of degree zero in prices alone and so cannot be affected even momentarily by the quantity of money, and that they sought thus to dichotomize the pricing process, explaining the movement of (equilibrium and non-equilibrium) relative prices in the "real sector" alone, and the price level in the monetary sector by means of a quantity theory (illegitimately) superimposed on the system;[14]

3. finally, that by Say's Law they meant Say's Identity which states that the supply of commodities will create its own demand irrespective of the behaviour of the stock of cash and the price level.

Clearly these charges are not unrelated. Yet it may be worth investigating the attitude of "the classics" on each of these points simply because the authors may conceivably have failed to see the connection and illegitimately have accepted one of these and yet rejected one of the others which follows from it.

In the discussion we trust we have avoided reading too much into the classics in concluding that many of them held views more acceptable than those which have been attributed to them. Certainly we do not mean to imply that they always fully understood the perils they thereby avoided. It may be added that we began our investigation expecting considerably weaker results, and were most surprised to find how clearly many of the classics had expressed themselves on these matters.[15]

V. THE UTILITY OF CASH

Here we may begin with no less an authority than J. B. Say who recapitulates his views on this question by stating, "I have . . . pointed out the various utility of gold and silver as articles of commerce, wherein originates their value; and considered their fitness to act as money, as part of that utility".[16] He had already noted that "paper (money) has a peculiar and inherent value", and, indeed, gone into this point at length.[17]

Ricardo was, of course, less interested in the question of the relation between utility and value. Nevertheless, Marget[18] takes this statement that its employment as money merely adds to the list of uses of bullion to imply that added utility is imparted to metal by its becoming money.

Senior can also be cited to this effect,[19] and Marget[20] points out that Jevons wrote of "the 'utility' of 'that quality of money' which a man 'will desire *not* to exchange' ". Wicksteed[21] speaks of the marginal significance of gold being raised by its use as a medium of exchange, as well as its use as a standard of value. And while Marshall, in speaking of the constancy of the marginal utility of money presumably referred to income rather than cash balances, there is at least one point in the *Principles* in which his money unmistakably means cash,[22] and in which he goes into detail on "the marginal utility of ready money".

Surely Patinkin is not justified in citing Walras as one of those to whom money has no utility. His only reference (indeed his only "damning" reference to Walras) is to the statement "Soit (U) la monnaie que nous considérerons d'abord comme un objet sans utilité propre . . . ".[23] This is hardly conclusive, and it may well be meant to indicate no more than the author's intention *at that point* to deal only with monies like paper rather than, for example, gold. In any case, it includes the phrase "d'abord" (to begin with). Indeed it would be most strange for one who has been hailed as a mighty protagonist of the cash balance approach,[24] to find Walras denying utility to cash. But we have better evidence than this. In his *Théorie de la Monnaie* he makes it abundantly clear that he is most pleased that the theory of money provides such a fine and important application of the theory of marginal utility[25] and more than once speaks of the *rareté* of money[26] after having pointed out that this is the term he had appropriated from his father to designate marginal utility.[27]

Pareto is another of the only five "classics" (Walras, Pareto, Wicksell, Cassel and Divisia) whose work is specifically cited by Patinkin as an example of the mishandling of monetary theory. No doubt Pareto's monetary theory is considerably more superficial than that of Walras. Nevertheless even in his case the charges are questionable. As with Walras, Patinkin provides us with only one specific reference to prove that any of his charges apply to Pareto, and again this reference is intended to show that in the Paretan system money has no utility. But the choice of passage is here even more strange. The only reference to money on the page cited is the following: "La monnaie étant une marchandise doit avoir pour quelques individus une ophélimité propre; mais elle peut ne pas en avoir pour d'autres".[28] Surely this is the contradictory of Patinkin's allegation! Indeed, Pareto goes further – in effect reprimanding those others (?) who maintain that money has no utility:

"La monnaie remplit deux rôles principaux: 1° elle facilite l'échange des marchandises; 2° elle garantit cet échange . . . C'est parce qu'on n'a pris parfois en considération que son premier rôle qu'on n'a vu dans la monnaie qu'un simple signe sans valeur intrinsèque".[29]

The list is by no means exhausted, but there seems little point in going on. "The classics" did not generally believe that the holding of cash balances adds nothing to utility beyond that which will eventually be derived by spending the money.

Of course there are those who might appear in some looser statements to have argued otherwise. J. S. Mill did argue that "money, as money, satisfies no want",[30] but he wanted only to point out that money is valuable only because commodities can be bought for it,[31] a homily that should find few dissenters. Divisia more explicitly[32] and Knight by implication[33] have clearly denied a utility to money. In general, however, it seems rather difficult to find classicists taking the extreme form of the position attributed to them by Patinkin.

It may be remarked that the sort of statics which would be required to deprive money of utility in Patinkin's sense would be very special indeed. Transactions demand would be eliminated only if wage payments and all other receipts were staggered in time and amounts so as just to cover the transactions which the recipient desires to make at the moment he desires to make them. This would happen in particular if receipts and payments coincided in a steady stream.[34] Where these requisites do not hold, money derives a "utility" from the goods it can buy, it is true, but because it can buy them at the moment the buyer considers convenient.

VI. HOMOGENEITY OF DEMANDS AND SUPPLIES IN PRICES ALONE

The "Pigou effect"[35] consists of a rise in the quantities of goods and services demanded with a fall in absolute prices, arising from the resulting increase in purchasing power of all cash holdings. This is a complete denial of the homogeneity postulate, for it permits the demands for goods to be affected by a change in the price level alone, relative prices remaining unchanged. If we are not to call the title of Professor Pigou's article misleading, this effect is part and parcel of the classical stationary state, and there is no more to be said upon the subject.

However, the homogeneity (dichotomization) allegation is really at the heart of the charges under examination, and so is worth some further investigation.[36] First it should be noted that even an unqualified statement that the quantity of money may not affect the quantities of the various commodities demanded and supplied need not mean that the author believes in homogeneity of supplies and demands in prices alone. This may merely be the following (comparative statics) assertion which has been argued above (following Patinkin[37]). If all cash stocks are raised in proportion all prices will rise in proportion, and thus there will be no change in quantities demanded or supplied once a new equilibrium is attained, even in the "modified" classical system. This is not the same as the homogeneity assumption which would never have permitted the quantities of the commodity demanded and supplied to vary even temporarily with the changed stock of cash (no matter how it is injected). What we must then disentangle is which of these, if either, approximates the views of the writers in question.

The literature is quite rich on the effect of an injection of cash, going back to Cantillon and Hume, both of whom make it abundantly clear that they are having no truck with "the homogeneity postulate". Thus Cantillon wrote,

> "Through whatever hands the money which is introduced may pass it will naturally increase the consumption; but this consumption will be more or less great according to circumstances. It will be directed more or less to certain kinds of products or merchandise according to the idea of those who acquire the money. Market prices will rise more for certain things than for others however abundant the money may be".[38]

Similarly, Hume wrote,

> " . . . we find, that, in every kingdom, into which money begins to flow in greater abundance than formerly, everything takes a new face: labour and industry gain life; the merchant becomes more enterprising, the manufacturer more diligent and skilful, and even the farmer follows his plough with greater alacrity and attention . . .
>
> " . . . though the high price of commodities be a necessary consequence of the encrease of gold and silver, yet it follows not immediately upon that encrease . . . At first, no alteration is perceived; by degrees the price rises, first of one commodity, then of another; till the whole at last reaches a just proportion with the new quantity of specie . . . "[39]

Malthus seems to have accepted Hume's analysis, and indeed to have cited it with approbation, but Ricardo's attitude can at best be described as lukewarm.[40] McCulloch felt that Hume had exaggerated the beneficial effects of an influx of money, but nevertheless contested James Mill's out-and-out denial of the validity of Hume's argument.[41] Note, however, that even if McCulloch (like Walras, as Patinkin himself observes[42]) believed in "just a little non-homogeneity", e.g., believed that prices will rise sufficiently quickly and close to proportionately to render nugatory the impact effects of an influx of cash, he has escaped Patinkin's problems. He has accepted the "modified" classical system, the argument with Hume being only over the time path between the two equilibria which is irrelevant to the present discussion.

J. S. Mill also supported this sort of position,[43] but perhaps the clearest statement is to be found in Marshall's testimony before the Gold and Silver Commission to which the reader is referred.[44]

The case of Wicksell is worth special consideration, especially since he is under particular attack by Patinkin on this point.[45] Wicksell in his writings explicitly employed the device of proceeding from the (over) simple to the complex. Hence it is dangerous to attribute lack of sophistication to him on the basis of isolated passages, since these may be preceded by a warning and adequately qualified later. Thus, as Patinkin points out, at several points[46] Wicksell states that the demand functions for commodities will depend solely on relative prices. But on each occasion the assumption provisionally made is that money serves only as a unit of account and a medium of exchange, and its function as a store of value is explicitly abstracted from.

However, he knew well enough how to deal with homogeneity:

" . . . let us suppose that for some reason or other commodity prices rise while the stock of money remains unchanged, or that the stock of money is diminished while prices remain temporarily unchanged. The cash balances will gradually appear to be *too small* . . . I can rely on a higher level of receipts in the future. But meanwhile I run the risk of being unable to meet my obligations punctually, and at best I may easily be forced by shortage of ready money to forgo some purchase that would otherwise have been profitable. I therefore seek to enlarge my balance . . . through a *reduction* in my *demand* for goods and services, or through an *increase* in the *supply* of my own commodity . . . the universal reduction in demand and increase in supply of commodities will necessarily bring about a continuous fall in all prices. This can only cease when prices have fallen to the level at which the cash balances are regarded as *adequate*."[47]

It is true that Cassel did commit himself to (the macro-economic parts of) the model which Patinkin has called the classical system, and, indeed, the difficulties in which this involved him have been noted before.[48]

In sum there seems to be considerable ground for doubt about the validity of the attack on the classical system. Yet somehow Patinkin's argument is not completely pointless. Somewhere the impression seems to have arisen (and to have gotten into teaching) that this was indeed the nature of the classical system. Indeed, some of the classics themselves have, as we have seen, represented the contrary views as corrections of errors widely held. Keynes' polemics may have contributed considerably. One important source of confusion is, no doubt, the superficial resemblance between the valid comparative statics assertion that equilibrium relative prices may be unaffected by the quantity of cash (if injected into the system in an appropriate manner), and the position ascribed by Patinkin to the classics that relative prices can never be affected by the quantity of cash (however injected), even temporarily.

The nature of the mathematical notation employed may also partly be responsible. The demand and supply functions were usually written as functions of prices alone with no explicit cognizance taken of the quantity of cash or anything else, including money income, all of these having been held in abeyance via *ceteris paribus*. This may indicate merely that an author using this notation had for the moment not thought explicitly about the role of cash, or considered it unimportant at that point. Nevertheless, confusion about demands and supplies being homogeneous of degree zero in prices alone, may have arisen in this manner.

A particularly apt case in point is that of Lange himself who, as Patinkin shows, has gone wrong on just this point in the mathematical appendix to his book.[49] Yet much of the book itself is devoted to an examination of the effects of changes in the stock of cash and the price level on the quantities of individual commodities demanded and supplied, i.e., to a discussion of the effects of the absence of homogeneity in prices alone!

VII. SAY'S IDENTITY

This section will necessarily be the most inconclusive in our examination of the "classical views". This is largely because Say's Law seems to have been used ambiguously in most cases, the writers for the most part not having considered the relation between the law and the nature of the money market. Moreover, several different propositions have been referred to as Say's Law. Say himself, besides formulating the proposition[50] which has caused so much controversy, confused it with two different, considerably more innocuous, assertions.

The first is the tautological proposition that there will always be a market for all goods produced where we define a good to be something which can be sold at a price covering its costs.[51]

The second is the almost Keynesian view that demand will not exist without production since production creates the income with which goods can be bought.[52]

However, Say has also advocated the more familiar proposition, and at one place he makes it clear that he is thinking of the equality rather than the identity, but in a rather peculiar form.

> "Sales cannot be said to be dull because money is scarce, but because other products are so. There is always money enough to conduct the circulation and mutual interchange of other values, when those values really exist. Should the increase of traffic require more money to facilitate it, the want is easily supplied, and is a strong indication of prosperity . . . In such cases, merchants know well enough how to find substitutes for the product serving as the medium of exchange or money [by bills at sight, or after date, bank-notes, running-credits, write-offs, etc. as at London and Amsterdam] and money itself soon pours in, for this reason, that all produce naturally gravitates to that place where it is most in demand".[53]

Thus Say is operating with a nearly Wicksellian credit economy in which price level is indeed indeterminate. But this is so not because the quantity of money (and credit) has no influence, but rather because the quantity of circulating medium will vary by just the amount necessary to maintain any price level!

James Mill, on the other hand, makes a statement typical of many which were to follow, and which might be used to defend the view that most of the classics believed in Say's Identity: "When a man produces a greater quantity of any commodity than he desires for himself, it can only be on one account; namely, that he desires some other commodity".[54] Unless he here means money to be considered a commodity or unless, and this is a possibility we cannot rule out, he is assuming implicitly that the price level is adjusted to the quantity of cash, this would appear to imply acceptance of the identity. It is, of course, also possible that the problem did not occur to him.

If we compare this with McCulloch (who is sometimes considered the least subtle "classic") it becomes clear that it is not entirely far-fetched to argue that James Mill's statement need not mean that he believed in the identity rather than the equation. Thus McCulloch first argues very much like Mill, only more specifically excluding money:

"It is, however, the acquisition of [other commodities] . . . and not of money, that is the end which every man has in view who carries anything to market".[55]

and argues that therefore the redundance of individual produce must occur because production is misdirected and "is independent of the value of money". However, he at once makes it clear (and repeats this point in detail on the following page) that this is only a long-run equilibrium statement and is so *because the value of money has had time to adjust to the quantity:*

"It must, however, be borne in mind, that in the previous statements we have taken for granted that the value of money . . . has been invariable, or that, at all events, it has not been sensibly affected by sudden changes in its quantity and value. These changes may, as already stated, exert a powerful influence; and have frequently, indeed, occasioned the most extensive derangement in the ordinary channels of commercial intercourse . . . any sudden diminution of the quantity, and consequent rise in the value of money . . . may be such as materially to abridge the power of the society to make their accustomed purchases; and thus to occasion a glut of the market".[56]

Could there be a more forceful rejection of the identity?

J. S. Mill, in the *Principles,* speaks similarly of the "under-supply of money" during a commercial crisis,[57] this again in connection with a discussion of Say's Law, and after having just made the statement (quoted by Keynes in the *General Theory*) that "All sellers are inevitably, and by the meaning of the word, buyers" etc.[58] But the clearest statement on this point is that in J. S. Mill's second essay in his *Unsettled Questions.* We shall offer no quotations from there – it must be read *in extenso.* It is all there and explicitly – Walras' Law, Say's Identity which Mill points out holds only for a barter economy, the "utility of money" which consists in permitting purchases to be made when convenient, the possibility of (temporary) oversupply of commodities when money is in excess demand, and Say's Equality which makes this only a temporary possibility.[59] Indeed, in reading it one is led to wonder why so much of the subsequent literature (this paper included) had to be written at all.

It thus appears that the classics may have been taken too literally by Lange and Patinkin. As was the case in other connections, some of the classics may simply not have considered it worth the effort to point out that they were speaking about long-run equilibrium tendencies. Certainly the cases cited lend support to this view, and we have not found a "classic" who was explicit to the contrary.

The case of Wicksell is also particularly interesting in this connection because of Lange's comments. Lange himself points out that Wicksell (in our terminology) was driven to reject Say's Identity in favour of the Equality. After pointing out how Wicksell was forced to abandon the Identity in order to establish any monetary theory at all, he states,

> "He finally appeased his conscience by stating that total demand and total supply must be equal only 'ultimately' but may differ 'in the first place'. With this observation Wicksell, and with him all monetary theorists, gave up Say's law by substituting for the identity an equation which holds only in equilibrium. . . . But this tendency toward equilibrium . . . should not be confused with Say's law."[60]

POSTSCRIPT

We have made several minor changes in this article. Most of these changes are expository, and a few are intended to take account of some of Professor Patinkin's critical comments, in correspondence and in his subsequent writings.[61]

It should be admitted from the outset that this article does Patinkin a serious injustice in that, prior to its publication, he had announced a substantial modification in his position in a long footnote whose significance we had overlooked.[62] He now conceded that the *neo*-classical writers did indeed recognize the role of the value of the stock of cash in determining supplies and demands for commodities in those parts of their writings *where they discussed monetary theory*. But, he maintained, they failed ". . . to carry over recognition of this effect from monetary theory to demand theory."[63] On this issue, we believe that no one has found any conclusive evidence.

To us this is not really surprising because we do not believe that either the classical or neoclassical economists had gone into the problem in any detail. For the issue only arises in conditions of disequilibrium where the cash balance (Pigou) effect provides an adjustment mechanism (see above, pp. 761–64. But the classics were almost exclusively interested in comparative statics (equilibrium questions). It is, therefore, to be expected that classical pronouncements on such matters will be difficult to find.[64]

Our basic position therefore remains unchanged.

1. The classics never really concerned themselves in detail with the issues under discussion and were therefore not in error with respect to them. Moreover, they sometimes did use the real balance effect and they used it correctly. This is not meant to imply that they fully understood the issues and had a fully integrated analysis of the role of cash balances in disequilibrium. But whatever their errors on these matters, they were sins of omission, not sins of commission.

2. The classical and neoclassical analyses of problems of comparative statics are essentially valid, and the Lange-Patinkin discussion is not directly relevant to them.

3. In many well known contemporary writings the dichotomisation fallacy does occur and represents a serious error.

4. Patinkin's work in this area represents a very noteworthy contribution both because of the errors which pervaded recent monetary writings, and, more important, because it fills a major gap in our understanding of the role of money and other assets in the equilibrating mechanism of general equilibrium theory.

NOTES

1. The authors are indebted to Professors Viner and Brunner for their comments and suggestions.

2. See references [1], [8], [12], [13], [14], [31]–[35], and cf. [17], [18] and [36]. But note Patinkin's reservation: "To minimise this [the problem of textual interpretation] . . . I shall confine myself to the mathematical economists of this ['classical'] school". ([31], p. 4).

3. "Commodities" are also considered "goods". Paper money is "a good" only.

4. [13], p. 50.

5. [34], pp. 140–145.

6. This equilibrium possibility is suggested by Brunner ([1], footnote 20, pp. 167–168). Patinkin ([32], footnote 7, p. 135) has argued that infinite prices are not economically meaningful. But surely they can be interpreted to mean that money is not wanted. For when money is worthless, the money price of any useful good must be infinite. Thus, economically, this is identical with the Phipps solution (see [35]) which requires that the price of money be zero. In this case people will throw money away because it will buy nothing. This alone should already raise doubts as to whether any classic ever meant that money has no utility in this sense. But Knight ([11], p. xxii) does believe that money has no utility in a static economy and anticipates Patinkin in pointing out the consequences of this view. Cf. also, e.g., P. N. Rosenstein-Rodan [39], Part II.

7. Note that Say's Identity does not *require* that money have no utility, i.e. that demand (rather than *excess* demand) for money be zero.

8. Cf. Neisser [29].

9. See Lange [13], p. 65, Patinkin [31], pp. 12–16, [32], p. 138. Patinkin's contention goes somewhat further than this, pointing out that with Say's Identity no matter how the stock of cash behaves, the quantity of cash (flow) demanded and supplied must both increase in proportion with prices, i.e. they must both be homogeneous of degree one in absolute prices. This is true since the quantity of money (flow) supplied is the money demand for goods, which is the sum of the demands for the various goods each multiplied by its price. Since the quantity of each good demanded is unaffected by a proportionate change in prices, the sum of these demands each multiplied by its price, i.e. the quantity of money supplied, must change in proportion with the change in prices. The same argument holds for the demand for money, and hence for the excess supply of money. Now the Cambridge equation does not call for the excess supply of cash flows to behave in this manner *irrespective of the level of the stock of cash.* The *form* of the Cambridge relationship is thus in contradiction with the *form* assumed for the money excess supply function. It is this which Patinkin has called "Invalidity I" ([32], p. 138). The next paragraph in this paper summarizes his "Invalidity II" (*Ibid.*, p. 141).

10. [31], pp. 23–26, [32], pp. 143–150 and [33].

11. We require that *every* stock of cash doubles, and not just that the total quantity of cash in the system double, since the effects of an injection of cash will obviously vary with the method employed to introduce it. If given to the miser who sews it into a mattress, the effect will evidently be quite different from that of a gift to someone who spends it at once.

12. There have been some recent attempts to resurrect a system with demand functions that are unaffected by changes in the price level and yet contains a Cambridge-type of equation (see G. C. Archibald and R. E. Lipsey, "Monetary and Value Theory: A Critique of Lange and Patinkin," *The Review of Economic Studies,* Vol. XXVI, October 1958, pp. 1–22; and S. Valavanis, "A Denial of Patinkin's Contradiction," *Kyklos* (1955), pp. 351–368.

For a criticism of the Archibald-Lipsey paper by one of us, see W. J. Baumol, "Monetary and Value Theory: Comment," *The Review of Economic Studies,* to appear in a forthcoming issue. Valavanis' error appears to lie (see p. 356) in treating the Cambridge equation as a technological restraint on the turnover of cash instead of as a behavioral relation. At the very most, purely technological considerations can provide an upper limit to the turnover of cash; they cannot specify an exact value for the price level.

13. We have dropped from the originally published version a section on the role of non-monetary assets because it contained some errors (see D. Patinkin, "Dichotomies of the Pricing Process in Economic Theory," *Economica,* Vol. XXI, May 1954, p. 118) and because it is not important for our purposes. A correct analysis can be found in D. Patinkin, [33], pp. 42–62, and his *Money, Interest and Prices* (Row-Peterson, Evanston, 1956), pp. 137–145.

14. This is what Brunner [1] has called "the complementarity property," meaning thereby that a separate money equation is superimposed on the system to complement the real sector.

15. The authors decidedly do not consider themselves experts in *Dogmengeschichte,* and so are forced to rely heavily on pilfered references coming largely from those extraordinary two volumes ([19]) where, conveniently, Professor Marget subjects closely related allegations to most painstaking examination (see esp. Vol. II, pp. 8–124). No attempt has been made at an exhaustive survey of the literature.

16. [42], p. 228. He is arguing against Garnier, translator of the *Wealth of Nations.* Locke had said this by implication [16], pp. 578–582.

17. *Ibid.,* p. 227, but cf. p. 133, esp. the footnote. It is noteworthy that in later French editions Say decided paper money was of sufficient importance to warrant a separate chapter (see the 6th edition, p. 256, and Chapter XXVI).

18. [19], Vol. II, p. 31, footnote 81, where Turgot and Law are cited to the same effect. For the Ricardo references see [37], pp. 9–10.

19. [43], p. 23 ff. McCulloch argues that coins "exchange for other things, because they are desirable articles, and are possessed of real intrinsic value" [21], (p. 135), but by this he may mean their value as metal, and is willing, though not without hesitation, to exempt drafts, checks and bills from this conclusion. Indeed, elsewhere (p. 217) he has sellers lend or spend their money immediately upon receipt.

20. [19], Vol. II, p. 56, footnote 14.

21. [48], p. 600 (Vol. II).

22. [24], p. 335 and footnote.

23. [44], p. 303.

24. See Marget [17] and esp. [18] for a spirited defence of Walras on these points written some twenty years before the Patinkin articles. After writing this the authors found that Professor Jaffé had, in a paper delivered at a meeting of the Econometric Society, pointed out Patinkin's misinterpretation of Walras on the utility of cash balances. For a summary see [10], pp. 327–8.

25. [45], esp. the introduction, pp. 65–70.

26. *Ibid.,* esp. p. 102. He is presumably speaking of the utility of availability of cash which he distinguished from the utility of money *per se.*

27. *Ibid.,* p. 66.

28. [30], p. 593. It is cited by Patinkin in [34], p. 140, footnote 5.

29. [30], p. 451.

30. [28], p. 6 (Preliminary Remarks). See also Hume [9] ("Of Interest"), p. 321 to the effect that money has "chiefly a fictitious value".

31. Thus compare [27], pp. 69–70.

32. [5] Chapter XIX and the Appendix.

33. [11], p. xxii.

34. This can to some extent be arranged artificially by investing money the moment it is received with provision for repayment the (perfectly foreseen) moment it will be needed. But this would only by done to the extent necessary to eliminate demand for cash completely if there were no transactions cost of making and then calling in the investment, and if, in addition, no effort were required in carrying out this transaction. Where these are not abstracted from, it will pay to hold at least small quantities of cash for payments planned for a time shortly after the money has been received, "perfectly" static world or no. It is true that if loans were perfectly safe (the outcomes perfectly foreseen) the distinction between cash and securities might disappear, but not the distinction between the "money-securities" and "real assets", and the latter would still have a positive yield because they are not convenient means of payment and so not perfectly liquid.

35. [36], pp. 349–350. Note the relation to Say's Equality.

36. Various kinds of dichotomization accusations and denials always seem to have flown thick and fast. Locke ([16], p. 582) and Say ([42], p. 226) most emphatically insisted that dichotomization is illegitimate, arguing that, " . . . money . . . is a commodity, whose value is determined by the same general laws, as that of all other commodities". (Say, *op. cit.,* p. 226). Ricardo accuses Malthus and others (not completely specified) of saying that money is a commodity " . . . subject to the same laws of . . . value . . . as other commodities", yet reasoning in an erroneous manner which showed "that they really consider money as something peculiar, varying from causes totally different from those which affect other commodities". [37], pp. 72–3. See also [38], p. 292, and [37], pp. 9–10). Yet this same charge is brought against Ricardo by Cannan ([2], p. 182) and, in effect, Leontief ([15]). Similarly Senior attacked James Mill on this ([43], pp. 8–9), while J. S. Mill explicitly affirmed that the value of money was determined like that of other commodities ([28], Book III, Chapter VII, Section 3, p. 488). To Walras the theory of money provided

". . . une des premières et des plus décisives applications de mon système d'économie politique pure" (i.e. his marginal utility theory). (See [45], p. 69); while Ohlin has lauded Wicksell for "this 'new approach (!)' to monetary theory", for "Until then, and as a matter of fact for long afterwards, it was regarded as self-evident that . . . a change in the general price level must be due to entirely different circumstances from a change in individual prices". ([46], Ohlin's introduction, p. xiii).

37. [31], p. 23, [33], p. 53.

38. [3], p. 179.

39. [9], p. 313.

40. [38], pp. 387–388 and the reference to Malthus given there. For a case of non-homogeneity in Ricardo, see [38], p. 179.

41. [21], pp. 556–557. But note that James Mill did not commit himself to homogeneity but argued rather that if the additional money were used to augment demand, prices would rise at once and rob this money of its value. See [26], pp. 160–161.

42. [31], p. 12, footnote 5.

43. [28], Book III, Chapter VIII, Section 2, and the second essay in [27].

44. [23], esp., pp. 38–52. It is noteworthy that at one point Marshall even included the stock of assets among the determinants of the demand for cash ([22], p. 44, as cited by Hansen [7], p. 2). However, Marshall never seems to have done much with this.

45. [31], p. 12, footnote 5, and [32], p. 149, footnote 30.

46. [46], p. 23, [47], Vol. I, p. 67, and Vol. II, p. 22.

47. [46], pp. 39–40 (Wicksell's italics).

48. See the excellent discussion by Marget [19], Vol. II, pp. 338–341, also Wicksell [47], Vol. I, pp. 224–225; Cassel [4], pp. 150–152.

49. See Lange [12], pp. 99–103. The Patinkin discussion of this point is in [31], pp. 18–20. This is not to deny that some recent mathematical theorists have adopted monetary analyses involving dichotomization of the real and monetary systems throughout their works. Indeed Brunner may well be right when he maintains in a letter to the authors that such an approach had recently become well entrenched.

50. Say's Law has been attributed to James Mill, but this judgement is not universally accepted. Though most of its components can be found there, the first edition of the *Traité* which appeared in 1803 had no well organised discussion of the "Law" (but McCulloch ([20], p. 21), seems not to have noticed this—note also the incorrect date given there). Before the second edition with its extended discussion of the Law appeared in 1814, James Mill had published his *Commerce Defended* ([25]) in which the argument is developed at length.

51. For references see Lange [13], p. 60, footnote 15, and Neisser [29], p. 385, footnote 4. In particular see Say's last two letters to Malthus (published posthumously) and Malthus' reply to the first of these in [41], pp. 502–515, esp., pp. 504–505, 508 and 513.

52. This argument is found in many places in Say's discussions of the Law. See [42], pp. 136–137, reproduced in [40], pp. 340–342, and [41], p. 441.

53. [42], p. 134. The insertion in brackets is Say's footnote.

54. [26], p. 222.

55. [21], p. 217.

56. *Ibid.*, pp. 218–219. The unabridged passage is even more forceful. He adds, "It is almost unnecessary to lay any examples of what is, unfortunately, so common before the reader."

57. [28], Book III, Chapter XIV, Section 4.

58. *Ibid.*, Sections 2 and 3.

59. [27], pp. 46–74, esp., pp. 69 ff. Mill remarks (p. 74) ". . . these well-known facts . . . were equally well known to the authors of the doctrine (Say's Law) who, therefore, can only have adopted from inadvertence any form of expression which could to a candid person appear inconsistent with it."

Note that on p. 71 a general fall in commodity prices decreases the demand for cash not through the transactions demand, but via the expectation that the price fall will not be permanent.

60. Lange [13], p. 66, Wicksell, [47], Vol. II, pp. 159–160. See also the passage quoted above.

61. See "Dichotomies," *op. cit.*, and *Money, op. cit.*, esp. pp. 373 ff.

62. [32], footnote 30.

63. "Dichotomies," *op. cit.*, p. 117.

64. This interest in comparative statics also explains why the demand for money was said to have unit elasticity, for this is the relevant function in finding the change in equilibrium resulting from shifts in the money supply. This is exactly analogous with the role of commodity demand functions which were developed to analyze the change in equilibrium resulting from shifts in commodity supply functions. For this reason we cannot agree with Patinkin that the classical monetary demand curve is different in form from their commodity demand curves. Patinkin's distinction between *ceteris paribus* (or individual) and *mutatis mutandis* (or market) demand curves seems to us misleading in this respect. For a similar criticism of Patinkin, see J. M. Buchanan, "*Ceteris Paribus*: Some Notes on Methodology," *Southern Economic Journal*, Vol. XXIV, January 1958, pp. 262–264.

BIBLIOGRAPHY

[1] BRUNNER, KARL, "Inconsistency and Indeterminacy in Classical Economics", *Econometrica,* Vol. 19, April, 1951.

[2] CANNAN, EDWIN, *A Review of Economic Theory,* P. S. King, London, 1929.

[3] CANTILLON, RICHARD, *Essai Sur La Nature Du Commerce En Général,* Higgs Translation, Macmillan, London, 1931.

[4] CASSEL, GUSTAV, *The Theory of Social Economy,* translated by Joseph McCabe, Unwin, London, 1923.

[5] DIVISIA, F., *Économique Rationnelle,* Gaston Doin, Paris, 1917.

[6] FISHER, IRVING, *The Purchasing Power of Money,* Revised Edition, Macmillan, New York, 1911.

[7] HANSEN, ALVIN, *Monetary Theory and Fiscal Policy,* McGraw Hill, New York, 1949.

[8] HICKMAN, W. BRADDOCK, "The Determinacy of Absolute Prices in Classical Economic Theory", *Econometrica,* Vol. 18, January, 1950.

[9] HUME, DAVID, *Essays Moral, Political and Literary,* Longmans, Green and Co., London, 1875.

[10] JAFFÉ, WILLIAM, "The *Élements* and its Critics", Abstract of a paper delivered before The Econometric Society, Chicago, December 27, 1950, *Econometrica,* Vol. 19, July, 1951, pp. 327–328.

[11] KNIGHT, F. H., *Risk, Uncertainty and Profit,* London School of Economics and Political Science Series of Reprints of Scarce Tracts in Economic and Political Science, No. 16, London, 1933.

[12] LANGE, OSCAR, *Price Flexibility and Employment,* Cowles Commission Monograph No. 8, The Principia Press, Bloomington, Indiana, 1944.

[13] LANGE, OSCAR, "Say's Law: A Restatement and Criticism" in *Studies in Mathematical Economics and Econometrics; in Memory of Henry Schultz,* edited by Oscar Lange, Francis McIntyre and Theodore O. Yntema, Chicago University Press, Chicago, 1942.

[14] LEONTIEF, WASSILY, "The Consistency of the Classical Theory of Money and Prices", *Econometrica,* Vol. 18, January, 1950.

[15] LEONTIEF, WASSILY, "The Fundamental Assumptions of Mr. Keynes' Monetary Theory of Employment", *Quarterly Journal of Economics,* Vol. LI, November, 1936.

[16] LOCKE, JOHN, *An Essay on the Consequences of the Lowering of Interest and Raising the Value of Money,* Ward, Lock and Co. Edition of *The Works of John Locke,* London, (no date).

[17] MARGET, ARTHUR, "Léon Walras and the 'Cash Balance Approach' to the Problem of the Value of Money", *Journal of Political Economy,* Vol. XXXIX, October, 1931.

[18] MARGET, ARTHUR, "The Monetary Aspects of the Walrasian System", *Journal of Political Economy,* Vol. XLIII, April, 1935.

[19] MARGET, ARTHUR, *The Theory of Prices,* Prentice Hall, New York, Vol. I, 1938, Vol. II, 1942.

[20] MCCULLOCH, J. R., *The Literature of Political Economy,* London, 1845.

[21] MCCULLOCH, J. R., *Principles of Political Economy,* Fourth Edition, London, 1849.

[22] MARSHALL, ALFRED, *Money, Credit and Commerce,* Macmillan, London, 1923.

[23] MARSHALL, ALFRED, *Official Papers,* Macmillan, London, 1928.

[24] MARSHALL, ALFRED, *Principles of Economics,* 8th Edition, Macmillan, London, 1920.

[25] MILL, JAMES, *Commerce Defended,* Second Edition, London, 1808.

[26] MILL, JAMES, *Elements of Political Economy,* Second Edition, London, 1824.

[27] MILL, JOHN S., *Essays on Some Unsettled Questions of Political Economy,* London, 1844, No. 7 in the Series of Reprints of Scarce Works on Political Economy, London School of Economics and Political Science, London, 1948.

[28] MILL, JOHN S., *Principles of Political Economy,* edited by W. S. Ashley, Longmans, Green, London, 1909.

[29] NEISSER, HANS, "General Overproduction", in *Readings in Business Cycle Theory,* Gottfried Haberler, editor, American Economic Association, Blakiston, Philadelphia, 1944.

[30] PARETO, VILFREDO, *Manuel D'Économie Politique,* 2nd edition, Giard, Paris, 1927.

[31] PATINKIN, DON, "The Indeterminacy of Absolute Prices in Classical Economic Theory", *Econometrica,* Vol. 17, January, 1949.

[32] PATINKIN, DON, "The Invalidity of Classical Monetary Theory", *Econometrica,* Vol. 19, April, 1951.

[33] PATINKIN, DON, "A Reconsideration of the General Equilibrium Theory of Money", *Review of Economic Studies,* Vol. XVIII, 1950–51.

[34] PATINKIN, DON, "Relative Prices, Say's Law, and the Demand for Money", *Econometrica,* Vol. 16, April, 1948.

[35] PHIPPS, CECIL G., "A Note on Patinkin's 'Relative Prices' ", *Econometrica,* Vol. 18, January, 1950.

[36] PIGOU, A. C., "The Classical Stationary State", *Economic Journal,* Vol. LIII, December, 1943.

[37] RICARDO, DAVID, *Letters of David Ricardo to Thomas Robert Malthus,* edited by James Bonar, Oxford, London, 1887.

[38] RICARDO, DAVID, *The Works of*

David Ricardo, McCulloch-Edition, London, 1876.

[39] ROSENSTEIN-RODAN, P. N., "The Coordination of the General Theories of Money and Price", *Economica,* N.S., Vol. III, August, 1936.

[40] SAY, J. B., *Cours Complet D'Économie Politique Pratique,* Third Edition, Paris, 1852.

[41] SAY, J. B., *Oeuvres Diverses,* Paris, 1848.

[42] SAY, J. B., *A Treatise on Political Economy,* Prinsep Translation, Philadelphia, 1853.

[43] SENIOR, NASSAU W., *Three Lectures on the Value of Money,* London, 1840, London School of Economics and Political Science Reprints of Scarce Tracts in Economic and Political Science, No. 4, London, 1931.

[44] WALRAS, LÉON, *Éléments D'Économie Politique Pure,* Édition Définitive, Pichon et Durand-Auzias, Paris, 1926.

[45] WALRAS, LÉON, *Études D'Économie Politique Appliquée,* Second Edition, Pichon et Durand-Auzias, Paris, 1936.

[46] WICKSELL, KNUT, *Interest and Prices,* Translated by R. F. Kahn, Macmillan, London, 1936.

[47] WICKSELL, KNUT, *Lectures on Political Economy,* Translated by E. Classen, Edited with an introduction by Lionel Robbins, Routledge, London, Vol. I, 1934, Vol. II, 1935.

[48] WICKSTEED, PHILIP H., *The Common Sense of Political Economy,* Edited with an Introduction by Lionel Robbins, Routledge, London, 1933.

[40]

On Marx, the Transformation Problem and Opacity
Baumol – Samuelson – Morishima

Editor's Note: *Few articles in the history of the* JEL *have stirred the controversy that Paul A. Samuelson's "Understanding the Marxian Notion of Exploitation: A Summary of the So-called Transformation Problem between Marxian Values and Competitive Prices,"* J. Econ. Lit., *June 1971,* 9 *(2), pp. 399–431, did. We have already had one "terminal" discussion of the reaction—Bronfenbrenner, M. "Samuelson, Marx, and Their Latest Critics," and "Samuelson's 'Reply on Marxian Matters',"* J. Econ. Lit., *March 1973,* 11 *(1), pp. 59–63. Professor Baumol has found a history of thought approach to the topic which deserves the attention of all economists who have an interest in Marx, Marxism, or the evolution of classical economic thought. We print his essay here. Professor Samuelson sought to comment on Baumol's work, and we give his views, as well. In the course of Samuelson's reply, he "took on" Professor Morishima, who quite naturally wanted to add a few words of further explanation. We have finally allowed Professors Baumol and Samuelson to share in what we hope are the "last words." M.P.*

The Transformation of Values: What Marx "Really" Meant (An Interpretation)

By William J. Baumol
Princeton and New York Universities

I would like to thank the students in my seminar on doctrinal history at Princeton University whose discussions contributed greatly to the ideas in this paper. I am also grateful to Elizabeth Bailey, Fritz Machlup, Michio Morishima and Paul Samuelson for their very helpful comments on earlier drafts of this paper. I am particularly indebted to Professor Samuelson for an extensive, illuminating and delightful correspondence on the subject.

This paper will suggest that the meaning of the relationship between values and prices described in *Capital* has been widely misunderstood. Commentators as eminent as Mrs. Robinson and Professor Samuelson have sought in the transformation discussion issues which Karl Marx never meant it to contain. Writers on "the transformation problem" since L. Bortkiewicz have focussed on an issue that is largely peripheral; and others like E. Böhm-Bawerk have asserted that there is a contradiction between the analyses of Volumes I and III which is certainly not to be found there unless 1ne reads into them an interpretation different from that which Marx repeatedly emphasized.

Interpretation of the intentions of the writings of the dead is always a questionable undertaking, particularly since defunct authors cannot defend themselves. Yet there are some cases in which a careful rereading of the pertinent writings indicates that the author *did* speak for himself and spoke very clearly—the trouble in such cases seems to be that something about the original presentation prevents most readers, even some very careful ones, from seeing what the writer intended.[1]

A notable case in point is D. Ricardo's discussion of the labor theory of value. It is hard to understand how a careful reader of any edition of the *Principles* can overlook Ricardo's recognition of the role of the quantity and the durability of capital in the determination of price. The labor theory is explicitly proposed as a remarkably good approximation to the determination of competitive price. But, ultimately, Ricardo holds to a cost of production theory of pricing, not to a pure labor theory. Yet until Stigler's fine article on the subject (1958),[2] in which this is documented beyond any shadow of a doubt, virtually any text was prepared to ascribe to Ricardo the purest of labor theories, and even J. H. Hollander and E. Cannan (see G. J. Stigler for references) suggested that Ricardo retreated grudgingly under fire to the cost of production model of the third edition. Only a few commentators, notably A. Marshall, J. Viner, and P. Sraffa, saw Ricardo's analysis for what it so plainly was from the first edition on.[3]

I emphasize this case for two reasons; first, because I will try to show that the correct interpretation of Marx' intentions is equally evident, and second, because I will suggest that the false analogy between Ricardo's and Marx' value theories may help to explain our misunderstanding of the latter.

[1] I must emphasize that it is not the purpose of this paper to attack or defend the substance of Marx' transformation discussion or to argue the significance of the insights it offers. This issue can be discussed profitably only after clarification of the content of his analysis—which is the only objective of this article.

[2] Obviously, I disagree emphatically with Samuelson's judgment that "It is a sad reflection on the decadence of literary economics that so much printer's ink has been wasted on the sterile and ambiguous question of whether Ricardo had or didn't have a labor theory of value, or a 93 percent labor theory, or . . ." [13, 1971, p. 405]. If an author speaks for himself as clearly as Ricardo did, it is surely more appropriate to discuss what he did say than what some commentator has somehow inferred he ought to have said.

[3] For references on these matters, see Stigler [15, 1958]. Note that Marx himself understood Ricardo correctly on this issue. Thus in a letter to Engels dated July 6, 1863, Marx wrote "You know that according to *Adam Smith the 'natural' or 'necessary price'* is composed of wages, profit (interest), rent. . . . This nonsense was taken over by Ricardo, although he excludes rent, as merely accidental. . . ." (Marx' italics.) All translations, unless otherwise noted, are taken from [8, 1956]. The preceding quotation appears on p. 174.

I have chosen to follow the published translations of the correspondence, which seem to be reasonably accurate. In a few cases some of the English phrases that Marx scattered through his letters have been edited by the translator.

Marx' Interpretation of the Transformation Problem: Summary

In Ricardo, the labor theory of value *was* meant as a good approximation to a full explanation of the determination of prices. However Marx probably never intended to produce such an approximation and it certainly was not his intention when he wrote about the transformation problem; yet that objective, or something close to it, is often attributed to Marx.

I will provide evidence that Marx did not intend his transformation analysis to show how prices can be *deduced* from values. Marx was well aware that market prices do not have to be deduced from values (nor, for that matter, values from prices). Rather, the two sets of magnitudes which are derived more or less[4] independently were recognized by Marx to differ in a substantial and a systematic manner.[5] A subsidiary purpose of the transformation calculation was to determine the nature of these deviations. But this objective and, indeed, any explanation of pricing as an end in itself, was of very little consequence to Marx, for the primary transformation was not from values into prices but, as Marx and Engels repeatedly emphasize, from *surplus* values into the non-labor income categories that are recognized by "vulgar economists," *i.e.*, profits, interest, and rent.

Thus we must surely reexamine the implications of Samuelson's conclusion:

> The truth has now been laid bare. Stripped of logical complication and confusion, anybody's method of solving the famous transformation problem is seen to involve returning from the unnecessary detour taken in Volume I's analysis of values. . . . [S]uch a "transformation" is precisely like that in which an eraser is used to rub out an earlier entry, after which we make a new start to end up with the properly calculated entry [13, 1971, p. 421].

[4] Not entirely, since labor time (Marxian value) is a technological datum which enters the determination of cost and, hence, competitive price.

[5] R. L. Meek [9, 1956] and M. Morishima [10, 1973, Chapter 7] in my view may be the only current authors who have described the transformation problem correctly.

I will argue that this conclusion represents no real conflict with Marx' intentions, as Samuelson seems to suggest. Marx knew perfectly well that price determination can be explained in terms of the competitive process by itself, just as the classical economists had done, so that if the objective were an analysis of pricing, Volume I would indeed represent an "unnecessary detour." But Marx' interests were not focused on price theory, and as I will show, he was well aware that competitive prices can be deduced without prior recourse to Marxian values.

My contention is that Marx' interest in the transformation analysis as a sequel to his value theory was not a matter of pricing. Rather it sought to describe how *non* wage incomes are *produced* and then how this aggregate is *redistributed*, the first of these being the substantive issue to Marx and the one he discusses in Volume I, while the latter is the surface manifestation known to all bourgeois economists and which Marx only deigns to consider in Volume III.

The substance of Marx' analysis can be summarized in a simple parable, in which the economy is described as an aggregation of industries each of which contributes to a storehouse containing total surplus value. The contribution of each industry is its total output minus the consumption of its labor force. If we use labor units to measure these quantities, each industry's contribution is proportionate to the quantity of labor it uses, for reasons to be noted in a later footnote. This, then, is how society's surplus value is *produced*.

The *distribution* of society's surplus value from the central storehouse now takes place via the competitive process which assigns to each industry for profit, interest payment, and rent an amount strictly proportionate to its capital investment. This is the heart of the transformation process—the conversion of surplus value into profit, interest, and rent. It takes from each according to its work force, and returns to each according to its total investment.

The object of the discussion of the conversion of surplus value into "average profit" is then straightforward. Given the contribution of some one industry to the social surplus (as described by the value analysis) and the largely independent determination of that same industry's withdrawals in the form of profits, interest payments, and rent, the question is how those two compare. Put another way, the question is, under what circumstances will a given industry withdraw more than it has contributed, and when will the reverse be true?

This is a question which cannot, I believe, be answered with the aid of an eraser. Marx proposed part of the answer, but his argument for even that portion was incomplete. Morishima, (especially pp. 80–84) in his excellent book, is, as far as I know, the first to have supplied a careful answer [10, 1973].

The Value Theory Reconsidered

In Volume I, Marx does occasionally speak of values as if they were meant to approximate prices. For example, he asserts "It is true, commodities may be sold at prices deviating from their values, but those deviations are to be considered as infractions of the laws of the exchange of commodities . . . ."[6] He goes on to describe these deviations as "temporary" ascribing them to "Market disturbances." However, his comments must be interpreted in context: at this point Marx is merely arguing that profits or surplus values cannot be *ascribed* to a process of inflation of prices above values since in such a universal inflation no one can gain. His language at such points generally seems to be explainable primarily in terms of his expository objectives. Certainly by the time we come to Volume III, values and prices are clearly dissociated, with "cost prices" based on equality of rates of return on investment in different industries.

There seem to be three plausible ways to account for the distinction between the role of value in the two volumes. The first is that Marx originally intended his values as equilibrium relative prices and only retreated from this position when he began to realize it was untenable, doing his best to explain away his retreat as a planned regrouping of his forces.[7] This view has been implied by a number of writers.[8] The second and more common interpretation is that Marx intended the value theory as a simplified approximation to the correct analysis

[6] Volume I. [6, 1906], Chapter V, pp. 176–77—all references to *Capital* are to the Charles Kerr edition.

[7] R. Hilferding (p. 155) seems to ascribe this view to Böhm-Bawerk but I have not been able to find any such assertion by the latter. Böhm-Bawerk does assert that there is an irreconcilable contradiction between the value theory of Volume I and the price theory of Volume III (p. 29 and Chapter III in general). However, he does not attempt to account for its origin [2, Böhm-Bawerk, 1949].

[8] For an illustrative reference see Sweezy [16, 1942, p. 111].

of prices (somewhat in the manner of Ricardo) and that the transformation calculation of Volume III is his way of producing the appropriate correction.[9] The third explanation, which I suspect is the correct one, is that the value theory was never intended as a theory of price, which, as a superficial manifestation of the bourgeois economy, Marx considered worth very little attention, but was instead designed to explain something to him far more fundamental: the process of production, *i.e.,* the extraction of surplus values in the various sectors of the economy.

Turning to the first of the hypotheses, we cannot hope to prove that Marx never changed his mind on the relation of his values to prices. But we do know that at least half a decade before the completion of the preface to Volume I his views of the transformation problem were quite fully formed. A letter from Marx to Engels, written five years before the publication of Volume I, provides a clear statement of the transformation problem and Marx' proposed solution.[10] Moreover, Engels tells us that "Volume III . . . was written for the greater part in 1864 and 1865" (Preface to Volume II, p. 9), that is, two years before the appearance of Volume I.[11] In fact, in that same place Engels states Marx had reached his solution "even in his manuscript for His 'Critique of Political Economy' " on which Marx had worked in the 1850's (p. 28).[12]

But substance rather than tedious arguments about dating is our real purpose here. Later, I will show explicitly that what Marx had revealed in his Volume III analysis of price he considered to be no improvement over his Volume I analysis of value. On the contrary, from his point of view the price analysis of Volume III dealt with the "outward

[9] See M. Bronfenbrenner [3, 1973] where Marx' "approximation" is explicitly likened to Ricardo's. P. M. Sweezy also argues in a way that tempts the reader to impute this position to him:

> It is perfectly legitimate to postulate a capitalist system in which organic compositions of capital are everywhere equal and hence the law of value does hold. . . . Whether or not this procedure is valid . . . must be tested by dropping the assumption. . . . [I]n Volume III [Marx] abandons this assumption and attempts to show that, from the point of view of the problems which he was attempting to solve, the modifications which result are of a relatively minor character. (*Ibid,* p. 70.)

However, in a very helpful letter to me, Sweezy rejects this interpretation of his views:

> I never had any inclination to accept what you call the "second and more common interpretation . . . that Marx intended the value theory as a simplified approximation to the correct analysis of prices." On certain assumptions, most importantly equal organic compositions of capital, value theory was *also* a valid price theory; but of course Marx never for a moment entertained the notion that the equal organic compositions assumption was realistic, from which it follows that for him the notion of values "approximating" prices was nonsense.

[10] For example, Marx writes in this letter:

> . . . with *equal* exploitation of the worker in *different* trades, different capitals of the *same size* will yield very *different* amounts of surplus value in different spheres of production and therefore *very different rates of profit,* since profit is nothing but the proportion of the surplus value to the total capital advanced. This will depend on the *organic composition* of the capital, *i.e.,* on how it is divided into constant and variable capital. . . . And capitalists are brothers. Competition (transfer of capital or withdrawal of capital from one trade to another) brings it about that *equal sums* of capital in *different* trades, despite their different organic compositions, yield the *same average* rate of profit. In other words: the *average* profit which a capital of £100, for instance, yields in a certain trade it yields not as the capital employed in this particular way, nor in the proportion, therefore, in which it itself produces surplus value, but as an *aliquot part* of the aggregate capital of the capitalist class. It is a share on which, in proportion to its size, dividends are paid from the total sum of surplus value (or unpaid labour) which the total variable capital (laid out in wages) of the class produces [8, 1956, pp. 158–59, Marx' italics].

[11] On p. 209 of Volume III in a footnote, Engels explicitly dates at least that portion of the transformation discussion as 1865.

A bit of chronology may be helpful in following the dating issue.

Marx' preface to Volume I is dated July 24, 1867. The letter telling Engels he had finally finished reading proof for the volume is dated 2 A.M., August 16, 1867. There are at least four letters in which Marx and Engels discuss the transformation problem. The first is dated August 2, 1862, five years before the publication of Volume I. There is an exchange dated June 26 and June 27, 1867, written while Marx and Engels were reading proof for the volume and one dated April 30, 1868, less than one year after publication of Volume I [8, 1956].

Quotations from all four letters are offered later in this paper. They show clearly that there was no significant change in Marx' position on the subject over the period.

[12] Hilferding and Sweezy are among those who have previously pointed out that Marx had worked through the transformation issue before Volume I was published. See Hilferding [2, 1949, p. 155] and Sweezy [16, 1942, p. 111fn].

disguise" assumed by the subject of his discussion. Only the analysis of the relation of profit and surplus value permitted "the actual state of things [to be] revealed for the first time" (Vol. III, Chapter IX, p. 199). Thus Marx tells us he had something more in mind than mere revision of the value theory in accord with the workings of competitive equilibrating forces.

One must also reject the assertion that Marx thought prices had to be *deduced* from values via his transformation calculation. Marx knew very well that his "prices of production" were the same as the "natural values" of classical economics. He apparently ascribes to Malthus the basic observation underlying their construction: "The theoretical conception . . . according to which every part of the capital yields uniformly the same profit. . . ." [6, 1909, Vol. III, Chapter IX, p. 200; see also, Chapter I, pp. 48–49]. In his first letter on the transformation problem (1862), Marx is quite explicit on the identity of his prices with the classical prices based on cost of production: "*Price* regulated in this way [*i.e.,* via the transformation process] = the expenses of capital + the average profit . . . is what Smith calls the *natural price, cost price,* etc." (p. 160, Marx' italics). Thus, he does *not* accuse the classical authors of having erred in deducing their price relationships without using Marxian values in the process. Rather, the charge repeatedly reasserted is that they dealt only with "this form of appearance."

Prices and values are, in short, not the same thing. Values are not approximations to prices nor a necessary step in their calculation. Rather, one is a surface manifestation, while the latter is intended to reveal an underlying reality. But what are these values and what is their rationale?

An Interpretation of Marxian Values

T. B. Veblen calls to our attention a mystery which no one since seems to have attempted to clear up. Veblen writes

> It is scarcely worth while to question what serves as the beginning of wisdom in the current criticisms of Marx; namely, that he offers no adequate proof of his labor-value theory. It is even safe to go farther, and say that he offers no proof of it. The feint which occupies the opening paragraphs of the *Kapital* and the corresponding passages of *Zur Kritik,* etc., is not to be taken seriously as an attempt to prove his position on this head by the ordinary recourse to argument. It is rather a self-satisfied superior's playful mystification of those readers (critics) whose limited powers do not enable them to see that his proposition is self-evident [17, 1919, pp. 419–20].

This failure to attempt any rationalization should be evident to anyone who rereads carefully the few pages in Volume I that are ostensibly devoted to an explanation of the workings of his value theory. (See especially Chapter I, section 1, pp. 44–46.)

Now, this lacuna seems strange in light of two facts: Marx' near-talmudic skill in conducting an argument and his avowed intention to write *Capital* in as prolix a style as possible.[13] If Marx had in mind or felt he needed some substitute for the competitive mechanism in the Ricardian analysis of prices, why does he not bring it out? In the discussion of values such a mechanism is never mentioned while, by contrast, it plays a clear and explicit role in the determination of prices in Volume III and in the justification of the premise that the rate of surplus value tends to be equal in all industries.[14]

Presumably, the reason Marx attempts no rationalization of his theory of value is, in Veblen's words, that at least to him it was "self-evident."[15] This

[13] Letter to Engels, June 18, 1862. "I am stretching out this volume, since those German dogs estimate the value of books by their cubic contents" [8, 1956, p. 156].

[14] The argument for the equality of rates of surplus values in all industries is straightforward, and applies only to a capitalist economy in which labor is free to move. On Marx' assumption (which is shared by Ricardo as well as J. von Neumann, R. Solow, H. Uzawa and many other contemporary writers) that labor is homogeneous and receives equal wages and if all work is equally unpleasant, the working day in all industries must tend to equality, for otherwise workers would move from industries with long working days to those in which working days are shorter. With working days everywhere equal, total value production per laborer (measured in hours of "socially necessary labor") must also be equal. Subtract from this in every industry the same subsistence wage (also measured in value units), and we are left with the same surplus value per worker everywhere. (See Volume III, p. 206.)

[15] In his *Critique of political economy,* the fragment published eight years before Volume I of *Capital,* Marx stated explicitly that he took his value theory to be a tautology:

> Since the exchange value of commodities is, in fact, nothing but a mutual relation of the labours of individuals . . . it is a tautology to say that labour is the *only* source of exchange value and consequently of wealth, in so far as the latter consists of exchange values. Similarly, it is a tautology to say that matter in its natural state has no exchange value, because it does not contain any labour. . . .

(pp. 31–2, Marx' italics). In other words, "ex-value theory was intended to explain the gestation, *i.e.*, the production of total surplus value, describing the contribution of each activity in the economy to that total. The tautology used by Marx in this explanation is that each industry contributes to the total surplus its entire output minus the amount used up in supporting labor. The part of the assertion that is not tautological or self-evident is that the "freedom" (mobility) of labor, which Marx stresses so heavily in Volume I as a prerequisite of the historical stage of capitalist production, guarantees a tendency toward equality of surplus value per laborer in every industry, when value is measured in terms of labor.

Moreover, as is now generally recognized, certainly the determination of the magnitudes of the values is straightforward on the Ricardo-Marx-Leontief assumption of fixed production coefficients. To summarize the standard interpretation of the matter as described, *e.g.,* by Morishima, a set of input-output equations can be used to express the value of each output as the amount of labor used directly in its production plus the amount of labor used up indirectly in the form of capital ("congealed labor"), where that indirect labor component is determined by the unit values of the capital inputs.[16]

These values are entirely determined by technological relationships and, under the simple fixed coefficient assumptions shared by both modern and classical models, are entirely independent of pricing.[17] That is, the input-output formulation of the problem puts to rest Joan Robinson's suggestion [11, 1959, p. 362] that ". . . the *values* which have to be 'transformed into prices' are arrived at in the first instance by transforming prices into values."

Values into Prices or Surplus Values into Profits?

Let us turn now to the textual evidence for the preceding discussion. If the interpretation proposed here is valid, Marx was concerned primarily with the relationship between profits and surplus value and only incidentally (as a means to get at the former) with that between prices and values. As a first piece of evidence, I reproduce in full Engels' famous challenge in the preface to Volume II, the first public statement of the transformation problem, in which it will be noted that the word "price" does not appear even once:

> According to the Ricardian law of value, two capitals employing the same and equally paid labor, all other conditions being equal, produce the same value and surplus-value, or profit, in the same time. But if they employ unequal quantities of actual labor, they cannot produce equal surplus-values, or, as the Ricardians say, equal profits. Now in reality, the exact opposite takes place. As a matter of fact, equal capitals, regardless of the quantity of actual labor employed by them, produce equal average profits in equal times. Here we have, therefore, a clash with the law of value, which had been noticed by Ricardo himself, but which his school was unable to reconcile. Rodbertus likewise could not but note this contradiction. But instead of solving it, he made it a starting point of his utopia (Zur Erkenntniss, etc.). Marx had solved this contradiction even in his manuscript for his "CRITIQUE OF POLITICAL ECONOMY."
> According to the plan of "CAPITAL," this solution will be made public in Volume III. Several months will pass before this can be published. Hence those economists, who claim to have discovered that Rodbertus is the secret source and the superior predecessor of Marx, have now an opportunity to demonstrate what the economics of Rodbertus can accomplish. If they can show in which way an equal average rate of profit can and must come about, not only without a violation of the law of value, but by means of it, I am willing to discuss the matter further with them (Vol. II, pps. 27–8).[18]

Turning to Marx' own words, we notice that he entitled the two books in Volume III that are devoted to the subject "Part I: The Conversion of Surplus-value into Profit and of the Rate of Surplus-

change value" is, *by definition,* related to labor content, and consequently not necessarily the same as price [5,1904].

[16] For an explicit discussion of this construction, see Morishima, [10, 1973, Chapter 1]. Of course, this interpretation also appears in various other writings.

[17] Note also that by treating the training of labor as investment in human capital it removes any difficulty of comparing the value contribution of different *qualities* of labor. When the coefficients of production of different types of labor are constant, the Ricardian and Marxian treatment of an hour of skilled labor as several hours of unskilled labor, with their ratio based on relative training costs, runs into no logical difficulty.

[18] In a letter to me Samuelson writes:

> By the way, Engels' 'challenge' is absurd; there was no 1830's crisis of the Ricardian system; there was no contradiction in it, for as you remind people, when Ricardo is not assuming the labor theory of value he is not assuming it and there is no reason why such cases should not disagree with the labor-theory-of-value cases. . . . When you revise your paper you might point this out.

value into the Rate of Profit" and "Part II: Conversion of Profit into Average Profit." Pricing is again not mentioned. It is true that in Chapter IX of Part II he does get around to dealing with prices and says so in the title "Formation of a General Rate of Profit (Average Rate of Profit) and Transformation of the Values of Commodities into Prices of Production." But is should be clear from the ordering which issue has the star billing.

Finally, we may note how Marx described the issue to Engels in his 1868 letter:

> . . . it is proper that you should know the method by which the rate of profit is developed. I will therefore give you the *most general features* of the process. . . . In Book III we come to the transformation of surplus value into its different forms and separate component parts. . . .
>
> *Profit* is for us first of all only *another name* or another category of *surplus value* . . . *surplus value* gets the form of *profit, without any quantitative* difference between the one and the other. This is only the illusory form in which surplus value appears [8, 1956, pp. 245–6; all italics are Marx'].

The Parable: "Capitalist Communism"

I have attempted to explain the transformation process in terms of a parable in which the economy's total surplus value is first aggregated[19] and then redivided by the competitive process. It is easy to show by a quotation from *Capital* that this parable describes Marx' intentions accurately.[20]

> . . . the capitalists in the various spheres of production . . . do not secure the surplus-value, and consequently the profit, created in their own sphere by the production of these commodities, but only as much surplus-value, and profit, as falls to the share of every aliquot part of the total social capital out of the total social surplus-value, or social profit produced by the total capital of society in all spheres of production . . . . *The various capitalists, so far as profits are concerned, are so many stockholders in a stock company in which the shares of profit are uniformly divided for every 100 shares of capital,* so that profits differ in the case of the individual capitalists only according to the amount of capital invested by each one of them in the social enterprise, according to his investment in social production as a whole, according to his shares. (Vol. III, Chapter IX, pp. 186–7. My italics.)

The Transformed Profits as a Mere Surface Manifestation

We economists have always had a somewhat warmer spot in our hearts for Volume III, and have tended to treat Volume I as an "unnecessary detour" to the issue that really matters—the explanation of competitive pricing. But that is merely a reflection of our own prejudices as bourgeois (shall I say, "vulgar"?) economists. From the point of view of the objectives of Marx' analysis, what is all that important about an explanation of the determination of competitive prices?[21] To Marx, indeed, it was worth discussing only to reveal its irrelevance

[19] To Marx this aggregation was of fundamental importance. He lists it as the first of

> . . . the three fundamentally new elements of the book [*Capital*, Vol. I] . . . that in contrast to *all* former political economy, which *from the very outset* treats the particular fragments of surplus value with their fixed forms of rent, profit, and interest as already given, I first deal with the general form of surplus value, in which all these fragments are still undifferentiated—in solution, as it were (Marx to Engels, January 8, 1868, p. 238).

The other two fundamentally new contributions of Volume I, are, in Marx' view, the difference between the use value and the exchange value of labor, and the evaluation of wages as an "irrational form in which a relation hidden behind them appears." Note these are all matters relating to income distribution, not pricing of commodities in general.

[20] The parable is also described several times in Marx' correspondence. For example in his later 1868 transformation problem letter he wrote:

> What competition between the various masses of capital—differently composed and invested in different spheres of production—is striving to produce is *capitalist communism,* namely that the *mass of capital belonging to each sphere of production* should snatch an aliquot part of the total surplus value proportionate to the part of the total social capital which it forms [8,1956, p. 248, Marx' italics].

Recall from our first quotation from that letter, that the parable also appears in the earliest (1862) transformation letter, which uses the phrase "and all capitalists are brothers" for what has here become "capitalist communism." In the text of Volume III it becomes the metaphor about proportionate dividends on shares in a joint stock company, a metaphor that had also been used in the 1862 letter.

[21] Note that to Marx, Volume I deals with "The *Process of Capitalist* Production" (Marx' italics), that is, not (primarily) with *price* theory (Marx to S. Meyer, April 30, 1867, p. 224). Similarly, in two letters to Engels, dated August 24, 1867 and January 8, 1868 (the one cited in the preceding footnote) Marx gives his lists of the main contributions of Volume I, none of which relates to the pricing of commodities [8, 1956].

and to tear away the curtain it formed before our eyes, so that the basic truth about the production of surplus value could be revealed. *That* is why the first volume is indeed the important one for Marx and his followers. To argue that he and Engels stuck by Volume I in order to put up a brave show when they had realized the weakness of its analysis is to reveal one's own misunderstanding of Marx' purpose.

Once again it is easy to document this conclusion. I quote a rather long but very significant passage from *Capital:*

> . . . the mass of the surplus-value produced in any particular sphere of production . . . has any importance for the individual capitalist only to the extent that the quantity of surplus-value produced in his line plays a determining role in regulating the average profit. But this is a process which takes place behind his back, which he does not see, nor understand, and which indeed does not interest him at all. The actual difference of magnitude between profit and surplus-value—not merely between the rate of profit and of surplus-value—in the various spheres of production now conceals completely the true nature and origin of profit, not only for the capitalist, who has a special interest in deceiving himself on this score, but also for the laborer. By the *transformation of values into prices of production, the basis of the determination of value is itself removed from direct observation* . . . The fact that the actual state of things is here revealed for the first time; that political economy up to the present time . . . [has clung] to the obvious phenomena of these differences—this confusion of the theoretical economists demonstrates most strikingly the utter incapacity of the capitalist, when blinded by competition, to penetrate through the outward disguise into the internal essence and the inner form of the capitalist process of production. (Volume III, Chapter IX, pp. 198–99, my italics.)

The Significance of the Transformation to Marx

If Marx considered pricing an unimportant phenomenon which only served to obscure the relevant relationships, then why did he devote so much effort and space to the transformation problem? The answer has already been suggested in the preceding section—it must be explained in order to get it out of the way. It is important because it had misled so many people—capitalists, laborers (see the preceding quote), vulgar economists and even economists as considerable as Ricardo.

But—and this is the essential issue—what is this truth that Marx is trying to reveal? In other words, what is the value theory really about? Is it just a bit of revolutionary propaganda, or mere playing with persuasive definitions, or a bit of Hegelian mysticism?[22]

I believe that the answer is none of the above, but to see why, it is suggestive to look ahead in time. Think of the economists at the turn of the century who were seeking evidence of justice in the capitalistic process of distribution with the aid of marginal productivity theory. It is not totally unfair to characterize their argument as proceeding from the position that labor, land,[23] and capital each contributes toward the production of society's output. It is surely only just, therefore, that each of these should share in that output. Since, regrettably, mother nature is not available to collect her share, it is indeed fortunate that the landlord is willing to accept it in her stead.[24]

Such nonsense is precisely what Marx' analysis anticipates and what it is intended to expose. Again, let Marx speak for himself.

> In Capital—Profit, or better Capital—Interest, Land—Rent, Labor—Wages of Labor, in this economic trinity expressing professedly the connection of value and of wealth in general with their sources, we have the complete mystification of the capitalist

[22] "Taken on the Hegelian (neo-Hegelian) ground, and seen in the light of the general materialistic conception, the proposition that value = labor-cost is self-evident, not to say tautological. Seen in any other light, it has no particular force." (Veblen, *loc. cit.*)

[23] Marx was at pains to emphasize the contribution of land to the *productive process:*

> The use-values, coat, linen, etc., *i.e.,* the bodies of commodities, are combinations of two elements—matter and labour. If we take away the useful labour expended upon them, a material substratum is always left, which is furnished by Nature without the help of man. . . . As William Petty puts it, labour is its father and the earth its mother. (Vol. I, Chapter I, section 2, p. 50.)

Why Marx denied that "land" contributed *value* to the product should soon become clear.

[24] Marx' objections to Adam Smith on this score presumably arise out of passages such as the following:

> . . . rent may be considered as the produce of those powers of Nature, the use of which the landlord lends to the farmer. . . . It is the work of Nature which remains after deducting or compensating every thing which can be regarded as the work of man [14, 1937, Book II, Chapter V, pp. 344–5].

mode of production. . . . It is an enchanted, perverted, topsy-turvy world, in which Mister Capital and Mistress Land carry on their goblin tricks as social characters and at the same time as mere things . . . it is . . . natural that the actual agents of production felt completely at home in these estranged and irrational forms of Capital—Interest, Land—Rent, Labor—Wages of Labor, for these are the forms of the illusion, in which they move about and in which they find their daily occupation. It is also quite natural that vulgar economy, which is nothing but a didactic, more or less dogmatic, translation of the ordinary conceptions of the agents of production and which arranges them in a certain intelligent order, should see in this trinity, which is devoid of all internal connection, the natural and indubitable basis of its shallow assumption of importance. This formula corresponds at the same time to the interests of the ruling classes, *by proclaiming the natural necessity and eternal justification of their sources of revenue* and raising them to the position of a dogma. (Volume III, Chapter 48, pp. 966–67, my italics.)

This discussion is clearly pertinent to an understanding of the significance of the value theory to Marx. But if it is relevant for the transformation analysis it may well be asked why he let some 700 pages intervene between this passage and the transformation discussion in Volume III. We can never be sure of the answer but it must be remembered that Engels tells us (in the preface to Volume II) that the manuscript from which he produced Volumes II and III was made up of many bits and pieces which he fitted together as best he could. Part VII of Volume III, from which the preceding quotation is taken, is one of the most fragmentary, with sentences reported to have been illegible, (*e.g.*, Ch. 48, p. 948) and pieces of manuscript left uncompleted, (*e.g.*, p. 950). It might only have been natural for Engels to have put it off to the end.[25]

But we are not forced to rely on conjectures on this issue either. Once again, Marx tells us about the matter; for in his later transformation letter to Engels (1868), he juxtaposes the two issues very clearly, completing his discussion of the transformation issue thus:

V. We have now reduced profit to the form in which it appears in practice . . . *Next comes the splitting up of this profit into entrepreneur's profit and interest. Interest-bearing capital. The credit system.*

VI. *Transformation of surplus profit into ground rent.*

VII. At last we have arrived at the *forms of appearance* which serve as the *starting point* in the vulgar conception: ground rent coming from the earth, profit (interest) from capital, wages from labour. But from our point of view the thing is now seen differently. The apparent movement is explained. Moreover, Adam Smith's nonsense, which has become the *main pillar* of all economics hitherto existing, that the price of a commodity consists of those three revenues, *i.e.*, only of variable capital (wages) and surplus value (ground rent, profit (interest)), is overthrown. Then—the whole movement takes place in this form of appearance. Finally since these three (wages, ground rent, profit (interest)) constitute the respective sources of income of the three classes of landowners, capitalists and wage labourers, we have, in conclusion, the *class struggle*, into which the movement and the smash-up of the whole business resolves itself. . . .[26]

The point of the value theory may then be summed up as follows: goods are indeed produced by labor and natural resources together. But the relevant *social* source of production is labor, not an inanimate "land." Thus profits, interest, and rent must also be attributed to labor, and their total is equal (tautologically) to the total value produced by labor minus the amount consumed by labor itself. The competitive process, that appears to show that land is the source of rent and capital the source of profits and interest, is merely a distributive phenomenon and conceals the fact that labor is the only socially relevant source of output. This is the significance of the value theory and the transformation analysis to Marx.

Conclusion: Sources of Misunderstanding

Having come to so unequivocal a conclusion about what Marx hoped to accomplish through his notion of a transformation process one may well ask how the apparent misunderstanding of so many commentators might have arisen. But before turning to this it should be noted again that Meek and Morishima are very clear cut exceptions and that my interpretation is very close to theirs. Thus, Morishima reminds us of Samuelson's remark that

[25] Engels also reported that the transformation discussion "(relation of Mehrwertsrate to Profit rate)" required "a great deal of work" on his part to prepare it for publication (Letter to N. F. Danielson, November 13, 1885.) [8, 1956, p. 464].

[26] The (anonymous) Russian translator exhibits some delicacy in this rendition. The word he translates as "business" is *"scheisse"* in the original [8, 1956, p. 250].

"the proportionality of market price to labor content applies validly only when surplus value is zero and not worth talking about!" [12, 1957, p. 888].

On this Morishima remarks:

> . . . in the transformation problem Marx did not intend to establish a proportionality between values and prices but, on the contrary, to show that individual exploitation and individual profit are disproportional unless some restrictive conditions are imposed. . . . Thus it is clear that the transformation problem has the aim of showing how 'the aggregate exploitation of labour on the part of the total social capital' is, in a capitalist economy, obscured by the distortion of prices from values; the other aim is to show how living labour can be the sole source of profit" [10, 1973, pp. 85–6.].

Meek begins his discussion with a statement of the issue that is just as clear. However, he does go on to treat the transformation problem as though it were primarily a matter of explaining *price* determination.

Sweezy [16, 1942, esp. pp. 125–130] also comes close to the Meek-Morishima position arguing that prices and profits of individual capitalists are micro issues while Marxian values are intended to deal with the macro issues of distribution in which Marx is interested (pp. 125–6). He notes that the "price calculation . . . mystifies the underlying social relations of capitalist production. Since profit is calculated as a return on total capital, the idea inevitably arises that capital as such is in some way 'productive' " (p. 129).

His book does follow the Bortkiewicz tradition in treating prices as magnitudes to be determined from values. However, Sweezy's letter to me also casts additional light on this matter. He writes:

> To the best of my recollection, I never treated 'the transformation problem primarily as a matter of determining prices from values.' Values are in fact an abstraction from capitalist reality, not an observable phenomenon, and could not possibly 'determine' prices of production (which are also an abstraction albeit on a lower level). The justification for such abstractions, esp. value, is that they reveal the essence of capitalist reality as opposed to the appearance—an argument which orthodox economics of course is totally unable to comprehend.

In any event, it is clear that with these and perhaps a few other exceptions, the interpretation I have offered and sought to document is hardly the view that is held universally. I have already suggested one explanatory hypothesis—that many readers may have been misled by the analogy with Ricardo. Ricardo tells us explicitly when he gets to the role of capital in price determination that the "labor theory" model gives us answers that are still very nearly correct, so that in his view it remains a good model to use in explaining the determination of individual prices. Marx, on the other hand, points out that the deviations between the two models are systematic and significant enough to conceal the underlying relationships from other observers. Moreover, as we have seen, at this point, at least, Marx is not even interested to any significant degree in the theory of price.

Yet Marx himself must bear a good share of the blame for the confusion. Since it seems true that Volume I and Volume III were written with perfectly consistent intentions he should surely not have adopted the word "value" for the magnitude on which he focuses his discussion. He was perfectly aware that "value theory" was used in the economic literature to refer to the theory of price determination (though he felt that Ricardo had also groped, albeit unsuccessfully, for a deeper phenomenon when he discussed values). Consequently, if he deliberately used the term to denote a magnitude that differs from price in a significant and systematic manner he was certainly asking for the sort of misunderstanding to which the work has been subject. Moreover, in the bulk of Volume I Marx does speak as though the "exchange value" which he explains in terms of labor were a normal market price. If he meant otherwise he hardly hinted at it.[27]

[27] There seem to be only three points in Volume I where the reader is given some warning on the matter; on pp. 184–5, footnote, p. 244, footnote, and on pp. 335–6. In the second of these, he writes "We have in fact assumed that prices = values. We shall, however, see, in Volume III, that even in the case of average prices the assumption cannot be made in this very simple manner."

Similarly on p. 335–6 we have the statement

> This law [that the masses of surplus value produced by different capitals vary directly as the variable constituents of these capitals] clearly contradicts all experience based on appearance. Everyone knows that a cotton spinner, who, reckoning the percentage on the whole of his applied capital, employs much constant and little variable capital, does not, on account of this, pocket less profit or surplus-value than a baker, who relatively sets in motion much variable and little constant capital. For the solution of this apparent contradic-

This too constitutes something of a mystery. Since Marx did have his transformation analysis worked out before Volume I was published, why is there no clear statement of the issue there? But this mystery does have a known solution. The definitive answer is provided in an exchange of letters between Marx and Engels. As they were making the final corrections for Volume I, Engels (gently) rebuked Marx for his failure to deal with the issue in Volume I. In a letter dated June 26, 1867 he wrote

> . . . As for the origin of surplus value, the following: The manufacturer, and with him the vulgar economist, will at once object: If the capitalist pays the worker only the price of 6 hours for his 12 hours of working time, no surplus value can originate from this, for then every hour of labor of the factory worker is only equal to half an hour of labor—equal to what is paid for it—and enters into the value of the product of labor as worth only that much. . . . No matter how terribly shallow this argument is, no matter how much it identifies exchange-value and price, value of labor and wages, no matter how absurd its assumption that one hour of labor enters into value as only half an hour if it is paid for as only half an hour, I marvel that you have not taken this into consideration already, for it will *quite certainly* be held up to you at once and it is better to dispose of it in advance. Perhaps you will return to it in the next [printer's proof] sheet . . . (Engels' italics).

To this Marx replied on the next day . . .

> . . . As for the inevitable objections you mention of the philistine and the vulgar economist . . . [The answer to this problem] presupposes [among other matters] . . . that the *conversion of surplus value into profit, of profit into average profit,* etc., is set forth. This presupposes a previous account of the *process of the circulation of capital,* since the turnover of capital, etc. plays a part here. Hence this matter can be set forth only in the third book. . . .
>
> If I were to *silence* all such objections *in advance,* I should ruin the whole dialectical method of development. On the contrary, this method has the advantage of continually *setting traps* for these fellows which provoke them to untimely demonstrations of their asininity. (Marx' italics.)[28]

tion, many intermediate terms are as yet wanted. . . . It will be seen later how the school of Ricardo has come to grief over this stumbling-block. Vulgar economy which, indeed, "has really learnt nothing" here as everywhere sticks to appearances in opposition to the law which regulates and explains them [6, 1906].

References

1. Blaug, M. *Economic theory in retrospect.* Revised edition. Homewood, Ill.: Richard D. Irwin, 1968.
2. Böhm-Bawerk, E. von *Karl Marx and the close of his system and Böhm-Bawerk's criticism of Marx by Rudolf Hilferding with an appendix by L. von Bortkiewicz.* Edited by P. Sweezy. New York: Augustus M. Kelley, 1949.
3. Bronfenbrenner, M. "Samuelson, Marx and Their Latest Critics," *J. Econ. Lit.,* March 1973, *11* (1), pp. 58–63.
4. Engels, F. *Engels on capital: Synopsis, reviews, letters, and supplementary material.* Translated and edited by L. Mins. New York: International Publishers, Inc., 1937.
5. Marx, K. *A contribution to the critique of political economy.* Translated by N. I. Stone. Chicago: Charles H. Kerr and Co., 1904.
6. ——— *Capital. A critique of political economy.* Chicago: Charles H. Kerr and Co., Volume I (1906); Volumes II and III (1909).
7. ——— and Engels, F. *Correspondence 1846–95; with explanatory notes.* Translated by Dona Torr. New York: International Publishers, [1934, 1936] 1942.
8. ——— and ——— *Selected corrrespondence.* Moscow: Foreign Languages Publishing House, 1956.
9. Meek, R. L. "Some Notes on the Transformation Problem," *Econ J.,* March 1956, *66,* pp. 94–107.
10. Morishima, M. *Marx's economics: A dual theory of value and growth.* New York: Cambridge University Press, 1973.
11. Robinson, J. "Review of Sweezy, P., *Karl Marx and the close of his system . . . ,*" *Econ. J.,* June 1950, *60,* pp. 358–63. [see ref. 2.]

[28] I came across this exchange of letters quite accidentally (thanks to a fortunate find by my secretary in a 6th Avenue trash can!) after an earlier draft of this paper had been completed. Note how remarkably it confirms Veblen's conjecture about Marx' attitude toward some of his expected readers, as well as several of the hypotheses of this article. The translation here is taken from Mins, in whose little volume (presented to me by my secretary) I first came across the exchange [4, 1937].

12. SAMUELSON, P. "Wages and Interest: A Modern Dissection of Marxian Economic Models," *Amer. Econ. Rev.*, Dec. 1957, *47*, pp. 884–912; reprinted in SAMUELSON, P., *Collected scientific papers*, edited by J. STIGLITZ. 2 vols. Cambridge, Mass.: M.I.T. Press, 1965, Ch. 29, pp. 341–69.

13. ——— "Understanding the Marxian Notion of Exploitation: A Summary of the So-called Transformation Problem Between Marxian Values and Competitive Prices," *J. Econ. Lit.*, June 1971, *9* (2), pp. 399–431.

14. SMITH, A. *An inquiry into the nature and causes of the wealth of nations.* Edited by EDWIN CANNAN. New York: Modern Library, [1776] 1937.

15. STIGLER, G. J. "Ricardo and the 93% Labor Theory of Value," *Amer. Econ. Rev.*, June 1958, *48* (3), pp. 357–67.

16. SWEEZY, P. M. *The theory of capitalist development.* New York: Oxford University Press, 1942.

17. VEBLEN, T. B. *The place of science in modern civilization, and other essays.* New York: Viking Press, 1919.

BIBLIOGRAPHY

I. BOOKS

Economic Dynamics (with a contribution by Ralph Turvey) New York: Macmillan, 1951. 2nd Edition 1959. 3rd Edition 1970.
(Spanish translation) Barcelona, 1964. 2nd Edition 1971.
(Japanese translation) Tokyo, 1961. 2nd Edition 1973.
(Greek translation) 2nd Edition, Athens, 1974.

Welfare Economics and the Theory of the State. London: Longmans Green, 1952. 2nd Edition Cambridge: Harvard University Press, 1965.

Economic Processes and Policies (with Lester V. Chandler). New York: Harper, 1954.
(Spanish translation) Bogota: 1963
(Arabic translation) New York: Harper and Bros., 1954.

Business Behavior, Value and Growth. New: Macmillan, 1959. Revised edition New York: Harcourt, Brace and World, 1966.
(Japanese translation) Tokyo, 1963. Revised Edition 1969.
(Italian translation) Milan, 1972.

Economic Theory and Operations Analysis. Englewood Cliffs, New Jersey: Prentice-Hall, 1961. 2nd Edition 1965. 3rd Edition 1972. 4th Edition 1976.
(Maruzen Asian translation) Tokyo, 1961.
(Russian translation) London: Prentice-Hall International 1962. 2nd Edition Moscow, 1965.
(French translation) Paris, 1963.
(Indian translation) New Delhi, 1963.
(Spanish translation) Mexico, 1964.
(Japanese translation) 2nd Edition Tokyo, 1965.
(Italian translation) Rome, 1968.
(Hungarian translation) Budapest, 1968.

What Price Economic Growth? (co-edited with Klaus Knorr). Englewood Cliffs, New Jersey: Prentice-Hall, 1961.

The Stock Market and Economic Efficiency. New York: Fordham University Press, 1965.

Performing Arts: The Economic Dilemma (with William G. Bowen). New York: Twentieth Century Fund, 1966.

Precursors in Mathematical Economics: An Anthology (co-edited with Steven M. Goldfeld). London: London School of Economics Series of Reprints of Scarce Works on Political Economy, No. 19, 1968.

Portfolio Theory: The Selection of Asset Combinations. New York: McCaleb-Seiler, 1970.

Environmental Protection, International Spillovers and Trade. Wicksell Lectures, Stockholm: Almqvist and Wicksell, 1971.

Study of the New York Theater. New York: New York City Cultural Council, 1972.

Economics of Academic Libraries (with Matityahu Marcus). Washington, D.C.: Mathematica, Inc. American Council on Education, 1973.

Last-Minute Discount on Unsold Tickets (with Hilda Baumol). New York: Theater Development Fund, 1974.

The Theory of Environmental Policy (with Wallace E. Oates). Englewood Cliffs, New Jersey: Prentice-Hall, 1975.

Economics and the Quality of Life (with Wallace E. Oates). Englewood Cliffs, New Jersey: Prentice-Hall (forthcoming).

II. ARTICLES AND COMMUNICATIONS TO TECHNICAL JOURNALS

"Community Indifference", *Review of Economic Studies,* XIV, (1946-47), 44-8.

"Notes on the Theory of Government Procurement", *Economica,* N.S., XIV, (February, 1947), 1-18.

"Notes on Some Dynamic Models", *Economic Journal,* LVIII, (December, 1948), 506-21.

"Formalization of Mr. Harrod's Model", *Economic Journal,* LIX, (December, 1949), 625-9.

"The Community Indifference Map: A Construction", Review of Economic Studies. XVII, (1949-50), 189-97.

"The Analogy Between Producer and Consumer Equilibrium Analysis" (with H. Makower), *Economica,* N.S., XVII, (February, 1950), 63-80.

"The Neumann-Morgenstern Utility Index—An Ordinalist View", *Journal of Political Economy,* LIX, (February, 1951), 61-6.

"Yet Another Note on the Harrod-Domar Model", *Economic Journal,* LXII, (June, 1952), 422-7.

"The Transactions Demand for Cash: An Inventory Theoretic Approach", *Quarterly Journal of Economics,* LXVI, (November, 1952), 545-56.

"The Classical Monetary Theory: The Outcome of the Discussion" (with Gary S. Becker), *Economica,* N.S., XIX, (November, 1952), 355-76. (See Section III for revised version, 1960).

"Firms with Limited Money Capital", *Kyklos,* Band 6, Article 2, (1953), 119-33.

"Economic Theory and the Political Scientist", *World Politics,* VI, (January, 1954), 266-77.

"More on the Multiplier Effects of a Balanced Budget" (with Maurice H. Peston), *American Economic Review,* XLV, (March, 1955), 140-8. "Reply", *American Economic Review,* XLVI, (March, 1956), 160-2.

"Acceleration Without Magnification", *American Economic Review,* XLVI, (June,

1956), 409-12.
"Variety in Retailing" (with Edward A. Ide), *Management Science,* 3, (October, 1956), 93-101.
"On the Role of Marketing Theory", *Journal of Marketing,* XXI, (April, 1957), 413-8.
"Interactions Between Successive Polling Results and Voting Intentions", *Public Opinion Quarterly,* XXI, (Summer, 1957), 318-23.
"Speculation, Profitability, and Stability", *Review of Economics and Statistics,* XXXIX, (August, 1957), 263-71. "Reply", *Review of Economics and Statistics,* XLI, (August, 1959), 301-2.
"Marketing Costs and Mathematical Programming" (with Charles H. Sevin), *Harvard Business Review,* , (September-October, 1957), 52-60.
"A Warehouse-Location Problem" (with Philip Wolfe), *Operations Research,* 6, (March-April, 1958), 252-63.
"Topology of Second Order Linear Difference Equations with Constant Coefficients", *Econometrica,* 26, (April, 1958), 258-85.
"On the Theory of Oligopoly", *Economica,* N.S., XXV, (August, 1958), 187-98.
"Marginalism and the Demand for Cash in Light of Operations Research Experience", *Review of Economics and Statistics,* XL, (August, 1958), 209-14.
"Activity Analysis in One Lesson", *American Economic Review,* XLVII, (December, 1958), 337-73.
"The Cardinal Utility Which Is Ordinal", *Economic Journal,* LXVIII, (December, 1958), 665-72.
"On Professor Neisser on Magnification," *Review of Economics and Statistics*, XLI, (February, 1959), 69-70.
"Integer Programming and Pricing" (with Ralph E. Gomory), *Econometrica,* 28, (July, 1960), 521-50.
"Monetary and Value Theory: Comments", *Review of Economic Studies,* XXVIII, (October, 1960), 29-32.
"Pitfalls in Contracyclical Policies: Some Tools and Results", *Review of Economics and Statistics,* XLIII, (February, 1961), 21-6.
"What Can Economic Theory Contribute to Managerial Economics?" *American Economic Review,* LI, (May, 1961), 142-6.
"Stocks, Flows and Monetary Theory", *Quarterly Journal of Economics,* LXXVI, (February, 1962), 46-56.
"An Approximative Algorithm for the Fixed Charges Transportation Problem" (with Harold W. Kuhn), *Naval Research Logistics Quarterly,* 9, (March, 1962), 1-15.
"Reappraisal of the Doctrine of Consumers' Sovereignty - Discussion", *American Economic Review,* LII, (May, 1962), 288-90.
"The Role of Cost in the Minimum Pricing of Railroad Services" (with Burton N. Behling, James C. Bonbright, Yale Brozen, Joel Dean, Ford K. Edwards, Calvin B. Hoover, Dudley F. Pegrum, Merrill J. Roberts and Ernest W. Williams, Jr.), *Journal of Business,* XXXV, (October, 1962), 1-10. "Statement of Clarification", *Journal of Business,* XXXVI, (July, 1963), 348-51.
"The Theory of Expansion of the Firm", *American Economic Review*, LII, (December,

1962), 1078-87.

"On Dividend Policy and Market Imperfection", *Journal of Business*, XXXVI, (January, 1963), 112-5.

"An Expected Gain-Confidence Limit Criterion for Portfolio Selection", *Management Science*, 10, (October, 1963), 174-82.

"Rules of Thumb and Optimally Imperfect Decisions", *American Economic Review*, LIV, (March, 1964), 23-46.

"Monopolistic Competition and Welfare Economics", *American Economic Review*, LIV, (May, 1964), 44-52.

"External Economies and Second-order Optimality Conditions," *American Economic Review*, LIV, (June, 1964), 358-72.

"Decomposition, Pricing for Decentralization and External Economies" (with Tibor Fabian), *Management Science*, 11, (September, 1964), 1-32. "Comments on Maiti and Sengupta's Note," *Management Science*, 19, (August, 1973), 1461-2.

"Oligopoly Theory and Retail Food Pricing" (with Richard E. Quandt and Harold Shapiro), *Journal of Business*, XXXVII, (October, 1964), 346-63.

"Baumol's Sales-Maximation Model: Reply," *American Economic Review*, LIV, (December, 1964), 1081.

"On the Performing Arts: The Anatomy of Their Economic Problems" (with William G. Bowen), *American Economic Review*, LV, (May, 1965), 495-502.

"Investment and Discount Rates Under Capital Rationing—A Programming Approach" (with Richard E. Quandt), *Economic Journal*, LXXV, (June, 1965),

"Informed Judgment, Rigorous Theory and Public Policy" *Southern Economic Journal*, XXXII, 2, (October, 1965), 137-45.

"Enterprise et Societe," *Economie Applique*, Presses Universitaires de France, (1965), 211-22.

"The Valuation of Convertible Securities" (with Burton G. Malkiel and Richard E. Quandt), *Quarterly Journal of Economics*, LXXX, (February, 1966), 48-59.

"Mathematical Analysis of Portfolio Selection, Principles and Application," *Financial Analysts Journal*, (September-October, 1966), 1-5.

"The Demand for Abstract Transport Modes: Theory and Measurement" (with Richard E. Quandt), *Journal of Regional Science*, 6, (1966), 13-26.

"Macroeconomics of Unbalanced Growth: The Anatomy of Urban Crisis", *American Economic Review*, LVII, (June, 1967), 415-26. "Comment", *American Economic Review*, LVIII, (September, 1968), 896-7. "Comment on the Comment", *American Economic Review*, LIX, (September, 1969), 632. "Reply", *American Economic Review*, LXII, (March, 1972), 150.

"Error Produced by Linearization in Mathematical Programming" (with Robert Bushnell), *Econometrica*, 35, (July-October, 1967), 447-71.

"Calculation of Optimal Product and Retailer Characteristics: The Abstract Product Approach", *Journal of Political Economy*, LXXV, (October, 1967), 674-85.

"The Firm's Optimal Debt-Equity Combination and the Cost of Capital" (with Burton G. Malkiel), *Quarterly Journal of of Economics*, LXXXI, (November, 1967), 547-78

"Entrepreneurship in Economic Theory", *American Economic Review*, LVIII, (May, 1968), 64-71.

"Sales Maximization vs. Profit Maximization, Are They Consistent?: Comment", *Western Economic Journal,* VI, (June, 1968), 242.

"The Dual in Nonlinear Programming and its Economic Interpretation" (with M.L. Balinski), *Review of Economic Studies,* XXXV, (July, 1968), 237-56.

"Thoughts on the Present State of Economic Theory", *Indian Economic Journal,* XVI, (July-September, 1968), 69-70.

"On the Social Rate of Discount", *American Economic Review,* LVIII, (September, 1968), 788-802. "The Social Rate of Discount: Comment on the Comments", *American Economic Review,* LIX, (December, 1969), 930.

"The Demand for Abstract Transport Modes: Some Hopes," (with Richard E. Quandt), *Journal of Regional Science,* 9, (1969), 159-62.

"An Inventory Theoretic Model of Freight Transport Demand" (with H.D. Vinod), *Management Science,* 15, (March, 1970), 413-21.

"Optimal Departures from Marginal Cost Pricing" (with David F. Bradford), *American Economic Review,* LX, (June, 1970), 265-83. "Optimal Taxes and Pricing: Reply" (with David F. Bradford), *American Economic Review,* LXII, (March, 1972), 175-6.

"Input Choices and Rate of Return Regulation: An Overview of the Discussion" (with Alvin K. Klevorick), *Bell Journal of Economics and Management Science,* 1, (Autumn, 1970), 162-90.

"Earnings Retention, New Capital, and the Growth of the Firm", (with Peggy Heim, Burton G. Malkiel and Richard E. Quandt), *Review of Economics and Statistics,* LII, (November, 1970), 345-60. "Efficiency of Corporate Investment: Reply", (with Peggy Heim, Burton G. Malkiel and Richard E. Quandt), *Review of Economics and Statistics,* LV, (February, 1973), 128-31.

"The Analysis of Public Policy in Dynamic Urban Models" (with Wallace E. Oates and E.P. Howrey), *Journal of Political Economy,* LXXIX, (January-Febuary, 1971), 142-53.

"The Use of Standards and Pricing for Protection of the Environment" (with W.E. Oates), *Swedish Journal of Economics,* 73, (March, 1971), 42-54.

"Les Decisions Multivariees dans la Theorie de l'Oligopole", *Revue d'Economie Politique*, (Mars-Avril, 1971), 171-88.

"Economics of Athenian Drama: Its Relevance for the Arts in a Small City Today," *Quarterly Journal of Economics,* LXXXV, (August, 1971), 365-76.

"Optimal Depreciation Policy: Pricing the Products of Durable Assets", *Bell Journal of Economics and Management Science,* 2, (Autumn, 1971), 638-56.

"Environmental Protection at Minimum Cost", *American Journal of Economics and Sociology,* 30, (October, 1971), 337-44.

"Jacob Viner at Princeton", *Journal of Political Economy,* LXXX, (January-February, 1972), 12-25.

"On the Economics of the Theater in Renaissance London" (with Mary I. Oates), *Swedish Journal of Economics,* 74, (March, 1972), 136-60. "Reply", *Swedish Journal of Economics,* 76, (September, 1974).

"Detrimental Externalities and Non-Convexity of the Production Set" (with David F. Bradford), *Economica,* N.S., XL, (May, 1972), 160-76.

"On Taxation and the Control of Externalities", *American Economic Review,* LXII,

(June, 1972), 307-22. "Reply", *American Economic Review,* LXIV, (June, 1974), 472.

"The Cost Disease of the Personal Services and the Quality of Life" (with Wallace E. Oates), *Skandinaviska Enskilda Banken Quarterly Review,* 2, (1972), 44-54.

"J.R. Hicks' Contribution to Economics," *Swedish Journal of Economics,* 74, (1972), 503-27.

"Full Costing, Competition, and Regulatory Practice" (with Alfred G. Walton), *Yale Law Journal,* 82, (March, 1973), 639-55.

"Income and Substitution Effects in the Linder Theorem," *Quarterly Journal of Economics,* LXXXVII, (November, 1973), 629-33.

"Competitive Pricing and the Centralized Market Place," *Eastern Economic Journal,* I, (January, 1974), 11-19.

"The Transformation of Values: What Marx 'Really' Meant," *Journal of Economic Literature,* XII, (March, 1974), 51-62. "Comment," 74-5.

"An Overview of the Results on Consumption, Health and Social Behavior," *Journal of Human Resources,* IX, (Spring, 1974), 253-64.

"Payment by Performance in Rail Passenger Transportation: An Innovation in Amtrak's Operations," *Bell Journal of Economics,* 6, (Spring 1975), 281-98.

III. CHAPTERS IN BOOKS AND CONTRIBUTIONS TO PROCEEDINGS

"Discussion" (of papers at a session of the 1952 A.E.A. Christmas meetings on recent developments in mathematical economics and econometrics), *American Economic Review*, XLVII, (May, 1953), 415-6.

"Selecting an Appropriate Model for an Operations Research Problem", *Cost and Profit Outlook.* VIII, (November, 1955).

"Experimental Research in Consumer Behavior", *Cost and Profit Outlook*, IX, (February, 1956).

"Consumer Information and Rational Choice", *Cost and Profit Outlook,* IX, (March, 1956).

"Solution of Management Problems Through Mathematical Programming", *Cost and Profit Outlook,* IX, (May, 1956).

"Analyse Graphique de Modeles de Cycles non Lineaires de Premier Ordre", *Les Modeles Dynamiques En Econometrie,* Colloques Internationaux, LXII. Paris: Centre National de la Recherche Scientifique, 1956.

"Cost Reduction Through Mathematical Programming", *The Frontiers of Marketing Thought and Science,* American Marketing Association, 1957.

"Operations Research Applied to Marketing Problems", *Cost and Profit Outlook,* X, (March, 1957).

"A Guide to Operations Research Methods", *Cost and Profit Outlook,* X, (April, 1957).

"Marginalism and the Demand for Cash in Light of Operations Research Experience", (Early version of 1958 article). *Trends in Economics.* Second Conference of Pennsylvania Economists, Pennsylvania State Economists, 1958.

"Price Behavior, Stability and Growth". *The Relationship of Prices to Economic Stabil-*

ity and Growth. Washington: U.S. Government Printing Office, 1958.

"Statement (on a Proposal to Increase Rate of Growth)". *Hearings, U.S. Congress, Joint Economic Committee,* Part 9a. Washington: U.S. Government Printing Office, 1959.

"Orientation Toward Optimality in Business Planning", *Cost and Profit Outlook,* XII, (May, 1959).

"The Classical Monetary Theory: The Outcome of the Discussion" (with Gary S. Becker), (Revision of 1952 article with new postscript). *Essays in Economic Thought: Aristotle to Marshall.* Edited by Joseph J. Spengler and William R. Allen. Chicago: Rand McNally, 1960.

"Comment." *Demographic and Economic Change in Developed Countries.* Princeton, New Jersey: Princeton University Press, 1960.

"Mathematical Models and Thinking in Marketing". American Marketing Association, *Proceedings of the 1960 Winter Conference,* Chicago, 1961.

"Economic Theory and the Marketing Curriculum". American Marketing Association, *Proceedings of the 1960 Winter Conference,* Chicago, 1961.

"Proposals for Increasing the Rate of Growth of National Output". *What Price Economic Growth?* Edited by W.J. Baumol and Klaus Knorr. Englewood Cliffs, New Jersey: Prentice-Hall, 1961.

"The Appropriate Rate of Growth of National Output". *What Price Economic Growth?* Edited by W.J. Baumol and Klaus Knorr. Englewood Cliffs, New Jersey: Prentice-Hall, 1961.

"The Economic Status of the Profession, 1960-61", *AAUP BULLETIN,* 47, (June, 1961).

"Annual Report by Committee Z", *AAUP Bulletin,* 48, (Summer, 1962).

"The Economic Status of the Profession, 1961-62" (with Peggy Heim), *AAUP Bulletin,* 48, (Summer, 1962).

"On the Fringe: Retirement Contributions and Other Faculty Benefits", *AAUP Bulletin,* 48, (December, 1962).

"Physical Distribution Systems: Discussion", in "The Social Responsibilities of Marketing", *Proceedings of the American Marketing Association,* 1962.

"Prerequisites for Economic Growth", from Hearings before Joint Economic Committee (Part 9a, 1959, 2792-96). *Contemporary Economics.* Edited by R.E. Slesinger and A. Isaacs. Boston: Allyn and Bacon, 1963.

"From Problem to Model to Computer to Solution". *Marketing and the Computer.* Edited by Wroe Alderson and Stanley J. Shapiro. Englewood Cliffs, New Jersey: Prentice-Hall, 1963.

"Toward the Construction of More Useful Models". *Models of Markets.* Edited by A.R. Oxenfeldt. New York: Columbia University Press, 1963.

"Dual Prices and Competition" (with Richard E. Quandt). *Models of Markets.* Edited by A.R. Oxenfeldt. New York: Columbia University Press, 1963.

"Urban Services: Interactions of Public and Private Decisions". *Public Expenditure Decisions in the Urban Community.* Edited by Howard G. Schaller. Washington: Resources for the Future, 1963.

"Economic Status of the Profession" (with Peggy Heim), *AAUP Bulletin,* 49, (June, 1963).

"Linear and Integer Programming", *Proceedings of a Symposium on Decision Theory,* Division of Research, College of Business Administration, Ohio University, Athens, 1964.

"Company Goals, Growth and the Multiproduct Firm". *Theory in Marketing.* Edited by Reavis Cox, Wroe Alderson, and Stanley J. Shapiro. American Marketing Association. Homewood, Illinois: Irwin, 1964.

"Economic Status of the Profession" (with Peggy Heim), *AAUP Bulletin,* 50, (June, 1964).

"Economic Status of the Profession: Taking Stock" (with Peggy Heim), *AAUP Bulletin,* 51, (June, 1965).

"Models of Economic Competition". *Models, Measurement and Marketing.* Edited by Peter Langhoff. Englewood Cliffs, New Jersey: Prentice-Hall, 1965.

"The Economic Status of the Profession, 1965-66" (with Peggy Heim), *AAUP Bulletin,* 52, (June, 1966).

"Salary Structures in Public Junior Colleges Which do Not Have the Usual Academic Ranks" (with Peggy Heim), *AAUP Bulletin,* 52, (December, 1966).

"Economic Models and Mathematics". *The Structure of Economic Science.* Edited by Sherman R. Krupp. Englewood Cliffs, New Jersey: Prentice-Hall, 1966.

"The Escalated Economy and the Stimulating Effects of Inflation". *Etudi in Onore Marco Fanno,* Vol. II. Edited by T. Bagiotti, Padua: Cedam, 1966.

"The Ricardo Effect in the Point Input-Point Output Case". *Essays in Mathematical Economics in Honor of Oskar Morgenstern.* Edited by Martin Shubik. Princeton: Princeton University Press, 1966.

"On Contracting with Publishers: or What Every Author Should Know" (with Peggy Heim), *AAUP Bulletin,* 53, (March, 1967).

"Economics" (with F.H. Knight). *Encyclopedia Brittanica,* 1967 edition, Volume VII.

"Further Progress: The Economic Status of the Profession, 1966-67" (with Peggy Heim), *AAUP Bulletin,* 53, (June, 1967).

"On the Appropriate Discount Rate for Evaluation of Public Projects". U.S. Senate, *Congressional Record,* September 26, 1967.

"Discussion" (on Tax Policy and Business Investment). *Fiscal Policy and Business Capital Formation.* Washington: American Enterprise Institute, 1967.

"Statics and Dynamics in Economics". *International Encyclopedia of the Social Sciences,* Vol. 15. New York: Macmillan Co. and the Free Press, 1968.

"On the Financial Prospects for Higher Education" (with Peggy Heim), *AAUP Bulletin,* 54, (Summer, 1968).

"Reasonable Rules for Rate Regulation: Plausible Policies for an Imperfect World". *Prices: Issues in Theory, Practice and Public Policy.* Edited by Almarin Phillips and Oliver E. Williamson. Philadelphia: University of Pennsylvania Press, 1968.

"Performance of the Firm and Performance of Its Stocks". *Economic Policy and the Regulation of Corporate Securities.* Edited by H.G. Manne. Washington: American Enterprise Institute, 1969.

"Some Approaches to Urban Problems", 2nd Annual Report of the Economic Policy Council, Department of the Treasury of the State of New Jersey, June, 1969.

"On the Discount Rate for Public Projects". *The Analysis and Evaluation of Public Ex-*

penditures: The PPB System. Joint Economic Committee. Washington: U.S. Government Printing Office, 1969.

"Mathematics in Economic Analysis". *The Spirit and the Uses of the Mathematical Sciences.* Edited by T.L. Saaty and F.J. Weyl. New York: McGraw-Hill, 1969.

"On the Discount Rate for Public Projects", *Public Expenditures and Policy Analysis.* Edited by R.H. Haveman and Julius Margolis. Chicago: Markham, 1970.

"The Firm with Inelastic Demands". *Induction, Growth and Trade: Essays in Honour of Sir Roy Harrod.* Edited by W.A. Ellis, M.F.G. Scott and J.N. Wolfe. Oxford: Clarendon Press, 1970.

"Enlightened Self-Interest and Corporate Philanthropy". *A New Rationale for Corporate Social Policy.* New York: Committee for Economic Development, 1970.

"Competition and Monoply in Telecommunications Services" (with Otto Eckstein and Alfred E. Kahn). New York: AT&T Co., 1970.

"On the Behavioral Theory of the Firm" (with Maco Stewart). *The Corporate Economy.* Edited by Robin Marris and Adrian Woods. London: Macmillan, 1971.

"Rate Making: Incremental Costing and Equity Considerations". *Essays on Public Utility Pricing and Regulation.* Edited by Harry M. Trebing. East Lansing: Michigan State University, 1971.

(Translation) M. Boiteux, "On the Management of Public Monopolies Subject to Budgetary Constraints", (with D.F. Bradford), *Journal of Economic Theory,* 3, (September, 1971).

"Utility and Value". *Encyclopedia Brittanica,* 1971 edition. 1974 edition. 1977 edition.

"The Dynamics of Urban Problems and its Policy Implications." *Essays in Honor of Lord Robbins.* Edited by Maruice Peston and Bernard Corry. London: Weidenfield and Nicolson, 1972.

"Environmental Protection and Distribution of Incomes." *Problems of Environmental Economics.* Paris: OECD, 1972.

"Business Responsibility and Economic Behavior." *Managing the Socially Responsible Corporation.* Edited with commentaries by Melvin Ansher. New York: Macmillan, 1974.

"The Instruments for Environmental Policy" (with Wallace E. Oates). *Economic Analysis of Environmental Problems.* Edited by Edwin Mills. New York: National Bureau for Economic Research, 1974.

"Environmental Protection and Income Distribution." *Redistribution Through Public Choice.* Edited by Harold M. Hochman and George E. Peterson. New York: Columbia University Press, 1974.

"Acceleration Incentives and X-Efficiency." *Econometrics and Economic Theory: Essays in Honor of Jan Tinbergen.* Edited by Willy Sallekaerts. London: Macmillan, 1974.

"Scale Economies, Average Cost and the Profitability of Marginal Cost Pricing." *Essays in Urban Economics and Public Finance in Honor of William S. Vickrey.* Edited by Ronald E. Grieson. Lexington, Massachusetts: D.C. Heath, 1975.

IV. BOOK REVIEWS

California Business Cycles, by Frank L. Kidner, *Economica*, N.S., XIV, (May, 1974), 162-3.

Elementary Mathematics for Economists and Statisticians, by W.L. Crum and Joseph A. Schumpeter. "Mathematics for Economists", *Economica,* N.S., XIV, (November, 1947), 310-3.

Price Quantity Interactions in Business Cycles, by F.C. Mills, *Economica,* N.S., XIV, (November, 1947), 327-30.

Foundations of Economic Analysis, by Paul A. Samuelson. "Relaying the Foundations", *Economica,* N.S., XVI, (May, 1949), 159-68.

Expectation in Economics, by G.L.S. Shackle. "Three Notes on Expectation in Economics" (with Ralph Turvey, J. de V. Graaff, and G.L.S. Shackle), *Economica,* N.S., XVI, (November, 1949), 336-46.

La Courbe D'Offre, by Jane Aubert, *Journal of Political Economy,* LVIII, (August, 1950), 361-2.

Recent Developments in Welfare Economics, by Tibor Scitovsky, *Econometrica,* 19, (July, 1951), 350.

Social Choice and Individual Values, by Kenneth J. Arrow, *Econometrica,* 20, (January, 1952), 110-11.

Conference on Business Cycles, National Bureau Committee for Economic Research, *Econometrica,* 20, (April, 1952), 346-47.

The Theory of Inter-Sectoral Money Flows and Income Formation, by J.S. Chipman, *American Economic Review,* XLII, (September, 1952), 614-15.

International Economic Papers, No. 1, *Journal of Political Economy,* LX, (October, 1952), 449-50

Application of Linear Programming to the Theory of the Firm, by Robert Dorfman, *Journal of Political Economy,* LX, (October, 1952), 459-60.

Readings in Business Cycles and National Income, Hasen and Clemence, eds., *Econometrica,* 21, (October, 1953), 627-8.

Economic Stability in a Changing World and *Trade not Aid,* by John H. Williams, *Review of Economics and Statistics,* XXXVI, (February, 1954), 114-5.

A Study of Moneyflows in the United States, by Morris A. Copeland. "Professor Copeland's Study of Money Flows", *Review of Economics and Statistics,* XXXVI, (February, 1954), 102-4.

An Essay in the Theory of Profit and Income Distribution, by B.S. Kierstead, *American Economic Review,* XLIV, (June, 1954), 402-3.

Economic Essays, by R.F. Harrod, *Econometrica,* 22, (October, 1954), 539-40.

Essays in Positive Economics, by Milton Friedman, *Review of Economics and Statistics,* XXXVI, (November, 1954), 462-5.

Elements of Pure Economics, by Leon Walras, translated by William Jaffe, *Journal of Political Economy,* LXIII, (February, 1955),77.

A Study in the Theory of Economic Evolution, by Trygve Haavelmo, *Econometrica,* 25, (July, 1955), 359-60.

Economic Theory and Method, by F. Zeuthen, *Journal of Political Economy,* LXIV, (December, 1956), 536-7.

Economic Policy: Principles and Design, by Jan Tinbergen, *American Economic Review,* LXIV, (September, 1957), 688-9.

Mathematical Economics, by R.G.D. Allen, *Economica,* N.S., XXIV, (November, 1957), 364-6.

Theoretical Welfare Economics, by J. de V. Graaf, *Econometrica,* 27, (April, 1959), 317-8.

Introduction to Mathematical Economics, by D.W. Bushaw and R.W. Bushaw and R.W. Clower, *Econometrica,* 27, (July, 1959), 512-3.

Studies in Linear and Nonlinear Programming, by K.J. Arrow, L. Hurwicz, and H. Uzawa, *Kyklos,* Fasc. 4, (1959), 666-8.

The Corporation in Modern Society, edited by Edward S. Mason, *Journal of Political Economy,* LXIX, (February, 1960), 74-5.

Essays in Economics and Econometrics: A Volume in Honor of Harold Hotelling, edited by William Pfouts, *Southern Economic Journal,* XXVII, (April, 1961), 363-4.

Essays in Value and Distribution and *Essays on Economic Stability and Growth,* by Nicholas Kaldor, *American Economic Review,* LI, (June, 1961), 409-13.

Management Models and Industrial Application of Linear Programming, Vol. I, by A. Charnes and W.W. Cooper, *Naval Research Logistics Quarterly,* 9, (March, 1962), 63-4.

A Behavioral Theory of the Firm, by R.M. Cyert and J.G. March. *Journal of Marketing Research*, I, (February, 1964), 74-6.

Full Employment or Stagnation?, by J.M. Culbertson. *Journal of Political Economy,* LXXII, (November, 1964), 633-4.

Essays in Normative Economics, by Abram Bergson. *Journal of Political Economy,*LXXIV, (August, 1966), 410-11.

Higgledy Piggledy Growth Again, by I.M.D. Little and A.C. Rayner. *Economica,* N.S., XXXIV, (August, 1967), 326-29.

The Years of High Theory, by G.S.L. Shackle. *American Economic Review,* LVIII, (June, 1968), 565-6.

The Theory of the Firm: Production, Capital and Finance, by Douglas Vickers. *Journal of Economic Literature,* VII, (June, 1969), 428-9.

Cost and Choice, by James Buchanan. *Journal of Economic Literature,* VIII, (December, 1970), 1210-11.

Welfare and Competition, by Tibor Scitovsky. *Economica,* N.S., XXXIX, (February, 1971), 89-90.

Economic Dynamics, by Roy Harrod. *Economica*, N.S., XL, (May, 1973), 218-9.

Marx's Economics: A Dual Theory of Value and Growth by Michio Morishima. *Monthly Review,* (February 1975), 57-64.

On Economic Inequality by Sen. *Economica,* N.S., 42, (May, 1975), 211-2.

AUTHOR INDEX

A

B

C

D

E

F

G

H

I

J

K

L

M

SUBJECT INDEX

D

E